Who's Who
IN GAY AND LESBIAN HISTORY

Who's Who
IN GAY AND LESBIAN HISTORY

From Antiquity to World War II

Edited by
Robert Aldrich and
Garry Wotherspoon

London and New York

First published 2001
by Routledge
11 New Fetter Lane, London EC4P 4EE

Simultaneously published in the USA and Canada
by Routledge
29 West 35th Street, New York, NY 10001

Second edition first published 2002

Routledge is an imprint of the Taylor & Francis Group

Typeset in Sabon by RefineCatch Limited, Bungay, Suffolk
Printed and bound in Great Britain by
TJ International Ltd, Padstow, Cornwall

British Library Cataloguing in Publication Data
A catalogue record for this book is available from the British Library

Library of Congress Cataloging in Publication Data
A catalogue record for this book has been requested

ISBN 0–415–15983–0

Contents

Introduction

What do Sappho, Michelangelo, Queen Kristina of Sweden, Oscar Wilde, Magnus Hirschfeld, Colette, Henry James and Sigmund Freud have in common? Nothing at first glance, but there is one commonality: they are all significant in the history of homosexuality, and as such they feature in this *Who's Who in Gay and Lesbian History*.

A *Who's Who* in some ways can seem a rather quaint sort of book – potted biographies of the rich and famous, the worthy and the nefarious, or those with some exalted position in society which gets them included. The assumption is that someone must be relatively important or well known as well as meritorious to appear in a *Who's Who*; yet even being written about in such a volume itself provides at least a few lines of fame. It is thus by very definition élitist – unknown people do not make it into a *Who's Who*. Indeed, it would be rather pointless if they did, because those who consult the book need to know the name of a specific figure in order to read about her or him. Except for those admirable eccentrics who derive great pleasure simply from browsing through encyclopedias and dictionaries, readers of a *Who's Who* are interested in biographical information on identifiable figures.

Professional historians may well have certain reservations about the approach to the past implied by a *Who's Who*: it smacks of the 'great men in history' attitude of the nineteenth century (needless to say, our professional forebears were less concerned about 'great women' in history). Furthermore, those of us reared in the 'new social histories' of the *Annales* sort, or even the old or new Marxist history, may raise our eyebrows about a project that is necessarily based solely on individuals, with only limited scope for discussion of social context, general trends and the activities of groups or classes, or the impact of impersonal forces in history. As well, the overwhelming amount of discussion in recent years about 'identity' and the related arguments by postmodernists and queer theorists have raised questions about any categorisation of individuals by a single trait, in this case that of sexual orientation. Especially with 'deviant' sexuality, given its long-held taboo status in many Western societies, there seems also the danger of degenerating into high-class gossip: was one or another figure *really* lesbian or gay?

Nevertheless, reference books such as *Who's Who* directories are essential – they are often the first port of call for students embarking on research, for scholars needing to check basic facts, and for general readers looking for brief introductions. Undoubtedly more people consult, and certainly learn more from, a range of such reference books than they do from many ponderous monographs. Given the limits but recognising the imperatives, putting together a *Who's Who* is therefore a useful undertaking.

The idea of reference works on homosexuality, including biographical ones, is not new. After all, early writers on homosexuality, including most of those in the late 1800s and early 1900s, listed as precursors of our tribe the great 'gays' – or homosexuals, sodomites, inverts, Urnings, Uranians or whatever other colloquial terms were used – of Antiquity and afterwards. Having such illustrious predecessors could 'justify' what society saw as reprobate emotions and behaviours. This approach continued well into the twentieth century. One of the most widely circulated of the books on homosexuality written in the 'second wave' of scholarly works, in the 1970s and 1980s – the time that such pioneering scholars as Kenneth Dover, John Boswell, Lillian Faderman and Jeffrey Weeks were giving gay and lesbian historical studies real legitimacy – was A. L. Rowse's *Homosexuals in History*. Rowse was an eminent Elizabethan scholar, and the subtitle of his work – '*A Study of Ambivalence in Society, Literature and the Arts*' – appeared to indicate an imaginative perspective.[1] However, as many critics have noted, the work seemed largely a project of 'recuperation' (as postmodernists might say): a wide range of famous persons might be read as gay, and Rowse certainly had ample anecdotes (some of rather doubtful provenance) to prove his point. Chapter after chapter moved through century after century in a great gay genealogy.

Enjoyable and important as it was, Rowse's book suffered from flaws that a number of other writers would repeat. It presupposed that it was critical to prove that a range of famous people were homosexual and to find the 'stains on the sheets', and it supposed that almost anyone who strayed from the straight and narrow was probably 'one of us'. Even today, there continues to be much work that assumes that paintings of two men gazing at each other are automatically a gay *mise en scène*, or that lines expressing even the most comradely or amical bonding are proof of at least a covert or latent homosexual relationship. This sort of approach quickly turns into chauvinism. Some works, in fact – as in several recent American publications – do not even try to hide their inspirational intentions and verge on the hagiographical. Not all succumb to these faults; the two-volume *Encyclopedia of Homosexuality*, published in 1990, remains a valuable resource, despite criticisms of certain aspects of its scholarship.[2]

Available biographical compendia display various limitations. Curiously, many such books, explicitly or implicitly, try to provide rankings, as do the lists that come out in *Gay Times*, *The Advocate* and other publications which list the 'Top 100' of gays and lesbians of the past or present. One 1995 American publication was indeed called *The Gay 100: A Ranking of the Most*

Influential Gay Men and Lesbians, Past and Present, while in the following year appeared the revised *Gay Men and Women Who Enriched the World*.[3] Another problem is that many of these books are heavily weighted to the history of homosexuality in the English-speaking world. Several are remarkably Americanocentric. While they each generally include the usual suspects, like Sappho and Leonardo da Vinci, they are overbalanced towards the moderns and towards the Americans; figures from regions such as the Nordic countries and eastern Europe, for instance, almost never appear. This is notably true of the recent *Completely Queer*.[4] Furthermore, the scholarly apparatus of footnotes and bibliographies is usually rudimentary.[5] Directories in languages other than English, of which few have been published, have been little better. Two gay encyclopedic dictionaries in French published in recent years have a most eclectic choice of figures and only the briefest of references.[6]

We have tried to learn from these earlier examples, and to avoid their weaknesses. We have set certain clear criteria. First, we have taken as our parameters only the Western world, where concepts such as lesbian and gay (but also homosexual) have a specific cultural meaning. Also, it has been argued that – with notable exceptions – it is primarily in the West that human worth has come to be valorized largely in individual terms; in many non-Western cultures, individuality is downplayed, being subsumed under wider social demands. Thus we focus on Europe and societies of European settlement – North and South America, Australia, New Zealand and southern Africa. We considered that it would be inappropriate to include entries, by name of individual, for India or Africa or China or other non-Western regions, except in those very few cases where the persons have become – like Yukio Mishima – part of the cultural canon of the West. Moreover, the construction of sexuality in non-Western societies makes it hardly appropriate to apply such terms as 'lesbian' and 'gay' (or earlier variants) there. Even in this work, there are variations in the way in which the term 'gay' (or other terms) has been applied, indicating how language can be transformed when moving between cultures and periods, or even as used by different historians.

Similarly, the very nature of a *Who's Who* – a dictionary organised only by the names of individuals – effectively vetoed the approach of using group entries (say, Danish politicians, Portuguese writers or British activists). Although group entries may have aided some readers, the inclusion of figures by their individual names gives greater recognition to men and women who, though not always well known outside their own societies, have played significant roles in gay and lesbian cultures in various countries.[7]

Despite being an English-language book, this volume includes as many non-Americans and non-Britons as possible, even at the risk of slighting the US and UK in overall distribution. Our argument is that English-speaking readers already have much material available on the history of sexuality in those two countries, but know relatively little about homosexuality elsewhere in the West (including other English-speaking countries). Thus the book provides in effect an overview of how homosexuality has been perceived, and dealt with, in the Western world over the past three thousand years. Some of the entries on the non-English-speaking figures are also more detailed than those on Americans and Britons, and thus provide further background on historical development and social contexts in these countries. More extensive 'plot summaries' present information on writings that may not be accessible to those unable to read various European languages. We also hope that this greater representation from the wider world will remind readers that gay and lesbian history did not start in Christopher Street in 1969 and was not just a product of the invention of the word 'homosexuality' by Kertbeny a century earlier.

The question of gender balance has been a serious one. Women have generally been under-represented in most reference books and in many studies of gay and lesbian history. However, after discussions with a number of women scholars, we decided that it would be unreasonable to expect gender parity in this volume. The criminalisation of male homosexuality in many Western societies has meant that men were thrust into the public arena, often through court cases, in a way that women were not. Furthermore, the domination of public life by men until very recent years has meant that many of the 'famous' people who warrant inclusion in a *Who's Who* are male. A number of women historians have lamented the dearth of studies of lesbianism, and even pointed to a lack of primary materials in some areas. We can only repeat calls for further explorations of public archives and personal papers to reveal the history of lesbians around the world.

The sexual orientation of a person has also been an issue, somewhat paradoxically for a *Who's Who in Gay and Lesbian History*. This book contains those figures of importance to gay and lesbian history, whether themselves homosexual, heterosexual, bisexual or none of the above. For example, it seemed absurd to exclude such important figures as Freud, who was heterosexual; even prominent homophobes such as St Paul rate an entry. So what the figures actually did in bed is really of little relevance: indeed it seems pointless to include a figure in this *Who's Who* simply because he or she is or was famous *and* homosexual, unless homosexuality had some particular bearing on the person's public or creative life or his or her life story is in some way representative of wider trends in history. It seemed unnecessary, for instance, to include every Renaissance painter whose portrayal of men together might suggest homosexual interpretations, or every Arcadian poet who wrote verses about comradely affection, or every famous person who has been 'outed'. Indeed, our goal is certainly not to 'out' people from the past, to repeat tittle-tattle about famous people's sexual habits, to propagate rumours with little historical basis, or to try to claim as homosexual legions of the great and famous of the world. Having said that, it is still interesting to note how many figures of importance in the Western cultural pantheon are included here.

Another issue of importance we faced in compiling this work was the need to have a thorough coverage of both what used to be called 'high' culture and 'popular' culture: to include those who wrote for the broadsheet as well as those who wrote classics, to include some from the 'lower orders' as well as those from the upper and middle classes, and to give attention to the music hall as well as to the opera and concert hall. However, reliable biographical material on many figures is simply not available, and this has acted to limit somewhat the coverage of persons from backgrounds different from those who 'created' and recorded our 'high' culture in the past. The work of artists and writers is preserved in their media, that of political leaders chronicled in the public record. Many of the more ordinary men and women who figure here appear, ironically, because they were 'caught': arrested for sodomitical offences, cross-dressing or some other crime, tried and convicted and, sometimes, executed. Those who, with great luck, got away, those who 'passed' with great discretion, remain anonymous.

As any editors of similar compendia know, there are an infinite number of entries that one might include, but only a finite number of pages. We went through many books and drew up lists of possible entries, which we then discussed with a variety of colleagues around the world. There was unanimity on some figures – Sappho, Tchaikovsky, Wilde, Radclyffe Hall, of course – but much difference of opinion. The list of *possibly* significant others then became very long – far too long to include everyone in a book that must, after all, cover Western history from Antiquity to the middle of the twentieth century. Eventually, we worked out a group that we hope is both representative and comprehensive. Here, we would particularly like to acknowledge the vital assistance provided by our editorial advisers, specialists in particular fields, who counselled us on the choice of figures to be included.

Readers may well feel that the list is not perfect, and some reviewers may find that favourite figures are absent; specialists may be concerned about the representation from their areas, whether national groups, professional fields or other divisions. Indeed, one of the perverse pleasures of reading this book might well be searching for – and not finding – some favourite figures.

Apart from being interesting individual stories, these biographies are also a window through which to view wider issues: at their most basic level, they tell us much about attitudes and behaviours in the past. For example, they suggest that, even in the West, and within its multiple cultures, attitudes to same-sex relations have varied extensively, both within any society and over time. This has become increasingly obvious over the past decade, as growing amounts of scholarship have brought to light the great diversity that existed, and still exists, in attitudes towards sexuality. We have resisted the urge to make generalisations – which, in any case, might be dubious – about this vast procession of 'gay' characters on the historical timeline. We do note, however, how certain clusters appear – from humanist philosophers in Renaissance Italy to African-American writers and performers in Harlem in the jazz age. We also note how homosexuality has sometimes emerged – and been studied – in different ways in various societies. There seems, for instance, little evidence of homosexuals in nineteenth-century Canada, though whether this relates more to the lack of historical research than to objective historical conditions remains to be seen. Theorists of homosexuality seem particularly numerous in late nineteenth- and early twentieth-century Germany, while poets and novelists taking homosexual themes are more common in France. Further east and north – for Nordic and Eastern Europe – writers account for the bulk of these areas' entries. Such configurations deserve further research.

This *Who's Who*, then, shows how much gay and lesbian history there is to explore, how many individuals need to be brought to greater public attention – whether as demons, angels or simply 'ordinary' people; how many figures have not received appropriate full-length treatment, how much archival work, primary research and empirical history remains to be done. Furthermore, it also suggests how unfamiliar many of us are with the gay and lesbian history of such regions as Scandinavia, or the Iberian peninsula, or Australia, despite the significance and importance of a number of figures from those regions. Third, it provides convincing evidence of the merits of biographical study as a lens through which to view the history of sexuality and gender, and the usefulness of studies of individuals as a way to see into entire historical milieux and epochs. Such a compilation of material from different societies allows for interesting comparisons, and speculation as to what any similarities and differences might signify. Finally, it confirms the vitality of gay and lesbian studies throughout the Western world today.

Note: Those figures who are most often associated with the period before World War II, or whose major activities of relevance to the history of homosexuality occurred in the years before 1945, are included in this volume, even when they lived past 1945. Those whose activities took place mainly in the post-war period are included in the companion volume, *Who's Who in Contemporary Gay and Lesbian History*. This division across two volumes has necessitated some difficult decisions, such as placing W. H. Auden and Stephen Spender in the first volume while placing their colleague Christopher Isherwood in the second volume, as Isherwood went on to write gay-relevant works well into the second half of the twentieth century.

This work of reference covers figures who have had an impact upon gay and lesbian life throughout history, and not merely individuals who were or are themselves homosexual. Unless explicitly stated, no inferences should be made about subjects' sexual orientation.

Notes

1 A. L. Rowse, *Homosexuals in History: Ambivalence in Society, Literature and the Arts* (London, 1977).
2 W. R. Dynes (ed.), *Encyclopedia of Homosexuality*, 2 vols (New York, 1990). It should also be noted that the encyclopedia did not contain entries on living persons.
3 P. Russell, *The Gay 100: A Ranking of the Most Influential Gay Men and Lesbians, Past and Present* (New York, 1995); T. Cowan, *Gay Men and Women Who Enriched the World* (Boston, 1988; rev. edn, 1996). The second of these books has only 47 profiles, but contains no references. An even smaller number of figures – entries on 11 women – are included in R. Collis, *Portraits to the Wall: Historic Lesbian Lives Unveiled* (London, 1994).

4 S. Hogan and L. Hudson, *Completely Queer: The Gay and Lesbian Encyclopedia* (New York, 1998).

5 W. Stewart, *Cassell's Queer Companion* (London, 1995), is a seemingly random selection of names, terms and other entries and contains no references whatsoever.

6 M. Larivière, *Homosexuels et bisexuels célèbres* (Paris, 1997); L. Povert, *Dictionnaire Gay* (Paris, 1994). The former did not include women; the latter was not limited to entries on individuals.

7 There is a valuable discussion about finding balances between men and women, the living and the dead, the famous and the unknown, and other issues that editors of biographical directories face in I. Calman (ed.), with J. Parvey and M. Cook, *National Biographies and National Identity: A Critical Approach to Theory and Editorial Practice* (Canberra, 1996).

Contributors

Scott Bravmann, San Francisco, United States

Alan Bray, Birkbeck College, University of London, United Kingdom

David J. Bromell, Christchurch, New Zealand

Diana L. Burgin, Cambridge, Massachusetts, United States

Andrea Capovilla, Oxford University, United Kingdom

Chistopher Capozzola, Columbia University, United States

Adam Carr, Melbourne, Australia

Vitaly Chernetsky, Columbia University, United States

Lucy Chesser, Melbourne, Australia

Joseph Chetcuti, Melbourne, Australia

Jens Damm, Free University, Berlin, Germany

Ken Davis, Sydney, Australia

Dennis Denisoff, University of Waterloo, Canada

Elizabeth de Noma, University of Washington, United States

Maria Di Rienzo, Treviso, Italy

Graham N. Drake, State University of New York at Geneseo, United States

Helen Driver, Melbourne, Australia

Karen Duder, University of Victoria, Canada

Ianthe Duende, London, United Kingdom

Justin D. Edwards, University of Copenhagen, Denmark

Greger Eman, Johanneshov, Sweden

C. Faro, University of Sydney, Australia

Ruth Ford, La Trobe University, Australia

Krzysztof Fordoński, Adam Mickiewicz University, Poznan, Poland

Kathleen E. Garay, McMaster University, Canada

David Garnes, University of Connecticut, United States

Jan Olav Gatland, University of Bergen, Norway

Didier Godard, Paris, France

Ken Gonzales-Day, Scripps College, United States

Michael Goodich, Univeristy of Haifa, Israel

James N. Green, California State University, Long Beach, United States

Hanna Hallgren, Stockholm, Sweden

Melissa Hardie, University of Sydney, Australia

Johan Hedberg, Göteborg, Sweden

Linda Heidenreich, University of California, San Diego, United States

Seán Henry, University of Kansas, United States

David Hilliard, Flinders University, Australia

Clifford Hindley, London, United Kingdom

Michael Morgan Holmes, Toronto, Canada

Sarah Holmes, Salem, Massachusetts, United States

Keith Howes, Sydney, Australia

Helle Jarlmose, Bagsvaerd, Denmark

James W. Jones, Central Michigan University, United States

Tuula Juvonen, Tammersfors, Finland

Marita Keilson-Lauritz, Bussum, The Netherlands

Hubert Kennedy, San Francisco State University, United States

Roman Koropeckyj, University of California, Los Angeles, United States

Lena Lennerhed, Södertöm University College, Sweden

Andrew Lesk, University of Montreal, Canada

Kate Lilley, University of Sydney, Australia

Martin Loeb, Stockholm, Sweden

Jan Löfström, University of Jyväskylä, Finland

Suzanne MacAlister, University of Sydney, Australia

Erin E. MacDonald, University of Waterloo, Canada

Peter McNeil, University of New South Wales, Australia

Ian Maidment, Adelaide, Australia

William E. Martin, University of Texas, Austin, United States

Clive Moore, University of Queensland, Australia

Michael J. Murphy, Washington University, United States

Stephen O. Murray, San Francisco, United States

Kati Mustola, University of Helsinki, Finland

Axel Nissen, University of Oslo, Norway

Åke Norström, Lund, Sweden

Rictor Norton, London, United Kingdom

Harry Oosterhuis, University of Maastricht, The Netherlands

Salvador A. Oropesa, Kansas State University, United States

Annette Oxindine, Wright State University, United States

Johanna Pakkanen, Helsinki, Finland

David Parris, Trinity College, Dublin, Ireland

David L. Phillips, University of Western Sydney, Australia

George Piggford, Tufts University, United States

Gerald Pilz, Korwestheim, Germany

Roger Pitcher, University of New England, Australia

Neil A. Radford, Sydney, Australia

Tim Reeves, Canberra, Australia

Graeme Reid, University of Johannesburg, South Africa

J. Z. Robinson, Dunedin, New Zealand

Monique Rooney, University of Sydney, Australia

Johan Rosell, Stockholm, Sweden

Tiina Rosenberg, University of Stockholm, Sweden

Matthew M. Roy, University of Washington, United States

Jens Rydström, University of Stockholm, Sweden

Philippe-Joseph Salazar, University of Cape Town, South Africa

Mark Seymour, Trinity College, Rome, Italy

Charley Shiveley, University of Massachusetts, Boston, United States

Gary Simes, University of Sydney, Australia

Graeme Skinner, Sydney, Australia

Paul Snijders, The Hague, The Netherlands

William J. Spurlin, University of Cardiff, United Kingdom

John Stanley, Toronto, Canada

Lisbeth Stenberg, Gothenburg University, Sweden

Ingrid Svensson, The Royal Library, National Library of Sweden, Stockholm, Sweden

Victoria Thompson, Xavier University, United States

Juha-Heikki Tihinen, Helsinki, Finland

Lutz van Dijk, Amsterdam, The Netherlands

Maurice van Lieshout, Utrecht, The Netherlands

A. M. Wentink, Middlebury College, United States

David West, Australian National University, Australia

Elizabeth A. Wilson, University of Sydney, Australia

Garry Wotherspoon, University of Sydney, Australia

Øystein S. Ziener, Copenhagen, Denmark

Acknowledgements

We would like to thank, at Routledge, Kieron Corless for having suggested this volume, Roger Thorp, who encouraged us through the work and saw the book to publication, also Ruth Jeavons and Hywel Evans. The volume benefited from Rictor Norton's work as copy editor. Our Editorial Advisers, in addition to writing a large number of entries themselves, have provided regular counsel on which figures ought to be included here, helped us locate contributors, and aided greatly in sorting out questions about the appropriate balance between various countries, periods and domains of activity. A particular word of thanks should go to Wilhelm von Rosen for helping us to put together a group of Nordic entries and contributors, and to David William Foster for advising us on Latin American entries. Henny Brandhorst at Homodok in Amsterdam helped line up writers and entries on the Low Countries, and Vicki Feaklor, in the United States, kindly circulated our draft lists and appeals for contributions through the e-mail list of the Committee on Gay and Lesbian History. The contributors themselves have put together entries which, though confined by strict word limits, often provide small-scale essays not just on the individuals about whom they have written but on broad historical contexts. Many contributors have willingly taken on extra entries at our request – sometimes when other authors, alas, did not come through with the pieces they promised – and we are most grateful.

Robert Aldrich translated the entries by Giovanni Dall'Orto, Maria Di Rienzo and Didier Godard; Nicholas Haldosen translated the entry by Hanna Hallgren.

Julie Manley, at the start of this project, and Ruth Williams, during the last stages of editing, provided truly invaluable secretarial assistance, and cheerfully and efficiently handled various versions of entries, countless changes made while we edited them, and a constantly evolving list of contributors and entries. Patrick Ferry kindly helped with the final checking and collation.

A

Achilles, legendary Greek figure. In the first line of the *Iliad*, Homer announces his poem's central theme: the wrath of Achilles. This anger arose from the insult suffered by Achilles, leader of the Myrmidons, when Agamemnon, the Greek commander-in-chief, robbed him of his concubine, Briseis. In response, Achilles, the Greeks' greatest champion (without whom they could not win), withdrew from battle. He sulked in his tent until his friend, Patroclus, fighting in Achilles' armour, was killed by the Trojan prince, Hector. Only then was Achilles roused to fight – to avenge his friend's death. He massacred Trojans without mercy, until finally Hector was slain and his corpse dragged into the Greek camp behind Achilles' chariot.

Achilles is a legendary figure, son of the goddess Thetis and the human Peleus. He had affairs with several women, including the princess Deidamia, who bore him a son, Neoptolemus. His friendship with Patroclus was variously regarded. Homer never says explicitly that they were lovers, though he portrays an emotional bond between them which is far more intense than that between any other pair of heroes. According to XENOPHON, Socrates held that Patroclus was Achilles' 'companion' rather than his 'lover'. But for others (both ancient and modern), episodes such as the overflowing grief exhibited by Achilles at his friend's death, and the desire of Patroclus's ghost for a common tomb, have implied an erotic relationship.

This was the commoner view in classical times. It is movingly expressed in one of the few fragments to survive from Aeschylus's lost play, *The Myrmidons*, where Achilles reproaches Patroclus for having deserted him by dying: 'You showed no regard for [my] pure worship of [your] thighs – so lacking in gratitude for so many kisses!'

It was also disputed whether Achilles or Patroclus was the older. For Aeschylus, it was Achilles. Similarly for Aelian (*c.* AD 200), the visit of ALEXANDER and Hephaestion to the heroes' tombs at Troy makes coded reference to the parallel between the relationship of Hephaestion (as the younger beloved) to Alexander and that of Patroclus to Achilles. On the other hand, Phaedrus, a speaker in PLATO's *Symposium*, says (using the current terminology) that Homer makes Patroclus the older ('lover' – *erastes*) and Achilles the younger ('beloved' – *eromenos*).

Faced by Homer's opaqueness, later writers interpreted the legend in terms of their own times, thus providing icons for themselves and their successors. This process is particularly discernible in AESCHINES' speech *Against Timarchus*, where the Achilles–Patroclus relationship appears as an example of legitimate *eros*, though it is viewed rather differently by Aeschines and by his opponents. For the latter, the story provides a precedent for physical intimacy, whereas Aeschines sees Homer 'concealing' (but not 'denying') the physical passion and emphasises the heroes' affection and mutual devotion.

W. M. Clarke, 'Achilles and Patroclus in Love', *Hermes*, 106 (1978); D. M. Halperin, 'Heroes and their Pals', in *One Hundred Years of Homosexuality*, New York, 1990: 75–87.

Clifford Hindley

Acosta, Mercedes de (1893–1968), American writer. The youngest daughter of a fashionable family who lived in turn-of-the-century New York City, as a child de Acosta believed that she was a boy. Her mother wanted a son, so she dressed de Acosta in boy's clothing and encouraged her to play with boys. Axel Madsen notes that an early, unpublished version of de Acosta's memoirs describes how the 7-year-old learned her biological sex. '"You're deformed", I shouted. "If you're a boy and you haven't got this, you are the one who is deformed", he shouted back. By this time other boys had joined us, each boy speedily showing me the same strange phenomenon the first boy had exhibited. "Prove you're not a girl," they screamed.'

Unlike four of her older sisters, de Acosta spurned debutante balls and grand marriages. She married painter Abram Poole in a small ceremony. As a feminist, writer and lesbian, de Acosta retained her surname, lived apart from her husband while working on productions, and had loving relations with famed artistic women, including dancer Isadora Duncan and actresses Eva Le Gallienne, Alla Nazimova, Greta GARBO and Marlene Dietrich.

Dressed in tailored suits and walking shoes, de Acosta enjoyed the speakeasies, homosexual clubs and theatrical circles in 1920s New York City. She published two books of poems, two novels and the plays *Jeanne d'Arc* (1924) and *Jacob Slovak* (1928). Her theatre connections led to RKO hiring her in 1930. Though the Pola Negri movie she was hired to write never appeared, de Acosta quickly integrated herself into the circles of Hollywood actresses and screenwriters who held same-gender sexual interests. Similar to Paris' salons, these 'sewing circles' included actresses such as Constance Collier and Beatrice Lille and socialites Elsa Maxwell and Elsie de Wolfe. De Acosta's fortunes as a screenwriter did not improve. She battled unsuccessfully with MGM production chief Irving Thalberg to put Garbo in pants for a movie titled *Desperate*, then watched the star don them in *Queen Christina* (1933).

Several newspaper and magazine representations of the screenwriter described her masculine attire. Although similar to the 'mannish lesbian' image that demonised lesbians in medical textbooks and pulp fiction, the depictions made de Acosta into what historian Carroll Smith-Rosenberg labelled a second-generation New Woman. These women used male language and images to defy gender conventions, and de Acosta's attire helped her form a *persona* that one article described as strikingly handsome. This image looks manly and dignified, instead of having the delicate and graceful attractiveness associated with females in the culture. These representations presented de Acosta's New Woman attitudes and interests. The screenwriter decried marriage, noting that 'matrimony is out of date. I don't approve of it at all.' After questioning the role that society offers women, de Acosta demonstrated her ability in foreign relations, an area that the culture of her time considered a male province. The screenwriter attempted to put her interest into action and tried to serve in the Spanish Civil War during the mid-1930s.

De Acosta returned to the New York theatrical and art worlds in the early 1940s. Her memoirs, *Here Lies the Heart*, appeared in 1960 to mixed reviews and limited public interest. Years of failing health drained her finances and curtailed her activities by the mid-1960s.

A. Madsen, *Forbidden Lovers: Hollywood's Greatest Secret – Female Stars Who Loved Other Women*, New York, 1996; K. Swenson, *Greta Garbo: A Life Apart*, New York, 1997; H. Vickers, *Loving Garbo – The Story of Greta Garbo, Cecil Beaton, and Mercedes de Acosta*, New York, 1994.

Brett L. Abrams

Acton, Harold (1904–1994), British writer. Acton was born at the Villa La Pietra in Florence, Italy, the son of American Hortense Mitchell, Illinois Bank and Trust heiress, and Englishman Arthur Mario Acton, a failed artist turned avid art collector, by virtue of his wife's fortune and subsequent investments. A younger brother, William, a gay artist of modest achievement, died an apparent suicide in 1944.

Raised in a household of connoisseurs, young Acton met DIAGHILEV, Jean COCTEAU, Max Beerbohm, Reggie Turner (Oscar WILDE's friend and disciple) and artist Charles Ricketts while still an adolescent. Already, an avowed aesthete before entering Eton in 1918, he and classmate Brian HOWARD were devotees of Diaghilev and rebels against British philistinism and old-guard 'manliness'. Champions of RIMBAUD and the French symbolist poets, modern American poetry, Osbert, Satcheverell and Edith SITWELL, jazz and everything connected to the modern aesthetics of the Ballets Russes, Acton and Howard wielded enormous social, artistic and intellectual influence during their years at Eton (1918–1922). Together they promoted modern dandyism and founded the Eton Society of the Arts (whose membership included Anthony Powell and Cyril Connolly), and published the *Eton Candle*, a literary magazine (1922). Acton's poetry attracted the attention of the Sitwells and led to the publication of his first two books of poems, *Aquarium* (1922) and *An Indian Ass* (1925), works now undeserving of their initial critical acclaim.

Unabashedly gay, Acton entered Christ Church, Oxford, in 1922, succeeding as planned to dictate fashion and taste and to 'rule' as he and Howard had at Eton. At Oxford he founded the iconoclastic literary magazine the *Oxford Broom*. He was immortalised by fellow Oxonian Evelyn WAUGH as the flamboyant and decadent dandy 'Anthony Blanche' in *Brideshead Revisited* (1944), a 'smear' which to his disgust followed him throughout most of his life. During his homosexual phase at Oxford, Waugh was one of many students to have an affair with Acton, to whom he dedicated his first novel, *Decline and Fall* (1929).

With his writing career floundering, and finding Depression-era England inhospitable to his style of dandyism, Acton travelled to Peking in 1932 to lecture, write and translate Chinese poetry. In Peking, he lived like a mandarin, finding a new Buddhist serenity as well as opium and fulfilment with numerous Chinese youths. It was during this period, however, that he met Desmond Parsons, a young Englishman who, according to some friends, was the one true love of his life. After only a brief affair with Acton, Parsons became ill, returned to London and died of Hodgkin's disease at age 26. In 1939, on the eve of World War II Acton was forced to return to Britain. During the war he served in the Royal Air Force and tried unsuccessfully to return to China, where he felt he would have been of most value, but instead was sent briefly to India.

Despite his youthful brilliance, Acton ultimately lacked the discipline and individuality to apply his literary and scholarly talents to lasting value or acclaim. His contribution to twentieth-century culture was having introduced modernist aestheticism to a generation of British writers and intellectuals, many of whose attainments ultimately were far greater than his own. For more than half his life, Acton remained internationally famous as a brilliant raconteur and devoted time between travels to writing fiction and scholarly studies, and lecturing on art history. But his prime life's work became the preservation of the five villas, libraries and precious art collection of his 57-acre Florentine estate, where he entertained such notables as Bernard Berenson, Cecil BEATON, Winston Churchill, D. H. LAWRENCE, George Orwell, Aldous Huxley, Graham Greene, Henry Moore and Prince Charles. At his death, he bequeathed La Pietra, along with investments valued at $250–$500 million and $25 million in cash, to New York University.

Acton's books include works of history, *The Last Medici* (1932), *The Bourbons of Naples*, *The Last Bourbons of Naples*, fiction, *Peonies and Ponies* (1942), and the multi-volume autobiography, *Memoirs of an Aesthete* (1948, 1971).

M. Green, *Children of the Sun*, New York, 1976; J. Lord, *Some Remarkable Men*, New York, 1996.

A. M. Wentink

Addams, Jane (1860–1935), American social reformer. Addams was born in Cedarville, Illinois, where her father was a mill owner, devoted Quaker and a representative to the state legislature. Her mother died when Jane was young. She was a top student at the Rockford Female Seminary, and after graduating, entered medical school, withdrawing because of back trouble to return to Illinois.

In 1888 she and a close friend, Ellen Gates Starr, went to live in a poor neighbourhood in Chicago to learn more about how they might reduce the suffering created by poverty. In 1889 they purchased a house on the West Side of the city, Hull House, which grew to become the first settlement house in America. It was a focal point for neighbourhood social welfare programmes, advocacy, the arts and education, and a decentralised, anarchistic organisation that later developed a reputation for radicalism.

Hull House provided playgrounds, literary clubs, an art gallery, a chorus, a theatre, a summer school for women, a day nursery, a kindergarten, public baths, a library, a chemist, an employment bureau, a cooperative apartment for young working women and a Juvenile Protective Association working on issues of sexual morality, prostitution and drug abuse.

Addams is the most well known American social reformer and a model for many generations of social workers and advocates for disempowered people. She was the key person to convince the American public that welfare and social programmes were both right and practical, developing a theory and practice of social ethics that said that people are essentially good, but that society has the potential to be corrupt and that it is the collective responsibility of a culture to see that the environment protects and nurtures each individual's best qualities. Her work with low-income people set a new standard for charitable work and helped create the concept of social welfare.

Throughout her life Addams was close to many women and was very good at eliciting the involvement of women from different classes in Hull House's programmes. Her closest adult companion, friend and lover was Mary Rozet Smith, who nurtured and supported Addams and her work at Hull House, and with whom she owned a summer house in Bar Harbor, Maine.

Addams also took part in political activities in the Chicago area, nationally and internationally. She authored ten books, and in 1915 became a founding member of the Women's Peace Party. However, by 1917 she became constantly ill and her activism was somewhat curtailed. By 1926 she was a semi-invalid as a result of a heart attack, but continued to receive numerous commendations for her work. In 1931, along with Nicholas Murray Butler, she won the Nobel Peace Prize. She died of cancer in Chicago.

J. Addams, *Twenty Years at Hull House*, New York, 1910; J. B. Elshtain, 'A Return to Hull House: Reflections on Jane Addams', *Feminist*

Issues, 15, 1/2 (1997): 105–13; K. S. Lundblad, 'Jane Addams and Social Reform: A Role Model for the 1990s', *Social Work*, 40, 5 (1995): 661–9.

Sarah Holmes

Adelswärd-Fersen, Baron Jacques d' (1880–1923), French author. D'Adelswärd-Fersen became one of the most notorious of Europe's *fin de siècle* homosexuals, principally because he was at the centre of a major French pederasty scandal. His family, descended from the Baron Fersen who had been Swedish ambassador to France in the reign of Louis XVI, was wealthy, royalist and socially very well established, and he was originally destined for the diplomatic corps. But a trip to Capri with his mother in 1897, when he may have met Oscar WILDE, seems to have led to his decision to become a writer. He duly published his first work, a book of poems titled *Chansons légères*, in 1901, and continued to write, mostly novels, for the next twenty years. Although never receiving much critical acclaim or public interest, his writings did have admirers, notably the influential woman novelist and critic Rachilde. A more decisive influence on his life and work than Wilde was probably the poet and novelist Jean LORRAIN, whom he encountered in Venice in 1902, and who describes d'Adelswärd-Fersen's racy lifestyle in *Pelléastres* (1910). In July 1903 d'Adelswärd-Fersen was arrested, together with another aristocrat, Hamelin de Warren, and charged with indecent assault and 'exciting minors to debauchery'. The importance of the scandal derived from the fact that the minors in question were boys of good family from well known Parisian schools: the Lycée Carnot, the Lycée Condorcet and the Lycée Janson-de-Sailly. The occasion of the supposed offence was a series of *tableaux vivants* organised at his house in which a number of the schoolboys took part, including one to whom he had written indiscreetly passionate letters. The assault charge was thrown out, but he was found

guilty of the lesser offence and sentenced to a fine, a six-month prison sentence and 'forfeiture of family rights'. Consequently, he went to Capri, where he became a central figure in the island's homosexual expatriate colony until his death in 1923. His writings include a novel, *Une Jeunesse* (1906), which has a pederastic subplot; he was also founder of the short-lived homoerotic periodical *Akadémos* (1909), to which he contributed under the pseudonym 'Sonyeuse'. But his real significance derives from his status as an archetype of the turn-of-the-century aesthete–pederast, an image embodied in the biographical novel *L'Exilé de Capri* by Roger Peyrefitte.

R. Aldrich, *The Seduction of the Mediterranean*, London, 1993; P. Cardon, *Dossier Jacques d'Adelswärd-Fersen*, Lille, 1991; R. Peyrefitte, *L'Exilé de Capri*, Paris, 1959.

Christopher Robinson

Adrian-Nilsson, Gösta (1884–1965), Swedish painter. Better known as GAN, Adrian-Nilsson was born in a working-class area of the Swedish university town of Lund. In his early poems and pictures, he was obviously influenced by Oscar WILDE and Aubrey Beardsley. He soon came to discover Cubism and Futurism and painted his first modernistic paintings in 1913. After spending time in Berlin and Köln, he returned to Lund in 1914. During GAN's absence, his lover Karl Edvard Holmstöm had died of pneumonia, a loss from which GAN never recovered. When GAN exhibited his new work in Lund, he was met by scepticism and was labelled 'expressionist', which was meant to be derogatory.

After moving to the capital, Stockholm, GAN focused on painting sailors in what he himself referred to as his 'wild' style. But sailors were not only a motif for GAN. He also had them as lovers and friends. One of them, Edvin Andersson, who later changed his last name to Ganborg, was to become a lifelong friend and promoter of

GAN's work. At this time, modernistic painting in Sweden was dominated by pupils of Matisse, and GAN's synthesis of Cubism and Futurism influenced by German painting (especially Franz Marc) was not well received by the art critics or by the public. In 1920 GAN moved to Paris, where he rented a studio in the building where Léger worked. GAN was never a pupil of Léger, but under Léger's influence he started moving away from his 'wild' style towards a more rigid one, though the motifs remained the same – athletes, bullfighters, soldiers and sailors. In the latter half of the 1920s GAN moved back to Lund and did a series of illuminations and paintings in an affected 'Gothic' style. In 1930 he took on geometric abstraction, collaborating with his younger follower Erik Olson. He once again moved to Stockholm, where he was to live in the same flat for the rest of his life.

After having been one of the painters introducing Surrealism in Sweden and once again being ridiculed, GAN became bitter and chose to live in voluntary isolation. After 1940 he produced very little of value. In 1984, a grand retrospective exhibition finally made GAN celebrated and recognised as a unique painter who had created numerous modernistic syntheses in which his homosexual identity was by far a more important element than any purely artistic influence.

N. Lindgren, *GAN*, Halmstad, 1949; J. T. Ahlstrand, *GAN*, Lund, 1985.

Martin Loeb

Aelred of Rievaulx, St (*c.* 1110–1167), English monk, writer. Saint Aelred of Rievaulx is one of the most passionate and engaging medieval commentators on friendship (*amicitia*) between men. Many of Aelred's writings and the biography written shortly after his death attest to the centrality of homoerotic affection to his conception of enlightened spirituality.

Aelred was born about 1110 in Hexham, Northumberland. He came from an upper-rank family which had a long history of holding important positions in the pre-Norman Church. When Aelred was about 15 years old, he was sent to be educated at the court of King David of Scotland, where he became a valued member of the royal household and received an excellent education.

Had he pursued a worldly course, Aelred would likely have been offered a prominent bishopric. However, on a journey to Yorkshire on the king's business he was spiritually drawn to the recently founded Cistercian monastery, Rievaulx Abbey. Aelred entered the Rievaulx community in 1134. On a journey to Rome in 1142 he met St Bernard of Clairvaux, at whose command Aelred, upon his return to England, wrote his first major work, the *Speculum Caritatis* (*The Mirror of Love*). The *Speculum* is a treatise on love which carefully distinguishes between worldly and spiritual varieties, the latter – referred to as *caritas* – being a complete and loving surrender to Christ's authority. This is an important document in the history of medieval homoeroticism, for in it Aelred celebrates an intimate friendship he had enjoyed with a fellow monk named Simon, a dear companion who had recently passed away. In some of the biographical sections of the *Speculum* (and in another work, *De Institutione Inclusarum*), it appears that Aelred felt some anxiety over the likely carnal dimension of friendships he had enjoyed while at the Scottish court. His love for Simon, however, seems to have shown him a way to integrate love for one's friends and love for God in a spiritual prefiguration of heavenly bliss.

In 1143 Aelred became the first abbot of Rievaulx's new daughter-house at Revesby. Four years later he returned to Rievaulx as its abbot, a position he held until his death over twenty years later. While leader of the Rievaulx community, Aelred composed his most moving celebration of amity, *De Spirituali Amicitia* (*Spiritual Friendship*).

In terms of form and content the most

important influence on this treatise was Cicero's *De Amicitia* (*On Friendship*); one can also perceive the impact of Augustine's *Confessions* and the Bible (especially Solomon's Canticles, and the stories of DAVID and JONATHAN, and JESUS and John). Friendship, Aelred posits, 'is that virtue by which spirits are bound by ties of love and sweetness, and out of many are made one'. *De Spirituali Amicitia* rejects 'puerile' carnality and movingly elevates friendship to a quasi-divine status. Drawing on the Gospel of John, one of the dialogue's interlocutors offers the famous Aelredian epigram: 'God is friendship'.

The third and final part of *De Spirituali Amicitia* returns to the subject of Aelred's friendships with particular men. Here we again find mention of Simon, which is followed by a lengthy discussion of Aelred's passionate camaraderie with a younger, unnamed monk who 'mounted with me through all the stages of friendship, as far as human imperfection permitted'. Waxing enthusiastic, Aelred goes on to recount that 'love increased between us, affection glowed the warmer and charity was strengthened, until we attained that stage at which we had but one mind and one soul to will and not to will alike'.

A major theme of Aelred's paean to friendship is the connection between this world and heaven. Describing his experience of sublime friendship, Aelred rhetorically asks: 'Was it not a foretaste of blessedness thus to love and thus to be loved; thus to help and thus to be helped; and in this way from the sweetness of fraternal charity to wing one's flight aloft to that more sublime splendor of divine love, and by the ladder of charity now to mount to the embrace of Christ himself; and again to descend to the love of neighbor, there pleasantly to rest?' This passage and others like it attest to a profound connection between embodied homoerotic desire and the attainment of transcendent spiritual states. 'Fraternal charity' is, in this life, both the starting point for divine love and, importantly, the benefactor of such good-

ness as may be obtained from more spiritual fulfilment. In Aelred's writings and, it would seem, his life, earthly and spiritual love are not separate and opposed but, rather, are united in Christ who is 'the inspiration of the love by which we love our friend'. Perhaps we can recognise here a triangulation model of desire whereby Christ is the mediator of passion between men. When death came for Aelred in 1167 he was, says his friend and biographer Walter Daniel, appropriately surrounded by 'twelve, now twenty, now forty, now even a hundred monks . . . so vehemently was this lover of us all loved by us'.

In 1980, John Boswell argued that there 'can be little question that Aelred was gay'. Subsequent developments in sexuality studies lead one to question the use of a modern identity category for the Cistercian saint. Aelred's devotion to male friends seems to span with ease the 800 years between our time and his; however, the ascetic quality and ultimate spiritual orientation of these bonds likely differs from that of most 'gay' men today. Boswell also noted, though, that Aelred's treatment of friendship (along with that of St ANSELM) differs markedly from the monastic precepts which severely censured 'particular friendships'. Aelred's break with tradition opens a window on a still-familiar conjunction of homoeroticism and cultural dissidence.

Aelred of Rievaulx, *Spiritual Friendship*, trans. M. E. Laker, Kalamazoo, Michigan, 1977; J. Boswell, *Christianity, Social Tolerance, and Homosexuality*, London, 1980; W. Daniel, *The Life of Ailred of Rievaulx*, trans. F. M. Powicke, London, 1950; K. C. Russell, 'Aelred, The Gay Abbot of Rievaulx', *Studia Mystica*, 5, 4 (1982): 51–64.

Michael Morgan Holmes

Aeneas, Greek mythological figure. Aeneas is the hero of the *Aeneid* of VIRGIL, an epic poem in twelve books which recounts the fall of Troy to the Greeks and the subsequent flight of Aeneas and other

Trojans to Italy where they become the ancestors of the Romans. Aeneas was the son
of Venus, goddess of love, and the Trojan
Anchises, and was the husband of Creusa,
one of the daughters of King Priam. It was
the rape of Helen, wife of Menelaus of
Sparta, by Priam's son Paris which precipitated the Greek expedition to Troy and the
ten-year siege which ended only when the
Greeks built a wooden horse inside which
they hid soldiers and persuaded the Trojans to take the horse into their city. Aeneas was in the thick of the fighting, but is
persuaded by his mother to flee. Shipwrecked after various adventures on the
coast of North Africa, Aeneas finds himself at Carthage, a city being built by its
queen, Dido, with whom Aeneas falls in
love. Reminded by Mercury, messenger of
the gods, that his destiny lies not in Africa,
but Italy, Aeneas abandons Dido, who
commits suicide as he sails away. Having
reached Italy, Aeneas visits the future site
of Rome where he is entertained by
Evander, a Greek from Arcadia who has
settled on the Palatine Hill. Evander's son
Pallas, awestruck by the visitor, joins the
Trojans as they fight the Rutulians under
Turnus. In one of the battles, Turnus kills
Pallas and takes his baldric as a trophy,
much to the distress of Aeneas, who had
promised Evander to take care of his son.
The climax of the story comes in single
combat between Aeneas and Turnus: Turnus, who cannot resist the will of the gods
that Aeneas should be victor and rule in
Latium, is forced to admit defeat. Aeneas,
hovering on the point of sparing his life,
catches sight of Pallas's baldric and des-
patches Turnus to the underworld. Thus
the work ends with the hero exacting revenge for the life of Pallas, a conclusion
which has led to debate about the character of Aeneas and the behaviour of a
hero.

The importance of Aeneas lies in his
humanity and susceptibility to human
emotions and feelings, as shown especially
in his relationship with Dido. While there
is no evidence of any sexual relationship

with Pallas, the language used suggests an
intensity of feeling which goes beyond that
which Aeneas shows to his own son Ascanius, though similar to that which he shows
his father. Virgil's reticence on this may
reflect contemporary values; though Aeneas has a faithful companion, Achates, he
does not provide a primary emotional
focus for Aeneas.

C. J. Mackie, *The Characterisation of Aeneas*,
Edinburgh, 1988; E. Oliensis, 'Sons and Lovers:
Sexuality and Gender in Virgil's Poetry', in C.
Martindale (ed.) *The Cambridge Companion
to Virgil*, Cambridge, 1997: 294–311; M. C. J.
Putnam, 'Possessiveness, Sexuality, and Hero-
ism in the *Aeneid*, in *Virgil's Aeneid: Interpret-
ation and Influence*, Chapel Hill, 1995: 27–49.

Roger Pitcher

Aeschines (*c*. 390–*c*. 322 BC), classical
Greek orator. The Athenian orator Aeschines was a leading player in the diplomatic and military manoeuvres which
reached their climax in the battle of
Chaeronea (338 BC), where Philip of Macedon defeated a Greek alliance (led by
Athens and Thebes), and effectively ended
the age of independent Greek city-states.
Aeschines entered politics late, having first
served in the army (for which he was decorated), and then worked as a clerk to
various magistrates and as a tragic actor.
The latter experience honed his skills as an
orator in the democratic Assembly,
through which lay the route to political
leadership. In 346 BC he emerged as a
member of two delegations, the first seeking (unsuccessfully) to negotiate a common alliance with other Greek states, and
the second commissioned to treat with
Philip for a settlement – the short-lived
'Peace of Philocrates' (346 BC).

At this stage Demosthenes, the greatest
orator of the age, was associated with Aeschines in the search for peace, but a fundamental split soon developed between
them. Aeschines came to stand for peace-
ful coexistence with Philip, whereas Demosthenes, distrusting Philip's intentions,

advocated resistance by force. The split turned to bitter enmity when (later in 346 BC) Demosthenes, assisted by a lesser figure named Timarchus, prepared to prosecute Aeschines for his part in the peace negotiations, charging him with accepting Macedonian bribes. (The twists and turns of the ensuing diplomacy over several years cannot be pursued here, but Demosthenes finally won the political argument at the cost of military defeat on the field of Chaeronea.) It is against this background that we must view Aeschines' speech against Timarchus – one of the key documents for understanding homosexual practice in classical Athens, and the basis for K. J. Dover's epoch-making book on the subject.

Aware of Demosthenes' bribery charges, Aeschines resolved to get his legal blow in first. He prosecuted Timarchus under a law which forbade any citizen who had engaged in prostitution to speak in the assembly or exercise other civic rights, the belief being that no one prepared to sell himself could be trusted not to betray the state's interests for gold. The aim of the prosecution was not to uphold public morality but to destroy Timarchus politically and weaken his associate, Demosthenes. In view of this, and the flimsiness of the evidence, the truth of some of the charges may be open to question. But to support Aeschines' case they must have been believable as pertaining to the life-style adopted by some upper-class Athenians, and therein lies their interest for us.

Aeschines' speech begins with a catalogue of the laws which regulate the behaviour of young boys and those put in charge of them: opening hours of schools and gymnasia, the supervision of attendants and trainers, the ban on parents or other relatives hiring out their kin for prostitution. As for adults, though a moral distinction is drawn between the role of the kept man (*hetairos*) or prostitute (*pornos*) on the one hand and 'honourable love' (*dikaios eros*) on the other, there

seems to have been no law banning prostitution as such on the part of a citizen: indeed it emerges later in the speech that the state exacted a tax on prostitutes.

Aeschines claims that by common repute, Timarchus practised prostitution in several forms over many years. His reports are graphic. Once past puberty, Timarchus went to live with a doctor in the Piraeus, pretending to be a medical student, but in fact living as a rent boy. He attracted the attentions of an apparently respectable and wealthy (older) citizen named Misgolas, who paid Timarchus a large sum to come and live with him. Devoted to music and amazingly keen on boys, Misgolas found Timarchus ready for every kind of sensuality, whether in sex or gluttony. So claims Aeschines, though his recognition that had Timarchus done no more than stay as Misgolas's lover his conduct would have been 'reasonable' suggests a degree of exaggeration in the charges of unbridled dissipation.

Leaving Misgolas, Timarchus took up with a certain Anticles, and after him a wealthy slave in the public services named Pittalacus, whom he met while dicing and cock-fighting. Once again nameless abuses of Timarchus's body are mentioned. There next appeared a man named Hegesandrus, an eminent citizen who had been paymaster with a general in the Hellespont. Returning to Athens, Hegesandrus lured Timarchus away from Pittalacus. The ensuing bad blood erupted in a drunken public brawl, in which Pittalacus received a whipping. Lawsuits followed, but Pittalacus, recognising that his money could not win against Hegesandrus and his upper-class friends, withdrew. Aeschines damns Hegesandrus with the claim that as he now kept Timarchus as a woman, so he had previously lived as the wife of a man named Leodamas. Here (and elsewhere) the severest censure is due to a man who allows himself to be used as a woman.

But while Aeschines lambasts Timarchus and his friends for sexual excesses, he is careful not to condemn 'honourable eros'. He imagines a general coming to the rostrum to attack him for undermining the basis of Athenian culture. His critic will recall the great heroes who were lovers – HARMODIUS AND ARISTOGITON, ACHILLES and Patroclus. Aeschines endorses friendships of this kind, quoting Homer, and capping the reference with a couplet of Euripides in praise of an *eros* which leads to virtue. He also recognises that parents pray for handsome sons, and expect them to have lovers. He even names five mature men of eminent beauty among his contemporaries, who had many lovers without attracting censure, and three youths and boys of whom the same could be said. Perhaps most remarkably, Aeschines acknowledges that he himself is *erotikos* (a lover of boys), and has been involved in quarrels on that account. He had also written poems (by implication, of an amatory nature), though they had sometimes been misrepresented.

The charges of prostitution were supplemented by accusations of wasting a substantial patrimony and, in the event, Timarchus was found guilty of speaking unlawfully in the Assembly. As for Aeschines, his political career continued until he lost his final oratorical encounter with Demosthenes – over the question whether the latter deserved a 'crown' for his services to the state (330 BC). He died around 322 BC.

K. J. Dover, *Greek Homosexuality*, London, 1978; R. L. Fox, 'Aeschines and Athenian Democracy', in R. Osborne and S. Hornblower (eds) *Ritual, Finance, Politics*, 1994; E. M. Harris, *Aeschines and Athenian Politics*, New York, 1995: Chap. 5.

Clifford Hindley

Agathon (and **Pausanias**) (*c.* 450–399 BC), classical Greek dramatist. As a leading poet and writer of tragedies, Agathon would have qualified for a substantial entry in any Athenian *Who's Who* published in the early fourth century BC. He was ranked next to the three great tragedians, Aeschylus, Sophocles and Euripides, whose work is still celebrated today. But none of Agathon's plays has survived, and his work is known only through a handful of brief fragments. He is also remembered as the lover of Pausanias in a relationship which (by ancient Greek standards) was of exceptional longevity.

The son of Tisamenus of Athens, Agathon was born around 450 BC. In his poetry he developed a florid style under the influence of the sophist Gorgias (a style reflected by PLATO in the encomium on love assigned to Agathon in the *Symposium*). He was the first to write interludes for the chorus unconnected with the plot of the play; he also sometimes invented plots and characters rather than follow the earlier custom of drawing upon well known mythological stories.

Agathon won first prize for tragedy at the festival of Lenaea in 416 BC, and the banquet described in Plato's *Symposium*, hosted by Agathon himself, was held to celebrate this victory. Also present was Pausanias, by then long recognised as Agathon's *erastes* (lover). We first meet this couple at a distinguished gathering in the house of Protagoras the Sophist, dated to 433 BC. Here Agathon is referred to as a youth in his late teens, possessed of a noble nature and great beauty. He reclines next to Pausanias, and, says the narrator, 'I would not be surprised if he turned out to be Pausanias's boyfriend' (Plato, *Protagorus* 315). As for Pausanias, he is clearly already a grown man, and in Plato's *Symposium* (set some fifteen years later), it is clearly acknowledged that he and Agathon are lovers. Indeed, ARISTOPHANES in the dialogue refers to them as perhaps an example of those homosexual couples who (in his myth) result from the bisection of an originally all-male creature.

Virtually nothing is known of Pausanias outside of Plato's *Symposium*. It seems, however, fair to assume that his contribution to the dialogue represents the kind of thing the historical Pausanias might have said. It describes an ideal of boy-love, including physical intimacy, provided that the relationship serves a pedagogical purpose and is untainted by the expectation of financial or political gain. As for Agathon, tradition depicts him as effeminate and sexually passive. In Aristophanes' play of 411 BC, *Thesmophoriazousae* (in the Penguin translation, *The Poet and the Women*), not only is Agathon's literary style parodied, but the poet himself appears in drag and (in Aristophanes' uninhibited way) is said to be readily available to be fucked.

It seems that Agathon and Pausanias remained together in the following years. When, some time between 411 and 405 BC, Agathon settled in Macedon under the rule of King Archelaus (a noted patron of the arts), Pausanias followed him. Also resident there was the poet Euripides, who himself had an erotic interest in Agathon (though by this time Agathon was aged 40 and Euripides was 72). Of this period Aelian records that when king Archelaus rebuked Agathon for constantly quarrelling with his lover, he replied that it was because the pleasure of making up was so great. On another occasion, the king admonished Euripides for kissing the bearded Agathon at a banquet. He replied that with handsome men, the autumn was as fair as the spring.

Many questions about these *amours* are unanswerable, but the history of Agathon and Pausanias may remind us, in the continuing debate about the norms of Greek pederasty, that the experience of long-lived relationships was not unknown.

K. J. Dover, 'The Date of Plato's *Symposium*', *Phronesis*, 10 (1965): 2–20, reprinted in K. J. Dover, *The Greeks and Their Legacy*, Oxford, 1988: 86–101; K. J. Dover, *Greek Homosexuality*, London, 1978; D. Ogden, 'Homosexuality and Warfare in Ancient Greece', in A. B. Lloyd (ed.) *Battle in Antiquity*, London, 1996: 107–68.
Clifford Hindley

Aguiar, Asdrúbal António d' (1883–1961), Portuguese medical doctor. Aguiar was born in Lisbon; he graduated in 1912 and immediately entered the Institute of Forensic Medicine of Lisbon as an assistant. He made his career in this institution, rising to a senior position. He also held a number of other posts, including a teaching post in the Faculty of Medicine, and, as an Army captain, was responsible for the medico-legal services of the Lisbon Garrison.

Aguiar became Portugal's leading expert on forensic medicine. He published extensively on the subject, both as a practical discipline and as an aid to interpreting history. Many of his works relate to sexual offences, including rape and indecency. He wrote accounts of the female sexual organs and described sexual and gender anomalies of various types. These included male homosexuality and lesbianism, to which he devoted several works.

In *Evolução da Pederastia e do Lesbismo na Europa* (*Evolution of Pederasty and Lesbianism in Europe*), written in 1918 and published in 1926, he described the situation of homosexuals, both male and female, in the countries of Europe, including Portugal. The opening chapter summarises contemporary knowledge about manifestations of homosexuality, noting that homosexuals were to be found in all social classes, and listing the slang terms, meeting-places, occupations, average ages of male prostitutes, examples of blackmail, ways of dressing and talking, physical characteristics, emotional relationships, sexual practices and social behaviour of male homosexuals and lesbians. The sources are the medical and forensic treatises of the late nineteenth century. The rest of the work comprises a vast compendium of historical information about male and female homosexuality, divided by period and country. Although most of the content is drawn from published works, the section on contemporary Portugal includes a number of recent anecdotes and reproduces case notes on prisoners arrested for

homosexuality whom Aguiar had personally interviewed. The final part summarises Portuguese law on homosexual acts.
This work is written from a detached,
professional viewpoint and is relatively
objective.

Aguiar's work complemented that of
another author published under the
auspices of the Lisbon forensic institute.
Arlindo Camilo Monteiro was a doctor
interested both in the history of medicine
and in artistic and literary matters who
gave a number of papers at scientific conferences before moving to Brazil. His
*Amor Sáfico e Socrático (Sapphic and So-
cratic Love)*, published in 1922, is a com-
pendious work containing information on
all aspects of homosexuality but concentrating on Portugal. In the first part, Monteiro describes the historical evidence for
homosexuality in Antiquity and in the
countries of Europe and the rest of the
world, before going into more detail about
the Iberian Peninsula and Portugal. The
longer second part of the work covers contemporary scientific knowledge about
homosexuality. Drawing extensively on
French, German and Italian writers, Monteiro discusses aspects of male and female
homosexuality, bisexuality and hermaphroditism, psychiatric and medical
theories, therapeutic and preventative
measures, and the legislation of foreign
countries and Portugal.

Monteiro's work is more impassioned
than that of Aguiar. He frequently uses
negative moralistic terms to describe
homosexual activity and even defends the
Inquisition against its nineteenth-century
critics, yet the sheer amount of detail and
the care with which documents are
transcribed suggests a labour of love. Occasionally he slips into a defence of homosexuals against the more extreme attacks
of writers such as Francisco Ferraz de
MACEDO, and he acknowledges the widespread prevalence of the phenomenon.

The two works show how far contemporary medico-scientific knowledge
about homosexuality had been absorbed

in Portugal by the 1920s. Their greatest
interest today, however, lies in their tran-
scription of legal texts and references to
historical events. With their detailed footnotes, they serve as invaluable guides to
historians.

Other Portuguese doctors who wrote on
homosexuality during the first half of the
twentieth century include Egas Moniz,
one of the leading medical authorities of
the day, who thought that homosexuals
could be cured, and Luís A. Duarte
Santos, a lecturer at the University of
Coimbra. Writing in 1943, Duarte Santos
rejected the idea that homosexuality was
inborn, arguing that it was caused by external factors and that homosexuals were
responsible for their actions. He ap-
plauded the recent dismissal of the poet
António BOTTO from his government post.

A. A. d'Aguiar, *Evolução da Pederastia e do
Lesbismo na Europa: Contribuição para o Estudo da Inversão Sexual* (published in *Arquivo
da Universidade de Lisboa*, 11 (1926): 335–620,
and separately as the author's *Sciencia Sexual:
Contribuições para o seu Estudo. Livro V. Ho-
mosexualidade* [1927?]); A. C. Monteiro, *Amor
Sáfico e Socrático*, Lisbon, 1922; E. Moniz, *A
Vida Sexual: Fisiologia e Patologia*, 4th edn,
Lisbon, 1918; L. A. Duarte Santos, *Sexo Inver-
tido? Considerações sobre a Homossexuali-
dade*, Coimbra, 1943.

Robert Howes

Alan of Lille (*c.* 1128–1203). Alan studied
at Paris, and taught at both Paris and
Montpellier, joining the Cistercian order
towards the end of his life. Named a
doctor universalis of the Church because
of his learning, he produced literary,
theological, penitential, exegetical and
pastoral works that exercised considerable
influence at the nascent University of
Paris. Some of his work has been subject
to conflicting interpretation, such as the
rather obscure poetic *De planctu naturae*,
written sometime before 1171 in accordance with the strict rules of classical rhetoric revived in the twelfth-century schools.

It has been argued that the work was directed against the allegedly scandalous behaviour of Archbishop Roger of York, an opponent of the martyred Thomas à Becket. Alan attacks the weakening of mankind through subjugation to the senses, and sodomy is taken particularly as a metaphor for the denial of the natural aim of humankind, i.e. the bearing of children.

In his sermons on capital sins, Alan argued that sodomy and homicide are the most serious sins, since they call forth the wrath of God, which led to the catastrophic destruction of Sodom and Gomorrah, so vividly described in Scripture. The continuing absence of life at the Dead Sea is proof of the destructive results of such sin. His *Ars praedicandi*, a manual for preachers, suggested the use of Biblical, classical and patristic sources in the composition of the ideal sermon directed against sins and providing parallel virtues in order to combat them. His chief work on penance, the *Liber poenitentialis* (1201/3?), dedicated to Henry de Sully, the Archbishop of Bourges, exercised great influence on the many manuals of penance produced as a result of the Fourth Lateran Council of 1215, which required every Christian to confess and undergo suitable penance at least once a year. Alan's identification of the sins against nature included bestiality, masturbation, oral and anal intercourse, incest, adultery, rape, sexual relations with nuns and 'sodomy', and provides detailed accounts of the proper penance to be prescribed for such acts. In addition to his battle against moral decay, Alan wrote a work against Islam, Judaism and Christian heretics (i.e. the Waldensians and Cathars), dedicated to Guillaume VIII of Montpellier, an area in southern France where heresy abounded.

M. D. Jordan, *The Invention of Sodomy in Christian Theology*, Chicago, 1997; G. R. Evans, *Alan of Lille, the Frontiers of Theology in the Later Twelfth Century*, Cambridge, 1983.
Michael Goodich

Alcuin (*c.* 732–804), English teacher. Possibly born of a noble family, Alcuin was educated in the cathedral school at York and ordained a deacon in his youth. Ælberht, his teacher, friend and patron, had been in turn a pupil and friend of Bede. Alcuin succeeded Ælberht as master of the school of York in 767, and accompanied him on various journeys to the Continent.

In 781, he met Charlemagne at Parma, and was invited to head up Charlemagne's Palatine School, which he did from 782. Charlemagne's court, itinerant from 782 to 793, eventually settled at Aachen, where Alcuin occupied an eminent place amidst an international élite of scholars, including Theodulf of Orléans, Angilbert, Einhard, Peter of Pisa, Paulinus of Aquileia and Paul the Deacon. He made only two return visits to England, in 786 and 790–793. In 796, Alcuin was asked to provide leadership to the troubled Abbey of St Martin's at Tours, where he remained until his death.

Alcuin's achievements included his considerable effectiveness as a teacher and educational administrator, regulation of the liturgy of the Frankish church, collating and re-editing the Latin Bible, reforming continental script, and presiding over the first phase of the Carolingian Revival. He was not an original thinker, and his legacy of Latin verse is competent but scarcely distinguished.

Some of his poetry (all of which is dated prior to 781–782) is homoerotic, emphasising the spiritual and idealistic aspects of his love for his friends and pupils. At Aachen, his pupils were given pet names, derived from classical allusions, chiefly from VIRGIL's *Eclogues* (themselves frequently homoerotic in tone).

Of 300 surviving letters, written in Latin, most date from the last decade of his life, and furnish very little information on his childhood, youth or early adulthood. The tone of 'passionate friendship', not uncommon between the religious in the early Middle Ages, can be gauged from the following letter (Epistle 10): 'I think of your love and friendship with such sweet memories, reverend bishop, that I long for that lovely time when I may be able to clutch the neck of your sweetness with the fingers of my desires. Alas, if only it were granted to me ... to be transported to you, how would I sink into your embrace, ... how would I cover, with tightly pressed lips, not only your eyes, ears, and mouth but also your every finger and your toes, not once but many a time.'

At the end of his life, Alcuin had a reputation for holiness, yet he is not included in the canon of saints and never advanced to holy orders beyond those of deacon.

J. Boswell, *Christianity, Social Tolerance, and Homosexuality: Gay People in Western Europe from the Beginning of the Christian Era to the Fourteenth Century*, Chicago, 1980; P. Goodman (ed.) *Alcuin, the Bishops, Kings and Saints of York*, Oxford, 1982.

David J. Bromell

Aleramo, Sibilla (1876–1966), Italian writer. The carefree and happy childhood of Sibilla Aleramo, who was born Rina Faccio in Alessandria, came to a dramatic end at the age of 16, when she was forced to marry the man who had raped her. The future author of the novel *Una donna* (1906), her masterpiece and a true and accurate denunciation of the condition of women in Italy at the beginning of the century, attended only primary school. In *Una donna* Aleramo recounts her own life down to her decision to leave both the husband who had been imposed on her and their son. She moved to Rome, where she lived with the poet Giovanni Cena, did voluntary social work, worked in the cause of Italian feminism, was active in the National Women's Union and organised evening and holiday schools for the poor and for women.

In 1908, at a women's congress, she met Cordula (Lina) Poletti, a student nine years younger than herself. It was Poletti who declared her love for Aleramo and, a year later, they began the relationship which the author described in the novel *Il passaggio* (1919). *Il passaggio* won flattering praise from COLETTE, Romaine BROOKS and Anna de Noailles, but Italian critics were divided between supporters and detractors. Aleramo and Poletti were too different from each other; even as Aleramo continued to remain fascinated by the one who seemed the very incarnation of the 'new woman' and whose freedom, assertiveness and pride she appreciated, she remarked with increasing annoyance on Poletti's efforts to 'masculinise' herself. 'She felt she had a man's heart', Aleramo wrote in *Il passaggio*, 'but I – no one can judge whether more dementedly or clairvoyantly – was instead touched by what remained in her of that which was identical to my own self.'

In one of the one hundred letters which remain of their correspondence, Aleramo exhorted Poletti not to reject her own femininity and to live out her love for women as a woman. Their relationship came to an end after about a year. In 1910, Poletti entered a marriage of convenience, quickly followed by a separation. Aleramo meanwhile in 1913 went to Paris, where she frequented the salon of Natalie Clifford BARNEY and wrote the story 'La Pensierosa' (collected in *Andando e stando*), in which, proceeding from feminist theory, she delineated a visionary apologia for feminine spirituality separate from and independent of masculine spirituality. In *Andando e stando* (1921), Aleramo vividly described the world of Parisian lesbians through impassioned portraits of Colette ('Listen to her song, and ask for nothing else'), Barney (a spirit 'of amber and steel') and de Noailles ('a delightful miracle: a woman and a genius, a queen and a fawn'). For the rest of her life, Aleramo wandered between Paris and Capri, from Corsica to Assisi. As a Communist activist in the post-war period, she incessantly travelled around Italy giving lectures to worker and peasant groups. Her contacts with the modest people who came to hear her and showered her with affection and gratitude moved her deeply, and reinforced her great dream of one day being able to see a better life for all of humanity: 'on our earth worthy at last of grain, olive and rose' (as she said in the last verses of her poem 'Va lontano il nosto sorriso' in *Luci della mia sera*, 1956).

B. Conti and A. Morino (eds) *Sibilla Aleramo ed il suo tempo*, Milan, 1981; *Sibilla Aleramo. Coscienza e scrittura*, Milan, 1986; A. Buttafuoco and M. Zancan (eds) *Sibilla Aleramo: una biografia intelletuale*, Milan, 1988.

Maria Di Rienzo

Aletrino, Arnold (1858–1918), Dutch author. This doctor and novelist belonged to the second generation of the literary bent of the 1880s that brought modern literature to The Netherlands.

Aletrino wrote some very sombre novels on the life of hospital nurses. He specialised in criminal anthropology and wrote his first essay on 'uranism' in 1897. It was a review of M. A. RAFFALOVICH's *Uranisme et unisexualité* (1896). He was the first Dutch figure of some repute to defend the naturalness of homosexual desire, and would continue to write on the topic, shifting his position from the stance of Raffalovich – that homosexuals can be as masculine as normal men – to the position of Magnus HIRSCHFELD – that they are a third sex. In 1901 he addressed the fifth conference of criminal anthropology, held in Amsterdam. His position that uranism is natural and should be accepted was opposed by most other participants, foremost by Cesare Lombroso, the Italian founder of the discipline. After the conference, the Calvinist prime minister raged against the University of Amsterdam, where Aletrino, he claimed, would teach the sins of Sodom. When his friend Jacob Israël DE HAAN published the first gay novel, dedicated to him and having him as a leading character, Aletrino was not amused and bought all available copies to save his reputation. His subsequent booklet on uranism was published under a

pseudonym. In 1912 he belonged, but only in name, to the founders of the Dutch chapter of the Wissenschaftlich-humanitäre Komitee. Aletrino was married twice and laboured under severe addiction to morphine. There is reason to assume that his portrait by de Haan as bisexual and slightly sadist was not far from the truth.

K. Joosse, *Arnold Aletrino. Pessimist met perspectief*, Amsterdam, 1986.

Gert Hekma

Alexander the Great (356–323 BC), Hellenistic ruler. Alexander became king of Macedon in 336 BC, shortly after his father, Philip, had won hegemony over the Greek states at the battle of Chaeronea (338 BC). The young prince had been given a Greek education under the philosopher Aristotle, and among his classmates was a young Macedonian named Hephaestion, who was to become his lifelong friend.

Alexander himself was possessed with the ambition to lead Macedonians and Greeks in a great war of revenge against the Persian Empire. Launching his invasion of Asia Minor (modern Turkey) in 334 BC, he had within ten years established himself as king, by force of military conquest, from the Aegean seaboard to the northwest frontier of India. In 324 he returned to the Persian capital, worn out by the unremitting pursuit of glory (and, it must be said, alcohol). The following spring he fell ill of a fever and died on 13 June 323 BC.

One ancient writer claims that Alexander was madly keen on boys, but only two names of possible male lovers are known to us – Hephaestion and Bagoas. Hephaestion remained a devoted companion until his death in 324 BC, and also played an important military and public role, first as commander of the Companion Cavalry, and later as 'Chiliarch', second in rank only to the king himself. No ancient source declares unequivocally that they were lovers, though a number of anecdotes show that they were extremely close. Thus, on a visit to Troy, Alexander laid a wreath on the tomb of ACHILLES, while Hephaestion similarly honoured that of Patroclus. Following Hephaestion's death, Alexander exhibited an extravagant grief. He lay long hours on the corpse, and would not be comforted. He ordered public mourning, funeral rites on a gigantic scale, and the payment of semi-divine honours to Hephaestion.

Being about the same age, the two men did not conform to the usual pattern of Greek pederasty. We may surmise, however, that in their youth they had had a love affair whose physical passion matured into a close friendship of mutual esteem and affection – an evolution which Aristotle noted in his *Ethics* as a common occurrence.

Far less prominent, but high in Alexander's affections, was the Persian eunuch, Bagoas, described by Plutarch as the king's *eromenos* (beloved boy). A youth of outstanding beauty, Bagoas was brought to Alexander as a gift by a high-ranking Persian, who hoped to secure favours for himself. Bagoas's influence over the king could be turned to intrigue – as when he plotted the destruction of a courtier who publicly called him the king's whore. The troops, however, seem to have relished the relationship. In a great public dancing contest, the prize was (unsurprisingly) awarded to Bagoas. But when he took his seat beside Alexander, the crowd insisted that the king kiss his favourite – which he did, apparently with gusto.

Alexander also married at least three wives, two of them for political reasons. His last marriage, to the Bactrian Roxane, was, seemingly, a love match. She bore him a posthumous son.

That an absolute ruler should enjoy multiple sexual affairs was unremarkable, but Alexander's love for Hephaestion was no mere dalliance, and it must have provided significant support for him in all his frenetic activity. As for Bagoas, beyond the sex and the sinister intrigues, one can perhaps see here one of many indications of Alexander's desire to transcend the racial divisions of his empire.

Alexander was not the only Greek general to have pederastic relationships. Many instances can be quoted, both honourable and the reverse: from lovers standing by one another in battle, to commanders deserting their posts for their lovers' embrace. An honourable military pederasty was supported by the belief that a lover's presence would inspire a man to avoid the shame of cowardly action. This was the rationale for the famous Sacred Band of Thebes, which was composed of pairs of lovers. Numbering 300, the Band was established around 378 BC. It fought in many campaigns culminating at the battle of Chaeronea, where its warriors died to a man defending the Greek alliance against Philip of Macedon.

P. Green, *Alexander of Macedon*, London, 1991; E. Badian, 'The Eunuch Bagoas', *Classical Quarterly*, NS 8 (1958); T. Africa, 'Homosexuals in Greek History', *Journal of Psychohistory*, 9, 4 (1982); D. Ogden, 'Homosexuality and Warfare in Ancient Greece', in A. B. Lloyd (ed.) *Battle in Antiquity*, London, 1996.

Clifford Hindley

Algarotti, Francesco (1712–1764), Italian essayist, popular science writer, poet and diplomat. Born in Venice, the son of a merchant, Algarotti attended excellent schools, showing interest in both science and literature. Indeed he won acclaim as a writer of books on science for the general public; one of his most famous works was *Il newtonianesimo per le dame* (*Newtonism for Ladies*), published in 1737.

In 1734 he had visited Paris, where he made friends with the leading figures of the French Enlightenment, among them VOLTAIRE. Two years later he was in London, where he was made a fellow of the Royal Society. Algarotti also met Lord John Hervey (1696–1743), a politician notorious for his bisexuality, who, according to Rictor Norton, 'fell passionately in love with him. Unfortunately Hervey's very good friend Lady Mary Wortley Montagu proved to be his rival . . ., for Algarotti was also bisexual. Thus began one of the silliest love-triangles in the eighteenth century. After a brief summer in London, . . . Algarotti returned to Venice. . . . Soon he received an avalanche of *billets doux* from both of his devoted English admirers. Lord Hervey wrote, 'Je vous aime de tout mon coeur' ['I love you with all my heart']; Lady Mary wrote, 'Je vous aimerai toute ma vie' ['I will love you all my life']. Hervey and Lady Mary boasted to one another how frequently they were receiving letters from Algarotti. In one pair of letters that must have been a source of great amusement to the young Italian, Hervey invited Algarotti to come to him in England while Lady Mary invited herself to go to him in Italy. Algarotti returned polite encouragements to both, but had his own affairs to attend to. At this precise moment he had taken up with a young man named Firmaon in Milan, with whom he made a leisurely tour of southern France. Lord Hervey playfully scolded Algarotti for not writing more often; Lady Mary sent agonizing pleas for more missives. Lord Hervey wisely controlled his hurt; Lady Mary foolishly kept posting *cris du coeur*. Lord Hervey grew jealous; Lady Mary became distraught.'

Algarotti expressed thanks to Hervey, dedicating to him six of the letters which make up one of his most celebrated works, *Viaggi di Russia* (1739–1751). When he returned to London in 1739, he stayed with Hervey, who thereby saw him again. Only three months after arriving, however, Algarotti left for Russia, whence he wrote to Hervey and asked the Englishman not to forget him and to continue to love him. Hervey put on a good face, but Lady Mary, by contrast, left her home, family, friends, husband and country and fled to Venice, hoping to be reunited with her lover as soon as he had returned from his journey.

On his way back to London, Algarotti stopped for eight days at the Prussian court, where he made the acquaintance of the heir apparent, Frederick (1712–1786), his exact peer, who found him irresistible. Eight months later, after the death of the old king, the new King FREDERICK II of Prussia (later called 'Frederick the Great') asked Algarotti to attend his coronation. Again abandoning Hervey (Algarotti was never to see him again), Algarotti moved to Prussia. He became the king's intimate friend – soon replacing his previous lover, Baron Keyserling – and, over the next decade, amassed honours, political appointments (notably as court chamberlain), the title of count and diplomatic postings. He nevertheless did not renounce affairs with other men, as evidenced by a letter from Voltaire, who joked on 15 December 1740 that seeing 'tender Algarotti strongly hugging handsome Lugeac, his young friend, I seem to see Socrates reinvigorated on Alcibiades' back'. (Charles-Antoine de Guérin, Marquis de Lugeac, was an attaché at the French embassy in Berlin.) Algarotti and Frederick's idyll lasted for two years; in 1742, when their relations cooled, the Italian joined the court of the King of Poland in Dresden. In 1746, the two made up and Algarotti returned to Frederick in Potsdam, though not to the king's bedchamber, which was now filled with grenadiers.

In 1753, in declining health because of tuberculosis, Algarotti left for Italy, where he dedicated himself to writing and study, and continued to exchange courteous letters with Lady Mary. The search for a healthier climate in the last years of his life led Algarotti to Pisa, where he eventually died. Frederick the Great, in memory of their relationship, constructed an imposing mausoleum for him; it is still visible in the southern wing of the famous Camposanto.

G. Dall'Orto, 'Socrate veneziano', *Babilonia*, 165 (April 1998): 88–9; M. Elliman and F. Roll, *The Pink Plaque Guide to London*, London, 1986: 100–1; R. Halsband, *Lord*

Hervey: Eighteenth-Century Courtier, Oxford, 1973; R. Norton, *Mother Clap's Molly House*, London, 1992: 146–58.

Giovanni Dall'Orto

Alger, Jr, Horatio (1832–1899), American author. Born the son of a Harvard-educated Unitarian minister in Chelsea, Massachusetts, Alger's name is synonymous with the American dream of rags-to-riches personal success. He owes his place as a cultural symbol more to biographers and historians than to the reality of his life and achievements.

Only five-feet-two-inches in adulthood, Horatio was a frail child and was educated at home until age 10. Entering Harvard in 1848, he was an excellent student, eighth in his class in 1852. Encouraged by receiving the Bowdoin Prize for his writing efforts at Harvard, Alger first attempted to establish himself as a poet while moving through a variety of teaching, writing and editing jobs. Although a number of his stories and poems were published in *Harper's* and *Putnam's* magazines, he was unable to make a living as a writer. He entered Cambridge Divinity School in 1857, graduating in 1860, after which he toured Europe. Returning from Europe, he settled in Cambridge and continued to teach and write. In 1864, the year *Frank's Campaign*, his first juvenile fiction, was published, he was appointed minister of the Unitarian Society in Brewster, Massachusetts. Alger's tenure as Brewster's popular Unitarian minister came to a sudden end in 1866, when he was ignominiously dismissed for having 'indecent relations' with a number of local youths, allegations which he made no effort to deny.

After a quiet 'disappearance' from Brewster, Alger relocated to New York City, which would remain his home for the next three decades. There he began to write in earnest, producing nearly one hundred juvenile novels. In 1867, *Ragged Dick*, Alger's most popular and only best-selling novel, was published, followed by a seven-book series, including *Mark the Match Boy* and *Ben the Luggage Boy*, titles which, regardless of Alger's intentions, seem aimed at an audience which shared his sexual preferences. Over the next decade, the prolific writer produced numerous multi-volume juvenile series with individual titles such as *Tattered Tom*, *Phil the Fiddler*, *The Young Outlaw*, *Luck and Pluck* and the Pacific Series, for which he made the first of two tours of the American West to gather local colour. The tone of these novels, in which Alger poses as a highly moralistic teacher of young boys, seems to reflect a conscious effort to atone for his early shame as well as to counteract what were surely persistent desires. Personal motives aside, Alger's social consciousness was genuine and throughout his life he espoused environmental, temperance and children's aid reforms. Despite his constant stream of publications, he was never financially secure and for many years augmented his income by tutoring the children of wealthy New Yorkers, including banker Joseph Seligman. In 1896, when years of overwork precipitated a decline in his always poor health, Alger retired to South Natick, Massachusetts, where he died.

The pervasive Horatio Alger myth, in which the author is lionised as a champion of capitalism and personal financial success, is in direct contrast to his moral tracts in which young boys, virtuous by nature, struggle against temptation, including the mercenary evils of the Gilded Age, to lead successful and morally upright lives. Were it not for a misrepresentation in a turn-of-the-century edition of the *Dictionary of American Biography* of the significant influence of works such as *Struggling Upward* and *The Store Boy*, Alger might have receded into historical obscurity. Instead, mid-century historians picked up on the exaggeration and created a myth. Reputable scholars, including Samuel Eliot Morrison, Henry Steele Commager and Frederick Lewis Allen, credited him as one of the great mythmakers of the modern world with a cultural influence surpassed only by Mark Twain's. In reality, his modestly successful, albeit prolific, output could lay no such claims on culture in his own lifetime, and throughout his career he struggled without success for acclaim as a major writer not of juvenile novels but adult fiction. Alger, who never married, was successful, however, in shrouding his personal life in complete privacy. Other than respectable relationships with young students, relatives and wards, it remains unsubstantiated that he ever continued or found fulfilment in the kind of relationships for which he was banished from Brewster.

E. P. Hoyt, *Horatio's Boys*; *The Life and Works of Horatio Alger, Jr.*, Radnor, Penn. 1974; G. Scharnhorst, *The Lost Life of Horatio Alger, Jr.*, Bloomington, Ind. 1985.

A. M. Wentink

Andersen, Hans Christian (1805–1875), Danish author. Born into the lowest proletariat of the Danish provincial town of Odense, Andersen in 1819 travelled to Copenhagen in order to pursue a career in the theatre. A process of upward social mobility that was remarkable for his times now began. He lived by himself, had very little money, but was financially supported by patrons to whom he had introduced himself. His strange ability to gain entrance into the families of the middle and upper classes, even the royal family, probably owed much to his talent for being sweetly and weirdly entertaining and amusing. One of these houses was the Collin family, which for the rest of his life became the centre of his existence. Jonas Collin, a prominent civil servant and co-manager of the Royal Theatre, took charge of Andersen's education and secured a royal grant through which Andersen was a boarder at the high school (gymnasium) from 1822 to 1828. In 1829 he published his first novel. From then on he was a well known literary figure in Copenhagen. Novels,

poems, travelogues and plays followed. In 1833–1834 he travelled on a royal grant through Germany and France to Italy. From 1840 travelling became an almost compulsive habit which took him (in 30 trips) to all corners of Europe and made him the most cosmopolitan of Danish authors. 'To travel is to live', he said.

In 1835 Andersen published his first collection of the fairy tales that made him immortal among poets. In an autobiographical sketch two years earlier, he had written of his own life as a fairy tale, in which the hand of God directs everything for the best. In 1847 he published his autobiography, *The Fairy Tale of My Life*. By then he had achieved the fame as a poet and an artist that he had longed for since childhood, and honours were bestowed upon him nationally and internationally. More than most authors, Andersen saw the connection between life and art as decisive. 'Reality [is] the most beautiful fairy tale.'

Andersen's life is like an open book. His amazing desire to communicate was embodied in intimate diaries, autobiographies and thousands of letters to his many friends. In his fiction he is nearly always present in a highly personal manner. Clearly, Andersen conceived of himself as being different from others.

Eighteen years after Andersen's death a newspaper in 1893 for the first time hinted at his homosexuality. In 1901 the Danish author Carl HANSEN FAHLBERG published an article in Magnus HIRSCHFELD's *Jahrbuch für sexuelle Zwischenstufen*, 'H. C. Andersen. Beweis seiner Homosexualität' ('H. C. Andersen: Proof of his Homosexuality'). The analysis of Andersen's conception of himself as a homosexual and of his management of his sexuality in Hans Mayer's *Aussenseiter* (1975) is perceptive, although not always founded in fact. Mayer's stern judgement of Andersen as a suppressed 'homosexual' is heavy-handed and influenced by his concept of homosexuality as a transhistorical essence.

Andersen scholarship concurs that Andersen, who remained unmarried, probably never experienced genital sex with anybody, man or woman. He fell in love with women as well as men. Most of the correspondance with the women he fell in love with (Riborg Voight, Louise Collin) was destroyed in his own lifetime. His love for men was probably considered less improper than his romantic feelings for women and his love letters to men have been preserved and are to a large extent published. The most important love of his life was undoubtedly Edvard Collin (1808–1886), son of his benefactor, Jonas Collin. Although Andersen and Edvard remained close friends all their life, Andersen's feelings for Edvard were not reciprocated. Edvard maintained an emotional distance that hurt Andersen deeply. Contemporaries saw Andersen's overt and unmistakable affection for Edvard and his yearning for 'warm friendship' with Edvard, as well as with other men, as childish, morbid, unmanly, overwrought, sentimental and romantic. Andersen himself wrote to Edvard in 1833 that it was his own 'softness and half womanliness' that made him cling to Edvard, and in the draft of an 1835 letter to Edvard that was not sent, he wrote that his love for him was not overwrought sentimentality but 'a pure, noble feeling'. Edvard's wedding in August 1836 made Andersen review their relationship. The fairy tale The Little Mermaid (1837) is an existential and poetic reflection and clarification of his love for Edvard – the impossible and fatal love of a little mermaid for a prince who never really sees her, except for her art, her dancing on the small feet that hurt as if she were treading on knives. Andersen wrote no more love letters to Edvard.

Andersen's infatuation with young men led to a number of sentimental friendships lasting several years, rather one-sided 'love-affairs', notably with divinity student Ludvig Müller (1832–1834), hereditary Grand-Duke Carl Alexander of Saxe-Weimar-Eisenach (1844–1848), ballet dancer Harald Scharff (1860s) and theatre manager Robert Watt (late 1860s).

In the farce Hr. Rasmussen (1846), Andersen anonymously presented a model of close friendship between two men by having them enter a formal engagement. The play was performed only once, at the Royal Theatre, and failed.

In 1860 Karl Maria KERTBENY, who later became one of the early pioneers of homosexual emancipation – and inventor of the word 'homosexual' – looked up Andersen in Geneva. Although Kertbeny, according to Andersen, was 'extremely kind and highly spiritual', their meeting made Andersen feel 'inexplicably sinister' and seems to have triggered an almost suicidal depression. Andersen hurried home. Their meeting was an encounter of two very different concepts of men's love for men, a meeting between two historically separate ages.

Although Andersen cannot be labelled 'homosexual', his personality and his lifestyle make him easily identifiable as a precursor of the homosexual man who emerged soon afterwards.

H. Bech, 'A Dung Beetle in Distress: Hans Christian Andersen Meets Karl Maria Kertbeny, Geneva 1860', Journal of Homosexuality, 35, 3/4 (1998); E. Bredsdorff, Hans Christian Andersen: The Story of His Life and Works, London, 1975; H. C. Andersens Dagbøger 1825–1875 I–XII, Copenhagen, 1971–1976; H. Ringblom, 'Om H. C. Andersens påståede homosexualitet', Anderseniana 1997, Odense, 1997: 41–58; W. von Rosen, Månens Kulør. Studier i dansk bøssehistorie 1628–1912, Copenhagen, 1993: 323–73, 618–28.

Wilhelm von Rosen

Anderson, Margaret (1886–1973), American editor and novelist. Anderson was born and raised in Indianapolis, Indiana, leaving to attend the Western College for Women in Oxford, Ohio. After college, she moved to Chicago, Illinois, where she began reviewing books for a religious weekly and was subsequently hired by the

Dial, a literary review where her editorial skills were noted.

In 1914 she founded the *Little Review*, a periodical featuring writings, photos and illustrations by both US and expatriate authors on modernism, feminism, avant-garde art, psychoanalysis and philosophy. She featured a notable group of writers in the magazine, including James Joyce, Amy LOWELL, Emma Goldman, Ezra Pound, Gertrude STEIN, Tristan Tzara, Ernest Hemingway, Djuna BARNES and Sherwood Anderson. The motto of the magazine was 'Making No Compromise with the Public Taste' and this attitude periodically cost her financially. At one point she lost her office and home and established a campsite on the shores of Lake Michigan, but continued to issue the publication. She later appointed Jane Heap Assistant Editor for the magazine.

The *Little Review* began serialising James Joyce's *Ulysses* in 1918, but the four issues containing the novel were seized by the US Post Office and burned because of the sexually explicit material they contained. Anderson and Heap were brought up on charges of publishing obscenity and fined $50, but this did not discourage them and the magazine stayed in print for another 11 years. In 1924 Anderson moved to Paris and became an integral part of the literary and lesbian communities there.

Heap and Anderson met during the early years of the magazine's publication, and Anderson found Heap to be both fascinating and a wonderful literary commentator. The two women fell deeply in love and stayed together for many years, living in Chicago, California and Paris. Anderson was also closely attached to Georgette Leblanc, a French actress and singer, and promoted the work and relationships of many women in her life. The last major love of her life was Dorothy Caruso, an American woman in the publishing industry.

Anderson was primarily an editor, publisher and literary mentor for numerous modern writers, but she also published a novel, *Forbidden Fires* (1996), and a three-volume autobiography, *My Thirty Years' War* (1930), *The Fiery Fountains* (1951) and *The Strange Necessity* (1962). She died in France.

M. Anderson, *My Thirty Years' War*, New York, 1930; M. Anderson, *The Strange Necessity*, New York, 1962.

Sarah Holmes

Andrade, Mário de (1893–1945), Brazilian writer. Mário Raul Moraes de Andrade was a leading figure of the modernist movement that débuted in São Paulo in 1922 and revolutionised Brazilian literary, artistic and cultural production. Born to a lower middle-class family in the city of São Paulo, Andrade first worked as a piano teacher and journalist. He become one of the most versatile Brazilian writers of the twentieth century, producing poetry, short stories and novels. Andrade also excelled as a music, art and literary critic, as well as a folklorist, musicologist and ethnographer. His collection of poems *Paulicéia Desvairada* (*Hallucinating São Paulo*), published in 1928, is the seminal statement of the modernist movement, and his novel *Macunaíma*, appearing the same year and based on extensive research of Brazil folklore and popular culture, analyses the Brazilian national character. The author also served as the Director of São Paulo's Department of Culture from 1935 to 1938.

Andrade remained very protective of his private life. In 1929 he severed contacts with Oswald de Andrade, another titan of the modernist movement (and no relation to the author), after Oswald publicly imputed Mário's effeminacy in the *Revista de Antropofagia* ('Cannibalist Review'), a literary supplement of the *Diário de São Paulo*. Referring to Mário de Andrade as 'our Miss São Paulo, translated into the masculine', Oswald de Andrade signed the article with the pseudonym Cabo Machado in an allusion to a sensuous and nationalistic poem, 'Cabo Machado'

(Corporal Machado), that Mário de Andrade had written in 1926 about a soldier by that name.

Moacir Werneck de Castro, a member of a group of young Bohemians who socialised with Mário de Andrade when he lived in Rio de Janeiro from 1938 to 1941, later recalled that he and his cohorts had no idea that Andrade had led a double life or was a homosexual. The famous author would spend endless hours with this new generation of aspiring writers and intellectuals, savouring their company while apparently never initiating any sexual contacts with his youthful colleagues. Yet in retrospect, when learning about Andrade's homoerotic desires, Castro recognised the profoundly homosexual content of some of his writing.

Indeed, Andrade led a discreet private life. Although it is currently widely acknowledged that he experienced strong sexual attractions towards other men, few details have been published about this aspect of his life. One of his short stories, 'Frederico Paciência', however, deals rather directly with his own homosexuality. Written and revised many times between 1924 and 1942, it was published posthumously in 1947. The story describes the romantic friendship of two students (one presumably being the author) who drift apart without consummating their desires other than through furtive kisses and affectionate embraces. The narrator expresses relief that the friendship has dissolved and the two are separated by distance, as if to imply that he, therefore, does not have to face his own homosexual feelings for Frederico Paciência. Although Andrade did not create a sick and pathetic protagonist, he nevertheless left the reader with the impression that it was far better to repress homoerotic feelings than to express them openly. In many ways, this short story paralleled the real life of the modernist writer who also attempted to contain his sexual desires for other men and shrouded his personal life in a veil of secrecy.

M. de Andrade, 'Frederico Paciência', in *Contos Novos* (*New Stories*), São Paulo, 1947, republished in *My Deep Dark Pain is Love: A Collection of Latin American Gay Fiction*, ed. W. Leyland, trans. E. A. Lacey, San Francisco, 1983; W. Martins, *The Modernist Idea: A Critical Survey of Brazilian Writing in the Twentieth Century*, New York, 1970; M. W. de Castro, *Mário de Andrade: exílio no Rio*, Rio de Janeiro, 1989.

James N. Green

Andræ, Poul (Georg) (1843–1928), Danish civil servant, author. Andræ was a son of Prime Minister C. G. Andræ and independently wealthy. He graduated in law in 1868 and became a civil servant in the colonial and finance administration. In 1894 he obtained an early discharge from the civil service, with a pension, by producing a medical certificate issued by the Austrian psychiatrist Richard von KRAFFT-EBING, probably for 'nervousness' caused by 'contrary sexuality'. Andræ's literary production centred on the history of his father's political career. As the son of a prime minister he was appointed Cavalier of the Chamber in 1884; in 1912 he became (titular) Councillor of State.

The publication in 1891 of a lecture on 'perverted sexuality' by the prominent psychiatrist and professor Knud Pontoppidan – the first medical treatise in Denmark on homosexuality – incited an anonymous Danish 'contrary sexual' to publish a very long and learned article, 'The Feeling of Contrary Sexuality', in the leading journal of medicine. It is virtually a certainty that Andræ was the author behind the pseudonym 'Tandem' (Latin: 'at last'). The article was based on the author's own experiences as one who 'more than anyone else in this country, knows of contrary sexuals in the most varied professions'. Tandem relied heavily on Krafft-Ebing's understanding of contrary sexuality as an illness connected with a neuropathological condition. However, as the editor of the journal remarked, the author was somewhat one-sided. With

great skill he managed to interpret Krafft-
Ebing to mean that genuine 'contrary sexuals' were absolutely never attracted to the
sexually immature, nor did they – in the
main – commit sodomy (anal intercourse).
Instances of such behaviour were not
caused by congenital contrary sexuality,
but should be understood as perversities
committed by otherwise heterosexual
men. Tandem's account of the experiences
of 'a patient who cannot avoid ejacula-
tions' while watching naked young men on
a nearby bathing raft was an example of
the abnormally early and strong sexual
drive of the 'contrary sexual', but may also
have been a personal memoir.

Indirectly the author demonstrated that
'contrary sexuality' was not opposed to
respectability and could be combined with
learning, insight and intelligence, and
found in society's better classes. Thus
Andræ was the first in Denmark to publicly defend homosexuals. This he did by
allying himself as an emancipationist
with psychiatry.

In later life Andræ became a well known
character in Copenhagen's café milieu,
odd, awkward and generous. In his will he
left a sum of money for the translation
and publication (in 1928) of Magnus HIR-
SCHFELD's 1901 pamphlet *What Should
The People Know About The Third Sex?*

S. C. Bech, 'Poul Andræ', *Dansk biografisk
Leksikon*, 1, Copenhagen, 1979: 245; Tandem
[Poul Andræ], 'Den kontrære Sexualfornem-
melse. Fragmenter til Oplysning', Bibliothek for
Læger, 1892: 205–25, 247–81; W. von Rosen,
*Månens Kulør. Studier i dansk bøssehistorie
1628–1912*, Copenhagen, 1993: 505, 674–9.

Wilhelm von Rosen

Anneke, Mathilde Franziska (1817–1884),
German-Swiss-American author, journalist and women's rights activist. Anneke
was born Mathilde Giesler in Blanken-
stein, Germany. The family was not entirely secure financially, and it was a
matter of some relief when, in 1836, the
19-year-old Mathilde married a wealthy

wine merchant, Alfred von Tabouillot.
Three years later she sued for divorce, but
lost her case and was instructed by the
court to return to her husband. At a second
hearing she swore on oath that von Tabouillot had physically mistreated her, and was
granted the divorce with custody of their
daughter, but without alimony: Mathilde
was judged to be the guilty party in the separation because she had failed to return to
her husband when so instructed by the
court. To earn a living for herself and her
daughter, she began to work as a writer. As
well as a large number of journalistic articles
on politics and the women's movement, she
produced in the course of her career a number of short stories (two on the slave trade),
poetry, memoirs and a drama, *Oithono oder
Die Tempelweihe* (*Oithono or the Consecration of the Temple*, 1842). *Oithono* was
performed in Münster, and earned a scornful review from the distinguished German
writer Annette von Droste-Hülshoff, in a
letter to Levin Schücking. Droste had not
seen the piece, but intended to resist the
social advances of the admiring but penniless Mathilde von Tabouillot.

In Münster, Mathilde became a member
of the Democrat's Club, where she met a
politically active ex-officer of the Prussian
army called Fritz Anneke. They married in
1847. In the same year Mathilde published
a pamphlet in defence of the women's
rights activist Louise Aston, who had been
banished from Berlin in 1846; its title was
*Das Weib im Conflict mit den socialen
Verhältnissen* (*Woman in Conflict with
Social Structures*).

In the year of revolutions, 1848, Mathilde and Fritz Anneke edited a democratic
newspaper, the *Neue Kölnische Zeitung*.
Fritz, who was in regular contact with Karl
Marx and Friedrich Engels, was arrested,
leaving Mathilde to run the newspaper.
When it was banned, she launched a replacement, which she called the *Woman's
Paper* (*Frauen-Zeitung*); the name was
merely a cover, and it, too, was censored
after its third appearance. In 1849,
after the defeat of the Baden-Palatinate

uprising, the couple fled to the US via France and Switzerland.

In the United States, Mathilde founded another women's newspaper, this time the real thing, called the *Deutsche Frauen-Zeitung*. Fritz returned to Europe in 1859, and Mathilde, after ten years of marriage and five children, established a love relationship with Mary Booth, a younger woman of American Indian parentage. In 1860 they moved to Switzerland, a country that was soon to become a centre for German-speaking lesbians and emancipated women, especially when the first women were admitted to Swiss universities. But after Booth's death in 1865, Anneke returned to the United States with her new parner, Cäcilie Kapp; the two women founded a girls' school in Milwaukee. Anneke became a prominent activist in the American women's rights movement, working side-by-side with women such as Elizabeth Cady Stanton and Susan B. ANTHONY. In 1869 she became vice-president of the National Women's Suffrage Association in Wisconsin. She died in Milwaukee.

Mathilde Anneke's literary works include *Memoiren einer Frau aus dem badisch-pfälzischen Feldzuge* (*A Woman's Memoirs of the Baden-Palatinate Campaign*, 1853); *Die Sclaven-Auction* (*The Slave Auction*, 1862); and *Gebrochene Ketten* (*Broken Chains*, 1864).

M. F. Anneke, *Gebrochene Ketten. Erzählungen, Reportagen und Reden 1861–1873*, ed. M. Wagner and H. Mück, Stuttgart, 1983; M. Gebhardt, *Mathilde Franziska Anneke: Madame, Soldat und Suffragette*, Berlin, 1988; M. Henkel and R. Taubert, *Das Weib im Conflict mit den socialen Verhältnissen: Mathilde Franziska Anneke und die erste deutsche Frauenzeitung*, Bochum, 1976; I. Kokula and U. Böhmer, *Die Welt gehört uns doch! Zusammenschluss lesbischer Frauen in der Schweiz der 30er Jahre*, Zurich, 1991.

Sarah Colvin

Anselm of Canterbury, St (1033/4–1109), Italian-French-British philosopher and prelate. Born in Italy, Anselm entered the Benedictine monastery at Bec, in Normandy, France in 1060, to study under the prior, Lanfranc. Anselm was himself elected prior (1063) and then abbot (1078) of Bec when Lanfranc became abbot of Caen. Anselm was a highly original thinker, the founder of Scholasticism, author of both the ontological argument for the existence of God and the satisfaction theory of Christian atonement, and a fine Latinist.

In 1066 William the Conqueror established Norman overlordship of England. William was a benefactor of Bec, and gifted lands in both England and Normandy to the monastery. Anselm made three visits to England on account of these lands. William's son and successor, William II Rufus, named Anselm Archbishop of Canterbury in March 1093. Anselm reluctantly accepted, with the intention of reforming the English church. His consecration on 4 December 1093 resulted in an investiture contest.

John Boswell portrays Anselm as having prevented the promulgation of the first anti-gay legislation in England. R. W. Southern, the leading contemporary historian and interpreter of Anselm's life and work, has strongly challenged Boswell's assumptions, and specifically his interpretation of the Council of London in 1102. Southern argues that in the Middle Ages, no one knew anything of, or had any interest in, 'innate homosexual tendencies': 'In so far as they were known to exist, they were seen simply as symptoms of the general sinfulness of mankind, which led to every kind of sin . . . . In dealing with these matters, legislators were concerned only with practical actions arising from these evil intentions'.

Penitential codes down to the eleventh century treated 'sodomy' on the same level as bestiality. Severe penances were specified for every kind of sexual act except intercourse between persons married to each other and for the strict purpose of procreation. However, no procedures were established to enforce the penances. Horrified by the incidence of 'sodomy' in William Rufus's court, Anselm himself initiated legislation to bring a limited range of common homosexual practices to the notice of parishioners in every parochial church in England, with penalties attached. He was severe in his condemnation of 'sodomy', and of any behaviour (including males wearing long hair or effeminate clothes) which might encourage it. According to Southern, he only wrote to Archdeacon William prohibiting publication of the decree because he was rightly anxious that he did not have the support of his fellow bishops, who had well justified doubts about the practicability of his proposals on this and other matters.

Boswell and Southern are agreed that Anselm was personally committed to the monastic ideal of celibacy, and that he integrated into his theological system the clerical tradition of 'passionate friendship'. Human love and spirituality were, in Anselm's thought, intimately related ideas. Southern challenges Boswell's assertion, however, that the style of language used in Anselm's letters to his friends (*dilecto dilectori* - 'beloved lover') could pass for correspondence between lovers in any society. Southern maintains that letters like Anselm's from Bec could not have been written in the next century, when language of this sort had been appropriated by the poets of romantic love. Anselm's talk of 'kisses and hugs' is figurative of unity in spiritual endeavour, fusion of souls and a peculiarly intense imaginative projection of personal ties.

Anselm does appear to have 'toned down' his correspondence after he left Bec. Southern suggests that this, a *Meditation* on his 'lost virginity', his later demands for total self-abnegation and his exaggerated sensitivity evidenced at the Council in 1102 may all indicate some personal struggle, and possibly a homosexual orientation in the modern sense of the word. If this is taken to be the case, then Anselm's story is more an all-too-familiar saga of internalised homophobia acted out through clerical power, rather than that of a 'gay' hero from the Middle Ages single-handedly stemming a rising tide of ecclesiastical intolerance.

J. Boswell, *Christianity, Social Tolerance, and Homosexuality: Gay People in Western Europe from the Beginning of the Christian Era to the Fourteenth Century*, Chicago, 1980; R. W. Southern, *Saint Anselm: A Portrait in a Landscape*, Cambridge, 1990; R. W. Southern, *Saint Anselm and His Biographer: A Study of Monastic Life and Thought 1059–c. 1130*, Cambridge, 1963.

David J. Bromwell

Anthony, Susan Brownell (1820–1906), American social reformer and feminist activist. Anthony was born into a Quaker family in Adams, Massachusetts. Her early years were spent as a teacher at a Quaker boarding school and later as headmistress of girls at an academy in New York state.

By the 1850s, Anthony had become active in anti-slavery and temperance movements, founding the Women's State Temperance Society in 1852. Her work as reformer then began to focus on women's suffrage, and for the entire second half of the nineteenth century she was one of the key players in efforts to achieve social equality for American women. She worked closely and for many years with her contemporary, Elizabeth Cady Stanton, herself an internationally known women's rights activist. Although the exact nature of their physical relationship is unknown, Stanton is without doubt the person with whom Anthony formed her closest emotional and affectional bond.

Anthony served as president of the influential National Women's Suffrage Association from 1892 to 1900 and remained active in the cause until her death in Rochester, New York. Fourteen years later, the 19th Amendment to the Constitution, guaranteeing American women the right to vote, was passed. It is still popularly known as the 'Anthony Amendment'.

K. Barrie, *Susan B. Anthony: A Biography of a Singular Feminist*, New York, 1988; J. E. Harper, 'Susan B. Anthony', *Gay & Lesbian Biography*, Detroit, 1997; L. Sherr, *Failure Is Impossible: Susan B. Anthony in Her Own Words*, New York, 1995.

David Garnes

Antinous (110/112–130), favourite of the emperor Hadrian. The most famous homosexual relationship in Roman history is the love of the emperor Hadrian for Antinous, a youth from Bithynium in Bithynia (northern Asia Minor) who drowned in the Nile in 130. The early history of the relationship is unknown, but it is likely that the emperor met Antinous during a visit to Bithynia and took him into his household. The lack of details about the relationship suggests that it aroused no comment; Hadrian's grief after Antinous's death indicates the depth of the attachment between them, for it is said that Hadrian wept for him like a woman. Antinous was deified, a new city, Antinoopolis, was founded near the site of his death, and numerous statues were erected in his honour throughout the empire, statues which embody a particular Hellenic ideal of youthful beauty.

Controversy surrounds the death of Antinous, as even at the time there were rumours that his death was no accident, and some believed that Antinous offered himself as a sacrifice to the gods to ensure Hadrian's prosperity. Whatever the truth, Antinous's manner of death gave him a prominence he may not have enjoyed had he continued as Hadrian's beloved and outlived him, as would have been expected. It was only his death which unleashed a public outpouring of grief on the part of Hadrian, thus exposing to view emotions more often confined to the less visible world of private relationships.

R. Lambert, *Beloved and God: The Story of Hadrian and Antinous*, Secaucus, New Jersey, 1988; M. Boatwright, *Hadrian and the City of Rome*, Princeton, 1987: Appendix, 'The Obeliscus Antinoi', pp. 239–60.

Roger Pitcher

Aquinas, St Thomas (*c.* 1225–1274), Italian philosopher and theologian. Thomas Aquinas was born near the town of Aquino, which is situated between Naples and Rome. He studied at Naples, where he joined the Dominican order, and with Albertus Magnus at Cologne and Paris, eventually gaining employment as a university teacher in 1252. The rediscovery, from mainly Arabic sources, of Aristotle's discussions of natural philosophy, metaphysics, ethics and politics represented an important challenge to Christian thought in the thirteenth century. Though controversial in his day, Aquinas forged a magisterial synthesis of Christian and Aristotelian ideas, above all in his *Summa theologiae* (1266–1273), which was to become Catholic orthodoxy and make Aquinas the most influential Catholic philosopher and theologian since Augustine. In this capacity, unfortunately, Aquinas made a decisive contribution to the consolidation of homophobia in Western thought.

At the heart of Aquinas's synthesis of faith and reason is his view that philosophy and the particular sciences of nature provide knowledge of the material world which, though derived independently of faith or revelation, serves to complement rather than contradict our knowledge of God. In the area of morality, human reason can discover universal values and principles of justice by considering the order of the natural world. This 'law of nature' reflects the will of God and so complements Christian teaching. The emphasis on nature leads Aquinas to accept that the pleasures of sex, like those of eating and drinking, are essential to that part of our nature 'which men have in common with other creatures'. Less happily, Aquinas understands sex exclusively in terms of procreation. Only monogamous heterosexual activity obeys both the natural necessity to bear and rear children and the divine injunction to 'Be fruitful, and multiply.' By the same token, homosexual activity is deemed 'unnatural'. Not squeamish in such matters, Aquinas carefully ranks sins of 'lechery' according to the extent to which they depart from the natural aim and object of sexual activity: 'And so, to compare unnatural sins of lechery, the lowest rank is held by solitary sin, where the intercourse of one with another is omitted. The greatest is that of bestiality, which does not observe the due species . . . . Afterwards comes sodomy, which does not observe the due sex. After this the lechery which does not observe the due mode of intercourse, and this is worse if effected not in the right vessel than if the inordinateness concerns other modes of intimacy'.

Although Aquinas's catalogue of sexual sins is impressively thorough, there were serious problems with his reasoning. As earlier medieval writers had observed, some animals *do* engage in homosexual activity, so it cannot be unnatural. Again, as a member of a celibate religious order, Aquinas is only too ready to admit that reproduction has to be regarded as the duty of the human *species* as a whole, not of every individual human being. He even admits that 'unnatural' acts may be natural for a particular man if 'in him nature is ailing'. According to John Boswell's account, even Biblical condemnations of homosexuality, which Aquinas also cites, are open to alternative interpretation. And even if these passages are accepted at face value, it is not clear why the proscription of homosexuality has outlived similar Biblical pronouncements against eating pork, intercourse during menstruation, the cutting of beards and partaking of rabbits and shellfish. What is more, the recognition that human reason is *beyond* nature is fundamental to Aquinas's Aristotelian conception of the distinctiveness of human beings, 'who alone can recognise as good and fitting something which is be-

yond the requirements of nature'. The arts and sciences and, of course, knowledge and love of God are presumably beyond nature in this sense. So why not homosexual love and desire?

Alas, Aquinas does not contemplate this possibility. Deeming all sins to be, by definition, 'against reason', Aquinas regards sins 'against nature' as at least doubly vicious, since they violate both our rational and our animal natures. Even worse, since 'the plan of nature comes from God', any 'violation of this plan, as by unnatural sins, is an affront to God, the ordainer of nature'. The result is that homosexuality is classed with cannibalism and bestiality as the worst of all possible sins. According to Boswell, Aquinas's hostile view of homosexuality is best understood as the rationalisation of an intense wave of prejudice against 'sodomites', Muslims, Jews, lepers and heretics, which swept across Europe in the late thirteenth century, with the result that 'Between 1250 and 1300, homosexual activity passed from being completely legal in most of Europe to incurring the death penalty in all but a few contemporary legal compilations'. The baneful effect of Aquinas's moralising was certainly exacerbated by the simultaneous rise of the Catholic Inquisition, with its increasingly systematic, fanatical, cruel – and profitable – imposition of religious orthodoxy.

St Thomas Aquinas, *Summa theologiae*, ed. T. Gilby, London, 1964; J. Boswell, *Christianity, Social Tolerance, and Homosexuality*, Chicago, 1980; F. C. Copleston, *Aquinas*, Harmondsworth, 1955.

David West

Aristophanes (*c*. 460/450–*c*. 386 BC), classical Greek dramatist. Aristophanes did not begin writing until after the death of the great Athenian statesman, Pericles, and his active life thus covered the period of Athens's political and military decline, through the Peloponnesian War (431–404 BC), oligarchic revolution and the restoration of democracy, and its return to a degree of prosperity in the decade before the poet's death. Almost nothing is known of his private life, except that he was an Athenian citizen and that he had a son, Ararus, who produced two of his father's plays after the latter's death and also wrote plays of his own.

Of Aristophanes' plays, 11 survive entire out of some 40 titles attributed to him. They provide (with uninhibited enthusiasm) much information about Athenian sexual mores, though in drawing conclusions about behaviour in general some allowance must no doubt be made for the exaggeration endemic to comedy and to political and social satire, with which, under the buffoonery, the plays are seriously concerned. It is, also, not always clear whether sexual language is being used with specific meaning or for the purpose of general abuse.

The world of these plays is very different from that of PLATO's dialogues: instead of upper-class leisure and sophisticated discussion of the acceptable love of boys, there is a good deal of slapstick and straightforward bawdy with appeal to the working mass of the poorer citizenry, who had neither time nor resources for the self-indulgence of the wealthy. The same-sex element is treated as on a par with the heterosexual, though it is the latter which predominates. It can be broadly characterised in three ways. There are jokes about the genitals, as when (in *Knights*) a boy detailed to fetch a folding stool is described as well hung, and may then himself be used as a stool. Then there are social observations, such as the speech of 'Right' (in *Clouds*), who recalls the possibilities of titillation in the gymnasium – the 'dew' appearing on a boy's penis, or the impression of his buttocks left on the sand where he has been sitting; or the man (in *Birds*) who chides his neighbour for being stand-offish in not chucking the speaker's son under the balls.

But the most prevalent same-sex theme is the ridicule and indeed contempt shown for male acceptance of anal penetration.

The 'wide arse' said to result from such activities is frequently referred to as characteristic of corrupt politicians or despised effeminates. Such verbal abuse is allied with accusations of prostitution, the continuing message being that it is through such practices that politicians make their way in the world. This contempt for the passive sexual role is found throughout the classical period. But K. J. Dover (who emphasises this point) also argues that men are never criticised in comedy for aiming at sexual copulation with beautiful young males. Also, it is Aristophanes who records the word which denotes the *acceptable* form of homosexual copulation: the thrusting of the penis between the thighs.

In addition to the comedies, Aristophanes is credited with a contribution to the debate on love in Plato's *Symposium*. His speech, while remote from the satirical bawdy of the real Aristophanes, is in the form of a comical allegory, which recognises the power of sexual love and the ideal which it seeks of union with another person, whether of the same or the opposite sex.

K. J. Dover, *Aristophanic Comedy*, London, 1972; K. J. Dover, *Greek Homosexuality*, London, 1978, especially section III C; K. J. Dover, 'Aristophanes' Speech in Plato's *Symposium*', *Journal of Hellenic Studies*, 86 (1966); D. M. Halperin, 'Platonic *Erôs* and What Men Call Love', *Ancient Philosophy*, 5, 2 (1985).

Clifford Hindley

Arondeus, Willem (1895–1943), Dutch painter, writer, resistance fighter. Born in Amsterdam as one of seven children, of tailors who worked for theatres, Arondeus ran away from home at age 18 and sought the friendship of several artists, while visiting an art school for painters. The conflict with his family was so strong that contact was never established again.

For almost ten years he struggled to survive with almost no recognition. His first paid work was at the age of 28: he did a huge wall painting in the city hall of Rotterdam. Two more works followed, along with the first positive newspaper reviews. Nevertheless he stopped painting in 1928 and started writing, but his first poems and short stories did not sell well. Through all these years he kept writing a diary, in which he openly expressed his unsatisfied longing for friendship and love towards other men.

In 1933 – at the age of 38 – he met Jan, a young delivery boy from a grocery shop in the countryside close to Apeldoorn, where he lived at the time. Jan soon moved in with Willem and although both were very poor, they enjoyed a deep love and gave each other much support. Unfortunately their financial problems grew, and often they did not have enough to eat or to pay their rent. Arondeus felt deeply ashamed that he – as the older one – could not care better for his young lover.

Finally in 1938 he started writing the biography of the Dutch painter Matthijs Maris (1839–1917), who fought on the barricades in 1871 for the Communards in Paris. With each word, Arondeus identified himself strongly with Maris. The sales of this book assured him for the first time a certain income.

After the German occupation of The Netherlands in May 1940 Arondeus became one of the first artists to join the resistance. Not much later he split up with Jan, who returned to Apeldoorn while Arondeus remained in Amsterdam. He took part in several smaller activities in the resistance before he started to realise his own plan: the destruction of the citizen registration building of Amsterdam, where copies of all identity cards of each citizen were held. This meant that fake identity cards or passports (which were made by some artists for persecuted Jews or political activists) could be proved as false when checked with the official registration.

On the evening of 27 March 1943 Arondeus set out with a group of students, artists and two young doctors, all wearing German uniforms. Arondeus himself was dressed as a 'Hauptmann'. They asked the guards of the building to open for a special inspection. Within seconds the guards were handcuffed and given injections by the doctors to make them sleep. Shortly after that the whole building was set on fire. The sleeping guards were put into the courtyard, so that none was harmed. The whole group escaped before the police, firemen and real German soldiers arrived.

This attack inspired more activists to set registration buildings in other cities on fire. However, via an unknown betrayer all 15 members of Arondeus's group were arrested on 1 April 1943. Two other gay men were also members of his group: the tailor Sjoerd Bakker, who made the uniforms, and the writer Johan Brouwer. During the trial Arondeus took the main responsibility for the action. The two doctors were sentenced to life in prison, while the other 13 men were shot on 1 July 1943.

Bakker requested a pink shirt as his last wish. Arondeus asked his lawyer to make public after the war that he and two other men were gay: 'Tell the people that gays are no cowards!'

After the war Arondeus's family – with whom he had no contact since he was 18 – received a medal of honour from the Dutch government. Only in 1990, in the TV documentary by the Dutch filmmaker Toni Bouwmans, did it become known to the public that Arondeus was gay.

T. Bouwmans, ' "Na het feest zonder afscheid verdwenen" – notities uit het leven van Willem Arondeus', TV documentary, The Netherlands, 1990; L. van Dijk, 'Homosexuelle sind keine Schwaechlinge . . .! – Willem Arondeus', Reinbek, 1992; M. Entrop, *Onbewaam in het compromis, Willem Arondeus, kunstenaar en verzetsstrijder*, Amsterdam, 1993.

Lutz van Dijk

Astell, Mary (1666–1731), British writer. Astell was the daughter of a prominent coal merchant in Newcastle, the centre of the English coal trade. She was fortunate to be educated by her uncle, Ralph Astell, a curate associated with the Cambridge Platonists. The family fortunes failing after the death of her father, Astell took up residence in London in 1688 and was close to destitute when she successfully appealed for financial assistance to Archbishop Sancroft. It may have been through his recommendation that Astell came into contact with the publisher Rich Wilkin, who in 1694 issued her impressive first book, *A Serious Proposal to the Ladies, For the Advancement of their true and greatest Interest By a Lover of Her Sex*, and most of those which followed.

Astell is a crucial figure in the history of feminism both for her specific advocacy of women as a group and her notable contributions to the political, religious and philosophical debates of her time. She was the author of nine titles including *An Impartial Enquiry into the Causes of Rebellion and Civil War* (1704), *The Christian Religion as Profess'd by a Daughter of the Church* (1705) and *Bart'lemy Fair: or, An Inquiry after Wit* (1709). She is now best remembered for two powerful and influential feminist tracts: *A Serious Proposal to the Ladies* (1694; Part II, 1697) and *Some Reflections on Marriage* (1700), a stern but sympathetic warning to all women occasioned by the infamous example of her neighbour in Chelsea, the Duchess of Mazarin.

Astell campaigned eloquently for women's intellectual and moral education from a High Church, Tory standpoint. Her arguments are separatist, ascetic and idealist, combining conservative political and religious views with radical sexual critique in complex ways. Astell denounces 'Custom, that merciless torrent that carries all before it' and especially women's complicity in their own sexual commodification and oppression: 'How can you be content to be in the World like Tulips in a Garden, to make a fine show and be good for nothing'. Not surprisingly, she was as hostile to sensualists like Aphra BEHN who had distinguished themselves in popular drama and fiction as she was to the women who patronised their work.

Even in her earliest writing, a collection of manuscript poetry (1689) published for the first time in Ruth Perry's valuable modern biography, Astell repudiates both masculinised worldly ambition and feminised vanity in the service of 'Heroic Virtue': 'I wou'd no Fame, no Titles have, / And no more Land than what will make a grave. / I scorn to weep for Worlds, may I but reign / And Empire o'er my self obtain' ('Ambition').

A Serious Proposal to the Ladies imagines a flexible separatist community where middle- and upper-class women would live and study at a cost of £500 each, either as a prelude to marriage or, preferably, a genuine alternative to it. Astell figured this 'monastery without vows' as 'a Type and Antepast of Heav'n': 'Here are no Serpents to deceive you, whilst you entertain yourselves in these delicious Gardens'. When the proposal failed to garner the necessary financial backing, Astell turned her attention to Part II, 'Wherein a Method is offer'd for the Improvement of their Minds'. In this pragmatic sequel to the *Serious Proposal*, the need for a literally separate and separatist building is obviated. Astell revises her argument in terms of the enclosed garden of active contemplation, 'a natural Liberty within us'. She urges women to 'Retire a little, to furnish our understandings with useful Principles, to set our inclinations right, and to manage our Passions, and when this is well done, but not till then, we may safely venture out'. The 'Master within' is sarcastically contrasted with those masters without, whose 'Lawful Privileges' Astell equally affirms and repudiates: 'The Men therefore may still enjoy their Prerogatives . . . nor can they who are so well assur'd of their own Merit entertain the least Suspicion that we shall overtop them'.

The women Astell addresses are chiefly women of her own kind, but her closest friendships were with much wealthier and often younger women known for their intellect and charitable work, like Lady Elizabeth Hastings, Lady Catherine Jones (neither of whom married), the widowed Lady Ann, Countess of Coventry, Lady Mary Wortley Montagu and Elizabeth Hutcheson, Astell's executrix. Undoubtedly these were the primary relations of Astell's life and there is, as Ruth Perry puts it, 'a libidinous energy in her pleas for women'. Indeed, Astell's rigorous devotion to the passions of the mind, combined with her frank avowal of a preference for female company and distaste for marriage, can be read as a symptomatic response to the problematic of desire disclosed in *Letters Concerning the Love of God* (1695): 'Though I have in some measure rectified this Fault, yet still I find an agreeable Movement in my Soul towards her I love'. With the help of her circle of wealthy female friends, as well as middle-class subscriptions, Astell opened a charity school for the daughters of outpensioners of the Royal Hospital in Chelsea in 1709 and retired from public controversy.

B. Hill (ed.) *The First English Feminist*, New York, 1986; R. Perry, *The Celebrated Mary Astell*, Chicago, 1986; M. Astell, *A Serious Proposal to the Ladies*, P. Springborg ed., London, 1997; *Astell: Political Writings*, P. Springborg ed., New York, 1996; H. Smith, *Reason's Disciples*, Urbana, 1982.

Kate Lilley

Atherton, John (1598–1640), Irish bishop. Born near Bridgwater in Somerset, the son of an Anglican parson, Atherton was educated at Oxford. He served as Anglican rector of Huish Comb Flower, Somerset; and became prebendary of St John's, Dublin in 1630; chancellor of Killaloe in 1634; chancellor of Christ Church and rector of Killaban and Ballintubride in 1635. In 1636, under the patronage of Thomas Wentworth, Earl of Strafford, Lord Lieutenant of Ireland, Atherton was appointed as Lord Bishop of Waterford and Lismore, but he was not welcomed by the Roman Catholic majority in his see.

In 1640 he was accused of buggery with his steward and tithe proctor, John Childe. Though his fellow clerics tried to prevent the trial so as to avoid disgrace to the reformed religion of Ireland, the verdict of guilty was hailed by cheers in court, and he was nearly murdered on his way from the bar to the gaol in Cork. On the day of execution, he read the morning service for his fellow prisoners, and then was placed in a carriage with his arms pinioned to prevent escape, and, while Christ Church tolled the Passing Bell, in a great company of halberds led by three sheriffs, he passed through the thronged streets to Dublin Castle, where he was hanged on Gallows Green on 5 December. In court he denied the specific charge of sodomy, and did so once again from the gallows, though he had virtually admitted his guilt to the divine who attended him in prison. His lover, Childe, was hanged in March 1641 at Bandon Bridge, Cork. The anonymous pamphlet *The Life and Death of John Atherton* (1641) has illustrations of both men hanging on the gallows. (This was the second pair of men executed for sodomy in UK history; the first men executed for sodomy were Lord Audley, Earl of Castlehaven, and his two menservants, in 1631.)

In 1710 Atherton was defended as a victim of a conspiracy, on evidence gathered from people recently living. The main reason for the Bishop's disgrace may have been his political zeal in opposing the Articles of Irish Convocation in 1634, and the personal enmity of the Earl of Cork, whom he had successfully sued in a dispute over land rights. Atherton's patron, the Earl of Strafford, also an enemy of the Earl of Cork, was executed for treason in May 1641. The conspiracy may have been organised by a lawyer named Butler, who was disputing with Atherton over the ownership of some land at Killoges, near Waterford. Butler went mad soon after Atherton's execution, and claimed to see the latter's apparition constantly before him. Even as late as 1710 Butler's former house was said to be haunted by the Bishop's ghost.

Anon., *The Life and Death of John Atherton*, London, 1641; N. Barnard, *The Case of John Atherton*, London, 1710; Anon., *The Case of John Atherton . . . Fairly Represented*, London, 1710.

Rictor Norton

Auden, W(ystan) H(ugh) (1907–1973), British-American writer. Regarded as one of the best poets of the English language in the twentieth century, successor to William Butler Yeats and T. S. Eliot, author of a large body of poems, plays, librettos, translations and literary criticism and essays, he was born in York, but grew up in the Midlands, the youngest child of George Augustus Auden and Constance Rosalie Bicknell (there were two older brothers). After Cambridge, he spent 1930–1935 as a schoolmaster. In 1935, at the instigation of his close friend Christopher Isherwood, Auden married Erika MANN (1905–1969), eldest child of Thomas MANN, to give her a British passport. In 1937, he went to Spain to fight fascism during their civil war. He emigrated to the United States in 1939 and became a citizen in 1946, though he spent many restless years in Europe including a five-year stay as Professor of Poetry at Oxford (1956–1961). His companion, Chester Kallman (1921–1975) – whom he met in 1939 – and he maintained a stormy relationship all their adult lives.

Auden's first book was *Poems* (1930); his collected poems were edited by Edward Mendelson in 1994, and his *Complete Works* were issued in 1989. Notable collections of his essays are *The Dyer's Hand* (1962) and *Forewords and Afterwords* (1973). His librettos were collaborations with Kallman, and his plays were co-authored with Isherwood. Strongly influenced by Marx and Freud in the 1920s and 1930s, he became interested in Søren Kierkegaard and Reinhold Niebuhr in the 1940s; this led to a renewed interest in Anglo-Catholic Christianity.

Auden said that a writer's private life 'is, or should be, of no concern to anybody except he himself, his family, and his friends'. He never wrote about his homosexuality except for a few poems which he did not publicly acknowledge, and he was conservative about issues related to gay politics, but he was not closeted in his life outside the public sphere. Auden was a poet, a great poet, who happened to be homosexual rather than a gay writer.

E. Mendelson, *Early Auden*, New York, 1981; H. Carpenter, *W. H. Auden*, Boston, 1981, 1992; C. Osborne, *W. H. Auden: The Life of the Poet*, New York, 1979, 1995; R. Davenport-Hines, *Auden*, New York, 1995; D. Farnan, *Auden in Love*, New York, 1984.

Seymour Kleinberg

B

Bacon, Sir Francis (1561–1626), British king's counsel, essayist, philosopher. Bacon was born into a middle-class family, became a practising lawyer in 1582, and was appointed Queen Elizabeth's Counsellor in 1591. He rapidly rose to fame under King JAMES I, who confirmed his position as king's counsel in 1604. He was knighted in 1603, made Solicitor General in 1607, Attorney General in 1613, and Lord High Chancellor in 1618. He received the titles of Baron Verulam in 1618 and Viscount St Albans in 1621. In that same year King James fell from grace by trying to abolish Parliament, and Bacon was found guilty of having accepted bribes while serving as a judge. Bacon acknowledged receiving gifts (it was common practice for judges to accept gifts from the winning parties) but maintained that this custom never influenced his judgments; no one ever demanded a retrial of any of the suits in question.

Bacon retired to his estate at Gorhambury, outside St Albans, to write and to conduct scientific research. *New Atlantis*, utopian fiction about the ideal society, had been published in 1617; the *Novum Organum*, a theory for organising knowledge, in 1620; *The Advancement of Learning*, an argument for empirical research and against superstition, in 1623; his famous *Essays* were expanded from 10 in 1597 to 58 in 1625. He also wrote poetry and plays; some claim that he wrote some

of SHAKESPEARE's plays (*Hamlet* re-uses a line from Bacon's essay 'Of Wisdom for a Man's Self' – 'be so true to thyself as thou be not false to others'). In 1626 Bacon tested the effect of freezing on the preservation of meat by going out in a blizzard and stuffing a chicken with snow; the chicken was preserved, but Bacon caught pneumonia and died.

Bacon married Alice Barnham in 1606, when he was 45 years old; they had no children. Contemporary figures relate that he was a 'sodomite'. John Aubrey in his *Brief Lives* says quite bluntly that Bacon 'was a pederast' and had 'ganimeds and favourites'; the Puritan moralist Sir Simonds D'Ewes in his *Autobiography and Correspondence* discusses Bacon's love for his Welsh serving-men; in particular he says that when Bacon had to resign in 1621 he kept 'one Godrick, a verie effeminate faced youth, to bee his catamite and bedfellow, although hee had discharged the most of his other household sevants: which was the moore to bee admired, because men generallie after his fall begann to discourse of that his unnaturall crime, which hee had practiced manie yeares, deserting the bedd of his Ladie' (diary entry for 3 May 1621). His mother, Lady Ann Bacon, complained especially about 'that bloody Percy' whom her son kept 'yea as a coach companion and a bed companion'. Many of the youths in his service were left legacies at his death. His closest friend was Tobie Matthew (later knighted), actor, spy and the inspiration for Bacon's famous essay 'On Friendship': 'If a man have not a friend, he may quit the stage'.

His brother, Anthony Bacon (1558–1601), a spy in the service of the Earl of Essex, was also homosexual. He was charged with sodomy in the summer of 1586, in Montauban, France. But the case was not pursued, and he was granted mercy through the efforts of Henri, King of Navarre. After this scandal, Anthony returned to England and lived for a time with Francis, and then set up a bachelor establishment at his estate in Redbourn.

D. du Maurier, *Golden Lads: A Study of Anthony Bacon, Francis, and their friends*, London, 1975; D. du Maurier, *The Winding Stair: Francis Bacon, His Rise and Fall*, London, 1976; R. Norton, *Mother Clap's Molly House*, London, 1992.

Rictor Norton

Baden-Powell, Robert (Stephenson Smyth), 1st Baron (1857–1941), British soldier. Baden-Powell was the British soldier who founded the Boy Scout and Girl Guide movements. During the Boer War (1899–1902) he won national fame for holding Mafeking against a Boer siege for a grisly 217 days, and later reorganised the South African constabulary. He formed the Boy Scouts in 1908 and, with his sister, Agnes Baden-Powell, the Girl Guides a year later. In 1910 he retired from the Army and devoted his life to the scouting movement, writing over thirty books and travelling the world.

Born at Paddington, London, he was the eighth child of the Reverend Baden-Powell, a Professor at Oxford University, who died when Baden-Powell was just three years old. Baden-Powell attended Charterhouse School, where his interest in woodcraft was born. In 1876 he went to India as a young Army officer, and his unorthodox but successful methods soon led to his training others in scout techniques.

In 1907 he held a pioneering summer camp on Brownsea Island, Dorset, to try to bring together a mix of 22 boys from private upper-class schools and working-class schools. This, together with his best-selling *Scouting For Boys* (1908), was the spark which led within two years to the almost spontaneous formation of a Scouting movement in Britain, which quickly spread throughout the British Empire.

Much of the evidence for Baden-Powell's homosexuality can be found in Tim Jeal's monumental and definitive biography, *Baden-Powell* (1989), in which Jeal states frankly: 'The evidence available points inexorably to the conclusion that Baden-Powell was a repressed homosexual', although it seems that, like the majority of homosocial men at that time, he 'managed to follow Plato's prescription glorifying the love of man for man, or man for boy, while remaining physically chaste'. A complex and creative man of the utmost integrity, 'Baden-Powell was in a position of trust which made watching, at one remove, the only way to satisfy his interest'. Jeal gives several detailed instances of Baden-Powell's pleasure in seeing naked boys, his emotional enjoyment gained from living alongside them, and his delight in contemplating the clandestine 'artistic' nude photography of boys which was at that time circulating among English pederastic public school circles.

He did, eventually, marry, in 1912. Olave Soames was a 'strange compound of child and grown woman ... That he thought of her as a mixture of young woman, male comrade and child-friend is apparent in his earliest letters'. She also altered her appearance to suit Baden-Powell: 'Apart from flattening her breasts and concealing any hint of cleavage with handkerchiefs, she promised herself that she would cut off most of her hair ... With every hint of sex removed from a relationship he could get on reasonably well with women'.

Baden-Powell was made a baron in honour of his services. In 1938, he returned to his beloved Africa, to live in semi-retirement at Nyeri, Kenya. He died there three years later.

T. Jeal, *Baden-Powell*, London, 1989.

Ianthe Duende

Balbi, Giròlamo (1450?–1535), Italian humanist. Balbi probably studied in Rome with POMPONIO-LETO but, by 1485, was in Paris, where he obtained a university chair four years later. His severe and uncompromising character brought him into conflict with several colleagues whom he accused of incompetence. The quarrel became increasingly bitter and in 1490 or 1491, accused of sodomy and heresy, Balbi had to flee Paris. One of his rivals, Publio Fausto Andrelini (1462–1518), in a Latin eclogue, 'De fuga Balbi' (1491–1493), also published the accusations of sodomy against him. One of Balbi's former students, Jacques Morlin, wrote a defence, *Invectiva in Fausti Balbi calumniatorem*, in which he accused Andrelini of homosexual tastes. One Guillaume Tardif, in *Antiabalbica*, also claimed that Balbi had been tried for sodomy. Meanwhile, Balbi took refuge in England, then travelled to Vienna (1493) and on to the court of King Ladislas of Bohemia in Prague. In 1497, faced with new accusations of sodomy, he was again obliged to take flight. Balbi's erstwhile protector, Bohuslaw von Hassenstein (Baron Lobocovicz), published a Latin composition proclaiming that perhaps the Bohemians were not so cultured as the Italians, but at least they knew nothing about the love for GANYMEDE. Balbi found a haven in Hungary, where he was ordained to the priesthood, obtained important political and diplomatic posts and, in 1523, was made bishop of Gurk; he eventually died there.

Balbi was most appreciated during his life (in certain ways similar to Filippo BUONACCORSI) for spreading humanism in eastern Europe. His poetry, letters and philosophical tracts, written in Latin, reveal Balbi's vast learning. A number of the compositions that have homosexual themes are included in his published works. (Others, such as those in the Manoscritto Marciano Latino (No. 4689) in the Marciana Library in Venice, remain unpublished and unstudied). One published letter sent to Pomponio-Leto speaks of his new love for a youth. In another, he says that women were not allowed into his house (which he had consecrated to Hercules) but only a 'chaste' youth whom he called 'Illa' after Hercules' male lover. Such remarks suggest that the accusations against Balbi were at least partly based on fact.

G. degli Agostini, *Notizie istorico-critiche intorno le vite e le opere degli scrittori viniziani*, Venice, 1752–1754, Vol. 2, pp. 240–80; Publio Fausto Andrelini, *The Eclogues of Faustus Andrelinus and Ioannes Arnolletus*, Baltimore, 1918: 53–7, 113–14; G. Balbi, *Opera poetica, oratoria ac politico-moralia*, Vienna, 1781–1792.

Giovanni Dall'Orto

Bang, Herman (Joachim) (1857–1912), Danish novelist, journalist and theatre director. After graduating from high school in 1875, Bang arrived in the rapidly expanding city of Copenhagen. He had no success in his ambition to become an actor, but very soon established himself as a *feuilletonniste*, a journalist and an author of critical essays inspired by French naturalism. His excessively mannered and pointed style both delighted and offended readers. Whatever subject he touched was made sensational. His early reportage included detailed descriptions of the horrifying living conditions in the slums of Copenhagen. Bang's journalism was and still is considered a pioneering achievement.

His early novel, *Haabløse Slægter* (*A Generation Without Hope*, 1880), described the life of a young degenerate and failed actor, the victim of neurotic parentage, of congenital tuberculosis, and of Countess Hatzfeldt's and other women's sexual inclinations: 'The Countess loves children so much'. The book was banned by the Supreme Court as immoral. At the same time, as a very young man, Bang developed the persona of a decadent dandy whose homosexuality was strongly implied and widely known or suspected. He established himself as Denmark's most notorious and exemplary homosexual man.

Undoubtedly Bang was the most modern of the authors of the so-called 'Emergence of Modernity' from 1875 to 1890. His major novels, *Ved Vejen* (*At the Roadside*, 1886), *Stuk* (1887), *Tine* (1889), and *Ludvigsbakke* (1896), are still widely read and admired. They have given Bang a place in the foremost rank of Danish novelists. The less important novel, *Mikaël* (1904), is traditionally viewed as his most explicit representation of homosexuality.

Bang's position as an exemplary homosexual made him vulnerable to slander. In order to escape from this nerve-racking lifestyle he spent long periods as a quasi-exile in the Danish provinces, and in France and Germany. During a stay in Paris from 1893 to 1895 he was engaged by Aurélien Lugné-Poë at the experimental Théâtre de l'Œuvre, where he introduced the plays of his Nordic contemporaries Henrik Ibsen, Bjørnstjerne BJØRNSON and August STRINDBERG to the Parisian audience. The crowning point of his success was to direct the primadonna Gabrielle Réjane as Nora in Ibsen's *A Doll's House*. However, also outside of Denmark Bang was persecuted and defamed as a sexual pervert in anonymous letters 'from home'.

Nowhere in Bang's novels is homosexuality explicitly represented. Still, it is possible to read his *œuvre* as a continuous endeavour to express, implicitly, the homosexual's terms of existence by the *fin de siècle*, at the transition from premodernity to modernity. In Bang's novels the trauma of this transition is explained, even caused, by the lost War of 1864 between Denmark and Prussia, and by the ensuing secession of large parts of Denmark. The emergence of modern urbanity in the following period was also

an emergence of sexuality. Bang described life in Denmark's pre-modern agricultural society as a pre-war paradise of innocence contrasted to the unbearably painful modern existence. The contrast is explained by the emergence of 'sexuality'. Sexuality for Bang is separated from love, it is a force, independent of and existing beyond the will of the individual. It is *fate*, and mythologised as fate it cannot constitute identity. It dissolves identity with its dark and horrible Dionysian insanity devoid of meaning. Instead of giving life, sexuality can only cause death – and art. Therefore, to be a loving person in Bang's universe is to be a longing and a suffering, even a dying person, because man's deepest longing, the longing for love, can never be satisfied. The only way to survive, for Bang and for his characters, is to become an artist, a writer. Only through the paradox of the literary narrative is it possible to express, with meaning, the impossible longing for love.

Late in life, he collaborated with his German doctor, Max Wasbutzki, on a factual essay on homosexuality, *Gedanken zum Sexualitätsproblem* (*Thoughts on the Problem of Sexuality*) which was published posthumously in 1922. From the privileged position of a homosexual artist and aristocrat he described and interpreted homosexuality as a social and scientific problem. Explicitly he subjected himself to 'medical control' in order to contribute to the prevention of homosexuality, 'not least out of urgent consideration for propagation'. The one love affair in Bang's life was with the German actor Max Eisfeld (Appel), whom he met in Berlin in 1885. Their relationship lasted for a little more than a year.

With great sophistication Bang exploited the new possibilities of modern mass society. He cast himself as the protagonist in a highly visible tragedy and acted out his life between the poles of success and scandal. He had the courage to be offensively effeminate; his consumption of perfume was legendary to the point where 'perfume' – as in 'perfumed literature' – became synonymous with 'homosexual'. As a poseur and a victim of satire, disparagement and calumny, Bang has had no equal. In later life his friends and admirers gave him the sobriquet 'The Little Fakir'. Bang's talent for manipulating the exchange of surfaces was supreme, although it was probably more a compulsion than voluntary. In his youth his dark-coloured fringe accentuated the pallor of his skin; 'his weird whiteness made the light from his darkly burning, sad eyes secretly phosphorescent'. When he aged, he assumed the figure of an infinitely wise man of the world who carries the heavy burden of knowledge of the human condition: suffering as man's inexorable master. Although Bang died a natural death from exhaustion, on a train near Ogden, Utah, while on a lecture tour in the US, the public and some of his aquaintances believed that he had committed suicide, the only natural death for a homosexual.

C. Rimestad, 'Herman Bang', *Dansk Biografisk Leksikon*, Vol. 1, Copenhagen, 1979: 403–7; Pål Bjørby, 'The Prison House of Sexuality: Homosexuality in Herman Bang Scholarship', *Scandinavian Studies*, 58 (1986); Wilhelm von Rosen, *Månens Kulør. Studier i dansk bøssehistorie 1628–1912*, Copenhagen, 1993: 628–54; H. Bech, *When Men Meet: Homosexuality and Modernity*, Cambridge, 1997; H. Jacobsen, *Herman Bang*, 5 vols. Copenhagen, 1954–1974.

Wilhelm von Rosen and Øystein S. Ziener

Barnes, Djuna (1892–1982), American writer, journalist. Barnes was born in New York; a legendary recluse, she led a secluded life in Greenwich Village at odds with the reputation that she earned during the 1910s, 1920s and 1930s as a reporter, writer, artist and habitué of Bohemian circles in New York and Paris. However, her account of Bohemian life, written in a style which ranged from mordantly acerbic humour to hyperbolic and nostalgic sentimentality, might be understood as a natural precedent to the shut-in life she adopted from the 1950s to her death.

Barnes's career in journalism followed her unorthodox private schooling and formal education at the Pratt Institute in Brooklyn and the Artists' Student League in 1912–1913. In her popular journalism and short fiction, she developed some of the idiosyncratic narrative techniques that typify her later work; at the same time she wrote decadent poetry and plays for the Provincetown Players, and developed a Beardsleyesque illustrative style. *The Book of Repulsive Women* (1915), a chapbook of poems and drawings, documents the lives of women living in a Bohemian and economic twilight world on the streets of Manhattan, and adopts a vocabulary reminiscent of Baudelaire to describe lesbians and their ways.

Barnes travelled to Paris in 1921, becoming both a peripatetic journalist and the denizen of bars, cafés and artistic salons as she published *A Book* (1923), *Ryder* (1928), *A Night Among the Horses* (1929) and a variety of stories, journalistic essays and poems in publications ranging from *Vanity Fair* to *transition*. *Ladies Almanack*, a chapbook privately published in Paris in 1928, documents the circle of women who frequented the salon of Natalie BARNEY. In it, Barnes parodies the adventures and passions of these women, adopting the form of an almanac which recounts the cycle of the seasons as a narrative of love, contest and digressive anecdote. This *roman à clef*, sold privately and a *succès de scandale* in Barnes's own literary and personal circles, offers one of the best if more eclectic contemporary portraits of Barney's salon, and the lives and personae of such women as Barney, Romaine BROOKS, Janet Flanner, Solita Solano and Mina Loy.

Barnes's fame undoubtedly rests, however, on her novel *Nightwood*. Its dark reimagining of the 1930s as a time of dislocation and social stigmatisation, its baroque narrative style, and its extended elaboration of the fate of the so-called 'third sex' attracted attention equally for its literary innovation and its sexually explicit consideration of lesbianism. Written over a protracted period through the late 1920s to mid-1930s, and greeted with ambivalence as Barnes sought publication, *Nightwood* was eventually published in 1936 and has remained in print ever since, developing a significant coterie readership as well as considerable academic interest. Her work raises many questions about the assumed style and purpose of modernist innovation; always backward-looking, Barnes's work raises the spectre of decadence and *fin de siècle* aesthetics and politics as the uncomfortable but ineluctable companion of the pared-down aesthetic of literary and cultural modernism.

Barnes's personal life has been the topic of considerable attention, most particularly in the 1983 biography *Djuna: The Life and Times of Djuna Barnes* by Andrew Field, Philip Herring's 1995 biography *Djuna: The Life and Work of Djuna Barnes*, and Hank O'Neal's '*Life is painful, nasty, and short – in my case it has only been painful and nasty*': *Djuna Barnes, 1978–1981: An Informal Memoir.* Her relationships with men and women, and especially her relationship with Thelma Wood, which serves loosely as the model for the lesbian relationship which structures the narrative of *Nightwood*, have all been read in terms of larger questions of sexual definition and identity within modernist writing, and woman's writing in general. Carolyn Allen goes so far as to suggest a 'tradition' of darkly contemplative narrative within lesbian fiction deeply indebted to Barnes's work. Barnes herself was at best ambivalent about the question of lesbian self-identification, and in later years expressed a variety of sentiments from disinterest to disgust when questioned on the topics of lesbianism and feminism. Without doubt, however, Barnes's writing, and *Nightwood* in particular, has had a sustained and invigorating effect on the development of lesbian fiction in the latter half of the

twentieth century, and her coterie publication, *Ladies Almanack*, remains a valuable document in the history of avant-gardes and salon culture in Paris through the first half-century.

C. Allen, *Following Djuna: Women Lovers and the Erotics of Loss*, Bloomington, 1996; S. Benstock, *Women of the Left Bank: Paris, 1900–1940*, London, 1987; M. L. Broe (ed.) *Silence and Power: A Reevaluation of Djuna Barnes*, Carbondale, Illinois, 1991.

Melissa Hardie

Barney, Natalie Clifford (1876–1972), American-French author. Barney saw her life itself as her true work and her writings as merely the result of that life. In almost every respect her life represents not just a conscious refusal to accept patriarchal norms but a positive choice of values and practices which she considered superior. At the same time, in inverting the then fashionable view of art as superior to life, she was both reacting against the standard tenets of contemporary aestheticism and expressing her faith in the importance of the expression of the self through the body. It is indeed as the figure at the centre of the major lesbian social and cultural groups in early twentieth-century Paris that she is principally remembered, but her writings are now attracting attention again as an important expression of the philosophy at work within that group.

Born in Dayton, Ohio, the daughter of a successful American industrialist, Barney grew up in Cincinnati and Washington, and received an effective cultural and linguistic education and travelled widely in Europe from the age of 10. An ability to speak and write fluent French and an interest in both French and classical Greek literature were notable features of her adolescence. French she learnt through two years at a French finishing school; it was probably Eva Palmer, heiress to the Huntley and Palmers biscuit fortune and future wife of the Greek poet Anghelos Sikelianos, who introduced the young Natalie to the delights of both all-female eroticism and Greek culture. Efforts to marry her off came to an end when she impishly declared her determination to marry Lord Alfred DOUGLAS. Her lesbianism was then made clear to her family in the *Quelques portaits, sonnets de femmes* which she published in Paris in 1900, a book which upset her father sufficiently for him to buy up all the copies he could lay his hands on, together with the printing plates. At the same period she made a name for herself by a lesbian relationship with the bisexual courtesan Lyane de Pougy (described in the latter's novel *Idylle saphique*, where Barney appears under the pseudonym Florence Temple-Bradford, which she herself had used). It was on another trip to Paris with her family in 1901 that she became involved in a passionate but ill-starred *affaire* with the poet Renée VIVIEN which was to mark her life until Vivien's death in 1909. But despite the turmoil of this failed relationship, Barney rapidly set about becoming the centre of a literary and social circle – a task facilitated by the financial independence which she derived from her father's death in 1902. First at her home in Neuilly and from 1909 onwards in her house at 20 Rue Jacob, she created a *salon* which was to last for almost sixty years. Her guests from the world of recognised literature included Pierre LOUŸS, Anatole France, André GIDE, Marcel PROUST and Paul Valéry, and her friendship with the bisexual novelist Lucie Delarue-Mardrus introduced her to such aristocratic lesbians as the Princesse de Polignac and the Duchesse de Clermond-Tonnerre (with whom she was to have a long-lasting relationship). For a while, COLETTE was a notable presence. Without excluding men, Barney's *salon* was consciously designed as a separate 'women's space' from a cultural point of view: it focused on all-female entertainments and on presenting the works of women writers, a project strengthened by Barney's foundation, in 1927, of the Académie des Femmes as a place for women writers to try out unpublished works and an institution for subsidising the printing of commercially unviable works.

Lesbianism is not, for Barney, an adjunct to her values; it is at their centre. From her earliest works she argues for the separate and superior nature of female values against any form of male domination or manipulation of women, and that separateness and superiority have their origins in the female body. In *Cinq petits dialogues grecs* (1901) she represents heterosexual sex as a violation of women's wholeness, whereas lesbianism allows the maintenance of both purity (non-penetration) and sensuality. Maternity she saw as a sapping of a woman's potential for any other form of creativity, and her plays and poems consistently reflect that view. Her post-World War I prose works *Pensées d'une amazone* (*Thoughts of an Amazon*, 1920) and *Nouvelles pensées d'une amazone* (*More Thoughts of an Amazon*, 1989) confirmed and expanded her position. The rejection of the male in general and of heterosexuality in particular, coupled with a systematic redefinition of female sexuality and female creativity, is at the heart of these works – paradoxically perhaps, in that they are cast in the form of epigrammatic maxims, a genre exclusively masculine up to that time. Barney uses the naturally paradoxical form of the maxim to show the inherent connections which she sees within such conventionally opposed pairs as love and war, birth and death, sensuality and brutality, in the forms in which those phenomena manifest themselves in contemporary straight society. The belatedly published *Traits et portraits* (1963) shows that her belief in the rightness of her position never wavered to the very end.

S. Benstock, *Women of the Left Bank: Paris, 1900–1940*, London, 1987; K. Jay, *The Amazon and the Page: Natalie Clifford Barney and Renée Vivien*, Indianapolis, 1988; C. Robinson, *Scandal in the Ink: Male and Female*

Homosexuality in Twentieth-Century French Literature, London, 1995.

Christopher Robinson

Barnfield, Richard (1574–1620), English poet. Barnfield was born in 1574 to a well-to-do family in Norbury, Staffordshire. He entered Brasenose College, Oxford, in 1589 and was graduated BA in 1591/2. Although no record survives, Barnfield was probably admitted to Gray's Inn, London, to study law. During the 1590s he was likely a member of the Countess of Pembroke's literary circle.

Barnfield's first book of poems, *Greenes Funeralls* (1594), honours the recently deceased Elizabethan pamphleteer Robert Greene. Later that year Barnfield published *The Affectionate Shepherd*, swiftly followed in early 1595 by *Cynthia, with Certaine Sonnets*. His fourth volume, *The Encomium of Lady Pecunia* (1598), was reissued in 1605. A poem from this work, 'As it fell upon a Day', was for centuries attributed to William SHAKESPEARE, a mix-up which likely stemmed from its inclusion in *The Passionate Pilgrim* (1599). With *Lady Pecunia* Barnfield appears to have ceased writing and to have retired from London to lead the life of a country gentleman (though an impoverished one) at Darlaston.

Barnfield's importance to the history of homosexuality lies primarily in his middle two books. *The Affectionate Shepherd* and *Cynthia* are important contributions to the flowering of homoerotic literature in England during the 1580s and 1590s. Barnfield's lush representations of same-gender male desire keep company with Shakespeare's *Sonnets* and Christopher MARLOWE's *Edward II* and *Hero and Leander*.

In the first two long poems in *The Affectionate Shepherd* we encounter the shepherd Daphnis's deep passion for a younger man named GANYMEDE (who is, allegorically, likely the handsome courtier Charles Blount). Drawing on a centuries-old tradition of pastoral homoeroticism and Ovidian sensuality, Daphnis promises his beloved a world of eroticised abundance, such as a 'pleasant Bower / Fild full of Grapes, of Mulberries, and Cherries'. In this over-heated environment, Daphnis expostulates to Ganymede: 'O would to God (so I might have my fee) / My lips were honey, and thy mouth a Bee. / Then shouldst thou sucke my sweete and my faire flower / That now is ripe, and full of honey-berries'. Alas, Ganymede is unresponsive and Daphnis has the added burden of contending with Queen Guendolen's rival enticements of the disdainful lad.

Barnfield's next book, *Cynthia*, contains a prefatory letter which indicates that certain readers were quite critical of *The Affectionate Shepherd*. Barnfield defends his work, however, by claiming that his poetic 'conceit' was 'nothing else, but an imitation of *Virgill*, in the second Eglogue of *Alexis*'. Commentators on Barnfield have often assumed that the author's reference to the Roman poet VIRGIL's second eclogue was a way to defuse criticism of *The Affectionate Shepherd*'s blatant homoeroticism. George Klawitter has persuasively argued, however, that Barnfield's citation of Classical precedent was his way of avoiding censure for the text's thinly veiled and offensive political allegory in which Guendolen is Lady Penelope Rich, and the ugly old man who pursues the queen is her actual husband, Lord Robert Rich. If homoeroticism had been the problem with *The Affectionate Shepherd*, one would certainly be quite astonished to find *Cynthia*'s sequence of 20 sonnets dealing again, in luxurious and affective language, with Daphnis's sustained yearning for beauteous but unresponsive Ganymede.

For many years it was believed that Barnfield had passed away in 1627; Andrew Worrall has recently proved, however, that the poet actually died in 1620. Worrall also argues that Barnfield's disinheritance in 1598 suggests a reaction by his father against his eldest son's course down a 'perilous path through the literary and social conventions of his time'.

The homophobia which possibly engendered this family quarrel certainly characterises many subsequent appraisals of Barnfield's literary corpus. Edmund GOSSE's entry in the *Dictionary of National Biography*, for instance, informs us that Barnfield's 'best early pieces, and especially his sonnets, are dedicated to a sentiment of friendship so exaggerated as to remove them beyond wholesome sympathy'. As Klawitter notes, this attribution of 'unwholesomeness' (which sadly persists in some later twentieth-century studies) stems largely from modern homophobia. Read with a more open mind, meanwhile, Barnfield's Arcadian dalliances can challenge readers to re-evaluate prejudicial understandings of 'natural' desire and sexuality, and thereby broaden their understanding of the varieties of human experience, past and present.

S. Giantvalley, 'Barnfield, Drayton, and Marlowe: Homoeroticism and Homosexuality in Elizabethan Literature', *Pacific Coast Philology*, 16, 2 (1981): 9–24; G. Klawitter, Introduction to *The Complete Poems*, by Richard Barnfield, Selinsgrove, 1990: 12–58; B. Smith, *Homosexual Desire in Shakespeare's England: A Cultural Poetics*, London, 1990; A. Worrall, 'Richard Barnfield: A New Biography', *Notes and Queries*, 237 (1992): 370–1.

Michael Morgan Holmes

Barrie, J(ames) M(atthew) (1860–1937), British writer. After a strict upbringing in the Scottish village of Kirriemuir, Barrie attended Edinburgh University and then worked as a journalist in Nottingham. A piece extolling the delights of 'Pretty Boys' was rewarded with the sack, and he moved to London as a freelance writer. His fierce work-ethic and prodigious output carried him to the top of his profession within three years.

Barrie began 'worshipping from afar' young actresses of the 1890s London stage, despite his being scarcely five feet tall and having a legendary shyness and reserve broken only in the presence of children. In 1894, dangerously ill with pleurisy and pneumonia, he married actress Mary Ansell. During the convalescent honeymoon it became apparent that Barrie had little real interest in women. The childless marriage was a sham and his wife became increasingly bitter.

Barrie 'went back to the silence of his study' and began his first novel of boyhood, *Sentimental Tommy*, finding a life-model in his close friendship with Arthur Quiller-Couch's son, Bevil – the first of a lifelong string of intimate friendships with young boys. After success as a novelist, Barrie then made his name as a playwright, his dramatic reputation firmly established with the biting social satire on the English class system, *The Admirable Crichton* (1902).

Peter Pan or the Boy Who Would Not Grow Up was first performed in 1904, with huge success. *Pan* grew from tales told for the five sons of Arthur and Sylvia Llewelyn Davies: Barrie first met the boys on his daily walks among children and their nannies in Kensington Gardens, and they soon became the loves of his life. After their father died he became a surrogate father, and after their mother died he effectively adopted the boys. Further tragedy followed – his beloved George was killed in action at Flanders in 1915, and his adored Michael drowned with an Oxford friend while swimming in the Thames.

A. Birkin, *J. M. Barrie and the Lost Boys*, London, 1970; J. Kincaid, *Child-Loving; The Erotic Child and Victorian Culture*, London, 1993.

Ianthe Duende

Beach, Sylvia (1887–1962), American publisher, bookseller. Beach was born in Baltimore, Maryland, as Nancy Woodbridge Beach. When she was six months old her family moved to Bridgeton, New Jersey, where her father was the pastor of the

Presbyterian church. Unhealthy and frail as a young child, she was a committed reader at a young age of poetry, philosophy, languages and history. She developed a strong sense of morality and the need for service from her family, but rejected a more specific religious practice.

When Sylvia was 15 the family moved to Paris for three years and she became acquainted with the city which was to be her home for most of her adult life. In 1918 she studied typing and shorthand with an eye to working in business, but instead decided to travel to Serbia to work for the Red Cross. She was profoundly moved by her six months there, and returned to Paris a feminist after seeing the disempowerment of women in Red Cross decision-making, and a socialist and pacifist as a result of viewing damages wrought by World War I.

In Paris in 1917 she met Adrienne Monnier, the woman who was to be her lover and close friend throughout her life. Monnier, the proprietor of the Left Bank bookstore La Maison des Amis des Livres, was a stalwart and committed beacon in the French literary community, and introduced Beach to Paris's thriving lesbian community.

In 1919, Beach opened Shakespeare and Company, the first English lending library and bookstore in France, with a gift of $3,000 from her mother. First located at 8 Rue Duputien on the Left Bank, the store quickly became a gathering place for writers, artists and readers from the US, Britain and the continent. She was known for fostering writers and giving them, or locating, the support they needed to continue with their work. She provided food, housing, loans, a postal service, and translation, editorial and administrative consultations. Beach was an agent and translator for numerous little magazines and publishers and included amongst her friends James Joyce, Paul Valéry, André GIDE, T. S. Eliot, Ernest Hemingway, Ezra Pound, Mina Loy, John dos Passos, Janet Flanner, Harriet Weaver, Jean Prevost,

Carola Giedion-Welcker, Samuel Beckett, Brancusi, Alexander Calder, Gertrude STEIN, Alice B. TOKLAS, H. D. Bryer (Annie Winifred Ellerman) and Natalie BARNEY.

She was most noted for publishing Joyce's groundbreaking novel *Ulysses*. After encountering censorship concerns in the US and England because of the explicitly sexual passages in the novel, she found a typesetter in France who did not understand English and was therefore willing to bring the book into print. The publication of *Ulysses* fomented an artistic revolution far more significant than even Beach and her associates had envisioned.

In 1941 the Germans occupied Paris and she closed the bookshop on short notice, moving all of its contents to safety before taking refuge with friends in Touraine, where she remained sequestered until after the war. She then returned to Paris where she lived until her death.

N. R. Fitch, *Sylvia Beach and the Lost Generation: A History of Literary Paris in the Twenties and Thirties*, New York, 1983; C. Summers (ed.) *The Gay and Lesbian Literary Heritage*, New York, 1995.

Sarah Holmes

Beaton, Sir Cecil (Walter Hardy) (1904–1980), British photographer, stage and costume designer. Born to a middle-class Hampstead family, Beaton always had aristocratic tastes and ambitions. He became an international celebrity, composed thousands of stylish portrait and publicity shots, designed sets and costumes for Broadway and the movies, and led a thoroughly camp life. Stephen Tennant called him 'a self-created genius'. Beautiful as a child, he identified with the world of the stage from an early age, collecting fashion plates and images of female stars. As was usual, he performed female roles in school plays and theatricals, but rather too well. He entered Harrow in 1918, where he dressed flamboyantly and wore make-up. Later he wrote, 'Most people were frightfully naughty and used to go to bed with tons of people but I didn't'. From 1922 to 1925 he studied history and architecture at Cambridge, but did not graduate. He had a number of flirtations, designed sets for amateur theatricals and acted in female roles.

In the 1920s Beaton commenced a life-long photographic career, using baroque and sometimes surrealist props and mannered gestures for his sitters. He also posed for famous 'queer' photographs, such as Beaton with Tennant in striped jerseys, by Maurice Beck and Helen Mac-Gregor. On his first trip to New York, in 1928–9, Beaton met society figures including the couple Elizabeth Marbury and Elsie DE WOLFE. He secured a contract with *Vogue* to provide photographs and sketches; in 1931 he photographed Hollywood stars. Criticised for painting his face at this time, Cecil denied the charge, noting: 'I adore *maquillage* and so wish that young men could paint their faces, but they definitely can't without being branded as social nuisances'. Beaton was conservative and naïve regarding gay sexual expression on this trip, and was surprised to learn from bachelor journalist Beverley NICHOLS of New York's gay working-class subcultures and of the homosexuality of men such as Oliver MESSEL and Noel COWARD. Beaton later had numerous infatuations with men and a close relationship with Greta GARBO.

Back in England Beaton created in the 1930s a set-like fantasy stage on which he and his many male friends performed. He created remarkable spoofs. *My Royal Past* was published in 1939, the 'auto-biography' of Baroness Von Bülop, née Princess Theodora Louise Alexina Ludmilla Sophie von Eckermann-Waldstein. It included photographs of cross-dressed friends such as Antonio Gandarillas as the Baroness in Second-Empire style, Francis Rose in a dress with his moustache painted out, and Frederick Ashton and Michael Duff in full evening dress – all in vulgar gilded frames. During World War II Beaton worked for the Ministry of Informa-tion shooting memorable images in Britain and North Africa. In the 1950s and 1960s his career was boosted by the regular patronage of the British royal family, to whom he had provided flattering images since 1939.

Beaton designed for a number of plays, musicals and films, such as the stage and film version of *My Fair Lady* and the film *Gigi*. A retrospective of his portraits was held at the National Portrait Gallery in 1968; in 1971 he organised a fashion exhibition at the Victoria and Albert Museum. Throughout his career Beaton put a thoroughly camp aesthetic at the centre of fashionable imagery. He occupied the position of someone wishing to be 'in' society but always nervous of reactions to his homosexuality; when the Wolfenden Report was accepted in 1967 he was delighted and relieved. He was knighted in 1971.

D. Mellor (ed.) *Cecil Beaton*, London, 1986; H. Vickers, *Cecil Beaton: The Authorized Biography*, London, 1985; D. Souhami, *Greta and Cecil*, New York, 1994.

Peter McNeil

Beauchamp, William Lygon, 7th Earl (1872–1938), British colonial governor and politician. Beauchamp was born in London, the elder son of a wealthy and influential family. He was raised in the conservative High Church tradition and educated at Eton and Oxford, succeeding his father as seventh earl in 1891. He was elected mayor of Worcester at the age of 23. The offer of the governorship of New South Wales four years later surprised him; he 'scarcely knew where was the colony & certainly nothing about it'.

Beauchamp, a bachelor, arrived in May 1899 and took up residence at Government House in Sydney. Although inexperienced, he carried out his gubernatorial duties soberly and without complaint. However, to the chagrin of Sydney society, he also sought the company of a Bohemian circle of artists and writers. The poet Henry

Lawson described him as a 'fine, intelligent, cultured gentleman'.

The following year Beauchamp went on leave, eventually returning to England and commencing a political career. Marriage to Lady Lettice Grosvenor produced seven children. He visited Australia many times and was a regular diner at Sydney's Latin Café, a smart homosexual haunt known for its washroom assignations. He occasionally wrote for the Australian press, and in one article lyricised that the local men were 'splendid athletes, like the old Greek statues. Their skins are tanned by sun and wind, and I doubt whether anywhere in the world are finer specimens of manhood . . . The life-savers at the bathing beaches are wonderful'.

In 1931 Beauchamp's wife petitioned for divorce, and he was threatened with criminal proceedings which would reveal his homosexuality. Upon hearing of the matter, King George V made his infamous remark: 'I thought men like that shot themselves.' Beauchamp, who had been Liberal leader in the House of Lords, resigned all of his offices but one and went into exile. He died of cancer in New York on 14 November 1938.

C. Hazlehurst, 'Beauchamp, seventh Earl', in B. Nairn and G. Serle (eds) *Australian Dictionary of Biography*, Melbourne, 1979.

Tim Reeves

Beccuti, Francesco ('Il Coppetta') (1509–1553), Italian poet. Born to a noble family in Perugia, Beccuti held public office and lived the uneventful life of a provincial literary figure there; he died and was buried (in the church of San Francesco al Prato) in his native city. The interest of his poetry, which did not develop far beyond the contemporary models of Petrarch and BERNI, lies not so much in its considerable formal quality as in its content. Beccuti profited from the enormous tolerance of homosexuality, which existed in Italy just before the start of the Counter-Reformation, to discuss his own homosexual loves with a frankness which would become unthinkable only a few decades later. Suffice it to say that among his poems number two long compositions on the 'pros' and 'cons' of homosexual sodomy. A reading of his poems reveals the 'outing' of an entire generation of the upper classes of Perugia in this period; even if the names are disguised, the fact that the true identity of the persons of whom he speaks has come down to us implies that in Beccuti's time they were not a mystery.

For instance, a composition published under the title 'Contro la pederastia' (1545–1553) was a plea to Francèsco Colòmbo ('Il Platòne', 1515?–1553), a professor at the University of Perugia, to abandon his sexual relations with men; however, the final verse says: 'But I know I am wasting my time and this sheet of paper as well'. 'In lode della pederastia' was addressed to a certain Bino (who has been identified as Captain Baldino Baldinèschi), asking him to come to his senses and break off a relationship with a woman, since such a (heterosexual) love was against his true nature. To convince Bino to do so, Coppetta vaunted the beauty of the youth of Perugia – Boncambio, Crispoltino, Contino, Valeriano, Turno, Alcide and Francesco Bigazzini (with whom Beccuti himself was in love). Two further sonnets addressed to Baldinèschi then warned him not to fall too much in love with a certain Pietro, a handsome youth, but with a diamond-hard heart. A comic sonnet chided one Bernàrdo Giùsti for his excessive 'kindness' (which in the comic slang of the time meant 'preference for passive sodomy').

Although three sonnets from around 1553 lauded the virtue and the beauty – more the beauty than the virtue – of a Berardino Alfàni, most of the homosexual verse of Beccuti concerns his love for Bigazzini (whom he called 'Alessi'), which lasted from 1547 to 1553. It is noteworthy that in a time in which it was understood that homosexual love would be pedophilic, Beccuti fell in love with a young adult – one of the sonnets celebrates Bigazzini's twenty-third birthday. The great interest of this 'songbook', which is written in a Petrachian style, is the way in which Beccuti chronicles the phases of his relationship: Beccuti's approaches and Bigazzini's rejection – he was heterosexual and did not appreciate the declarations of Coppetta's 'chaste' love – through rivalry with other homosexuals (Agnolo Felìce Mansuèti, Pellìno Pellìni, Fàbio Stràtta), right to the end. Every phase is presented in explicit terms (though Beccuti was indeed married). The verses constitute a social, personal and even anthropological document, as well as a literary work, which is practically unique in its genre, and merit a detailed study from the point of view of homosexual history.

E. Chiòrboli, 'Di alcune questioni intorno alle rime del Coppetta', *Giornale storico della letteratura italiana*, 75 (1920): 234–47; C. Mutini, 'Beccuti, Francesco, detto il Coppetta', *Dizionario biografico degli italiani*, Vol. 7, Rome, 1965: 498–503; Abd-El-Kader Salza, 'Francesco Coppetta de' Beccuti, poeta perugino del secolo XVI', *Giornale storico della letteratura italiana*, suppl. no. 3 (1900), especially pp. 30–1 and 113–16; J. Wilhelm (ed.) *Gay and Lesbian Poetry: An Anthology from Sappho to Michelangelo*, London, 1995: 315–17.

Giovanni Dall'Orto

Beckford, William (1760–1844), British writer and collector. Beckford's father, twice Lord Mayor of London and owner of Jamaican sugar plantations, died in 1770, leaving his 10-year-old son the wealthiest man in England. Beckford received a brilliant education, and was widely learned in French, Latin, Greek, Italian, Spanish, Portuguese, philosophy, law, literature and physics by the age of 17; legend has it that Mozart was his private piano teacher. At the age of 19 he fell in love with 10-year-old William Courtenay, later 3rd Viscount and 9th Earl of Devon.

To silence rumours about the relationship, Beckford's family persuaded him to marry Lady Margaret Gordon in 1783 (she died giving birth to their second child in 1786). But in 1784 'strange goings on' between Beckford and Courtenay were alleged to have taken place in Courtenay's bedroom at Powderham Castle, Devon, and scandalous hints about 'Kitty' Courtenay appeared in the newspapers. The scandal was partly fabricated or at least exaggerated by Courtenay's vindictive uncle Lord Loughborough, whose persecution ensured that Beckford was systematically ostracised by the English for the rest of his life. No criminal charges were filed, but King George III dismissed Beckford's application for a peerage. After a year of such abuse Beckford finally went abroad, where he remained for the next ten years (living mainly in Portugal), followed by a magnificent entourage of servants. These were his happiest years, and he had several homosexual relationships with young Portuguese noblemen, especially the young son of the Marquis of Marialva. His longest-lasting lover and friend was Gregorio Franchi, a choirboy whom he brought back with him from Portugal. (Courtenay seems to have led a dissolute life; in 1811 a warrant was issued for his arrest for committing 'unnatural crimes', and he fled to France. He never returned to England, and died in Paris 24 years later.)

In his oriental-Gothic novel and thinly veiled fantasy-autobiography, *Vathek* (written in French but published in an unauthorised English translation in 1786), Beckford portrayed himself as a villainous caliph satiated with sensual pleasures. The deliberately decadent style of the novel directly influenced the novels of Ronald FIRBANK, Joris-Karl Huysmans, and the poetry of Mallarmé and Swinburne. Several additional *Episodes* contain explicitly homosexual tales.

Upon his eventual return to England, Beckford secluded himself behind an eight-mile-long, twelve-foot-high wall surrounding his estate at Fonthill Gifford, Hampshire, attended by a small army of boy-servants which gave rise to rumours of orgies. He devoted much of his wealth towards building Fonthill Abbey, designed by James Wyatt, with a 300-foot central tower and enfilades of Gothic rooms with 300-foot uninterrupted interior vistas. But except for a notable reception for Lord Nelson and Emma, Lady Hamilton at Christmas 1800, his guests were painters, writers, artisans and book dealers, for he was never accepted by polite society. Within this fabulous mansion Beckford gathered together one of the world's finest collections of paintings, books, furniture and *objets d'art*: 20,000 books in his own binding; paintings by Titian, Bronzino, Raphael, Velasquez, Rembrandt, Rubens and Canaletto (20 of the paintings he once owned now hang in the National Gallery, London) as well as the major contemporary artists; a table from the Borghese Palace whose centre consisted of the largest onyx in the world; Jacobean coffers; Venetian glass; Japanese lacquer; and thousands of objects of porcelain, bronze, jewellery, silver, gold and agate, including many silver-gilt settings made to his own exquisite neo-Renaissance designs. Beckford overspent himself and had to sell the Abbey, and in 1823 the central tower collapsed due to inadequate foundations, destroying most of the building. He moved to Bath, where he built another tower, in a chaste Classical-Byzantine design overlooking the town, in whose grounds he was buried.

Beckford also assembled scrapbooks of newspaper cuttings about homosexual trials and scandals, which he discussed with Franchi, for example, 'Tomorrow (according to the papers) they are going to hang a poor honest sodomite. I should like to know what kind of deity they fancy they are placating with these shocking human sacrifices.' He has become a potent symbol for the homosexual outcast who defends himself with arrogant disdain for propriety.

B. Alexander, *England's Wealthiest Son*, London, 1962; B. Alexander, *Life at Fonthill*, London, 1957; B. Fothergill, *Beckford of Fonthill*, London, 1979; M. Jack, *William Beckford: An English Fidalgo*, New York, 1996; R. Norton, *Mother Clap's Molly House*, London, 1992.

Rictor Norton

Behn, Aphra (1640?–1689), British writer. Behn's prolific and versatile career as a professional author in London spanned at least 17 plays and an equally prodigious quantity of poetry, fiction and nonfiction. Turning her hand to whatever was saleable in the literary marketplace, Behn also produced translations from the French and edited anthologies which provided a venue for other women writers. Behn's reputation was made in the theatre in the 1670s and 1680s with such plays as *The Forc'd Marriage*, *The Lucky Chance*, *The Feign'd Curtezans* and *The Widow Ranter*. Her skilful and topical woman-centred dramas of sexual passion and intrigue provided multiple star vehicles for actresses, still a highly eroticised novelty on the Restoration stage. In Behn's best known play, *The Rover*, first performed in March 1677, Elizabeth Barry took the part of the virginal Hellena and, in a later revival, appeared as the charismatic courtesan, Angellica Bianca.

Despite her many successes in print and on the stage, Behn was often in financial difficulty and was imprisoned for debt in 1668. One of the earliest women writers to attempt to earn her living by writing, Behn challenged patriarchal ideology not just as a woman writer unambiguously on the market, but one expressly associated with sexual critique and the sophisticated genres of the theatre, scandal fiction and amatory poetry. Often styled as 'Astrea' or 'Sappho' because of her self-appointed role as advocate of women and scourge of sexual hypocrisy, Behn also had strong links with the libertine aesthetes and privileged amateur writers of the Restoration court, especially the infamous Earl of Rochester. However, Behn's attraction to aristocratic ideology and an epicurean ideal of sensual pleasure and diversity always incorporated a powerful critique of its misogyny in practice. In poems such as 'The Disappointment', 'On Desire' and 'The Willing Mistress', Behn wittily refigures lyric convention and hierarchy to foreground the experience of those occluded by gender and/or rank, specifically replying to the work of her male contemporaries. 'On a Juniper Tree Cut Down to Make Busts' plays on the myth of Daphne, personifying the tree as 'a joyful looker-on' and mute actor in multiple sexual encounters: 'The shepherdess my bark caressed, / Whilst he my root, love's pillow, kissed'. Behn's enigmatic Ovidian lyric, 'To the Fair Clarinda who Made Love to me, Imagin'd More than Woman', has become a key text in contemporary discussions of the complexity of aims, identifications and object-choice in early modern sexualities: 'Thou beauteous wonder of a different kind, / Soft Cloris with the dear Alexis join'd, / When e'er the manly part of thee would plead / Thou tempts us with the image of the maid, / While we the noblest passions do extend / The love to Hermes, Aphrodite the friend.'

Middle-class and mercantile in background, Behn was probably married to John Behn, a tradesman and shipowner of Dutch origin who died of the plague in 1665. Capitalising on the relative autonomy and assertiveness inherent in the legal status and cultural imaginary of the widow, Behn's writing offers a polemical representation of the agency and potential self-marketing of women not limited to the variously hypersexualised figures of the widow, courtesan or mistress but equally disclosing the desires of wives and virgin daughters. Much of Behn's work draws directly on contemporary sexual and political scandal to create racy, commercial texts designed to appeal to a sensation-seeking metropolitan audience. *Love Letters Between a Nobleman and his Sister* (1684–1687), her triple-decker epistolary novel based on the notorious court-room scandal of Forde, Lord Grey's elopement with his sister-in-law, Lady Henriette Berkeley, was a bestseller which ran into at least 16 editions in the century after its first printing. One of Behn's most famous short tales, 'The Fair Jilt', features a cloistered virgin's unsuccessful attempt to seduce and then falsely accuse a chaste Franciscan, climaxing with a journalistic rendition of the spectacularised culture of public execution.

Behn was herself something of a tabloid figure, partly by her own design. Contemporary gossip most commonly linked her to John Hoyle, a lawyer, rake and 'known bisexual' who was unsuccessfully tried for sodomy, and much salacious speculation on the nature of her 'friendship' with Oroonoko, the 'slave prince', followed the publication of *Oroonoko, or the Royal Slave* (1688), Behn's eye-witness narrative of a slave rebellion in colonial Surinam in the West Indies. In recent years this text has galvanised critical attention with its contradictory and yet subtle attempt to inscribe the lurid dynamics of gender, hierarchy and 'race' in the trade between Africa, Surinam and Europe.

Throughout her career as a writer Behn stages a canny and necessarily complicit enquiry into the cultural hegemony of heterosexual relations, but also acknowledges the heterogeneity, perversity and instability of desire. At her most utopian she gestures towards the reciprocity and fluidity of desire between and across the divisions of sex, gender, rank and 'race' in such a way as to call into question both the priority of heterosexuality and the truth of gender, always returning to a shrewd analysis of the multifarious operations and seductions of power. Critical analysis of Behn's work is a cornerstone of current feminist and queer analysis of the performance of subjectivity and sexuality during the Restoration. Her poems are standard inclusions in even the most traditional anthologies, her collected works have been reissued and many of the individual plays and prose texts mentioned here are available in multiple editions.

S. Wiseman, *Aphra Behn*, London, 1996; H. Hutner (ed.) *Rereading Aphra Behn*, Charlottesville, 1993; J. Todd, *The Secret Life of Aphra Behn*, London, 1998; R. Ballaster, *Seductive Forms*, Oxford, 1992; J. Goldberg, *Desiring Women Writing*, Stanford, 1998.

Kate Lilley

Benedict, Ruth F. (1887–1948), American scholar. Benedict was a prominent anthropologist who popularised characterisations of whole cultures as having particular personalities. Unsatisfied with a marriage contracted in 1914, she enrolled in the New School for Social Research in 1919 and was influenced by students of Franz Boas (1858–1943) to study with the master himself at Columbia University. She earned her PhD in 1923 with a thesis on the distribution of the concept 'guardian spirit' in native North America. In subsequent years as Boas's 'right hand', administrative subordinate and chosen successor, she did fieldwork among the Zuni and Cochiti in the American Southwest.

Although her collections of folklore are known to specialists, it was her book *Patterns of Culture* (1934), applying the concept 'Apollonian' to the Zuni – and contrasting them to the 'Dionysian' Knwagiutl studied by Boas and the 'treacherous' Dobu studied by Reo Fortune – that made her famous. It introduced simplistic characterisations of primitive cultures to a wide audience as a means of demonstrating the variability (and, thus, malleability) of 'human nature' – with passing mention of different conceptions of homosexuality.

Benedict was noted for a lack of sympathy for male students. She had a coterie of younger women around her, including her most famous student, Margaret MEAD (1901–1978), with whom she was sexually, intellectually and politically involved during the last two decades of her life (both had relationships with other women as well, and Mead with several men, including her three husbands). Aiming to contribute to psychological war efforts, the two pioneered 'the study of culture at a distance' during World War II, working with persons in New York who had been raised in cultures of strategic interest. Benedict wrote about Rumanian and Thai culture, as well as her famous discussion of militarism and aestheticism in Japanese 'national character', *The Chrysanthemum and The Sword*. As with her characterisation of Zuni as free of conflict, her interpretation of Japan has had numerous specialist critics and many readers.

M. C. Bateson, *Through a Daughter's Eyes*, New York, 1984; M. Mead, *An Anthropologist at Work*, Boston, 1959; J. S. Modell, *Ruth Benedict*, Philadelphia, 1983.

Stephen O. Murray

Benson, E(dward) F(rederic) (1867–1940), British novelist. The third son of Edward White Benson, Archbishop of Canterbury from 1883 to 1895, he was born at Wellington College, where his father was then headmaster. He was educated at Marlborough College and at King's College, Cambridge University, where he graduated BA in 1891. A brilliant classical scholar and a natural athlete, he was on the staff of the British School of Archaeology in Athens from 1892 to 1895 and of the Society for the Promotion of Hellenic Studies, in Egypt, in 1895. From 1895 he was a full-time writer, living in the fashionable West End of London. In 1919 he acquired the lease of a house formerly owned by Henry JAMES at Rye in Sussex, which increasingly became his home. He was mayor of Rye from 1934 to 1937.

Like his two brothers, Arthur and Hugh, 'Fred' Benson was a prolific writer. From 1893 he published a stream of novels (70 in total) which were very popular among the upper classes, in which real people were often disguised by fictional names. The best known of these are his *Mapp and Lucia* series. These record, with cynical amusement, the petty snobberies and social clashes of small-town life between the wars. Many of his works, although elegantly written, are superficial. More substantial are his later works: biographical sketches, histories and reminiscences. Despite the scale of his literary work, and the fame it brought him, Benson successfully concealed his private opinions and private behaviour from everyone else. However, there is no doubt that, like his brothers, he was homosexual. The entry on Benson in the *Dictionary of National Biography* observes that he had 'a generalized dislike of women'. He enjoyed the company of handsome and intelligent young men, regularly holidayed in Capri and in several of his novels wrote about fervent schoolboy friendships. After the publication of his schoolboy novel *David Blaize*, an anonymous admirer sent him a square piece of paper on which was written 'I know your secret'. There is no direct evidence that Benson ever had sexual relationships with other men; disinterested affection without sexual expression was his ideal. In the way he dealt with his homosexuality he was representative of many gay men of his generation and class.

B. Askwith, *Two Victorian Families*, London, 1971; B. Masters, *The Life of E. F. Benson*, London, 1991; G. Palmer and N. Lloyd, *E. F. Benson – as he was*, Luton, 1988; D. Williams, *Genesis and Exodus: A Portrait of the Benson Family*, London, 1979.

David Hilliard

Bentham, Jeremy (1748–1832), British moral philosopher and legal reformer. Born in London as the son of an attorney, Bentham was the founder of utilitarianism. According to Boralevi he was also responsible for 'the earliest scholarly essay on homosexuality presently known to exist in the English language'. His voluminous but, until recently, sadly unpublished writings on 'pederasty' were radical for his own time, and remained radical at least until gay liberation. Unlike

his Enlightenment predecessors, VOLTAIRE and Montesquieu, Bentham was daringly consistent in his application of the principles of rationality to the still unmentionable sin.

Bentham's attempt to found morality on rational and enlightened principles takes human well-being, pleasure or 'utility' as its ultimate standard. But in contrast to the Marquis de SADE, who celebrated the pleasure of the agent at the expense of his victim, 'utilitarianism' enjoins us to maximise the pleasure and minimise the suffering of humanity as a whole. At a time when the punishment for sodomy was either hanging or the pillory – a punishment often no less fatal – Bentham's ethical principle had radical implications indeed, since 'pederasty' gives obvious pleasure to its willing practitioners and causes no obvious harm. The central pillar of Christian homophobia, which deems pederasty unnatural, is also revealed to be without foundation. Apart from the fact that pederasty is less common than the more 'prolific appetite', 'All the difference would be that the one was both natural and necessary whereas the other was natural but not necessary. If the mere circumstance of its not being necessary were sufficient to warrant the terming it unnatural it might as well be said that the taste a man has for music is unnatural'. Bentham proceeded, over the course of a long and productive career, to assemble an impressive array of arguments to the effect that sexual relations between men are harmless and may even be useful. He rehearses free-thinking arguments against religious morality, which eagerly offers human pleasures as sacrifices to a spiteful God. At the same time, attacking religion on its own terms, Bentham rebuts standard homophobic interpretations of the Bible. Thus the story of Sodom and Gomorrah is a lesson against inhospitality rather than sodomy. Nor can the exceptional acts of a vengeful Providence be intended to establish everlasting moral laws, as the story of Abraham and Isaac surely confirms. Tracing much of the problem with Christianity to ST PAUL, Bentham maintains that 'Asceticism is not Christianity but Paulism'. This claim was elaborated in a book titled *Not Paul but Jesus* (1816–1818), which was eventually published, but only pseudonymously and without the chapters on pederasty.

Bentham also conscientiously refutes any suggestion that pederasty causes harm or suffering and so is unacceptable according to his own utilitarian principles. Against Montesquieu, Bentham cites the example of the ancient Greeks and Romans to show that even passive sodomy neither feminises its devotees nor diminishes the manly strength of the nation. And pederasty is never likely to unduly deprive women of their venereal pleasures, since it is usually a transient relationship between older and younger men, which excludes neither heterosexual intercourse nor marriage. In any case, the sexuality of women is surely more restricted by the demands of modesty than by the abstention of pederasts. Voltaire's fear that the human race would disappear if homosexuality were to become the universal rule – itself, perhaps, a revealing fear – is ridiculous: 'The apprehension of a deficiency of population for want of the regular intercourse between the sexes in the way of marriage is altogether upon a par with an apprehension of the like result from a general disposition in mankind to starve themselves'. The Church's commitment to fertility also rests on shaky ground. Or as Bentham acidly remarks, 'If then merely out of regard to population it were right that pederasts should be burnt alive, monks ought to be roasted alive by a slow fire'. Bentham also recognises the legal obstacles to the enforcement of sexual morality, which would eventually play an important role in the decriminalisation of homosexuality. Material evidence is inevitably scarce and the dangers of malicious prosecution and blackmail are considerable. Nor, finally, are prejudice and 'antipathy', which reflect differences

merely 'in point of taste and opinion', any reason to punish an otherwise harmless activity. Prejudice, Bentham optimistically assumes, can be alleviated by his own rational utilitarian arguments. As a ground for punishment, antipathy might justify the prohibition of almost anything.

Bentham goes so far as to propose an 'all comprehensive liberty' in matters of sexuality, for 'If there be one idea more ridiculous than another, it is that of a legislator who, when a man and a woman are agreed about a business of this sort, thrusts himself in between them, examining situations, regulating times and prescribing modes and postures'. Greater sexual freedom might even remove one of the causes of pederasty. It is the excessive constraint of young men's desires which, along with feather beds – 'implements of indulgence and incentives to the venereal appetite with which the antients were unacquainted' – drives them to 'improper' sexual outlets. By the time of his later writings, Bentham has abandoned earlier concessions to popular prejudice regarding this 'perverted taste' and 'abomination'. His newly acquired Malthusian views, concerning the inevitable tendency of population to exceed the resources available to sustain it, even led him to acknowledge the positive usefulness of this 'improlific appetite'.

J. Bentham, from 'Offenses against Oneself: Pederasty' (*c.* 1785), and from 'Offenses Against Taste' (1814–1816), in M. Blasius and S. Phelan (eds) *We Are Everywhere: A Historical Sourcebook of Gay and Lesbian Politics*, London, 1997: 15–33; L. C. Boralevi, *Bentham and the Oppressed*, Berlin, 1984; J. E. Crimmins, *Secular Utilitarianism: Social Science and the Critique of Religion in the Thought of Jeremy Bentham*, Oxford, 1990; L. Crompton, *Byron and Greek Love: Homophobia in 19th-Century England*, Berkeley, 1985.

David West

Berber, Anita (1899–1928), German dancer and silent movie actress. Berber is an icon of modern expressive dance and German silent film of the 1920s. She was born into an artistic family; her father was a violinist and her mother an actress and singer. Berber grew up in Munich and Berlin and made her début as a ballet dancer in Berlin at the age of 17. With Valeska Gert and other young dancers she performed modern avant-garde dance soirées to the music of Debussy, Saint-Saëns and Sibelius. Her costumes were innovative, too, designed, for example, by doll-maker Lore Pritzel. A tour of Germany in 1919 was extremely successful and received enthusiastic reviews in the quality press. Along with Expressionist silent film, to which it was aesthetically related, modern expressive dance was regarded as a new and exciting art worthy of serious attention.

In 1919, in order to escape the restrictions of the maternal household, Berber entered a marriage of convenience to a certain Nathusius (his first name remains unknown). Two years later she left her husband to live with her lover Susi Wanowski. Berber became part of the lesbian social and cultural scene which established itself in the Berlin of the Weimar Republic. She had a large circle of female friends and lovers and regularly performed in women-only bars.

Berber acted in many classics of the German silent film era, including Richard Oswald's *Peer Gynt* and Fritz Lang's *Dr. Mabuse der Spieler* (*Dr. Mabuse the Player*). She lived excessively, drank heavily and from the early 1920s was addicted to the fashionable drug of the day, cocaine. Otto Dix painted a famous portrait of Berber in her mid-twenties, which caricatured her as a worn-out old woman. Another, perhaps more significant, reason for her decline was her inability to hold her ground as a dancer in the increasingly conservative Weimar Republic of the mid-1920s. In order to survive, she was ever more frequently forced to appear in late-night bars in front of an audience exclusively interested in her nudity. She

became infamous for the scandals she caused, smashing champagne bottles over the heads of punters sitting near the stage.

In 1925 she married the gay American dancer Henri Chatin-Hofmann, and together they tried to live a less excessive life and to build up a collaborative career. They toured The Netherlands with a successful repertoire in 1926, but following this, Berber collapsed physically and was taken in by her friend, the doctor and psychoanalyst Magnus HIRSCHFELD. In 1928 on a trip to North Africa she collapsed again and died from the effects of tuberculosis. The gay German film-maker Rosa von Praunheim paid homage to Berber in his 1987 film *Anita – Tänze des Lasters* (*Anita – The Dances of Sin*).

L. Fischer, *Tanz zwischen Rausch und Tod*: *Anita Berber 1918–1928 in Berlin*, Berlin, 1996; A. Meyer, *Lila Nächte*, Cologne, 1981.

Andrea Capovilla

Bergerac, Savinien Cyrano de (1619–1655), French writer. He was born in Paris, in spite of his Gascon-sounding name which accounts for the theatrical character created by Edmond Rostand (1897), a fictitious personnage who has come to obscure the real Cyrano. In fact, far from being the quixotic buffoon imagined by Rostand and perpetuated by the French tradition (that of a ridiculous and bombastic duellist in love with priggish Roxane), Cyrano was an incisive and cutting-edge thinker. Recent studies have exploded the French and Hollywood myth of a philandering, boisterous yet pathetic Cyrano (unfortunately sustained by actor Gérard Depardieu in a 1990 film) and restored this original thinker to his prominence among the *libertin* avant-garde of the first half of the seventeenth century, in the great Paduan tradition.

The *libertins* were intellectuals who, in the face of Calvinist rigourism and Counter-Reformation propaganda, found in Greek and Roman scepticism materials and methods to debunk dogmas and develop 'free-thought' and, often by implication, to reinvent what was then labelled 'pagan' morality, sex. The best example is by another *libertin*, François de La Mothe Le Vayer, who extolled Greek love in his *Hexaméron rustique* (1670), having laid the foundations for it in his early and anonymous *Dialogues* (1630), and who was a friend of Molière, whose *Don Juan* is strongly marked by *libertinage*. Cyrano the homosexual cannot be taken in isolation. Well known at the time for his satirical plays (and a tragedy), more known today for his two famous cosmic voyages (*L'Autre monde* or *Histoire comique des Etats et Empires de la Lune et du Soleil*, in two separate parts, published posthumously in 1656 and 1661), he developed a scathing critique of French society.

His work has recently been repositioned within a network of homosexual friendships. Cyrano entertained a relationship with notorious *libertin* writers Charles Coypeau d'Assoucy (1605–1677) and Chapelle (1626–1686), all three of them close to Molière and, in one way or another, students of Epicurean philosopher Pierre Gassendi (1592–1655), whose own passionate biographies of celebrated savants of the time point towards the importance of homosocial friendships in such circles. Whether an atheist or not, it is certain that Cyrano's rejection of Catholic dogmas regarding nature, society (he stood against absolutism) and morality found its source in his homosexuality as a subversive force. He had to exercise caution in concealing his 'atheism' (the sum total of the above) since such random accusation had cost the life of a forerunner, Lucilio Vanini (1585–1619), burnt at the stake in Toulouse, and brought to the pyre an effigy of fellow poet and homosexual Théophile de VIAU (1590–1626), as well as it frightened sympathiser René Descartes enough to have him escape to Holland.

Yet, in the central episode of *Les Etats du Soleil*, Cyrano lifts the veil on his homosexuality: a comely youth appears, whose bodily beauty resonates through the universe, cosmetic appearance and cosmic arrangement being one in the raptured contemplation of male assertiveness. Cyrano does not rework here the commonplace of Renaissance 'harmonic man', as his philosophy is a materialistic one, steeped in atomism. The young man does not fulfil the function of an allegory for an orderly universe. It is an erotic vision, powerfully sexual and seminal, which signs, as it were, that unfinished manuscript, held back by the author at the time of his death.

Cyrano de Bergerac, *Œuvres complètes*, ed. M. Alcover, 3 vols, Paris, 1998.

Philippe-Joseph Salazar

Berni, Francesco (1497–1536), Italian author. Born in the Florentine hinterland, Berni studied in Florence and developed a love of playful, populist poetry in the tradition of Burchiello. In 1517 he moved to Rome and entered the service of his distant relative, the cardinal and literary figure Bernardo Dovizi da Bibbiena (1470–1520), after whose death he worked for his nephew, the Apostolic Proto-Notary Agnolo Dovizi da Bibbiena. In 1523, Bibbiena exiled Berni to the abbey of San Giovanni in Venere, in Abruzzo, to punish him for a homosexual scandal about which little is known. Since the scandal had cost him his job, when Berni returned he entered the service of the austere reformist bishop Giovan Matteo Giberti (1495–1543), with whom he went to Verona in 1527. Five years later, tired of Giberti's rigour, Berni found employment with Cardinal Ippolito de' Médici, whom he followed to Bologna, Florence and Rome. In 1534, he returned to Florence and engaged with the Médici court. Such frequentations proved fatal, as he was drawn into intrigues and the struggle between Ippolito and Alessandro de' Médici for control of the Florentine government: Berni was himself poisoned when he refused to poison Ippolito's supporter, Cardinal Giovanni Salviati.

Berni's fame rests on his comic compositions (called 'chapters'), which are written in two registers. On the surface, the poems offer either praise to objects of trifling importance (a needle, fennel, fish) or disdain (the plague). The words, however, are always used with a double meaning which is sexual and very often homosexual. This type of poetry enjoyed a great success and was called 'Bernesque poetry' after the writer; among other practitioners were Angelo Firenzuola (1493–1543), Andrea Lori (sixteenth century), Matteo Franzesi (sixteenth century) and Giovanni DELLA CASA (1503–1556), who was rumoured to have written a book titled *De laudibus sodomiae seu pederastiae* ('In praise of sodomy, that is to say, pederasty'), a volume which in fact never existed. These poems were collected in three volumes. Several of Berni's followers as well showed a preference for homosexual themes, such as Benedetto VARCHI (1503–1565), Lodovico Dolce (1508–1568), Francesco Maria Molza (1484–1544) and Anton GRAZZINI ('Il Lasca') (1503–1584).

The most shocking aspect of Berni's poetry is that not only did he celebrate sexuality in all of its forms (including homosexuality), but he breached the machismo rule of the Renaissance (according to which sodomy could only be written about in the voice of the 'active' partner). Berni's poetry, in contrast, also exalts passive sodomy. For instance, in a 1533 poem in which he discusses the danger of being captured by Turkish pirates while travelling by sea, Berni declares: 'I already warned several officers / and prelate friends of mine: "Be careful / because in these countries prisoners are impaled". / And they replied: "We are not frightened; / if this is the only harm we shall receive / we shall consider it an advantage and a piece of good luck; / furthermore for such a pleasure / we shall intentionally go as far as to Trebizond / so that what has to be done be done as soon as possible". / While I was writing this, I was reminded / about our dear Molza, who once told me / about them in a very solemn way: / somebody

once told me: "Molza, I am that crazy / that I would like to become a vineyard / to have plenty of stakes and change them as frequently as possible". / . . . / Molza replied: "Therefore haste to put our hand on oars / . . . / let's sail, since I would also like / to be that gloriously impaled"'.

Berni went so far as to use his coded language to ask a friend of his for 'hams' (i.e. both 'buttocks' and 'catamites') in private letters of 1550–1551. (The friend, Vincilao Boiano [1485/1490?–1560], who as a young man had also written love poems to Giovan Matteo Giberti, seems to have been particularly skilled in spotting young men who were available for sex.) Berni even praised as an 'utterly lucky man above any other man he who / can both give and take "peaches" [i.e. "pricks"]'.

His Latin poetry, in which he no longer needed to resort to *doubles entrendres* to write about his love for a youth, is particularly explicit. These verses, which were written in a moment of desperation, when Berni's beloved was stricken with plague and seemed to be on his deathbed, are among his most sincere and delicate works. The unexpected recovery of the youth provided the occasion for a Latin poem in which Berni gave vent to his joy. Berni is, in sum, one of the most interesting poets of the Italian Renaissance, not only for what he wrote, but also for his network of friends, which included several outspoken homosexually inclined men.

Carmina quinque illustrium poetarum, Florence, 1562: 137–59, 164–5); F. Berni, *Rime burlesche*, Milan, 1991; G. Dall'Orto, 'Bernesque Poetry' and 'Burchiellesque Poetry', in W. Dynes (ed.) *Encyclopedia of Homosexuality*, New York, 1990: 131–2, 173–4; G. Dall'Orto, 'Chiamiamoli prosciutti', *Babilonia*, 123 (June 1994): 71–3; J. Wilhelm (ed.) *Gay and Lesbian Poetry: An Anthology from Sappho to Michelangelo*, London, 1995: 311–13.

Giovanni Dall'Orto

Bernstein, Eduard (1850–1932), German journalist and socialist politician. Born in

Berlin to a lower-middle-class Jewish family, Bernstein joined the German Socialist Democratic Party in 1872, was exiled in 1878 and finally returned to Berlin in 1901, where he became the leader and principal theorist of the 'revisionist' wing of the socialist movement. Most notably in his book *Evolutionary Socialism* (1898), Bernstein parts company with the insurrectionary socialism of contemporaries like V. I. Lenin, advocating a gradual and parliamentary or 'evolutionary' path to socialism. Bernstein's views on homosexuality can be found in two short pamphlets written after the Oscar WILDE trial of 1895. Bernstein deplores the fact that the socialist movement unscientifically harbours a wide range of incompatible views on sexuality: 'There is more *pre*-judging than *judging*, and extreme libertarianism borrowed from philosophical radicalism alternates with an almost pharisaical, ultra-puritan, morality'.

Bernstein's historical-materialist convictions, inspired by Marx, require him to judge sexual mores (according to Weeks) 'in historical perspective rather than in absolute terms'. This approach leads Bernstein to a number of relatively enlightened conclusions. 'Male love' should be regarded as statistically abnormal rather than 'unnatural' or immoral. In any case, many good things are unnatural or uncommon. And most sexual acts are non-procreative and so, by the strict Christian standard, immoral. 'Abnormal' sex, Bernstein notes, has flourished in diverse cultures throughout history without being associated with decadence. Bernstein adopts the essentially liberal position that 'sodomy' is an issue of individual morality, which lies beyond the legitimate concern of the state and law. Society should not condemn homosexuality but, as KRAFFT-EBING, HIRSCHFELD and most of those in the homosexual reform movement in Germany argued, treat it as an unchosen, 'pathological' and, therefore, guiltless condition.

Unfortunately, Bernstein's uncomfortable defence of homosexuality as an unchosen affliction is further compromised: 'As long as social conditions which, so to speak, threaten natural sexual pleasure with punishment, as long as our entire way of life does constant injury to the requirements of health of body and spirit, then so long will abnormal sexual intercourse not cease. On the contrary it will reveal a tendency to become the normal'. A more enlightened sexual morality and legislation would, he implies, help to eradicate the 'problem' altogether. Nor does Bernstein conceal his distaste for the decadent 'cult of cynicism, paradox and refinement' surrounding Oscar Wilde. Indeed, Bernstein regards the corrupt and pernicious doctrine of 'art for art's sake' as far more dangerous than the 'inconsequential' actions that led to Wilde's imprisonment.

E. Bernstein, *Evolutionary Socialism* (1898), New York, 1961; E. Bernstein, *Bernstein on Homosexuality: Articles from 'Die Neue Zeit', 1895 and 1898*, Belfast, 1977; J. Weeks, *Coming Out: Homosexual Politics in Britain from the Nineteenth Century to the Present*, London, 1977.

David West

Bjørnson, Bjørnstjerne (1832–1910), Norwegian author and public figure. Bjørnson, a Lutheran minister's son, was born in the parish of Kvikne in the rural part of central Norway, and followed his family to Romsdalen in the western part of the country when his father was appointed vicar of another rural parish. At the age of 18, he moved to Christiania (Oslo) to continue his education, and from then on spent much of his life moving from place to place, spending long periods of time in Rome and Paris, and at his estate, Aulestad, in the Gudbrandsdalen valley north of Oslo. In his younger years, Bjørnson combined his writing career with shorter engagements as a magazine and newspaper editor in Christiania and working for several years as a theatre director in Christiania and Bergen, before devoting himself primarily to writing and public debate (particularly on social and political issues) from the 1870s. His works includes poetry (his most famous poem being the Norwegian national anthem, 'Ja, vi elsker dette landet'), numerous novels, short stories, plays, essays and letters. In 1858, he married the actress Karoline Reimers (1835–1934). Bjørnson was awarded the Nobel prize for literature in 1903.

From 1856 onwards, Bjørnson maintained what might perhaps be called a platonic love relationship with Clemens PETERSEN (1834–1918), a Danish critic, who in 1869 had to flee Denmark and settle in the USA, after having been exposed as a homosexual. After this incident, Petersen lost all his friends, except Bjørnson; their friendship and correspondence lasted until Bjørnson's death. Their letters are full of declarations of a special friendship.

Bjørnson also befriended and took care of the Norwegian actor and dresser Ivar Bye (1824–1863), and, when 'the time was ripe', he wrote a very touching story about him (*Ivar Bye*, 1894), in which he describes how Bye falls in love with another man. Bjørnson also wrote a beautiful poem to his friend, called 'Alene og i anger' ('Alone and regretful').

Bjørnson corresponded with several men who fell in love with other men, such as the Danish authors Hans Christian ANDERSEN and Herman BANG. In 1892, he publicly defended the latter against what Bjørnson himself called 'slanderous coarseness'. Five months earlier, in December 1891, Bjørnson published an article titled 'Synd og Sygdom' ('Sin and Illness'), in which he argued against punishment of sexual deviants: 'such persons are impervious to punishment'. In 1901, Bjørnson also openly supported Magnus HIRSCHFELD's campaign against the German anti-gay laws.

Male friendship is a theme in his novel *Arne* (1859), which tells the story of the young farmboy Arne and his friendship with Kristian. When Kristian emigrates to America, he promises to write and to send his address and money, so that Arne can follow him. But Arne's mother hides the letters and the money, in order to keep her only son at home. When Arne's mother finally confesses her sin to the local minister, he takes pity on her and forgives her. Both agree not to tell Arne anything about Kristian, and they decide to try to couple Arne with a girl. They succeed.

J. O. Gatland, 'Enn om vi kledde fjellet – Bjørnson og mannleg vennskap', *Edda*, 82, 1 (1995): 24–39; J. O. Gatland, *Mellom linjene. Homofile tema i norsk litteratur*, Oslo, 1990.

Jan Olav Gatland

Blank, Klaas (*c.* 1705–1735), South African figure. Klaas Blank, a Khoi youth, was sentenced in 1718 to 50 years' imprisonment on Robben Island for reasons which remain unknown. He became the first recorded instance of someone sentenced to death for sodomy in Cape Town. He was executed by drowning in Table Bay in 1735 together with his co-accused, Rijkhaart Jacobz (*c.* 1700–1735) of Rotterdam, when both were in their mid-thirties. Evidence was given that they were seen committing sodomy as early as 1724 on Dassen Island, where they had been sent by prison authorities to collect seal blubber. The sergeant in charge on Robben Island was, according to the court record, informed of these acts but turned a blind eye. He was relieved of his post partly for this reason. His replacement was less tolerant and through severe beating obtained a confession from Jacobz relating to other occasions on which he and Klaas were seen having sex together. These confessions were confirmed in court, leading to their conviction and execution. Their case was not an isolated one. Between 1705 and 1792 more than 200 men were tried, under Dutch law, in 150 sodomy trials conducted by the Court of Justice in Cape Town. Sentences were determined by the nature of the crimes – the death sentence for actual sodomy, and milder punishments, such as flogging, banishment and forced labour, for the crimes of attempted sodomy and mutual masturbation.

J. Oosterhoff, 'Sodomy at Sea and at the Cape of Good Hope During the Eighteenth Century', in K. Gerard and G. Hekma (eds), *Male Homosexuality in Renaissance and Enlightenment Europe*, New York, 1989; Civiele en Crimenele Regstrolle benevens de Processtucken van de Raad van Justitie des Casteels de Goede Hoop, archival nos. VOC 10907 to VOC 10992 (1705 to 1792), General States Archives, The Hague; Court of Justice Records in the Cape Archives.

Graeme Reid

Blüher, Hans (1888–1955), German writer and psychoanalyst. As a young man of 24, Blüher caused a sensation in 1912 with his book *Die deutsche Wandervogelbewegung als erotisches Phänomen* (*The German Wandervogel Movement as an Erotic Phenomenon*), in which he asserted that homoerotic friendships, fostered by the sex-segregated education in Wilhelmine Germany, were essential for the cohesion and popularity of the German youth movement of the Wandervogel. In his autobiography Blüher wrote that between the age of 14 and 20, he was an adept of the 'love of friends'. He was one of the pioneers of the Wandervogel, which emerged around 1900 and which grew out of a romantic form of protest against modern industrialised and urbanised society as well as against the authority of parents and school. Youths set off together in pursuit of unspoiled nature, and their shared experiences on such hiking expeditions facilitated close bonds of friendship. Blüher introduced to the movement Wilhelm Jansen, a wealthy landowner and supporter of Adolf BRAND's Gemeinschaft der Eigenen, who became the centre of a more or less homoerotically orientated circle within the Wandervogel, until he was accused of 'pederasty' and had to resign his position in 1910. Thereupon he, Blüher and others founded a new group, the Jung-Wandervogel, which in contrast to the rest of the youth movement never admitted girls as members.

Blüher grew up in a middle-class milieu in Berlin and studied philosophy, literature, biology and theology, but he completed none of these studies. He read the work of FREUD closely and established himself as a psychoanalyst and writer of cultural and philosophical essays. Following Freud, Blüher elaborated a theory according to which sublimated homosexual feeling was an important factor in binding groups together, from the sanctity of religious orders to the youthful spirit of the Wandervogel and the masculine ethos of military organisations. He projected himself as an independent, revolutionary thinker who courageously raised his voice against a lethargic bourgeoisie. He was undoubtedly intelligent, but also conceited, arrogant and self-centred. Moreover, quite quickly his youthful anti-bourgeois attitude developed into dubious political views.

With his two-volume *Die Rolle der Erotik in der männlichen Gesellschaft* (1917) Blüher became one of the most important right-wing ideologues of the nationalist Männerbund, propagating a purification of German society under the guidance of all-male brotherhoods, in which members would be devoted to each other on the basis of homoeroticism and charismatic leadership. From a cultural perspective he considered male homoeroticism superior to heterosexual relations: women, according to Blüher, were completely at the mercy of their sexual drive, which is inherently aimed at procreation and care, and intellectually they had nothing to offer to men. He was also vehemently against equal rights for men and women. He felt that women's emancipation meant a fatal infringement on the autonomy of the male world and true masculinity, which constituted the foundation of culture and politics. Blüher saw feminisation and cultural levelling as dominant characteristics of the Weimar Republic and these were diametrically opposed to his ideal of male brotherhood. He called himself a Prussian monarchist and corresponded with the former Emperor Wilhelm II, whom he visited in Dutch exile. In 1933 Blüher welcomed the Nazi rise to power, not only because it put an end to the 'Jewish spirit' of Weimar, but also because he expected that the Third Reich would realise his idea of a state based on an élitist male brotherhood. This hope evaporated with the liquidation of Ernst RÖHM in 1934. Blüher was obviously not acceptable to the Nazis because of his plea for homoerotic bonds. Yet, although his work was forbidden under the Nazi regime, he was not persecuted for his views. The remaining years of his life he devoted primarily to philosophical study. He tried but failed to win acclaim with his main work, *Die Achse der Natur* (1949). Right before his death in 1955, Blüher made some of his admirers solemnly promise to fight for a 'rehabilitation of homoeroticism'.

H. Blüher, *Die Rolle der Erotik in der männlichen Gesellschaft. Eine Theorie der menschlichen Staatsbildung nach Wesen und Wert*, Jena, 1919; H. Blüher, *Die deutsche Wandervogelbewegung als erotisches Phänomen. Ein Beitrag zur Kenntnis der sexuellen Inversion*, Berlin, 1912; H. Blüher, *Werke und Tage*, Jena, 1920, 1953; U. Geuter, *Homosexualität in der deutschen Jugendbewegung*, Frankfurt am Main, 1994.

Harry Oosterhuis

Boisrobert, François Le Métel de (1592–1662), French poet and playwright. Born in Caen, Boisrobert, a priest, became a significant figure in the history of both French literature and homosexuality. His passion for the theatre helped him win the favour of Cardinal Richelieu, the all-powerful minister of Louis XIII. The author of 18 plays, Boisrobert contributed to the establishment of the French Academy, of which he was elected a member, and he was appointed a state counsellor. Boisrobert made his career without dissimulating his homosexuality, like numerous other figures in the *ancien régime*. He was notorious for his relationships with

his servants. When he stopped at a hotel, the chambermaid was to prepare 'a bed for Monsieur de Boisrobert and for his lackey'. A contemporary witness affirmed that 'Boisrobert's lackeys never ran the risk of being hanged, but only had to fear being burned at the stake' – the punishment for sodomites. At the age of 60, he still boasted about his sexual conquests of men. Ninon de Lenclos, a celebrated *courtisane*, after staying with nuns who had treated her particularly well, quipped, 'I think that I will follow your example and start to love my own sex.'

Boisrobert's life shows that the history of homosexuality in pre-revolutionary France must not be reduced to one of repression. Though represssion certainly existed, many sodomites pursued their affections openly without scandal or legal troubles.

T. des Réaux, *Historiettes*, Paris, 1970; E. Magne, *Le Plaisant abbé de Boisrobert*, Paris, 1909; M. Lever, *Les Bûchers de Sodome*, Paris, 1985.

Didier Godard

Bonfàdio, Jàcopo (1508?–1550), Italian humanist and historian. Born in Gazano on the Garda River and studying in Verona and Padua, from 1532 Bonfàdio worked as secretary to various cardinals and bishops in Rome and Naples, then in 1540 became tutor to Torquato, the son of the humanist cardinal Pietro Bembo (1470–1547). In the meantime, Bonfàdio's writings had gained him fame; in particular, he was praised for his elegant poetry, and his *Lettere famigliari* (first published in part by Aldo Manuzio in 1543) went through numerous editions. His fame brought him the offer of a position teaching philosophy at the University of Genoa in 1544. In the same year, the government of the Republic of Genoa offered him the prestigious post of official historian of the state. He wrote a meticulous history of Genoa from 1528 to his own time, but his integrity in researching historical 'truth' had fatal consequences. According to the most reliable reconstruction of events, several powerful families, who did not appreciate the way in which Bonfàdio had written about them, took advantage of the fact that the historian had been accused of having seduced one of his students to have him condemned to death for sodomy and beheaded on 9 July 1550; his body was then burned at the stake.

Bonfàdio was one of the very few humanists tried for sodomy to be executed. The connivence of influential persons, which in similar cases was generally successful in at least allowing the accused to escape, in Bonfàdio's case did not happen because of the hatred of the noble families which were offended by his work. The scandal produced by his death sentence was great, and intellectuals throughout Italy mobilised, in vain, to try to save his life. Bonfàdio's execution remained alive in the memory of Italian intellectuals as an unjust act to such a degree that it was still used as a reproof against the Republic of Genoa as late as the end of the eighteenth century. The Genoese government, to save itself from embarrassment, engineered the disappearance of the trial papers at some undetermined moment. With the 'loss' of the documents, from the seventeenth century onwards it was possible for 'patriotic' scholars to deny that the real cause of Bonfàdio's conviction was sodomy. An enormous number of writings appeared on the issue, and as late as 1970, R. Urbani, in the *Dizionario biografico degli italiani*, maintained that the charge of sodomy in reality masked an accusation of heresy. This, however, would have been without parallel, since at the time there was no need to mask accusations of heresy. In reality, recent studies, especially the work of Giovanni Delfino, show that contemporary documents agree on the accusation of sodomy. Thus the idea that the scandal was exploited, if not actually framed, for political reasons appears more likely.

Bonfàdio left two moving 'last letters'

written while he was awaiting the executioner. In one of them, he did not protest his innocence but stated that he did not merit such a heavy penalty. In the other (which some scholars argue to be apocryphal), he wrote: 'Don't bother to plead for me as best you can against human facts and rumours, because this is a manifest error, since they and we and the memory of those who were or will be, will all be devoured by Time. As for my body, I never had a care about entering the grave, nor do I feel it now. The same care displayed by Nature in making my body, she will display in unmaking it. And if I die now, so will those who make me die now, so that eventually either more or fewer days will settle our accounts.' They were prophetic words: time has indeed settled the accounts and erased the memory of those who executed Bonfàdio, but not that of Bonfàdio himself.

J. Bonfàdio, *Le lettere e una scrittura burlesca*, Rome, 1978: 155–6; G. Delfino, 'Dei martirii e delle pene: il caso Bonfàdio', *Sodoma*, 1, (1984): 81–92, which includes further references.

Giovanni Dall'Orto

Bonheur, Marie Rosalie (1822–1899), French painter. Bonheur's parents struggled hard to make ends meet. Her father, a painter, was head of a drawing school for young girls in Paris, a position Bonheur and her sister would hold jointly after his death in 1849. Her mother, a merchant's daughter who gave piano lessons and sewed garters to earn extra income, died when Bonheur was young.

Bonheur's early education was erratic. Most of it took place at home where she, her sister and two brothers all worked to produce artwork that could be sold. At 16, Bonheur enrolled at the art school of the Louvre, and spent long days copying the works of the great masters. At the same time, she began frequenting the slaughterhouses of Paris, studying the anatomy of animals. For such expeditions, Bonheur dressed in male clothing so as to be more comfortable and less remarked upon. Although cross-dressing was illegal, the police eventually granted Bonheur permission to dress in men's clothing for 'health' reasons.

Bonheur had her first painting accepted for the Paris salon in 1841. Within three years, she began to sell paintings, and in 1848 she won the gold medal at the Paris salon. Her growing reputation was further enhanced by the exhibition in 1849 of *Ploughing the Nivernais*, which won great critical acclaim. Her increased independence and the death of her father allowed Bonheur to move into the house of her childhood friend and lover, Nathalie Micas. Bonheur and Micas would remain together until Micas's death in 1889. Bonheur's fame was secured with the 1853 exhibition of *The Horse Fair*. Thousands of lithographic prints of the painting were sold in France, Britain and eventually the United States, where the painting was shown in 1857. With her growing income, Bonheur was able to buy a manor house outside of Paris, the Château de By, where she and Micas lived with a menagerie that included gazelles, a yak and lions. Bonheur was known by this time as the foremost painter of animals, and critics praised her ability to capture the drama of the natural world. In 1864, the Empress Eugénie presented Bonheur with the Legion of Honour. In the 1890s, despite her reputation as one of the century's great painters, Bonheur was increasingly targeted by anti-Semitic attacks. These attacks, formulated when anti-Semitism was on the rise in France and was often invoked to explain perceived moral 'degeneration', were no doubt prompted by her independence and unconventional lifestyle. Bonheur found a second love late in life; in 1897, two years before she died, she met and 'married' the much younger American painter Anna Klumpke. Bonheur, Micas and Klumpke are buried side-by-side in Père Lachaise cemetery in Paris, under a tombstone reading 'Friendship is Divine Affection'.

D. Ashton, *Rosa Bonheur: A Life and A Legend*, London, 1981.

Victoria Thompson

Borgatti, Renata (1894–1964), Italian pianist. The daughter of the famous Wagnerian tenor Giuseppe Borgatti, Renata made her début as a ballerina at a very young age; but her inability to wear tight shoes soon caused her to abandon dance. Borgatti then made a career as a pianist, especially as the most renowned performer of the works of Debussy. She settled in Capri, the 'homosexual paradise' of the 1920s and 1930s, wore her hair short and was recognised for her beautiful face and long eyelashes, her wiry figure, large 'masculine' feet and a throaty deep voice. At age 24, she developed an unrequited love for Lica Riola, a heterosexual woman. Riola was affable but too preoccuped with her own financial reverses; although she had a great affection for Borgatti, she had little time to devote to her, and neither could, nor wanted to, return her feelings.

Against the background of these frustrations, in May 1918, in Capri, Borgatti met Mimì Franchetti, the beautiful daughter of a Venetian baron, Alberto Franchetti, whose arrival had thrown the lesbian world of Capri into commotion. Franchetti, in fact, was stupendously egocentric, unable to keep herself from interfering in any relationship between two other women for the sole purpose of testing her own attractions. Borgatti, given the state of her dissatisfaction with her friendship for Riola, could not but be easily fascinated by Franchetti. Their tempestuous and impassioned relationship lasted about a year. Meanwhile, Franchetti was living in Capri with her own friend Francesca Lloyd, who was hopelessly, and to no avail, in love with her. The relationship between Franchetti and Lloyd paralleled that of Borgatti and Franchetti – flying bottles, furious quarrels, separations, reconciliations and rare periods of harmony. Franchetti, an untameable *femme fatale*, was long the moving spirit behind lesbian parties in Capri, during one of which, when she was completely inebriated, she almost fell off the cliff above the Villa Solitaria. She continued to be surrounded by women who were madly in love with her.

Borgatti, however, in 1919, took up with Romaine BROOKS, then aged 45, who painted an intense portrait of *Renata Borgatti at the Piano*. Franchetti then tried, without success, to conquer Brooks, who possessed such fame and charisma that any girl able to spark her interest boasted that this was almost like being loved by SAPPHO herself! However, Brooks's interest in Borgatti was short-lived; the year after they met, Brooks was already writing to Natalie BARNEY that she was trying to avoid a visit by Borgatti and no longer had any intention of aiding her financially.

Also in 1920, Borgatti's studio at Punta Tragara was demolished to make room for the building of a mansion, and the pianist left the island. She then had to undergo a hysterectomy (in a public hospital in Rome since she could not afford a private clinic), and for several months was prey to a major depression. She settled in Bologna in 1921, but then moved to Paris, where she spent most of her time in social engagements which ultimately disgusted her. She thereupon moved to Monaco, where she enrolled in a music school in order to devote herself once again to the piano. She subsequently taught music, first in Switzerland (until the second half of the 1950s), then in Rome. Generous and uninterested in her own promotion, she aided pupils at her own expense; at the beginning of the 1930s, she even cut her finger so that the Romanian pianist Clara Haskil could perform in her place – Haskil later gained world fame. In February 1964, in Rome, Borgatti fell ill with leukemia. Since she had expressed a desire to die while listening to Bach's *St Matthew's Passion*, her pupils played this work from dawn to dusk on the following 8 March, the day Borgatti died.

C. Mackenzie, *Vestal Fire*, London, 1927; J. Money, *Capri: Island of Love*, London, 1986; R. Peyrefitte, *L'Exilé de Capri*, Paris, 1959.

Maria Di Rienzo

Borghese, Scipione Caffarelli (1576–1633), Italian cardinal and art patron. The son of Ortensia Caffarelli, who was the sister of Camillo Borghese, he was adopted by his uncle (whose name he then took) and made a cardinal at the age of 29, when his kinsman became Pope Paul V (reigned from 1605 to 1621). His uncle's favours allowed Borghese to accumulate an immense fortune, which he used to acquire the vast land-holdings with which he constituted the Villa Borghese and a collection of art masterpieces which form the nucleus of today's Museo Nazionale di Villa Borghese in Rome. He was also the patron of numerous artists, among them Bernini, who sculpted two famous busts of the cardinal in the Galleria Borghese.

In his private life, Scipione was described by some contemporaries as orientated towards his own sex, a condition which led to full-blown scandals, one of which is particularly well known because of the repercussions it engendered. In 1605, Borghese, soon after being made a cardinal, wanted to bring to Rome Stefano Pignattelli (?–1623), his intimate 'friend'. The scandal which resulted was so great that even an official Catholic writer, Gaetano Moroni, was only able to blur the details and not disguise the episode. According to Moroni, Scipione, 'mindful for Stefano's affection, invited him to Rome and admitted him to his court, where Stefano acquired such an ascendency over the cardinal that he did everything according to his advice. It was enough for envy and jealousy among courtiers to utter malicious and venomous calumnies against him, which prompted cardinals and ambassadors to report to the pope that Stefano was full of loathsome vices, and that for his nephew's honour, it was necessary to banish him entirely. Paul V therefore deceived him and compelled him to move out of Cardinal Scipione's house. But the cardinal, knowing he was innocent, doubled his love for the oppressed man, and more than that, he succumbed to a severe melancholy because of his disgrace, which resulted in a long and serious illness.' Only when Pignattelli returned to Rome to look after Scipione did the cardinal recover.

Scipione's uncle, the pope, thereupon decided that in order to keep a check on Pignattelli he must co-opt, rather than combat, him; he had him ordained, the beginning of a career which led to his becoming a cardinal in 1621. On this occasion, a lampoon was written, revealing the rumours to which Moroni alluded; it stated that the king of Spain wanted his 'men' to be appointed cardinals, just as did the king of France, and in sum everyone desired his partisans to become cardinals. Therefore, it was no wonder that Cardinal Scipione's prick wanted 'his' man to become a cardinal. As can be seen, the accusation that the two men maintained a homosexual relationship was made explicit at the time. The cardinal is buried in the Borghese chapel, next to his uncle, in the basilica of Santa Maria Maggiore in Rome.

V. Castronovo, 'Borghese Caffarelli, Scipione', *Dizionario biografico degli italiani*, Vol. 12, Rome, 1970: 620–4; G. Dall'Orto, 'Il trionfo di Sodoma. Poesie erotiche inedite dei secoli XVI–XVII', *La Fenice di Babilonia*, 2 (1997): 37–69; G. Moroni, 'Pignattelli, Stefano, cardinale', *Dizionario di erudizione storico-ecclesiastica*, Vol. 53, Venice, 1851: 50–1.

Giovanni Dall'Orto

Bosco, St Giovanni (1815–1888), Italian priest. Giovanni Bosco was born to an impoverished rural family in the Piedmont: patronage from clerics allowed him to enter the seminary and be ordained priest in 1841. Bosco's religious activity focused on unskilled and homeless peasant teenage boys, hundreds of whom were attracted to Turin by the Industrial Revolution.

Inhumane living conditions led the youths to crime and social marginalisation. Bosco consecrated his life to preventing crime and providing for adolescents the necessities of lodging, food and vocational training. In return, Bosco asked them to submit to Catholic indoctrination in the 'oratories' which he founded.

Bosco's paternalistic but basically humanitarian efforts meant that already in 1846 over 300 youths attended his first oratory. In 1864, he founded a religious order, the Society of St Francis de Sales (The 'Salesian Fathers'), as well as the auxiliary Daughters of Mary, dedicated to helping female adolescents. In 1875 the order began sending missions overseas (notably to South America).

Success came despite the hostility of the Catholic leadership, for whom the fact that the Salesian priests played football in the oratories alongside youths from the lowest social classes was a scandal, and contrary to the hierarchical vision they cherished.

The Salesian oratories nevertheless numbered 250 at Bosco's death, and his reputation for holiness led to his being beatified in 1924 and declared a saint a decade later.

Bosco is one of many homosexuals who found in the Catholic church a family and a 'mission'; he was a pedophile who succeeded (perhaps) in sublimating his attraction to young boys into an accepted and socially useful undertaking. This emerges, surprisingly, from the opinion of Girolamo Moretti, the priest who began the study of graphology in Italy. Analysing Bosco's handwriting, he declared: 'The character of the subject tends to be dominated by an insincerity carefully constructed in order to ruin an entire generation, and it would be better if such an individual had never been born . . . . The subject has a great capacity for sexual tenderness, a tendency towards languid affection for which every effort is made to strike at the vulnerability of the soul and bend it to his sick intentions.' This view received unexpected confirmation from Giuseppe Cafasso, Bosco's confessor: 'Were it not that he worked for the glory of God, I would say that he is a dangerous man, more for what he did not reveal than for what he let on about himself.' There is other evidence of Bosco's tenderness towards boys, and of his horror of contact with women.

Bosco's repressed sexuality also appeared in the approaches towards caring for the youths which he instilled in his followers: the teacher was to love the child, teach him that he was loved ('in Christ'), guide his soul and direct him towards Christian values. Such a pedagogical theory was considered revolutionary at the time. Bosco's sexual ideal for his wards was chastity verging on asexuality, but this was mediated by an obsessive attention to everything touching on sex in order to avoid masturbation or homosexual activities.

Church authorities have strongly denied that Bosco was a practising homosexual, much less a pedophile, especially as present-day Catholic authorities have faced increasing incidence of pedophilia among the clergy.

G. Dall'Orto, 'Il santo dei fanciulli. Ritratto di don Bosco come gay', *Babilonia*, 52 (December 1987): 26–8; S. Quinzio, *Domande sulla santità*, Turin, 1986: 31–9; G. Ceronetti, 'Elementi per una anti-agiografia (don Bosco)', in *Albergo Italia*, Turin, 1985: 122–33; G. Dacquino, *Psicologia di don Bosco*, Turin, 1988: 124–9.

Giovanni Dall'Orto

Botelho, Abel (1855–1917), Portuguese army officer, diplomat and writer. Born near Viseu in central Portugal, Botelho was educated in the Military College, Polytechnic School and Army School in Lisbon, going on to make a successful career as an army officer, reaching the rank of colonel, then Parliamentary deputy, senator and finally Portuguese ambassador to the Argentine Republic, dying in post in Buenos Aires. He took an active interest in art as a critic, participated in various artistic groups and official bodies and received a number of official honours. At the same time he was active as an author, publishing a range of poetry, plays, short stories and novels. His plays were controversial because of their direct political references and one was banned because of its allusions to a government minister of the time.

Today Botelho is best known for a collection of short stories about rural life in his native region of central Portugal, *Mulheres da Beira* (*Women of Beira*, 1898) and for his cycle of five naturalist novels which were published under the collective title of *Patologia Social* (*Social Pathology*). To these should be added a further three novels which were similar although not formally part of the cycle. The most famous, or at least notorious, of these novels is titled *O Barão de Lavos* (*The Baron of Lavos*), written in 1888–1889 and published in 1891, which is one of the earliest major full-length novels published in any European language to have a male homosexual as its main character and homosexuality as its central, overt theme. The second novel in the cycle, *O Livro de Alda* (*The Book of Alda*, 1898) is about a heterosexual nymphomaniac but includes a brief lesbian scene.

O Barão de Lavos recounts the triangular erotic relationship between the Baron of Lavos – a rich, artistically inclined Lisbon aristocrat, his wife Elvira and a 16-year-old street-urchin called Eugénio. The Baron picks up Eugénio in the park outside the circus, seduces him and sets him up in a small apartment, where he is able to visit him easily. The Baron soon becomes infatuated with Eugénio and the latter, realising the hold he has over his protector, begins to exploit him financially with increasing ruthlessness. The Baron nevertheless insists on inviting him to his house and this soon causes gossip to spread about the relationship. Elvira is also attracted to Eugénio, who seduces her, and the two embark on a passionate affair. Eugénio begins to extort money from Elvira as well, using a mixture of wheedling and blackmail. The Baron, hitherto blissfully ignorant, is alerted by a vindictive maid and surprises the two together. The marriage comes to a sudden and acrimonious end. Elvira returns to her mother and Eugénio becomes a celebrated music-hall star, while the Baron enters a spiral of decline, taking pornographic photographs, having sex with young boys, suffering from syphilis and sinking deeper into destitution and ignominy until he is accidentally killed by a group of vagabonds in the street.

Although the appearance of O Barão de Lavos caused a stir and some newspapers declined to review it, the novel was generally treated seriously by the critics, even those who disliked it. One critic noted that there were homosexuals in various walks of life who managed to live their lives successfully. Others interpreted the novel as a moralistic work, warning of the dangers of homosexuality and the sad, degraded end awaiting homosexuals. This is the view that has come to predominate and explains why the novel has continued to be published under successive political systems, including the repressive Salazar regime.

O Barão de Lavos is heavily influenced by late nineteenth-century degeneration theory in the extreme form popularised by the Italian criminologist Cesare Lombroso. Botelho explains the Baron's homosexuality as a result of heredity and atavism, the ultimate stage in the degeneration of a Portuguese aristocratic family. The novel charts the Baron's decline in great detail, from a prosperous businessman, husband and art connoisseur to a squalid child-molester who dies in the gutter. As such, it reinforces traditional Christian views about the immorality of homosexuality. It also has a veiled political undercurrent, representing a critique of the decadent monarchical regime, which was overthrown by a Republican military uprising in 1910. There is, however, no sense of outrage at the corruption of youth, such as can be found in some French novels of the period. Eugénio is presented as a thoroughly venal character, who mercilessly exploits his position for mercenary purposes.

Two points are noteworthy about the novel's treatment of homosexuality. First, without being pornographic, the novel is quite explicit about the physical relations between the two males. It is clear that, initially, the Baron is the active partner and the younger Eugénio the passive one. This is in line with the classical Mediterranean model of pederasty. Later, when the Baron begins to take the passive role, this is seen as a further step in his decline. Second, both male characters are presented as bisexual rather than exclusively homosexual. The Baron is married and has had sexual relations with women before engaging regularly in homosexuality. Eugénio's reasons for taking part in a homosexual relationship are purely opportunistic. He also has a girlfriend and later relishes the chance to seduce the Baron's wife. The Baron thus resembles other literary heroes of the time such as Huysman's Des Esseintes and WILDE's Dorian Gray. It seems that while Botelho clearly had some acquaintance with contemporary medical writings of the period, he was less influenced by the German sexologists, such as Richard von KRAFFT-EBING and Albert Moll, who recognised a category of exclusive homosexuals. This is reflected in his use of the traditional words 'pederast' and 'sodomite' to describe the Baron rather than the more modern 'uranist' or 'homosexual', which were in use in Portugal a few years later.

The novel offers some interesting glimpses of gay life in Lisbon of the period. It opens with a description of the Baron cruising the area outside the Circus and later there is a description of homosexuals cruising the dark streets at night. The Baron picks up a young newspaperboy and takes him to a dilapidated house which rents rooms for sexual purposes. To the Baron's surprise, however, when asked if this is his first time, the boy calmly replies that he has done it only the day before, with a priest. The Baron reflects, 'So it was not just him! There were others who also . . . Many perhaps, who knows? . . . Yes, probably many. Many! Far more than he, than anyone imagined!'

O Barão de Lavos was translated into Spanish in 1907 but has not been translated since. The occasional insights into gay life at the time are overwhelmed by a welter of pseudo-scientific terminology and a contorted narrative style, deriving from its degenerationist thesis, which render the novel almost unreadable at times. The detracting effect of this discourse was noted in some of the original reviews and was summed up by Aubrey Bell in 1922: 'This may be magnificent pathology, but it is not art or literature.' *O Barão de Lavos* remains a historical curiosity, fatally flawed by its underlying philosophy and its language, but nevertheless interesting for being one of the first novels to deal with homosexuality explicitly.

The lesbian scene in *O Livro de Alda* occupies only four pages. In it the heroine tells her lover, the narrator, about her relationship with a rich aristocratic woman who effectively keeps her. She visits the woman's garden studio and after some sketching they shut the door and 'do mystic things'. To underline the point, the narrator refers to this as Alda's 'lesbian revelation' but the novel does not go into any further detail.

M. Benoit-Dupuis, 'Contribution à la bibliographie d'Abel Acácio de Almeida Botelho', *Sillages*, 5 (1977): 49–78; M. Saraiva de Jesus, 'Erotismo Decadentista e Moralismo Romântico n'*O Livro de Alda* de Abel Botelho', *Diacrítica*, 6 (1991): 141–62; M. Moisés, *A Patologia Social de Abel Botelho*, São Paulo, 1962; J. G. Simões, *História do Romance Português*, Vol. 3, Lisbon, 1972: 79–91.

Robert Howes

Botto, António (1897–1959), Portuguese writer. Botto was born in provincial Portugal but soon moved with his family to the picturesque working-class district of Lisbon known as the Alfama. His increasingly obvious homosexuality led to difficulties with his family. Despite his humble background, a job in a bookshop brought him into contact with the writers and intellectuals of the day, including Fernando Pessoa, now considered the greatest twentieth-century Portuguese poet, who became a close friend. Botto then got a job in the civil service and, despite the notoriety gained by the publication of his verse in the early 1920s, was posted to Africa where he did a two-year stint as a senior government official in a Portuguese colonial enclave near Angola from 1924 to 1926. Back in Lisbon, he affected the pose of an elegant dandy. Botto was highly sociable and was well known for his Bohemian life-style, his taste for sailors and his wicked tongue, which made him many enemies. In 1942, he was dismissed from his government post by the increasingly repressive and moralistic Salazar regime, and from then on led a precarious existence, beset by financial difficulties and ill health. During this time, despite his open homosexuality, he married and his wife, Carminda, stood by him to the end. In 1947 he decided to rebuild his fortunes by emigrating to Brazil. After some initial success he appears to have fallen on hard times. He died after a traffic accident in 1959; in 1965, his remains were returned to Portugal.

Botto is best known for his collection of poems known as *Canções (Songs)*, which contained some love poems clearly addressed to males. Originally published as a slim volume in 1920 as *Canções do Sul (Songs of the South)*, the first edition with the title *Canções* appeared in 1921 and a second, revised edition, which was published by Pessoa under his Olisipo imprint, came out in 1922. A couple of months later Pessoa wrote an article for the leading literary and artistic magazine, *Contemporanea*, in which he praised Botto as the only true aesthete in Portugal.

This was the subject of a bitter attack in the following issue of *Contemporanea* in an article titled 'Literatura de Sodoma' ('Literature of Sodom') by the journalist Álvaro Maia, who attacked Botto's book and Pessoa's article for their praise of Greek love. The main response to this was a pamphlet, again published by Pessoa's Olisipo publishing imprint, written by the openly gay but mentally unstable amateur philosopher Raul Leal. This defended idealised pederasty in inflamed but abstruse language and appeared under the provocative title of *Sodoma Divinizada* (*Sodom Deified*). The polemic then got caught up in the politics of the last chaotic years of the First Portuguese Republic and the repercussions of a police raid on a drag ball during the 1923 Carnival. A group of Catholic students led by Pedro Teotónio Pereira, later an important political figure in the Salazar regime, demanded the banning of immoral books. Botto's and Leal's works were seized, although some booksellers continued to sell them under the counter. Botto kept quiet throughout this period but both Pessoa and Leal issued leaflets attacking the students.

Botto published more books of verse, including many poems with homoerotic overtones: *Motivos de Beleza* (*Motives of Beauty*, 1923), *Curiosidades Estéticas* (*Esthetic Curiosities*, 1924), *Piquenas Esculturas* (*Small Sculptures*, 1925), *Olimpyades* (1927) and *Dandysmo* (1928). Many of these poems were republished in a further edition of *Canções* (1930), which from then on in successive editions became effectively his collected verse, although the poems included and their texts were frequently altered. During the 1930s, Botto continued to publish books containing gay love poems, such as *Ciúme* (*Jealousy*, 1934), and prose, such as *Cartas que me Foram Devolvidas* (*Letters Which were Returned to Me*, 1932). In 1933 he published *António*, a dramatic novel intended for reading rather than performance. The plot revolves around the relationship

between an adolescent dancer, António, and an aristocratic young man, Duarte.

Botto subsequently wrote less on gay themes and turned more to the popular traditions associated with the district where he was brought up. He wrote a play, *Alfama* (1933), which had a successful production, and became involved with the night-life world of the *fado* singers. He also enjoyed some success as a writer of children's stories, some of which were translated into English by Pessoa.

Botto's poetry is written in deceptively simple language. Rejecting the rhetorical flourishes of much Portuguese poetry, he opted for a colloquial style which makes his work immediately accessible. Love, and particularly gay love, forms the subject of much of his work from the 1920s and early 1930s. Some poems recount a chance encounter or a one-night stand, but the majority form part of an ongoing dialogue with an anonymous lover or lovers, in which only the voice of the poet is heard. The poems chart the poet's desire, both physical and emotional, his awareness of the intransience of love and his sense of disillusion, suffering and loss, as each time his hopes are dashed. References to masculine beauty, kisses, embraces and beds make clear that Botto is not talking about platonic love, but the emphasis on emotional states and feelings ensures that the poems remain within the long Portuguese tradition of love poetry. The emphasis, however, is on the poet's need to be loved and the impossibility of satisfying this need. Botto's poetic voice, based it seems on his own personality, is narcissistic and insecure, with more than a hint of misogyny. His sense of beauty, both his own and others, is imbued with transience and doom. His physical needs may be met but his emotional aspirations remain unfulfilled, although this failure is sometimes undercut by irony.

The reception of Botto's work is revealing. Pessoa saw him as an aesthete whereas João Gaspar Simões thought his open assertion of his homosexuality was a way of drawing attention to himself, and José Régio analysed the complex way in which Botto's verse dealt with homosexuality. Botto himself acknowledged the effect of his open avowal of homosexuality on his poetry. Botto continues to produce mixed reactions, acknowledged as the epitome of the gay poet and as an important but secondary figure in the mainstream tradition of Portuguese lyric poetry.

A. Botto, *As Canções de António Botto*, Lisbon, 1980; L. P. Moitinho de Almeida, 'António Botto, Fernando Pessoa, Outros e Eu', in *Fernando Pessoa no Cinquentenário da sua Morte*, Coimbra, 1985: 69–82; R. W. Howes, 'Fernando Pessoa, Poet, Publisher and Translator', *British Library Journal*, 9, 2 (Autumn 1983): 161–70; R. Leal, *Sodoma Divinizada* ed. Aníbal Fernandes, Lisbon, 1989; A. Augusto Sales, *António Botto, Real e Imaginário*, Lisbon, 1997.

Robert Howes

Boulton, Ernest, and **Park, William Frederick**, also known as, respectively, 'Mrs Stella Graham' (also 'Lady Arthur Clinton') and 'Miss Fanny Winnifred Park', British transvestites. The two young men during their 1871 trial became notorious for their blatant public transvestitism.

On the evening of 28 April 1870, the 22-year-old Boulton and the 23-year-old Park, attired as women, were arrested on leaving the Strand Theatre. They were charged with appearing in public in women's clothes – but, after an illegal physical examination by the police surgeon, the charge was amended to sodomy. When it became clear that the medical evidence (or, more precisely, the ignorance of the doctors concerning what constituted physical evidence of sodomy) could not support the felony charge, the indictment was again amended to 'conspiracy to commit a felony' (sodomy).

The morning after the arrest, Boulton's and Park's rooms were searched, and their extensive correspondence was discovered. This led to the arrest of others who were charged as co-conspirators, including Louis Charles Hurt of Edinburgh, employed in the surveyor's department of the General Post Office; John Safford Fiske of Edinburgh, the American consul at Leith; and Lord Arthur Pelham Clinton, Member of Parliament and third son of Henry Pelham, the fifth Duke of Newcastle. Two weeks after he was committed for trial, on 18 June, Clinton died, reportedly of exhaustion resulting from scarlet fever.

The trial opened on 9 May 1871. The evidence for the prosecution consisted of witnesses who had seen them in public both made-up and provocatively dressed as 'gay women' (prostitutes) and effeminately dressed as men (tight trousers, low-necked shirts opened at the front, wearing powder and rouge). A witness also claimed that Boulton had posed as Lady Clinton, Lord Arthur's wife. Effusive letters exchanged between the charged parties were also produced.

The case for the defence was that Boulton and Park's transvestitism had ample justification given their theatrical performances at fashionable watering-holes and stately country houses, performances which were immensely successful. The rest – going out in public in drag, the effusive letters – was simply to be put down to idiotic foolishness, which merely showed youthful high spirits unchecked by proper judgement.

The legal point in favour of the defence was that the charge, conspiracy to commit sodomy, was weakened by the fact that, given that the defendants had been examined with no conclusive evidence that sodomy had been committed, the Crown could only prove their case by arguing that the defendants' lives were indicative of people who would commit or intended to commit sodomy. This led the jury to return a verdict of 'Not Guilty' for all defendants on all counts.

The preliminary hearings and trial generated such public interest that not only was it extensively reported and editorialised about in the newspapers, but it found its way into more popular formats, such as a broadsheet titled *Stella: Star of the Strand* (1870), and the following limerick: 'There was an old person of Sark, / Who buggered a pig in the dark; / The swine in surprise / Murmured: 'God blast your eyes, / Do you take me for Boulton or Park?' A decade later, Boulton and Park were among the characters featured in Jack Saul's fictionalised memoirs *The Sins of the Cities of the Plain; or the Recollections of a Mary-Ann* (1881). Nothing is known of their lives after the trial.

The Boulton and Park trial is a significant moment in the history of the hesitant emergence of a public discourse of the homosexual as an identity. Perhaps more importantly, the case is significant in its revelation of a 'pre-homosexual' subculture which was obviously extensive, varied and flourishing, involving, in differing roles and degrees, men of all walks of life.

The Trial of Boulton and Park, with Hurt and Fiske. A Complete and Accurate Report of the Proceedings extending over Six Days, from Tuesday, May 9th, to Monday, May 15th, 1871, Manchester, 1871; J. Weeks, *Sex, Politics and Society*, 2nd edn, London, 1989; N. Bartlett, *Who Was That Man?*, London, 1988; A. Sinfield, *The Wilde Century*, London, 1994.

Jason Boyd

Boye, Karin (1900–1941), Swedish writer. Boye was born into an upper-middle-class environment in Gothenburg. In 1909 her family relocated to Stockholm, where she grew up and studied at the city's university college. Further studies followed at Uppsala University, from which she graduated in 1928. Her professional activities consisted mainly of teaching, since writing alone could never fully sustain her.

Boye's literary début came in 1922 with *Moln* (*Clouds*), a book of poetry, which was followed by a mixture of poetry and prose writing. Her breakthrough as an author came with the collection of poetry titled *Härdarna* (*The Hearths*, 1927).

Boye's most important prose writings are considered her modernist novels *Kris* (*Crisis*, 1934) and *Kallocain* (1940). In *Kris* she openly portrayed lesbian love.

Boye was one of the most prominent intellectuals of her time and was deeply engaged in contemporary thought and debate. She was a member of the socialist organisation Clarté and, in 1931, was a founder of the psychoanalytic modernist journal *Spektrum*. There she published her important literary work on poetics, 'Språket bortom logiken' ('Language beyond logic'), in which she strove to unite intellect with emotion and stated that 'it is all but rational to disregard the irrational'. Boye also did translation work. She was a fervent opponent to Nazism.

Boye's life partner was Margot Hanel, a German Jewess. They met in Berlin in 1932 and lived together as a couple in Stockholm. In 1941 Boye committed suicide, due to circumstances that are not altogether clear. Shortly thereafter Hanel killed herself.

Hanna Hallgren

Bradford, Edwin Emmanuel (1860–1944), British clergyman and poet. Born in Torquay, Devon, England, in 1860, Bradford was educated at Castle College School in Torquay and at Exeter College, Oxford University. He entered Exeter College in 1881 and graduated BA in 1884 with third-class honours in Theology, proceeding to MA in 1901, BD in 1904 and DD in 1912. After ordination in the Church of England in 1884 he served curacies at High Ongar and Walthamstow in Essex, from where he went to St Petersburg as assistant chaplain to the English church in 1887–1889 and then to Paris where he was assistant curate of St George's Church in 1890–1899. Back in England, after two more curacies, at Upwell and Eton, in 1909 he was appointed to a parish of his own. He remained as vicar of Nordelph, a small village in Norfolk, until his death.

Bradford's career in the Church of

England was undistinguished. As an author, however, he achieved a modest reputation. He was one of an informal group of English 'Uranian' poets who wrote on the theme of boy-love. Between 1908 and 1930 Bradford published 12 volumes of bouncy cheerful verse. His poems had titles such as 'To boys unknown', 'Joe and Jim', 'The kiss' and 'When first I fell in love with you'. In these he expounded his ideas on the pre-eminence of masculine bonding and male beauty. He extolled the high spiritual status of romantic love between adult men and adolescent boys and advocated a new chivalry that transcended the boundaries of class. In England, at a time when there was considerable hostility to homosexuality, it is remarkable that Bradford's uncomplicated celebration of male love in verse was well received and favourably reviewed in newspapers and journals.

E. E. Bradford (selected by P. Webb), *To Boys Unknown*, London, 1988; T. d'Arch Smith, *Love in Earnest: Some Notes on the Lives and Writings of English 'Uranian' Poets from 1889 to 1930*, London, 1970; P. Webb, 'Not one is as pretty as he', *Spectator* (London), 27 February 1988: 14–16.

David Hilliard

Brand, Adolf (1874–1945), German activist and publisher. Brand was one of the most controversial activists in the pre-World War II German homosexual movement and publisher of the first homosexual journal, *Der Eigene* (1899–1931). After abandoning his profession as a teacher because of his anarchist opinions, Brand started a publishing firm and began publishing *Der Eigene*, a literary and artistic homosexual journal 'for male culture'. He advocated 'a revival of Greek times and Hellenic standards of beauty after centuries of Christian barbarism', and attacked medical sexologists – among them Magnus HIRSCHFELD – because their scientific research on homosexuality, Brand maintained, 'took away all beauty

from eroticism'. In addition to editing the journal, Brand contributed homoerotic poems, political essays and photographs of nude boys and young men. He associated with Bohemians and free-thinkers in Berlin and politically he was influenced by a particular kind of anarchism, formulated by the philosopher Max Stirner. Stirner strongly rejected any subordination of individuality, be it to ecclesiastical and secular authorities, or to morality, rationalism and ideology.

Brand was a militant and quick-tempered man who often became involved in public quarrels, scandals and trials. He was prosecuted several times on immorality charges because of the homoerotic prose, poetry and illustrations he published. In 1907 Brand's name appeared in the national and foreign press because of his involvement in the sensational Harden–EULENBURG scandal in which two advisers of Emperor Wilhelm II were accused of homosexuality (in order to obstruct their political influence). Brand, who believed that the disclosure of homosexual relationships among high-ranking men would eventually bring about the abolition of the legal ban on homosexual intercourse, published a pamphlet in which he asserted that the German Chancellor, Bernard von Bülow, was having a homosexual relationship with one of his assistants. Bülow sued Brand for libel and Brand was sentenced to prison for a term of 18 months. He was in fact the only one who was actually imprisoned as a result of the scandal, and this strengthened his role as a martyr for the homosexual cause.

To gain moral and financial support for his publishing and political activities, Brand founded the Gemeinschaft der Eigenen in 1903. This society was not so much a political organisation like Hirschfeld's Wissenschaftlich-humanitäres Komitee, but a literary circle. Again and again Brand and his supporters stressed that the 'male eros' they advocated had nothing to do with the branch of the human species psychiatrists and sexologists were labelling as a third sex and for whose rights Hirschfeld's Committee pleaded. They tried to counterbalance medical stereotypes of homosexuality by glorifying various forms of male bonding and the cultural model of classical Greece. Brand liked to present himself as the leading man of an élite of masculine and culturally sophisticated homosexuals. Although the circulation and frequency of *Der Eigene* and some other journals he published were greater than ever in the 1920s, he became disappointed with Weimar democracy and the liberties of Berlin, because homosexuality continued to be punishable by law. Hitler's rise to power put an end to his activism. Soon after Hitler's nomination as Chancellor, storm troopers raided Brand's house five times and seized his journals, books and photos. Although Brand was well known as a homosexual activist, he was not arrested during the Nazi regime. It is likely that he would have survived the war were it not for the American bombardment which killed him together with his wife at home in 1945.

M. Keilson-Lauritz, *Die Geschichte der eigenen Geschichte: Literatur und Literaturkritik in den Anfängen der Schwulenbewegung*, Berlin, 1997; H. Oosterhuis and H. Kennedy, *Homosexuality and Male Bonding in Pre-Nazi Germany. The Youth Movement, the Gay Movement, and Male Bonding before Hitler's Rise. Original Transcripts from* Der Eigene, *the First Gay Journal in the World*, New York, 1991.

Harry Oosterhuis

Breker, Arno (1900–1991), German sculptor. Born the son of a stonemason and sculptor, Breker studied art in Düsseldorf. He spent a brief period in Rome (where he helped restore one of MICHELANGELO's statues), then lived in Paris between 1927 and 1933, returning to Germany the year that Hitler became Chancellor. Soon Breker became the most renowed sculptor of the Nazi regime and one of Hitler's favourite artists. Indeed in 1937 Hitler made Breker 'Official State Sculptor', gave him a large property and provided a studio where the sculptor employed a thousand assistants; he was also exempted from military service.

Breker's work exalted the ideology of the new order and the image of the Teutonic 'superman'. *The Army* and *The Party*, sculpted for the Reich Chancellery in Berlin designed by Albert Speer, were meant to embody the twin pillars of the National Socialist regime. *The Warrior's Departure* and *The Avenger* glorified aggressive militarism, while such works as *Daring* and *Comradeship* lauded the virtues prized by the authorities. *Prometheus* and *Dionysus* recalled the ancient Greek world, the heroism and racial purity of which the Nazis imagined they were restoring. The statues of athletes Breker and others produced for the stadium hosting the 1936 Olympic games are paeans to brawny German prowess.

Most of Breker's statues are of naked men – invariably muscular and flawlessly handsome 'Aryans'. Their nudity was intended to symbolise the healthiness, classlessness and lack of puritanical shame of the 'supermen' of the Nazi society. According to Adam, they are 'pin-ups of sexual fantasies'. These ideal types of fierce Germanic masculinity, by the prominent display of their sexual attributes, are subliminally homoerotic images, though critics note that the sculptures are cold, lifeless and bombastic.

Despite persecution of homosexuals, some of the totalitarian regimes of the 1920s and 1930s remained fascinated with masculine nudity and physical perfection. Leni Riefenstahl's film of the Berlin Olympics dwelt on the beauty of the young athletes, and Nazi propaganda often portrayed heroic bare-chested male workers. In Rome, the Foro Italico stadium constructed by Mussolini is surmounted by several dozen larger than lifesize statues of naked athletes (each representing an Italian city or region) pointing to the

Duce's ambition of recreating a Roman empire and exalting Italian manhood.

Breker's own sculptures were often reproduced and shown in Germany and in occupied Europe; the catalogue for a 1942 exhibition in Paris included a preface written by Jean COCTEAU. After the war, Breker continued work, sculpting heads of (among others) Cocteau, Henry de MONTHERLANT, Jean Marais and Salvador Dalí. In 1961, he purchased many of his own sculptures from other private collections and placed them in the garden of his Düsseldorf house.

Breker's work transformed the Greek-inspired male nude common in pre-twentieth-century sculpture into a tool of Nazi propaganda. His obsession with perfect male form also foreshadowed images of buffed blond muscle-men common in post-war gay pornography, though most of the creators of those images did not share the ideology which ultimately sent homosexuals to concentration camps.

P. Adam, *Art of the Third Reich*, New York, 1992; I. Golomstock, *Totalitarian Art in the Soviet Union, the Third Reich, Fascist Italy and the People's Republic of China*, London, 1990.

Robert Aldrich

Brooke, Rupert (1887–1915), British poet. Athletic, highly intelligent, strikingly handsome, Brooke seemed to embody every ideal of English manhood in that troubled time that began with the accession of George V and ended in the trenches of World War I.

Brooke was born into an affluent academic family; his father was a housemaster at Rugby school, which Brooke attended before moving on to King's College, Cambridge. Keeping in mind that King's even at the turn of the twentieth century was affectionately known as 'Queens', he found himself to be the object of considerable romantic attention from fellow Kingsmen and members of the secret society of 'Apostles', including E. M. FORSTER and John Maynard KEYNES.

His most intimate undergraduate relationship was with James Strachey, brother of Lytton STRACHEY and later (with his wife Alix) translator of FREUD. According to their letters (recently edited by Keith Hale), the romance was intense but short-lived, complicated by Brooke's close attachment to his mother.

Brooke began writing poetry as a neo-Romantic of the Georgian school but is most famous for his handful of war sonnets, notably 'The Soldier'. Filled with sentimental patriotism, these are poems of innocence rather than, as in the case of Siegfried SASSOON and Wilfred OWEN, of actual experience with trench warfare. Brooke enlisted at the beginning of the war, but saw only one day of action, during the evacuation of Antwerp. He died of blood poisoning on his way to Gallipoli and was buried on the island of Skyros. The reaction to his death was immediate and strong: D. H. LAWRENCE swooned ('bright Pheobus smote him down. It is all in the saga. O God, O God'); Dean Inge read 'The Soldier' from the pulpit of St Paul's in London on Easter 1915; and Winston Churchill, then the First Lord of the Admiralty, eulogised him in the London *Times*. In death as in life he continued to be an object of erotic, often homoerotic affection. Even Churchill could not help referring to Brooke's 'classic symmetry of mind and body'.

P. Fussell, *The Great War and Modern Memory*, New York, 1975; K. Hale (ed.) *Friends and Apostles: The Correspondence of Rupert Brooke and James Strachey, 1905–1914*, New Haven, 1998.

George Piggford

Brooks, Romaine (1874–1970), American painter. Brooks was born in Rome but spent much of her early childhood in and around New York. She attended school in New Jersey, Italy and Switzerland, eventually studying voice in Paris and art in Rome. By 1908, after the deaths of her mother and brother, Brooks had become financially independent and was able to establish residence in a fashionable section of Paris. Today this American expatriate is best known for her portraits of the French élite of the arts and letters, but Brooks began her career as an interior decorator for the well-to-do, a position which would ultimately facilitate her role as a portraitist.

She had her first solo exhibition in 1910 at the Galeries Durand-Ruel in Paris. In 1912 she painted Gabriele d'Annunzio, the poet in exile, and in 1914 she painted a little known Jean COCTEAU, indications of the artistic milieu within which she travelled. Addressing the influence of World War I and the changing social conditions for women, Brooks received critical attention for her painting La France Croix (1914), which depicted a young nurse on the front lines – a cathedral half-visible in the distance. Stylistically her work was more closely linked to earlier painting styles than to the emerging avant-garde that found its way into the nearby salon of Leo and Gertrude STEIN who were busily collecting the works of Picasso, Matisse and even the young Marsden HARTLEY. Brooks travelled in different circles, being frequently found among the likes of Ida Rubinstein of the Russian Ballet and Natalie BARNEY, who was also known as L'Amazone, and whose salon was frequented by the such figures as Marcel PROUST, André GIDE and COLETTE.

Brooks is perhaps best known for her portrait, painted in her typically muted palette, of Una Lady Troubridge (1924), which portrayed a close friend of the author Radclyffe HALL, whose novel The Well of Loneliness remained a cornerstone of lesbian literature for more than half a century. For historians of gay and lesbian culture, Brooks provides a small glimpse into lesbian portraiture of the 1920s. Historical accounts acknowledge that several of Brooks's sitters were self-identified lesbians who lived openly as such. It is now widely acknowledged that Hall had modelled several of the characters from The Well of Loneliness after Troubridge and Brooks herself. Brooks died in Nice.

A. Breeskin, Romaine Brooks: 'Thief of Souls', Washington, 1971.

Ken Gonzales-Day

Bukh, Niels (Ebbesen Mortensen) (1880–1950), Danish physical education pioneer. Bukh grew up in the traditions of the particularly Danish educational system of 'Folk High Schools' where his father taught. After some years as a farmer, he was educated as a schoolteacher, specialising in physical education. He was leader of the Danish gymnastics team that won the Silver Medal at the Olympic Games in Stockholm in 1912. In 1914 he became a teacher at the Ollerup Folk High School where his brother-in-law was principal. Based on 'Swedish gymnastics' (developed by P. H. Ling), he developed his own style: rythmical and fast movements in long series. This appealed to his pupils and in 1920 he opened the Ollerup Physical Education Folk High School, the first of its kind. In the early 1920s he began a long series of international tours of lectures, seminars and shows with the Ollerup Gymnastics Team. Thereby Bukh's style of gymnastics was introduced worldwide, and he and the Ollerup Gymnastics Team became the most prominent 'ambassadors' for Denmark during the following decades. He won large numbers of adherents, not only within the popular physical education movements but also within the Danish army and the educational system in general. Visits to the beautifully located Ollerup became fashionable.

Bukhs's insight into the intimate relationship between mind and body led him to see the teaching of gymnastics as something 'much larger and beautiful', a means towards national revival which to Bukh meant radical right-wing and anti-democratic politics. In the 1930s he had close contacts with the armed wing of the German Nazi Party, the SA (Sturmabteilung), until 1934 under the leadership of Ernst RÖHM. In Denmark he became a vocal supporter of Nazi ideology.

The combination of nationalism, Nazi ideology and athletics as propagated by the internationally renowed Bukh was much more of a danger to Danish parliamentary democracy than the small and insignificant Danish Nazi Party. Within the Social Democratic Party, however, it became known that Bukh was a homosexual. He was spied upon and the reports and affidavits pertaining to his relationship in the 1920s with a teacher at Ollerup, Kristian Krogshede (later the founder of the Gerlev Physical Education Folk High School), and his alleged attempt to seduce a pupil were presented to the Minister of Education (F. J. Borgbjerg, a Social Democrat) in October 1933. Officially, there was no reaction. However, Bukh's school at Ollerup depended on the authorisation and the subsidies administered by the Ministry of Education. He was discreetly threatened with exposure and agreed to put a halt to his public endorsement of Nazism. From then on he was more discreet in his politics. Bukh's collaboration with the German authorities during the German occupation of Denmark from 1940 to 1945 must now be seen as treasonable, but the details and the extent of his contacts with Nazi organisations were not known at the time. He was briefly arrested in 1945, but was then able to reestablish his school in Ollerup and from 1947 to resume the annual international tours of the Ollerup Gymnastics Team.

Bukh's style and method of gymnastics constituted a radical new vision of masculinity. Naked and sweaty torsos, the touching, supporting and lifting of men by men, challenged the norms of propriety for masculine behaviour at the time. The Ollerup aesthetics of masculine healthiness, strength and muscularity should probably be seen as inspired by Bukh's homosexuality, but it was conceived of as elevated above sexuality. It therefore also permitted the incorparation of elements of tenderness.

N. Bukh, *Primary Gymnastics*, trans. F. N. Punchard, London, 1939; L. Vangdrup, 'Niels Bukh', *Dansk Biografisk Leksikon*, Vol. 3, Copenhagen, 1979: 71–2; H. Bonde, *Danmarks store ungdomsfører. Niels Bukh og hans Gymnastik 1880–1950*, Copenhagen, forthcoming.

Wilhelm von Rosen

Buonaccorsi, Filippo (Callìmaco Esperiente) (1437–1496), Italian humanist and political figure. Following a scandal that was both political and homosexual, most of Buonaccorsi's career took place in Poland, where, among other posts, he was tutor to the future King Jan Olbracht and where he is important for having spread the ideas of humanism.

Born in San Gimignano, Tuscany, Buonaccorsi moved to Rome in 1462 and became a student of the (homosexual) humanist POMPONIO-LETO (in whose house he also lived); he also became a member of the Accademia Romana founded by Pomponio-Leto. Buonaccorsi's life took a dramatic turn in 1468, when he was accused of having conspired against Pope Paul II. He managed to avoid arrest by flight, but the homosexual verses which were found in his papers then earned him a reputation for sodomy. Among the youths hailed in his poems was Antonio Lepido, another of Pomponio-Leto's students, whom 'Callìmaco' (Buonaccorsi's humanist name) called 'his Ganymede' (*phrygius amor*). The poems also referred to Lucio Fazini, who became Bishop of Segni in 1481, as 'Lucidus Phosphorus' ('Bearer of Light').

After various peregrinations, Callìmaco took refuge in the court of the king of Poland, who named him tutor to the royal princes. Thus began a meteoric rise. In 1474, Buonaccorsi was named royal secretary, in 1476–1477 he served as ambassador to Constantinople, and in 1486 he became the king's representative in Venice. With the accession to the Polish throne of his former pupil Jan Olbracht, Buonaccorsi's influence peaked. He reciprocated the royal favour in his writings by arguing the necessity of a reinforcement of the king's power at the expense of the aristocracy. He died and was interred in Cracow, where his tomb can still be seen.

Buonaccorsi was the author of poetical, philosophical and historical works – which, after the scandal which led to his exile, prudently became exclusively heterosexual. The fact that much of the research on him has appeared in Polish (and which in part remains unpublished) has meant that his life and work is little known outside of Poland, though it merits rediscovery.

L. Pastor, *Storia dei Papi*, Rome, 1911. Vol II, p. 746; L. Calvelli, 'Un umanista italiano in Polonia. Filippo Buonaccorsi da S. Gimignano', *Miscellanea storica della Valdelsa*, 22 (1914): 45–65, and 23 (1915): 45–66; F. Buonaccorsi, *Epigrammatum libri duo*, Wratislaw, 1963; K. Kumaniecki, 'Il periodo italiano dell'opera poetica di Filippo Buonaccorsi: i suoi epigrammi romani', in *Il mondo antico nel Rinascimento*, *Atti del V convegno internazionale di studi sul Rinascimento*, Florence, 1958: 65–73; G. Paparelli, *Callìmaco Esperiente (Filippo Buonaccorsi)*, Salerno, 1971; G. Uzielli, 'Filippo Buonaccorsi "Callìmaco Esperiente" di San Gimignano', *Miscellanea storica della Valdelsa*, 6 (1898): 114–36, and 7 (1899): 84–112.

Giovanni Dall'Orto

Burra, Edward (1905–1976), British artist. Born in London, Burra grew up and spent much of his life at his parents' home near Rye in east Sussex. Continuing ill health (rheumatic arthritis and anaemia) prevented him from receiving the education his parents had planned, but they encouraged his interests in drawing and painting with instruction from a local teacher.

During 1921–1923 Burra studied life drawing, illustration and architectural drawing at the Chelsea Polytechnic and then for two years at the Royal College of Art, while he also pursued his interests in films (a favourite actor was Mae West) and jazz. A fellow student at the Chelsea Polytechnic was William Chappell (ballet dancer, choreographer, theatre producer and director), who became a close and lifelong friend. Burra's parents encouraged him to adopt painting as a profession and provided financial support. He travelled regularly to Mediterranean France and Spain and later to Boston and New York, often with Chappell or other friends from his student days. Burra was particularly affected by a visit to Spain during the Civil War and this was magnified by his experience of World War II which evoked a sombre and pessimistic mood in his work.

Burra's vision of the world was influenced by the Spanish artists El Greco, Zurbaran and in particular Goya. He also admired artists as disparate as COCTEAU, Grosz, Beardsley, de Chirico, Wyndham Lewis and Dalì. Early in his career Burra gave up using oil paint and developed his own technique of thickly applying watercolour.

During the 1930s Burra's subjects were taken from the 'red-light' life of Boston, Harlem, and Mediterranean port cities, especially the French naval base port of Toulon. Burra especially admired the physicality of black men in dance halls. He enjoyed the atmosphere of European pre-war nonconformity in waterfront entertainment places, which he found again in post-war American clubs and cabarets.

In his manner and conversation Burra was camp. 'Hello dearie' or 'well dearie' were usual expressions. He was a dandy at heart, although his usual crumpled corduroys and bulky jumper belied it. Though he was not a church-going Christian, his subjects conveyed the religious tension of evil and good. His working life was disciplined and his paintings were exhibited regularly in London and occasionally in Europe and the United States and he is represented in major public collections of British painting. Between the 1930s and 1950s Burra also designed six ballets, an opera and a musical play.

In his paintings and drawings Burra depicted the contrasting worlds of alienation, isolation and destruction brought about by malevolent bureaucracies, with the warmth, comfort and promise of sexual satisfaction he saw amongst people of cultures or classes other than his own. He used few overtly homosexual subjects, although his figures often convey the potential for sexual liaisons of various kinds. Burra was awarded a CBE in 1971 and died at Rye.

A. Causey, *Edward Burra: Complete Catalogue*, Oxford, 1985; W. Chappell (ed.) *Edward Burra: A Painter Remembered by His Friends*, London, 1982; J. Rothenstein, *Edward Burra*, London, 1945; Arts Council, *Edward Burra*, London, 1985.

Ian Maidment

Burton, Sir Richard (Francis) (1821–1890), British explorer and writer. Born in Devon and educated at Oxford (though he was expelled from the university), in 1856 Burton set out with John Speke (with whom he later fell out) to explore eastern Africa, where he was the first European to reach Lake Tanganyika. Burton also travelled in Abyssinia, Arabia, India and America. He served in consular positions and carried out intelligence work for the British government, receiving a knighthood for his work. Burton also brought the Indian classic of sexual practice, the *Kama Sutra*, to the West, and he produced a multi-volume translation of the *Thousand and One Nights* (1884–1886).

In 1845, British authorities in India asked Burton to investigate brothels in the Sind, and he provided precise information about the homosexual bordellos he found in Karachi. Although his report was lost (or, it has been speculated, was never even written), even his association with such places of ill repute temporarily tarnished his reputation. Footnotes and commentary in Burton's later translation of the *Arabian Nights* discussed sexual posture, venereal disease and male and female homosexuality. The 'Terminal Essay' of the work, published in 1885, put forward Burton's theory of a 'Sotadic Zone' where male homosexuality was common. Burton held homosexuality 'to be geographical and climatic, not racial', though he did not explain why this was so. The Sotadic Zone encompasses the northern and southern shores of the Mediterranean, much of the Middle East, all of China and Japan, the islands of the South Seas and the indigenous cultures of the Americas. After reviewing the history of pederastry in Antiquity, Burton described 'Le Vice' (as he usually called it) in various parts of the world, complete with footnotes and quotations in Latin and other languages. The theory did not gain great currency, but undoubtedly confirmed the opinion of some that 'perversion' was endemic in the tropical and Oriental world.

Burton's research and writing, as well as rumours spread by his rivals, such as Speke, led some to believe that he was homosexual, but no evidence suggests that this was the case. He was happily married, and his wife Isabel collaborated on his scholarly undertakings. However, she did destroy many of his papers, including private letters, after his death.

E. Rice, *Captain Sir Richard Francis Burton*, New York, 1990; M. S. Lovell, *Rage to Live: A Biography of Richard and Isabel Burton*, London, 1998.

Robert Aldrich

Butler, Eleanor (1737–1829), and **Ponsonby, Sarah** (1755–1831), known as the Ladies of Llangollen, Anglo-Irish gentlewomen, 'romantic friends'. Butler was a descendant of an old Anglo-Irish family. The Garryricken Butlers were Catholic and had lost their early status as influential gentry and were, by the eighteenth century, financially impoverished. Butler was born in Cambrai during one of the family's periods of self-exile during the years of the Penal Code. The Butlers returned to Garryricken the next year, but she travelled frequently between Cambrai and Ireland, spending several years boarding at the convent in which she had been born. In 1768, the Butlers, through a complex inheritance line, succeeded to Kilkenny Castle. Ponsonby was the daughter of Chambre Brabazon Ponsonby, a member of the Irish Protestant Ascendancy in Inistiogue, and Louisa Lyons, his second wife. Both parents were dead by the time she was 7 and her stepmother, Ponsonby's third wife, died when Sarah was 13, leaving her orphaned and destitute. Ponsonby was sent to the care of her father's cousin, Lady Betty Fownes, and her husband, Sir William, then to Miss Parkes's boarding school at Kilkenny. Lady Fownes asked Miss Butler of the Castle to keep a watchful eye on her while she was at Miss Parkes's school.

Butler and Ponsonby met in 1769 and gradually developed a close friendship. What is known of their relationship comes largely from Butler's journals from the period 1784–1821, Ponsonby's few remaining personal records, and the records of family and friends. It would appear that a secret correspondence developed between the two women. In 1778, when Ponsonby was living with Fownes, she became the object of his unwanted attentions. Butler, meanwhile, was being pressured by her mother, who feared that she would never marry, to join a convent. They wrote repeatedly to each other, perhaps with the assistance of servants as messengers. On 30 March 1778 they eloped. Both wore men's clothes, Ponsonby taking also a pistol and her small dog. They aimed for Waterford, where they hoped to catch a boat to England. They were discovered, however, and returned home. It soon became apparent that the two were determined to continue their relationship, and their families allowed them to travel to Wales, where they settled in 1780 in a small house, Plas Newydd, in Llangollen Vale. They were by no means wealthy, but each of the women had a small income from her family. Plas Newydd attracted many renowned visitors, including William Wordsworth, Sir Walter Scott and the Duke of Wellington. The two women became the subject of much public attention and were well known for their hospitality and charm.

In the relationship of the Ladies of Llangollen, as they have become known, we can see the acceptable characteristics of the 'romantic friendship': lifelong devotion, mutual respect and moral and spiritual uplift. It was deemed acceptable, and even desirable, for young women to form strong emotional attachments as a prelude to marriage, and it was often accepted that these might continue into later life in the absence of the marriage of one or both of the partners. Romantic friendships were held to embody the finest of qualities, particularly those of loyalty and devotion, and the Ladies' relationship was widely publicised as a model of such qualities. The eighteenth-century poet Anna Seward called the Ladies' relationship a 'sacred Friendship, permanent as pure'.

Not all their contemporaries were inclined to see their relationship as entirely respectable. An article written about the Ladies in the *General Evening Post* described the elopement of the two women in relatively neutral terms, but then went on to state that 'Miss Butler is tall and masculine, she always wears a riding habit, hangs her hat with the air of a sportsman in the hall, and appears in all respects as a young man if we except the petticoats which she still retains. Miss Ponsonby, on the contrary, is polite and effeminate, fair and beautiful ... Miss Ponsonby does the duties and honours of the house, while Miss Butler superintends the gardens and the rest of the grounds.' The Ladies were not pleased, and enquired about suing the author. Their friend Edmund Burke advised against it and offered as consolation that they 'suffer only by the baseness of the age you live in'.

Whether or not the Ladies had a physical relationship remains unclear. It would appear that at least some of their contemporaries thought that they were 'Sapphists'. Also a matter of debate is the degree to which they themselves conceived of their relationship in terms that acknowledged its 'lesbian' nature. Lillian Faderman has argued that Butler, like other women in romantic friendships, did not see her sexuality as deviant. She bases this assumption on the fact that Butler, after reading an Anthony Hamilton novel containing a lesbian character, failed to comment on the lesbian component. Faderman contends that 'it is probable that one who was concerned with the difficulties that female homosexuals might encounter would have noted the case'. But as Emma Donoghue argues, it is equally likely that, like the lesbian character in the novel, Butler may have recognised herself as at risk of persecution for her sexuality, and thus might have avoided mentioning it in a journal which might have been read by other people. Whether or not the Ladies had a genital relationship or a lesbian identity as we would now know it, they nevertheless serve as one of the preeminent examples of same-sex love between women in the eighteenth century.

Plas Newydd is now a tourist attraction, described as the home of 'the two most celebrated virgins in Europe'. Advertising information does not explore the issue of the women's sexuality.

E. Donoghue, *Passions Between Women: British Lesbian Culture 1668–1801*, London, 1993; L. Faderman, *Surpassing the Love of Men: Romantic Friendship and Love Between Women from the Renaissance to the Present*, New York, 1981; E. Mavor, *The Ladies of Llangollen: A Study in Romantic Friendship*, London, 1971.

Karen Duder

Butler, Samuel (1835–1902), British-New Zealand writer. Butler was 25 years old when he stopped praying, the night he boarded the *Roman Emperor* bound for New Zealand and a new life as a sheep farmer. His background was the church; both his father and grandfather were Anglican clergymen. He had been brought up in Langar Rectory, Nottinghamshire, and educated at Shrewsbury School and St John's College, Cambridge, where he gained a classics degree in 1858.

His early years were characterised by the brutal attentions of his father and the emotional undermining at which his mother excelled. As an adult, Butler professed to loath his parents and three siblings, but dutifully corresponded with them all. With quill, he quibbled and quarrelled with them for nearly 40 years.

Getting away to New Zealand in 1860 seems to have been the making of him. The farm prospered. In the evenings he studied Handel, Darwin and the Gospels, wrote letters home, and penned articles for the Christchurch papers. He also met a sub-editor, the handsome young Charles Pauli. Their friendship flourished and by 1864 they were living in London. Butler fancied himself as a painter – it was not until 1877 that he would say that his career as an art student was over – and he continued to write. He paid for Pauli to study law; as well, he agreed to pay him regular sums and keep his distance. This arrangement only ended with Pauli's death 37 years later when it was discovered that he had other (male) benefactors and quite a fortune; he had not willed Butler a penny.

The satirical and utopian *Erewhon* came out in 1872. It was Butler's only popular success. Though it is unlikely his mother read a word of it, his father blamed the shock of it for her death. About this time, work commenced on *The Way of All Flesh*, his attack on Victorian life and social values. It was practically an autobiography and he opted for posthumous publication. Not only would the family members recognise themselves, he hinted, but there was clearly the danger to him of mentioning in print anything resembling what the Marquis of Queensbury later referred to as 'somdomites'. During the mid-1870s he made some disastrous investments in Canada. His writing and publishing continued.

Butler had by now a new companion, Henry Jones, who had been persuaded to give up law in return for a pension from

Butler, a sort of Boswell/Johnson arrangement. The two men got on famously, and Jones eventually wrote a biography of Butler and edited his notebooks. With Jones and his married manservant Alfred, Butler explored much of rural Kent and Sussex. They wrote music together, *faux*-Handel pieces which Butler published. They ventured further afield to the Alps, the Aegean, the plains of Troy. Travel books appeared and Butler translated Homer. They met young Hans, a Swiss man who spent two years with them brushing up on his English, eventually leaving them for Singapore. The two older men wept openly when Hans's train pulled out, and Butler went home to write what he considered to be his finest poem, 'In Memoriam H R F'.

He then turned to SHAKESPEARE's sonnets, perhaps seeing in the situation between Shakespeare and 'Mr W. H.' similarities with his own and Mr Pauli. His essay and rearrangement of the sonnets was published in 1899.

The end came in 1902; having picked up a stomach complaint abroad, he was brought back to London and nursed by Alfred and Jones. Removing his spectacles, he said, 'I don't want these anymore', and died.

S. Butler, *The Way of All Flesh*, London, 1903; P. Henderson, *Samuel Butler: The Incarnate Bachelor*, London, 1953.

J. Z. Robinson

Byron, George Gordon, Lord (1788–1824), British poet. Few writers embody the idea of the tragic Romantic – young, brave, passionate and bold, yet doomed – as well as Byron. His death at the early age of 36 merely ensured that his already legendary reputation lived on.

Born in London to a Scottish mother and an English aristocratic father (who died when Byron was 3), at the age of 8, on the death of his uncle, Byron inherited both the title and the ancestral estate of Newstead Abbey, Nottinghamshire. Educated at Harrow (where he was mocked because of his club foot) and at Trinity

College, Cambridge, Byron experienced the usual crushes on fellow students: some of his earliest poems were dedicated to John Edleston, whose gift of a cornelian Byron kept with him for the rest of his life. On Edleston's death in 1811, Byron wrote a series of elegies, 'Thyrza', whose pronouns he changed for publication in the homophobic world of Georgian England.

Undertaking his 'Grand Tour' of the continent in 1809, Byron discovered the Mediterranean and its delights, particularly its adolescent males, with several of whom he formed liaisons. On his return to England, he became involved in a series of spectacular emotional entanglements – with Lady Caroline Lamb, with Lady Oxford, and with his half-sister, Augusta Leigh, finally in 1815 marrying Annabella Milbanke. Her leaving him within the year, amid much rumour about his homosexuality, merely added to his reputation as 'mad, bad and dangerous to know'.

He continued with a peripatetic existence, both emotionally and geographically, travelling extensively in Europe, and settling into occasional *ménages*, as with the Shelleys in Switzerland, and later with the Countess Teresa Guiccioli in Italy. In 1823, he became involved in Greece's war of independence from Turkey; while on the island of Cephalonia he met and fell in love with the 15-year-old Loukas Chaland-routsanos, who was his travelling companion for the remaining months of his life. The following year, in Missolonghi, Byron caught a fever and died, apparently bereft that his last love was unrequited.

His works include *Hours of Idleness* (which includes his translations of homoerotic classical poems), *Child Harold's Pilgrimage* and *Don Juan*. As Louis Crompton has noted, critics, scholars and public managed, despite overwhelming evidence, to ignore Byron's blatant bisexuality until recent years.

L. Crompton, *Byron and Greek Love*, London, 1985.

Garry Wotherspoon

C

Caesar, Julius (Gaius Julius Caesar), (100–44 BC), Roman general and politician. Born in Rome into an old patrician family, Caesar's early political sympathies lay with the 'popular' side, being related to the 'popular' leader Gaius Marius (married to his aunt Julia) who, after a brilliant military career, marched on Rome, took it in 87 BC and died the following year. The civil unrest of the early first century BC shaped Caesar's early career; after serving his first military campaign in Asia in 81, he left Rome and did not return until 73. Elected to the senate before 70, he supported Pompey in repealing the constitutional reforms of Marius's opponent Sulla. His career developed steadily: after serving as quaestor (a junior magistracy) in Further Spain (68) he was elected aedile in 65, pontifex maximus in 63, and praetor in 62, after which he returned to Further Spain as governor in 61. Back in Rome, he entered into an informal alliance with Pompey and Crassus which secured his election to the consulship for 59. In the following year he took the governorship of Illyricum (Dalmatia), Gallia Cisalpina (northern Italy) and Gallia Transalpina (southern France), which he used as a base for his campaigns over the next nine years to conquer the remainder of Gaul. Caesar's account of these campaigns, including expeditions to Britain, survive.

As the term of his governorship came to an end in 49, Caesar, contrary to the convention of magistrates laying down one command before standing for another, attempted to secure election to another consulship for 48. Pompey chose not to support Caesar, and when Caesar in defiance of the senate crossed the Rubicon (the boundary between Italy and Cisalpine Gaul) with his army on 10 January 49, Pompey was given command of the senatorial forces. Caesar later published his account of the civil war which ensued. Defeated in 48 at Pharsalus in Greece, Pompey fled to Egypt where he was murdered. It was in Egypt at this time that Caesar met Cleopatra VII, who became his mistress and later accompanied him to Rome. Caesar conducted a successful campaign against Pharnaces, the king of Pontus, in 47, and defeated Pompeian supporters at Thapsus in Africa in 46 and Pompey's sons at Munda in Spain in 45. Appointed to a dictatorship for ten years in 46, Caesar embarked upon a programme including a reform of the calendar which remained unchanged until adjustments were made in the sixteenth century. Though Caesar was enormously popular with the army and the people, opposition persisted within the senate, resulting in a conspiracy which led to his assassination at a meeting of the senate on the Ides of March (15th) 44. Although this action prevented Caesar making himself king, as some feared he would do, it could not prevent further civil war between the Republicans (led by

Brutus and Cassius) and Mark Antony which would end with the Republican defeat at Philippi in Greece in 42.

Caesar was married three times: Cornelia, the mother of his daughter Julia (later married to Pompey); Pompeia, granddaughter of Sulla, whom he divorced following a political scandal in 62; and Calpurnia. The tradition is unanimous that he was notorious as a womaniser, his most famous mistress apart from Cleopatra being Servilia, the mother of Brutus. The elder Curio is quoted by Suetonius as describing Caesar as 'every woman's man and every man's woman', an allusion to the report that as a young man on his first campaign Caesar had enjoyed a sexual relationship with Nicomedes, the king of Bithynia. Suetonius in his life of Caesar (§49) records the persistent attacks on Caesar because of this relationship, condemned as much for the alleged submission to a foreigner as for submission to a man. That Caesar could thereafter be insulted as a 'queen' demonstrates the seriousness with which Romans regarded questions of masculinity and were prepared to use this in pursuit of political ends. In the context of prevailing attitudes to sexual behaviour, it is remarkable that there are no other reports of Caesar enjoying male sexual company, and that a single foreign affair was never forgotten.

Suetonius, 'Divus Iulius', in *Lives of the Caesars and Extracts from Lives of Illustrious Men*, trans. J. C. Rolfe, 2 vols, London, 1914, and *The Twelve Caesars*, trans. R. Graves, Harmondsworth, 1957; M. Grant, *Julius Caesar*, London, 1969; C. Meier, *Caesar*, trans. D. McLintock, London, 1995.

Roger Pitcher

Cahun, Claude (1894–1954), French photographer. Born Lucy Renée Matilde Schwob, she was educated at Oxford and the Sorbonne, and it is currently believed that she began making photographic self-portraits sometime around 1912. By 1917 she had adopted her pseudonym, Claude

Cahun. In 1922, Cahun moved to Paris with her stepsister and lifelong partner, Suzanne Malherbe, also know as Marcel Moore.

Cahun has been of particular interest in recent years because her work is so easily read in relationship to contemporary debates around gender and gender performativity. Cahun's photographs create a series of characters or personae which were then incorporated into her collages. Avant-garde, Dada and Surrealist artists all made use of collage, and it was generally seen as responding to one or more of the following conditions: as a means of asserting the surface plane, as responding to modernist claims of form and function, as a rejection of the *status quo* notion of art as an extension of bourgeois ideology. Collage was used as a technique for disrupting the conventional passivity of the picture plain by literally disturbing its surface. This rather literal disruption of the picture-as-window metaphor provided collage with a recognisably modern technique that allowed for the incongruous combinations of images, which liberated the artist from many visual conventions. Collage was particularly well suited to Cahun's interest in disrupting static notions of gender, manifested both on the literal level of the image surface as well as on a metaphoric level. Among Cahun's cast of characters are a giant doll-like figure and a Bavarian folk dancer; another sports a hand-drawn hairline. Cahun herself appears in a dark suit with a shaved head – clearly intended to be read as a young man. Regardless of the specific changes to gender theory since its emergence in the first decades of the twentieth century, Cahun's gender-bending characters clearly stand as some of the earliest examples of gender play within the visual arts. Even within Cahun's own time a handful of scholars had begun to explore the notion of gender as masquerade. What is particularly significant about Cahun's work is its critical response to static gender models.

F. Leperlier, *Claude Cahun: Masks and Meta-morphoses*, trans. Liz Heron, London, 1999.

Ken Gonzales-Day

Cambacérès, Jean-Jacques-Régis de (1753–1824), French statesman. Cambacérès was born into a noble family of magistrates in Montpellier in southern France. He pursued a legal career in the 1770s and 1780s, supported the French Revolution in 1789, and won election as deputy to the National Convention (1792–1795). He avoided taking any clear-cut political stand in the assembly, lest it compromise him with one or another of the rival factions, and instead laboured discreetly to reform and codify French law. He stayed in politics under the Directory (1795–1799), becoming Minister of Justice in June 1799. After Napoleon Bonaparte's *coup d'état* in November 1799, he became Second Consul, the second personage in the State. When Napoleon was proclaimed Emperor in May 1804, he named Cambacérès Arch-Chancellor of the Empire. He presided over the Senate and supervised the administration during Napoleon's frequent absences on military campaigns. He worked hard, showing skill, tact and good judgement, but was indecisive by nature and always totally subservient to the Emperor. Napoleon made him duke of Parma in 1808.

Cambacérès's affected mannerisms, pomposity, haughtiness and gluttony made him a subject of ridicule both during his lifetime and after his death. Although he was always discreet, he remained unmarried, kept to the company of other bachelors and was almost certainly homosexual. Many people, including Napoleon himself, joked openly about Cambacérès's presumed sexual proclivities. In 1814, after Napoleon's fall, Royalist caricatures portrayed him as a cowardly 'auntie' (dubbing him '*Tante Urlurette*') and a lubricious pursuer of handsome young men. In 1859, the municipal council of his home town voted against raising a statue to Cambacérès because of his alleged morals.

Many wrongly give credit to Cambacérès for the decriminalisation of homosexuality in France. In fact, the Constituent Assembly (1789–1792) decriminalised sodomy (along with such other 'imaginary crimes' as bestiality, heresy, blasphemy and witchcraft) in 1791, when Cambacérès was still only an obscure provincial judge. He did oversee much of the drafting of the Civil Code of 1804 (the celebrated Code Napoléon), but had no part in writing the Penal Code of 1810, which, in the case of sodomy, followed the Code of 1791.

In 1815, the restored royal government expelled Cambacérès from France and he spent three years in Holland and Belgium. Allowed to return in May 1818, he lived in obscure retirement in Paris until his death.

J.-L. Bory, *Les cinq girouettes*, Paris, 1979; P.-F. Pinaud, *Cambacérès*, Paris, 1991; P. Viallès, *L'Archichancelier Cambacérès (1753–1824)*, Paris, 1908.

Michael Sibalis

Caminha, Adolfo (1867–1897), Brazilian novelist, journalist and literary critic. Born in Ceará in northern Brazil, Caminha studied at the Navy School in Rio de Janeiro and then began a career as a naval officer, including a training voyage to the Caribbean and United States in 1886. In 1889, he became involved in an affair with the wife of an Army officer in the provincial city of Fortaleza. In the ensuing scandal Caminha resigned his commission rather than give up the relationship. He later moved to Rio and lived in relative poverty and obscurity, working as a minor civil servant and literary critic. He died of tuberculosis at the age of 29, leaving his common-law wife, Isabel, and two young daughters, one of whom died shortly afterwards.

Apart from some juvenile works, Caminha published three novels, a travel book about the United States and a collection of literary reviews and criticism. He is best known as the author of the novel *Bom-*

Crioulo (*Good Darkie*, 1895), the first major Latin American literary work to have male homosexuality as its explicit central theme, which appeared in the same year as the Oscar WILDE trials. It is also one of the earliest Brazilian novels to have a pure black as its hero, although Caminha was white. It seems unlikely that Caminha was homosexual, given the obvious strength of his commitment to Isabel, but the social ostracism he endured, coupled with his rebellious and combative temperament, appears to have made him sympathetic towards transgressive sexual relationships. Caminha may also have witnessed homosexual relationships during his time as a naval officer.

Bom-Crioulo tells the story of an escaped black slave, Amaro, nicknamed Bom-Crioulo, who enlists as a sailor in the Brazilian navy. Onboard ship, he befriends a 15-year-old white cabin-boy, Aleixo, and then seduces him after undergoing punishment by flogging on his behalf. When the ship reaches Rio, Bom-Crioulo rents a room in a boarding house belonging to a friendly Portuguese washerwoman, Dona Carolina, where he and Aleixo spend their free time together. This idyllic situation comes to an end when Bom-Crioulo is transferred to another ship where he cannot easily get shore leave. Left to his own devices, Aleixo, who has tired of his male lover's physical attentions, is seduced by Dona Carolina, who wants a young lover to enliven her flagging middle age. Aleixo begins to assume a more assertive masculine role and forgets Bom-Crioulo. Meanwhile, the increasingly desperate Bom-Crioulo absents himself without leave from his ship in an unsuccessful attempt to meet Aleixo. He gets drunk, picks a fight with a Portuguese dockworker and, as a punishment, is flogged till he collapses, ending up confined in hospital. With no news from Aleixo, Bom-Crioulo is increasingly consumed by a mixture of love, hatred and jealousy. He finally escapes from hospital after learning that Aleixo has got a girlfriend and makes his way to the house where a shop assistant tells him that Aleixo is living with Dona Carolina. At this moment, Aleixo arrives. Bom-Crioulo seizes him and slashes his throat with a razor. The novel ends with the murderer being led away while a crowd gathers to see the corpse.

Bom-Crioulo is a curiously ambiguous work and has inspired many different interpretations for its treatment of race and gender as well as homosexuality. At one point Caminha refers to anal intercourse as a 'crime against nature' and occasionally uses condemnatory language, but generally he assumes a detached and non-judgemental authorial stance towards the relationship he describes. This prevents facile interpretations of the novel as a pro- or anti-gay work. In its treatment of homosexuality, *Bom-Crioulo* incorporates elements both of classical pederasty and late nineteenth-century European medical theories. The relationship between Bom-Crioulo and Aleixo is very much that of the older lover or *erastes* educating and guiding the younger beloved or *eromenos* in return for sexual favours. At the same time, without going into great physical detail, Caminha makes clear that Bom-Crioulo is the active and Aleixo the passive partner. The hero, Bom-Crioulo, is perhaps the first homosexual character in modern literature to be portrayed as masculine rather than effeminate and as exclusively homosexual rather than bisexual. This reflects the influence of contemporary European sexologists such as Richard von KRAFFT-EBING and Albert Moll, whom Caminha cited in an article defending the novel against hostile critics.

Traditionally described as a naturalist novel because of its controversial and explicit sexual theme and its lower-class setting, *Bom-Crioulo* is essentially a tragedy of passion. The engine which drives the plot is sexual desire and jealousy. There is an obvious debt to Shakespeare's *Othello* but the novel draws more profoundly on the structure of classical Greek tragedy.

Through this it appears to invite reflection rather than moralisation.

Bom-Crioulo nevertheless caused a scandal when it was first published. The hostile, homophobic reaction of two of the major critics of the period and the early death of the author caused it to lapse into obscurity for the next forty years. In the second half of the twentieth century, it has increasingly been recognised by mainstream critics and literary historians as one of the major nineteenth-century Brazilian novels. Gay critics have been more ambivalent because of the difficulty of interpreting its attitude towards homosexuality. Nevertheless, it has now been translated into English, Spanish, German and French. As critics begin to unravel its many threads and nuances, the novel's very ambiguity is coming to be recognised as one of its great strengths.

S. de Azevedo, *Adolfo Caminha: Vida e Obra*, 2nd edn, Fortaleza, 1999; A. Caminha, *Bom-Crioulo: The Black Man and the Cabin Boy*, trans. E. A. Lacey, San Francisco, 1982; D. W. Foster, *Gay and Lesbian Themes in Latin American Writing*, Austin, Texas, 1991: 9–22; R. Howes, 'Race and Transgressive Sexuality in Adolfo Caminha's Bom-Crioulo', *Luso-Brazilian Review*, forthcoming; Oficina Literária Afrânio Coutinho, *Enciclopédia de Literatura Brasileira. Vol. 1*, Rio de Janeiro, 1990: 370; S. Ribeiro, *O Romancista Adolfo Caminha, 1867–1967*, Rio de Janeiro, 1967; A. Caminha, 'Um Livro Condemnado', *A Nova Revista*, 1, 2, (February 1896): 40–2.

Robert Howes

Campanella, Tommaso (1568–1639), Italian writer and philosopher. Born the son of an illiterate cobbler in Reggio Calabria, Campanella entered the Dominican order at the age of 13 and began studies in grammar and philosophy. He developed an anti-Scholastic philosophy which, after the publication of his first work (*Philosophia sensibus demonstrata*, 1591), earned him condemnation by the Inquisition. Campanella, however, refused to submit and, disobeying the order to return to Calabria, travelled around various Italian cities. A second condemnation for heresy and insubordination followed in 1597, and the Inquisition commanded him to return to his native region. Here he became the spokesman for those discontented with social injustices, the overweening power of the church and Spanish domination; Campanella figured among the organisers of a general populist uprising. However, he was betrayed, arrested in 1599 and tortured. He saved his life by feigning madness, but remained imprisoned in Naples for 27 years. During this time he managed to write numerous works and maintain a vast network of relations with scholars throughout Europe. Freed in 1626, he was obliged by the Holy Office in Rome to account for his actions and ideas, and held in jail for a further two years. Once out of prison, he again took up his political and religious battles, struggling for social equality and for missionary endeavours – Campanella conceived of Christianity as a perfectly rational creed derived from Christ, the absolute First Reason. In 1634, when he learned that the Neapolitan government was going to accuse him of leading another conspiracy, Campanella fled to Paris, where he lived for the rest of his life.

The discovery of Campanella's homosexual tendencies is very recent, notwithstanding reports by his contemporaries. In 1985, Luigi Firpo published the transcript of conversations held between Campanella and his cellmate, which had been overheard by a spy sent during his trial in Naples to determine whether the philosopher's madness was only simulated. On the night of 14 April 1600, Campanella said to his cellmate: 'O Father Pietro, why don't you do something so that we may sleep together, and we may get pleasure?' Pietro replied: 'I wish I could, and I'd even bribe the gaolers with ten ducats. But to you, my heart, I would like to give twenty kisses every hour.'

Before the discovery of this document

only the condemnation of sodomy in the most famous of Campanella's books, *La città del Sole* (1602), was known. In this work, the inhabitants of a utopian 'sun city', who are surprised in the act of committing sodomy, are forced as punishment to wear a shoe around their neck because they have 'perverted the order [of nature] and put feet where the head should be.' Convicted a second time, they are sentenced to death. Such sanctions occurred even though in the same work, *bardascismo* – a taste for passive sodomy – and effeminacy are explained as caused by the astrological influences of Venus and the moon.

Following the publication of the transcript of Campanella's prison conversation, a new meaning was read into the presence of two love sonnets contained in his highly regarded and heterosexual poetical work. The poems 'Sonetto fatto al signor Petrillo' and 'Sonetto fatto al medesimo' date from July 1601 and were composed when Campanella was in jail. They were written for Petrillo Cesarano, the adolescent nephew of the doctor who cared for Campanella after his torture. In the first of them, Campanella praised the youth's beauty and apostrophises him: 'Glorious lad, who pricks my heart / with very chaste love using an arrow / adding new sense to my lost sense'. In the second, he remembered that physical beauty is fated to disappear in a short while unless, as the expression of inner beauty, it turns towards the God who has created it: 'Therefore be careful to give it in exchange / to the one who gives you virtue, goodness and sense / not vain words in return'. Despite this evidence, the question of Campanella's sexual preferences remains open.

T. Campanella, *Tutte le opere*, Milan, 1954: I, 261–2; L. Firpo (ed.), *Il supplizio di Tommaso Campanella*, Rome, 1985.

Giovanni Dall'Orto

Campiglia, Maddalena (1553–1595), Italian poet. Campiglia was born in Vicenza,

the daughter of Polissena Verlato and the nobleman Carlo Campiglia; her parents, widow and widower, were not married to each other, but already had two sons together. Such a situation, scandalous at the time, was 'normalised' only in 1565, when the couple wed. Her parents gave Campiglia the upbringing of a lady, teaching her poetry, literature and music; in various letters written as an adult, Campiglia declared her passion for 'viols, lutes and harpsichords'. Her future, as clearly planned by her father himself, was to be for marriage. To this end, her brothers were charged with finding her a husband, and her father each year increased Campiglia's dowry – if she had not succeeded in marrying by the age of 25, she would find herself in possession of a considerable fortune. However, this eventuality was averted two years earlier when she was probably compelled to marry Dionisio Colzè. She left him in 1580 to return to her parents' house, where she lived until she died, probably from a long and painful eye illness.

She and her husband had no children, and in her will she tried to deny her husband hereditary rights to her belongings because, she declared, 'in conscience and according to God's laws' he had never been a proper husband to her. At the time, indeed, popular opinion retained the idea that only physical union between the partners made a marriage legally valid; it is likely, given the celebration of virginity in all of Campiglia's works, that this had never occurred in her case.

Finally freed from an unwanted marriage, courageous, careless of conventions and yet much admired in the society in which she lived, Campiglia now devoted her attention to the writing of prose and poetry. Her first published work, in 1585, was a religious tract, *L'Annonciatione della Beata Vergine e la Incarnatione del S.N. Giesù Christo*, dedicated to a woman, Suor Vittoria Trissino-Frattina, whose virginity Campiglia exalted as the sole feminine possession which allowed her an escape from the canonical roles of wife, widow and nun. She asked other women to trust in their own sex for their salvation, taking as 'chief' and 'sublime lady' the Virgin Mary. Only the verse prologue of another religious work, the *Vita di Santa Barbara*, survives, although in her will Campiglia expressed a desire for it to be published.

Her second published work was *Flori. Favola boscareccia* (1588), which earned the praise of Torquato TASSO. The verses of this pastoral fairy-tale tell the story of the nymph Flori who, driven mad with grief at the death of a beloved woman, the nymph Amaranta, decides to renounce love forever. Flori also figured as the heroine of a second fairy-tale, *Calisa: Egloga*, in which she is again in love with a woman, and this time gives a defence of lesbian love in an impassioned and convincing peroration. The woman for whom the work was written, the Marchesa di Soragna, Isabella Pallavinici Lupi, was most likely one of the women whom Campiglia loved and was certainly her protector and patron; Campiglia wrote numerous sonnets in praise of Lupi's beauty and spiritual virtues. Another woman with whom Campiglia was closely linked was Giulia Cisotti, abbess of the convent of Aracoeli, in whose tomb, at her own request, Campiglia was also buried.

S. Rumor, *Per una poetessa del sec. SVI, s.i.t.*, Vicenza, 1897; D. Sartori, *Le stanze ritrovate*, Mirano [Venice], 1994.

Maria Di Rienzo

Carafa, Carlo (1517/1519–1566), Italian cardinal. Born in Naples, Carafa was a younger son in a powerful noble family. He became a soldier and for 17 years took part in the bloody wars which ravaged Italy, first on the side of the Habsburg imperial armies, afterwards with French troops. Then his uncle, Gian Piero Carafa (1476–1559), was elected pope, as Paul IV (in office 1555–1559), and made Carafa a cardinal, entrusting him with important duties and for long periods leaving him in charge of the Papal States. Carafa profited from his power to spin a web of intrigues, orientating the papacy in a pro-French and anti-Spanish direction – a series of about-faces which aimed at securing a Tuscan state for Carafa's family to rule. The war against the Holy Roman Empire and Spain, however, had disastrous results for the Papal States (the southern parts of which were occupied by the Spanish). The Treaty of Cave (1557) returned the situation to the *status quo ante bellum*, crushing the ambitions, if not the intrigues, of Carafa, who now switched his loyalties to the imperial side.

These developments gave new wind to the pro-French opponents of Carlo and Giovanni Carafa, the nephews of the upright and moralistic Paul IV; their scandalous conduct was violently denounced to the pontiff. For instance, on 17 January 1558, Cardinal Charles de Lorraine (1525–1574) asked the French ambassador in Rome to report to the pope scandals concerning his nephews. In his letter he stated that the courtiers had been scandalised by what they had witnessed, 'and among the culprits were openly numbered, to my great regret, those who were closest in blood relations to our Holy Father the pope'. They had engaged in 'that sin so loathsome in which there is no longer a distinction between the male and female sex'.

These rumours cannot be explained away as political slander. Already, in about 1555, the poet Joachim du Bellay (1522?–1560), who was then in Rome, wrote a sonnet mentioning one Ascanio (presumably recently deceased) as the beloved of Carafa. In Sonnet CIII of *Les Regrets*, he invites Love to weep, 'for now you must not recall / his father to handsome Ascanio; now you should mourn / handsome Ascanio himself, Ascanio, O pity! / Ascanio, whom Carafa loved more than his own eyes: / Ascanio, whose face was handsomer / than that of the Trojan cupbearer [GANYMEDE], who pours for the gods'.

At first the pope refused to believe the numerous and varied accusations, but he was finally convinced of their veracity; furious with his nephews Carlo and Giovanni, he deprived them of their positions and exiled them in January 1559. Carlo Carafa's fall opened the way for lampoons which accused him of being a sodomite; one published at the time of the pope's death (1559) abhored Carlo's conduct: 'Look at this wicked bad man / who his incest and his sodomy notwitstanding / is in the cardinals' company'. After Paul IV's death, Carlo returned to Rome but immediately felt the effects of the disastrous political choices imposed on the Papal States. The new pontiff, Pius IV, had him arrested for a lengthy series of crimes ranging from homicide to heresy, among which was sodomy. A kangaroo court convicted Carlo with his brother Giovanni, and he was executed. It is worth noting, however, that the charges of sodomy were of little or no significance in the trial; politics provided the true motivation for their condemnation. Conviction of Paul IV's nephews amounted to a condemnation of the anti-Spanish politics of the former pope, the blame for which was laid entirely on their shoulders. When a *rapprochement* had been effected with Spain, the new pope, Pius V, reopened the case in 1567 and rehabilitated Carlo Carafa. The cardinal's tomb lies next to that of his uncle in the Carafa chapel in the church of Santa Maria sopra Minerva in Rome.

E. Cazal, *Histoire anecdotique de l'Inquisition en Italie et en France*, Paris, 1924: 85–100; D. Chiomenti-Vassalli, *Paolo IV e il processo Carafa*, Milan, 1993; G. Duruy, *Le Cardinal Carlo Carafa (1519–1561)*, Paris, 1882: 296–7; A. Prosperi, 'Carafa, Carlo', *Dizionario biografico degli italiani*, Vol. 19, Rome, 1976: 497–507.

Giovanni Dall'Orto

Caravaggio, Michelangelo Merisi da ('Il Caravaggio') (1571–1610), Italian painter. Caravaggio was born near Bergamo in northern Italy and had his early training there. He went to Rome in 1593, where, after a difficult start, he found a protector in Cardinal Francesco Maria Del Monte (1549–1627), who in 1597 housed him in his palace, commissioned several works from him, and in 1599 helped him secure his first large-scale commission, paintings of St Matthew for the San Luigi dei Francesi church. This proved to be the beginning of a successful career; within a short time, Caravaggio's realist style, marked by sharp contrast between light and darkness, was imitated by several other painters, and Caravaggio found himself much in demand.

Yet his criminal record prevented him from enjoying the fruits of his labours: on several occasions, he brawled and became involved in street-fighting, and he had to flee Rome after killing one Ranuccio Tommasoni. Caravaggio first went to Naples around 1606, then moved on to Sicily and Malta, where he was jailed for offending a Knight of Malta, after which in 1608 he fled. He returned to Sicily, only to be obliged to flee once more in 1609, then to Naples, where he was injured in a fight. He died, probably of malaria, on the Latium shore, not far from Rome, where he had most likely taken refuge while waiting for his powerful friends in Rome to obtain a pardon for him.

Caravaggio's criminal character and overall instability have sometimes been linked, especially in Herwarth Roettgen's 1975 psychoanalytic study, with the painter's unease with his homosexuality. Dubious as this bizarre explanation may be, it at least makes reference to his sexuality. Times have changed since the great art critic (and closeted homosexual) Roberto Longhi (1890–1970), who rediscovered Caravaggio after centuries of neglect, attacked a rival art critic (also a closeted homosexual), Bernard Berenson (1865–1959), for writing in 1951 that Caravaggio 'might' have been a homosexual. Only a homosexual himself, Longhi venomously replied the next year, could give credit to such an idea. More recently, Derek Jarman's film *Caravaggio*, interpreting the artist as a blatantly bisexual character, caused no eyebrows to be raised – except in Italy, where art critics such as Maurizio Calvesi insisted that 'actually Caravaggio's purported homosexuality, useful just to add an extra touch to the picture of his "cursed" life, is likely nothing but a blunder.'

However, outside Italy, art historians take for granted Caravaggio's homosexuality, which is so self-evident from his pictures that one of the first owners of the *Amore vincitore* now in Berlin – a completely naked pin-up teenager – prudently kept it hidden behind a curtain. Documents about Caravaggio's life that have been uncovered since the artist's post-war rediscovery confirm what previously was just an inference taken from the blatant homoeroticism of his pictures, especially the earlier works. Christoph Frommer has even reconstructed the milieu in which Caravaggio obtained his first commissions, showing that he addressed himself to a coterie sensitive to homoerotic themes. As Margaret Walters puts it: 'Caravaggio was catering to an openly homosexual subculture in Rome, sophisticated, confident and wealthy enough to indulge its fantasies and to develop its own codes and ironies. The tone of Caravaggio's work for this group is distinctive.'

Extant documents show that Cardinal Del Monte was himself inclined towards boys and young men, and even, according to Frommer, 'Del Monte was, for the young Caravaggio, something more than a protector who offered him lodging, commissions and a rich collection to gaze on.' In Del Monte's palace, Caravaggio shared rooms with a young 'friend' with whom he had settled in 1594, a second-rate Sicilian painter, Mario Minniti (1577–1640). They lived together until 1600, when Minniti left Caravaggio to get married. Frommer identifies as Minniti the sensuous model for several of Caravaggio's early paintings, among them the Uffizi *Bacchus*, the Hermitage *Lute Player* and the Louvre *Fortune-Teller*. When Minniti moved out, Caravaggio became so angry with him that, in a 1603 trial, he said that Minniti 'used to live with me in the past and three years ago, he went away and I never spoke to him again'. However, Minniti reappeared in Caravaggio's life in 1608, when Caravaggio stayed with him in his native Syracuse and obtained a commission in part thanks to him.

Incidentally, in the same 1603 trial, one witness, Tommaso Salini, called a boy named Giovan Battista, 'Caravaggio's *bardassa* [catamite]'; this might have been just slander, as Calvesi argues, yet it shows that Caravaggio's (bad) reputation was not a very heterosexual one. However, it is impossible to learn more from the trial records because the painter prudently denied having ever known the boy. Nevertheless, the earlier biographer and art historian Francesco Susinno (*c.* 1670/1680–*c.* 1739) said that the reason Caravaggio had to flee Messina, in Sicily, where his paintings were much appreciated, was that not everyone liked his habit of chasing boys in the street: 'On holidays he followed a grammar school teacher called Don Carlo Pepe, who used to lead his pupils to the shipyard so that they could amuse themselves. ... In such a place Caravaggio observed these boys, who were playing, to fulfil his fantasies. The teacher grew grimly suspicious and asked why he was always chasing after him. The painter fiercely disliked this question and became so enraged and furious that, confirming his notoriety as a foolish man, he hit that good man and hurt his head.'

Much has been said on the homoeroticism of Caravaggio's paintings, for instance, in Dominique Fernandez's novel *Dans la main de l'ange*; Fernandez finds sadomasochistic undertones in his pictures. Yet much remains to be said, since the exploration of the rich subculture in which Caravaggio found shelter (first explored by Posener and Frommer) still leaves much to discover.

M. Calvesi, 'Caravaggio', *Art & Dossier*, April 1986: 14; D. Fernandez, *Dans la main de l'ange*, Paris, 1982; C. Frommer, 'Caravaggios Frühwerk und der Kardinal Francesco del Monte', *Storia dell'arte*, 9–10 (1971): 5–29; R. Longhi, 'Novelletta del Caravaggio "invertito"', *Paragone*, March 1952: 62–4; D. Posener, 'Caravaggio's Early Homo-erotic Works', *Art Quarterly*, 24 (1976): 301–26; F. Susinno, *Le vite de' pittori messinesi e di altri che fiorirono in Messina*, Florence, 1950 [1724]: 114–15; H. Roettgen, *Il Caravaggio, ricerche e interpretazioni*, Rome, 1975; M. Walters, *The Male Nude*, Harmondsworth, 1978: 188–9.

Giovanni Dall'Orto

Carlier, Félix (*fl.* 1860s), French administrator. Carlier was head of the Parisian vice squad from 1860 to 1870. Nothing is known about Carlier's life or career. Some sources erroneously give his first name as François; others confuse him with Pierre Carlier (1794–1858), prefect of police for Paris from 1849 to 1851. In 1870, Carlier began writing a book on Parisian prostitution, which finally appeared in 1887. It included 230 pages on 'anti-physical [i.e. unnatural] prostitution'. Carlier declared that previous works on prostitution had intentionally omitted any discussion of 'anti-physical passions', but that 'we have overcome our disgust and have completed our work in the interest of public security'. Although homosexual relations were legal in France since 1791, Carlier argued that homosexuality was 'a vice that should be a misdemeanour, because of the dangers to morality and public safety', especially in Paris but also in the provinces. He urged that France follow the example of Germany and make homosexuality a crime.

Carlier reluctantly accepted the necessity of heterosexual prostitution ('without it, rape, public indecency [and] the corruption of young girls would be a public danger'), but he saw no such utility in homosexual prostitution. Although his book was supposed to be a study of prostitutes, Carlier also discussed homosexuals engaged in non-venal relations, for whom

he showed a marked distaste: 'The passion for pederasty [i.e. homosexuality] . . . extinguishes, among those of whom it takes hold, the noblest sentiments, love of country and of the family; it renders them useless to society'. He insisted that 'unnatural relations . . . do not derive either from affection or for genuine love; they are born exclusively from desire for sensual pleasures'. He expressed his shock that 'pederasty . . . leads to the most monstrous pairings from the social point of view. The master and his servant, the thief and the man without a criminal record, the beggar in rags and the dandy accept each other as if they belonged to the same social class.' Carlier believed that the homosexual could be easily recognised by 'an obsequious and exaggerated politeness, a [certain] intonation of the voice, a way of dressing, . . . a passion for showy jewelry, a languorous gaze, the movements of his body'.

Carlier's primary concern as a policeman was crime, and he devoted an entire chapter to the blackmail of homosexuals by unscrupulous criminals: 'Pederasty has this feature in particular, . . . it whets the appetites of all evil-doers. One could say that it provokes crime . . . Swindles, thefts, armed robbery, even murder, [the blackmailer] stops at nothing.' He implicitly blamed the victim as much as the blackmailer for this state of affairs.

Carlier was not the first French policeman to discuss homosexuality in print. For example, the memoirs of Louis Canler (1797–1865), first published in 1862, include a 30-page chapter titled 'The Anti-Physicals and Blackmailers'. But Carlier treated homosexuality more extensively than any of his predecessors and his book is a compendium of all the contemporary prejudices and preconceptions. It demonstrates the extent to which the French police constructed an unflattering image of homosexuals as social deviants even before medical science tackled the subject.

F. Carlier, 'Etude statistique sur la prostitution clandestine à Paris', *Annales d'hygiène publique et de médicine légale*, 2nd series, 36 (1871), and *Les deux prostitutions*, Paris, 1887.

Michael Sibalis

Carpenter, Edward (1844–1929), British writer and social reformer. Born into comfortable, upper-middle-class circumstances, Carpenter was educated at Trinity Hall, Cambridge, becoming a fellow and taking orders in 1870. His liberal Anglican and Christian socialist views led him into university extension lecturing; after a crisis of faith and seeking to simplify life, he abandoned this work, forsook the cloth, and moved to a cottage, Millthorpe, in rural Derbyshire, where he wrote and market-gardened. He had come under the influence of Walt WHITMAN, and visited him twice, in 1877 and again in 1884, publishing in 1906 an account of those visits, *Days with Walt Whitman, with Some Notes on his Life and Work*. His admiration for the good gray poet influenced the form and shape of his own utopian vision, Whitmanesque prose-poems titled *Towards Democracy* (1883; three further parts, 1885–1905), a work that with supporting social critiques such as *Civilisation: Its Cause and Cure* (1889) was widely influential. He met his lover, George Merrill, on a train in the winter of 1889–1890 when the working-class 20-year-old from the Sheffield slums was out of work. Carpenter found him the first of a number of jobs. In 1898 Merrill moved into Millthorpe, against the advice of all of Carpenter's friends, and remained with Carpenter until his death in 1928. Their living together brought them both happiness, and it is difficult now to conceive what a radically daring and courageous step it was in 1898. Millthorpe became a place of pilgrimage for supporters of all of Carpenter's many causes; many homosexuals wended their way there, with inspiriting and even liberating effect, notably E. M. FORSTER, who was prompted to write his overtly homosexual romance, *Maurice*.

In 1894 Carpenter issued *Homogenic Love*, the first openly published defence of homosexuality by a homosexual in England. Bravely defiant of the fear and hostility stirred up by the WILDE trials in 1895, he published another treatment of the subject, *An Unknown People*, in 1897, which became chapter 2 of *The Intermediate Sex* (1908), a collection of his papers on 'homogenic love' that remained continuously in print until the 1950s. It was also included in 1906 in an enlarged edition of *Love's Coming-of-Age: A Series of Papers on the Relations of the Sexes* (1896), a widely read sex-reform volume, where it served to introduce the subject of homosexuality sympathetically to a straight audience. *Ioläus: An Anthology of Friendship*, a work known unsympathetically in the second-hand book trade as the Bugger's Bible, came out in 1902, inspired by Elisàr von Kupffer's German anthology two years before, *Lieblingsminne und Freundesliebe in der Weltliteratur*. It, too, went through many editions.

In the meantime Carpenter pursued ethnographic and historical studies of homoeroticism in relation to religion and warrior castes, which were collected in *Intermediate Types among Primitive Folk* (1914). In 1916 Carpenter published his autobiography, *My Days and Dreams*, which, without of course being explicit, treats his ménage with Merrill with considerable frankness. Many understood perfectly what was implied in his idyllic portrait of the rural life of two bachelors. In 1913 he helped to found, with Laurence Housman and others, the British Society for the Study of Sex-Psychology, a forum for positive discussion of homosexuality. He addressed the society on Whitman, this time speaking explicitly of the US bard's homosexuality and its place in his work. *Some Friends of Walt Whitman: A Study in Sex-Psychology* (1924) usefully surveys earlier English-language treatments of the subject, but is in the end rather timorous in its conclusions.

Although a few others wrote privately, clandestinely, or anonymously in favour of same-sex behaviour, Carpenter was the only English writer before World War I who publicly and openly defended homosexuality and the homosexual's rightful place in society.

C. Tsuzuki, *Edward Carpenter, 1844–1929: Prophet of Human Fellowship*, Cambridge, 1980; S. Rowbotham and J. Weeks, *Socialism and the New Life: The Personal and Sexual Politics of Edward Carpenter and Havelock Ellis*, London, 1977.

                                        Gary Simes

Casement, Roger (David) (1864–1916), Irish patriot. Casement was born in Kingstown – now Dún Laoghaire – near Dublin. One should beware of the dichotomous choices through which Irish identity is often presented. Casement's father was a Protestant, his mother Catholic; he belonged to the Ascendancy, though his means were modest; he was a servant of the Empire, yet sought its dissolution and Irish independence; he wanted to be a Gael, yet knew little Irish; he lived a Protestant, yet died a Catholic.

After leaving what is now Ballymena Academy, Casement entered the British consular service, distinguishing himself in two reports on 'human rights abuses', first in the Congo, and then in Putumayo, Brazil. Though a convinced anti-slaver, his pronouncements on matters racial sometimes fall short of modern political correctness: 'Altogether the resultant human compost is the nastiest form of black-pudding you have ever sat down to.' He was rewarded with promotion to Consul-General and a knighthood. Most of his career was spent away from Ireland, and his conversion to nationalism was progressive and intellectual. There was an imperial dimension to his nationalism: he saw the plight of the rural poor in Connemara as parallel to that of the Amazonian Indian, and intended that Ireland, once independent, should come to the aid of the Egyptians. In his mind Ireland had a geopolitical role: 'The true alliance to aim at for all who love peace is the friendly union of Germany, America and Ireland. These are the true United States of the world. Ireland the link between Europe and America must be freed by both.' However, to attempt to bring this about by asking help in enemy territory during war-time was to seek martyrdom. This was hastened by a Norwegian manservant, doubtless his lover, but also a double agent. The German episode had elements of swashbuckling adventure but ended in farce as Casement landed from a U-boat in Kerry, was swiftly apprehended, taken to London and imprisoned in the Tower. There was little doubt that the charge of treason would be upheld. There remains the question of his homosexuality. Though there had been indiscretions throughout his career, these had led to no more than social opprobrium, and the British authorities had only discovered his proclivities shortly before his arrest. However, his diaries fell into the hands of the authorities, and were used once he had been convicted to prevent public sympathy for a plea of clemency. The diaries were an embarrassment to the Irish, and their authenticity was contested, but they are almost certainly genuine. Casement was stripped of his knighthood and was hanged in Pentonville prison in 1916. It has never been entirely clear whether Casement's infamy was his treachery or his sexuality. He took communion as a Catholic only once, just prior to execution; his request to be admitted to the Church had previously been made conditional on his expressing regret for his homosexual past.

A. Mitchell (ed.) *The Amazon Journal of Roger Casement*, London, 1997; R. Sawyer (ed.) *Roger Casement's Diaries–1910: The Black and the White*, London, 1997.

                                        David Parris

Cather, Willa (1873–1947), American writer. Born in Virginia and living most of her adult life in Pittsburgh, New York City and the island of Grand Manan, Canada, Cather is probably best known for writing about the vast landscape of the American heartland and those who immigrated and settled there in the late nineteenth and early twentieth centuries. In 1883, the Cather family moved to Nebraska, where she lived until a year after graduating from the University of Nebraska in 1895. The Nebraska landscape had a profound effect on her writing, especially her fascination for detail. This is most vividly expressed in her two most famous novels, *O Pioneers!* (1913) and *My Ántonia* (1918), the latter winning critical acclaim in the US and Europe.

Cather commented that art was something not extraneous to life, but 'must spring out of the very stuff that life is made of'. Yet the 'stuff' of her own life, and those for whom she felt the 'deepest affection' both in her life and in her work, have traditionally been ignored or overridden. While critics such as Mildred Bennett acknowledge her masculine haircuts and preference for men's clothes, as well as her assumption of a masculine narrative point of view in *My Ántonia*, what has often been elided, until recently, is Cather's emotional attachments to other women, both in her work and in her life. Cather herself often cultivated an image of celibacy and tried to give the impression that she rejected emotional ties for the sake of her writing. Around the turn of the century in the US, especially following the publicity of the WILDE trials in England, it was common for women in same-sex relationships to keep them private. This tension between same-sex desire and growing awareness of the building momentum of homophobia in the early twentieth century is evident not only in Cather's public rebuke of Oscar Wilde in one of her columns in 1895, but also in her short story 'Paul's Case' (1905), one of her most often republished and frequently taught stories. It is about the scapegoating of a feminine high school boy by his teachers for being different (though the second half of the

story detailing his flight to New York treats Paul more sympathetically). Cather herself taught English in a Pittsburgh high school from 1901 to 1906 which coincided, in part, with her 12-year relationship with Isabelle McClung. By concealing her relationships with the women she loved, including Louise Pound, McClung (whose later marriage devastated Cather) and Edith Lewis, with whom she shared a 40-year relationship, Cather also concealed, as Lillian Faderman notes, the ways in which these women contributed to and nourished her creative abilities.

Lesbian studies have questioned interpretations of Cather's work and her identification with her characters, particularly readings of *My Ántonia* as a classic heterosexual love story. Lesbian readings suggest, for instance, the strong possibility that the novel was not a capitulation to convention in spite of Cather's lesbianism, but a *resistance* to heteronormative relations. Judith Fetterley has argued that unlike Ántonia, who has traditionally been idealised as the pioneer heroine, the character of Lena Lingard, who resists marriage as restrictive to women, elicits desire in the fictional narrator and in the narrative voice (i.e. Cather's) that describes her. To merely focus on Cather's masculine masquerade in narrating the novel is to miss important connections to Cather as a lesbian novelist. Given homophobic speculation and suspicion of so-called 'female friendships' in the early twentieth century, Cather's use of the masculine fictional narrator may also have been a subversive way to write about women as objects of desire.

Cather wrote other novels including *The Professor's House* (1925) and *Death Comes for the Archbishop* (1927), and numerous poems and essays. She was awarded the Pulitzer Prize in 1923 for *One of Ours* and held honorary degrees from various universities. She was elected to the American Academy of Arts and Letters in 1938 and received a gold medal from the National Institute of Arts and Letters in

1944. She died in New York City; Edith Lewis, author of the biography *Willa Cather Living* (1953), died in 1972 in the apartment the couple had shared there.

M. R. Bennett, *The World of Willa Cather*, Lincoln, Nebraska, 1961; L. Faderman, *Odd Girls and Twilight Lovers: A History of Lesbian Life in Twentieth-Century America*, New York, 1992; J. Fetterley, '*My Ántonia*, Jim Burden, and the Dilemma of the Lesbian Writer', in K. Jay and J. Glasgow (eds) *Lesbian Texts and Contexts: Radical Revisions*, New York, 1990: 145–63; L. Johnson, 'Faithful Past in Continuous Present. What Endures: Visiting the Edith Lewis–Willa Cather Cottage on Grand Manan', in K. L. Osborne and W. J. Spurlin (eds) *Reclaiming the Heartland: Lesbian and Gay Voices from the Midwest*, Minneapolis, 1996: 176–89.

William J. Spurlin

Catullus (Gaius Valerius Catullus) (*c*. 84–*c*. 54 BC), Roman poet. Born in Verona, Catullus spent his adult life in Rome, where he was one of a number of poets who drew inspiration from Hellenistic poets like Callimachus, eschewing the more traditional forms of epic and drama. The 116 poems in the collection of his works range from two-line epigrams to the mini-epic Poem 64 of over four hundred lines. He moved in fashionable literary and political circles, mixing with the likes of Cicero and CAESAR, and falling in love with a married woman whom he calls Lesbia. Lesbia is the subject of numerous poems, which together make up a cycle chronicling the delights and the disappointments of love. The choice of the name 'Lesbia' to conceal the identity of his mistress (later identified as Clodia) is a tribute to SAPPHO of Lesbos, one of whose poems Catullus translates (Poem 51) to describe the physical effect on him of seeing Lesbia with another man.

The importance of Catullus lies in the personal dimension he introduces into his poetry, particularly in the area of relationships. Complementing the Lesbia poems is a cycle of eight poems (15, 16, 21, 24, 40, 48, 81, 99) concerning a youth, Juventius, which reveals that Catullus was comfortable working within the Hellenistic tradition of poetry in praise of boys. These poems do not share the same intensity as the Lesbia poems, which may indicate that whatever his involvement with Juventius, did not affect him as deeply as his affair with Lesbia. On details of Catullus's life it is impossible to be dogmatic, given the limited, and controlled, evidence of the poems themselves. Some of the poems reflect a year he spent abroad in the suite of Gaius Memmius, who was governor of Bithynia 57–56 BC. Poem 101, a tender address to his brother, who had died in the Troad, was probably written to commemorate a visit to his tomb during this period, while Poems 4, 31 and 46 suggest that Catullus was more pleased to be at home than abroad. Despite the evident affection he expresses for his property at Sirmio on Lake Garda (Poem 31) and the pride in his homeland, it is doubtless the stimulation of Rome which he, along with others, craved. The lack of allusion to any event later than Caesar's invasion of Britain in 55 BC (Poems 11, 29) provides the probable date of death in 54.

Catullus was influential on later poets, particularly VIRGIL and MARTIAL, and is quoted by many writers through to the second century AD. Thereafter he is cited infrequently, and it is a stroke of good fortune that his poetry survived into the modern world at all, via a single manuscript in Verona (now lost) in the early fourteenth century.

Catullus, *The Poems of Catullus*, trans. Guy Lee, Oxford, 1991; B. Arkins, *Sexuality in Catullus*, Hildesheim, 1982; K. Quinn, *Catullus: An Interpretation*, London, 1972; T. P. Wiseman, *Catullus and his World: A Reappraisal*, Cambridge, 1985.

Roger Pitcher

Cavafy, Constantine (1863–1933), Greek poet. Though Cavafy is the foremost homosexual poet in modern European literature, his life tells us little about his sexuality; the real importance of that is to be found in his work. He was born in Alexandria into a typical Levantine merchant family, with relations in Constantinople and business connections in London and Cairo. He held both English and Greek citizenship, his father being a naturalised British citizen. His father's death in 1870 left the family in straitened circumstances, as a result of which they moved from Egypt to Liverpool. They stayed in England for five years, allowing the young Cavafy to acquire a command of English and an interest in English literature which were both important to his development. Financial difficulties then forced the family back to Alexandria, where Cavafy was to spend the rest of his life. Thereafter the only significant period which he spent away from his home city was from 1882 to 1885, when he went to Constantinople to stay with his mother's relations (initially to avoid serious rioting in Alexandria). It seems that during his stay Cavafy was probably initiated into sex by his cousin George and that he also experimented a little with the sexual opportunities afforded by the night-life of the Turkish capital. On his return to Alexandria he found a variety of small jobs, but around 1889 he started to do part-time work, unpaid, for the Irrigation Office in the hope of obtaining a salaried post. He was appointed to such a post on a temporary basis in 1892 and stayed there for 30 years.

The Cavafys were a respected family within the Greek community, but their precarious finances prevented them from taking the place in society they might otherwise have done. Furthermore two of Cavafy's brothers got themselves into financial and personal difficulties – Aristides abandoned his wife after misusing her dowry and Paul, more notoriously homosexual than his younger brother, lived profligately, got into debt and defaulted on loans. Consequently, it was

relatively easy for Constantine to withdraw from social engagements in the way which his temperament encouraged. This became more true still after the death of his mother in 1899. It seems that in the 1890s he was discreetly frequenting the *quartier* around the Rue d'Anastasi, where it was easy to find poor young Greek men who would provide sexual favours in return for small amounts of cash. Though the biographical evidence for this is largely anecdotal, it is supported by the poetry. Certainly, after he moved into a flat in the Rue Lepsius with his brother Paul (1907), he was free to lead whatever private life he wished. Though he probably fell in love with young men from his own class from time to time, for example Alex Mavroudis, a poet and dramatist of sorts, whom he met in 1903 on one of his few trips to Athens, there is no evidence that he even made his feelings known to them. Some of the confessional notes among his papers show that he had difficulty coming to terms with his erotic appetites, but interestingly these 'confessions' stop about the very time that his more overtly erotic poems were beginning to be written (after 1911), as though the poems become a justification in themselves, an idea which is actually present in a poem such as 'Their beginning' (1921).

Cavafy really started to write poetry only when he reached his forties. The poems were for the most part privately circulated to a select group of his peers in a form which allowed him to add poems to (and on occasion subtract them from) the corpus. Though he himself placed much stress on the philosophical and historical dimensions of his material, the poems make no real sense without reference to his sexuality, a fact which makes it all the more remarkable that until the 1980s it was a factor which received little or no attention. Partly to blame was the extreme homophobic bias of the critic and minor poet Tinos Malanos, who produced what was for years treated (in Greece at least) as an authoritative reading of the Cavafean corpus, and who separated out the supposedly bad – overtly sexual – poems from the rest of the writings. In practice nearly every poem is an expression, at some level, of issues of marginality, of the gap between individual and social persona, of cultural separation and of the need for immediacy of experience, all of which are clearly connected with his sexual identity. Having read widely in the work of the French decadents and being familiar with some English poetry too, particularly Browning, Cavafy combined these European influences with his reading in the history and literature of the Greek East, particularly from the period of Alexander the Great through the early centuries of Roman occupation. (He had little interest in modern Greek literature and used the name of the greatest of the contemporary Greek poets, Palamas, as a synonym for second-rate: 'Don't drink that!' he was famous for saying, 'It's the Palamas whisky.') The Hellenistic and Roman periods offered him a society in which homosexual desire was taken for granted and in which the question of identity was more easily defined by culture than by politics or race. A small group of modern poems offers a contrast with this nostalgically explored Levantine past. His 'political' poems reflect the transitoriness of what society regards as important and the enduring quality of individual experience; his private poems insist on the centrality of love and desire. Few poets of any age have celebrated male beauty with such fervour or placed so much emphasis on the power of transitory sexual pleasure to be the creative force behind great art. Equally, few poets have more poignantly evoked the precariousness, the sense of isolation and of loss which can haunt those who are not central to a society's power structure. Nor surprisingly, then, Cavafy's influence on other gay writers, from FORSTER to PESSOA, and the attraction of his work for an artist such as Hockney, make him a seminal presence in twentieth-century gay 'high culture'.

R. Liddell, *Cavafy: A Critical Biography*, London, 1974; C. Robinson, *C. P. Cavafy*, Bristol, 1988.

Christopher Robinson

Cellini, Benvenuto (1500–1571), Italian sculptor, goldsmith and writer. Born in Florence, Cellini was apprenticed as a goldsmith and, working in this profession, moved to Rome in 1523. Apart from several trips to other Italian cities, he remained there until 1540, working in the papal mint from 1529 and executing various gold works (now all lost) for various cardinals and popes. Possessed of a violent and arrogant temper, Cellini had continuing problems with the law – he was implicated in three homicides – and he was being held in the Castel Sant'Angelo when King Francis I invited him to the French court. Cellini produced a number of gold works and sculptures (most of which have been lost) in Fontainebleau, which won admiration and contributed to the spread of Mannerism in France. His involvement in brawls and quarrels continued, though he was found innocent on a charge of heterosexual sodomy.

In 1545, Cellini returned to Florence, where Grand-Duke Cosimo commissioned what is unanimously considered his masterpiece, the bronze of *Perseus* in the city's Piazza della Signoria. Cellini now turned his attention largely to sculpture, and over the next five years produced the most conspicuous body of works with homosexual themes created by an Italian Renaissance sculptor: the marble statues of *Ganymede and an Eagle*, *Apollo and Hyacinth*, and *Narcissus*, all in the Museo del Bargello in Florence, as well as a bronze *Ganymede and eagle* in the Bargello (which is, however, also attributed to Tribolo).

Catastrophe suddenly struck in 1557; Cellini was sentenced to four years imprisonment for sodomy. The Grand-Duke commuted the sentence to four years of house arrest, during which time Cellini sculpted a *Crucifixion* (now in the Escorial in Spain) and began his celebrated

Autobiography. He worked on the auto-biography until 1565, recounting the events of his life to 1562 – omitting the convictions for sodomy but not his homicides. Once his sentence was served, Cellini returned to the straight and narrow and married his servant Piera Parigi, by whom he had (he claimed) five children. When he died he was buried in the church of the Santissima Annunziata in Florence.

The homosexual dimension of Cellini's life is among the best documented ones in Renaissance history, both because of his court convictions and from the hints made in his autobiography about other accusations (which he denied as slanders). For instance, as narrated in Book II, Chapter 61, of the autobiography, Cellini said that the mother of his assistant (one Cencio della Gambetta), a prostitute, tried to blackmail him by demanding money, pretending it was necessary to hush up the scandal arising from his sexual relations with her son; Cellini chased the woman away, insulting her and protesting his innocence, but nevertheless left Florence the following day.

On three occasions, Cellini was officially accused of sodomy. On 14 January 1523, he was sentenced to pay 12 *staia* of flour as a fine for sodomising a boy. In 1548 a certain Margherita denounced Cellini for relations with her son Vincenzo, but the trial was not carried out, and Cellini thus went free on this occasion. On 26 February 1557, Cellini was convicted for having sodomised Fernando di Giovanni di Montepulciano 'many times' and was ordered to pay the substantial fine of 50 gold *scudi*; he was also permanently banned from public office and sentenced to four years in jail (the sentence that was subsequently commuted to house arrest).

Furthermore, homosexuality appears several times in Cellini's autobiography. For example, in Book I, Chapter 23, he speaks of having frequented a youth named Luigi Pulci, also a friend of MICHELANGELO, in Rome; Cellini describes him as handsome, virtuous and highly intelligent, but, when the youth rejected his attentions in favour of a Giovanni Barbo, Cellini calls him a common hustler. In the same book, in Chapter 71, Cellini recounts the quarrel he had in Tuscany with a rival sculptor, Baccio Bandinello, who called him 'you dirty sodomite'. Surprisingly, Cellini responded with an apologia for homosexual love: 'You madman, you are going too far. But I wish to God I did know how to indulge in such a noble practice; after all, we read that Jove enjoyed it with Ganymede in paradise, and here on earth it is the practice of the greatest emperors and the greatest kings of the world. I'm an insignificant humble man, I haven't the means or the knowledge to meddle in such a marvelous matter' (Bull's translation).

It is noteworthy that such a defence was made not by an artist better integrated into mainstream society but by one whom it would not be an exaggeration to characterise as a delinquent. Cellini, the outsider, produced two homoerotic sculptures for his own enjoyment. A sculpture of *Apollo and Hyacinth* clearly shows the erotic link between the god and the youth, and one of *Narcissus* – an exhibitionistic *tour de force* – portrays the sexual attractiveness of an outrageously handsome naked youth. Cellini sculpted these works without a commission and never sold them; he left them to the Grand-Duke of Florence at his death.

The example of Cellini shows, in sum, that in this early period a lifestyle which consciously included homosexuality was not inconceivable, nor was it impossible to theorise about it within the cultural parameters of the day. However, such a life could only be practised on the margins of society, even over the boundary of the criminal edge. It was such a dangerous position that even a convinced outsider such as Cellini eventually found it intolerable.

I. Arnaldi, *La vita violenta di Benvenuto Cellini*, Bari, 1986: 129–43; B. Cellini, *Auto-*

biography, trans. G. Bull, Harmondsworth, 1956; L. Greci, 'Benvenuto Cellini nei delitti e nei processi fiorentini, ricostruiti attraverso le leggi del tempo', *Archivio di antropologia criminale*, 50 (1930): 342–85 and 509–42; J. Saslow, *Ganymede in the Renaissance*, New Haven, 1986: 142–74.

Giovanni Dall'Orto

Charke, Charlotte (1713–1760), British writer. Charke was the estranged youngest child of the infamous Colley Cibber, poet laureate and actor-manager at Drury Lane Theatre, and the actress Katherine Shore. She is now known for her extraordinary autobiography, *A Narrative of the Life of Mrs. Charlotte Charke, Written by Herself*, first serialised in the *Gentleman's Magazine* in 1755. In it she gives a highly entertaining 'Account of my UNACCOUNTABLE LIFE', documenting her 'natural propensity to a hat and wig', her education 'sufficient for a Son instead of a Daughter', and the misadventures of her itinerant and impoverished life 'en cavalier'.

In 1730 Charlotte Cibber entered into a short-lived marriage with Richard Charke, composer and dancing master at Drury Lane, and had a daughter, Katherine (who became an actress). She made a successful début at Drury Lane in *The Provok'd Wife* and for a time acted as general understudy to the company. After separating from her husband she went to work for Henry Fielding's rival Little Haymarket Company with her brother, Theophilus Cibber. Her first role for Fielding was a satirical representation of her father as Lord Place in Pasquin. This affront and her penchant for cross-dressing both on and off the stage led to a breach and a series of failed attempts at reconciliation.

'Gaping for a crust' and with only her 'projecting brain' to rely on, Charke tried numerous occupations in and out of London with varying degrees of success, including grocer, groom, manservant, sausage seller, pastrymaker, publican, waiter and puppeteer: 'As I found one Business fall off, I resolved to set up another'. For almost a decade she became a strolling actor, 'playing at Bo-Peep with the World', travelling and living as 'Mr. Brown' with her friend 'Mrs. Brown', 'a good natured gentlewoman'. On the reason for her passing as Mr. Brown and the nature of her relationship with Mrs. Brown, the autobiography is silent, while Charke does admit to a marriage proposal from an unsuspecting heiress: 'ever endeavouring to keep up the well-bred Gentleman, I became, as I may most properly term it, the unhappy Object of Love in a young Lady'. Teasingly she confirms that she 'might have been at once possessed of the Lady, and forty thousand pounds', but immediately alibis herself against the scandalous sexual implication: 'This was a most horrible Disappointment on both Sides; the Lady of the Husband, and I of the Money.' Charke's rejection in this episode of the sexual deceit and opportunism facilitated by passing as a man offers an implicit contrast to the relatively oblique narration of her long-standing partnership with Mrs. Brown, an intimacy involving counterfeit and deception but not of each other. Whether Charke could be termed a 'female husband' in the sensational and sexually active sense of that term remains an open question. In the wake of Fielding's *The Female Husband: or the Surprising History of Mrs. Mary, Alias Mr. George Hamilton* (1746), Charke takes the novel approach of deflecting but not resolving the potentially scandalous aspects of her career by enigmatically drawing attention to the fact that she is constrained not to explain. In its deadpan, evasive and comic style of incomplete disclosure, the autobiography flirts with the secret of having a secret: 'My going into mens Cloaths, in which I continued many Years; the Reason of which I beg to be excused'. As Straub comments, Charke's *Narrative* does not 'fram[e] the sexually ambiguous cross-dressed woman in a heterosexual narrative' but 'stop[s] short of the dangerous oppositionality of the female husband'.

As well as the *Narrative*, Charke wrote three plays, *The Carnival* (1735), *The Art of Management* (1735) and *Tit for tat* (1743), two tales, *The Lover's Treat; or Unnatural Hatred* (1758) and *The History of Charles and Patty* (nd), and two novels, *The Mercer; or Fatal Extravagance* (1755) and *The History of Henry Dumont, Esq. and Miss Charlotte Evelyn* (1756), which Straub calls 'viciously homophobic'.

In recent years Charke's life and work, especially her *Narrative*, have begun to attract renewed attention in the context of revisionist histories of gender and sexuality and contemporary fascination with performative subjectivity and passing.

P. E. Baruth (ed.) *Introducing Charlotte Charke*, London, 1998; F. Morgan, *The Well-Known Troublemaker: A Life of Charlotte Charke*, London, 1988; K. Straub, *Sexual Suspects: Eighteenth Century Players and Sexual Ideology*, Princeton, 1992.

Kate Lilley

Chaucer, Geoffrey (*c*. 1340–1400), English writer, royal official and diplomat. Chaucer is known historically as a married man with a proclivity for women that resulted in the *raptus* of one Cecily Champagne. Scholars have recently re-examined *raptus* as a possible sexual assault (for which Chaucer was officially exonerated). Chaucer's love stories and their characters are transparently heterosexual, whether in the tragic romances of *Troilus and Criseyde*, the lament for John of Gaunt's wife Blanche in *The Book of the Duchess*, the bawdy fabliaux of the *Canterbury Tales* or the libidinal pride of the Wife of Bath. One character among the pilgrims to Canterbury, however, has raised questions about same-sex desire: the Pardoner.

Though Chaucer's Pardoner sells indulgences or pardons for the remission of sin, he is no ascetic, riding with his hood fashionably undone. He is boastful, hypocritical, ecclesiastically current and moralising all at once, openly offering pardons, fraudulent relics and a sermon on the evils of lust, swearing, gambling and murder. Yet it is his body that separates the Pardoner from the other pilgrims. His fashionable clothes cannot detract from his glaring eyes likened to a hare's. His only body hair – long, blonde, smooth and thin – seems to be on his head. He cannot grow a beard – in fact, Chaucer's narrator says, the Pardoner will never be able to grow one – and his voice sounds as high-pitched as a goat's. Such an appearance leads the narrator to imagine the Pardoner as a 'gelding or a mare'.

To medieval readers, the Pardoner's physical description may well have suggested both a eunuch and passive homosexual, and Chaucerian scholars in this century have noted these resonances. In 1919, Walter Curry fastidiously dubbed the Pardoner a *eunuchus ex nativitate*. Others have seen him as a hermaphrodite or even an effeminate *heterosexual*. Monica MacAlpine looked the glaring hare in the eye and dealt straightforwardly (as it were) with the idea of the Pardoner's homosexuality.

Subsequent scholarship has supported MacAlpine's line of enquiry. Boswell notes that hares are associated in medieval bestiaries with anal intercourse, and a passage from the Pardoner's description lends credence for this predilection. In the *General Prologue* to the *Canterbury Tales*, the Pardoner rides with his huge, frightening, lustful companion, the Summoner, an ecclesiastical court officer. To pass the time, the Pardoner sings (in his goat-like tenor): 'Com hider, love, to me! / This Somonour bar to hym a stif burdoun / Was nevere trompe of half so greet a soun.' (Come hither, love, to me! / This Summoner replied to him with a strong "burden" / There was never a trumpet that had so great a sound)' (*Canterbury Tales, General Prologue*, lines A.672a–674).

While 'stiff burdoun' has usually been glossed as 'loud bass accompaniment', a 'burdoun' is also a club or staff. Readers of Chaucer have noted the *double entendre*: the grotesque Summoner as the active, penetrating partner to the woman-like body of the Pardoner.

Moreover, according to Steven Kruger, the linguistic perversion of the Pardoner's hypocrisy is linked in medieval tradition to homosexuality (notably in the *De planctu naturae* of ALAN OF LILLE), as is the literal-mindedness of the three immoral young thugs in the Pardoner's story who mistake Death for a heap of gold coins and end up dead anyway. Queer theorists such as Glenn Burger have more recently begun to see the Pardoner as a rich source of sexual ambiguity that troubles the easy distinctions readers may make between heterosexual and homosexual, virile and effeminate, material and spiritual.

J. Boswell, *Christianity, Social Tolerance, and Homosexuality: Gay People in Western Europe from the Beginning of the Christian Era to the Fourteenth Century*, Chicago, 1980; G. Burger, 'Queer Chaucer', *English Studies in Canada*, 20 (1994): 153–70; S. Kruger, 'Claiming the Pardoner: Toward a Gay Reading of Chaucer's *Pardoner's Tale*', *Exemplaria*, 6, 1 (1994): 115–39; M. MacAlpine, 'The Pardoner's Homosexuality and How it Matters', *PMLA*, 95 (1980): 8–22.

Graham N. Drake

Church, John (*c*. 1782–*c*. 1835), British cleric. A baby boy was discovered on the steps of the Church of St John in Clerkenwell, London, and sent to the Foundling Hospital, where he was named John Church. At the early age of 9 the Governors apprenticed him out after discovering him playing sexual games with his fellow orphan boys. He was apprenticed to a gilder for an 11-year indenture, but was released at the age of 15 after mistreatment by the gilder. He worked for a composition ornament maker in Tottenham Court Road, and began preaching the gospel and founded a Sabbath School. He joined the Baptist Society, the Expounding Society and the Westminster Itinerant Society of Dissenting Ministers. In 1801 Church married a Miss Elliott from Hampshire, who would bear him six children.

At Tottenham Court Chapel, Church fell in love with a devout young man named William Webster. He, Webster and another candidate for the priesthood hired out a garret in a brothel, where they practised their preaching. Another minister, who was noted as 'a notorious Sodomite', obtained for Church a living as the minister of the parish church of Banbury, north of Oxford. This ended in 1808, when the Banbury elders heard rumours that Church had been 'sodomitically assaulting' several of the devout young men in his congregation. In 1810 Church became the regular conventicle preacher at the Obelisk Chapel, St George's Fields in south London, where he remained for ten years.

In November 1809 Church performed the funeral services for Richard Oakden, a bank clerk who had been hanged for sodomy at Tyburn. After the funeral, the hearse and coach returned to a public house, where Church and other mollies ate a feast in honour of the dead. In the summer of 1810 a male brothel was set up at The Swan molly house in Vere Street, and Church was persuaded to officiate as the chaplain of their Marrying Room, which they called The Chapel. This room resembled a Christian chapel, but also included several beds. Church sometimes married three or four male couples simultaneously, and the nuptials were consummated by the 'bridesmaids' in drag as well as by the marriage partners. The Swan was raided by the police in July 1810 and 27 men were arrested; the landlord was found guilty of keeping a disorderly house, and he and six men convicted of attempted sodomy were sentenced to the pillory and two years' imprisonment, and two men were hanged for sodomy.

Church escaped, but was exposed by the landlord after his release from prison in 1813, and the *Weekly Dispatch* mounted a campaign against him, provoking riots outside the Obelisk Church. Church was charged with having sodomised Webster ten years before (with his consent), but was not convicted. Some 20,000 pamphlets, chapbooks and broadsheets abused his character. His notoriety grew, and in his own words, 'Vast crowds assembled round the chapel on Sunday nights, so that the congregation had to pass through them as the Israelites through the Red Sea.' Church's flock doubled in size, enabling him in 1814 to build a new meeting house, the famous Surrey Tabernacle. His wife died of drink in 1813, and Church remarried.

In 1816 Church was again charged with attempted sodomy, and convicted in 1817 after losing an appeal. He was sentenced to two years' imprisonment. His female disciples considered him a martyr, and every day they came to his prison bars with delicious food and drink. He spent his time writing sermons and his autobiography. On the night of his release he returned to the Obelisk to preach to a congregation of 1,000 persons. In 1822 it was reported that 'his Church is crammed whenever it is announced to be opened'. His last sermon was published in 1824, and there are no more records of him. His numerous sermons are informed by genuine Christian fervour. Some of his sermons, love-letters to a boyfriend and portions of his autobiography discuss the value of male friendship.

Anon., *The Trial and Conviction of that Infamous Hypocrite John Church*, London, 1817; J. Church, *The Foundling; or, The Child of Providence*, London, 1823; R. Norton, *Mother Clap's Molly House*, London, 1992.

Rictor Norton

Clap, Margaret, known as Mother Clap (*fl.* 1720s), British molly-house keeper. Mother Clap ran the best known and most popular molly house (pub for homosexual men) in eighteenth-century London, in Field Lane, Holborn. Clients would come from 30 miles outside London to be there, especially on Sunday nights, when more than 40 men regularly gathered to sing and

dance together, engage in camp talk and bawdy behaviour, and make assignations. In so far as Mother Clap went out to fetch liquor (probably from the Bunch o'Grapes pub next door), her molly house was probably a private residence rather than a public inn or tavern. It was not a brothel (indeed there is no evidence of payment for male sex work until the late eighteenth century), and may have been run more for pleasure than profit. One molly, Thomas Phillips, had lodgings at her house for two years. Mother Clap enjoyed her clientele, and took an active interest in supporting the homosexual subculture. Her (false) testimony at the trial before Judge Mertins helped get a molly acquitted of charges of sodomy. A police constable who infiltrated her house declared that 'The Company talk'd all manner of gross and vile Obscenity in the Prisoner's hearing, and she appear'd to be wonderfully pleas'd with it.' She was perhaps the first documented 'fag hag'.

Her house had been under surveillance for two years when it was raided in February 1726, with the help of the detective efforts of the Societies for Reformation of Manners. One constable testified that 'I found between 40 and 50 Men making Love to one another, as they call'd it. Sometimes they would sit in one another's Laps, kissing in a lewd Manner, and using their Hand[s] indecently. Then they would get up, Dance and make Curtsies, and mimick the Voices of Women. O, Fie, Sir! – Pray Sir. – Dear Sir. – Lord, how can you serve me so? – I swear I'll cry out. – Your're a wicked Devil, – and you're a bold Face. – Eh ye little dear Toad! Come, buss! – Then they'd hug, and play, and toy, and go out by Couples into another Room on the same Floor, to be marry'd, as they call'd it.'

Margaret Clap was found guilty of keeping a disorderly house in which she procured and encouraged persons to commit sodomy. She was sentenced to stand in the pillory in Smithfield Market, to pay a fine of 20 marks, and to serve two years' imprisonment. During her punishment, she fell off the pillory once and fainted several times. It is not known what became of her, if indeed she survived prison. Of the 40 mollies arrested in the raid, three were hanged at Tyburn for sodomy, two were pilloried, fined and imprisoned, one died in prison, one was acquitted, one was reprieved, and several were forced to go into hiding. A wave of popular outrage led during the next ten years to even more hangings and pilloryings.

There were more homosexual pubs and clubs in London in the 1720s than in the 1950s, and a very well organised molly subculture. The molly houses ranged from private back rooms in gin shops to three-story public houses run by male couples. 'Markets' or cruising grounds were well known in the Royal Exchange, St James's Park, Moorfields Gardens (which had a long walk popularly known as 'The Sodomites' Walk'), and Lincoln's Inn Fields (where men were arrested at the boghouse, London's first urinal, built in the 1680s). The men defined themselves as 'mollies', and many adopted female nicknames (called 'Maiden Names') such as Moll Irons, Flying Horse Moll, Pomegranate Molly, Black Moll, Primrose Mary (a butcher in Butcher Row), Orange Deb (Martin Macintosh, an orange seller), Pippin Mary (alias Queen Irons), Dip-Candle Mary (a tallow chandler), Nurse Mitchell (a barber), and Miss Sweet Lips (a country grocer). Specific male–female role-playing, however, is counter-indicated: Fanny Murray was 'an athletic Bargeman', Lucy Cooper was 'an Herculean Coal-heaver', and Kitty Fisher was 'a deaf tyre Smith'. An extensive 'Molly Dialect' existed (drawn partly from the 'Rogues' Lexicon' or 'Canting Dialect' used by thieves, highway robbers, vagabonds and female prostitutes), and some 40 terms are documented, such as mollies, molly-culls, mollying-culls, and mollying-bitches; queen and bitch; euphemisms such as 'the pleasant deed' and 'to do the

story'; and terms for anal intercourse such as 'caudle-making' and 'to indorse'. The mollies went 'strolling or caterwauling' in 'the markets', where they 'picked up' partners called 'trade' with whom they would 'make a bargain' or 'bit a blow' (meaning score a trick). By the 1780s the mollies, now called 'madge-culls', had developed special signals to communicate with one another while out cruising: 'If one of them sits on a bench, he pats the backs of his hands; if you follow them, they put a white handkerchief thro' the skirts of their coat, and wave it to and fro; but if they are met by you, their thumbs are stuck in the armpits of their waistcoats, and they play their fingers upon their breasts.'

A variety of 'gay' folk rituals took place at the molly houses, such as a 'mock birth' or 'lying-in' (when one man playing the role of a mother gave 'birth' to a doll while 'midwives' attended him/her, sometimes followed by a mock christening) and 'Wedding Nights' (some molly houses had a room called 'The Chapel' or 'The Marrying Room'; more formal 'gay' weddings had 'Bridesmaids', and half-a-dozen long-term relationships are documented; curiously, molly couples always referred to each other as 'husband' or 'spouse', never 'wife'). Many of the men dressed in drag on special 'Festival Nights' (apparently associated with holidays such as Christmas or Whit Monday), and many employed feminine mannerisms and signals. A few men dressed in drag quite regularly, such as the butcher John Cooper, known to all his neighbours as Princess Seraphina. It is nevertheless very clear that these men identified themselves as *mollies*, not as *women*.

The molly subculture (there was no lesbian subculture until about 1780) consisted almost entirely of members of the working classes: servants (messenger boy, chairman, coachman, footman, waiter, waterman), artisans or skilled craftsmen (cabinet maker, gilder, peruke maker, tailor, fan maker, upholsterer), tradesmen (fruit seller, butcher, hardware dealer,

woollen draper), suppliers of services
(barber, tavern keeper, porter, postboy),
workers of various skills (candle maker,
wool comber, silk dyer, blacksmith), and
not a few foot soldiers, but relatively few
schoolmasters and gentlemen of independent means. Class exploitation of
workers by aristocrats is undocumented,
as is payment for sex until the 1780s (male
brothels did not exist until 1810). Virtually
none of the mollies can be classified as bisexual libertines; most of them were not
married, and they clearly possessed a
homosexual self-identity. The molly subculture possessed every characteristic of
modern gay subcultures (shared friendship
networks, styles of clothing, slang and
semiotics, folk rituals, pubs and clubs
and cruising grounds, literary artefacts
such as songs, and self-identification as
homosexual) except for political self-
consciousness. But there were the first
stirrings of gay pride, as when William
Brown, when asked by the police in 1726
'why he took such indecent Liberties
with [another man], . . . was not ashamed
to answer, *I did it because I thought I
knew him, and I think there is no Crime in
making what use I please of my own
Body.'*

The English molly subculture closely resembles the Dutch gay subculture during
the same period, and there may have been
some cultural exchange. The widespread
appearance of 'gay' subcultures across Europe around the year 1700 is almost certainly linked not to the rise of capitalism
or a changing conceptualisation or ideology of homosexuality or sex roles, but to
the rise of surveillance. Efficiently organised 'police forces' hardly existed before
then. The subculture was uncovered as a
result of new social regulations rather
than constructed by them. In England the
discovery of the molly subculture exactly
coincides with the activities of the Societies for Reformation of Manners (formed
in 1690, disbanded in 1738) which led to
prosecutions. Our extra-legal knowledge
comes from newspapers and pamphlets;

that is, the rise of evidence of the subculture is closely linked to the rise of a
popular press at the turn of the century,
and the use of investigative reporters to
uncover sensational stories. The gay subculture was *exposed* rather than *emerged*,
and its features were already so distinct
and well organised that it must have
existed well before 1700.

Select Trials, 2nd edn, London, 1742; *The Lon-
don Journal*, 30 July 1726; R. Norton, *Mother
Clap's Molly House: The Gay Subculture in
England 1700–1830*, London, 1992.

Rictor Norton

Cocteau, Jean (1889–1963), French writer,
painter, film-maker. Cocteau participated
in nearly all the major art forms of his
day: in addition to writing poetry, prose
and drama, to painting and to making
films, he created dance libretti for the Ballets Russes and even the libretto for an ora-
torio, Stravinsky's *Oedipus Rex*. Given
that the period when he lived spanned in
aesthetic terms the heydays of decadence,
post-impressionism and modernism, he
thereby contrived to be at the hub of
French cultural activity for several decades. He was also at the centre of a very
visible group of homosexual figures in
inter-war Paris. His contribution both to
the publicisation of homosexuality and to
the creation of a particular image of it was
a very substantial one.

Yet there is little to be learnt about his
life in a direct way from his openly autobiographical writings. His father's suicide
when Cocteau was 9 years old, for example, is never mentioned, though the
theme of fatherlessness appears, either
literally or by effacing of the father-
character, in several of his prose works –
Le Grand Ecart (*Wide Apart*), *Thomas
l'imposteur* (*Thomas the Imposter*), *Les
Enfants terribles*. This is not chance. Cocteau was in essence a self-creation, best
evidenced in his works, yet whose life was
as much a work of art itself. In both work
and art, behind the determination to

dazzle and shock, the shadows of a bourgeois background and an oppressively doting mother are constantly to be found (the two things were indivisible, Mme Cocteau being 'an admirable woman but 'frrrightfully bourrrgeois', according to Coco Chanel).

Shocking was a pastime in which Cocteau indulged from very young, whether in the form of getting himself systematically expelled from a series of schools, or of running away to Marseilles for a year of initiatory debauchery when he was 15, or of joining the clique around an ageing theatrical queen (Edouard de Max) in order to get himself launched into Parisian society. His next stage was to learn to dazzle, and in this he had the best of masters. When the Ballets Russes took Paris by storm in 1909, the 20-year-old Cocteau used his connections to get himself an introduction to DIAGHILEV, and from there he never looked back. Though World War I necessarily caused something of a hiatus in his career – he was classified unfit for military service and worked for the Red Cross – it was not entirely a fallow period. Apart from the fact that the war itself inspired a volume of quite powerful poetry, *Le Cap de Bonne Espérance* (*Cape of Good Hope*, 1916), and supplied him with material for the novel *Thomas l'imposteur* (1922), it was also the period when he met Picasso and Eric Satie, with whom he collaborated on his first ballet, *Parade* (1916). Though never completely turning his back on the world of the salons, Cocteau now threw in his lot with the modernists. He wrote a little book on music, *Le Coq et L'Arlequin* (*The Cock and Harlequin*, 1918), by way of a modernist manifesto, he began to write avant-garde plays, and he launched into a passionate *affaire* with a 15-year-old schoolboy, Raymond Radiguet, whom he met through another well known homosexual of the day, the poet Max Jacob. This *affaire*, which lasted until Radiguet's tragic early death in 1923 (having himself written two exquisite novels, *Le Diable au corps* [*The Devil Within*] and

Le Bal du Comte d'Orgel [*The Comte d'Orgel's Ball*]), marked Cocteau's work overtly, in his collection of poems *Plain-Chant* (1922), in his novels of the same period, and in a particular thematic association between passion and death which was to stay with him throughout the rest of his creative life, from *Les Enfants terribles* (1930) to the ballet scenario *Le Jeune Homme et la Mort* (The Young Man and Death, 1946) and the film *Orphée* (1950).

The openness of his homosexuality is not in doubt. After Radiguet's death he had other relationships, the most important of which, (with Jean Marais (the most handsome French actor of the era), lasted 20 years. Nor is there any doubt as to the importance of his sexuality to his work. The spiritual motif of being fatally wounded by adolescent male beauty recurs in his poems, fiction and plays, whilst from the images of buggery in the opening poems of the opium-inspired collection *L'Ange Heurtebise* (1926) to his extremely explicit illustrations to Jean Genet's *Querelle de Brest*, he allowed himself to represent homoerotic desire with bravura. But he was curiously reticent on the subject in other respects. Notably, the autobiographical novel *Le Livre blanc* (*The White Book*, 1928), even in the later edition with his own erotic illustrations, he never acknowledged as his. Yet this is the work which gives us the key to the image of homosexuality which Cocteau projects in codified form, or translated into heterosexual symbols, in his other works. It is at one level a definitely erotic plea for social acceptance, but at another level it portrays homosexual love as doomed to disappointment or destruction. This sense of foredoomed emotional disaster was closely linked to his periods of opium addiction in the late 1920s and his flirtations with conversion to Catholicism, and is reflected in a different way in his fascination with the Oedipus legend – his most successful play of the 1930s was his reworking of that myth in *La Machine infernale* (*The*

Infernal Machine, 1935). It is difficult to believe that the Cocteau who aspired to, and achieved, social and intellectual success – he was elected to the the the Belgian Academy and the Académie Française in 1955 – and whose life was mostly characterised by a froth and glitter which all too often gives him the air of stepping straight from the pages of a Noel COWARD comedy – never quite came to terms with his sexuality, but this would seem to be the case.

F. Steegmuller, *Cocteau*, London, 1970.

Christopher Robinson

Colette, Sidonie Gabrielle (1873–1954), French author. The importance of Colette's lesbianism lies precisely in its ostensible unimportance. Sexuality in Colette's life as in her works offers a seamless continuum of desire, and the gender of the object choice only becomes significant for reasons beyond the relationship itself. She seems to have found all-female emotional and physical relations a necessary part of her development into independent womanhood and to have remained aware of the strength and value of such attractions throughout her life. But for separatist lesbianism as a social phenomenon she retained a certain suspicion, for reasons which sets out in her important volume of essays *Le Pur et L'Impur* (*The Pure and the Impure*, 1932).

Colette (the use of just her surname was one of the legacies of her first husband) was born in the Burgundian village of Saint-Sauveur en Puisaye, the second child of her mother's second marriage. She had a moderately comfortable rural childhood, which came to an end in 1890 with the need to move to Châtillon-sur-Loing, as a result of her father's financial ineptitude. Her marriage three years later to Henri Gauthier-Villars, better known as Willy, was in part contracted as a result of the need to escape from the confines of her family's new circumstances. But it led her into a different set of confines, both physical – her husband's cramped Parisian flat

– and social, in the obligations of a married life-style for which she was quite unprepared. Willy encouraged Colette in lesbian experimentation for his own titillation while demanding from her a heterosexual fidelity which he himself did not observe. She launched her career with the 'Claudine' novels, nominally in collaboration with her husband, though most of the work was her own. The first, *Claudine à l'école* (*Claudine at School*, 1900), is highly autobiographical and its treatment of the motifs of the lesbian headmistress and of all-girl passions, though reflecting a contemporary literary cliché, already suggests the gender-nonspecific sensuality which will be a distinguishing mark of Colette's approach to physical experience. It is, however, *Claudine en ménage* (*Claudine Settles Down*, 1902) which is the key text of the early period. In this novel Colette draws on her own *affaire* with another married woman. It both introduces the idea of lesbianism as a way of releasing feminine potential without the distorting influence of masculine control, and extends the critique of contemporary prejudices against male homosexuality which she had already aired in *Claudine à Paris* (1901). From here up to *La Retraite sentimentale* (*Sentimental Withdrawal*, 1907), Colette is constructing a critique of all relationships, regardless of their sexual label, which involve domination, manipulation or mere physical exploitation of another human being.

The date of publication of *La Retraite sentimentale* is significant, because it was in 1906 that Colette had left her husband and embarked upon a lesbian *affaire* with the Marquise de Belbœuf which was to show her the limits of social tolerance in matters sexual and to lead to her divorce. When (in January 1907) she and Missy (as her lover was known) took part in a mime act with definite lesbian overtones at the Moulin Rouge, the performance was brought to a standstill by the outraged audience, and the Prefect of Police instructed Missy to refrain from taking part in any further performances. Thereafter the two women were no longer socially acceptable. Colette seems to have been perfectly happy to turn her back on a society that was cold-shouldering her, and to explore the world of the lesbian *salons*: in the ensuing period she became friendly with both Renée VIVIEN and Natalie BARNEY. For several years she earned her living as a music-hall artist, thus doubling the *demi-monde* of lesbianism with that of the popular theatre, a life summed up in *La Vagabonde* (1910). What she gained from this precarious existence was independence – physical, economic, sexual and emotional.

Colette's period of primarily lesbian experience ended in 1911, when she fell in love with Henri de Jouvenel, whom she married the following year. This was the start of a period of what can roughly be defined as serial monogamy, the marriage breaking down when Colette had an affair with her husband's adolescent son by an earlier marriage, a relationship which was itself displaced by that with Maurice Goudeket, another man substantially younger than Colette, whom she eventually married in 1935. The works of the 1920s and 1930s, which are widely regarded as her greatest achievement – *Chéri* (1920), *Le Blé en herbe* (*While the Corn is still Green*, 1923), *La Fin de Chéri* (*The End of Chéri*, 1926) and *La naissance du jour* (*The Beginning of the Day*, 1928) – though all heterosexual in their focus, present issues of gender and physical relationships in ways which are unthinkable without the period of exclusive lesbian apprenticeship which Colette had undergone. It is significant that the set of essays in which she explores her ideas on homosexuality in a more discursive form, *Le Pur et L'Impur* (originally titled *Ces plaisirs*), should have appeared in 1932, just after the major novels. Colette herself regarded it as perhaps her best book, a judgement which critics too careless to read it properly or not equipped to understand it have consistently ridiculed. It is certainly a very

broad-ranging exploration of problems of sexuality, straight *and* gay, male *and* female, to which in Colette's view social pressures and biologically inherent gender differences prevent there being a single set of answers. Though she continued to publish a variety of works until the late 1940s, the best known probably being *Gigi* (1944) and the most moving *L'Etoile vesper* (*The Evening Star*, 1946), she certainly never wrote anything more thought-provoking than *Le Pur et L'Impur*.

D. Holmes, *Colette*, London, 1991; J. Richardson, *Colette*, London, 1983; C. Robinson, *Scandal in the Ink: Male and Female Homosexuality in Twentieth-Century French Literature*, London, 1995.

Christopher Robinson

Cooper, Lilian Violet (1861–1947) and **Bedford, Mary Josephine** (1861–1955), British-Australian public figures. Lilian Cooper and Josephine Bedford lived together for more than sixty years and are buried together in Toowong cemetery in Brisbane, Australia. Cooper was born in Kent, England, where she met Bedford in the early 1880s. They became friendly and persuaded their families to allow them to set up house together in Russell Square, London, while Cooper studied medicine at the London School of Medicine for Women and Bedford studied art at the Slade School, University of London.

In 1891 Cooper decided to take up a private practice in Brisbane and was accompanied there by Bedford. The first female medical practitioner in Queensland and only the second in Australia, she was the first woman to be a consultant at any Australian hospital (Brisbane's Hospital for Sick Children) and the first to be awarded a Fellowship of the Royal Australasian College of Surgeons. Associated with several Brisbane hospitals between 1896 and her retirement in 1945, she received a Doctorate in Medicine from Durham University in 1912. Her life companion, Bedford, was involved in the

National Council of Women and the Creche and Kindergarten Association.

L. M. Williams, *No Easy Path: The Life and Times of Lilian Violet Cooper*, Brisbane, 1991.
Clive Moore

Copland, Aaron (1900–1990), American composer and conductor. Born in Brooklyn, New York, Copland was the son of Russian Jewish immigrants who became successful retail-store owners. As a child, Copland studied music with his sister, who encouraged their parents to allow Aaron to pursue piano studies with Leopold Wolfsohn, Victor Wittgenstein and Clarence Alder. Following high school graduation in 1918, he studied music theory with Rubin Goldmark, under whose tutelage he began to compose, and from the outset he earned a reputation as a radical young composer. Bypassing university, Copland played piano in dance bands before travelling to Europe for study at the Fontainebleau School of Music. He was a pupil of Paul Vidal before becoming the first American student of Nadia Boulanger, with whom he studied for three years. Copland returned to the US, working as a piano teacher before being asked to join the League of Composers, who presented the first US performance of his work. His first major composition, the *Symphony for Organ and Orchestra*, was premiered by Walter Damrosch and the New York Symphony, with Nadia Boulanger, for whom the piece was written, at the organ. The piece brought Copland to the attention of Boston Symphony conductor Serge Koussevitsky, who thereafter became a champion and major interpreter of the young composer's works.

In the late 1920s, Copland turned to creating music with an American accent, including his famous *Music for the Theatre*, the *Concerto for Piano and Orchestra* and four blues pieces for piano. By the 1930s, Copland had become the acknowledged leader of young American composers, especially through the League of Composers and the Copland–Sessions concerts (1928–1931), which promoted not only Copland and Roger Sessions, but works by Virgil THOMSON, Roy Harris, Carlos Chavez and Walter Piston. Owing to his ability to compose quickly and successfully in a wide range of forms, from abstract to folk and popular music, Copland received many commissions for instrumental and theatrical scores. His score for *Hear Ye! Hear Ye!* (1934), a ballet by Chicago choreographer Ruth Page, paved the way for his acclaimed scores for *Billy the Kid* (1938), *Rodeo* (1942), and *Appalachian Spring* (1944). Copland also achieved success with film scores, including *Of Mice and Men* (1939), *Our Town* (1940), *The Red Pony* and *The Heiress* (both 1948). Among Copland's most popular works are the *Concerto for Clarinet*, the *Third Symphony*, *El Salon Mexico*, *Dance Symphony*, *Danzon Cubano*, *A Lincoln Portrait* and *Fanfare for the Common Man*. Copland lectured widely at colleges and universities, including Harvard, throughout his career, and published several books, including *What to Listen for in Music* (1939), and *Copland on Music* (1963). He died of respiratory failure in North Tarrytown, New York, in 1990.

A moral conservative by nature, Copland was an affable, modest and mild-mannered man who valued friendships and thrived in social settings. Like many of his contemporaries, he guarded his privacy, especially in regard to his homosexuality, but was one of the few composers of his stature to live openly and travel with his lovers, most of whom were talented, much younger men. Often described as 'stunningly ugly' or 'endearingly homely', Copland apparently was experienced and at ease with his sexuality even as a young man before leaving Brooklyn for Paris. Among Copland's love affairs, most of which lasted for only a few years yet became enduring friendships, were ones with photographer Victor Kraft, artist Alvin Ross, pianist Paul Moor, dancer Erik Johns and composer John Brodbin Kennedy.

With the possible exception of Leonard Bernstein, Aaron Copland is the most recognised twentieth-century composer of classical music in the US. His honours, fellowships and awards include the Congressional Gold Medal, the Kennedy Center Honors, the Pulitzer Prize, Grammy, Emmy and Oscar nominations and awards, Fulbright and Guggenheim fellowships, the Medal of Arts, the Medal of Freedom and the Prix de Paris.

A. Copland and V. Perlis, *Copland: 1900 through 1942*, New York, 1984, and *Copland since 1943*, New York, 1989; H. Pollack, *Aaron Copland: The Life and Work of an Uncommon Man*, New York, 1999.

A. M. Wentink

Còsmico, Niccolò (*c*. 1420–1500), Italian humanist and poet. Born Niccolò Lelio Della Comare in Padua, Còsmico spent his life moving from court to court; he lived in Milan, then Rome (where he had links with POMPONIO-LETO's academy), Florence, Mantua and Ferrara before returning to Padua, where he eventually died. He became famous among his contemporaries for playful compositions in Italian and Latin. Today he is considered only a minor author; critics judge that his (heterosexual) love poetry does not move past a Petrarchian style. They think more highly, however, of Còsmico's humorous verses in kitchen Latin.

Contemporaries accused Còsmico of sodomy, especially in an anonymous series of Italian sonnets, 'In Cosmicum patavinum' (partially published under the name of Antonio Cammelli, 'Il Pistoia', from 1436 to 1502). The author, who wrote during Còsmico's stay in Ferrara, placed the blame on the poet for the declining birthrate in the city: 'Don't be surprised if few children / nowadays are born in Ferrara; / there is Còsmico who corners all human seed / and he looks like amusing himself in

swallowing it. / No other food was ever so agreeable to him: / he likes it very much through his mouth and even more through his arse. / ... / Nature is ashamed and always weeps / for bearing such an Anfisbena [a mythical snake with a head at each end], who devours her seed with two mouths'. Vittorio Rossi has also published an anonymous Latin epigram in which Còsmico is accused of sodomising the kitchen-Latin poet Tifi Odoasi.

Such accusations might be considered part of a stock of insults which quarrelsome humanists habitually exchanged with each other had not Còsmico himself spoken about his homosexual experiences in a remarkably frank fashion. Thus in a long Latin composition, 'Ad Adrastum puerum' ('To the Boy Adrastus'), Còsmico addresses a black youth (perhaps the slave whom Lorenzo the Magnificent asked him to return to him in a 1483 letter). He declares that the colour of the youth's skin does not mar his beauty and pleads with Adrastus to give in to his advances, without worrying about his age, because many serious philosophers (such as PLATO) also loved youths at their advanced age. In another poem, 'Ad Ianum' ('To Janus'), remarkable for its hushed and intimate tone, he addresses his former lover Janus; the poem begins with the words, 'Janus, my crime certainly can be barely excused: / having lain with you so many nights, so many days'. (Both poems are published in Rossi.)

Còsmico's works remain partly unexplored, especially in terms of their homosexual aspects. It is hoped that further research will bring to light more insight on his life and poetry.

A. Cammelli, *Rime edite ed inedite*, Livorno, 1884: 223–40; V. Rossi, 'Di un poeta maccheronico e di alcune rime italiane', *Giornale storico della letteratura italiana*, 11 (1888): 12–14; V. Rossi, 'Niccolo Lelio Còsmico, poeta padovano del secolo XV', *Giornale storico della letteratura italiana*, 13 (1889): 101–58.

Giovanni Dall'Orto

Couperus, Louis (1863–1923), Dutch writer. Couperus was born in The Hague into a leading colonial family. He spent part of his youth in the capital of the Dutch East Indies, Batavia (now Jakarta, Indonesia). Many of the topics he would later write on stemmed from his experiences in the East Indies. He did not follow in the steps of his family, but chose a career in literature, becoming the most famous Dutch novelist of his time.

His first experiments with poetry were not successful, whereas his first novel, *Eline Vere* (1889), was an immediate bestseller. He later conceded that this story of a sensuous woman actually offered a self-portrait. The second novel, *Destiny* (1891), is about two close friends: Bertie, described as a weakling, is in love with Frank and when Frank is on the verge of marriage, Bertie destroys that relationship with a forged letter. When he later tells this to Frank, the latter kills the weakling. After having served his prison term, Frank returns to his fiancée, and they marry. But their relationship is doomed and together they commit suicide. The novel is a decadent play on a degenerate theme.

After 1900, Couperus wrote mainly classical novels. The most famous is *De berg van licht* (*Mountain of Light*, 1905–1906) on the androgynous polysexual Roman emperor ELAGABALUS. As in his later work, *Iskander* (1920), on ALEXANDER the Great, Couperus showed the struggle between East and West, between sensuousness and morality. In the end, sensuality has its Pyrrhic victory and the main characters die an early death. For his general perspectives, Couperus used Lucien von Römer's theories on homosexuality and androgyny. Critics were so harsh on *De berg van licht* that Couperus considered writing a pamphlet on their attitude towards homosexuality, but failed to do so. For some time, he wrote no more novels, only articles for newspapers. Some of his short stories of this period have a sensuous homoerotic quality.

Couperus enjoyed travel, and stayed for long periods in the Mediterranean and in the East Indies. During World War I he was forced to remain in Holland, where he began a successful career as a dandy speaker. His pink satin dress-coat still stands out in the museum devoted to him in The Hague. When he died, he was, according to his decadent successor Gerard Reve, probably still a virgin, having neither consummated his marriage with a cousin nor fulfilled his passions for masculine men. What remained unsatisfied in his life is portrayed with great elegance in his novels.

The work of Couperus is still regularly reprinted and his complete works were published in the past decade. Some of his novels have been adapted for television. He has a secure place among the classics of Dutch literature and still attracts many readers. A very active fan club started a museum in his honour, edits books and newsletters devoted to him, and organises guided tours in Couperus's The Hague.

F. Bastet, *Louis Couperus, een biografie*, Amsterdam, 1987.

Gert Hekma

Coward, Sir Noel (1899–1973), British songwriter and entertainer. Few people will be unfamiliar with at least some of Noel Coward's *risqué* songs and lyrics: 'Mad about the Boy' (1932), one of the better known, both epitomises these and sums up his sexual orientation.

Born at Teddington near London, he was on the stage at an early age, appearing in *The Goldfish* in 1911. His first play, *I'll Leave It to You* (1920), was followed by a constant output of songs, plays and other material. Although some of his early plays dealt with contemporary and contentious social issues – premarital sex and 'sophisticated' life were the focus of plays like *Fallen Angels* and *Easy Virtue* (both 1925) – most of his plays can be classed into two groupings. First were the comedies, light and frothy, with much witty dialogue, but all focusing on the doings of the young, rich and idle: as one writer noted, they were 'incarnations of vanity and selfishness', written at a time when the Great Depression was having such an impact on the lives of a majority of his fellow countrymen and women. Second were his more 'patriotic' offerings, such as *Cavalcade* (1931) and *This Happy Breed* (1942), appealing to the chauvinism of the nation.

His type of theatre fell from favour in the 1950s, when audiences sought more social realist comment, and the so-called 'kitchen sink' dramas of a new generation of playwrights – such as John Osborne and Joe Orton – drew in the crowds. In the face of this, Coward reinvented himself as a cabaret artist, establishing a whole new career.

Despite – or perhaps because of – his status as a major figure in the British theatrical world, Coward could never 'come out', although his homosexuality was widely known. His situation epitomises that of many major figures in the British establishment: as long as his sexuality was kept private, no one need do anything; or as it has more recently been put, in another context, 'Don't ask, don't tell.'

P. Hoare, *Noel Coward: A Biography*, London, 1995; C. Fisher, *Noel Coward*, New York, 1992.

Garry Wotherspoon

Cowell, Henry (1897–1965), American composer. As a professional pianist, Cowell was internationally celebrated during the 1920s for his imaginative and iconoclastic treatment of his instrument. In his many characteristic piano compositions, including *Aeolian Harp* (1923), *The Banshee* (1925), *Tiger* (1928) and *2 Woofs* (1930), he frequently combined folk-like modal melodies with newly devised harmonically and rhythmically dissonant effects. From the mid-1920s he sought to develop what he called an 'ultramodern' style based on a synthesis of Western, Asian and African folk musics, closely related to dance and other utilitarian forms. Some 20 symphonies (the last completed by his friend and pupil Lou Harrison) re-

main virtually unknown, somewhat overshadowed by the engaging series of *Hymns and Fuging Tunes* (over 18 works, mostly orchestral, some with choral participation) based on early American hymnody. Cowell's advocacy was perhaps more important than his own composition. An engaging writer, teacher, lecturer and editor, he popularised music by other American composers, notably Charles Ives, whose biography he authored together with his wife, the folklorist Sidney Robertson.

Cowell's own biography remained incomplete until Michael Hicks published the full facts surrounding the tragic event of Cowell's mid-career. On 21 May 1936, at the age of 39, he was arrested for having oral sex with a 17-year-old boy at his home in Menlo Park, California. He made a full confession, in which he admitted to other homosexual contacts, and was sentenced to serve 1–15 years in San Quentin prison, where he remained until winning parole in June 1940. In autobiographical notes prepared in support of an earlier parole request (in 1938), Cowell listed previous physical relations with ·14 young men, the youngest 16 and all consenting. Once, after the death of his fiancée Edna Smith in a train accident, the 25-year-old Cowell had a relationship with a man four years his junior. At the time of his arrest, he had been befriended by a group of local working-class youths who had free access to his home. The arrest followed an attempt by one of them to blackmail him.

Cowell was widely reputed to be enthusiastic, hardworking, honest and openhearted to the point of naïvety, traits that underlay his talents as a teacher and advocate which he continued to utilise even in prison as an extraordinarily successful instructor in musical appreciation classes. Paradoxically, of his homosexual activities, he said: 'Such things never occurred to me when I was working, playing, lecturing, but when I was idle, I just couldn't help myself', and at the time of his arrest he said he was 'in love' with a woman and engaged to be married. Lewis Terman, a Stanford psychologist who had taken an interest in Cowell over almost 20 years, believed that he was not a true homosexual, but was merely delayed in his heterosexual adjustment. A year after his release, Cowell married, and his wife was one of the petitioners for his eventual pardon. Granted in 1942, the pardon was essential to enable Cowell to travel overseas on wartime government propaganda work. However, contrary to Saylor's account, the authorities never came to the conclusion that he was innocent of the original 'morals' charge.

Though widely vilified in the Hearst press ('California Oscar Wilde Jailed'), Cowell received remarkably unequivocal support from family and many colleagues, including Nicolas Slonimsky, Martha Graham (who premiered a dance work of his during the prison term), and composers Edgard Varèse and Percy Grainger. Grainger, whose offer of employment enabled Cowell's parole, believed him to be 'wholly good . . . incapable of evil', adding that he himself would have been 'many times' jailed if his own (sadomasochistic) acts were publicly known. Ives, however, whose opinion mattered most to Cowell, damagingly cut off all relations with the composer until after his marriage in 1941. In the opinion of some, Cowell's loving marriage saved him; others, however, believed that he never recovered from the crisis.

M. Hicks, 'The Imprisonment of Henry Cowell', *Journal of the American Musicological Society*, 44 (1991): 29–119; N. Slonimsky, 'Jailed Friend', in *Perfect Pitch: A Life Story*, New York, 1988; B. Saylor, 'Cowell', in *New Grove Dictionary of Music and Musicians*, London, 1980.

Graeme Skinner

Crane, Hart (1899–1932), American poet. Crane was born Harold Hart Crane in Garretsville, Ohio, the only child of a successful candy tycoon, inventor of the Lifesaver. Until they divorced in 1916, the 'bloody battlefield' of his parents' unhappy marriage overshadowed his early childhood, leaving permanent psychological scars on their sensitive son. Shortly after Christmas 1916, the mostly self-educated 17-year-old left for New York City, where he planned to become a poet. For the next seven years, during which he worked intermittently for his father in Cleveland, he struggled to establish a writing career in New York City. Crane was introduced to gay sexual encounters soon after his arrival in New York, but his first great romance was with a man he met while working in one of his father's candy stores in Akron, Ohio (1919–1920).

Moving permanently to New York in 1923, he took the name 'Hart' (his mother's maiden name) in deference to his mother's support for his poetic ambitions. While struggling to produce his first mature poems, Crane supported himself with transient jobs writing advertising copy, loans from friends and handouts from his parents. His concentration was frequently distracted by his tormented relationship with his parents and by his increasing bouts of alcoholism. In 1926, a collection of his poems was published as *White Buildings*. Having courted the friendship and favour of Sherwood Anderson, Malcolm Cowley, Eugene O'Neill and others, in order to substantiate his place among the emerging literary luminaries of the day, Crane was never shy in asking for financial assistance. He succeeded in obtaining loans and outright gifts from financier Otto Kahn to support his work on *The Bridge*, the epic poem cycle which he struggled for years to complete.

Crane was openly gay to most of his New York friends, caring little that some tolerated his sexuality only in light of his genius. His preference also was understood tacitly by his mother, but the thought terrified him that she someday might expose his sexuality to his father. After years of his mother's excessive emotional manipulation, Crane accepted a position as companion to Herbert Wise, a wealthy young invalid relocating to Los Angeles, in order to be near her and his dying grandmother. When Wise returned East, Crane moved into a bungalow with his mother and grandmother, but his reckless pursuit of sailors on the Los Angeles waterfront and flirtation with Hollywood's debauched gay life led to a final split in 1928. He returned to New York and, rejecting his mother's frequent attempts at reconciliation, never saw her again. Drawing on a modest inheritance from his grandfather, Crane sailed for Europe in late 1928. With the encouragement of Harry and Caresse Crosby, publishers of the Black Sun Press, whom he met on that largely unproductive trip, Crane returned to New York in 1929 to finish writing *The Bridge*. Shattered by the negative critical response his *magnum opus* initially received, Crane never lived to witness its acclaim as one of the great American poems.

In his last four years, chronic alcoholism sabotaged Crane's attempts to produce poetry. In 1931, he left for a year in Mexico on a Guggenheim Fellowship, planning to write poetry inspired by the 'excitingly primitive, sensual', pre-Columbian culture. Despite fleeting moments of optimism derived from his first heterosexual affair, with artist Peggy (Mrs Malcolm) Cowley, the year produced only one completed piece, his final poem, 'The Broken Tower'. Returning by ship to New York, Crane spent a particularly debauched night, during which he was robbed and beaten by yet another sailor. The next morning, he left Cowley's cabin with the words, 'I'm not going to make it, dear. I'm utterly disgraced.' He went back on deck and, at noon, plunged into the sea.

There are conflicting accounts of Crane's last day and the motives for his suicide. 'If his life became literally unlivable for him by 1932', Thomas Yingling asserts, 'part of the reason for that was that homosexuality was central to his life but was itself socially and psychically designed as an unlivable existence.' Others find the cause in his shame over his scandalous behaviour in Mexico and not honouring the terms of his Guggenheim fellowship, or depression over mounting debts and the failure of his father (who died in 1931) to provide adequately for him in his will, or the fear that his poetic gifts had deserted him. Among the ironies connected with Crane's suicide are his death in the sea, an obsessive, often transmogrifying, image in his poetry, and the fact that it was his mother, herself one of the possible causes of his final despair, who dedicated the rest of her life (she died in 1947) to securing her son's reputation as one of the most important poets produced by the United States.

Crane's poetic influences ranged from John Donne and the seventeenth-century metaphysical poets to William Blake, Shelley, RIMBAUD, WHITMAN, Yeats, Pound, WILDE and T. S. Eliot. Ann Douglas, calling him 'the era's most intensely gifted poet', cites Mary Baker Eddy, whose theories were introduced to Crane by his Christian Scientist mother and grandmother, as yet another important influence and argues convincingly that much of the imagery in his poetry is a conjoining of gay love-making and Christian Science 'transmemberment'. In fact, Crane's dense imagery is replete with homoerotic themes couched in traditional poetic forms, as in 'Voyages', inspired by his intense love affair with Emil Opffer. His poetic output, though limited, has influenced American poets for generations. His poetic themes and imagery continue to stimulate new critical interpretations, many relevant to queer studies, relating especially to the interconnectedness of gay culture and modernism.

A. Douglas, *Terrible Honesty: Mongrel Manhattan in the 1920s*, New York, 1995; H. Langdon and B. Weber, *O My Land, My Friends: The Selected Letters of Hart Crane*, New York, 1997; J. Unterecker, *Voyager: A Life of Hart*

Crane, New York, 1969; T. E. Yingling, *Hart Crane and the Homosexual Text: New Thresholds, New Anatomies*, Chicago, 1990.

A. M. Wentink

Crevel, René (1900–1935), French writer. Themes of circumcision, suicide and homosexuality recur in Crevel's autobiographical novels. In *Le clavecin de Diderot* (*Diderot's Harpsichord*) he claims that circumcision is a consequence rather than a cause of the Oedipus complex, and a cure for it. Fascinated by psychology, Crevel denied his own Oedipal tendencies, and proclaimed he had a 'anti-Oedipus simplex'. Crevel described to his father how a perfect suicide might be presented as an accident, and his father killed himself in just that manner. Suicide is omnipresent in his novels. All Crevel's venom is reserved for mothers: 'for the young French bourgeois, a mother is a piece of furniture'. In *La mort difficile* (*Difficult Death*, 1926), Pierre Dumont (initials PD = *pédé*, 'queer' in French) overhears his mother saying he is not abnormal ('just a bit degenerate'). After the ensuing row, Pierre wants to have dinner with his American boyfriend, Arthur Bruggle, who refuses, leaving him to make do with his girlfriend instead. Pierre tells her he is more interested in Bruggle, but at a party later, Bruggle makes it clear he prefers some rough trade. Pierre commits suicide. This is an early portrayal of ordinary homosexuality, not presented as inversion. Much is made of Crevel's own bisexuality, but Pierre is definitely an undiluted homosexual: 'There was nothing about female flesh in itself that tempted him any more'. The girlfriend is a 'fag-hag' and Crevel's many female correspondents may in part have fallen into the same category. In *Êtes-vous fous?* (*Are You Crazy?*, 1929), Magnus HIRSCHFELD is caricatured under the name Optimus Cerf-Mayer and the hero Vagualame is alone in not applauding the sexologist's attempts at using surgery to correct identity. Of Cerf-Mayer's assistant, it is said: 'All his problems stemmed from a thus-far unsatisfied wish to sleep with a woman who had a penis.'

Embarrassingly good-looking and charming, Crevel frequented quite different strata of society: Surrealists, writers generally, the Communist Party and the rich and famous. At school with André GIDE's protégé Marc Allégret and Julien Green, a conscript with Marcel Arland and Roger Vitrac, he was a committed surrealist. He may have been the lover of the novelist Aragon long before the latter officially came out. Klaus MANN lusted after him. Tristan Tzara, Marcel Jouhandeau, Gertrude STEIN, Paul Éluard and Salvador Dali were among his friends. The way he supported a glittering life-style is not obvious. He seems to have had a succession of jobs in reviews and magazines. In the early evening, he attended the almost obligatory Surrealist meetings, and was able to create while asleep (automatic writing was a preoccupation of the Surrealists), going on later to society receptions, and ending up in gay bars. However, his activities were punctuated by long sojourns in sanatoria because of tuberculosis. The quest for a cure at last led him to travel to Switzerland and to Berlin, where he visited Hirschfeld's clinic, although he did not see Hirschfeld himself. In an attempt to shake off his illness, the vain and beautiful Crevel had several ribs removed to collapse the affected lung.

Crevel's absences from Paris gave rise to the best sections of his correspondence. Increasingly aware of the threat from fascism, he devoted himself to the anti-fascist struggle, embracing communism and moving away from his erstwhile Surrealist friends. When the communist ideologue Ilya Ehrenbourg described Surrealism as 'masturbation, pederasty, fetishism, exhibitionism and even sodomy', the homophobic Surrealist leader André Breton slapped his face, and Crevel found himself in an intolerable position. In failing health, he committed suicide, leaving a note saying 'Please cremate me – Revulsion'.

F. Buot, *René Crevel: biographie*, Paris, 1991; M. Carassou, *René Crevel*, Paris, 1989; J.-M. Devesa, *René Crevel et le roman*, Amsterdam, 1993; M. B. Rochester, *René Crevel: le pays des miroirs absolus*, Saratoga, Calif., 1978.

David Parris

Cruz, Juana Inés de la (1648?–1695), Spanish-Mexican nun. Juana Ramírez de Asbaje was born in San Miguel de Neplanta as an illegitimate child of the Spanish captain Pedro Manuel de Asbaje y Vargas Machuca and Isabel Ramírez de Santillana. She learned to read at the age of 3, and due to the socio-cultural conditions of the period, which did not allow women to attend universities, she had to satisfy her intellectual cravings with the books in the library of her maternal grandfather, Pedro Ramírez, in Panaoyán. After moving to Mexico City, the capital of the viceroyalty of New Spain, her fame as a gifted young woman opened the doors of the court to her. She was invited to live in the viceregal palace by Doña Leonor Carreto, Marquise de Mancera. In 1667, Juana entered the Carmelite convent, but she left a few months later, because of health problems. With the religious name of Sor Juana Inés de la Cruz, she made her profession in the convent of St Jerome, where she spent the rest of her life.

Sor Juana's unusual intellectual talent and writings, both religious and profane, aroused strong interest and violent reactions among her contemporaries. The introduction to the second volume of her works (1692) is proof of the unlimited praise her admirers were willing to express. However, her adversaries in the ecclesiastic hierarchy did whatever they could to prevent her from writing and publishing. In particular, the Jesuit Antonio Núñez de Miranda, Sor Juana's confessor from 1669 to 1689, tried to convince her to abandon her literary vocation. The relationship between them reached a point where the nun decided to dismiss him.

Considering a set of earlier poems expressing *amistad amorosa* (loving friend-ship) that Juana wrote to honour her protectors, first the Marquise de Mancera and later the Countess of Paredes, critics have speculated about the poet's lesbian sexual identity. Since it is not possible to support with actual documents any specific definition of the nature of the represented feelings, both the explanation of these love poems exclusively as a part of the literary tradition of platonic writing and their interpretation as manifestations of a lesbian desire are equally acceptable hypotheses. On a different level, in the context of the Spanish colonial culture, there is no historical documentation that could be used to open a way to research the existence of feminine homoeroticism, even though it is completely clear that convent life is a strong form of homosocial bonding.

The most bitter discussion among the commentators, dating back to the publication of *Fama y obras póstumas del Fénix de México* (*Fame and Posthumous Writings of the Mexican Phoenix*, 1700), centres on the presumed conversion of the poet after 1690. That year, the Bishop of Puebla, Manuel Fernández de Santa Cruz, published one of Sor Juana's religious writings, titled 'Crisis de un sermón' ('A Critique of a Sermon'), where the writer, refuting an old sermon by the Portuguese Jesuit Antônio Vieira, attacks the ideas of Núñez de Miranda. Her theological piece was published as 'Carta atenagórica' ('Athenian Letter'), preceded by a letter signed by Sor Filotea de la Cruz, a pen-name used by the bishop to address Sor Juana and to urge her to abandon her literary career. The nun answered, on the one hand, with the famous *Respuesta a sor Filotea de la Cruz* (*Reply to Sister Philotea of the Cross*), in which she courageously defended the right of women to learn and write; on the other hand, she wrote a satiric letter, signed with the pseudonym of Sor Serafina de Cristo, which contains a vehement and enigmatic attack against her former confessor. Although some Mexican critics consider this letter to be apocryphal, her editor, Elías

Trabulse, has proved beyond any doubt that the document is autobiographical. Nevertheless, the poet seemed to have been the victim of a secret trial, conducted under the rules of canon law. As a result, she was obliged to declare herself the worst of all women, was forbidden to publish any other writing, and had her library sold. The fact that she agreed to all these is evidence, for some, of her sincere conversion. However, the inventory prepared by Nazario López de la Vega, chaplain of St Jerome, in 1843, includes among other possessions kept in the nun's cell 189 volumes of selected works and 15 files of mystic and profane writings. As a consequence, it seems clear that Sor Juana carried on her intellectual interest, started rebuilding her personal library, and continued writing in spite of the prohibition set by the church authorities.

Modern scholarship has been able to reconstruct a feminist perspective with several of Sor Juana's writings: the bold self-defence of the *Respuesta*, the defiant content of the 'Villancicos a Santa Catarina de Alejandría' ('Christmas Carols to St Catherine of Alexandria', 1691), and the unlimited extolling of the Virgin Mary in other poems and, particularly, in the *Ejercicios devotos a la encarnación* (*Devotional Exercises to the Incarnation*).

D. Altamiranda, 'Juana Inés de la Cruz', in D. W. Foster (ed.) *Latin American Writers on Gay and Lesbian Themes: A Bio-Critical Sourcebook*, Westport, Conn., 1994: 192–8; M. S. Peden, *A Woman of Genius: The Intellectual Autobiography of Sor Juana Inés de la Cruz* (English translation of *Respuesta a Sor Filotea*), Salsbury, Conn., 1982; M. Glantz, *Sor Juana Inés de la Cruz: Hagiografía o autobiografía?*, Mexico City, 1995; D. Schons, 'Some Obscure Points in the Life of Sor Juana Inés de la Cruz', *Modern Philology*, 24 (1926): 141–62; E. Trabulse, 'Estudio introductorio', *Carta Atenagórica de Sor Juana (edición facsímile de la de 1690)*, Mexico Cuty, 1995.

Daniel Altamiranda

Cukor, George (1899–1983), American theatre and film director. The second child of a lower-middle-class non-religious Jewish family, Cukor grew up on Manhattan's tree-lined East 68th Street. He expressed more interest in the theatre and motion pictures than in schoolwork and found more enjoyment in Civil War stories than in sports or flirting with girls. Emmanuel Levy argues that the homosexual, Jewish and unattractive young man found the theatre a sanctuary for 'outcasts'.

Cukor began as a stage manager with a Chicago theatre company, became the resident director of a stock company in Rochester, New York, then reached Broadway in the mid-1920s. He forged a name as the director of prominent leading actresses, including Ethel Barrymore. Patrick McGilligan asserts that during this theatrical period Cukor accepted his homosexuality but remained guarded. He befriended many wealthy, educated gentlemen whose homosexuality was discreet.

By 1929, the sound motion picture required directors skilled in dealing with dialogue. Cukor moved from New York to Hollywood and coached the actors on *All Quiet on the Western Front* (1930). His early motion pictures with Paramount proved less-than-successful and the studio released him. In 1932, the director began a long professional relationship and friendship with producer David O. Selznick. The pair created several magnificent motion pictures, including *Dinner at Eight* and *Little Women*, both in 1933. Cukor moved to MGM and with some of the greatest female 'stars in heaven' helmed the classics *Camille* (1937), *The Women* (1939) and *The Philadelphia Story* (1940). His skill at capturing magnificent performances from Greta GARBO, Katherine Hepburn and other actresses earned him the label of a women's director. Many within the industry believed that Cukor's homosexuality made him a good women's director because the orientation made him pay attention to details of clothes and ambience, and enabled him to understand women and their emotions to a greater extent. This typecasting reportedly cost the director some prime projects because the studios believed he could not direct action, or male actors, as adeptly. A few other homosexual and heterosexual directors of the era, including Edmund Goulding, Irving Rapper and Vincent Sherman, were similarly typecast, but Goulding and Sherman battled against the label and directed projects outside of this genre as well.

While Hollywood's homosexuals – including actress Alla Nazimova, actor Nelson Eddy and director Edmund Goulding – gave noted parties, Cukor's Sunday soirées helped him forge a gay society. The parties followed a structured pattern with guests receiving their one drink at six-thirty, shortly before they moved into the dining room. Guests sometimes brought handsome, very masculine men to these parties for the pleasure of the host and other guests. This attraction to highly masculine men frequently led to trips with friends into the raucous section of cities like Long Beach. Once Cukor and actor William HAINES flirted too aggressively in a sailor's bar, prompting a fight. Cukor was arrested on a morals charge, but MGM's executives successfully suppressed the news. David Lewis, a producer and the long-time lover of director James WHALE, viewed Cukor's interest in and payment to these men as indicative of Cukor being loveless. However, the director enjoyed long-term friendships with many industry people, including Haines and Hepburn. He raised money for people such as Ethel Barrymore, and regularly telephoned long-forgotten figures in their nursing homes.

Cukor continued to make motion pictures into the 1980s. He received the best director Oscar for *My Fair Lady* in 1964. During his later years he provided off-the-record accounts of the industry's homosexual history to several journalists who later incorporated them into books on Nazimova and others.

B. Hadleigh, *Hollywood Gays*, New York, 1996; E. Levy, *George Cukor: A Master of Elegance*, New York, 1994; P. McGilligan, *George Cukor: A Double Life*, New York, 1991.
Brett L. Abrams

Cullen, Countee (1903–1946), American poet, writer, editor. Little is known about the details of Cullen's early life: he had been living in New York City, possibly with his grandmother, when he was adopted into a religiously conservative but politically active minister's family in Harlem and raised as an only child. Having enjoyed a successful beginning to his career while in high school, Cullen attended New York University and published his first volume, *Color* (1925), during his last year there. After receiving his Master's degree from Harvard, he took an editorial position at *Opportunity*, the magazine of the Urban League. Awarded a Guggenheim Fellowship in 1928, Cullen left for Paris to write and to study French literature.

An influential but stylistically atypical figure of the Harlem Renaissance, Cullen wrote lyric poetry in the manner of the English Romantics rather than the idioms of black vernaculars. While often expressing his desire to be considered a poet, rather than a Negro poet, Cullen consistently explored race matters and addressed the dilemma of 'this curious thing: / To make a poet black, and bid him sing!' ('Yet Do I Marvel', 1925) by writing of universal themes as constructed through the dynamics of race. Some of Cullen's poems also enable queer readings, such as 'The Black Christ' (1929), whose anti-racist message sings of black male beauty while referencing a homoerotic genealogy, and 'Tableau' (1925), whose youthful homoerotic miscegenation provokes both black and white disapproval. Cullen's gift to the poet Langston Hughes of an inscribed copy of his sensual poem 'To a Brown Boy' (1923) perhaps suggests an unrequited love.

Twice married – briefly to Nina Yolande

Du Bois, the daughter of the eminent scholar and activist W. E. B. Du Bois, and twelve years later to Ida Mae Roberson – Cullen also maintained a long-term relationship with Harold Jackman to whom he dedicated a number of his works and left a substantial share of his papers upon his death. In addition to Jackman and Hughes, Cullen's circle of friends in the 1920s included such queer writers as Alain Locke, Richard Bruce NUGENT, Wallace Thurman and Carl VAN VECHTEN.

In 1934, Cullen took a position teaching high school French and creative writing. While the demands of his new job restricted his literary output during the last 12 years of his life, he continued to write, pursuing different forms, including children's books in verse and prose, a prose translation of *Medea*, a novel and several plays. He died of high blood pressure and uremic poisoning in New York at the age of 42.

Though his initial reputation was eclipsed by other African-American writers from the 1920s, Cullen has begun to receive renewed biographical and critical attention which has led to the republication of his long-out-of-print works. In addition to more sustained studies of Cullen's exploration of black racial consciousness, gay scholars' projects of excavating and constructing gay cultural meanings in the Harlem Renaissance have prompted further re-evaluations of his poetry, his personal relationships and the social context of homosexuality during the period.

C. Cullen, *My Soul's High Song: The Collected Writings of Countee Cullen*, ed. G. Early, New York, 1991; B. E. Ferguson, *Countee Cullen and the Negro Renaissance*, New York, 1966; M. Perry, *A Bio-Bibliography of Countee P. Cullen*, Westport, Conn., 1971; A. R. Shucard, *Countee Cullen*, Boston, 1984.

Scott Bravmann

Custine, Astolphe de (1790–1857), French public figure. Custine was born into a wealthy noble family in Niderwiller in eastern France. Both his grandfather and his father were guillotined during the French Revolution, but his mother, the famous beauty Delphine de Sabran, recovered the family fortune and Custine enjoyed a pampered childhood. Rich, handsome, elegant, witty and intelligent, although always restless, nervous and physically frail, the young Custine was one of the most eligible bachelors in France; no one suspected his homosexuality. Custine married in 1821 and fathered a son the next year, but left immediately afterwards on a trip through England and Scotland, where he met Edward Sainte-Barbe (1794–1858), who returned with him to France. The two men remained inseparable companions for the rest of their lives. The death of Custine's wife (July 1823), followed by that of his son (January 1826) and his mother (July 1826), left him otherwise unattached.

Custine's homosexuality was revealed in 1824 by a scandal that shows the limits of public tolerance for sexual dissidence in nineteenth-century France. On the evening of 28 October, Custine turned up for an assignation with a young soldier in a barn north of Paris, whereupon several soldiers emerged from hiding to beat up and rob Custine, and then stripped him naked, leaving him for dead in a muddy field. The story soon came out and, in the words of one contemporary, Custine was henceforth 'a man sunk to the bottom, stigmatised, branded with the seal of [public] reprobation'. Another wrote: 'Never have I seen a more widespread outburst [of public outrage], a more burning and more verbose indignation; high society as a whole is furious . . .'.

If society turned its back on Custine, his wealth and his talent assured him a place in the literary world. He wrote plays, novels and memoirs of his travels, most notably a critical description of tsarist Russia, *La Russie en 1839* (published in English as *Russia in 1839*, 1843). He entertained lavishly in his Paris mansion and in his country house, and lent money to needy artists and writers. Nevertheless, as the Parisian literary critic C.-A. Sainte-Beuve wrote to a friend in 1844: 'Mr de Custine has such a bad reputation here . . .! One reads him; one enjoys him well enough; but nobody respects him. . . . His pretty house in the valley of Montmorency is a pure Sodom and Gomorrah.' At his death in 1857, Custine left his entire (but substantially diminished) fortune to Sainte-Barbe ('my best friend who has stuck with me for thirty years').

P. de Lacretelle, 'Un Charlus du Romantisme: Le Marquis de Custine', *La Parisienne*, January–March 1955; Marquis de Luppé, *Astolphe de Custine*, Monaco, 1957; Julien Frédéric Tarn, *Le Marquis de Custine*, Paris, 1985.

Michael Sibalis

Czechowicz, Józef (1903–1939), Polish poet and editor. Czechowicz created his own variety of avant-garde poetry, very personal, symbolic and visionary, rooted in myth, fairy tales and magic. In his final years his poems became permeated with an obsession with death, approaching catastrophism. Homoerotic traits were clearly visible in his lyrics; when their presence in the poem *Hildur, Baldur i czas* (*Hildur, Baldur and Time*) was pointed out by critics, the poet lost his job as teacher. He published six volumes of poetry, including *Kamień* (*The Stone*, 1927) and *nic więcej* (*nothing more*, 1936). He also edited avant-garde literary journals such as *Reflektor* and *Pióro*. Czechowicz was killed in a German air-raid in Lublin, during a visit to the hairdresser.

The poet's fascination with simple country boys was almost proverbial. Their reception sometimes led to rather ridiculous situations. One of the boys was so outraged by hostile reception of his friend's poems that he avenged the writer by breaking all the window panes in the building housing the editorial office of the journal which had published the critical review.

A. Selerowicz, *Leksykon kochających inaczej*, Poznań, 1994: 107; *Encyklopedia powszechna PWN*, Vol. 1, Warsaw, 1998.

Krzysztof Fordoński

D

Damian, St Peter (1007–1072), Catholic saint. Damian, born into a poor family at Ravenna, was abandoned and orphaned at an early age, and was employed by one of his brothers as a tender of pigs. Another brother, recognising his intelligence, sent Peter to study at Ravenna, Faenza and Parma. In 1035–1036, he entered the monastery of Fonte Avellana near Gubbio, where he reached the position of prior and was ordained a priest.

In about 1057, he was appointed cardinal-bishop of Ostia, one of the most important offices in the papal curia. Deeply involved in papal politics and in many of the theological and political controversies of the day, Damian was one of the most militant supporters of clerical celibacy and the reform of monastic life, and was himself known for his monastic austerity. His contemporary biographer, Peter of Lodi, reported that Damian was so troubled by carnal lust that he would frequently immerse himself naked in cold water in order to reduce his 'noxious passion'. Sexuality was often described in his writings in the most pejorative terms, as a product of 'the putridness of my flesh', thus condemning all forms of sexual expression. His works, which survive in over six hundred manuscripts, include saints' lives, sermons, hymns, legal studies and theological treatises dealing with such themes as clerical concubinage, monastic flagellation, and the various 'sins against nature'.

His treatise, *The Book of Gomorrah*, was written between 1048 and 1051 at the time of the Council of Rome (which condemned clerical sinfulness) and was dedicated to the reformer Pope Leo IX, whose candidacy he had supported. In this work he bemoans allegedly widespread sexual misbehaviour within the Church and focuses on what he regarded as the lax punishment applied to clergy and monks guilty of 'sins against nature' found in contemporary penitential manuals. Among the sins discussed are solitary and mutual masturbation, interfemoral and anal sex, pederasty, sex between confessors and their penitents, and possibly homosexual orgies. In support of contemporary efforts to reform canon law, Damian demanded the imposition of consistent, unequivocal, uniform and severe acts of penance on sexual offenders, asking the pope to exclude guilty clergy and depose those who had been promoted in ecclesiastical rank. Although various forms of same-sex behaviour were discussed in contemporary handbooks of penance, such as those by Burchard of Worms and Regino of Prum, and appear in poetry and treatises on friendship, this is the only theological tract which exclusively addresses this theme. It voices many of the standard medieval Christian charges: the men of Sodom were guilty of desiring sexual relations with Lot and the visiting angels, bringing down the wrath of God and their own destruction; same-sex relations are a more serious offence than bestiality, since two souls are damned, and should require imposition of the most severe penance on clergy and laity; and such behaviour may be likened to the infection of cancer and leprosy, an enormous 'crime' which destroys both the body and soul.

In his reply, Pope Leo IX admitted that deposition was the proper punishment for several of the sins outlined by Damian, but he was nevertheless willing to be more flexible with those who fully atone for their sins and are not long-term offenders. Damian speaks of the prevalence of these sins 'in our region', namely central Italy. This claim cannot be confirmed, although the late eleventh and early twelfth centuries were characterised by charges of sexual misbehaviour levelled against both high ecclesiastics and noblemen. Damian's feast day is 21 February, and he is placed by Dante in Paradise.

P. Damian, *Book of Gomorrah*, ed. and trans. P. Payer, Waterloo, Ont., 1982.

Michael Goodich

Damon and **Pythias** (fourth century BC). According to Valerius Maximus in *De Amicitiae Vinculo*, Damon and Pythias, legendary citizens of fourth century BC Syracuse, were initiates in the Pythagorean mysteries. When Pythias protested the tyranny of Dionysius I, he was condemned to death by the despotic ruler. The love of his friend Damon was so strong that he offered himself as hostage while Pythias returned to the home they shared together to arrange his affairs before death. Dionysius accepted the terms on the condition that Damon would be executed if Pythias did not return. When, on the final day of the allotted reprieve period, Pythias had not yet returned, Dionysius mocked Damon for a fool, but his faith in his friend did not falter. At the last moment, Pythias returned. Deeply impressed by this demonstration of loyalty, Dionysius not only remitted the sentence but asked to become their friend as well. 'Tyrants stand in awe of friends' concluded PLATO.

Through the ages Damon and Pythias have been venerated as symbols of the enduring power of loving male friendship, often with strong homoerotic overtones. In *The Faerie Queene*, for example, Edmund Spenser includes Damon and Pythias, 'whom death could not sever', as one of the mythic male couples immortalised in the temple of Venus. In the Victorian era, the pagan legend of same-sex love became Christianised with reference to the famous New Testament passage from John 11:53: 'Greater love hath no man than this, that a man lay down his life for his friend.' In an effort to heal the internecine conflicts of the Civil War in mid-nineteenth-century United States, Justus H. Rathbone founded the Supreme Order of the Knights of Pythias, in Washington, DC, in 1864. The organisation was founded on the principles of friendship, loyalty, peace, goodwill and public service as exemplified by the friendship of Damon and Pythias. By 1895, there were more than 250 lodges in the state of Missouri alone.

The love of Damon and Pythias has inspired theatrical works on stage and screen at least since the sixteenth century, from Richard Edward's *Damon and Pythias*, to Irish playwright John Bynum's 1821 play *Damon and Pythias: A Tragedy in 5 Acts*, to the 1915 film *Damon and Pythias* produced by Universal Pictures. Through the centuries, Damon and Pythias may well be considered the prototypes for such divergent loving male couples as Hamlet and Horatio, Don Quixote and Sancho Panza, Butch Cassidy and the Sundance Kid, the Lone Ranger and Tonto, the Cisco Kid and Pancho, Laurel and Hardy, and Abbott and Costello.

A. M. Wentink

Dauthendey, Elisabeth (1854–1943), Russian-German novelist and poet. Dauthendey, stepsister to the better-known poet and painter Max Dauthendey, was born in St Petersburg, where her father was court photographer to Tsar Nicholas I. From 1893 she lived in Würzburg, Germany. Dauthendey, who was influenced in her work by the writings of Friedrich NIETZSCHE, produced novellas, novels, poetry, fairy tales and essays; but her best-known work is *Vom neuen Weibe und seiner Liebe. Ein Buch für reife Geister* (*Of the New Woman and her Love: A Book for Mature Minds*, 1900). In this novel the narrator, Lenore, sets out to look for the perfect woman after having had a series of difficult relationships with men. She becomes involved with a beautiful Spanish-German woman called Rasti Tabera, and the two share a house. But Lenore avoids sexual contact with Rasti and finally insists on a separation when, one balmy night, the other woman wants to take her to her bed. Lenore explains that in her friendships with women she is repelled by 'impure motives'. After much searching for a 'pure' single-sex relationship, she finally finds happiness with her adopted daughter, Yvette, whom she left behind when she set out on her quest.

First published in Berlin in 1900, Dauthendey's novel appeared in 11 editions. One reason for its popularity lay in the fact that Lenore is an incorporation of the 'New Woman': the turn-of-the-century conception of (relatively) liberated womanhood. Having achieved a level of social and intellectual emancipation unknown to her historical predecessors, Lenore can no longer find fulfilment in men (who have not yet ascended to the same spiritual and intellectual heights as modern women), but only in other women like herself. Yet for all her liberation, Dauthendey feels the need to impose sexual prudery, or homophobia, on her heroine: Lenore may choose to share her life, even her bed, with another woman, but she must not indulge in 'Sapphic' physical love, which would render her impure.

Dauthendey's literary works include *An*

den Ufern des Lebens. Roman (*On the Shores of Life: a Novel*, 1919), *Ein Abend und andere Novellen* (*One Evening and Other Novellas*, 1914), *Hunger* (1901) and *Im Schatten* (*In the Shadows*, 1903).

L. Faderman and B. Eriksson, *Lesbians in Germany, 1890's–1920's*, Tallahassee, 1990 [1980].

Sarah Colvin

David and **Jonathan** (tenth century BC), Biblical figures. David was the youngest son of a Bethlehem farmer, who became the second king of Israel *c.* 1010 BC to *c.* 971–961 BC, founded the United Kingdom of Israel, and established its capital at Jerusalem ('the city of David'). David came to the attention of Saul, first king of Israel, as a skilled musician and resourceful warrior, having slain Goliath, the Philistine champion. Jonathan was the eldest son and presumptive heir of Saul. Very little is known of him historically. At the time of his death on Mount Gilboa in the failed Israelite campaign against Bethshan, he was about 30 years old. Jonathan was a heroic if somewhat idiosyncratic warrior, who lacked the qualities of leadership necessary to forge together the loose affiliation of Israelite tribes into a cohesive whole.

The story of the friendship between David and Jonathan is unusual, in that two individuals from very different family backgrounds 'covenant' together three times over without stipulated obligations. Their covenant did not concern power and politics, but rather mutual love and personal safety – Jonathan loved David 'as himself'. Although Jonathan continued to fight alongside his father, Saul experienced their alliance as profoundly anti-familial, perverted and shameful, and humiliated Jonathan on account of it.

David lamented Jonathan's death with the words: 'Greatly beloved were you to me; your love to me was wonderful, passing the love of women.' David had adequate basis for the comparison: his heterosexual experience included two 'wives of the wanderings', five wives and ten concubines at Hebron, various wives at Jerusalem and the adulterous (and eventually murderous) affair with Bathsheba.

The covenant of love between David and Jonathan is probably more literary than historical. Any homosexual and erotic significance in the story lies in the eye of the twentieth-century beholder. It has been widely used in Jewish and Christian theologies of gay and lesbian liberation as a positive role-model of personal affection and attachment in tension with patriarchy, social convention and familial responsibilities. On the other hand, it has been used to commend non-genital friendship between homosexuals. Thus the same text, in a religious context, may have power both to liberate and to oppress.

I Samuel 16: 1, to I Kings 2: 11, I Chronicles 10–29; C. Balka and A. Rose (eds) *Twice Blessed: On Being Lesbian or Gay and Jewish*, Boston, 1989; G. D. Comstock, *Gay Theology without Apology*, Cleveland, 1993; T. Horner, *Jonathan Loved David: Homosexuality in Biblical Times*, Philadelphia, 1978; R. Moss, *Christians and Homosexuality*, London, 1977.
David J. Bromell

Day, F(red) Holland (1864–1933), American photographer and publisher. Born in Norwood, Massachusetts, into a wealthy New England manufacturing family, Day remained financially independent throughout his life. An ardent bibliophile, he was especially an enthusiast of the English poet John Keats, whose memorabilia and first editions he avidly collected. In 1893 he co-founded, with Herbert Copeland, the Boston publishing house of Copeland and Day. The firm continued until 1899, publishing handsomely produced volumes of contemporary literature (especially poetry) using pre-industrial printing techniques, and it also imported Oscar WILDE's *Salome* (illustrated by Aubrey Beardsley) and the controversial English literary journal *The Yellow Book*.

Both Copeland and Day were associated with a group of poets and artists called the Boston Bohemians, who espoused the values of contemporary European aestheticism and decadence. Describing the group as 'smugly cliquish, enamoured of the exotic and the bizarre, contemptuous of the normal or average, in costume, in behavior, and in art', Stephen Maxfield Parrish wrote of Day, 'His manner swung from an exaggerated reserve that masked an absence of worldly ease, to a flamboyance carefully accentuated by an opera cloak, a broad black hat, a long cigarette holder with a flat Russian cigarette in it, and a convincingly esthetic bearing.'

Day had taken up photography at least by 1887, but most likely earlier, and within a decade he became a leading figure in pictorialist photography, despite the occasional technical unevenness of his work. Concerned principally with the overall design of the image, and employing a very restricted tonal range, he produced beautifully printed, soft-focus images that captured atmospheric moods rather than graphic detail. The self-conscious aestheticism of the photographs was accentuated by Day's wide-ranging art historical references (for example, many photographs were based on paintings by, among others, Hans Holbein, Guido Reni and William Holman Hunt) and by his frequent use of classical themes and motifs, especially in the later work, which were indicative also of his rejection of modernity and its values.

Day's early photographs included striking portraits of young men posed in various theatrical costumes. His sitters included one of his young protégés, the poet Kahlil Gibran, and he was one of the first photographers to use both male and female black models (who were often his servants), e.g. *Ebony and Ivory* and *African Chief* (1897). In 1898 Day produced a remarkable series of photographs of religious subjects (comprising some 250 negatives), including the *Crucifixion*, the *Descent from the Cross*, the *Entombment*, and the *Resurrection*, in which he himself posed as Christ (having fasted until he looked suitably emaciated and having let his hair and beard grow for over a year). Other models were attired in costumes that had been specially imported, as was the wood for the (historically accurate) cross. Despite Day's concern for accuracy, the series was clearly also a personal statement of his belief in the connection between art and suffering – the figure of St SEBASTIAN (who suffered for his love for Christ) was also one of Day's photographic subjects. In his later work, however, Day moved away from Christian themes, focusing instead on pagan subjects such as the legend of Orpheus. Although these photographs of nude youths in various pastoral settings recall those of his contemporary, Thomas EAKINS, Day's photographic technique and his highly poetic treatment of his subjects, e.g. *The Vision* (1910), are very different from Eakins's realist aesthetic. Day's final photographs, produced around 1911 while he was living in Maine, include a number of intimate and subdued portraits of sitters, including various boys in sailor suits, engaged in domestic pursuits such as playing checkers or else just gazing dreamily into space.

In 1895 Day was elected to the British photographic society the Linked Ring, which sought to promote photography as an art form, and in 1900 he went to England where he organised a major exhibition, 'The New School of American Photography', which opened in October before travelling to Paris the following year. Although Day shared with Alfred Stieglitz, America's leading art photographer, the aim of securing the artistic status of photography, Stieglitz did not support the 1900 exhibition. In turn, Day never joined the Photo-Secession group, founded by Stieglitz in 1902, and instead maintained his own independence. His somewhat marginal position was further compounded when a fire in November 1904 destroyed most of his work (includ-

ing his negatives). In 1917 Day withdrew from society and remained a bedridden recluse until his death in Norwood.

J. Crump, *F. Holland Day: Suffering the Ideal*, Santa Fe, 1995; M. Harker, *The Linked Ring: The Secession Movement in Photography in Britain, 1892–1910*, London, 1979; E. Jussim, *Slave to Beauty*, Boston, 1981.

David L. Phillips

De Haan, Jacob Israël (1881–1924), Dutch author. De Haan and his twin-sister, who later became famous as the novelist Carry van Bruggen, were born to a rabbi and his wife in Smilde in the northern part of The Netherlands. The family moved to Zaandam near Amsterdam and, later, Carry would write a poignant story of their childhood there in poverty. Jacob studied to become a teacher and continued his studies in law at the University of Amsterdam. He befriended the lecturer of criminal anthropology, Arnold ALETRINO, who helped him to come out as homosexual.

De Haan was a very intelligent but obstinate student who earned money by teaching and writing for the children's page of the socialist daily newspaper, *Het Volk*. In 1904, his first novel, *Pijpelijntjes*, was published. It contained a very realist description of the lives of two students in the new Amsterdam neighbourhood 'De Pijp' (whence the title; 'pijpen' also means 'to suck'). The students have a homosexual and quite sadistic relationship with each other, but find occasional lovers on the side in the streets of Amsterdam. There are rather explicit descriptions of sex with young men in their early teens. The names of the main characters are Joop and Sam (in fact the nicknames of De Haan and Aletrino) and the book was dedicated to 'dear Aletrino'. As Aletrino had always stated that doctors who wrote on homosexuality – like himself and HIRSCHFELD – were not necessarily subjectively involved, this novel endangered his reputation. Together with De Haan's betrothed – it was a time when gay men still married – he bought all the books from the publisher and shops to save their reputation. But none the less a scandal started which affected De Haan the most, as he lost his place as a teacher and on the socialist daily. A more sexually explicit second edition was published soon after, without the dedication and with different names for the main characters. This book was the first full-blown homosexual novel in Dutch.

In 1908 De Haan published his second and last novel, *Pathologieën*, which deals with a gay sadomasochistic relationship. This novel, with a foreword by De Haan's friend the Belgian gay author Georges EEKHOUD, caused less commotion. He also wrote short stories, one on a Faustian theme including the anal rape of JESUS by the main character, who sold his soul to the devil. De Haan's most important *œuvre* now became poetry with both gay and Jewish content. He published *Libertijnsche liederen* (*Libertine Songs*, 1914), *Liederen* (1917) and *Kwatrijnen* (1924). Some poems evoke Oscar WILDE's imprisonment and Eekhoud's novels. De Haan also wrote essays, journalism and developed in his dissertation *Rechtskundige significa* (1916) a linguistic theory for legal work focusing on criminal responsibility. He visited Russia and its jails and was horrified by the prisoners' situation. He wrote an indictment against their condition, *In Russische gevangenissen* (1913).

De Haan became a Zionist and after World War I went to Jerusalem in Palestine, where he taught law and wrote articles for the British and Dutch press. In one of his poems, he asks himself if he visits the Wailing Wall for God or for the Arab boys. His involvement with both Arabs and orthodox Jews made him critical of Zionist positions. As he started to disparage Zionist claims in the British press, where until then only Zionist views were heard, radical Zionists threatened him with death. In a beautiful letter, De Haan describes how it felt to awaken the day after he should have been killed. But assassinated he was, killed by Zionists. Isaac Ben Zvi, who later became president of Israel, was instrumental in De Haan's murder, although the actual murderer was never apprehended. Zionists spread the rumour that Arabs killed him because of his sexual relations with Arab boys. Until this day orthodox Jews honour De Haan's politics, but deny his homosexuality.

De Haan is nowadays considered one of the most accomplished Dutch poets. A line of his poetry, 'Such a boundless desire for friendship', decorates the Homomonument in Amsterdam. His collected poems were published in 1952, and many of his published and unpublished works were reissued in the 1980s. His life and work have been the subject of a play and an opera. No biography has yet been published that brings together the gay, Jewish, poetic, scholarly and political lines in De Haan's life.

J. Meijer, *De zoon van een gazzen*, Amsterdam, 1967.

Gert Hekma

Della Casa, Giovanni (1503–1556), Italian cleric and writer. Archbishop of Benevento (1544), papal nuncio to Venice (1544–1549) and papal secretary of state under Paul IV (1555–1556), Della Casa is now best known as author of a posthumously published manual of etiquette, *Il Galateo ovvero de' costumi* (1558), which enjoyed a great success.

Before entering the priesthood (in 1537), Della Casa had written various poetical works, in the style of Francesco BERNI, full of *doubles entendres*. Among his other youthful works is also always listed a prose work in Latin titled *In laudem pederastiae seu sodomiae* or *De laudibus sodomiae* (*In Praise of Buggery*). In fact, this work never existed, as was proved by Gilles Ménage, who in *Anti-Baillet* traced accounts about the work. He found that all of them, directly or indirectly, derived from propaganda spread by Protestants in order to discredit Della Casa and the Catholic

Church, of which Della Casa was an important defender. In particular, the charges about such a work were spread by Pier Paolo Vergerio, a church leader whom Della Casa had brought to court for 'heresy'; after his sensational conversion to Protestantism, Vergerio wrote a libelous work about Della Casa.

Indeed Della Casa, as a young man, had written a short comic work, *Capitolo del Forno* (*The Oven Chapter*), in which he pretended to sing the praises of a loaf of bread going into the oven – a comic *double entendre* about the act of sex. Although the composition was heterosexual in tone, several stanzas spoke of sodomy and these lines gave birth to the legend of *In laudem sodomiae*. Della Casa had defended himself in *Ad Germanos*, yet some observers said that the affair had cost Della Casa promotion to the cardinalate.

Catholics reacted by never letting the Protestant leader Théodore de Bèze (1519–1605) live down having published, in his *Juvenilia* (1548), a pair of Latin compositions in which he mentioned his love for a certain Audebert.

Others have remarked on homosexual behaviour occasionally hinted at in Della Casa's *Galateo*, confirming that, like the majority of the intellectuals before the Counter-Reformation, Della Casa maintained a detached and tolerant attitude towards love between persons of the same gender. Such an attitude was not unique to this author but was characteristic of an entire generation. The Protestant attacks on Della Casa were above all an attack against a whole class of Italian Renaissance intellectuals considered (with reason) too tolerant of homosexual behaviour.

G. Ménage, *Anti-Baillet*, The Hague, 1683.

Giovanni Dall'Orto

Demuth, Charles (1883–1935), American painter. The American-born Demuth is perhaps best known in the official chronicles of art history for his painting *The Figure 5 in Gold* (1928). Loosely modelled after Gertrude STEIN's word-portraits, and dedicated to William Carlos Williams (the American poet whose work inspired the painting's title and imagery), it is anything but illustrative. Influenced by the European avant-garde, Demuth's urban and industrial subjects are frequently interpreted as distinctly American. Though *The Figure 5 in Gold* marks a particularly notable achievement within the history and progression of modernist abstraction, it is a second body of Demuth's work that is of the most interest to gay and lesbian historians. This work received little critical attention until recently, and was mostly seen only in the private drawing rooms of its collectors; many of the works were never exhibited during Demuth's lifetime. Mostly done in watercolour and pencil on paper, they look at a flourishing gay lifestyle, if not an actual subculture, taking place in the baths and apartments, and on the beaches of this newest urban population. In *Eight O'Clock (Morning # 2)* (1917), Demuth depicts three men in various stages of undress – their scattered clothes suggesting something of an impromptu soirée. Identifiable within this particular interior, one can clearly see a top hat on one side and a bowler on the other, suggesting to art historians like Jonathan Weinberg considerably more than the social exchange between an upper-class gentleman and a street youth. Another work titled *Turkish Bath Scene with Self-Portrait* (1918) again presents three male figures. The first man stands suggestively draped in a towel before Demuth's own semi-nude self-portrait, his own towel visibly lying on the floor.

Demuth has also left a number of far less obscure works. His *Three Sailors on the Beach* (1930) depicts a sailor dressed only in a singlet and boots, his spread legs revealing an erect penis, his gaze turned to the man standing behind him. The second man, wearing only boxer-shorts, holds his own penis in one hand while directing the first man's head towards it with the other.

While titillating for gay historians and enthusiasts everywhere, Demuth must be remembered for the full breadth of his artistic contributions and not simply for his erotic watercolours. Clearly sexual identity does contribute something to our appreciation of his *œuvre*, as well as to the continuing struggle to establish gay scholarship within the academy, but the precise implications of such an aesthetic duality have yet to be fully theorised.

B. Haskell, *Charles Demuth*, New York, 1987; J. Weinberg, *Speaking for Vice: Homosexuality in the Art of Charles Demuth, Marsden Hartley, and the First American Avant-Garde*, New Haven, 1995.

Ken Gonzales-Day

De Pisis, Filippo (Tibertelli) (1896–1956), Italian painter. Born on the cusp of the *fin de siècle*, De Pisis might be expected to represent any number of the early twentieth century's rich array of avant-garde artistic movements. Instead, critics consider his painting, although revealing various influences, to have been noteworthy for its isolation from the main trends by which it was surrounded. De Pisis's own life was similarly unusual. Apparently unabashed by conventional morality, he assiduously cultivated his eccentricity from an early age, and carried a nineteenth-century tradition of dandyism well into the twentieth century, hand in hand with a reasonably open homosexuality. In short, De Pisis seemed to have a knack for taking full advantage of the fickle licence which bourgeois society has traditionally been prepared to grant to cultural figures.

The third of seven children, De Pisis was born into a rich, aristocratic and strictly Catholic family in Ferrara. Since the area's political life was dominated by liberal or socialist anti-clericals, the family had a somewhat isolated position in the town, and the young De Pisis spent his first years at home, where he was educated privately. He began art lessons at the age of 8, and indulged his intense curiosity about nature in the family's large garden. The protected and idyllic character of his childhood, as well as his emerging imagination, are evident in an early photograph which shows him dressed as a fourteenth-century scholar chasing butterflies. But De Pisis emerged from his own luxurious chrysalis, attending a public high school, and in 1916, relieved of military service because of a nervous problem, he enrolled at the University of Bologna. While at university, he continued to paint, and he frequented Bologna's artistic and café society circles. In 1920 he held his first exhibition of paintings, which was not a success. But he obtained his degree in letters the same year, and after graduating he moved to Rome.

Rome made Ferrara seem stuffy and provincial, and this impression was reinforced by the fact that Rome was where De Pisis appears to have had his homosexual awakening. He earned a living teaching art at a high school, and his diaries record sexual fantasies about his male students. In private he would sketch the way he imagined their torsos, based on what he had seen of other parts of their bodies, such as their knees. A more specific incident in his diary records a meeting with a 19-year-old oarsman in a boat on the Tiber, an account that glitters with barely suppressed homoeroticism. During this period De Pisis also painted continually, mostly still-lifes, but also landscapes when he went on holiday. In 1925 he exhibited paintings at the Third Rome Biennale.

By 1925 Italy was fully under the grip of Fascism, and De Pisis decided to move to Paris. Although initially he claimed that he was politically disinterested, and was no more an anti-fascist than he was a Fascist, it is probable that there were political as well as artistic motives for the move. Indeed, some years later he told a local Italian newspaper that he was not a fascist, and preferred to live in France. He was immediately attacked by several major Italian newspapers, and it was only the intervention of an old school friend and now Fascist minister, Italo Balbo, that saved De Pisis from being declared a traitor. Regardless of the political details, there is little doubt that in Paris De Pisis revelled in a lifestyle that the Fascists would certainly have considered degenerate.

The Parisian diaries are rich with details about the physiques of the many male models De Pisis recruited, mainly on the streets, and with details of the way the artist decked them out in classical costumes and posed them in the style of ancient Greece. But his sensual satisfaction was not limited to fetishising his models: De Pisis apparently also led a serene sensual life of unproblematic sexual encounters which were the envy of some of his friends. Beyond the satisfaction of his tastes and senses, De Pisis also worked hard during these years, and by the early 1930s was enjoying success as a painter. He had entered Parisian artistic and cultural circles, and among his friends and acquaintances were Matisse, Picasso, COCTEAU, Joyce, and the Italian writers Italo Svevo and Aldo Palazzeschi. Perhaps his most important friend was Giorgio De Chirico, whom he had known in Rome and who was an important mentor for him in Paris.

In 1935 De Pisis was invited to London by Anthony Zwemmer, an art dealer to whom he had sold several paintings. He stayed in London for some months, and Zwemmer arranged for him to work in Vanessa Bell's studio. The resulting exhibition of views of London was a success, and was reviewed favourably in *The Times*. In 1938 De Pisis made another trip from Paris to London, and was similarly successful. But once the war started in 1939 De Pisis was obliged to return to Italy. He spent most of his time in Milan, where he was kept under surveillance by the Fascists, and at one point was threatened with confinement by the prefect because he was viewed as a 'perturber of morals'. After the fall of the Fascist government in September 1943 he moved from Milan, which was badly damaged by bombs, to Venice.

De Pisis became something of a legendary figure in Venice, where his eccentricity generally went down well. He had the means to live in a large house, and to buy his own gondola. His most stable companion at this time was a parrot, never far from De Pisis's shoulder, especially when he was painting. But there was also the handsome gondolier Bruno, who fulfilled a multiplicity of other roles too: he would pose nude as a model, then dress in smart livery to serve tea at his employer's afternoon parties. De Pisis became well known for these occasions, to which he would invite cardinals and countesses, opera singers and army officers, not to mention down-at-heel artists and attractive young men. But De Pisis also became infamous for the parties he held later in the evening. In 1945, celebrating the end of the war, he was arrested in the small hours making merry with a group of 20 dancing boys dressed in G-strings. Although he suffered only the indignity of spending the remainder of the night locked in a cell rather than an embrace, it was a reminder that society's tolerance, even for artists, was far from unlimited.

De Pisis was also reminded of this professionally. His success as a painter continued, but in 1948 he was denied the grand prize at the Venice Biennale, apparently because of an intervention from Rome specifically referring to his homosexuality. Nevertheless, an entire room was dedicated to about 30 of his paintings, and he was clearly regarded by this stage as one of Italy's most important painters. This was recognised officially in the 1950s, when he won both the Premio Fiorino (1953) and the Mazotta prize (1954).

Despite this official success, De Pisis's final years were a sad contrast to his colourful life. As early as 1948 the nervous problems that had enabled him to avoid military service had developed into a chronic illness, and De Pisis spent much time and money going from clinic to clinic seeking a cure. Eventually he ran out of money and could not even afford a private room. In 1956 he died of an illness whose nature his doctors had still not agreed upon.

N. Naldini, *De Pisis. Vita solitaria di un poeta pittore*, Turin, 1991; S. Zanotto, *Filippo De Pisis ogni giorno*, Vicenza, 1991.

Mark Seymour

Deschauffours, Étienne-Benjamin (?–1726), French public figure. In many countries, homosexuality seems like a recent innovation, an American import or a symptom of a changing society. Doubtless, 'society' has been at pains to expunge the record, to deprive gay men of their history, to deny the perennial nature of homosexuality. Thus in France, all records of the trials of sodomites burned at the stake were consigned to the flames with them, obliterating all trace of their existence. However, by the eighteenth century, the police kept detailed records, obtained through a network of informers as well as on the basis of the denunciations of arrested sodomites, and many of these records were saved from the Bastille when it was sacked in the French Revolution. There were said to be 20,000 sodomites in Paris, but most of the victims of this surveillance seem to have had very ordinary sexual needs. However, a manuscript (Fonds Français 10970 at the Bibliothèque Nationale) gives a detailed account of investigations undertaken in 1725 and 1726 into one Étienne-Benjamin Deschaffours.

Under a variety of pseudonyms, and in various lodgings, Deschauffours earned a living by spotting 'likely lads' and supplying them on payment of commission to wealthy clients, both French and foreign (perhaps some 200 in all). Deschaffours frequently tried out his finds (young and very young), and found his pleasure in their pain (it is difficult not to think forward to the Marquis de SADE, or backward to Gilles de Rais). He castrated a young Italian whose admirer hoped this might render him more compliant. Deschauffours was burned at the stake on the Place de Grève (where sodomites had been executed for centuries) on 24 May 1726. Although as far as the spectators were concerned, the condemned were burnt alive, sometimes, especially when a noble was concerned, special instructions were given to the executioner in a letter called a *retentum*, which, as a mercy, allowed the executioner to strangle the victim before the flames got to him. Deschauffours ought to have been strangled, but the executioner bungled, and Deschauffours was seen gesticulating in the flames.

Whatever horror the manner of his death may inspire, the manner of his life can hardly inspire less. The Italian he had castrated, the children he sold into servitude, and the boy he killed deserved to be avenged. If one were bent on looking for an excuse, the most one might say in mitigation is that were homosexuality to have been less cruelly repressed, there would have been less call for Deschauffour's services.

Not all sodomites were burnt, and the treatment meted out to them varied according to their status, family connections and influence. A good proportion of ordinary 'perverts' were simply released with a caution. This was in part due to a genuine desire to rehabilitate offenders, but also to a fear that by exacting exemplary punishments, too much publicity would be given to the practice of homosexuality, and that rather than being a deterrent, the punishment would become an advertisement. Barely a year before Deschauffours's execution, VOLTAIRE's influence had been enough to secure the release of the Abbé Desfontaines, a libertine priest (whose ingratitude led him to publish satires against his benefactor after his release). It is difficult to discount totally the possibility that the time was judged right to burn a sodomite whose death would attract no protest, as an example. Louis XV, then still a minor, was on dangerously friendly terms with the Ducs de la Trémouille, d'Épernon and de Gesvres. This hypothesis is supported by the fact that the trial was not undertaken by the ordinary courts, but by a specially constituted body. Several of Deschauffours's associates were also punished, though only with prison terms. The least fortunate was Riotte de la Riotterie, who spent a quarter of a century in prison, largely at the behest of his father, who opposed his release by every possible means.

M. Lever, *Les Bûchers de Sodome*, Paris, 1985.
David Parris

Diaghilev, Serge (1872–1929), Russian impresario. Born Sergei Pavlovich Diaghilev, in Novgorod, the son of a Russian general and an aristocrat, who died in childbirth, as a child Diaghilev studied piano and through the musical connections of the family of his stepmother, met TCHAIKOVSKY and Mussourgsky.

A product of privilege, Diaghilev was a dandified young man, tall, with a large head and, by his own admission, a foppish manner. He studied law in St Petersburg from 1890, but soon gravitated to music, studying with Rimsky-Korsakov, who discouraged his ambitions to compose. Graduating in 1894, he determined, instead, to become a patron of the arts. Despite his meagre fortune, he began to organise exhibitions of Russian artists. In 1898, he co-founded with his cousin Dmitri Filosofovy *Mir Iskusstva* (World Art), a magazine of arts and letters. In 1899, he organised an exhibition of French Impressionists and, in 1901, the Society for Evenings of Contemporary Music. Appointed assistant to the Director of the Maryinsky Theater, St Petersburg, in 1899, he edited the theatre annual and participated in producing operas. In 1906, having depleted his own personal fortune and pressured by the homophobia of St Petersburg society, he left for the more tolerant and artistically progressive climate of Paris.

In Paris, he organized an exhibition of Russian art and, the following year, a concert series of music by Russian composers. Diaghilev's greatest triumph to date came in 1908, when he presented Fyodor Chaliapin in *Boris Godounov* at the Paris Opera. The success of this season led to an invitation to stage a season of Russian opera and ballet in Paris the next year. The extraordinary success of the first Paris season of the Ballets Russes, in 1909, not only introduced such immortal dancers as Pavlova, NIJINSKY, Karsavina, Fokine and Bolm, but heralded the birth of the most important artistic enterprise in the Western world. The masterworks produced for seasons in Paris, Berlin, Vienna, Budapest, Monte Carlo, London, Spain, North and South America represented nothing less than the birth of twentieth-century art. If Diaghilev had been responsible only for the 1913 premiere of Stravinsky's *Le Sacre du Printemps* with Nijinsky's revolutionary choreography, his position as a dominant force in the world of art would have been assured.

Diaghilev possessed perhaps the greatest gift of the century for 'sniffing out' unique talent, if not genius, in dancers, choreographers, composers and designers. Those who worked for him briefly or for long duration comprise a 'who's who' of twentieth-century art, music and dance: choreographers Fokine, Nijinsky, Massine, Nijinska and Balanchine; composers Stravinsky, Ravel, Poulenc, Milhaud, Satie, de Falla and Prokofiev; designers Bakst, Benois, Picasso, Roerich, Gontcharova, TCHELITCHEV, Matisse, Rouault and Jean COCTEAU. Among the ambitious young talents who sought his endorsement were Cole PORTER, George Gershwin, John Alden Carpenter, Kurt Weill, Vladimir Dukelsky (Vernon Duke) and Nicolas Nabokov. Under his guidance, the Ballets Russes produced, with the possible exception of the New York City Ballet, an unmatched repertoire of masterworks including *Les Sylphides, Carnaval, Schéhérazade, Firebird, Le Spectre de la Rose, Petrouchka, L'Après-midi d'un*

Faune, Jeux, Le Sacre du Printemps, Le Coq d'Or, Parade, La Boutique Fantasque, Le Tricorne, Le Chant du Rossignol, The Sleeping Princess, Les Femmes de Bonne Humeur, Les Noces, Les Biches, Le Train Bleu, Apollon Musagète, Le Bal and *Le Fils Prodigue*. So infallible was his artistic taste that even the most independent of artists, including Stravinsky and Richard Strauss, were persuaded to alter their compositions on his recommendation. Dancers, artistic collaborators and staff, whom he often pitted against each other, lived in fear of offending him and more often than not acquiesced to his wishes rather than their own.

The impact of Diaghilev's 20-year reign over Western art is immeasurable. The Ballets Russes was the wellspring not only of modern art, music and dance but of twentieth-century culture and aesthetics as well. Nothing, not even coming from his privileged and cultivated background, seems to explain the development of the greatest genius for artistic entrepreneurship of the century. Nothing, perhaps, except his homosexuality. Tirza True Latimer convincingly argues that Diaghilev's obsessive desire to succeed in the world of art was rooted in a fear that failure would bring the condemnation of a homophobic society down on his head. Diaghilev's homosexuality unquestionably influenced the artistic mission of the Ballets Russes, with its promulgation of the exotic, the sensual, the androgynous, the aesthetic of 'the other'. Diaghilev's glorification of the male dancer and the male body paved the way for the acceptance of male dancing and revolutionised ballet in the twentieth century.

Diaghilev paid dearly for his extraordinary successes. As with other men of genius, there was a touch of tragedy and madness to all his endeavours. Aside from his 14-year relationship with Dmitri Filosofov, Diaghilev never had a successful love affair. He had a propensity for falling in love with extraordinary artists, including Nijinsky, Massine, Anton Dolin, Serge Lifar and Igor Markhevitch, but none seemed capable of returning the same-sex love he craved. Those who might have returned that love he seldom found sexually attractive, his secretary Boris Kochno being a prime example. A lifetime of frustrated personal happiness made Diaghilev alternately and unpredictably generous and considerate, or vindictive and tyrannical.

After a particularly devastating bout with diabetes, Diaghilev left London after a triumphant Covent Garden season for Venice, where he died on 19 August 1929. Without its guiding force, the Ballets Russes disbanded, but the Diaghilev legacy survived through the subsequent work of its dancers, artists and choreographers in Europe and the United States, in particular through the Ballet Russe de Monte Carlo, Sadler's Wells (later Britain's Royal Ballet), Ballet Theater and the New York City Ballet.

S. Grigoriev, *The Diaghilev Ballet, 1909–1929,* London, 1953; R. Buckle, *Diaghilev,* London, 1979; L. Garafola, *Diaghilev's Ballets Russes,* New York, 1989; T. T. Latimer, *A Skirted Issue: Diaghilev's Sexual Orientation,* Pacific Grove, Calif., 1998.

A. M. *Wentink*

Dickinson, Emily (1830–1886), American poet. Unknown and virtually unpublished during her lifetime, Dickinson is now regarded as a writer of genius, arguably America's greatest poet. Along with Whitman, she embodies in her work a spirit of individualism, unconventionality and innovativeness that transcends the century in which she lived and wrote.

Dickinson was born in Amherst, Massachusetts into a prominent family: her grandfather was one of the founders of Amherst College, her father a distinguished lawyer and member of both the Massachusetts and the United States House of Representatives. One of three children, Dickinson attended Mt Holyoke Female Seminary for just one year, living the rest of her life in the elegant family homestead on Main Street in Amherst. Although she became a virtual recluse after the age of 30, the scope and grandeur of the subjects of her verse – love, death, nature, faith, immortality – belie the outward simplicity of her daily life.

Writing within the conventions of a variety of hymnal forms – usually the common metre – Dickinson experimented with off-rhyme, unorthodox punctuation, and a bold use of language and metaphor. After Dickinson's death in 1886, her sister Lavinia retrieved over 1,000 neatly bound poems from the poet's bedroom. With the help of their brother Austin's long-time lover, Mabel Loomis Todd, and Thomas Wentworth Higginson, a well known man of letters, a selection of poems was published in 1890. The critical and popular reception was immediate, but it was not until the 1950s that authoritative volumes of the poetry and letters, edited by Thomas Johnson, appeared. Since then, Dickinson's reputation, as well as the number of critical studies about her poetry, has steadily risen.

The eminence of Dickinson's position in the canon of American literature and the elusive nature of the details of her life have also resulted in much speculation and myth-making. A great deal has been written about the male 'masters' in Emily Dickinson's world, among them Higginson; the Reverend Charles Wadsworth, a Philadelphia minister; Samuel Bowles, newspaper editor of the *Springfield Daily Republican*, which published seven of Dickinson's poems; and Otis Lord, a Massachusetts judge with whom Dickinson formed a close attachment in her later years. More recent Dickinson criticism, however, has focused on her intense relationships with a number of women, especially Susan Gilbert Dickinson.

Often communicating to relatives and friends through short poems and letters, Dickinson lavished on 'Sue/Susie' literally hundreds of dense and often passionate communiqués. Even allowing for the liberal affectional conventions of nineteenth-century female friendship, Dickinson's expressed feelings for her school friend and later sister-in-law and lifelong neighbour argue for a lesbian interpretation. Whatever the exact nature of the relationship, however, what is indisputable is that Susan Dickinson provided the poet with the inspiration for some of her most deeply-felt writing.

J. Farr, *The Passion of Emily Dickinson*, Cambridge, Mass. 1992; S. Juhasz, *Feminist Critics Read Emily Dickinson*, Bloomington, 1983; R. B. Sewell, *The Life of Emily Dickinson*, 2 Vols, New York, 1974; C. G. Wolff, *Emily Dickinson*, New York, 1986.

David Garnes

Dickinson, G(oldsworthy) Lowes (1862–1932), British scholar. Born in London, the son of a portrait-painter, Dickinson spent most of his life at King's College, Cambridge, first as a student, then as a fellow. He lectured in history and political science, and his first published works were *Revolution and Reaction in Modern France* (1892) and *The Development of Parliament during the Nineteenth Century* (1895). He had read classics, however, and they remained his dearest scholarly love. *The Greek View of Life*, which went through several dozen editions after it was first published in 1896, was a widely hailed overview of ancient Athenian attitudes towards religion, the state, the individual and art. Dickinson argued that the ancients were profoundly modern in their views and that a study of Greek culture, even in translation, was of great importance to the contemporary world, a theme to which he returned in *After Two Thousand Years: A Dialogue between Plato and a Modern Young Man* (1930). Dickinson was also interested in Chinese culture and, even before he had visited China, published a successful volume of *Letters from John Chinaman* (1901), which critically appraised the potential negative impact of Western imperialism. During

World War I, Dickinson's attention turned to current affairs, as he wrote several studies of European politics, espoused pacificism and drafted plans for a 'league of nations' (a phrase which he probably invented).

Dickinson lived the quiet life of a Cambridge don, punctuated by regular sojourns in London, lecture tours of the United States and trips to the Mediterranean, China and (with his close friend E. M. FORSTER) to India. *The Autobiography of G. Lowes Dickinson*, published only in 1973, discussed in detail his homosexual passions. Dickinson fell deeply in love with a series of men, beginning with the Bloomsbury art critic Roger Fry, though it is unlikely that this or any of his affairs were fully consummated. (He also confessed to a lifelong boot fetish.) He remarked of his physical desire: 'Owing to frustration, it has continued to possess me without ever being able to fuse with the other currents of life.' That Forster's 1934 biography of his friend does not discuss his sexuality is revealing about both Forster and Dickinson himself, as well as about the social disapproval of homosexuality at the time.

Dickinson was a popular and very influential scholar and teacher, and the male camaraderie of his Cambridge college provided a congenial environment for close contacts and warm friendships with young men. His interest in ancient Greece, and the delight he experienced on his visits to Athens and Rome – where his descriptions evoke both VIRGIL and WINCKELMANN – are similar to the feelings of many classically trained scholars who found in Antiquity their spiritual and sexual home. The editor of his autobiography also suggests that his 'capacity for strong passion and the pain it brings … animated his lifelong concern for the suffering of humanity.'

E. M. Forster, *Goldworthy Lowes Dickinson and Related Writings*, London, 1973; G. Lowes Dickinson, *The Autobiography of G. Lowes Dickinson and Other Unpublished Writings*, ed. D. Proctor, London, 1973.

Robert Aldrich

Dobell, Sir William (1899–1970), Australian painter. Dobell was born in Newcastle, New South Wales, Australia, the youngest in a working-class family of three girls and three boys. At school Dobell showed some talent for drawing and later, as a young man, he preferred to pursue art rather than girls. In 1916 he began drafting work for a local architect and in 1923 moved to Sydney, drafting for a building supplies firm. In 1929 he won the Society of Artists' Travelling Scholarship which enabled him to study in London.

In Sydney Dobell studied at Julian Ashton's Art School evening classes and in London he enrolled in the Slade School of Fine Art; he also had private lessons. In late 1930 Dobell left the Slade and began exploring art museums in Europe. He shared Rembrandt's ability to see beauty and uniqueness in the commonplace. This was Dobell's most creative period. For a while he shared a studio with the Australian artist John Passmore, then with Eric Wilson. From 1936 to 1938 the Australian artist Donald Friend lived nearby and the two shared their interests in music, art and men.

At the end of 1938 Dobell returned to Sydney and took a flat in Bohemian Kings Cross, where he found the atmosphere similar to the London he had just left. He began part-time art teaching at East Sydney Technical College, which continued until he began war work in 1941. Dobell's painting was promoted by the publisher Sydney Ure Smith, who believed he had exceptional ability. The writer Patrick White saw Dobell's painting *The Dead Landlord* (1936), which was later to inspire his play *The Ham Funeral*. After White returned to Australia in 1948 he and Dobell were friends for some years. White saw in Dobell's work 'flashes of homosexual brilliance and insight'. The friendship soured after White's perceptive observation that Dobell had sold out to the society they had once criticised and that he had let the quality of his work suffer.

In 1942 Dobell was appointed an official war artist. For a time he shared a tent with a younger artist, Joshua Smith, who was later to be the subject of Dobell's 1943 Archibald Prize-winning portrait which led to Australia's most notorious art court case. He won the case against the claim that his portrait of Smith was not a portrait because it was a caricature. As a war artist Dobell depicted construction workers, lumpers and labourers involved in the war effort. His paintings of male figures show both strength and beauty and sometimes wry humour. His wartime portraits are his best: *Billy Boy*, *The Strapper*, *The Cypriot*. In 1948 and 1959 he again won the Archibald Prize for portrait painting. He also received a number of other prizes and commissions, including four covers for *Time* magazine. In 1949 and 1950, Dobell visited New Guinea, where he was intrigued by the unconscious sensuality of the highlanders. His New Guinea paintings were criticised so he returned to portraits.

In 1964 Dobell was given a retrospective exhibition at the Art Gallery of New South Wales. He was knighted in 1966 for his contribution to Australian art. After Dobell's death his estate went to the creation of the Dobell Foundation, which funds a chair of fine art at the Australian National University, a drawing prize and other grants. Dobell is one of Australia's most significant artists, but his homosexuality was known only to a small circle of friends.

B. Adams, *Portrait of an Artist: A Biography of William Dobell*, Melbourne, 1983; M. Eagle, 'William Dobell', *Australian Dictionary of Biography*, Vol. 14, Melbourne, 1996; J. Gleeson, *William Dobell*, London, 1964, rev. edn, Sydney, 1981; B. Pearce, *William Dobell, 1899–1970: The Painter's Progress*, Sydney, 1997.

Ian Maidment

Domitian (Titus Flavius Domitianus) (51–96), Roman emperor. The second son of Emperor Vespasian and brother of the Emperor Titus, Domitian was named praetor in 70 and succeeded his brother as emperor in 81. Domitian successfully promoted Roman expansion in Britain and on the Rhine, but failed to defeat the Dacians in an effort to move beyond the Danube. In domestic politics, he abandoned an alliance with the most conservative elements of the Roman aristocracy which had supported his father and brother. Instead he tried to win the favour of the populace in order to crush the old republican aristocracy's opposition to the empire. This strategy – including suits for *lèse-majesté* and confiscations – provoked a reaction from the oligarchy, which organised a conspiracy (in which Domitian's own wife took part) during which the emperor was killed.

Because of the opposition to Domitian, the accusation that he was homosexual, advanced by historians connected with the aristocracy, is dubious. Among such charges, SUETONIUS's report that the young Domitian prostituted himself to both the Emperor Nerva and the praetor Claudius Pollio appears to be calumny hurled at a political opponent. Philostratus the Lemnian Senior told the story of a very handsome Greek youth imprisoned for having resisted Domitian's advances who became celebrated for his virtue on his release. Yet this moralistic anecdote appears in the *Life of Apollonius of Tyana* (VII. 42), the biography of a Greek philosopher, that could only be hostile to Domitian because of his expulsion of all philosophers from Rome and Italy. Similar is an attack by Dio Cassius, who says in his *Roman History* that Domitian, despite his love for the eunuch Earinus, prohibited castration solely to impugn the memory of Titus, a lover of eunuchs. The hostility to Domitian was perpetuated at least until Tertullian, a Christian writer, who in *De pallio* (IV. 2–9) included him in a list of notoriously dissolute Romans.

Certainly more reliable are the accounts given in two works favourable to Domitian, which reveal his relationship with Earinus. The poet MARTIAL lauds Domitian for having outlawed castration, thus protecting youths from being seduced (IX. 4 and 7), and praises Earinus, who in a series of epigrams (IX. 11–13, 16–17, 36) is likened to GANYMEDE. Statius also (*Silvae*, III. 4) praises Earinus in a composition celebrating reaching adulthood. Earinus, according to Statius, changed sex in a painless operation effected by Apollo. The mythological parallels, however, do not obscure the violence to which the young eunuch had to submit.

C. Henriksen, 'Earinus: An Imperial Eunuch in the Light of the Poems of Martial and Statius', *Mnemosyne*, 50 (1997): 218–94; B. W. Jones, *The Emperor Domitian*, London, 1992; P. Southern, *Domitian: Tragic Tyrant*, London, 1997.

Giovanni Dall'Orto

Doolittle, Hilda (1886–1961), American poet and novelist. An Imagist poet, novelist and translator, Doolittle was born in Bethlehem, Pennsylvania. When she was 11, her father was appointed Professor of Astronomy at the University of Pennsylvania and the family moved to Philadelphia. She was 15 when she met the poet Ezra Pound and a close relationship developed between them. She then entered Bryn Mawr College to study Greek literature, and a year later became engaged to Pound, but she encountered health difficulties and withdrew from university. During this time she also fell in love with her first woman lover, Frances Josepha Gregg, but responded to Pound's requests that she move to London.

By 1912, H.D., as she had become known, had begun writing poetry and became a founder of the Imagist tradition. In 1913 she travelled to Italy with Pound and Richard Aldington and subsequently married Aldington. D. H. LAWRENCE became a close friend, housemate and literary com-patriot of the couple while he was writing *The Rainbow*, and his expressively sexual writing influenced her work. When Aldington joined the army during World War I, H.D. replaced him as the Assistant Editor of The *Egoist* and began publishing her first books.

Her poetry was known for its unusual beauty and special uses of language, grammar and punctuation. She used literal presentations in her work, and offered a very subjective orientation, with extensively crafted detail. She often depicted romantic relationships between women, sometimes including oblique erotic passages. Her poems are presentations of situations, and she drew upon her psychoanalysis by FREUD, nature, liberating images and views of women, Moravian history and doctrine, pagan mysticism and principles developed by other Imagist poets in her work.

Her marriage to Aldington floundered, and in 1918 she met Bryher (Annie Winifred Ellerman) who became her lover and closest companion for the rest of her life, though she remained formally married to Aldington until 1938. H.D. became pregnant by Cecil Gray, giving birth to a daughter in 1919, the same year she published *Choruses from the Iphigeneia in Aulis and the Hippolytus* and a translation of Euripides. Bryher provided emotional and financial support for her while she was raising her young daughter and proceeding with her writing and travels.

In 1922 H.D. moved into Bryher's home in Switzerland and wrote extensively, publishing over 20 books. She had a stroke and died in 1961 at a clinic in Switzerland, where Bryher had nursed her during the last months of her life.

J. S. Robinson, *H.D.: The Life and Work of an American Poet*, Boston, 1982; C. Summers (ed.) *The Gay and Lesbian Literary Heritage*, New York, 1995.

Sarah Holmes

Doone, Rupert (1903–66), British dancer and choreographer. Born Ernest Reginald

Woodfield in Redditch, England, the son of a Worcestershire needle factory foreman, at age 16 Doone ran away from home to find a career on stage. He became a pupil of leading ballet teachers in residence in London, including Serafina Astafieva and Margaret Craske, and worked with Michel Fokine. At 19, he left London for Paris, where he became a protégé and lover of Jean COCTEAU. An extraordinary performer, Doone was soon hailed the 'rage of Paris' and was a featured soloist in the 1923 Paris season of the Ballet Suédois. His partnering of the legendary Cléo de Mérode in a 1924 social dance recital reportedly encouraged the teenage Frederick Ashton to pursue a career in dance. That same year he appeared in Cocteau's *Roméo et Juliette* and partnered ex-DIAGHILEV ballerina Lydia Lopokova in Etienne de Beaumont's *Vogue* for 'Les Soirées de Paris'. But his terrible temper quickly alienated his fellow dancers. Despite Cocteau's pleas for sympathy, claiming that Doone 'clings to my coat-tails like a stray dog', he was dismissed from the company.

Returning to London in 1924, he understudied Massine in *Charlot's Revue*, once again partnering Lopokova, and, in 1925, staged the dance interlude for Nigel Playfair's production of *The Duenna* at the Lyric, Hammersmith. In 1926, Doone met and became the lover of painter Robert Medley with whom he returned to Paris. As members of the Ida Rubinstein company in its Paris season in 1928, Doone and Ashton became bitter rivals: Ashton longed to be a soloist like Doone, who in turn was harshly critical of Ashton's choreographic efforts. During this season, Doone was noticed by Diaghilev, who engaged him as principal dancer for the Ballets Russes' Covent Garden season in June 1929. His career with that legendary company was cut short when the impresario died in August and the company disbanded. At this point, Doone largely gave up dance to concentrate on theatre. Doone's other dance associations include the Nemtchinova–Dolin Ballet, the Camargo Society, the Ballet Club and the Vic–Wells Ballet, where he choreographed *The Enchanted Grove* (1932). In 1933, he arranged dances for the Cambridge Theatre, where he met the innovative director Tyrone Guthrie.

In 1930, Doone began an apprenticeship with Guthrie at the Festival Theatre, Cambridge, and thereafter worked primarily as a director of dramatic productions for the remainder of his career. In 1932, he and Medley formed the Group Theatre, intended as a slightly leftist creative enterprise which, they hoped, would be 'self-sufficient and independent of purely commercial considerations' and whose works would have 'directness yet fantasy'. W. H. Auden saw the Group Theatre as a progressive community 'who do everything and do it together'. Auden's first collaboration with Doone and Medley, *The Dance of Death* (1933), an anti-Nazi multimedia work featuring jazz orchestra and Doone as 'Death the Dancer', caused a sensation at its 1934 London performances. Doone also directed and produced *The Dog Beneath the Skin* (1936), *The Ascent of F6* (1937) and *On the Frontier* (1939) by Auden and Christopher Isherwood. Among other Group Theatre collaborators were Benjamin Britten, Henry Moore, T. S. Eliot, William Butler Yeats, Stephen SPENDER, Duncan GRANT, Adrian Stokes, Havelock ELLIS, Richard Masefield, Harold NICOLSON and Anton Dolin. Doone produced and directed for the group between 1932 and 1939, and again between 1946 and 1951. In addition to his work with the Group Theatre, Doone was director at Morley College (1939–1965), concentrating on revivals of restoration comedies and experimental plays by contemporary poets. Doone died of multiple sclerosis.

H. Carpenter, *W. H. Auden: A Biography*, Boston, 1982; R. Medley, *Rupert Doone Remembered by his Friends*, London, 1966; G. Morris,

'The Story of Rupert Doone', in the *Dancing Times*, April 1984.

A. M. *Wentink*

Dorval, Marie (1798–1849), French actress. Dorval's reputation for bisexuality is emblematic of the way that lesbianism was perceived in nineteenth-century France. What mattered was not what she *did*, but what she was and whom she knew. She was born Marie Delaunay, the illegitimate child of two members of a travelling theatre company that happened to be passing through the town of Lorient. She was abandoned by her father when she was barely 5 and her mother died of tuberculosis while she was still a child. Her marriage at the age of 15 to an actor-manager old enough to be her father, Allan-Dorval, resulted from a need for security rather than the fulfilment of a passion. It was a short-lived security, however, since in 1818 her husband died while on a trip to Russia, leaving Marie with two small children.

Though she had been on the stage since she was 4, it was only in 1827, at the Porte Saint-Martin theatre in Paris, that she had her first triumph, playing opposite the future matinée idol Frederick Lemaître in a popular melodrama called *Trente ans, ou La vie d'un joueur*. There were practical ways to protect her career, and they involved men. In 1829 she married the journalist Merle, who had been an owner of the Porte Saint-Martin at the time Dorval first obtained a contract there. Merle was a complacent husband and Dorval pursued the interests of her career determinedly. In 1831 she made the acquaintance of Alexandre Dumas (the elder), a notorious womaniser, and thus secured the plum role of Adèle in his high melodrama of illegitimate passion, *Antony*. This in turn secured her the even better and more prestigious title role in Hugo's verse drama *Marion Delorme*. From 1832 to 1838 she had an affair with Count Alfred de Vigny, which won her the role of Kitty Bell in his play *Chatterton* at the Comédie-Française in 1834. The play was one of the major on-stage successes of French Romantic drama – a success not unconnected with the sensation Dorval caused by an unrehearsed (but well planned) swoon down a flight of stairs at the dramatic high-point of the play, and this in turn earned her another role in a Victor Hugo play, *Angélo, tyran de Padoue*, for the same company.

That a woman with such a well publicised heterosexual life should be labelled a lesbian seems very odd to late twentieth-century eyes. But the fact is that as an actress, she was already a member of a class who were considered to be promiscuous and totally without moral scruples. When a poem titled *The Lesbians of Paris* began to go the rounds in 1845, for example, it was the practice to add new verses devoted to new actresses from year to year as a matter of course. Some rumours were true: Baudelaire's mistress, the mulatto actress Jeanne Duval, was certainly bisexual. Other rumours were almost certainly fanciful. Already in 1833 gossip associated Dorval with Juliet Drouet, Hugo's mistress. When, in the same year, George Sand – who not only wrote novels (another dangerously immoral activity for a woman in the eyes of 1830s society) but dressed in men's clothing and publicly conducted a liaison with a man scarcely out of adolescence (Jules Sandeau) – started to take an interest in Dorval, the 'obvious' explanation was the one that imposed itself. The truth of the matter cannot be known. The two certainly enjoyed a passionate friendship whose intensity is testified to by the surviving correspondence. Sand had a propensity for mothering people, her male lovers (Musset, Chopin) as much as anyone; at the same time, at nearly 30 she had never received any proper mothering herself. Dorval needed emotional support and female friendship; she was herself full of maternal feelings. (The resulting friendship was strong enough to last until Dorval's death: one of the first people to whom her daughter Caroline wrote with the news was Sand.) Arsène Houssaye, in his *Confessions*, dramatised the gossip of the period and gave it more tangible shape. The fact that from Balzac's *La Fille aux yeux d'or* (1834) to Pierre LOUŸS's *Chansons de Bilitis* (1895) male writers in nineteenth-century France were obsessed with the question of lesbianism says more about their own hangups than about contemporary female sexuality, just as the reputations handed out to actresses are a poor reflection on social prejudice and bourgeois hypocrisy.

Whether Dorval found a substitute mother, daughter or lover in Sand, her own sense of insecurity was in any case well justified. When theatrical fashions changed in the early 1840s she too went out of fashion. Despite her critical success in the title role of Ponsard's *Lucrèce* (1843) and a popular triumph in d'Ennery's melodrama *Marie-Jeanne ou la Femme du peuple* (1845), she was rapidly condemned to touring in the provinces, and died in poverty and neglect.

A. Gaylor, *Marie Dorval: Grandeur et misère d'une actrice romantique*, Paris, 1989.

Christopher Robinson

Douglas, Lord Alfred (Bruce) (1870–1945), British poet, editor. The third son of the eccentric and irascible ninth Marquess of Queensberry (compiler of the 'Queensberry Rules' for boxing), Lord Alfred Douglas was born near Worcester. From babyhood his mother called him 'Boysie', which became 'Bosie', the nickname by which he was known all his life.

When Douglas was 16 his parents divorced because of Queensberry's adultery. Douglas was very close to his mother and his relations with his father deteriorated irretrievably from that time. He entered Magdalen College, Oxford, in 1889. Although he never graduated, he was prominent in literary affairs, and his extraordinarily good looks won him numerous admirers who led him into sexual adventures, mostly homosexual.

In 1891 Douglas, then aged 20, met the celebrated wit, poet and playwright Oscar WILDE, 16 years his senior. They became intimate friends. Wilde was captivated by Douglas's youthful beauty and valued his ready entrée to aristocratic circles. Douglas, a conceited youth, was flattered to be a confidant of one of the country's most successful writers, and enjoyed the attention and respect this brought. Their relationship was primarily based on intellectual and emotional compatibility, but it was also homosexual. Douglas, the more experienced of the two in such matters, later admitted: 'So far from his leading me astray, it was I that (unwittingly) pushed him over the precipice.'

Embarrassing gossip about his son's relationship with Wilde caused Queensberry to pursue an irrational vendetta which led, in 1894, to his being sued by Wilde for libel. Wilde's friends had urged him to ignore what was, in reality, no more than a reckless outburst by a notorious eccentric, but Douglas, who hated his father and selfishly saw an opportunity to humiliate him, persuaded Wilde to sue. Wilde's judgement, clouded by his infatuation with Douglas, let him down fatally. Wilde lost the case and some of the evidence produced against him was so damning that he was promptly arrested, tried and imprisoned for gross indecency.

After Wilde's conviction, Douglas fled to France and published fervent letters and articles in defence of Wilde and of homosexuality. Upon Wilde's release in 1896 they resumed their friendship, and until Wilde's death in 1900 Douglas supported him financially and emotionally.

Queensberry also died in 1900 and Douglas inherited a modest fortune, which was soon dissipated through gambling. In March 1902 Douglas eloped with another poet, Olive Custance. Although she had private means, money became a persistent problem for Douglas after his inheritance dwindled away, and for most of his life he earned an erratic living as a poet, freelance writer, reviewer and editor of several literary magazines. Though happy at first, the marriage broke down about 1913, due primarily to Douglas's quarrels with Olive's father, who was upset by her choice of such a notorious husband. Alfred and Olive remained friends but never lived together again, though they never divorced (Douglas had converted to Roman Catholicism in 1911).

In the last decade of his life he lived alone in reduced circumstances in Hove, near Brighton, supported mainly by the generosity of friends. Some friends unsuccessfully petitioned the Prime Minister for a pension, pointing out that 'we have not his equal as a writer of sonnets'. In fact, as a poet he is generally judged to have been of modest ability and, although several of his sonnets have been highly praised, most of his work is unlikely to be remembered.

Douglas spent the majority of his life repudiating and regretting his youthful bisexuality. Although he never denied his homosexual relationship with Wilde, or his other homosexual activities at university and during his twenties, in later life he looked upon his old ways 'with utter repugnance and horror'. He once admitted that, until 1900, 'I was leading a bad life; an immoral, wicked man. I have regretted bitterly, and I have suffered from it all my life.'

He spent many years attacking Wilde's memory. In 1914 he published (but later repudiated) the autobiographical *Oscar Wilde and Myself*, in which he viciously attacked Wilde's morals. A few years later he called Wilde 'the greatest force for evil that has appeared in Europe during the last three hundred and fifty years', and regretted intensely ever having met him. But in the last 20 years of his life he abruptly changed his attitude and returned to proclaiming his loyalty to Wilde, saying that although the Wilde scandal had ruined his life he did not regret him or their friendship.

Douglas is remembered chiefly as Oscar Wilde's scandalous homosexual companion, and the cause of his spectacular downfall. His success in persuading Wilde to sue Queensberry for libel led almost certainly to the premature death of a considerable literary talent.

H. Montgomery Hyde, *Lord Alfred Douglas: A Biography*, London, 1984. Douglas published three autobiographies but they are not always reliable: *Oscar Wilde and Myself*, London, 1914 (mostly written by T. W. H. Crosland and later repudiated); *The Autobiography of Lord Alfred Douglas*, London, 1929; *Without Apology*, London, 1938.

Neil A. Radford

Douglas, Norman (1868–1952), British-German writer. George Norman Douglas was born at Thüringen in the Vorarlberg in Austria of mixed Scottish and German aristocratic lineage, and educated in England and at the Gymnasium in Karlsruhe, which gave him a sound scientific and classical education (hence his labour of love, *Birds and Beasts of the Greek Anthology* [1928]). After a brief stint in the British diplomatic service, he bought a villa at Gaiola on the Bay of Naples and later moved to Capri. In 1898 he married a cousin, Elsa Fitzgibbon, by whom he had two sons before he divorced her on the grounds of her infidelity in 1903. However, in 1897 he had become erotically involved with Michele, the 15-year-old brother of a temporary mistress, and after his divorce, his principal erotic and emotional interests were pederastic ('I've always liked a very small possessor attached to a very large possession', quotes Michael Davidson, paraphrasing him 'slightly'). From his Capri period onwards, there are records of a succession of boyfriends, named and nameless, some short-term, others who remained friends for life. In 1916 he chose, unlike WILDE in 1895, flight from England to Italy, skipping bail after he was charged with sexual assault of a 16-year-old. On at least two subsequent occasions, he had to leave Italy temporarily for similar prudent reasons, and on another, in 1930, he decamped post-haste from the Vorarlberg where he used to holiday in summer, when a policeman, come to check his passport, discovered him 'giving a lesson' to Fifo, his young Austrian friend of that season.

In 1904 he issued the first of a series of ten booklets on the topography, flora and fauna, and history of Capri, which were followed by his three best-known travel books, *Siren Land* (1911) on the Bay of Naples, *Fountains in the Sand: Rambles among the Oases of Tunisia* (1912) and *Old Calabria* (1915). Two further travel books, *Alone* (1921) and *Together* (1923), introduced a far more personal note. Indeed, the latter, an account of two summers in the Vorarlberg, features a travelling companion, Mr R, whom readers at the time were not to know was a 15-year-old Italian, René.

South Wind (1917), the novel for which he is chiefly remembered, is an amusing narrative of the fortnight's residence among the foreign colony on Capri of a colonial English bishop on his way home. Much of the action in the book, which Douglas largely wrote in London immediately before his exile, takes place in conversation, and he typically permitted himself the luxury of two characters, Mr Keith and Count Caloveglia, to express his philosophy, opinions and prejudices, although Keith, a wealthy, egoistical Scottish bachelor, is also sometimes satirized. Several of the characters might well be homosexual, but the Count is the only one of whom it is directly hinted. Unlike later novelists of Capri – Compton MACKENZIE and Roger Peyrefitte – Douglas did not deal explicitly with homosexuality but contented himself with creating an ambience in which it could well be flourishing.

The closest he came to expressing his views on homosexuality was his strange little volume *Paneros* (1930, 1931), which begins as an aphrodisiological investigation, but evolves into an exposition of his erotic philosophy, and specifically the art of getting sex. The discussion is notable for its not specifying the sex of the person one is seeking to bed. His principal volume of memoirs, *Looking Back* (1933), is likewise marked by a reticence about the sexuality of the multitudinous people who are remembered by their visiting cards. One learns, however, to read between the lines.

This absence of candour where we now expect it reminds us forcefully that for all the open confidence with which he lived his life and defied hypocritical custom, he was a child of Victorian times. His writing and his behaviour often reveal that he never escaped a sense of naughtiness, and his paganism is defined by contrast with Christianity. Moreover, his pride, egoism, hedonism and disdain for politics and democracy bespeak his aristocratic origins; he brooked no interruption of his pursuit of pleasure and the work that he chose to perform. It would never have occurred to him to involve himself in agitation for homosexual law reform (any more than for other causes); good manners dictated public reserve about essentially private matters. It sufficed that his condemnation of anti-homosexual law can be inferred from the general propositions he offers on individual freedom and sexual morality and custom.

M. Holloway, *Norman Douglas: A Biography*, London, 1976; J. Davenport, Introduction to *Old Calabria*, London, 1955; I. Greenlees, *Norman Douglas*, London, 1957.

Gary Simes

Druskowitz, Helene von (1856–1918), Austrian philosopher, literary theorist and writer. Aged only 16, Druskowitz was the first woman to sit the high school examination as a day pupil of the 'Piaristengymnasium' in Vienna. At the same time she graduated from her piano studies at the Conservatoire. Druskowitz was seen as a child prodigy with a glittering future ahead of her.

Since in 1872 the University of Vienna still did not admit women, Druskowitz's mother moved with her daughter to Zurich, where Helene, at the age of 22, was the first Austrian woman to complete a doctorate. In the following years she lectured in Vienna, Munich and Zurich, and travelled extensively in North Africa, France, Italy and Spain. Druskowitz was a committed atheist and categorically rejected marriage. She defended herself against all attempts to marry her off and proudly declared herself to be 'abnormal'.

Her literary output was extremely prolific; she published 11 plays, under various, mostly male, pseudonyms, but they were never performed. The protagonists were emancipated women – which set her at least a decade ahead of her time. She wrote literary studies on BYRON, Shelley, Joanna Baillie, Elizabeth Barrett-Browning and George Eliot, which achieved some recognition. But an academic career was not open to her. She was a friend of Rainer Maria Rilke, Lou Andreas-Salomé and Friedrich NIETZSCHE. Nietzsche wrote kindly of his admirer Druskowitz in an 1884 letter to his sister, saying that of all the women he had become acquainted with, she was by far the most earnest reader of his philosophy. However, when Druskowitz criticised his Zarathustra as a modern substitute for religion, their friendship came to an abrupt end. In 1887 Nietzsche wrote to Carl Spitteler: 'The little literature goose Druskowitz is anything but a "pupil" of mine.'

In 1887 Druskowitz began a relationship with the opera singer Teresa Malten. The two women lived together in Dresden. In 1891, at the age of 35, Druskowitz was forcibly admitted to the Dresden psychiatric hospital for reasons which are now unknown. Shortly thereafter, she was moved to the Mauer-Oehling psychiatric hospital near Vienna. She was compulsorily detained for 27 years until her death in May 1918.

Druskowitz carried on writing throughout her incarceration. In 1903 her *Pessimistische Kardinalsätze* (*Pessimistic Cardinal Propositions*) were published, available today in a new edition. She aims to show by means of logic that men are a historical and ideological failure, and that the two sexes therefore should live in divided towns. The Austrian author Elisabeth Reichert wrote a fictitious monologue for Druskowitz, which contains excerpts from her medical records.

H. von Druskowitz, *Der Mann als logische und sittliche unmöglichkeit und als Fluch der Welt. Pessimistische Kardinalsätze* (Man as Logical and Moral Impossibility and as a Curse on the World), ed. T. Hensch, Freiburg, 1988; E. Reichart, *Sakkorausch*, Salzburg, 1994.

Andrea Capovilla

Dumont, Franciscus (*c*. 1772–?), Danish-French milliner. Dumont immigrated to Denmark from France around 1800 and became a succesful and quite wealthy milliner, owning a shop on one of the main streets of Copenhagen and a factory producing artificial flowers. He married and had a daughter. Dumont was also the central figure of a small circle of men inclined to pederasty. The identity of 11 of these men is known. They were all from the middle bourgeoisie, mostly immigrant traders or men connected with the Royal Theatre. The social gatherings took place in their homes with wives and daughters present, or in taverns. Sexual activity was to a large extent directed towards young officers and soldiers. When the 16-year-old cadet Christian Fr. Schiøtt confessed in 1814 to his superiors that he had committed pederasty with most of these men (and a few others) they were, very discreetly, interrogated by a specially appointed judge. They all denied Schiøtt's allegation. Three men who did not belong to the group confessed to sodomy with Schiøtt. The government decided that silence on the matter had first priority and by Royal Order-in-Cabinet 'severe warnings' were issued. Schiøtt was exiled to the Danish West Indies. However, rumours circulated in Copenhagen of a 'Club of Infamous Pederasts', supposedly – and very unlikely – with the minister of justice, the commander of the Cadet Corps, and the unpopular head of the Royal Library as its members. Before Dumont could be officially warned, he left for France. He returned later and is known to have lived in Copenhagen in 1845.

Copenhagen was probably then a town that was still too small to sustain a sodomitical subculture. The group around Dumont could not establish continuity by recruiting new members in sufficient numbers, although several witnesses attested to attempts to do so. The investigation in 1814 was the end of the 'Dumont Circle'. There is no continuity with Copenhagen's pre-homosexual, pederastic subculture established in the 1850s. The circle around Dumont was inspired by immigrants who found a certain resonance in the world of the theatre. The consciousness of the Dumont Circle can only be deduced from the consistent denial of its members, whereas the three men who did not belong to the Dumont Circle confessed; they had no part in the collusion.

W. von Rosen, *Månens Kulør. Studier i dansk bøssehistorie 1628–1912*, Copenhagen, 1993: 270–98.

Wilhelm von Rosen

Duse, Eleonora (1859–1924), Italian actress. Duse was born in Vigevano, near Venice, of unknown parents; she had a nomadic and difficult childhood. She first went on stage as a young child and her great acting talents were already recognised by 1873, the year in which she played Juliet to great acclaim in Verona's famous arena. Her performance was bare and powerful with gestures reduced to the minimum and her lines delivered in a whispered voice. Her reputation was confirmed with her interpretation of Zola's *Thérèse Raquin* and afterwards with Dumas's *La Princesse de Baghdad*. In 1884, the year of her triumph in Verga's *Cavalleria Rusticana*, she met Arrigo Boito and entered into contact with Bohemian circles in Milan. Her repertory extended from Shakespearean characters to the heroines of nineteenth-century French drama. The last decade of the century saw an increasing interest in modern Italian and foreign drama; Duse was the first actress in Italy to perform Ibsen's *Nora* and *The Doll's House*, and thus present new images of women to the public. As well as a leading actress, she was a careful administrator of her own theatrical company, through which she aimed to expand the boundaries of the theatre and to 'raise' the standards of public taste. Her artistic and amorous relationship with Gabriele D'Annunzio was passionate but unhappy. Duse persisted in staging the works D'Annunzio wrote for her (*Il sogno di un mattino di primavera*, *La città morta*, *Gioconda*, *La figlia di Jorio*), although they did not enjoy popular appeal.

During a period in which she temporarily stopped performing after 1909, Duse began an affair with Lina Poletti (who had only just finished a relationship with the writer Sibilla ALERAMO). Their relationship was tempestuous and marked by frequent quarrels, though it left aftereffects. Poletti was considered to be a hardly respectable young woman (who dressed as a man and was a feminist and open rebel); her presence at the side of Duse, according to her own friends, compromised her integrity. Duse's friendship for the dancer Isadora Duncan was also rumoured to be a lesbian relationship. Duse maintained contacts with Italian feminism, but her political positions were relatively moderate – she could thus never keep on good terms with Aleramo. Aleramo tried to seek her favour and was particularly devoted to her (writing praises of her as a 'wandering magician', as 'adventurous in harmonies and dreams'), but the older and much more famous Duse tended to snub her.

Duse returned to the stage in 1921 – in 1916, for the only time, she had acted in a film, *Cenere* – with a repertoire centred on Ibsen and D'Annunzio; she now labelled Dumas 'rubbish', and said that the time of his plays' 'lost women' and their 'just punishment' was past. Death struck Duse on 21 April 1924 in Pittsburgh, where she was making a triumphant tour of the United States (during which the American poet Amy LOWELL was able to obtain for her all the champagne she desired: Lowell had previously fallen madly in love at first sight with Duse, in honour of whom she wrote her first lyrical verses). Duse was buried in Italy after a state funeral in the town of Asolo, a place she loved dearly and where she had bought a house in which, because of continuing renovation, she had never been able to live.

D. Danna, *Amiche, compagne, amanti*, Milan, 1994; L. Mariani, *Il tempo delle attrici, emancipazionismo e teatro in Italia tra Ottocento e Novecento*, Bologna, 1991; G. Olivieri, *Ladies Almanack. Artiste e scrittrici a Parigi e Londra negli anni Venti e Trenta*, Florence, 1992.

Maria Di Rienzo

E

Eakins, Thomas (1844–1916), American painter, sculptor and photographer. Born in Philadelphia, Eakins studied at the Pennsylvania Academy of the Fine Arts (where he would later teach) from 1862 before travelling to Paris where he enrolled at the École des Beaux-Arts, studying under the neoclassical painter Jean-Léon Gérôme from 1866 until late 1869. His final six months in Europe were spent in Spain, where the painting techniques of Velázquez made a great impression on him. Returning to Philadelphia in July 1870, he set himself up as a portrait painter with financial support from his father.

Although technically conservative, Eakins's portraits are notable for their directness and psychological presence, and his belief in the almost scientific status of realism is evident in paintings other than the portraits. For example, the *Gross Clinic* (1875) not only depicted the internationally renowned surgeon, Dr Samuel D. Gross, supervising surgery on a patient, but also portrayed the operation itself. Although the graphic realism of the painting shocked many contemporaries, Eakins again painted a similar subject, the *Agnew Clinic* (1889), which included various developments in surgery since the earlier painting such as the use of antiseptic, white operating gowns and the sterilisation of surgical instruments. Eakins's study of anatomy extended to the study of human movement and in 1884 he assisted

the photographer Eadweard Muybridge in his studies of human and animal locomotion at the University of Pennsylvania. Eakins himself was a keen photographer and, influenced by Muybridge and Etienne-Jules Marey, he produced a number of photographic studies of the figure in motion.

Many of Eakins's paintings are of sporting and leisure pursuits and depict the athletic male body in action – for example, early in his career Eakins produced a series of paintings of rowers, e.g. *Max Schmitt in a Single Scull* (1871), while boxers and wrestlers were depicted in the late 1890s, e.g. *Salutat* (1898). The importance of the male figure for Eakins is particularly evident in the many photographs that he took throughout the 1880s of himself and his (mostly male) students posing nude either in the studio or else engaged in various outdoor sporting activities. Nudity both inside the studio and beyond was intrinsic to Eakins's aim of fostering camaraderie amongst his students, as he sought to recreate within his circle the ethos and practices of an ancient Greek Academy. This self-conscious emulation of Greek life and art was evident also in the poses adopted in the photographs. The painting *The Swimming Hole* (*c.* 1883–1885), which was based upon photographs taken by Eakins and depicts a group of seven nude men comprised of Eakins and his students, can be viewed as a contemporary rendering of a classical Arcadian theme, and *Arcadia* was the title of both a painting and a plaster relief from 1883.

Although there is no evidence of any impropriety arising from the nudity of Eakins and his students (indeed, the practice was supported by both his wife, whom he married in 1884, and his father-in-law), it was none the less an unconventional practice and a number of negatives were destroyed after Eakins's death. Following a dispute between Eakins and the Pennsylvania Academy of Fine Arts over student admissions, the Board of Directors forced him to resign in 1886 – ostensibly over a claim that he had removed the loincloth from a male model in a mixed life drawing class. In 1887 Eakins met the poet Walt WHITMAN, then aged 68, and painted a highly empathetic portrait of him, which Whitman declared his favourite of the many portraits made of him. The two developed a close friendship based upon a shared disregard for social conventions and a belief that their contemporaries had misunderstood them. In his final years, however, Eakins did receive greater recognition by winning several prizes both in the US and overseas. He died in Philadelphia, his growing reputation as a key figure in American realist painting secured by memorial exhibitions held in New York and Philadelphia in 1917 and 1918.

S. Danly and C. Liebold, *Eakins and the Photograph*, Philadelphia, 1994; W. Davis, 'Erotic Revision in Thomas Eakins's Narratives of Male Nudity', *Art History*, 17, 3 (1994): 301–44; E. Johns, *Thomas Eakins: The Heroism of Modern Life*, Princeton, 1983.

David L. Phillips

Edward II (1284–1327), king of England. Edward was born at Caernavon and became King of England on the death of his father in 1307. His reign was dogged from without by an intractable war with Scotland and from within by a war of attrition with his own nobility that led to his mur-

der in 1327. But the opening of these troubles was Edward's love for his friend Piers Gaveston, the son of a Gascon nobleman. Edward had probably already met and fallen in love with Gaveston by 1301; and when he became king, Edward's nobles were to grow violently to resent the power that Gaveston's closeness to Edward gave over them and engineered his death in 1312.

In later centuries, Edward II's tragic love for Gaveston was to be the recurring subject of novels, poetry and drama; but in fourteenth-century chronicles (and in a contemporary royal document) he is characterised rather in terms that correspond to the Middle English expression 'wedded' or 'sworn' brother. Wedded brotherhood was a form of voluntary kinship: kinship formed not through blood but by promise and ritual. In modern society the only voluntary kinship is marriage. In the past there were others also, and wedded brotherhood was one of these.

It could be entered into in both a traditional customary form in which promises were exchanged and by being solemnised in church. A contemporary description early in the fifteenth century describes a Mass and Holy Communion together as being at that point at least a conventional part of the ritual. This is presumably the reason why, in the case of two English esquires in 1421, the promises are referred to as having been made in church and why the tomb monument of two such wedded brothers from the fourteenth century, William Neville and John Clanvowe, depicts them as exchanging the liturgical embrace that preceded Holy Communion in the Mass. One commentator implies that the Mass used was the same as the betrothal Mass; in Greek Christianity there was a distinctive liturgy, the *Adelphopoiesis*: literally a rite for 'the making of brothers' or 'sisters'.

Was the love between Edward and Gaveston homosexual? That would have gone beyond anything the Church's canon law intended to bless, but despite that fact

Edward and Gaveston's relationship probably was homosexual: canon law also did not countenance sexual relations between the ritual kin created through baptism, but jokes about the particular pleasure of sexual relations with one's 'spiritual kin' as they were called were common in medieval Europe. Late medieval canon law also disapproved of sexual relations before a betrothal was solemnised at church but was widely disregarded; and the formal unions in medieval and Renaissance Italy corresponding to English wedded brotherhood certainly in some cases did involve sexual relations, and the priests performing these blessings could hardly have been unaware of this. In Edward and Gaveston's case, the Meaux chronicle firmly records the conclusion drawn that their relationship was sexual.

Edward clearly loved Gaveston, and passionately: one contemporary chronicle says that Edward fell in love with Gaveston at first sight. Not all wedded brotherhoods were like this: some had purely pragmatic motives, such as that between King Edmund Ironside and his adversary Cnut in the eleventh century. But if Edward had been seeking that kind of alliance, he would have looked for it among his nobles, not in Gaveston, and a powerful love between wedded brothers was not unique to Edward and Gaveston. The Westminster chronicle records that the William Neville whose tomb monument was mentioned earlier died of grief a few days after his companion John Clanvowe died. Their surviving tomb monument still shows the dates of their death, a few days apart in October 1391.

It is difficult at this distance to know how common such relationships were. If the literary descriptions (such as the references in CHAUCER) are accurate, wedded brotherhood extended across society as far down as the level of peasant farmers. By the same kind of argument, the apparent absence of wedded sisters may similarly be misleading. Edward and Gaveston do, though, appear representative in having

become wedded brothers early in life: the bond created by wedded brotherhood was intended to persist across subsequent ties including those created by marriage, as it did when both Edward and Gaveston subsequently married. For most people wedded brotherhood fitted quietly into the matrix of society. Edward and Gaveston's tragedy was that theirs did not.

Wedded brothers remained a feature of English society well into the seventeenth century, and one of the last that can be discerned is that commemorated in the chapel of Christ's College, Cambridge in the joint tomb of Thomas Baines and John Finch. But by John Finch's death in 1682 a relationship like theirs was already becoming distinctly old-fashioned, and the wedded brothers of the past were soon to slip out of the collective memory of English society. Yet surviving monuments like those to William Neville and John Clanvowe or to John Finch and Thomas Baines tell a different story, and provide the historical context for the love of King Edward II of England for his wedded brother Piers Gaveston.

P. Chaplais, *Piers Gaveston: Edward II's Adoptive Brother*, Oxford, 1994; E. A. R. Brown, 'Ritual Brotherhood in Western Medieval Europe', *Traditio*, 52 (1997): 358–81; S. Düll, A. Luttrell and M. Keen, 'Faithful unto death: the tomb slab of Sir William Neville and Sir John Clanvowe, Constantinople 1391', *Antiquaries Journal*, 71 (1991): 174–90; J. Wilson, '"Two names of friendship, but one Starre"': Memorials to single-sex couples in the early modern period', *Church Monuments*, 10 (1995): 70–9; M. Rocke, *Forbidden Friendships: Homosexuality and Male Culture in Renaissance Florence*, Oxford, 1996: 170–2; J. Boswell, *Same-Sex Unions in Premodern Europe*, New York, 1994.

Alan Bray

Edwards, Albert Augustine (1888–1963), Australian hotel owner, philanthropist, politician. Born to a single mother in the depressed West End of Adelaide, South

Australia, 'Bert' Edwards believed he was the son of Charles Cameron Kingston, a radical politician and premier of South Australia in the 1890s. Edwards was brought up as a Roman Catholic. After primary schooling he worked in the city markets and by 1912 had saved enough money to open a tea shop. This became a meeting place for working-class men interested in football and gambling. Edwards took a keen interest in the local football teams, and in footballers. He soon became a successful businessman. In 1916 he bought the first of a series of hotels from where he distributed favours and patronage. On many occasions he gave employment and accommodation to young hard-up working-class men, from whom he obtained sex in return. Edwards also moved into politics. In 1914 he was elected to the Adelaide City Council and in 1917, standing for the Australian Labor Party, he won the seat of Adelaide in the South Australian state parliament. When Labor won government in 1924 Edwards became its spokesman on prisons and reformatories. In these areas he was an activist. He was responsible for setting up the state's first probation system and he abolished the inefficient State Children's Council. In the process he gained many enemies, who regarded him as a bullying troublemaker.

At the peak of his career, Edwards's homosexuality led to his political downfall. In 1930 he was charged with having committed an 'unnatural offence' upon a young man in Adelaide and an 'act of gross indecency' at a nearby seaside town. His trial in the state's Supreme Court before the Chief Justice attracted much public attention. In February 1931 the jury found Edwards guilty of having committed an unnatural offence but acquitted him on the other charge. When sentenced a few days later to five years' hard labour he created a sensation in the court by publicly attacking his accusers and the Chief Justice. Edwards's loyal supporters claimed that he had been framed and arranged three legal appeals, but without success.

Upon release from prison in June 1933 Edwards resumed hotel-keeping. He narrowly failed in several attempts to enter the state and federal parliaments. In 1948 he was re-elected to the Adelaide City Council. In his latter years he became one of the city's more flamboyant characters. He was a generous benefactor of the poor and destitute of Adelaide, and gave large sums to Roman Catholic charitable organisations. His requiem Mass in the Roman Catholic cathedral was attended by the auxiliary bishop. Edwards's career illustrated the dangers faced by homosexual men in Australian public life in the early twentieth century.

'Edwards, Albert Augustine', *Australian Dictionary of Biography*, Vol. 8, Melbourne, 1981: 415–16; R. Jennings, 'Rex v. Edwards: A Politician and the Law', *Journal of the Historical Society of South Australia*, 8 (1980): 92–8; R. R. St C. Chamberlain, 'Rex v. Edwards', *Journal of the Historical Society of South Australia*, 9 (1981): 118–20.

David Hilliard

Eekhoud, Georges (1854–1927), Belgian author. Eekhoud was to become a moving spirit in the literary world of *fin de siècle* Belgium and one of the earliest European novelists to address directly the subject of homosexuality, though his background was extremely provincial. He was born in Anvers, and though the town was in Flanders, he grew up, like all its middle-classes of the period, speaking French. Orphaned at an early age, he led a rather unsettled childhood, educated at the expense of an uncle who died while his nephew was still an adolescent. Eekhoud then joined the Ecole Royale Militaire but was expelled for unspecified disciplinary reasons after seven months. So, at the age of 19, he began a career of journalism, teaching and popular novel writing (under a pseudonym) which was to last until his death. Despite an early awareness of a taste for young working-class men, in 1883 he married a woman seven years older than himself, who had been in service in his grandmother's house. However, the marriage seems to have been based on a common of desire, in the sense that the couple would stroll in the old *quartiers* of Brussels admiring the healthy, unsophisticated young (male) peasants to whom they were both attracted

Most of Eekhoud's fiction, launched with a collection of short stories, *Kermesses*, in 1884, is set in Anvers, Brussels or the countryside around those cities, and it was as a recorder of the social and physical realities of his country that he gained his reputation. At the same time, a fascination with the sensuality of the young male, which was to come to a climax in *Voyous de velours* (1904 – originally titled *L'Autre vue*) is evident in all his writing, and as early as the story 'Le Quadrille du lancier' (*Cycle patibulaire*, 1892) the question of homosexuality is significantly raised. He also produced a translation of Christopher MARLOWE's homoerotic classic, *Edward II* (1896). It was, however, the novel *Escal-Vigor* (1899) which brought him international notoriety. This tale of the ill-fated passion of an aristocrat and a young country lad, devoid though it is of physical passion until the kiss which the unhappy couple share as they die, was the subject of a charge of corrupting public morals, in Bruges in 1900. Leading writers and public figures in both France and Belgium, including André GIDE, protested on Eekhoud's behalf, and the case was dismissed. What marks Eekhoud's portrayal of homoerotic passion both in *Escal-Vigor* and (more indirectly) in *Voyous de velours* is his sense of the homosexual as misfit, an attitude confirmed by his own reflections in his unpublished diary. None the less, the trial seems to have done him no harm, personally or publically, an outcome more or less unique for a European homosexual of the period.

M. Lucien and P. Cardon (eds) *Georges Eekhoud: un illustre uraniste*, Lille, 1996.

Christopher Robinson

Eisenstein, Sergei (Mikhailovich) (1898–1948), Russian film director and film writer. Scholars and politicians alike have been content to let Eisenstein remain a grand vizier of cinema, manipulating facts to create a series of sweeping historical events with people as icons representing basic human values, from innocence to corruption. To many, *Strike* (1924), *The Battleship Potemkin* (1925) and *October* (*Ten Days That Shook The World*) (1928) are the essence of cinema: spectacle brilliantly combined with human-scale pathos and beauty. There is perhaps now less consensus as to the merits of his two huge biographies, *Alexander Nevsky* (1938) and *Ivan the Terrible* (1945–1946), the third part of which was never filmed due to Stalin's disapproval of its increasingly obvious contemporary parallels.

For years after his death, books and television documentaries danced around one of the central themes of his life: Eisenstein's flight from disapproval on all sides because of his sexual orientation.

His seven completed films reveal an absorption and delight in the clothed and semi-clothed young male body. His passion was encouraged by the exigencies of Soviet revolutionary cinema with its emphasis upon physical fitness and comradely pursuits. His visit to Hollywood in the early 1930s and his period in Mexico making *Que Viva Mexico* (unfinished, though sections of it were assembled under the title *Time in the Sun*) enabled him to explore the fun-loving and sensuous parts of a nature often troubled and melancholic. He himself identified with Charles Dickens's autobiographical hero David Copperfield, filled with self-doubt and with strong attractions to men.

Few film artists have been able to harness all the elements of sound and vision so painstakingly for maximum consciousness and emotional impact. Eisenstein's development of montage was supremely influential on the world's film craftsmen. His collaboration with Sergei Prokofiev on

Alexander Nevsky brought about new flexibility and cunning in the use of music to underscore the image and to work (sometimes dishonestly) upon deep emotions.

Personal papers, long suppressed, have revealed an artist and a man at odds with society. His mother was openly contemptuous of his bachelorhood; innuendos about his decadent values assailed him from both bureaucrats and fellow directors. He was forced to marry his secretary at the age of 39. His 'scientific investigations' into Berlin gay bars and cafés and his (probably unconsumated) love for Grigori Alexandrov notwithstanding, he could not openly express the sexual libertarianism which had been one of the rallying calls of the Soviets in the 1920s. Often the target of suspicion and criticism, he managed to skate on bureaucratic thin ice to pursue his practical and theoretical ends in expressing feelings and ideas through the stimuli of film.

A visit to a circus as a child influenced the rest of his life. Fascinated by the clowns, he determined always to hide behind a mask so that his 'fatal weakness' would never be exposed. He wrote in a letter the day before his fatal heart attack: 'All my life, I've wanted to be accepted with affection. Yet I've felt compelled to withdraw and thus remain, forever, a spectator.'

R. Bergan, *Eisenstein: A Life in Conflict*, Boston, 1998.

Keith Howes

Elagabalus, (*c.* 205–222), Roman emperor. Every aspect of Elagabalus's life contains mystery and uncertainty except for his reign and death. He was born in Emesa (Homs in present-day Syria) to Soaemias, a cousin of Emperor Caracalla; she with her mother Julia Maesa (an aunt of Caracalla) had retired to an imperial outpost to be safe from the turmoil in Rome. Julia claimed that Elagabalus was the illegitimate son of Caracalla; the troops in Asia Minor proclaimed him emperor in 218. After a triumphant campaign, he entered Rome in 219 and ruled until 222.

While still only a teenager, Elagabalus attempted to transform the Roman Empire. Consecrated as a priest of the sun god Baal (hence his name Ela [god] Gabal [to form]: the sun-god in Syria, sometimes called 'Heliogabalus'), Elagabalus pursued three important goals which disturbed the Romans: mother-goddess worship, phallic worship and peace.

Romans notoriously welcomed many religions into Rome, but Elagabalus was the first priest to ascend to the throne. One tenet of his faith included worshipping women. He insisted that his grandmother Julia and his mother be seated in the Roman Senate, whose chambers excluded women. Only NERO had previously violated this taboo, when he had his mother enter the chamber, but she sat in the back and discreetly remained hidden by a curtain. The Senate taboo against women had been so strong that it had not been a law until after the fall of Elagabalus.

He tried to unite all the religions under one faith centred upon sexual exuberance and phallic worship. Thus he married one of the Roman Vestal Virgins and attempted to bring all the sacred objects of Rome into his own temple. When he first entered the city he carried a large phallus and pushed the worship of Baal by encouraging male castration (or, as in his own case, infibulation). He had contests to find men with the largest phalli and he formally married one of the greatest. Sex and even love between men never scandalised the Romans, but marriage was another matter. The union further scandalised the Romans because Hierocles had no royal blood, and because Elagabalus played the passive role.

His support for women and his phallic worship might have been tolerated, but his discouragement of war and his radical effeminism turned the army against him. Julia encouraged another nephew, Alexander, to foment a revolt; in 222 the soldiers brutally slaughtered Elagabalus and his mother. After hacking off his limbs, the soldiers tried stuffing the body down a sewer; failing that, they then threw the remains into the Tiber River. Statues, inscriptions and other memorials of Elagabalus were destroyed.

Both the Roman pagans and the Christians despised him, but his spirit has remained alive among poets and dramatists. Artaud wrote a celebratory work calling him *The Anarchist Crowned* (1934). Martin Duberman presented *Elagabalus* (1973) on the New York stage as a somewhat mad but remarkable Manhattan queen.

D. Magie (trans.), 'Elagabalus', *Historia Augusta*, Vol. II, London, 1980: 104–77; R. Turcan, *Héliogabale et le sacré du soleil*, Paris, 1985; M. Kleijwegt, *Ancient Youth: The Ambiguity of Youth and the Absence of Adolescence in Greco-Roman Study*, Amsterdam, 1991.

Charley Shively

Elbe, Lili (1886–1931), Danish painter. Elbe was born in Denmark and was identified as male at the time of birth. Her given name was Einar Wegener and she lived most of her life as a man. Under her given name of Einar Wegener, she became an accomplished artist, but abandoned her profession following sex reassignment surgery. Elbe's story is one of the first cases of sex reassignment to be recorded in modern history.

Prior to surgery and sex reassignment, Wegener was one-half of a marriage of artists – her wife Gerda Wegener also painted. According to the biographical work *Man into Woman*, the first time that Wegener cross-dressed was as a favour to her wife, who needed a female model to pose for one of her portraits. After cross-dressing for her wife, Wegener became convinced that she had another personality – a female one. In time, she began to feel that her female personality was dominating her person. She consulted two physicians, both of whom diagnosed her as homosexual. A third physician diag-

nosed her as intersexed and claimed she had rudimentary female sex organs. Elbe travelled to Germany for sex reassignment surgery, first to Berlin, then to Dresden and then back to Berlin. After the first four stages of the surgery, while she was living as Lili Elbe, the king of Denmark declared her earlier marriage to Gerda null and void. Elbe planned to marry after having a fifth operation performed to construct an artificial vagina, but died of heart problems before they were able to marry – her death was most probably related to the earlier surgeries.

Following Elbe's death, Ernst Ludwig Hathern Jacobson wrote the book *Man Into Woman* based on Elbe's life, letters and diary entries. In the work, Jacobson uses pseudonyms for both himself and for Wegener (Niels Hoyer and Andreas Sparre, respectively). Jacobson's biography of Elbe became one of the first popular works published that claimed that there were men who believed they were women yet were not homosexual. In this, *Man into Woman* was similar to the later work of Roberta Cowell and of Christine Jorgensen. In Jacobson's biography of Elbe, he constructed Einar Wegener's sexual desire as separate and different from that of Lili Elbe's. While a man, Einar Wegener is described as happily married to Gerda. Once Wegener becomes Lili, her sex interest is orientated towards men.

Man into Woman was read by transsexuals in the late twentieth century and received differently depending on the reader's expectations and subject position. For example, as a feminist, Sandy Stone critiqued the work for replicating socially enforced gender roles and playing into male fetishes. Renée Richards, on the other hand, read the book as a teenager and was relieved to learn that such a thing as sex reassignment surgery existed. The work *Man into Woman*, and the history of Elbe, remain important to the history of sexuality because of the distinctions they make between sexual orientation and gender orientation.

B. Bullough and V. L. Bullough, *Cross Dressing, Sex, and Gender*, Philadelphia, 1993; P. Califia, *Sex Changes: The Politics of Transgenderism*, San Francisco, 1997; N. Hoyer, *Man into Woman: An Authentic Record of a Change of Sex*, Essex, 1933; S. Stone, 'The Empire Strikes Back: A Posttranssexual Manifesto', *in Body Guards: The Cultural Politics of Gender Ambiguity*, London, 1991.

Linda Heidenreich

Ellis, Havelock (1859–1939), British sexologist and writer. Henry Havelock Ellis was the son of a sea-captain, and was largely raised by his mother, though as a child he twice sailed round the world on his father's ship. In 1875 he again travelled on his father's ship carrying emigrants to Australia, where he remained for four years teaching. During his lonely final posting at Sparkes Creek near Scone in the New South Wales bush, he had some sort of adolescent crisis, which he described as a mystico-ecstatic revelation, and he determined to devote his life to the study of sex. To this end he undertook medical training in London. His first books attracted the attention of John Addington SYMONDS, a homosexual historian and man of letters who had privately published a study of ancient Greek homosexuality in 1883 and whose last years were intellectually taken up with the defence of homosexuality against the morbidification of it in the new psychiatry of the 1880s. Symonds had published an apologia, *A Problem in Modern Ethics*, in 1891 and now wished to collaborate with a medical writer on a joint project; only thus did he believe he would gain serious consideration for his views from the medical and scientific communities. Ellis seemed to him an appropriate collaborator. After tentative soundings-out, they agreed to undertake a book, but Symonds died in 1893 before he had done much more than contribute his own and several other case-histories, a standard feature of medico-psychiatric texts of the time. Ellis went on to write the book, which was published

under both their names in German as *Das konträre Geschlechtsgefühl* (*The Contrary Sexual Sense*) in 1896 and in English as *Sexual Inversion* in 1897, volume one of his projected *Studies in the Psychology of Sex*. Symonds's family were horrified to see his name on the title-page, and his literary executor, Horatio Browne (himself gay), bought up almost all the copies. A new edition deleting Symonds's name and his named contributions (three appendixes, one of them the Greek study) was issued.

But that was not the end of the book's troubles: in 1898 a radical bookseller was charged with selling a 'lewd wicked bawdy scandalous and obscene libel' and convicted, thus making it illegal to sell the book in England. In consequence, Ellis refused to publish any more of the *Studies in the Psychology of Sex* in his native land; *Sexual Inversion*, renumbered Volume II, and the subsequent six volumes (1900–1928) were issued in the US and not openly sold in England until 1936.

Unlike most of the medico-psychological literature of the period, *Sexual Inversion* presented a non-pathological conception of homosexuality ('sexual inversion'), arguing that it is innate if also an anomaly, and not amenable to treatment. It began with a lengthy historical account, with good bibliographical support, much of the material for which had been provided by Symonds. After a survey of the existing scientific literature, Ellis then treated the subject medically, psychologically, sociologically and legally. Although Ellis was himself heterosexual, he took a sympathetic and tolerant stance, and over the next half-century many homosexuals came to an understanding and acceptance of themselves as a result of reading the book. In particular, the case-histories, many quite detailed and most positive (more gay ones were added in later volumes of the *Studies*), served to prove Ellis's argument that homosexuals were not mentally ill or neurotic and were frequently able – despite the level of social hostility and legal discrimination they faced – to lead normal, productive and satisfying lives. The greatly expanded and largely rewritten third edition of 1915 took advantage of the vast array of new material in Magnus HIRSCHFELD's magisterial *Homosexualität des Mannes und des Weibes* (1914), and in particular addressed and repudiated the defective-development ('nurture') conceptions of Freud and the psychoanalytic school. Although unfortunately the latter came to prevail for much of the twentieth century, *Sexual Inversion* remained, for long after, a humane bulwark of non-pathological thinking against the erroneous medico-psychiatric orthodoxy founded on unscientific theory.

H. Ellis, *My Life* (1939), with Introduction and detailed Bibliography by A. H. Walton, London, 1967; P. Grosskurth, *Havelock Ellis; A Biography*, London, 1980.

                                    Gary Simes

Enckell, (Knut) Magnus (1870–1925), Finnish painter. Enckell was born the sixth and youngest son in a vicar's family in a small provincial town in eastern Finland. He studied painting in Helsinki, then later in Paris at the Académie Julian, where he joined the Symbolist movement. Like other Symbolists, he was interested in Neo-Platonism and in Renaissance art, e.g. LEONARDO and MICHELANGELO. The most significant painting of Enckell's early period is *The Awakening* (1893), a youth sitting naked on a bed situated in a timeless and unrealistic space. An ascetic use of colour and simplicity are also characteristic of his other paintings during this period.

Thanks to his intellectual cosmopolitanism, Enckell became one of the leading figures in Finnish art circles. In 1907, he was asked to paint an altarpiece for the new cathedral in the city of Tampere. In the middle of this painting, which portrays the Resurrection, two men walk hand in hand – a detail that has often been ignored. Enckell's most famous works during this period are paintings of fauns. They were inspired by NIJINSKY's performance in the ballet *L'Après-midi d'un faune*, which Enckell saw in Paris at the invitation of Sergei DIAGHILEV, the manager of the Russian ballet. As a man of high repute, Diaghilev was an important contact for Enckell, and he helped Enckell arrange a section for Finnish art at the Salon d'automne exhibition in Paris in 1908. By now Enckell had turned to Post-Impressionism.

Enckell's work combines both classicism and the avant-garde of his own time. His works include various genres from murals to still-lifes. Reversibility between colour and plain line was the main feature of Enckell's work throughout his career. There was a close resemblance with Johann WINCKELMANN's views of beauty and the sublime in classical sculpture: also, to Enckell, beauty was masculine, the sublime was feminine.

Enckell died in Stockholm and his funeral was a national event. He was buried in the town of his birth. Enckell's private life has aroused fairly little interest. His love affairs with men have not been denied but they have been considered irrelevant. He never married his son's mother, Anna Emilia Holmlund, but the child was later adopted by Enckell's elder sister.

Enckell's art was perhaps too cosmopolitan to appeal to the nationalistic taste of the Finnish world of art in his own time. Yet he was a widely recognised artist. Scholars and critics have often downplayed the homoeroticism and celebration of male beauty in Enckell's work; it has been either ignored or explained in terms of sublimated emotion. In particular his little-known sketches have strong homoerotic overtones. In an original mixture of classical mythology and the modern avant-garde, Enckell's naked men and boys are openly erotic and sensual. The masculine nakedness in his paintings is never innocent.

J. Puokka, *Magnus Enckell: The Person and the*

Artist, Helsinki, 1949; S. Saraja-Korte, *Origins of Early Finnish Symbolism*, Helskinki, 1966.

Juha-Heikki Tihinen

Endymion, Greek mythological figure. Endymion was a beautiful youth, in some sources a king, in others a shepherd, who, as he slept on Mount Latmus, so moved the cold heart of Selene, goddess of the moon, that she came down and kissed him and lay with him. Upon waking, his dreams were so enticing that he begged Zeus to give him immortality and allow him to sleep perpetually on Mount Latmus. In *A Problem in Greek Ethics* (1883), John Addington SYMONDS proposes that it was Hypnos, god of slumber, who loved Endymion and put him to sleep with eternally open eyes. According to Bullfinch's *Mythology*, Endymion represents the aspirations of poetic love, 'a life spent more in dreams than in reality, and an early and welcome death'. Endymion has served for centuries as a literary symbol of eternal male youthful beauty and poetical yearnings in works such as John Lyly's comedy *Endimion, the Man in the Moone* (1585), in which the love of the moon goddess Cynthia for Endymion is chaste and platonic, and Keats' long allegorical poem *Endymion* (1817).

A. M. Wentink

Enrique IV de Castilla (1425–1474), king of Spain. Accounts of Enrique IV's reign are often influenced by the historian's attitude towards the monarch's sexual 'identity'. Impotence and homosexuality are often confused, as if it did not matter which was the case as long as sexual anomaly (*any* sexual anomaly) is involved. These personal flaws are then connected to some other personality traits such as indecisiveness and pusillanimity, and therefore blamed for the instability of the political situation. Clearly, he had to rule in politically turbulent times, face strong opposition from the aristocracy and several rival factions; these pressures together with his weak personality may have been responsible for his present status as one of the most maligned Spanish monarchs. (Curiously enough, homosexuality is less emphasised in the case of his father, Juan II, whose reign saw relative stability and economic and cultural wealth.) His relationships with noblemen were also confused and often misguided: he fought the powerful Álvaro de Luna in 1440 only to take his side six years later against other noblemen.

Enrique's alleged homosexuality seems to have been common knowledge at the time, although it is difficult to know how much was true and how much was just part of a campaign to tarnish his image in politically uncertain times. Enrique's sexual activities are often linked to the habits of the Arabs, who still held a few areas in southern Spain: in this way, the politically inconvenient king was related through accusations of sodomy to the loathed enemies, and homosexuality was used as a mark of otherness. Reports of numerous orgies and intense promiscuity do not square off with the often disseminated image of a physically weak man, impotent and prone to illness. And emphasis on perversion would later be used to justify a return to more conservative ideologies imposed by the 'Catholic monarchs' after Enrique's death. King Ferdinand of Aragon (who married Isabella, who succeeded Enrique IV to the throne) is reported to have mentioned Enrique's 'frivolousness and perversion' when told about his death. In life he was attacked in sets of rhymes that presented him having sex in the bushes and ignoring pressing matters of state. As in the case of other monarchs (both Juan II of Castille and EDWARD II in England), his 'favourite', Don Juan Pacheco, was one of the instruments used for attack. He was said to be an upstart who had sex with the king only to acquire social position, and when he was made Marquis of Villena animosity grew.

Enrique IV married twice. The first marriage was annulled when declared unconsummated. The question of succession was a pressing problem and rumours of impotence abounded. He then married Juana de Portugal, who did have a daughter, named after her mother. Court records suggest that mechanical devices were used to help the king fulfil his marital duties. But faith in the king's heterosexual abilities was damaged at this point and nobody really believed it was a legitimate child. Rumours of the queen's liaison with the nobleman Beltrán de la Cueva gave rise to the nickname of 'La Beltraneja' for her daughter. In any case one cannot dismiss political interests underlying the rejection of Juana: Isabella already had her supporters and illegitimacy seemed not to have been the issue, but something conveniently used for power machinations. There is something oddly symbolic in this shift in Spanish history: the king presented as homosexual and friend of the Muslims is regarded as unfit for government and succeeded by a xenophobic, conservative, imperialist regime that would dominate the next two centuries of Spanish history.

G. Marañón, 'Ensayo biológico sobre Enrique IV de Castilla y su tiempo', in *Obras completas*, Vol. V, Madrid, 1970: 87–165.

Alberto Mira

Eon de Beaumont, Chevalier d' (Charles Geneviève-Louise-Auguste-André-Timothée d'Eon) (1728–1810), French diplomat and 'cross-dresser'. The Chevalier d'Eon, if not necessarily a part of 'gay' or homosexual history, certainly qualifies as protoqueer. One of the most famous figures in eighteenth-century Europe, the Chevalier spent half his life dressed as a man and the second half as a woman; his contemporaries never investigated his sexual choices and he appears to have led a virginal life. Havelock ELLIS used the name 'eonism', in his *Studies in the Psychology of Sex* (1936), to denote transvestism, but Gary Kates's recent rereading of the d'Eon episode indicates that it is inappropriate to project modern psychiatric models backwards in order to understand the

significance of the Chevalier's cross-dressing.

Born in Tonnerre to an aristocratic family, d'Eon gained a law degree in 1749. In 1756 he joined the 'King's Secret' and travelled to Russia; some biographers claim that he cross-dressed there as a woman for purposes of espionage, but this claim is based on d'Eon's fabricated memoirs. From 1757 to 1760 he was Secretary to the French ambassador to Russia; in 1761 he was made Dragoon Captain and fought in the Seven Years War against England (1756–1763). In 1762 he travelled with the Duc de Nivernais to negotiate the Peace of Paris; he stayed in London until 1763, when he was recalled to France.

In 1770 rumours regarding his gender began to circulate; in 1775 he signed the 'Transaction' agreement worded by the playwright P. A. de Beaumarchais, cosigned by Louis XVI, stating that he was a woman. 'She' was henceforth forbidden to wear male garments or uniforms. The British Court recognised him as female in 1777, and he returned to France, where he at first dressed in his uniform but then was forced to dress consistently as a woman. He complained of the inanity of the female role and the expense of her wardrobe. In 1778 he attempted to join the army as a woman; the following year he was arrested and imprisoned briefly for disobeying the King and re-donning male uniform. From 1785 to 1810 he returned to England, where he performed as a 'female' fencer in women's clothes and wrote the memoirs published after his death by F. Gaillardet (1836). D'Eon continued to demand the right for women to serve as soldiers. He died in London and a board of five specialists determined that he was biologically 'male'; he lacked female breasts, and was not a 'hermaphrodite'. This was a different but perhaps a no-less-certain verdict than that delivered by the English Court and French King who had previously 'proven' he was 'female'.

The d'Eon incident indicates that ideas of the binary system of gender were considerably less stable in the eighteenth century than they were in the twentieth century. D'Eon convinced authorities that he had been born biologically female but had cross-dressed male as he wished to serve his country in a male role. Kates has advanced the theory that the Chevalier's adoption of female dress may have been induced by his Christian feminist belief that, as women were spiritually superior to men and also capable of serious intellectual thought, they were superior beings. The debate over the existence of the intellectual woman – the *querelle des femmes* – continued throughout the century, generating a huge literature; d'Eon owned one of the largest private libraries on this topic. Although Kates argues convincingly that d'Eon admired the character of women and made an intellectual decision to dress and live as one, the possibility that d'Eon derived satisfaction of some other kind from his double subterfuge should not be discounted.

F. Gaillardet, *The Memoirs of Chevalier d'Eon*, trans. A. White, London, 1970; M. Garber, *Vested Interests: Cross-Dressing and Cultural Anxiety*, New York, 1992; G. Kates, *Monsieur d'Eon is a Woman: A Tale of Political Intrigue and Sexual Masquerade*, New York, 1995.

Peter McNeil

Erauso, Catalina de (1592?–1650), also known as 'La Monja Alférez' (The Second Lieutenant Nun), Spanish-Mexican soldier, nun. The life of Catalina de Erauso illustrates the anomalous case of a woman who reached a prominent position in the masculine order in seventeenth-century Spanish culture and who enjoyed official recognition both from the Crown and the Catholic hierarchy. In appreciation for services rendered to Christianity, she was granted permission by Pope Urban VII to live her life dressing as a man and performing actively male-identified work in terms of the socio-cultural parameters of her time.

Born to Captain Miguel de Araujo (or Erauso) and María Pérez de Galarraga y Arce, Catalina was raised in a convent until she turned 15, when she decided to escape and start a life of adventure. In order to rid herself of her former identity, she cut her hair short, wore masculine clothing and adopted several male names. She travelled through Spain but finally crossed the Atlantic to the New World, in the same way many young and ambitious Spaniards did to obtain fame and wealth. Under the name of Antonio de Erauso, she fought in the wars against the Araucanian Indians in Chile, which won her the military degree of *alférez* (second lieutenant).

Back in Spain in 1625, Erauso got up a petition to the Spanish Crown asking for compensation for her heroic services. It is assumed that she wrote her memoirs to accompany this petition as proof of her merits. Her autobiography, commonly known as *Historia de la Monja Alférez escrita por ella misma* (*History of the Monja Alférez, Written by Herself*; English version by James Fitzmaurice-Kelly under the title *The Nun Ensign*, 1908), is a very problematic cultural document, both for the questions on authorship raised by criticism and for the shocking and sensationalist content of the book. According to some critics, there is no doubt that Erauso wrote the work herself, while others maintain that the text as we know it results from the intervention of a later writer who lengthened it by inserting various episodes. Finally, there are those who think that Erauso shared an oral account of her life with a writer who elaborated the narration in a literary fashion. Since no autographic manuscript stands, and there is no printed copy of the original (which is known to have been given to the printer Bernardino de Guzmán in 1625), most modern editions are based on a surviving copy, held by the Royal Academy of History in Madrid. To avoid the difficulties of attribution, Rima de Vallbona has titled her 1992 critical edition *Vida i sucesos de la Monja Alférez. Autobiografía atribuida a Doña Catalina de Erauso*

(*Life and events of . . . Autobiography attributed to D. C. de E.*).

In terms of content, Erauso is depicted almost as a fictional character, sharing aspects of the *pícaro* and the braggart soldier. Her attitude is unconventional and iconoclastic. As noted by Stephanie Merrim, she 'is presented as an incorrigible individualist and as a violent troublemaker and mannish woman who rejects feminine behaviour'. In the text, the contrast between being a nun and being a soldier, as an expression of the basic distinction female/male, is used to rouse the interest of the readers, underlining the sexual ambiguity of the character. In fact, the use of adjectives with their Spanish gender-marked forms is a regular device in the writing: masculine suffixes are used to characterise the subject in her more stereotypical masculine activities (such as boasting and flirting), while the feminine ones are exploited when the narrative adopts a more neutral tone. It has been said that this alternation of grammatical forms is due to the intervention of different writers and copyists in the partially known textual transmission of her memoirs. Moreover, it has been argued that such ambiguity mirrors the linguistic structure of Basque, Erauso's first language, in which there are no gender distinctions. However, the personality of the character as it is constructed in the narrative explains sufficiently the ambivalence of the discourse.

Erauso's life soon reached legendary proportions. Apart from many commentaries written by her contemporaries, the famous actor Pérez de Montalbán wrote a play titled *La monja alférez*, which opened in Madrid as early as 1626.

J. Berruezo (ed.) 'Prólogo', *Historia de la monja alférez, doña Catalina de Erauso, escrita por ella misma*, Pamplona, 1959: 7–24; S. Merrim, 'Catalina de Erauso y Sor Juana Inés de la Cruz: de la anomalía al ícono', *Y diversa de mí misma entre vuestras plumas ando. Homenaje internacional a Sor Juana Inés de la Cruz*, Mexico City, 1993: 355–65; M. E. Perry, 'Sexual Rebels', in *Gender and Disorder in Early Modern Seville*, Princeton, 1990: 118–36; R. de Vallbona (ed.) *Vida i sucesos de la Monja Alférez. Autobiografía atribuida a Doña Catalina de Erauso*, Tempe, Ariz., 1992.

Daniel Altamiranda

Erté (Romain de Tirtoff) (1892–1990), Russian-French designer, artist. Born in St Petersburg to a wealthy naval family, Erté moved to Paris in 1912, where he studied art briefly at the Académie Julian. He derived his name from the pronunciation of his initials in French, a pseudonym taken in order to avoid his family embarrassment when he began sketching female fashions for the Russian magazine *Damsky Mir*, providing fashion designs for Paul Poiret (including the famous orientalist 'Sorbet' design), and contributing illustrations to the luxury Paris magzine *La Gazette du Bon Ton*. Simultaneously he began his first costume designs; his work in all genres is marked by a swaggering Art Deco theatricality. He designed the costume for Mata-Hari in *Le Minaret* (1913). Erté claimed that his style was derived from Indian and Persian miniatures and the linear forms of Greek vase painting; his female figures tended to the androgynous, and he was partial to an Apollonian musculature and phallic props, such as in the illustration *Porteurs de Pierreries* (1927).

Erté became widely know to the public with his approximately 240 cover designs for the American *Harper's Bazaar* (1915–1936). He also provided line drawings of dresses, fashion accessories and furniture for the magazine, and for the store Henry Bendel's, in a bold graphic style which suited the mood of the times. He worked for Hollywood briefly in the 1920s. Erté claimed to have invented the *costume collectif*, group costumes linked to the set in which as much as six miles of gold lamé might be incorporated, a technique used to advantage in the Hollywood musical, and he matched coloured wigs to dresses in 1920s costume designs. As he continued to be prolific in a relatively unchanged idiom when the scholarly and market interest in Art Deco design revived in the mid-1960s, Erté and Art Deco became virtually synonymous. As late as 1974 he designed a line of knitwear for MagiFrance, and his drawings and designs for statuary and souvenirs of the Art Deco period commanded large sums.

Erté's autobiography provided a remarkably frank catalogue of his romantic liaisons, in marked contrast to the publicly closeted nature of most of his contemporaries in the field of fashion and design. This is partly because Erté lived an active life well past the beginning of Gay Liberation in the 1960s, partly because Paris was always more open sexually, and partly because he was less hidebound by convention due to the certainty of his class position. Never seedy and always amusing, Erté's catalogue of his sexual history begins at the age of 13; he described many other 'delightful adventures' and 'joys of the affairs of the heart', including a foray into a 1920s Hollywood orgy which was not to his refined taste, and descriptions of homosexual nightlife in 1920s Paris. He lived with Prince Nicolas Ouroussoff for close to 20 years until the Prince's premature death in 1933; later he had a close relationship with a Danish ex-champion swimmer and decorator named Axel.

When his designs incorporate young men, they are always strongly homoerotic, based on his enthusiasm for the male ballet-dancer's physique. An early venture into playful cross-dressing was so successful that he claimed Poiret asked him to model female clothes for the fashion house in an attempt to garner publicity. Interested in dress reform for men, his early years were smartly dandiacal, but he also wore rainbow colours and suits made and trimmed with female fabrics; his long curled hair caused consternation at customs. Late twentieth-century drag troupe performers probably owe their single biggest debt to the styling of Erté's music hall

costume designs; in this the Erté aesthetic has endured.

J. Cox, *Erté's Costumes and Sets for Der Rosenkavalier*, New York, 1980; Erté, *Things I Remember: An Autobiography*, London, 1975; T. Walters, *Erté*, London, 1978; Dover Publications, *Erté's Fashion Designs*, New York, 1981.
                                        Peter McNeil

Eulenburg, Philipp zu (1847–1921), German political figure. Born into one of Prussia's noblest Junker families, Eulenburg had a classical education, served in the army (during which he saw action in the Franco-Prussian War), and took a doctorate in law. He entered the civil service but then moved to the diplomatic corps, where he was Prussia's envoy to Bavaria and, subsequently, Germany's ambassador to Austria-Hungary, one of the highest ranks in the foreign service; in 1900, he was given the title of prince.

In 1886 Eulenburg met the future Kaiser Wilhelm II at a hunting party and the two became close friends; indeed, Wilhelm referred to Eulenburg as his best and only friend. They both had an interest in art, literature and music not always shared by others in the Kaiser's court. Eulenburg himself had written eight volumes of nationalist ballads inspired by Nordic mythology that counted among the emperor's favourite reading. Eulenburg and other members of the 'Liebenberg Round Table', who held regular hunts at Eulenburg's estate, formed a tight band of courtiers close to the emperor – 'all male, all noble, all university educated and entirely conservative', according to Hull. Eulenburg, who in particular had the emperor's ear, became extraordinarily influential in the 1890s, helping to bring about the downfall of Bismarck, promoting his allies (such as Chancellor von Bülow) and moving the German political system away from parliamentarianism towards the 'personal regime' of the Kaiser.

The Liebenberg group was also bound together by homoerotic bonds. Eulenburg championed intimate male comradeship and ideal friendship, and was particularly attached to Kuno von Moltke and Alex von Varnbüler, with both of whom he may have had sexual relationships; even his relationship with the emperor was highly emotional. He behaved indifferently to his wife, a Swedish countess, whom he had married in 1875, though he was a devoted father. According to Hull, 'his love of men was the central, shaping impulse of his private and public life'. For Röhl, he was 'not homosexual in the narrower sense of the term, certainly homoerotically inclined and therefore – since he was also drawn towards women – bisexual'. A scandal broke in the late 1890s, as Eulenburg was at the height of his influence, when the wives of Moltke and Eulenburg's brother Friedrich sued for divorce partly on the implicit or explicit grounds of their husbands' homosexuality; the scandal narrowly missed Eulenburg.

Eulenburg resigned his ambassadorial post in 1903 because of ill health and rising opposition to his court intrigues, but returned to public life several years later. Soon Germany became embroiled in a colonial conflict with France over influence in North Africa; the First Moroccan Crisis of 1905 was followed by a settlement that was disadvantageous to Germany at the Algeciras Conference. Criticism mounted that the negative results were in part because of Eulenburg's own 'soft' attitude towards France, opposition to colonial expansion and perceived pacifist orientation, and his by now numerous enemies moved to attack.

Maximilian Harden, a respected cultural critic and newspaper editor, in 1906 began publishing articles about the homosexual activities of leading court figures, especially Eulenburg and Moltke, including details of liaisons with labourers and a fisherman dating from the 1880s; several, including Moltke, resigned their positions, though Eulenburg told the Kaiser that he was free of guilt (even if he did not directly deny certain accusations). Moltke sued

Harden for libel, but the latter was acquitted in 1907; the verdict was then overturned on a technicality, and a second trial found Harden guilty. Harden appealed, but the trial was declared invalid; after a third trial, which again found Harden guilty, the journalist again appealed but then agreed to an out-of-court settlement. Meanwhile, in 1908, Eulenburg was arrested for perjury, accused of having lied in testimony about his homosexual activities. Friends counselled Eulenburg to commit suicide rather than face trial, a suggestion he refused. Eulenburg maintained in the witness box that he had not transgressed Paragraph 175 of the penal code, which had been interpreted to define only anal intercourse as illegal. Eulenburg's physical collapse ended the trial; the following year, he stood trial a second time, and again collapsed. For the next decade, medical doctors examined Eulenburg biannually to see if he was fit to stand trial, but he was never declared able to do so. He lived the rest of his life in relative tranquillity; though disgraced in public eyes, he never fully lost the Kaiser's sympathy and appeared as a guest at court receptions. Evidence from the Eulenburg trials was unaccountably destroyed by German authorities in 1932.

The Eulenburg–Moltke affair was a *cause célèbre* in Wilhelmine Germany, spreading further and lasting far longer than the scandal following the relevation of the homosexuality (and presumed suicide) of the businessman Alfred KRUPP only a few years earlier. Rumours of widespread homosexuality circulated – the homosexual emancipationist Adolf BRAND was sentenced to prison for alleging that Bülow was homosexual – and some even believed that the Kaiser himself had participated in homosexual activities as part of the Liebenberg circle, whose *soirées* sometimes extended to pantomines and cross-dressing. At the time when Magnus HIRSHFELD and other activists demanded reform of anti-homosexual laws and argued for social acceptance of homosexuals, questions of sexual irregularities assumed greater moment. The accusations that some of Germany's most important public figures consorted sexually with each other (and with working-class men) created scandal in a conservative, religious society. Yet the accusations of homosexuality, many of which were probably true, were used by journalists and politicians to discredit opponents whose power they wished to curb. Eulenburg had been instrumental in engineering a political environment which gave almost unlimited power to the emperor, though it was tempered by the relatively open ideas of Eulenburg's entourage; his exit opened the way for increased domination by the more conservative and militaristic camarilla which replaced Eulenburg's circle.

I. V. Hull, *The Entourage of Kaiser Wilhelm II, 1888–1898*, Cambridge, 1982; J. G. C. Röhl, *The Kaiser and his Court: Wilhelm II and the Government of Germany*, Cambridge, 1994.

                         Robert Aldrich

Evans, Edward De Lacy (1830–1901), Australian public figure. In September 1879 during a routine attempt to bathe him, Edward De Lacy Evans, a male patient at Kew Lunatic Asylum in Melbourne, was discovered to be a woman. Investigation quickly revealed that Evans had lived more than 23 years as a man, worked throughout that time as a miner, married three different women and was father to an 18-month-old daughter. This news created a sensation throughout the Australian colonies and details of the case were reported as far away as London and New York. Almost nothing is known with certainty about Evans's life prior to his/her emigration from Britain, but it is clear that he/she arrived in Victoria as a female passenger, Ellen Tremaye, aboard the *Ocean Monarch* in 1856. Passenger lists show she described herself as 26 years of age, single, a domestic servant, Irish, Roman Catholic and able to read and write.

In Melbourne Evans/Tremaye took a short engagement as a female servant at a country hotel, but shortly afterwards adopted male attire and married 34-year-old Mary Delahunty, with whom she had shared a berth on the *Ocean Monarch*. Several years later Delahunty left Evans, and in 1862 she remarried, telling all who questioned this apparent act of bigamy that her first husband was a woman. In 1862 Evans also remarried. Describing himself as a widower, he married a young Irishwoman called Sarah Moore. Moore died in 1867, and the following year Evans met and married his third wife, Julia Marquand, who was 25 years of age, French and a dressmaker's assistant. In 1877, after nine years of marriage, Julia Evans gave birth to a daughter, whom the couple named Julia Mary.

How Evans may have understood his/her own gendered and sexual subjectivity is difficult to determine, as he/she refused to speak on the matter. However, the facts of the case generated extraordinary public interest and speculation regarding both Evans's motivations, and those of his wives. Newspapers relayed numerous indications of Evans's sexual interest in women dating back prior to her adoption of male attire. That Evans married not once, but three times, implied a sexual motivation for what might otherwise be viewed as a curious fraud motivated by economics or eccentricity, and raised the issue of what had gone on between Evans and each wife in the privacy of the marriage bed. What the wives knew was of intense public interest. Generally, newspapers gave credence to the notion that Evans's wives were 'deceived' and that they were Evans's 'victims'. Yet clearly, far more speculation on the wives' motivations was privately engaged in. One rare indication of this is one newspaper's comment: 'The cause of none of the wives exposing the deception practised on them has been without doubt nymphomania.' The third wife told the press that she was unaware that her husband was a woman despite 11 years of marriage and the birth of a child. Evans, she said, never undressed or washed in front of her and, as for the child, she could only assume Evans had smuggled a 'real man' into the house one night at the time she usually expected him home.

Of course, such explanations created more problems than they solved: by being unable to pin-point an obvious occasion where something out of the ordinary had occurred, Mrs Evans was not only admitting that she and her husband regularly had sex, but that she had not been able to tell the difference when a 'real man' was substituted for her female husband. Evans was released as 'cured' three months after the sensation began. Shortly afterwards he/she appeared in court as a witness for Marquand, who sought child maintenance from her brother-in-law. Despite Evans's evidence, Marquand failed to prove paternity. It is not known how she managed to support herself and the child. She never remarried.

After the court case Evans moved away and gained a meagre living as a 'man–woman' exhibit in side shows. Within a year, and with failing health, she was taken in as an inmate of the Immigrants Home in Melbourne. She lived out the remainder of her life in female attire.

L. Chesser, '"A Woman who Married Three Wives": Management of Disruptive Knowledge in the 1879 Australian Case of Edward De Lacy Evans', *Journal of Women's History*, 9, 4, (1998): 53–77.

Lucy Chesser

Exler, Marie Jacobus Johannes (1882– 1939), Dutch writer, astrologer and farmer. Exler was born in Schiedam, the third child of a Roman Catholic gin distiller. In Brussels, where his family lived after Exler's twelfth birthday, he neither finished his training as a priest nor his study in

medicine. Starting a big project and not finishing it proved to be characteristic of Exler for the rest of his life. After many wanderings, he settled in 1925 in the Dutch village of Hattem. There he started a not very successful career as a chicken farmer and astrologist. He died of a heart attack in an Amsterdam tram on his way to collect a small prize in the national lottery. Only 12 friends attended his funeral.

Exler has his place in the history of Dutch gay liberation for two achievements. In 1912, together with Jacob Schorer, Lucien von RÖMER, Arnold ALETRINO and Joannes FRANÇOIS, he was co-founder of the Dutch branch of Magnus HIRSCHFELD's Wissenschaftlich-humanitäres Komitee, the first gay and lesbian organisation in The Netherlands. As far as we know, Exler did not play an active role on the committee. It probably was the novelist François who asked him to join the new organisation because of the publication, a year before, of Exler's novel *Levensleed* (*Life's Sorrow: A Book for Parents*). This novel, with a foreword by Hirschfeld, translated into German three years later and reprinted in Dutch in 1918, is a tendentious novel supporting the idea of homosexuality as a 'third sex'. The story, with its elaborations on contemporary ideas about same-sex relations, has no aesthetic value whatsoever, but still is interesting as a period document. What is remarkable is the fact that Exler did not use a pseudonym to publish his first and only novel. If this was an act of bravery or naïvety, we will never know.

M. van Lieshout, 'Uranist, optimist en astroloog. Marie Jacobus Johannes Exler', *Homologie*, 13, 1 (1991): 4–7; M. van Lieshout, 'Dutch and Flemish Literature', in C. J. Summers (ed.) *The Gay and Lesbian Literary Heritage*, New York, 1995: 211–16.

Maurice van Lieshout

F

Falleni, Eugenia (Harry Crawford) (1875–1938), Italian-Australian cross-dresser. Born in Italy in 1875, Falleni migrated to New Zealand with her family when she was 2 years old. As a young girl, she wore boy's clothes, and worked as a man. Falleni then left New Zealand, arriving in Australia in the 1890s. She had a child in 1898 in Newcastle, moved to Sydney and gave her baby, Josephine, to an Italian woman to be cared for – and then dressed and lived as a man.

In 1910, as 'Harry Crawford' she commenced employment as a 'useful' and began courting Annie Birkett, taking her on drives and bringing her flowers. They married in 1913 and lived together in Drummoyne, a working-class Sydney suburb. In 1917, Birkett disappeared and Crawford told neighbours 'his missus' had left him. In 1919, he married another woman, Lizzie Allison. When questioned by police in 1920, he claimed to be Harry Leon Crawford, a Scot born in Edinburgh, who migrated to New Zealand when 18 months old, and that at 18 he left his parents' home and worked his passage direct to New South Wales, where he worked in different jobs. Crawford told police that until he married Allison 'I was a single man.' On further questioning and impending arrest, Crawford admitted to being a woman, Eugenia Falleni. She was arrested and tried for the murder of her first wife (Birkett), found guilty and sentenced to death. The death sentence was later commuted to life imprisonment. After serving 11 years at Long Bay Gaol, Falleni obtained early release in 1931. She then lived under the name Mrs Jean Ford. It is likely that dressing and living as a woman was a strict condition of her parole. She died in 1938 after being hit by a car. Sensational stories about 'the man–woman murderer' have been retold in the tabloid press and crime story collections up to the present.

Although she was on trial for murder, Falleni was also on trial – in both the court room and in the press – for her gender-transgressions and subsequent marriages and sexual relationships with women. Newspaper headlines focused predominantly on Falleni's gender-crossing and marriages, and depicted the alleged murder almost as a secondary offence. Within the trial, much attention was paid to her masquerade as a man, her two marriages and the consequent 'deception' of her wives. The prosecution linked the murder directly to her cross-dressing, arguing that the motive for murder was Birkett's 'discovery' of Falleni's 'true sex'. The defence cast her as a sexual invert. Falleni's wives were constructed as sexual innocents, who had been deceived by an 'artificial phallus' found in a trunk under Falleni's bed by police and exhibited in court. Yet it is likely that Falleni's wives were aware of her sex. Members of the Italian community knew Crawford was a woman and

Falleni's daughter Josephine referred to her as 'mother'.

As well as depicting her as a man–woman freak, the press emphasised her Italian ethnic identity through reports of her appearance – 'dark complexion', 'black hair', 'small brown eyes' – while the prosecution cast her as devious and sly. These images drew on xenophobic views of southern European 'foreigners' in the midst of a 'White Australia'. Falleni's gender-crossing speaks of her desire to adopt a male identity and her sexual desires for women, while her ethnic 'passing' speaks of her desire to escape racial discrimination.

We do not know if Falleni murdered Birkett. Nor do we know if Falleni would have preferred to be known always as 'he'. Falleni marked himself as a man and perhaps saw this masculine identity as a fundamental part of himself. Yet Falleni also saw herself as a woman. In living as a man and marrying women, Falleni adopted a long tradition of passing women.

S. Falkiner, *Eugenia: A Man*, Sydney, 1988; R. Ford, ' "The Man–Woman Murderer": Sex Fraud, Sexual Inversion and the Unmentionable "Article" in 1920s Australia', *Gender and History*, 12 (2000): 158–96.

Ruth Ford

Farinacci, Pròspero (1554–1618), Italian criminologist. Farinacci was among the most important lay personalities in sixteenth-century Rome. As a political figure, he held various positions in the Papal States, and as a lawyer he participated in several sensational trials. (Particularly notable was the famous trial of Beatrice Cenci, and Farinacci appears in several eighteenth-century historical novels, including English ones, about the trial.) As a man of letters, Farinacci authored numerous works on jurisprudence and gained fame for a most ambitious project: to write a compendium for magistrates and lawyers which would sum up all previous works on the subject and make reference

to any other volume almost superfluous. This *Praxis et theorica criminalis*, published in Venice in 1608 and in Lyon in 1616, was both criticised and praised, but became the authoritative study for Italian (and to a minor extent foreign) tribunals and law faculties in the seventeenth century. Farinacci was also known to contemporaries for his inhuman severity as a judge – he invariably imposed the harshest sentences on offenders.

Farinacci condemned sodomy with great severity in his work, notwithstanding which he was implicated in activities which could have cost him his life if they had been brought before his court. A particular scandal occurred in 1595, when he was accused of having sodomised, on several occasions, 16-year-old Berardino Rocchi, a page in the Altemps palace, where Farinacci lived. The intervention of Pope Clement VIII, who pardoned him, saved Farinacci's life. In signing the pardon, the pope made a pun on Farinacci's surname – '*La farina è buona, ma il sacco che la contiene è cattivo*' ('The flour is good, but the floursack is bad') – which became famous.

L. Crasso, *Elogi d'huomini letterati*, Venice, 1666: 175–8; G. Dall'Orto, 'La farina era cattiva', *Babilonia*, 135 (July–August 1995): 24–6; A. Mazzacane, 'Farinacci, Prospero', *Dizionario biografico degli italiani*, Rome, 1995; N. Del Re, 'Farinacci giureconsulto romano (1544–1618)', *Archivio della Società romana di storia patria*, 98 (1975): 135–220.

Giovanni Dall'Orto

Farnese, Pier Luigi (1503–1547), Italian nobleman, first Duke of Parma and Piacenza. The illegitimate son of Alessandro Farnese (1468–1549), he was legally recognised by his father, who became Pope Paul III in 1534. Farnese took part in the wars which raged in Italy at the time and participated in the sacking of Rome in 1527. His father's election to the papacy guaranteed him several honours; he was successively named Duke of Castro, *gonfaloniere* (chief of the militia) of the church, and

Marquess of Novara. The crowning achievement of his father's 'nepotism' was, however, the scandalous separation of Parma and Piacenza from the Papal States and the concession of the territory, as a personal dukedom, to his son and his descendents. Thus was begun the Farnese dynasty in Parma, which remained on the throne even after local nobles, supported by Emperor Charles V, assassinated Pier Luigi Farnese; the family continued to rule until 1731.

Throughout his life, Farnese was rumoured to be a sodomite, and scandal exploded in 1537, when he was accused in what became known as the 'rape of Fano'. Farnese, while marching with troops through Fano, was alleged to have raped the young bishop of the city, Cosimo Gheri (1513–1537), who died 40 days afterwards. According to Mario Masini and Giuseppe Portigliotti, 'The Lutherans took great joy in this, saying that the Catholics had found "a new way of martyring saints".' The episode became widely known after it was recounted in Benedetto VARCHI's Storia fiorentina but was much used, as well, by Pier Paolo Vergerio, a bishop who converted to Protestantism. In his wake, the accusation of sodomy against Farnese was used by Protestant polemicists in the sixteenth century. The charges were then taken up by 'patriotic' Italian historians in the nineteenth century, some of them waging a long battle to prove that the accusations were a product of Protestant calumny, some others producing documents which gave evidence of Farnese's taste for men.

Among these was a private letter written on 17 October 1535 in which Pope Paul III strongly reproached his son for having taken his male lovers with him when he was sent on an official mission to the court of the emperor, who was known to be hostile to this type of love; the pope ordered his son to send his lovers away. Another letter, written by the chancellor of the Florentine embassy in Rome on 14 January 1540 (reprinted in Ferrai), recounted the 'manhunt' which Farnese had mounted in Rome to search for a youth who had refused his advances.

Such a debate awakened interest in Farnese among later Decadent writers, whose morbid fantasy was piqued by a figure with such an inflammatory reputation. Pierre Louÿs, a well known French writer of erotic literature, even used the ancient rendering of Farnese's first names as a pseudonym. A portrait of Farnese, painted by Titian in 1543, can be seen in the Museo di Capodimonte in Naples.

G. Dall'Orto, 'Un avo poco presentabile', Babilonia, 162 (January 1998): 26–7; L. Ferrai, 'Della supposta calunnia del Vergerio contro il Duca di Castro', Archivio storico per Trieste, l'Istria e il Trentino', 1 (1881–1882): 300–12; M. Masini and G. Portigliotti, 'Attraverso il Rinascimento: Pier Luigi Farnese', Archivio di antropologia criminale, 38 (1917): 177–92; B. Varchi, Storia fiorentina, Vol. 2 (Florence, 1858): 268–70.

Giovanni Dall'Orto

Ficino, Marsilio (1433–1499), Italian humanist and philosopher. The son of a medical doctor, Ficino was a student of philosophy. The flight to Italy of Byzantine scholars after the fall of Byzantium in 1453 provided Italian humanists with the opportunity to discover Greek works which were then unknown in the West; thus, young Ficino discovered and developed a passion for PLATO, learning Greek in order to study his works. Ficino earned the patronage of the Médicis, who protected and aided him throughout his life, and who gave him precious Greek manuscripts (which Ficino translated). In short, Ficino became a well known and respected cultural figure, gathering around himself a number of students at his Platonic Academy.

In 1473 Ficino was ordained a priest; he continued his philosophical work and undertook the onerous task of proving that Plato's philosophy was in harmony with Christian doctrine, just as Thomas

AQUINAS had done in the case of Aristotle. Among his most important works are *Theologia platonica* (published in 1482), as well as strictly religious works (*Commentarius in Epistolas D. Pauli*), philosophical commentaries (*Commentarius in Platonis Convivium*, published in the Platonic form of a dialogue in 1469) and an impressive number of translations of the works of Plato and other Greek philosophers. These translations made such works accessible to Western readers for the first time. Ficino is thus one of the most important figures in the Renaissance. His fame is linked to his loving and meticulous work in rediscovering, translating, commenting on and disseminating the works of Plato.

Of particular interest here is Ficino's restatement of Plato's ideal of love (as appears in the *Phaedrus* and the *Symposium*); in Ficino's wake, this would be taken up in countless sixteenth-century treatises on love to become the model of 'courtly love' *par excellence*. Under the name of *amor socraticus* (Socratic, or Platonic, love) or *verus amor* (true love), Ficino described a model of profound but highly spiritualised love between men who were linked by a common love for knowledge. According to Ficino's formulation in the *Commentarius in Platonis Convivium*, this love is illuminated by a vision of the beauty of the soul of the other person, a beauty which is itself a mirror of the Beauty of God. Through the physical beauty of a young man – women are unfit to inspire this sort of passion, and more apt to stimulate coition for the reproduction of the species – the wise man attains to the absolute Beauty which is an *idea* (in the Platonic sense) of the beauty which is God himself. Thus, the contemplation through love of the physical and spiritual beauty of a youth is a means of contemplating at least a fragment of the Beauty of God, the model for all earthly beauty.

Ficino practised his theory of love with the young and very handsome Giovanni Cavalcanti (1444?–1509), whom he made the principal character in his commentary in the *Convivium*, and to whom he wrote passionate love letters in Latin (published in 1492 in his *Epistulæ*). It is ironic that Ficino's beloved, as the philosopher himself lamented, responded with some embarrassment as if he had reservations about the true purity of *amor socraticus*.

There are numerous indications – not least these letters – which suggest that Ficino's erotic desire was directed towards men. Biographers had to begin soon after Ficino's death to rebuke those who alluded to his homosexual tendencies. However, during his life, the universal respect which Ficino enjoyed, his deeply felt and sincerely religious feelings and, also, his status in the Catholic clergy, sheltered him from the gossip and suspicions of sodomy which afflicted his later followers (such as Benedetto VARCHI). Furthermore, several men whose homosexuality is now a subject of debate formed part of Ficino's circle, among them Giovanni PICO della Mirandola and Angelo Poliziano.

Ficino himself camouflaged his homosexual preferences by taking advantage of the general misogyny of his time, as witnessed by Poliziano in his *Detti piacevoli*: 'Sir Marsilio says that women are to be used just as chamber pots: after man uses them, they shold be hidden and removed. . . . Sir Marsilio says that priests are worse than secular people, friars are worse than priests, monks are worse than friars, hermits are worse than monks and women are worse than hermits.'

After Ficino's death, the ideal of *amor socraticus* showed itself to be a powerful argument for justifying love between persons of the same sex, a screen which served numerous homosexual figures in the late fifteenth and early sixteenth centuries, among them LEONARDO da Vinci and MICHELANGELO Buonarrotti. This helped to discredit such an ideal in the eyes of the public, and it was viewed with ever-increasing discomfort with the passing of time, until, around 1550, *amor socraticus* was identified solely with sodomy. In consequence, in the mid-sixteenth century, the ideal of Platonic love was carefully heterosexualised, and in this form it survived in treatises on love and in Italian and European letters in general.

A. Chastel, 'Eros socraticus', *Art et humanisme à Florence au temps de Laurent le Magnifique*, Paris, 1961: 289–98; R. Marcel, *Marsile Ficin*, Paris, 1958; G. Dall'Orto, ' "Socratic Love" as a Disguise for Same-Sex Love in the Italian Renaissance', in K. Gerard and G. Hekma (eds) *The Pursuit of Sodomy*, New York, 1989: 33–65; J. C. Nelson, *The Renaissance Theory of Love*, New York, 1958; J. Saslow, *Ganymede in the Renaissance*, New Haven, 1986, especially pp. 187–200.

Giovanni Dall'Orto

Field, Michael (pseudonym of Katherine Harris Bradley, 1846–1914, and Edith Emma Cooper, 1862–1913), British poets. 'Michael Field' was the pseudonym used by Katherine Harris Bradley and Edith Emma Cooper, who were respectively niece and aunt. They lived together as atheists in what they called a 'female marriage', from the time when Cooper was a child: 'My love and I took hands and swore / Against the world, to be / Poets and lovers evermore'.

When Cooper turned 16 she took a degree at the University of Bristol, and Bradley attended classes with her. Their first volume of poetry was published in 1889. The poems were openly influenced by new overtly lesbian translations of SAPPHO, and sensual lesbian imagery concerning young women and girls became a central theme in their neo-pagan poetry. Bradley and Cooper also wrote plays, travelled together, and wrote a long journal which indicates that they were lovers. They claimed to have worked so closely together that they could not tell who had written which line in their work.

In 1906 they converted to Roman Catholicism and their work began to reflect their new religious world-view. These new-found religious beliefs, plus a social

atmosphere less tolerant than 'the naughty 90s', tended to stifle the sensuality of their earlier poetry.

Cooper died in 1913, of cancer. Bradley spent the next eight months compiling their poetry into several new books, before dying of cancer herself.

C. White, 'Lovers and Poets Forevermore – The Poetry and Journals of Michael Field', in J. Bristow (ed.) *Sexual Sameness – Textual Differences in Gay and Lesbian Writing*, New York, 1992: 26–43.

Ianthe Duende

Fiévée, Joseph (1767–1839), French novelist and bureaucrat. The son of a Paris restaurant-owner, Fiévée began his professional life as a printer. He survived the turbulent period of the Revolution and attracted attention at the end of the 1700s with a successful novel, *La Dot de Suzette*, a satire on parvenus under the new regime. Converted to Bonapartism, he was employed by Napoleon as a secret correspondent furnishing information on the French political situation. Fiévée was then made a state counsellor and named prefect of the Nièvre *département*.

Fiévée is interesting for the way in which he lived out his homosexuality in this period. Perhaps as a youthful indiscretion, he married, but his wife died in labour in 1790, leaving him a son. In a political club in the late 1790s, under the Directory, he met Théodore Leclercq, ten years his junior. Leclercq published a short book titled *Proverbes*, which is now forgotten but which was appreciated by such nineteenth-century critics as Sainte-Beuve. Leclercq and Fiévée lived together until the latter's death, and together they reared Fiévée's son. Contemporaries spoke about their 'Greek friendship', a relationship which was officially accepted. When Napoleon sent Fiévée on a mission to Britain, he took his friend and his son along with him. When Fiévée became a prefect, Leclercq moved into the official residence with him and acted as his 'hostess' during official receptions. Jean Tulard, Fiévée's biographer and a specialist of the First Empire, notes the absence of hostile reactions to his behaviour.

From the life and career of Fiévée, and that of CAMBACÉRÈS, one can conclude that French society at the time of Napoleon was not yet as homophobic as it would become after the Restoration of the Bourbon monarchy and subsequently.

J. Tulard, *Joseph Fiévée*, Paris, 1985.

Didier Godard

Firbank, Ronald (1886–1926), British novelist. Arthur Annesley Ronald Firbank was the second son of Sir Thomas Firbank, an MP, who had inherited the large railway-contracting business built up by his self-made father. A sickly child, Firbank spent only one year at school. In his teens he passed a year in Tours learning French and a period in Madrid learning Spanish before he went to a crammer in London to be prepared for Cambridge. He spent five terms at Trinity Hall from 1906 to 1909 (he was absent travelling during the other four terms), never sat one examination and left without a degree. Under the guidance of a fashionable Cambridge preacher, Hugh Benson, he converted to Roman Catholicism in 1907, but whether he maintained the faith is questionable. Having as an undergraduate had the most elegantly furnished rooms in college, in London he cut a figure as a rich, shy and utterly fastidious dandy, rather after the fashion of the aesthetes of the 1890s; he haunted the Café Royal and a fashionable Tottenham Court restaurant, the Tour Eiffel, drinking heavily and cultivating the eccentricity of manner and behaviour that his contemporaries so amply (and naïvely) recorded.

The sudden death of Sir Thomas in October 1910 revealed that the family fortunes had been declining; the widow and idle-rich son had to make some retrenchments in their style of living, but he was able to continue living in much the same manner until the outbreak of World War I.

After numerous medical examinations he was finally declared unfit for service and, finding war-time London too depressing, moved to Oxford where he lived reclusively for the duration of hostilities. After the war he led a peripatetic life alternately travelling and settling down for a few months to write. Whatever his reputation for eccentricity and ineffectuality might suggest, he always attended carefully to the management of the estates from which his and his mother's income derived. He died in Rome of pneumonia. Throughout his life he was as open about his homosexuality as it was then possible to be; he seems to have had no long-term relationships, relying on casual encounters. Their nature is perhaps indicated by his response to a comment that he must be lonely: 'I can buy companionship.'

The retreat to Oxford was beneficial for his health and literary output. The enforced quieter life allowed him to begin writing. *Vainglory* (1915), *Inclinations* (1916) and *Caprice* (1917) resulted from the Oxford period. They were followed by *Valmouth* (1919), his one play, *The Princess Zoubaroff* (1920), the serious but insubstantial novel *Santal* (1921), and the three final masterpieces, *The Flower beneath the Foot* (1923), *Prancing Nigger* (1924; also initially called *Sorrow in Sunlight* in England) and *Concerning the Eccentricities of Cardinal Pirelli* (1926). A few other works were published posthumously.

He had to pay for the publication of all his works, none of which was obviously successful. Yet the fey, simple-seeming novels gradually acquired discerning and appreciative readers, attuned to their peculiar qualities, and though their popularity has since waxed and waned they are now generally recognised as classics of their type. Firbank's fiction builds on and develops a peculiarly English comic tradition: beneath a deceptive appearance of lightness and insubstantiality, his novels are hard-headed, even cynical, unsentimental and unromantic; they are also gilded and scrupulously crafted, whilst seeming trifling and decadent. There are no ultimate values, everything is mocked or made to appear ridiculous, and yet one also senses sometimes the sadness behind things. Camp (the knowing, self-aware kind as opposed to the unintentional) enters literature in his work, and bawdiness and *double entendre* are prevalent to a still-surprising degree (many readers simply did not get his jokes). His approach allowed him great liberty with sex; lesbians and lesbianism and male homosexuality figure offhandedly in his writing to an extent unparalleled in contemporaneous authors in English.

M. Horder (ed.) *Ronald Firbank: Memoirs and Critiques*, London, 1977; M. J. Benkovitz, *Ronald Firbank: A Biography*, New York, 1969; B. Brophy, *Prancing Novelist: A Defence of Fiction in the Form of a Critical Biography in Praise of Ronald Firbank*, London, 1973.

Gary Simes

FitzGerald, Edward (1809–1883), British translator and scholar. FitzGerald is best known for his rendition into English in 1859 of the *Rubáiyát* (Quatrains) of the Persian astronomer–mathematician–poet Omar Khayyám (*c.* 1050–*c.* 1123), though scholars now regard the original work as an anthology written by different poets, and FitzGerald's version as an improvisaton rather than an exact translation. The gender of the 'beloved' in FitzGerald's version is obscured, though in the original text the 'beloved' is sometimes male, sometimes female. Nevertheless, FitzGerald's work, discovered by Dante Gabriel Rossetti and other contemporaries, became one of the classic renditions of Oriental literature and, with its evocations of wine, bread, roses, the moon and the desired companion, remains one of the best-known set of love poems.

FitzGerald was born in Suffolk and educated at Cambridge University, where among his friends he counted TENNYSON (who dedicated a poem to him). He mar-

ried at the age of 47 but his attitudes towards women approached misogyny. He may not have ever had sexual relations with anyone, though his voluminous correspondence is replete with expressions of 'love' to various close male friends. From his university days onwards, he had a continuing series of male companions, generally young and athletic. A particular friend was Edward Cowell, who was 18 (half FitzGerald's age) when the two met. The young man ran his father's counting-house but had taught himself several European languages, as well as Persian; that interest was the inspiration which ultimately led FitzGerald to the *Rubáiyát*. FitzGerald encouraged his protégé to go to Oxford, despite his previous lack of formal education, and Cowell gave FitzGerald a copy of the Persian poem cycle which he had copied from a manuscript in the Bodleian Library. Cowell lived up to his mentor's expectations and became Professor of Sanskrit at Cambridge.

Interest in Orientalism, the strength of male friendships, sexual reticence, and the links between emotional ties and literary endeavours – all characteristics of some nineteenth-century homosexuals – are thus well illustrated in the life and work of FitzGerald.

R. B. Martin, *With Friends Possessed: A Life of Edward FitzGerald*, London, 1985.

Robert Aldrich

Flandrin, Hippolyte (1809–1864), French painter. Born in Lyon, the most distinguished of three brothers who became painters, in 1829 Flandrin moved to Paris, where he studied with Ingres. In 1833, he won a fellowship to the French academy in Rome, where he remained for five years. He spent his entire life as a professional painter, completing allegorical and religious works, portraits and some landscapes. He was particularly known for his decorative paintings in churches, notably Saint-Germain-des-Prés in Paris. He was married and had several children.

Flandrin is known in the history of homosexuality for a single work, *Jeune homme nu assis sun un rocher* (*Nude Young Man Seated on a Rock*), begun in 1835 and finished the following year as a fourth-year study required by his fellowship. It portrays a curly haired ephebe seated with his arms wrapped around his legs and his forehead resting on his knees against a background of the sea and a rocky outcropping. Contemporary critics noted the influence of Piero della Francesca, MICHELANGELO and Ingres, and sometimes compared the painting to a medal or a cameo. Théophile Gautier wondered if the sad youth was a shepherd who had lost his flock or a voyager shipwrecked on a deserted island. The painting was purchased by Emperor Napoleon III in 1857 and it now hangs in the Louvre Museum in Paris.

The image entered the homosexual gallery when Wilhelm von GLOEDEN, around 1900, took a photograph of a young man in the identical pose as the figure in Flandrin's picture. Later photographers, including Robert Mapplethorpe, have reinterpreted the scene, sometimes with direct quotation from the original. Though painted by a heterosexual and without a specifically homosexual theme, Flandrin's painting has become one of the most widely recognised and appreciated gay icons – for the pictorial beauty of the Mediterranean youth and perhaps, too, the mood of solitude and reflection – through reproduction on postcards, posters and book jackets.

Hippolyte, Auguste et Paul Flandrin. Une Fraternité picturale au XIXe siècle, Paris, 1984; M. Camille, 'The Abject Gaze and the Homosexual Body: Flandrin's *Figure d'Étude*', *Journal of Homosexuality*, 27, 1/2 (1994): 161–88
                                                    Robert Aldrich

Foresythe, Reginald (1907–1958), British pianist, bandleader and composer. Born in London, Foresythe was the son of a Yoruba (Nigerian) barrister and an Englishwoman of German descent. Fore-

sythe received a public school education, and studied piano and composition. Throughout his life Foresythe used his upper-class British accent to achieve some measure of acceptance in an otherwise racially segregated world. In the 1930s in Britain he won respect in jazz circles for such bold and dazzling compositions as 'Serenade for a Wealthy Widow', 'Berceuse for an Unwanted Child', 'Greener the Grass', 'Melancholy Clown' and 'Dodging a Divorcee'. Charles Fox says: 'Foresythe's music frequently possessed wit as well as sophistication, charm as well as ingenuity, and certainly nobody in this country worked harder to expand the boundaries of jazz.'

On a visit to New York in 1937, Foresythe composed the music for some of the songs in that year's *Cotton Club Parade*, a lavish revue with a cast headed by Ethel Waters and Duke Ellington. In America in the 1930s, jazz giants such as Louis Armstrong and Fats Waller admired Foresythe and recorded his compositions. Earl Hines used Foresythe's 'Deep Forest' as a signature tune on his first radio series. Charles Fox says: 'If he had only stayed in the United States, instead of returning to Britain, he might easily have become an influential and important figure in jazz. Over here, of course, his ideas were considered to be "too far out", even by many musicians; he was looked on, in fact, as something of a musical eccentric. The result was that a very talented jazz composer failed to live up to his early promise.'

When the African-American singer Elisabeth Welch made London her home in 1933, she began looking for an accompanist. She recalls in *Brief Encounters* (1996): 'When I arrived in London I was offered cabaret engagements, but I didn't know anyone who could accompany me. I was given Reggie's name and of course I'd heard about him in America and Paris. He was a sweet, simple, charming person. His appearance was always immaculate and elegant. He loved good food and talked with that wonderful English upper-class accent. When we made fun of his accent, he didn't mind at all. He had a great sense of humour about himself. We all loved him. Reggie was a "confirmed bachelor". I do not recall a woman ever being associated with him. I know he had liaisons with men, but they were always very discreet.'

On his return to London from New York, Foresythe worked in Mayfair clubs until the outbreak of World War II. Overage for active service, he volunteered anyway. Drafted into the RAF in 1941, he became an Intelligence Officer, and served in North Africa.

In the 1930s Foresythe had been ahead of his time but, after the war, time seemed to have passed him by. He was soon leading bands in obscure West Country hotels, and playing solo piano in drinking clubs in London's Soho and Kensington. His career ended in obscurity and alcoholism. He died from heart failure after a fall at his home in London.

S. Bourne, *Brief Encounters: Lesbians and Gays in British Cinema 1930–71*, London, 1996; C. Fox, *Just Jazz 3*, London, 1959.

Stephen Bourne

Forster, E(dward) M(organ) (1879–1970), British writer. Born in London, Forster became one of the most important novelists of the Edwardian period. His novels, *Where Angels Fear to Tread* (1905), *The Longest Journey* (1907), *A Room with a View* (1908), *Howards End* (1910), and *A Passage to India* (1924), and his literary criticism and belletristic essays collected in *Aspects of the Novel* (1927), *Abinger Harvest* (1936), *Two Cheers for Democracy* (1951) and *The Hill of Devi* (1953), as well as short stories, established him as one of Britain's most beloved and respected authors. Politically liberal, personally charming and generous, he retired finally to Cambridge where he ended his long life, serene and honoured locally, nationally and internationally. After his death, his novel *Maurice* (written *c.* 1913), a story of homosexual love, as well as

many stories dealing with homosexuality were posthumously published (1975). Forster, who was publicly closeted, had struggled with the issue of coming out as both an artist and a man for many years, and though he did what he could to help create a climate of toleration for homosexuals, he could not in his lifetime bring himself into the public limelight as a gay man. When Lionel Trilling wrote his study of Forster, as part of *New Directions: The Makers of Modern Literature* series (1943), he did not suspect that Forster was homosexual.

Though Forster wrote many gay short stories, he also burned much of his earliest work sometime before the publication of *A Passage to India*. Some of the surviving stories are among his finest fiction. But *Maurice* was generally regarded by the public as inferior to his other novels. Critics complained that the novel was sentimental, but it seems more likely that the literary establishment was nonplussed by Forster's romanticism, his insistence on a happy ending and the depiction of homosexual love as guiltless and fulfilling. After *Maurice*, Forster did not think he could write novels anymore, having said all he had to about heterosexual love. It took him nearly ten years to return to the novel, his final work and masterpiece, *A Passage to India*, which is not about love at all, but about the crippling puritanism of colonial Britain. Then he announced he was finished with the novel as a genre. As a major novelist, Forster silenced himself in the name of decorum, and while his closetry might have been painful to bear, it was not intolerable. What it cost him as an artist is less clear. He lived 46 more years, many of them productive as a critic and essayist, but all the work was now in a minor key.

P. N. Furbank, *E. M. Forster, A Life*, London, 1978; F. H. King, *E. M. Forster*, London, 1978, rev. edn., 1988; B. J. Kirkpatrick, *A Bibliography of E. M. Forster*, Oxford, 1985; N. Beauman, *E. M. Forster, A Biography*, New York, 1993; M. Lago, *E. M. Forster, A Literary*

Life, New York, 1995; P. Bakshi, *Distant Desire: Homoerotic Codes and the Subversion of the English Novel in E. M. Forster's Fiction*, New York, 1996; R. K. Martin and G. Piggford (eds) *Queer Forster*, Chicago, 1997.

Seymour Kleinberg

Fowler, John Beresford (1906–1977), British interior decorator. Fowler, like other inter-war queer men such as Cecil BEATON, used the vehicle of eighteenth-century revivalism and escapist design to rise from humble origins to great success, selling back his version of patrician 'taste' to the English aristocracy: the Duchess of Devonshire called him 'the prince of decorators'.

Beginning his career painting decorative wallpapers, he commenced work at Peter Jones in London in 1931 before launching his own shop in the King's Road, Chelsea, in 1934. He joined forces with Lady Sybil Colefax in 1938, and then with Nancy Lancaster he founded a firm which is still in existence. His 1930s schemes had a camp swagger and Regency theatricality reminiscent of both Hollywood movies and the interiors arranged by Beaton. In the 1950s Fowler popularised a vision of country-house living in which fine antiques and fabrics and the symmetrical arrangements preferred in the eighteenth century were merged with more comfortable Victorian seat furnishings and informal chintz fabrics. This fashion for 'grand informality' employing principally English and French objects influenced town houses as well and enjoyed a strong revival amongst wealthy clients around the world in the 1980s. Knowledgeable about the history of interior design, he co-authored a seminal text with John Cornforth, *English Decoration in the 18th Century* (1974) and became adviser to the National Trust on the redecoration of its properties from 1956. He retired from Colefax and Fowler in 1969 but continued to work for the Trust.

His private life was as discreet as his design was about ebullient grandeur; perhaps for this reason he is generally less well known today than other inter-war designers such as Cecil Beaton.

R. Becker, *Nancy Lancaster: Her Life, Her World, Her Art*, New York, 1996; S. Calloway, *Twentieth-Century Decoration*, New York, 1988; C. Jones, *Colefax and Fowler: The Best in English Interior Decoration*, London, 1989.

Peter McNeil

François, Joannes Henri (1884–1948), Dutch writer and activist. François was the son of a gas and water-works manager. After a depressing high school period in The Hague, he found solace in Rein Leven, a sexual purity movement. Only 19 years old, he attended Dr Lucien von RÖMER's famous lecture 'Ongekend Leed' ('Unknown Sorrow'), from which he returned reborn, having realised he was a homosexual, and that there were many thousands like him, entitled to happiness through love, just like anyone else.

Shortly afterwards, he went to The Netherlands East Indies, to begin his career as a civil servant. François loved the East Indies, and also its population. He had an open eye for the injustice of the relations between the ruling Dutch and the Eurasians and Indonesians. Back in The Hague in 1908, he started writing, while supporting himself as a colonial civil servant in Holland. Almost all of his fiction, six novels and seven short stories, is permeated with idealism, the pursuit of a just society. François was a pacifist and a vegetarian, and fought for the equal rights of homosexuals as well as Eurasians. In 1909 he met M. J. J. EXLER, who showed him the manuscript of *Levensleed* (*Sorrow of Life*), a novel that sometimes reads like a lecture about homosexuality. François reviewed Exler's book, and as a result he was approached by Jacob Schorer, who founded the Dutch branch of HIRSCHFELD's Scientific-Humanitarian Committee in May 1912. From the beginning to the very end, François was Schorer's active co-worker. On his request, François reviewed *Die Bücher der namenlosen Liebe* by Sagitta (John Henry MACKAY). Afterwards, he courageously permitted his own name and address to be used to order Sagitta's works, which were forbidden in Germany.

His most important works were written in the next few years, in the service of homosexual emancipation. The first is a brochure, *Open Brief aan hen die anders zijn dan de anderen. Door een hunner (Open Letter to Them who are Different from the Others. By One of Them)*, published in 1916. It is a remarkable work, meant to comfort and cheer his fellow homosexuals – the first Dutch publication showing 'gay pride'.

François' first clearly homosexual novel, *Anders (Different,* 1918) was written under the pseudonym 'Charley van Heezen'. It possessed a didactic tendency, even to the extent of having a happy ending. Much more enjoyable than Exler's wooden tear-jerker, *Anders* exerted a beneficiary influence on several generations of shy homosexuals, continuing to be read until the 1960s. In 1922 under the same pen-name, he published a second homosexual novel, *Het Masker (The Mask)*, another key word for homosexuality.

Het Masker likewise is a didactic novel, but it is also a strong real-life report about being homosexual in the first half of the twentieth century. It tells us about the showing of Hirschfeld's movie *Anders als die Andern*, and there is a chilling account of the biggest homosexual scandal in The Netherlands, in The Hague in 1920.

François returned to Indonesia in 1921, and stayed there until 1935. He was very much interested in the Indonesian freedom movement. In 1936 he made a trip to India, where he had a talk with Gandhi and Nehru about Java. Still cooperating with Schorer, in 1939 he wrote a pamphlet about a shocking homosexual scandal in The Netherlands East Indies, in which several hundred men were involved. And on the day of the German invasion of The Netherlands, he assisted Schorer in destroying the archive of the Dutch Scientific-

Humanitarian Committee. Also, from the beginning, he was present in the group that later formed COC, the Dutch homosexual liberation association.

In a 1946 pamphlet he pointed out that the Dutch themselves were flagrantly guilty of causing Indonesian nationalism, eventually resulting in independence after a bloodily fought conflict. All his life, François was a champion of justice, be it for homosexuals, Indonesians or pacifists, courageously fighting to the end.

K. Joosse, 'J. H. François. Anders dan anderen', *Maatstaf*, 33, 5 (1985); G. Komrij, *Averechts*, Amsterdam, 1980; B. J. Stokvis, *De Homosexueelen*, Lochem, 1939, autobiography No. 11; H. van Weel and P. Snijders, 'Met trots en zelf-bewustheid', in H. Hafkamp and M. van Lieshout (eds) *Pijlen van naamloze liefde*, Amsterdam, 1988.

Paul Snijders

Frederick II (1712–1786), king of Prussia. Frederick the Great doubled the size of his northern German kingdom during his 46-year reign, establishing it as a military might and major European power. He was a cultivated Francophile, a writer and an accomplished musician. His homosexuality was an open secret, even during his reign. Born in Berlin, his parents were King Frederick Wilhelm I and Queen Sophie Dorothea, the sister of England's George II.

Frederick's youth was marked by his father's ill-treatment. Frederick Wilhelm, an intolerant, unloved king, was disgusted with his small, pretty son who curled his hair in the French style and played the flute. He exposed Frederick to frequent public beatings and other humiliations. At age 18, Frederick could stand no more, and planned to flee to France with his favourite companion, Hans von Katte, a handsome officer who shared Frederick's French tastes. The king, already suspicious of a sexual relationship between them, intercepted their escape plans, and had them both arrested. He ordered Katte to be beheaded outside Frederick's prison window. The weeping prince blew Katte a kiss and asked for forgiveness. Katte replied, 'No need of forgiveness, sir, I die for you with the greatest joy', then knelt for his decapitation. Frederick fainted dead away, and suffered hallucinations for two days following.

After Katte's death, Frederick's father forced him to marry Elizabeth Christine of Brunswick, niece of the Austrian Empress Maria Theresa. He immediately separated from his wife when Frederick Wilhelm died in 1740. Frederick was no woman-hater. He had had at least two affairs with women during his youth, and was very close to his sister, Wilhelmine. Nevertheless, he had very little in common with his bride. Moreover, he resented his political marriage as an example of the Austrian interference which had plagued Prussia since 1701. Their marriage produced no children. In later years, Frederick would pay his wife formal visits only once a year.

When he became king, Frederick introduced civil reforms, including the abolition of torture, religious discrimination and press censorship. He even wrote *L'Antimachiavel* (1740), an enlightened political treatise refuting the despotic principles endorsed by Machiavelli. On the international front, however, he had a score to settle with Austria. Upon accession he seized Silesia, an Austrian dominion in Poland. This led to a number of ensuing conflicts, culminating in the Seven Years War (1756–1763), in which Frederick thwarted attempts to regain Silesia by a coalition of Austrian, French, Swedish and Russian forces. After the war, Frederick appeased his Russian and Austrian foes by proposing that they divide Poland among themselves, extending Prussia's territory even further.

Outside the military milieu, Frederick spent much time in Potsdam at Sans Souci, his favourite residence, built in 1745–1747, pursuing erotic interests in regal seclusion. The grounds there even included a Friend-

ship Temple celebrating the homoerotic attachments of Greek Antiquity, decorated with portraits of Orestes and Pylades, among others. At Sans Souci, Frederick entertained his most privileged guests, especially the French philosopher VOLTAIRE, whom he had asked in 1750 to come to live with him and be his love. The correspondence between Frederick and Voltaire, which spanned almost 50 years, was marked by mutual intellectual fascination and homoeroticism. In person, however, their friendship was often contentious. Voltaire abhorred Frederick's militarism. On the other hand, Frederick, whom Voltaire once described as 'a loveable whore', was unnerved by the Frenchman's way of flirting with him and then backing off. Voltaire's jealous attack in the press on one of Frederick's literary companions made him no longer welcome in Prussia; on his return to France in 1753 he anonymously published *The Private Life of the King of Prussia*, wittily exposing Frederick's homosexuality and parade of male amours. Frederick neither admitted nor denied the contents of the book. Voltaire and Frederick soon thereafter amicably resumed their correspondence, only able to love each other from a distance.

Frederick became misanthropic and withdrawn during his old age, having outlived the ones dearest to him. After a long illness, he died at age 74, accompanied in his last days by a young Italian count, whom he rewarded with an ambassadorship.

S. W. Henderson, 'Frederick the Great of Prussia: A Homophile Perspective', *Gai Saber*, 1, 1 (1977): 46–54; N. Mitford, *Frederick the Great*, New York, 1970; L. Reiners, *Frederick the Great*, trans. L. P. R. Wilson, New York, 1960; J. D. Steakley, 'Sodomy in Enlightenment Prussia', *Journal of Homosexuality*, 16, 1/2 (1988): 163–75.

Seán Henry

Freud, Sigmund (1856–1939), Austrian founder of psychoanalysis. Born in

Moravia, Freud lived for most of his life in Vienna. There he founded the approach to the study of mental life and illness known as psychoanalysis. Central to Freud's approach is his theory of the 'unconscious', an idea implicit in both the pessimistic philosophy of SCHOPENHAUER and the sceptical psychological analyses of NIETZSCHE. Freud's use of hypnosis, 'free association' and dream analysis suggested that our unconscious mind has aims and intentions which sometimes require that our conscious mind be deceived. Freud exploits this fundamental idea to explain a wide range of mental phenomena from 'Freudian slips' to psychological illness. Neurosis and psychosis are traced to childhood experiences of psychological shock or 'trauma', resulting in the 'repression' of unassimilable material and the construction of unconscious 'defence mechanisms'. The symptoms of mental illness in later life are the unintended consequences of these now redundant psychic devices.

Less palatable to the *bourgeoisie* of *fin de siècle* Vienna was Freud's belief that the unconscious mind is mostly interested in sex. He attracted particular odium for attributing sexual motivations to children. The traumatic childhood scenes uncovered by the psychoanalyst typically involve experiences of sexual frustration and abuse, whether real or imagined. Children exhibit the sexual instinct both in the pleasure they take from 'erogenous' zones of the body, such as the mouth, anus and genitals, and in the intensity of their loving attachments to parents. The fate of these attachments plays a crucial role – via 'Oedipus' and 'Electra' complexes – in the subsequent mental life of the individual.

The idea of childhood sexuality is less shocking, however, once Freud's considerable broadening of the concept of sexuality is understood. Crucial to Freud's revised conception of sexuality is the distinction between 'sexual aim' and 'sexual object', which serves to undermine the common assumption that sex essentially involves reproductive behaviour. 'Let us', he says, 'call the person from whom sexual attraction proceeds the *sexual object* and the act towards which the instinct tends the *sexual aim*.' As such conscientious researchers into the startling variety of sexual experience as the Marquis de SADE and Richard von KRAFFT-EBING had already shown, sexual activity can involve a seemingly endless variety of 'aims' – active, passive, penetrative and non-penetrative, pleasurable and painful – employing every part of the body with a variety of 'sexual objects' – of the same and opposite sex, human, animal and fetish, living, dead, adult, adolescent and child.

Freud's extended concept of sexuality corresponds to a radical theory of the 'sexual aberrations' as a universal potential that is more or less prominent at different stages in the life of the individual, in different cultures and at different times. Thus both historical and anthropological evidence confirms that homosexuality, or 'inversion', has been tolerated, if not celebrated, in many societies including, of course, ancient Greece. Indeed this is to be expected, because sexual aberrations are anticipated in the 'polymorphously perverse' desires of the child, which are eventually pressed by society into the limiting mould of 'normal', reproductive adult sexuality. According to a lengthy footnote added in 1915 – both the length and number of revisions at this point suggest a certain anxiety on Freud's part – 'psychoanalysis considers that a choice of an object independently of its sex – freedom to range equally over male and female objects – as it is found in childhood, in primitive states of society and early periods of history, is the original basis from which, as a result of restriction in one direction or the other, both the normal and the inverted types develop'. The radical implication of this postulation of an original bisexuality is, as Freud recognises, that heterosexuality stands as much in need of explanation as any other manifestation of the sexual instinct.

Two factors, however, serve to blunt Freud's radicalism. In the first place, his theory of sexuality still posits a normal path of sexual development or maturation. At puberty the sexual aim is normally subordinated to the reproductive function, just as oral and anal 'erotogenic zones' are 'subordinated to the primacy of the genital zone'. By the same token, perverse sexuality is seen as a sign of arrested development: 'In inverted types, a predominance of archaic constitutions and primitive psychical mechanisms is regularly to be found.' As Neu tersely puts it, 'Perverse sexuality is, ultimately, infantile sexuality.' A second factor qualifying Freud's radicalism is his theory of 'sublimation'. Accused of dragging civilisation into the mire of base sexuality, Freud preferred to emphasise our ability to 'sublimate' libidinous energies, redirecting them to more refined artistic and intellectual activities necessary for civilisation. Freud's back-handed defence of the sexual perversions is, then, that 'by being suppressed or by being diverted to higher, asexual aims – by being 'sublimated' – [they] are destined to provide the energy for a great number of our cultural achievements'. It is in this sense that he can claim that 'the enlarged sexuality of psychoanalysis coincides with the Eros of the divine PLATO'.

S. Freud, *On Sexuality: Three Essays on the Theory of Sexuality and Other Works*, Harmondsworth, 1977; J. Neu, 'Freud and Perversion', in R. M. Stewart (ed.) *Philosophical Perspectives on Sex and Love*, Oxford, 1995: 87–104.

David West

Friedländer, Benedict (1866–1908), German biologist and philosopher. The son of a professor of economics, Friedländer studied natural sciences and graduated as a zoologist. He also published on political theory. Influenced by the philosophies of SCHOPENHAUER and NIETZSCHE, he advocated a combination of socialism and individual freedom, but he strongly rejected Marxism. Conducting biological and geological research, Friedländer travelled in Italy, the Pacific, India and Ceylon for many years. During the last period of his life he became involved in the homosexual movement and wrote several works on homosexuality.

A co-founder of BRAND's Gemeinschaft der Eigenen, Friedländer was at the same time a prominent member of HIRSCHFELD's Wissenschaftlich-humanitäres Komitee, until he headed a secession from the Committee in 1906. He planned to found a 'movement for a male culture', which was not realised, however, because, suffering from an incurable disease, he committed suicide in 1908. The main cause of the dramatic rupture in the early German homosexual movement was, according to Friedländer, Hirschfeld's biomedical theory of homosexuality. Friedländer refuted two important presuppositions in medical thinking: the existence of a natural homosexual category, independent of morals and culture, and the biological identification of male homosexuality with femininity in men. His reasoning, reminiscent of the Kinsey scale (according to which exclusive homosexuality and heterosexuality are mere abstractions), pointed to eroticism in male friendships and male bonding in general, since he believed men to be essentially bisexual. Friedländer argued that homosexuality in men, and masculinity, were in many cases inextricably connected.

In his main work, *Renaissance des Eros Uranios* (1904), Friedländer explained that medical interference with homosexuality was rooted in Christianity: the feeling of being sick and aberrant, the sense of belonging to a different human species originated in the Christian condemnation of homoeroticism as sinful and criminal. Supported by women, Friedländer maintained, priests had imposed an ascetic morality upon males, forcing them to suppress their omnipresent homoerotic leanings. Christian matrimonial morals, which were 'affirmed' by biomedical science, established the idea that only heterosexual love was natural and, consequently, 'physiological friendship' – a fundamental human passion, according to Friedländer – was no longer respected or cultivated. He stressed the social and cultural value of homoeroticism. In addition to examples taken from literature and history, Friedländer followed the example of Heinrich Schurtz's ethnological study *Altersklassen und Männerbünde: Eine Darstellung der Grundformen der Gesellschaft* (1902). In this book Schurtz maintained that the 'instinctive sympathy' between men was the precondition for social life and political institutions. Although Schurtz did not interpret this sympathy as erotic, Friedländer invoked his findings to assert that social organisations beyond the family could not exist if men restricted their emotional and erotic relations to women. He considered homoeroticism not only as fundamental for the unfolding of man's creative and intellectual qualities, but also for instilling in men patriotism and military virtues. He believed that in bourgeois society the female sphere of the family had become overdeterminant.

Like Otto WEININGER, Friedländer was obsessed by the notion that women exerted too much influence in modern society. Women's emancipation was the most objectionable consequence of democratisation, and since they thwarted male bonding, he held women, being materialistic and superstitious, responsible for cultural decline. For Friedländer, a healthy culture was inherently masculine, aristocratic and militaristic. Although he was a Jew himself, he also gave voice to racism in general and anti-Semitism in particular. He argued that countries such as the United States, Britain and France had already fallen victim to 'feminisation' and '*Verjüdung*', which he considered dangerous for the supremacy of the white race. It was clear to Friedländer that the German nation had to stop further feminisation of Western culture by making the *Män-*

nerbund the core of the state, thus safeguarding the exalted goals of male friendship including moral strength, self-sacrifice and *esprit*.

B. Friedländer, *Renaissance des Eros Uranios. Die physiologische Freundschaft, ein normaler Grundtrieb des Menschen und eine Frage der männlichen Gesellungsfreiheit*, Berlin, 1904; New York, 1975; B. Friedländer, *Die Liebe Platons im Lichte der modernen Biologie*, Berlin, 1909; G. Hekma, 'Een omstreden voorvechter van een homosociale maatschappij', in H. Hafkamp and M. van Lieshout (eds) *Pijlen van naamloze liefde. Pioniers van de homo-emancipatie*, Amsterdam, 1988: 155–8.

Harry Oosterhuis

Fullerton, Mary Eliza (1868–1946), Australian poet. Fullerton was born in Victoria. Raised in a Scots-Presbyterian pioneering community in Gippsland, she moved to Melbourne in the 1890s and joined the women's suffrage movement. She was also involved with literary societies and wrote articles for the *Socialist*. Her poetry, fiction and autobiographical writing were published in many periodicals, as well as in book form. In 1909 Fullerton met Mabel Singleton through their positions within the Women's Political Association. In 1910 Fullerton wrote a sonnet, ending with the words: 'heart of my heart, my soul clears and warms / I see you: and come to the harbour of Trust'. By 1911, Singleton had left her husband, and when she and her son left for England in 1921, Fullerton followed. Sylvia Martin has uncovered a wealth of letters and poems celebrating their relationship, offering another layer of meaning to Fullerton's declaration that she was a 'go-alone'. In Fullerton's own view, female friendship was pure. This discourse of ideal love being celibate created a space for the expression of love in terms acceptable to the society in which they lived. A strong, modernist poet, her poems are a reminder of those women who had the courage (and means) to express their love in an age in which physical desire between women was just beginning to be spoken. Fullerton died in Sussex, England.

K. Chadwick, "'Sweet Relief': The Politics of Erotic Experience in the Poetry of Lesbia Harford, Mary Fullerton and Zora Cross', in S. Lever and C. Pratt (eds) *Association for the Study of Australian Literature, Sixteenth Annual Conference 3–8 July 1994: Proceedings*, Canberra, 1995: 71–8; J. Hooton, 'Mary Fullerton: Pioneering and Feminism', in K. Ferres (ed.) *The Time to Write: Australian Women Writers, 1890–1930*, Melbourne, 1993: 38–53; S. Martin, 'Rethinking Passionate Friendships: The Writing of Mary Fullerton', *Women's History Review*, 2, 3 (1993): 395–406.

Helen Driver

Fuseli, Henry (1741–1825), Swiss artist and writer. Fuseli was born in Zurich, Switzerland, second of five children of Johann Füssli, a portrait painter, town clerk and writer on art, and his wife Elizabeth, who died when Henry was an adolescent. He grew up surrounded by drawings and engravings of sixteenth-century Swiss mannerist artists, absorbed his father's appreciation of WINCKELMANN and Mengs, and learnt about the emerging cult of the antique, centred in Rome. During his education at the Zurich Collegium Humanitatum he became an enthusiastic classical philologist and was introduced to the works of Homer, the *Nibelungenlied*, Dante, SHAKESPEARE and Milton, which later provided many of the subjects for his paintings.

Fuseli's autocratic father decided that his son would not develop his artistic talent but should train to be a minister in the Reformed Church of Zurich: he was ordained in 1761. A fellow theological student, Johann Lavater, remained a close lifelong friend, and later, Lavater's son also close to Fuseli. After a confrontation with the local bureaucracy, Fuseli, Lavater and two others recently ordained left Switzerland for Berlin. Fuseli then went

on to London in 1764 and abandoned theology but retained a formal respect for Christianity.

In 1768 Fuseli met Sir Joshua Reynolds, who urged him to take up painting. Two years later Fuseli went to Rome to train as a painter with financial support from his friend and patron, Thomas Coutts. In Rome Fuseli was impressed by the paintings of MICHELANGELO in the Sistine Chapel and by antique sculpture. The style he developed in Rome remained almost unchanged for the rest of his working life. In particular, classical statues and Greek vase paintings of nude men with legs apart and genitals exposed became for Fuseli an unselfconscious expression of either male strength and dominance or male vulnerability and submission. In his completed paintings, however, he usually bowed to convention and contemporary sensibilities by covering male genitals with either 'tights' or drapery.

Fuseli's heroes were derived from the lithe, athletic and youthful Apollo Belvedere or the solid, muscular, more mature Hercules. He is credited with creating the ideal of an implacable, resolute and wholesome man with steady gaze and clenched fist, much used by twentieth-century image-makers. The image of his other hero, the feminised, taunted and traumatised 'Apollo', has had more limited appeal.

Fuseli's drawings of erotic subjects for private circulation were not unusual for his time, but his constant theme of the dominant female was. His illustrations of episodes from literature, which described men submitting to, or being taunted by, women, appealed to both masochists and misogynists.

In 1782 Fuseli exhibited *The Nightmare* at the Royal Academy in London and made his name. The image became widely known through engravings and was satirised by caricaturists of the day. About this time Fuseli met the English artist William Blake. Until they fell out in 1810 they collaborated on projects and used images from each other's work in their own. They shared an imaginative intensity, but Fuseli rejected Blake's mysticism.

Fuseli held important positions in the Royal Academy and was an influential figure during his lifetime as a painter, art historian and writer and lecturer in art theory. His work was soon dismissed and neglected until twentieth-century Expressionists, Surrealists and post-Freudian scholars 'rediscovered' it. Fuseli married in 1788, but his sexuality is confused. His frank celebration of maleness has appealed to many gay men.

E. Mason, *The Mind of Henry Fuseli*, London, 1951; P. Tomory, *The Life and Art of Henry Fuseli*, London, 1972; Tate Gallery, *Henry Fuseli*, London, 1975.

Ian Maidment

G

Ganymede, classical Greek mythological figure. Ganymede is well known as a mythological figure from the heroic age of ancient Greece. His story and its development are viewed here as an important artistic and literary icon for boy-love.

The story begins with Homer, who names Ganymede as one of the three sons of Tros, founder of Troy. Because of his beauty, the boy was carried off by the gods to be cup-bearer to Zeus and to share the life of the immortals. Homer makes no mention of his role as Zeus's bed-mate, though later tradition clearly drew this inference from the emphasis on the boy's beauty, and the primary motive for the abduction became Zeus's sexual desire. As is common with Greek myths, various forms of the story developed – several heroes are named as Ganymede's father; the abduction is carried out by 'the gods' generally, or by Zeus himself, or on his instructions; when Zeus is the abductor he either appears in person, or takes the form of an eagle, or commands an eagle to snatch the boy up while tending his flocks on Mount Ida.

From an early period god and boy were regarded as archetypal lovers. Sophocles (fifth century BC) speaks of Ganymede 'setting Zeus's power aflame with this thighs'. The pair also served to validate the homoerotic tradition. Thus THEOGNIS, in the sixth century BC, speaks of Zeus and Ganymede as exemplars of the joys of boy-love, and ends his short poem with the words, 'And so, Simonides, do not be surprised that I have shown myself vanquished by love for a beautiful boy.' The myth belonged to a storehouse of poetic imagery drawn upon by Ibycus in the sixth century and by Pindar and Euripides (in the earlier and later fifth century). When XENOPHON (fourth century) represents SOCRATES as condemning copulation between men, he finds it necessary to deflect any appeal to the Ganymede myth by etymologising the name to mean 'attractive in judgement', not 'attractive in body' (though 'genitals' is an equally probable meaning for the second part of the name). Most interesting in the classical period are PLATO's two references to the myth. When, in *Phaedrus*, he is still (reluctantly) willing to allow an occasional lapse from the rule of celibacy, he describes the attraction between lovers as the stream of 'desire' felt by Zeus for Ganymede. When later (in the *Laws*) he condemns homosexual copulation altogether as 'unnatural', he claims that the Cretans are to be blamed for inventing the Ganymede myth in order to justify their 'perverse' indulgence in homosexual pleasure.

Not surprisingly, Ganymede survived Plato's strictures, though in the Hellenistic age he became little more than a light-hearted literary conceit. Several poets in the Greek Anthology express concern that Zeus might snatch away their boyfriends as he did Ganymede: MELEAGER, for example, is perturbed even by a passing fly, lest it turn out to be an eagle in disguise! Later still (in the Attic revival of the second century AD) Ganymede, as the object of Hera's jealousy, features in a kind of soap-opera about the court of the gods on Olympus (Lucian's satirical *Dialogues of the Gods*).

Alongside the literary allusions, there are many representations of Zeus and Ganymede in ancient Greek vase-painting, figurines, and so on, and in the Renaissance the myth was dramatically given renewed life in art and literature.

K. J. Dover, *Greek Homosexuality*, London, 1978; J. M. Saslow, *Ganymede in the Renaissance*, New Haven, 1986.

Clifford Hindley

Garbo, Greta (1905–1990), Swedish actress. The image of the mysterious and uncommunicative Greta Garbo has drifted around the edges of various sexual definitions. She was discovered by the Finnish/Russian-Jewish and avowed homosexual film director Mauritz STILLER in 1922 when he was looking for a lead to his forthcoming film, *The Story of Gösta Berling*. Greta Louisa Gustafsson, as she was born, had in 1921–1922 appeared in two short publicity films, *How Not to Dress* and *Daily Bread*, and as the feminine lead in the slapstick comedy film *Peter the Tramp*. Encouraged by this modest success, she applied for and won a scholarship to the Royal Dramatic Theatre Training School and soon began playing small roles on the stage as part of her training. Stiller introduced Greta Gustafsson to his social circle and coached her tirelessly from Stockholm to Hollywood where he was offered a contract in 1924, but where she was to become a superstar and a myth renamed Greta Garbo.

Garbo's biographer Barry Paris notes that she was technically bisexual, predominantly lesbian, and increasingly asexual as the years went by. She converted her enigmatic sexual status into power and her career profited from the curiosity and titillation that the mysterious, independent woman always aroused. With a potential bisexual star image, Hollywood did not address lesbian audiences in the first instance, but male voyeuristic interest. The Hollywood studios not only required lesbian and gay male stars to remain in the closet for the sake of their careers, but also desperately created the impression of a heterosexual romance, as MGM did for Garbo in the 1930s.

Garbo's aggressive independence, her identity of being unlike anyone else, went along with her reputation for sexual ambiguity and lesbianism. But the fact, as Paris points out, that she did not fullfil the social–sexual script the world had prepared for her was the world's problem, not hers. The assumption of her lesbianism or bisexuality was also fueled by her gender confusion in speech and dress, on and off-screen. There is as much humour as sexual revelation in Garbo's constantly masculine self-references. Garbo's off-screen wardrobe of 'male' clothing defined her androgynously in the media and created a powerful fashion statement. Garbo's sexual ambivalence was confirmed over the years, in both the public and Hollywood mind, by the male roles she always said she wanted to play – Dorian Gray, Hamlet and St Francis of Assissi, to mention a few.

Paris notes that virtually all the reports and 'common knowledge' of Garbo's affairs with women (or men, for that matter) are gossip. Garbo, of course, never told *anyone* whom she went to bed with. Socially she seems to have been more comfortable with women and gay men than heterosexual men. But it seems to be true that Garbo discreetly moved on to women after Stiller's death and the end of her liaison with John Gilbert. That double separation about 1928 marked the end of heterosexuality or its pretence in her life. A full inventory of Garbo's alleged affairs with women would still merely be based on rumours, but there are 181 letters from

Garbo to Mercedes de ACOSTA in repository at the Rosenbach Museum in Philadelphia. They might shed much further light on their relationship but were sealed until the year 2000. Future historians might find further details.

More significant than with whom and with which sex Garbo slept is *how* sex and gender were integrated into her life and films. What the public knew, or what the gay subculture knew about Garbo's real life, cannot be separated from her star image. Her star persona was ambiguous and paradoxical. Garbo often asserted movements in her films that were inconsistent with the narrative and even posed an ideological threat within it. Garbo's melancholic performance as Queen Christina (KRISTINA) with its intertextual connotations to the famous Swedish cross-dressing queen created a particular dynamic in this film. Garbo tells Gilbert that there is something inside her that will not allow her to rest. 'It is possible', she says, 'to feel nostalgia for a place one has never seen.' Similarly, 'the film *Queen Christina* created in gay people a nostalgia for something they had never seen onscreen', writes Vito Russo. Star and diva behaviour, as gay scholars Richard Dyer and Wayne Koestenbaum have pointed out, has an enormous power to dramatise the problematics of self-expression. Garbo's enigmatic and ambivalent gender performance was an appealing departure from heterosexual images and made it possible to identify both *as* gay and *with* other gay people across invisibility and disgrace. This might be her greatest contribution to lesbian and gay history.

K. Swenson, *Greta Garbo*, New York, 1997; B. Paris, *Garbo: A Biography*, New York, 1995; H. Vickers, *Loving Garbo*, London, 1995; V. Russo, *The Celluloid Closet: Homosexuality in the Movies*, New York, 1981.

Tiina Rosenberg

Gémito, Vincenzo (1852–1929), Italian sculptor. Gémito was born in Naples,

where he died. He began his artistic career in inauspicious circumstances: he was a foundling adopted by a poor Neapolitan family of carpenters. Already at the age of 9, he had shown precocious talent as a sculptor and, thanks to the goodwill of patrons, was able to take art lessons; nevertheless he remained largely self-taught. His first works were figures, generally in terracotta, of Neapolitan street urchins and folk scenes. In 1868 the purchase of one of Gémito's terracottas by the king of Italy propelled him to fame at an early age. He was thus able to sell a vast production of terracottas and bronzes in a realist style, most of them figures of nude or half-clothed children and adolescents.

The erotic appeal of such works undoubtedly derived from the sculptor's own tastes, but at the same time perfectly embodied the 'Mediterranean obsession' which Robert Aldrich suggests homosexual clients from northern Italy and northern Europe sought to indulge with southern Italian youths at this time. Contemporaries who were not homosexual were not unaware of the homoerotic character of Gémito's work, as admitted by Salvatore Di Giàcomo, writing about Gémito's sculpture in 1905: 'The working-class youths whom he took back [to his studio], for the price of a few coins a day, presented before the appreciative mixture of his wax and modeling-clay their magnificient nudity, burned by our torrid sun and tinted the colour of bronze. The quickness of their limbs shaped the bodies of these ephebes into a singularly gracious form. . . . In his observant wanderings, Gémito had always noticed the movements and passion of these semi-nude youths, whose smooth and flawless skin seemed already coloured with a metallic patina.' If Gémito's erotic enthusiasm remained relatively reserved in his sculptures, it was blatant in his drawings (which are less well known).

The years from 1870 to 1885 are those in which Gémito produced his best works and enjoyed the greatest success. There followed a period of artistic and personal crisis. Success, which had earned Gémito important 'official' commissions, drew him away from the less 'respectable' vision of fishermen, water-carriers and nude and seductive urchins. (In one of the most famous of Gémito's statues, *L'Acquaiolo*, a nude adolescent offers a drink with a gesture and a smile which go beyond the simple proposition of some water.) Gémito responded to the new market demands with increasingly cold and academic works.

His personal crisis, precipitated by a determination to make a heterosexual life and create the traditional and 'normal' family which, as an orphan, he had been denied – indeed, at his age and with his social position he was no longer one of the urchins whom he portrayed – left him mentally unbalanced by 1887. For the next 20 years, he alternated stays in mental asylums with periods of more or less regular work. His fate thus paralleled that of his contemporary realist painter Antonio Mancini (1852–1930), who shared with him a homoerotic enthusiasm for Neapolitan youths, and who also shared Gémito's studio and, possibly, his bed. Mancini's family also committed him to an asylum, which he left a broken man. The dilemma for Gémito and Mancini lay in the fact that the realist artistic approach pushed them towards ever more sincerity – that is, towards an ever more shameless homosexual inspiration – from which their 'bourgeois' success was distancing them.

Gémito was finally released from the asylum in 1909; though he had not lost his artistic virtuousity, he would never regain the inspiration and spontaneity (and success) of his youth. A commission for some portraits of Antonio ('Nino') Cesarini (1889–1943), the life-partner of Jacques d'ADELSWÄRD-FERSEN, proved that Gémito's work still held an attraction for a homosexual clientele, which Gémito, because of his situation, however, could (or would) no longer satisfy. On the other hand, for bourgeois patrons, the homoeroticism of his superb drawings was now too obvious – especially with a change in the social and artistic climate.

This is particularly well illustrated in one episode. In 1904, Gémito's friend and patron Achille Minozzi, trying to find a little work and some money for Gémito, who had just been temporarily discharged from the asylum, obtained for him from the newspaper *Il Mattino* a commission for an advertising poster. The editor of his biography recounts that 'whether by chance or bizarre choice [Gémito] chose for the model Roberto Pane – then an adolescent, but later an accomplished and well-known architect – whom he painted nude on the back [of a racing horse]. The board of directors of *Il Mattino*, despite their respect for Minozzi, did not feel at ease staking its reputation on such a daring poster; they rejected the work, and the artist received no payment.' No more explicit message could have been sent to Gémito about the unacceptability of his 'daring' nudes and about the end of an age of which he had been one of the greatest heralds. The acquisition by the Museo Nazionale di San Martino in Naples of an important number of the best works of Gémito has allowed his *œuvre* to be safeguarded and appreciated. However, its homoerotic aspect still awaits a full evaluation.

R. Aldrich, *The Seduction of the Mediterranean*, London, 1993; S. Di Giacomo, *Vincenzo Gémito*, Naples, 1905, and, rev. edn, 1988; R. Peyrefitte, *L'Exilé de Capri*, Paris, 1959.

Giovanni Dall'Orto

George, Stefan (1868–1933), German poet. Stefan Anton George was born in Büdesheim, a village near Bingen (his parents moved when he was 5 years old). His father was a landlord and became a fairly wealthy wine merchant in Bingen. His mother was the daughter of a miller from Büdesheim. George – like his elder sister and younger brother, who also became a wine merchant like his father – never married. The poet kept his room at the family house in Bingen until his death. Throughout most of his adult life, however, he lived abroad, including in London, Paris, Berlin, Vienna, Munich, Heidelberg, Basel, Kiel and Minusio, staying in boarding-houses or with various friends.

George wrote his first poems as a schoolboy. During his time at the classical secondary school (in Darmstadt) he started his first journal/literary review with a number of class-mates. On graduating in 1889, he travelled to London, Montreux (Switzerland) and Paris (perhaps with one of his teachers), where he made friends with the poet Albert Saint-Paul. He visited Stéphane Mallarmé, and met Pierre LOUŸS, Paul VERLAINE and other French and Belgian poets. According to George, it was from the French Symbolists that he learned to speak about the unspeakable in terms of religion. By the end of the same year, he went to Berlin to study modern languages. In Berlin, George met Carl August Klein, with whom in 1892 he started his review *Blätter für die Kunst* (12 volumes, mainly poetry, the last one published in 1919).

In 1891, George moved to Vienna, where he met the 17-year-old poet Hugo von Hofmannsthal. Although both were very impressed with one another, the young Hofmannsthal was soon frightened off by the claim George laid on him. What exactly transpired between the two is not very clear. Eventually, however, Hofmannsthal's father wrote to George, asking him to leave his son alone. George left Vienna. All the same, Hofmannsthal later had his poems published in George's *Blätter für die Kunst*.

Although George considered emigrating to Mexico with friends during this period, he decided instead to continue his studies in Munich. There he made many friends, the most important of whom were the poet Karl Wolfskehl (1869–1948), and a young student, Friedrich Gundelfinger (1880–1931), who later changed his surname to Gundolf and became a famous professor of literature at Heidelberg. It was also in Munich that George met the

philosopher Ludwig Klages (1872–1956), and the curious Alfred Schuler (1865–1923), the most open homosexual of what was a fairly homoerotic circle.

In 1902, George became fascinated by a young Bavarian boy, Maximilian Kronberger (1888–1904), whom George renamed Maximin. When Kronberger died in 1904, George took the opportunity to mythologise his memory; that is to say, he masked his love for the boy in terms of religion. There were other boys in George's life. The first in the series to follow Maximin was Hugo Zemik (Ugolino), who made his appearance in George's life and poetry only one year after the beloved boy-god's death. Zernik, then 14 years old, was visiting Berlin with his parents from Argentina. On the occasion of this reunion (they had met during an earlier visit in Berlin), George wrote some very passionate love poems, one of which was rendered into English by Stephen SPENDER ('My boy came home . . .').

Although George obviously loved young men and boys, and wrote many exciting love poems for them or about them, he disliked being called a homosexual, and probably did not think of himself or his friends as homosexuals in the sense of a 'third sex'. Perhaps he corresponded better with the more cultural model of Adolf BRAND and his 'Gemeinschaft der Eigenen'. While George himself never published any poems in *Der Eigene*, some of his followers/admirers did: the Swiss poet Siegfried Lang (1887–1970) and Hanns Meincke (1884–1974, also known as 'Olaf Yrsalon'). Peter Hamecher (1879–1938), one of Brand's most devoted contributors, wrote an article on George's 'manly love', which was published in Magnus HIRSCHFELD's *Jahrbuch für sexuelle Zwischenstufen* in 1914. Otto Kiefer, another contributor to both the *Jahrbuch* and *Der Eigene*, published an article on George's 'Eros' in 1926 *(Geschlecht und Gesellschaft*, 14/7).

George published his first volumes of poems privately in 1890 (*Hymnen*), 1891

(*Pilgerfahrten*) and 1892 (*Algabal*) in Berlin, Lüttich and Paris. His most famous volume, *Das Jahr der Seele* (Berlin, 1897), was also privately published. Although dedicated to his sister, it contained a cycle of poems telling a homoerotic tale of love between men (*Sieg des Sommers*). From 1898 onwards, all of his poems were published by the Berlin publishing house Georg Bondi (*Der Teppich des Lebens*, 1900; *Der siebente Ring*, 1907; *Der Stern des Bundes*, 1914; *Das neue Reich*, 1928).

When Hans-Dietrich Hellbach published his dissertation in 1931 on *Die Freundesliebe in der deutschen Literatur*, he hailed George as the fulfiller of German homoerotic poetry and referred to his last volume, '*Das neue Reich*, as not a political lesson but a lesson on love and love only'.

George's academic/official interpreters usually deny the homoerotic implications of his poetry (and, of course, every homosexual activity of the poet). One of George's fierce enemies, the writer Rudolf Borchardt (1877–1945), hinted at George's homosexuality as early as 1909, referring to it in terms of a danger to Germany's youth. In *Aufzeichnung Stefan George betreffend* (*Notes on Stefan George*), written in Italy in 1936 and published posthumously in 1998, Borchardt 'outs' George and some of George's friends (as well as some of his own friends, including the poet Rudolf Alexander Schröder) in a most awkward way. (If we can believe Borchardt, the German press and publishing houses were under the heavy domination of 'the homosexuals'.) Perhaps the publication of this text will force a long overdue academic discussion of the role of homosexuality in George's life and works.

S. George, *The Works of Stefan George*, trans. O. Marx and E. Morwitz, New York 1966; R. Borchardt, *Aufzeichnung Stefan George betreffend*, Munich, 1998; P. Hamcher, 'Der männliche Eros im Werke Stefan Georges', *Jahrbuch für sexuelle Zwischenstufen*, 14 (1914): 10–23; H. Dietrich [Hellbach], *Die Freundesliebe in der deutschen Literatur*, Leipzig, 1931; reprint, Berlin, 1996; M. Keilson-Lauritz, *Von der Liebe die Freundschaft heisst. Zur Homoerotik im Werk Stefan Georges*, Berlin, 1987; H.-J. Seekamp, R. C. Ockenden, M. Keilson [-Lauritz], *Stefan George. Leben und Werk. Eine Zeittafel*, Amsterdam, 1972.

Marita Keilson-Lauritz

Gerhard, Karl (1891–1964), Swedish actor, cabaret entertainer and songwriter. Gerhard started out as a dramatic actor, but from the 1920s onwards he rose to fame by introducing a new form of revue in which he satirised contemporary trends, politicians and society figures. Gerhard both wrote and starred in all his revues, producing over 60 of them and writing more than 4,000 songs. Elegant and urbane in style and attitudes, he has been described as a cross between ARISTOPHANES, Maurice Chevalier and Noel COWARD. During the 1930s he became a staunch opponent of Nazism and fascism, and in 1941 one of his revues was censored after an intervention from the German embassy. Gerhard, who was married three times, spent the latter part of his life living with another man and an adopted daughter. An inspired female impersonator, Gerhard also dealt with the themes of homosexuality and sexual inversion in some of his songs, and did so very openly despite homosexuality being illegal at the time. Notable examples are his signature number 'Jazzgossen' ('The Jazz Boy') from 1922 in which he satirises the effeminate homosexual dandies of the 1920s, and 'La Garçonne' and 'Flickan i frack' ('The Girl in Tails'), which deal with masculine ideals among women.

S. Ahlgren, *Den okände Karl Gerhard*, Stockholm, 1966; Å. Pettersson, *Ett bedårande barn av sin tid. Några kapitel om Karl Gerhard*, Falköping, 1977.

Johan Rosell

Ghislandi, Vittore (Fra Galgario) (1655–1743), Italian painter. Ghislandi was born in Bergamo and received his initial training from his father, a painter. He then studied with Giacomo Cotta and subsequently moved to Venice, where he remained for 13 years and became a friar. He returned to Bergamo around 1688, but moved back to Venice and on to Milan, working as a portraitist. He spent the last years of his life in Bergamo at the Galgario monastery – whence the name by which Ghislandi is generally known – and died there.

Fra Galgario's *œuvre* – in which portraits of women are rare and so pitiless that critics agree that he was misogynist – divide into two groups. His portraits of nobles, which mercilessly reveal their narrow-minded provincialism and empty-headed arrogance, border upon (and sometimes become) caricatures. Quite different are a group of portraits generically titled 'Ritratto di giovinetto' ('Portrait of a Young Man'): portraits of young priests and friars, painters and other artists, in which an affectionate approach triumphs in conveying the beauty and grace of the models. Among these, one large series stands out: portraits of the same model whom he obsessively painted from about the age of 10 until the boy reached adulthood. The model has been identified with 'Il Cerighetto' ('the little clerk'), spoken of by Fra Galgario's contemporaries as his 'favourite disciple', who died aged only 22. Giovanni Testori (1923–1993) remarks of this *œuvre*: 'Indeed, here, a wonder calls for a wonder; a caress, a caress; a kiss, a kiss; sweetness, sweetness.'

The contrast between the two kinds of painting clearly emerges when they are examined side by side, as the art critic Federico Zeri has noted in amusement: 'Realism is what one finds in Fra Galgario's painting, but . . . at the same time it is a pretext to . . . give vent through the paintbrush to the priest-painter's sexual inclinations. It cannot be denied that the most memorable [a word Zeri is here using ironically] portraits by Ghislandi are those with a female subject, especially in old age; as for men, the qualitative intensity of his pictures decreases with the subjects' age, and his many specimens of

lads and boys move along concentric orbits around an ideal model with wide eyes and thick curved lips.'

Moreover, Ghislandi's first biographer, Tassi (as quoted in Testori), wrote: 'He was very modest in every action of his; therefore, he was always little inclined towards portraying women; when he had to do it, he portrayed them completely clothed, painting in their portraits either lace-trimmings, or bizarre ribbons, or other fancy inventions, to adorn the pictures, and at the same time to cover the figure in those parts that neither his eye nor his very chaste mind wanted to explore.'

Fra Galgario had been almost completely forgotten until recent decades; today his work attracts ever increasing attention from both critics and the public. It may be mentioned that his homosexual inclination, unusually, is discussed as a self-evident fact. A large number of his paintings remain in private collections, but an important sample of his highest-quality work can be seen in the Accadmia Carrara in Bergamo and in the Museo Poldi-Pezzoli in Milan.

Fra Galgario (1655–1743) (exhibition catalogue), Bergamo, 1967; G. Testori (ed.) *Fra Galgario*, Turin, 1970, especially pp. 20–4 and 54–6; *Painting in the Eighteenth Century* (exhibition catalogue), Chicago, 1970.

Giovanni Dall'Orto

Gide, André (1869–1951), French writer. Gide was born in Paris into an affluent Protestant family which left him the means to pursue a literary career. More than almost any figure, Gide is a link between the nineteenth century and the twentieth: he was only 15 years RIMBAUD's and WILDE's junior. Since KERTBENY invented the word 'homosexual' in 1869, we can say Gide was born with homosexuality. In any event, he came to represent it for several generations (in a way that PROUST never did), and twentieth-century French literature is littered with tributes to Gide's role in restoring to gay men a sense of self-respect and reassuring them that they were not alone. Yet the champion of free thought and love, married (to his cousin) in 1895 and only widowed in 1938, was in many ways an unadventurous homosexual: his early memory of masturbation with (but not *of*) a young neighbour set a pattern for the rest of his life. It is easy to understand Gide's very mixed feelings about Wilde (his first instinct was to run), but his judgement is generous if *nuancé* ('despite all of Wilde's obvious failings, what I see above all is his greatness').

Gide reflected long on homosexuality, his thoughts eventually seeing the light of day in *Corydon*, a series of Socratic dialogues, thought out in the 1900s, drafted in 1911, and published in 1924. The argument is close and subtle, involving distinction between 'normal' and 'permissible', 'nature' and 'culture', parallels between various animals and humans (common at the time) and discussions of the Darwinian role of the sexes. As so often in homosexual thought, the Greek ideal is extolled, especially pederasty *stricto sensu*, which is seen as a protection against unchastity (because men could start with boys and graduate to women). *Corydon* is now a difficult book to read, and even when it was published, given that homosexuality was widely explained as 'inversion' or a sexual in-between stage, its omission of discussion of effeminacy must have made it seem incomplete. But it was a unique, public, reasoned plea for tolerance.

If Gide became a role-model for generations, his own inspiration was WHITMAN. The evocation of homosexuality is timid, often (as in *Corydon*) using a technique that distances the narration from the narrator. Thus, in *L'Immoraliste* (1902) a first narrator introduces Michel, a second narrator; though there are allusions to lithe limbs under flowing robes, and an increasing desire to enjoy the company of peasants and workers, the first homosexual kiss comes on page 196 (out of 214), and very little happens thereafter. In an age of

repression, only the most oblique references were possible, but were well understood. Gide inaugurated two themes that have permeated twentieth-century gay writing in France: North Africa as a liberating experience, and tuberculosis – both still to be found in work by Roland Barthes. Gide had other literary and political interests. Although a rather austere figure, his *Les Caves du Vatican* (1914) is thought by some to be the funniest book in French: a conventional (and hence ridiculous) bourgeois is thrown to his death from a moving train (the *acte gratuit* precursor of existentialism) by the handsome, amoral love-child Lafcadio, who, like Goethe's Werther, became a role model for a generation (not least René CREVEL). Gide was also preoccupied with the moral dimension of social issues like colonialism (*Voyage au Congo*, 1927). Like almost every French thinker of any note, he flirted with Marxism. His attempt at persuading the Soviets to reduce their anti-homosexual repression ran up against a blunt refusal, and disillusionment set in (*Retour de l'URSS*, 1936). The great love of his life was Marc Allégret (a classmate of Crevel and son of a Protestant pastor), and Gide and Allégret figure in Gide's *Les Faux monnayeurs* as Édouard and Olivier. Gide won the Nobel prize in 1947.

Gide is often compared with other authors – Joyce, Valéry, Rilke, Verhaeren – and often, in purely literary terms, the comparison would be to their advantage. It is difficult to define the essence of Gide: he was one of those French intellectuals for whom greatness was a profession. Barthes sums it up by suggesting that he was everyone's idea of a writer. And growing up in the 1920s, Barthes read, not the Surrealists, but Gide, 'just Gide'. Perhaps the best part of Gide for the gay reader would be his autobiographical writings and voluminous correspondence.

J. Fryer, *André and Oscar: Gide, Wilde and the Gay Art of Living*, London, 1997; M. Lucy, *Gide's Bent: Sexuality, Politics, Writing*,

Oxford, 1995; P. Pollard, *André Gide: The Homosexual Moralist*, New Haven, 1991; E. S. Apter, *André Gide and the Codes of Homotextuality*, Saratoga, Calif., 1987.

David Parris

Girodet-Trioson, Anne-Louis (1767–1824), French painter. Girodet's parents, part of the administrative bourgeoisie, did not intend for their son to become a painter, but he manifested a talent for drawing at a young age. He studied with the celebrated painter Jacques-Louis David, who recognised him as one of his more talented students. In 1789, Girodet won the prestigious Grand Prix de Rome for his painting *Joseph reconnu par ses frères*. This painting revealed Girodet's mastery of the stylistic conventions of the era. The painter demonstrated a more creative and innovative side in the work he produced while in Italy during the years 1790–1794. In particular, his *Sommeil d'Endymion* (1791) was heralded as an original interpretation of the classic myth. In his painting, Girodet replaced the goddess Diana, being brought by Cupid to gaze upon the sleeping youth, ENDYMION, with a ray of moonlight. The result is a sensual and suggestive painting of the meeting of two young men, as it is, in Girodet's version, Cupid who gazes upon the sleeping Endymion. Girodet insisted that this painting distinguished his work from that of David, and argued that he had drawn on his own experience to paint it. Indeed, during the time he worked on this painting, he had established a close relationship with another painter, Jean-Pierre Péquignot. Although the two were separated when Girodet returned to France, he remained devoted to his friend's memory following his death in 1807. Critics have speculated that his poem 'The Painter' was dedicated to this friend of his youth.

The success of the paintings Girodet produced in Italy established his reputation. On his return to France, he continued to display an interest in the unreal, fantastic and dreamlike, a sharp departure

from the realism of David's school. This approach characterised *Endymion*, as it did one of Girodet's best-known works, *Ossian* (1802), a depiction of the mythic warrior god of the Scots welcoming the heroes of the French revolutionary wars into paradise. Though this painting reportedly left David 'speechless', it inspired a new school of painting, Romanticism, which privileged emotion over reason. Girodet's position as one of the founders of Romanticism was cemented with his celebrated depiction of *Les Funérailles d'Atala* (1808), inspired by Chateaubriand's novel. Girodet's interest in Orientalism, seen in *La Révolte du Caire* (1810) and *Odalisque* (1812), as well as his penchant for capturing moments of great emotion, as in *Le Déluge* (1806), influenced painters such as Ingres, Géricault and Delacroix. Both the Empire and the Restoration celebrated Girodet. He was named a knight of the Legion of Honour in 1808 and an officer on the day of his death. Girodet's close friendship with Péquignot, his repeated refusal to let his long relationship with the actress Julie Candeille become sexual, and his extreme caution in the conduct of his private life (he had all of his love letters burnt before he died) have led some to speculate about Girodet's sexual orientation.

G. Bernier, *Anne-Louis Girodet, 1767–1824: Prix de Rome*, Paris, 1975; G. Levitine, *Girodet-Trioson: An Iconographical Study*, New York, 1978.

Victoria Thompson

Glassco, John (Buffy) (1909–1981), Canadian writer. Born in Montreal, Quebec, Glassco has become known as the expatriate Canadian who participated in 'the lost generation' of 1920s Paris. A bisexual poet and prose writer, he moved to Paris in 1927 with his partner, Graeme Taylor. While in Paris, Glassco had sexual relationships with Robert MCALMON, Kay Boyle, Claude MCKAY and many others. During his life in Paris, Glassco began writing his memoirs, a chapter of which, 'Extract from an Autobiography', was published in the literary journal *This Quarter* in 1929. In his later years he became a man of letters and an important literary figure in Canada, publishing numerous collections of poetry and his very amusing *Memoirs of Montparnasse* (1970).

Although he was never open about his homosexuality, Glassco frequently wrote about same-sex desire. His memoirs, for instance, describe him sharing a bed with Graeme Taylor and McAlmon. Moreover, Glassco's pornographic writings – *Squire Hardman* (1966), *The Temple of Pederasty* (1970), *Fetish Girl* (1972), *The Fatal Woman* (1974) – often depict characters with fluid sexual desires, engaged in sexual acts with partners of ambiguous gender. One of Glassco's more passionate relationships was with the American writer McAlmon. Between 1927 and 1929, the two men lived in Paris and travelled together throughout Europe. Neither man ever openly admitted his homosexuality publicly. However, Glassco, in a section of the manuscript that was expunged from the published text of his *Memoirs of Montparnasse*, records his overtly sexual relationship with McAlmon.

P. Kokotailo, *John Glassco's Richer World: Memoirs of Montparnasse*, Toronto, 1988.
Justin D. Edwards

Gloeden, Baron Wilhelm von (1856–1931), German photographer. Born into the minor nobility of northern Germany, Gloeden studied art and art history before falling ill with tuberculosis. After spending a year in a sanatorium, he decided to move to the warmer climate of Italy. He settled in Taormina, a seaport in Sicily known for its striking location near Mount Etna and its Greco-Roman amphitheatre. Gloeden began taking photographs as a hobby; after his father was implicated in a financial scandal, and he lost his allowance, Gloeden turned photography into a profession.

Many of Gloeden's pictures focused on typical Sicilian peasant scenes – young girls and old men, fishermen, water-carriers and priests, country roads and town squares. These were turned into postcards and achieved widespread popularity for their engagingly sentimental and charmingly 'typical' views of Mediterranean life. Gloeden also took hundreds, if not thousands, of photographs of Sicilian boys, often in states of partial or complete undress. He posed his ephebes against arcadian backgrounds or antique ruins, sometimes clothing them in mock togas or laurel crowns or using such props as small classical statues. His models were robust though poor boys whom Gloeden envisioned as the inheritors of classical beauty: 'My wish was to do artwork through photography. . . . Reading from Homer and THEOCRITUS' Sicilian poetry stimulated my fantasy. . . . My models were peasants, shepherds, fishermen.' None of the photographs portray sexual activities, yet the homoerotic message is strong. Those which highlight the masculine physicality of the subjects (the boys' genitalia or buttocks are usually clearly visible) could be classified as soft-core pornography; scenes of two or more adolescents imply homosocial camaraderie. Gloeden's most famous photograph, inspired by a painting by Hippolyte FLANDRIN, is a profile of a comely nude man sitting with his head resting on his arms and knees; titled *Kain* or *Solitude*, the picture has sometimes been seen as a metaphor for the homosexual condition in the late 1800s. In almost all of Gloeden's work, the dark-haired, dark-eyed muscular Sicilians were undoubtedly intended both to evoke homosexual fantasy and embody cultural references; *National Geographic* captioned one photograph in 1916: 'The present day descendants of the early Greek colonists of Sicily retain the grace of pose and the symmetry of form which distinguished their ancestors of two thousand years ago. Here is a youth who might have been the original for one of the matchless marbles of Praxiteles or for a figure on a Phidian frieze.'

Partly because of Gloeden's fame, Taormina became a great tourist resort, attracting such homosexuals as WILDE and KRUPP, and a number of other celebrities. Gloeden lived a comfortable life, surrounded by the protégés whom he photographed. He established bank accounts for a number of his models, and set others up in business. His closest associate, Pancrazio Bucini ('Il Moro'), served as a major domo and was possibly his lover. Although rumours circulated that other boys in Taormina of whom he took nude photographs also became Gloeden's bedfellows, he remained a respectable resident of the town. During World War I, he was classified as an enemy alien and returned to Germany, while Il Moro was conscripted into the Italian army. Many of Gloeden's photographic plates were destroyed by the facist authorities as being obscene. At the end of the war, Gloeden returned to Taormina, where he lived until his death.

R. Aldrich, *The Seduction of the Mediterranean: Writing, Art and Homosexual Fantasy*, London, 1993; C. Leslie, *Wilhelm von Gloeden, 1856–1931: Eine Einführung in sein Leben und Werk*, Innsbruck, 1980.

Robert Aldrich

Gluck (Gluckstein, Hannah) (1895–1978), British artist. Gluck was born into great wealth as a member of the J. Lyons & Co. catering and food manufacturing family. Despite the conservative pressures of a large extended family, Gluck's rebellious individualism, cojoined with her class status, allowed her to pursue an extraordinary public life as an artist who wore 'male' garments from London establishment outfitters and had relationships with women. She made such an effort to circumvent conventional notions of gender that she changed her name to the monosyllabic Gluck and refused 'prefix, suffix, or quotes'. Gluck had numerous relation-

ships with women, some married. Between 1932 and 1936 she formed a relationship with the society florist Constance Spry. Gluck in her paintings and frame-design and Spry in her floral arrangements promoted the bleached neoclassical 1930s aesthetic; they shared many of the same fashionable society clients. From 1944 to 1976 Gluck lived with the journalist Edith Shackleton Heald.

Following her schooling, Gluck attended St John's Wood Art School, near the family home, and met the Newlyn School artists in Cornwall. After an initial rift with her family, her father gave her economic independence in the form of trusts. This financial freedom permitted her to pursue an unorthodox life in considerable style, at one stage wearing androgynous clothes by Victor Stiebel and Elsa Schiaparelli. Romaine BROOKS painted her as *Peter, A Young English Girl* in 1926, but Gluck was not part of and disliked the Paris 'lesbian haut-monde' as she called it. She painted landscapes, still-lifes, genre scenes and portraits, in an Art Deco manner with an elegant calcified light, which were fashionable and sold well in the 1930s. Many of the flower-pieces are sexual: Gluck described 'loving them and stroking them with my most chosen brushes'.

Gluck's portraits of women are powerful and include famous inter-war lesbians such as the Austrian Mariette Lydis, Comtesse de Govonne. The *Medallion* painting (1937), a double portrait of Gluck and her lover Nesta Obermer, is justly famous as a paradigmatic representation of a female couple's 'marriage', as Gluck called it. In 1932 she patented the 'Gluck' frame, a stepped frame designed to make her paintings an integral part of a room's architecture. Indicating her love of craftmanship, from 1953 to 1967 she also conducted a long battle with paint manufacters over the fugitive nature of modern painting materials. Her last exhibition in 1973 proved immensely popular, coming as it did when the art and design of the

1930s were enjoying new attention in the academy and the marketplace.

D. Souhami, *Gluck 1895–1978: Her Biography*, London, 1988.

Peter McNeil

Gogol, Nikolai (Vasil'evich) (1809–1852), Russian writer. Born into a family of minor Ukranian nobility in the region of central Ukraine that was the cradle of the Ukranian literary revival at the beginning of the nineteenth century (his father was a playwright who wrote in Ukranian), Gogol chose, however, a literary career in Russian since that answered his strong personal ambitions. In 1828, after graduating from a Lyceum in the town of Nezhin, he moved to the imperial capital, St Petersburg, where he immediately sought, unsuccessfully at first, the acquaintance of Aleksandr Pushkin and other prominent Russian writers. His first book, a pseudonymously published long narrative poem that appeared in 1829, proved a fiasco (he bought up and burned most of the published copies), as did his brief appointment as an adjunct professor of history at St Petersburg University. Within a few years, he found his unique literary voice; encouraged by the success of the works of other Ukranian-born Russian writers who used their native land as an exotic locale for their Romantic and Gothic tales, he published a two-volume collection of short stories, *Evenings on a Farm Near Dikanka* (Part One, 1831, Part Two, 1832), which combined elements of the comic and the Gothic in an exoticised Ukranian setting; this work established his reputation as one of Russia's leading prose writers. Several other books soon followed: *Arabesques*, a miscellany of stories and essays; *Mirgorod*, consisting of four long stories, one of which, *Taras Bulba*, was later reworked into a historical novel of Walter Scottian type (both 1835); and a comedy, *The Inspector General* (1836). The year 1836 proved to be an abrupt turning point in his life. Dismayed at his failed

attempts at becoming a greater influence in Russian literary politics, and especially as a result of his conviction that his play was a sensational success for all the wrong reasons, Gogol left Russia for a prolonged stay abroad. He divided his time between travels around Europe and residence in Rome, working on his most ambitious project, the novel *Dead Souls*, which was conceived as a monumental work on the scale of Dante's *Commedia*.

It was in Italy that Gogol's repressed sexuality found an outlet. His more relaxed attitude to sexuality may be due to his friendship with the prominent Russian painter Aleksandr Ivanov, who lived in Rome for over 20 years and was known for his many portraits of nude teenage boys in open-air settings. In December 1838, Gogol met at the villa of a Russian princess the young Count Iosif Vielhorsky. A friend and former playmate of the future Tsar Alexander II, Vielhorsky had fallen ill with tuberculosis and was sent to Italy for treatment; he died in May 1839. The few months Gogol and Vielhorsky spent together were the happiest and most fulfilling in Gogol's life. His deep attachment to the young man proved to be Gogol's only experience of a meaningful emotional union with another person. He spent all his time with Vielhorsky, nursing him until the end; deeply disturbed by the loss of his beloved, he later proposed to the Count's sister, but was rejected. Gogol captured the experience of their time together in a cycle of diary-like fragments, 'Nights at the Villa', which in their tone and style are unlike anything else he ever wrote. They were not published in his lifetime, and were later discovered in the archive of one of this friends. Only a few pages have survived, and critics have speculated that they constitute part of a larger, now lost, text.

The subsequent years of Gogol's life and work show a darkening of his tone and an intensifying personal crisis. In 1842 he published, among other works, the first volume of *Dead Souls* and the short story

'The Overcoat', the two works that are generally considered his masterpieces. No new significant artistic works by him appeared after that year: the rest of his life is a chronicle of ever-growing frustration and desperation. He burned several versions of the manuscript of the second volume of *Dead Souls* and manuscripts of other unpublished works, and turned increasingly to quasi-religious writing, producing a bizarre book titled *Selected Passages from Correspondence with Friends* (1847), which was rejected by religious conservatives and liberals alike. In 1848, after a pilgrimage to Jerusalem which also proved a failure, he returned to Russia. In his final years, he repeatedly complained of an inability to write and of what he called 'a serious nervous disorder'. A priest he came to know and towards whom he developed what may be described as a masochistic attachment prescribed strict fasting and prayer as the cure for his spiritual malaise, and basically starved him to death. Shortly before dying, Gogol burned the manuscript of the second volume of *Dead Souls* one last time.

Gogol's lasting fame proved to be as that of Russia's first great prose writer. In subsequent years, realist and symbolists, modernists and socialist realists alike claimed him as a founding father of their traditions and as a key influence. One of his great achievements is the vitality of his language, ranging from the lyrical to the comic and the grotesque. Nowhere else in Russian prose of his time does one find such a rich play with sound, rhythm and allusion. A sexually repressed and deeply tormented person, he left in his 'Nights at the Villa' a document of the transformation effected by the release of one's true feelings, even though we will likely never know if he had ever consummated them.

S. Karlinsky, *The Sexual Labyrinth of Nikolai Gogol*, Cambridge, 1976; G. Luckyj, *The Anguish of Mykola Hohol, a.k.a. Nikolai Gogol*, Toronto, 1997; R. Maguire, *Exploring Gogol*, Stanford, 1994; V. Nabokov, *Nikolai Gogol*, New York, 1944.

Vitaly Chernetsky

Goodsir, Agnes Noyes (1864–1939), Australian painter. Goodsir was born in Portland, Victoria, the daughter of the commissioner of customs in Melbourne. Her art training in Australia was with Arthur Woodward, and in 1899 an art union of her work was held in Bendigo to enable her to study in Paris. She studied in several studios in Paris until 1912, after which she alternated between London and Paris. Her work was extremely successful, being shown at the New Salon, the Salon des Indépendants, the Société Nationale des Beaux-Arts, the Royal Academy and the Royal Institute. She returned briefly to Australia in 1927 to exhibit at Macquarie Galleries, Sydney, and the Fine Arts Gallery, Melbourne.

Her major interest was in painting portraits and some of her sitters were Count Leo Tolstoy, Dame Ellen Terry, Bertrand Russell and Banjo Patterson. Her many figure studies and portraits of women stressed their androgynous image and their use of male clothing, such as *Miss G in Pyjamas* (c. 1924) or *Type of the Latin Quarter* (c. 1926). Following her death in 1939 her studio model and close companion, Mrs Rachel Dunn, sent several of her works back to Australia to be given to state and regional galleries.

K. Quinlan, *In a Picture Land Over the Sea: Agnes Goodsir, 1864–1939*, Bendigo, 1998.

Elizabeth Ashburn

Gorani, Count Giuseppe (1740–1819), Italian soldier, writer, ambassador and adventurer. Gorani was born into an impoverished but noble Milanese family. After completing his studies, he enlisted in the army and took part in the Seven Years War. Taken prisoner, he remained in Prussia until 1763; there he studied law and took an interest in the reforms of FREDERICK II. Thanks to this experience, he became a figure of the Lombard

Enlightenment on his return home, promoting an idea of enlightened despotism modelled on the rule of Frederick the Great, and writing studies of the French physiocrats, economics and politics. He also made a number of trips to various European countries, collecting material for the memoirs he wrote in later life.

The oubreak of the French Revolution attracted Gorani's unconditional support and inspired his move to Paris, where he obtained French citizenship in 1793 and frequented political moderates such as Mirabeau, Condorcet and Bailly. The advent of the Terror caused a change of heart. Sent to Geneva to prepare for French annexation of the Swiss city, Gorani counselled the inhabitants to resist the French – leading him to be branded a traitor in Paris. Yet Gorani also made enemies among the counter-revolutionaries, especially after the publication of writings attacking the queen of Naples, Maria Carolina.

Gorani, now despised and forgotten by his former associates, settled in Geneva and spent the remainder of his life writing his monumental and amazing *Mémoires pour servir à l'histoire de ma vie*, which were published posthumously (albeit in truncated form). The work, in which Gorani showed no scruples in reporting intimate details and gossip about his contemporaries, constitutes an important account of eighteenth-century private life. Such a willingness to write about sexual life makes this work and his other memoirs (among them, *Memorie di giovinezza e di guerra (1740–1763)* and *Mémoires secrets et critiques*) significant documents generally overlooked in gay and lesbian history.

Gorani's sincerity extended to confessions about his own homosexual tendencies. He recounted how he 'acquired' (in his view) a taste for male youths during his studies at the Collegio dei Barnabiti in Milan, though such sentiments tormented him throughout his life. According to Gorani, 'My behaviour and my comely appearance earned me the friendship of my schoolmates in the college, as well as the immoderate love of several of the Barnabite priests who controlled us. Two of them developed a violent passion for me and, unable to obtain anything from me through flatteries and presents, wanted to try to use force. Certainly, if at the age of twelve I had not had great courage, my modesty would have been brutally assaulted. Two of those who wanted to corrupt me – and who had succeeded in their intentions with several of my friends – were finally punished, though with excessive leniency. In this college only the puerile sorts of religious practice were displayed – they taught me to chant psalms like a monk, but one received no lessons on true morality and proper conduct; one acquired depraved tastes, deplorable habits and a sad inclination which is rather common in Italian colleges. Notwithstanding what is said by its apologists to justify it by giving illustrious examples both classical and modern, it never ceases being a vice for which is felt a profound execration and which will be eradicated from society. Now, in my old age, I feel the inner consolation of having gained diverse victories over my dissolute passions. None of these victories cost me so dearly as the triumph over a sad inclination for the youth of my own sex. It was always to distance myself from this sinister inclination that I often pursued acts of gallantry with women of all manner, though I do not need to reproach myself with having seduced a single one or having distracted any of them from their wifely duties. I did, however, profit with alacrity from those who showed a favourable disposition for my gallantry.'

In addition to confessions about his own homosexual tastes, Gorani also wrote about those of Henry STUART; he recorded rumours about Queen Maria Carolina's alleged lesbianism and love for the English beauty Emma Lyons-Hamilton, and, in a famous description, he recounted the homoerotic fascination for *castrati* in Roman theatres.

To this day, Gorani's memoirs have never been fully explored from a gay and lesbian perspective, and it is possible that they contain further material about the homosexuality of well known personalities of the eighteenth century.

G. Gorani, *Memorie di giovinezza e di guerra (1740–1763)*, Milan, 1936; G. Gorani, *Mémoires secrets et critiques des cours, des gouvernements et des moeurs des principaux Etats de l'Italie*, Paris, 1793, 2 vols.

Giovanni Dall'Orto

Gosse, Edmund (1849–1928), British literary critic, biographer and poet. Although most highly regarded during his lifetime as a voluminous and catholic literary critic, Gosse's lasting achievement is *Father and Son* (1907), a moving remembrance of himself as a sensitive, artistic boy growing up under the dominion of his father, a strict clergyman belonging to the evangelical Plymouth Brothers sect, which espoused extreme Calvinism. Also of interest is a novel, *The Secret of Narcisse* (1892), which, although set in sixteenth-century France, explores the 1890s theme of the aesthete suffering in a phillistine society, and *Critical Kit-Kats* (1896), which contains insightful portraits of WHITMAN and Walter PATER. Gosse was notable for his friendships and correspondence with many of the leading writers of his time, including Henry JAMES, André GIDE and John Addington SYMONDS.

Symonds was the only correspondent to whom Gosse confided his love for men. Although Symonds's 1876 attempt to ascertain whether Gosse had 'Urning tendencies' met with an unfavourable reaction, at the end of 1889 Symonds sent Gosse a copy of his *A Problem in Greek Ethics* (1883). This treatise so affected Gosse that he at last confessed to Symonds his 'homosexual tendencies': 'I know of all you speak of – the solitude, the rebellion, the despair. . . . Years ago I wanted to write to you about all this, and withdrew through cowardice. I have had a very

fortunate life, but there has been this obstinate twist in it! I have reached a quieter time – some beginnings of that Sophoclean period when the wild beast dies. He is not dead, but tamer; I understand him and the trick of his claws.'

It is unfortunate that Gosse's admiration for Symonds's courage and pioneering efforts in the cause of homosexual emancipation did not inform his actions when he was left Symonds's papers upon the death of Symonds's literary executor, Horatio Forbes Brown. Janet Vaughan, Symonds's granddaughter, describes her reaction upon Gosse's telling her that he and a friend had burnt everything except Symonds's autobiography: 'I thought of those two old men destroying, one could only guess, all the case histories and basic studies of sexual inversion that J.A.S. is known to have made, together no doubt with other letters and papers that would have thrown much light on J.A.S.'s work and friendships. Gosse's smug gloating delight as he told me, the sense that he had enjoyed to the full the honour fate had given him, was nauseating.'

Gosse's life is an interesting study of the accommodation of 'homosexual' desire within social mores. Unlike Henry James – a perpetual bachelor and utterly circumspect about his passions – he acknowledged and was willing to discuss his desires, and, unlike Symonds, his married life was happy and the unfulfilment of his desire for men did not torture him to the extent it did Symonds. His ability to find a tolerable medium between the extremes of James and Symonds provides another example of how such men lived their lives in an intolerant society.

R. S. Moore (ed.) *Selected Letters of Henry James to Edmund Gosse, 1882–1915*, Baton Rouge, 1988; L. F. Brugmans (ed.) *The Correspondence of André Gide and Edmund Gosse, 1904–1928*, London, 1960; H. M. Schueller and R. L. Peters (eds) *The Letters of John Addington Symonds*, 3 vols, Detroit,

1967–1969; A. Thwaite, *Edmund Gosse: A Literary Landscape, 1849–1928*, London, 1984.

Jason Boyd

Grant, Duncan (1885–1978), British artist. Born in Inverness-shire to a distinguished (though not wealthy) Scottish family, Grant spent part of his childhood in India and Burma, where his father was posted with the army. He returned to England for preparatory school, then studied art in London, where he lived with the Strachey family, his cousins. Grant also studied in Paris and travelled in Italy, where he explored the work of Piero della Francesca, Byzantine murals, Matisse and Picasso, all of which were to influence him. Back in England, Grant began painting in earnest and, around 1905, he became a member of the Bloomsbury group presided over by Virginia and Leonard WOOLF, her sister Vanessa and Vanessa's husband, Clive Bell.

Bloomsbury is now almost as well known for the personal, and sexual, links among its members as for its writings and paintings. Grant had a significant but rather brief affair with Lytton STRACHEY, biographer of *Eminent Victorians*, then a longer-lasting relationship with the economist John Maynard KEYNES. He also fell in love with Lytton's brother, John Strachey, and with Virginia and Vanessa's brother, Adrian Stephen. Another deeply passionate affair was with David Garnett (who eventually married Angelica, the daughter of Grant and Vanessa Bell). Throughout his life, in addition to his relatively brief sexual affair and long, close friendship with Vanessa – with whom he shared a house, Charleston, in Sussex, where they lived together until Vanessa's death and were often visited by various Bloomsbury friends and sexual partners – Grant continued to enjoy numerous homosexual liaisons. He neither hid his homosexual side nor seemingly ever suffered from concerns about it, though he was disappointed that his love for several heterosexual protégés was not physically reciprocated.

Grant produced a substantial number of paintings and also designed fabrics, ceramics and other items (some in connection with Roger Fry's Omega Workshops) which blend a variety of influences in a brightly coloured modernist style. Homoeroticism was one of a continuing number of themes. *Bathing* (1911), one of his most important paintings, portrayed seven naked men diving, swimming and climbing into a boat in a way reminiscent of a multiple-exposure photograph. A number of male nudes, including other pictures of bathers, followed in the 1920s and later. In the 1950s, murals for a chantry in Lincoln Cathedral showed Christ (modelled on one of Grant's young friends) as a handsome bare-chested shepherd and pictured sturdy semi-nude dockers unloading wool. A collection of Grant's erotic drawings was published posthumously.

Simon Watney remarks on a 'tendency to dismiss him as no more than Bloomsbury's semi-official court painter', and Grant's portraits of Bell, Keynes and Strachey do form a gallery of Bloomsbury figures. Yet he is now seen as one of the key translators of modernism into British art. His personal attachments also typify the tolerant and dissident sexuality of Britain's early twentieth-century avant-garde.

F. Spalding, *Duncan Grant: A Biography*, London, 1997; S. Watney, *The Art of Duncan Grant*, London, 1990; D. B. Turnbaugh, *Private: The Erotic Art of Duncan Grant*, London, 1989; P. Stansky, *On or about December 1910: Early Bloomsbury and its Intimate World*, Cambridge, Mass., 1996.

Robert Aldrich

Gray, Eileen (1879–1976), Irish architect and interior designer. Born in Ireland, Gray studied at the Slade School of Art, London, in 1898, before moving to Paris in 1902. The store Gray owned in Paris from 1922 to 1930 with the ambiguous title Jean Désert retailed high-style Art Deco furnishings, notably lacquer, then from 1925 the pristine chrome and glass furnishings of her own design which attracted international recognition. Gray designed many iconic pieces of modern furniture, such as the 'Satellite' mirror (1927) and a tubular armchair of leather and chromed steel (1929); many continue to be manufactured under the Ecart label.

In Paris Gray mixed in lesbian circles which included Romaine BROOKS, Gabrielle Bloch and her lover Loïe Fuller, the singer Damia and Natalie BARNEY. Evelyn Wyld, who formed a relationship and established a shop with Eyre de Lanux (Elizabeth de Lanux, American painter and furniture designer) around 1924, supervised the production of Gray's rugs, later designing her own range. Although Gray's principal biographer is coy regarding the designer's sexuality, the patronage of her lesbian associates undoubtedly assisted her venture, with Bloch taking charge of the business matters. Gray's customers included Brooks and Damia; the Duchesse de Clermont-Tonnerre wrote a positive review of Gray's furniture for the *Feuillets d'Art* in 1922. Gray's architectural designs, exercises in modernist practicality and space, included her own villa at Roquebrune (1927); a studio for Jean Badovici, in Paris (1930–1931); and another villa for herself near Menton (1934).

P. Adam, *Eileen Gray, Architect/Designer: A Biography*, New York, 1987.

Peter McNeil

Gray, John (1866–1934), British poet and priest. Born into a working-class family in Bethnal Green in the East End of London, Gray began his working life at the age of 13 as a metal-turner at the Woolwich Arsenal. In 1882 he entered the British civil service as a clerk, initially in the Post Office and then in the more prestigious Foreign Office, and gained a knowledge of languages, music and painting. Always keen to move into literary and artistic circles, his upward mobility, despite his working-class accent, was assisted by his good looks. Contemporaries agreed that he was remarkably beautiful. He published his first writings in an avant-garde literary journal in 1889, collected influential friends and lived beyond his means. About the same time he met Oscar WILDE and for the next three years was a member of his inner circle of friends, probably a lover. It was during this period that Wilde wrote his novel *The Picture of Dorian Gray*. Gray was a model for 'Dorian' and Wilde chose the subject's surname to flatter his new friend. Gray himself delighted in the notoriety and signed at least one letter to Wilde as 'Dorian'.

Gray's book of poems, *Silverpoints*, designed by the artist Charles Ricketts, with exquisite typography and unusually wide margins, was published in a limited edition in 1893. One reviewer, unimpressed, described Gray as 'a young man with a promising career behind him'. Increasingly disillusioned with Wilde, and supplanted in his affections by Lord Alfred DOUGLAS, Gray moved away from his former circle; the final break with Wilde occurred early in 1893. At the same time, he established a close friendship with André RAFFALOVICH, who wanted to be his lover and became his patron. The trials of Oscar Wilde in 1895 brought Gray close to disaster. Like many others, he feared being mentioned in court, though he survived unscathed. His personal life, however, took a new direction. In 1890, he had been received into the Roman Catholic Church, though this step had not disrupted his way of life. In the mid-1890s, however, his religious faith revived and he felt he had been called by God to become a Catholic priest, which meant a life of celibacy. In 1898 he began studies for the priesthood at the Scots College in Rome. He was ordained in 1901. He served for the remainder of his life in the diocese of St Andrews and Edinburgh, initially as curate of a poor parish in Edinburgh and then, from 1907, as first parish priest of the middle-class suburb of Morningside.

There he was responsible for the building of St Peter's Church. Designed in Romanesque style by Sir Robert Lorimer, the leading Scottish architect of the day, its interior furnishings and art-works were selected with care so that it became the most 'artistic' Catholic church in Scotland. Part of the cost was borne by Raffalovich, who in 1905 had moved to Edinburgh to be close to Gray.

As a Catholic priest Gray lived a strictly disciplined life. His manner was always reserved and formal and he was careful to avoid close personal relationships. Many of his fellow clergy regarded him as rather precious. Although he rarely spoke about the literary figures he had once known, he remained attached to the styles of the 1890s and slept in his bed between black linen sheets. He died in June 1934, four months after Raffalovich. Gray was a minor literary figure. Much of the interest in him arises from the contrast between his early 'decadent' years and his later life as an austere Catholic priest.

J. H. McCormack, *John Gray: Poet, Dandy and Priest*, Hanover, New Hampshire, 1991; B. Sewell (ed.) *Two Friends: John Gray & André Raffalovich: Essays Biographical and Critical*, Aylesford, Kent, 1963; B. Sewell, *Footnote to the Nineties: A Memoir of John Gray and André Raffalovich*, London, 1968; B. Sewell, *In the Dorian Mode: A Life of John Gray, 1866–1934*, Padstow, Cornwall, 1983.

David Hilliard

Grazzini, Anton Francesco (1503–1584), Italian writer. Grazzini was born in Florence into a family of pharmacists (though his father was a notary). Despite irregular studies, and his failure to learn Greek and, apparently, Latin, he became a man of enormous culture. As a writer, Grazzini was an important enough figure in Tuscan culture to count among the founders of the Accademia degli Umidi and the most famous Italian academy, the Accademia della Crusca – established in 1582 to defend the purity of the Italian language and

still active today. Grazzini earned his reputation for seven comedies and a collection of stories.

Grazzini was a 'bourgeois' and anticlassical writer at a time when the Italian élites were being absorbed by the aristocracy. He defended the 'democratic' use of Italian against the noble and courtly preference for Latin and Greek, leading his campaign with irony, humour and satire. He was the inheritor of a Florentine tradition of playful and popular poetry in the tradition of BERNI and Burchiello and their followers.

In his verses, Grazzini confessed his own homosexual tastes (the only evidence remaining of his behaviour). Homosexuality appears in diverse, sometimes contradictory ways in Grazzini's work. In a set of burlesque poems, he makes fun of the poet Benedetto VARCHI for his pretence to 'enoble' his homosexual loves with a patina of Neoplatonism and Petrarchan style. Using crude and direct popular language, Grazzini demolishes Varchi's claims to 'spirituality', which he charged simply covered Varchi's sexual desires. In another group of poems, Grazzini praises the beauty of young men and boys with a frankness which he accuses Varchi of avoiding. In the 'Madrigalessa IX' (in the *Rime*), he speaks about his love and obsessions for a certain Liliano. In another poem, he talks about being enamoured of Donatello's statue of St George; in addition to being a most fetching youth, the statue, in contrast with flesh-and-blood youths, he says, does not ask for money, does not frequent taverns and brothels, is not concerned about those who spend hours admiring his beauty, is not the object of pursuit by other 'buggers', and never ages.

Grazzini's poetry was able to introduce the theme of homosexuality in surprising situations. A poem on bathing in the Arno evokes the possibility of touching and playing unawares with semi-nude swimmers; another poem lauds football, since matches provide an opportunity to tackle and hold handsome youths under the pretext of keeping them from getting the ball. In yet other poems Grazzini made use of *double entendre* to show his crudely sexual feelings, affirming for example in verses 'In praise of Sausage' that 'a sad, bad, ungrateful man is he / who does not kiss, grasp and hug it, / and does not keep it behind him night and day'. (Such ambivalent meanings are indeed present in other poems, where 'bathing in the Arno' or 'playing football' are metaphors for having sex.) Yet Grazzini also wrote satirical verses in which, in order to attack his literary rivals, he accuses them of sodomy; for instance, his epitaph for one writer was 'Here lies the knight so fond of sucking, / who milked Florentine dicks when alive: / now in Paradise cherubs make fun of him / because they have a handsome face, but no prick at all'.

Attention to homosexuality formed part of his 'bourgeois' polemics against a courtly literature which was increasingly rarefied and anti-realist, but also reflected an autobiographical motive which Italian Renaissance traditions allowed him to present in a socially accepted fashion. Grazzini, in fact, belonged to the last generation of Italian men of letters who could benefit from this tradition before the Counter-Reformation ended the possibilities of writing about homosexuality in such a way.

G. Dall'Orto, 'Bernesque Poetry' and 'Burchiellesque Poetry', in W. R. Dynes (ed.) *Encyclopedia of Homosexuality*, New York, 1990; G. Davico-Bonino (ed.) *Opera di Anton Francesco Grazzini*, Turin, 1974; A. F. Grazzini, *Le rime burlesche edite e inedite*, Florence, 1882; P. Lorenzoni, *Erotismo e pornografia nella letteratura italiana*, Milan, 1976.

Giovanni Dall'Orto

Grimké, Angelina Weld (1880–1958), American writer. Born in Boston, Grimké was the only daughter of Archibald Grimké, an emancipated slave, Harvard Law School graduate and executive director of the National Association for the Advancement of Colored People, and Sarah Stanley, a white woman from a wealthy and prominent family. Stanley left her husband and daughter soon after Angelina's birth. In many ways, Grimké followed in the footsteps of her namesake, her white great aunt, Angelina Emily Grimké Weld (1805–1879). The latter and her sister Sarah were famous abolitionists and women's rights advocates who publicly acknowledged their mulatto nephews, Archibald (Angelina Grimké's father) and Francis. Archibald and Francis were the sons of a Southern white man, Henry Grimké, and his slave, Nancy Weston.

Grimké completed a degree in physical education at the Boston Normal School of Gymnastics, became a gymnastics teacher at the Armstrong Manual Training School in Washington, DC and then an English teacher at Dunbar High School in Washington. Her work, which was mostly written between 1900 and 1920, was published in Harlem Renaissance journals, *Opportunity* and *The Crisis*, and important black anthologies, *Caroling Dusk* and *American Negro Poetry*.

Grimké's plays and prose demonstrate her interest in racial protest and politics. Although much of Grimké's poetry is made up of love poems, the theme of fame and literary inheritance is present in her elegiac verse as well as in her poems that commemorate famous people, many of them women. These poems include one about her aunt, Charlotte Forten Grimké, one to a fellow black poet and teacher, Clarissa Scott Delaney, and another, 'Where Phillis Sleeps', possibly alludes to the first known black poet, Phillis Wheatley.

The positive treatment of a literary and racial inheritance and genealogy in Grimké's poetry offsets the often agonistic theme of biological reproduction in her plays and short stories. The play *Rachel* is about a black woman who rejects her two strongest desires, motherhood and marriage, because she cannot conscientiously bring a black child into a society in which racial intolerance and violence, such as lynching, still exists. 'The Closing Door' is even more extreme; it is a short story about a black woman who kills her child and then herself after her brother is lynched in the South. Another story, 'Goldie', about a black man's lynching, was published in the *Birth Control Review*.

Carolivia Herron writes that Grimké's polemical use of controversial issues such as infanticide, racial suicide and genocide allow for the repudiation of heterosexuality as a valid choice for Grimké's heroines. Like the author Nella LARSEN, whose treatment of passing as white coincides with the theme of homosexual passing, Grimké's treatment of issues relating to race crosses over with her treatment of sexuality and gender. Although Grimké's prose and drama take the form of political and racial protest, they are also sentimental in structure. Sentimental novels, which centre on the domestic sphere, have traditionally portrayed relationships between women. Grimké thematises the issue of passing as white in her short story 'Jettisoned', one of her only optimistic racial and sentimental stories. It is about a black woman, Miss Lucy, who decides not to live with her biological daughter who is passing for white. Miss Lucy's daughter will only have her mother live with her on the condition that she pose as her 'mammy' and dress in a maid's uniform. At the end of the short story, Miss Lucy rejects her daughter's demeaning offer and decides to stay in a boarding house with her severe but drily humorous landlady, Miss Robinson, and her friend, Mary Lou, whom she saves from suicide and who becomes the equivalent of an adopted daughter.

Many of Grimké's love poems have been seen to be lesbian in content. Homosexual love is portrayed as an idealised, often purely specular love which is not able to be spoken or consummated by touch. The desire for contact with the beloved is thwarted in 'A Mona Lisa' by the allusion to the famous painting which distances spectator from spectacle as well as the actual author from the abstracted image of woman: 'I should like to creep / Through the long brown grasses / That are your lashes / I should like to poise / On the very brink / Of the leaf-brown pool / That are your shadowed eyes'. The use of a white male as narrator of these love poems covers over the lesbian content and suggests a thematic crossover between passing as a man and passing as straight. However, this masking of lesbianism has led to the evaluation of her work as a failure of expressivity by literary critics such as Barbara Christian. Gloria Hull similarly writes that she 'lived a buried life' and that when she did write 'she did so in shackles . . . chained between the real experience and convention that would not give her voice'. Several of Grimké's diary entries as well as her letters, which waver between using a male and female pronoun to designate her lover's gender, are directed to unnamed female lovers and also register her father's disapproval of her affairs.

Grimké moved to New York in 1926 and is said to have stopped writing in 1930 after the death of her father.

C. Herron (ed.) *Selected Works of Angelina Weld Grimké*, Oxford, 1991; B. Christian, *Black Feminist Criticism: Perspectives on Black Women Writers*, New York, 1985; G. Hull, *Color, Sex and Poetry: Three Women Writers of the Harlem Renaissance*, Bloomington, 1987.

Monique Rooney

Grove, Frederick Philip (1879–1948), Canadian writer. In 1909, in order to escape mounting debts, Felix Paul Greve faked his suicide and moved to the US; it is here we first encounter the Frederick Philip Grove who eventually settled in Canada. Grove had met André GIDE, whose work Grove was translating, in Paris. Yet the pressures of failure were too much, and the dissembling Greve left the continent.

He published a number of novels,

including the semi-autobiographical *In Search of America* (1927) and the rather ironically titled 'fictionalised' autobiography *In Search of Myself* (1946), for which he received a Governor General's Award. Other works include *Settlers of the Marsh* (1925), arguably the first work of Canadian prairie realism. It concerns an immigrant Swede, a pioneer who falls into a marriage with a woman he clearly does not love; rather, it is the mannish Ellen for whom he professes admiration, and the novel ends with their consolidation of a platonic friendship. *In Fruits of the Earth* (1933), the solitary protagonist rises to power while alienating his family; his eldest son is a sensitive, trusting boy who, we are given to believe, is a budding homosexual. *In Search of America* contains rather matter-of-fact depictions of the novel's narrator sleeping with other men, but only for the sake of sharing a mattress and presumably nothing else.

Grove's importance lies in his being a key Canadian literary figure, one whose work will, in the future, be much reinterpreted in the light of his (homo)sexuality.

Andrew Lesk

Guez de Balzac, Jean-Louis (1597–1654), French writer. Born in Angoulême, Guez deserves a mention as Théophile de VIAU's sometime lover, and as an innovative French stylist, forging the classical form that Bossuet was later to make famous.

He never put his oratorical talents to the service of his sexuality, however. Since this sexuality had led others to a horrible death at the stake, his silence should not be judged too harshly. On the contrary, it may be taken as a paradigm of the fate of the homosexual. When he suspected that his private life was exposing him to risk, he left Paris. He exercised a great influence on a group of writers among whom 'preciosity', an early form of feminism, was evolving; this was a refuge from the coarse heterosexuality of the court of Henri IV, and therefore drew to itself many homosexuals. He was a founding member of the Académie Française. Perhaps his gift was for reformulating other people's ideas, but one cannot quite help feeling that had he been more confident with his sexuality, his talent would have flowered.

C. Rizza, *Libertinage et littérature*, Paris, 1996.
David Parris

Gustav III (1746–1792), king of Sweden, 1771–1792. The son of a weak father and a strong-willed, cultured mother (the sister of FREDERICK the Great of Prussia), Gustav's youth was dominated by the conflict between the powerless monarchy and the ruling aristocracy. However, in 1772 he managed to stage a successful and very popular *coup d'état* and thereafter ruled in a mildly authoritarian fashion. Highly intelligent and reared in the French Enlightenment tradition, Gustav's reign was characterised by reforms and a flowering of the arts, manifested in the neoclassical style known as 'Gustavian'. Gradually, however, the aristocratic opposition against him grew, culminating in his assassination at a masked ball (the incident that inspired Verdi's opera *Un ballo in maschera*). The writers of contemporary diaries and memoirs noted the king's sexual indifference to women, including his wife, and his sexual preference for men, most notably displayed by the entourage of male favourites (foremost among them Gustaf Mauritz Armfelt) who surrounded him, and whose speedy career advancements gave rise to much criticism. Many writers, including his own sister-in-law, claimed that, 'through his own exalted example', he helped to spread in Sweden 'this vice of men sleeping with men, which hitherto had been almost unknown here' (as recorded by L. von Engeström, minister of justice in an unpublished memorandum).

Hedvig Elisabeth, Charlottas dagbok I-III, Stockholm, 1902–1907; L. von Engeström, *Minnen och anteckningar I*, Stockholm, 1876.
Johan Rosell

H

Hadrian (Publius Aelius Hadrianus) (76–138), Roman emperor. Cultivated and intellectual, Hadrian ruled Rome and its empire during a period which came to be regarded as the highpoint of the Roman Empire (117–138) before serious problems developed with peoples beyond the frontiers.

Born in Spain, Hadrian, on the death of his father in 85, became the ward of Marcus Ulpius Traianus and accompanied him to Rome in 99 after he had been proclaimed emperor. In the following year he married Vibia Sabina. Thereafter he held a series of offices in the service of the emperor Trajan, culminating in the governorship of Syria, and was held in such favour that Trajan on his death-bed adopted him as his son and designated successor, to the surprise of more experienced generals. Hadrian's position as emperor was confirmed by the senate, but he did not visit Rome until 118. He spent most of the years 120 to 131 touring the empire, making him the most widely travelled of Roman emperors. During these travels Hadrian became enamoured of the youth ANTINOUS, from Bithynia, who then accompanied him until he drowned on a trip up the Nile in 130. Back in Rome, Hadrian devoted himself to a building programme which left a permanent mark on Rome: to his reign belong the Pantheon, the Castel S. Angelo (built as his mausoleum) and the Temple of Venus and Rome. Near Tivoli Hadrian built a sprawling 'villa' (in reality a vast complex of buildings and gardens) which was decorated with outstanding mosaics and sculptures and other works of art. Another building project, a temple to Capitoline Jupiter in Jerusalem on the site of the Temple, provoked a major rebellion which lasted from 132 to 135 and culminated in the final expulsion of the Jews from Judaea, which became the Roman province of Syria Palaestina. Elsewhere, the provinces were generally stable during Hadrian's reign. Hadrian's health began to fail in about 136, and he died in 138, having adopted as his successor Antoninus Pius, by whom he was deified.

'Hadrian', in *Lives of the Later Caesars* (= Historia Augusta), trans. A. Birley, Harmondsworth, 1976; A. Birley, *Hadrian The Restless Emperor*, London, 1997; M. Boatwright, *Hadrian and the City of Rome*, Princeton, 1987.

Roger Pitcher

Hāfiz (Mohammad Shams Od-Dīn Hāfiz) (c. 1319–c. 1389), Persian poet. The great Persian Sufi poet was born and died in Shirāz, a city in the southwest of what is now Iran. His father, a merchant who had moved to Shirāz from Isfahan, died when Hāfiz was young. Although poor, and at some point a baker's apprentice, Hāfiz had a traditional Islamic education, working as a copyist into his thirties. 'Hāfiz' means someone who has memorised the *Qur'ān*, and Hāfiz's Arabic was sufficient to both write and lecture about classic religious texts and theology.

Very little is known about his life, although it is known that he was invited to Bengal and Baghdad courts, and his elegy for a dead son is taken by many as autobiographical. Shirāz was a Sufi centre and Hāfiz was a Sufi, although the particular group to which he belonged is not clear. He was an eulogist (not the official court poet) for the Muzaffarid Shah Shuja (ruled 1358–1385) and is supposed to have met the conqueror Timūr (Tamerlane) in Shirāz in 1378. For reasons now obscure, Hāfiz was out of favour from 1366 to 1376. He appears to have laid low during the five-year reign of Shah Shuja's father, with its rigid Sunni orthodoxy (whether Hāfiz was a Shi'ite is uncertain).

Busy in scholarship and teaching, Hāfiz did not collect and order his poems. The *Diwan* was organised just after his death. It is supposed to have been consulted soon thereafter, when some orthodox Shirāzi objected to his burial because of his sensualist, anti-orthodox poetry. The *Diwan* has been the only book other than the *Qur'ān* used for prognostication in Persia/Iran, although some Muslims have always considered his poetry not merely too hedonistic, but outright impious. Hāfiz is viewed by Sufis as a Qutub, a Perfect Master of his age, and his tomb remains a pilgrimage destination. Sufi understand the *Diwan* as describing all the stages and processes of inner unfolding that transform human love into divine love. For the illuminati, every complete ghazal refers to a specific spiritual state. Others appreciate the colloquial music of the verses.

His greatest and most lasting fame is for perfecting the ghazal, a lyric poem comprised of between six and fifteen couplets on a subject. The surface content is generally the love of boys and wine, though it is union with the divine that these ecstasies are widely supposed to symbolise. In col-

loquial, albeit lyrical Persian, Hāfiz wrote of the quest for God. His poetry influenced not only Ottoman poets, but German romantic poets, with Goethe's admiration being particularly notable.

As Sir Richard BURTON noted, 'almost all the poetry of Hâfiz is addressed to youths', a feature that is obscured by the lack of obligatory indication of gender in Persian, though the occasional introduction of Arabic in the poems leaves no doubt that the beloved is male. The Divine Beloved Who Acts as He Will, adored by the poet 'slave of love', is incarnated as a Turkic boy: beardless, with light skin, a round face and a dot of a mouth.

Hāfiz's poems were available in a German translation from the early 1800s, and translations (sometimes bowdlerised) into other languages followed. A number of Western writers, notably the homosexual German Romantic poet August von PLATEN, were influenced by his verses about youths. Among other Middle Eastern poets celebrating young men who later became known in the West were Abū Nuwās, Jāmī, Al-Mutanabbi, 'Obeyd-e-Zakani, Rūmī and Sa'di. Sir Richard Burton's translation of *The Thousand and One Nights* also popularised 'Oriental' eroticism.

P. Smith, *Diwan of Hāfiz*, Melbourne, 1986; A. Schimmel, 'Hāfiz and his Critics', *Studies in Islam*, 16 (1979): 1–33.

Stephen O. Murray

Haijby, Kurt (1897–1965), Swedish public figure. Son of a fish merchant, Haijby worked as a waiter in France and as a steward aboard America liners, and spent a short time in the French Foreign Legion. He married for the first time in 1922, and a second time in 1931. In 1936, his wife filed an application for divorce on grounds of adultery. Haijby himself notified the judge who handled the case that the adultery had been committed with King Gustav V, at the time 78 years old and still reigning monarch. Officials of the royal court decided to pay 15,000 kronors to Mrs Haijby in exchange for her withdrawing the application, and 1,500 kronors to Haijby on condition that he emigrated to America. Another 3,000 kronors would be paid to him on his arrival in New York. Since the money did not arrive there, Haijby returned and asked the court to help him settle as a hotel owner. By 1938, the court had paid at least 78,000 kronors (the equivalent today of US$220,000) to Haijby in exchange for his silence, each payment signed and approved by the King.

In 1938, Haijby was arrested, suspected of indecent behaviour with two teenage boys. During police investigation, a psychiatric forensic statement was prepared, and he was kept for observation in a mental asylum for two weeks. The psychiatrist declared that Haijby was not mentally ill. There was no trial, and when Haijby was released he went to Germany and was given a monthly subsidy of 500 kronors by the royal court. Shortly after arriving in Berlin, he was sentenced to nine months in prison for homosexual acts, and after the prison term was transferred to Gestapo headquarters where he was kept for another four months. During this period, the Swedish Foreign Office at one point asked the Gestapo to keep him under arrest while King Gustav passed through Berlin on his way to Nice, but declined the Gestapo's offer to put Haijby in a concentration camp. Finally released, he returned to Sweden in 1939. In January 1941 the security police recorded a telephone conversation in which Haijby discussed with an author the possibility of writing a book about his experiences. As a result of this, the police recommended that he voluntarily commit himself to a mental asylum. He spent almost two months in the asylum, and later claimed that this proposal was presented as an ultimatum.

In 1947, Haijby wrote a *roman à clef*, *Patrik Kajson går igen* (*Patrik Kajson Returns*), revealing the details of his relation with 'the fine old man'. Haijby's book was

not officially seized by the authorities, but the Stockholm Police bought the entire stock for 5,000 kronors, thus preventing it from being distributed. By now, the Governor of Stockholm took over the affair, and the Government was officially notified. According to the memoirs of Prime Minister Tage Erlander, Minister of Interior Mossberg opened a meeting bluntly announcing, 'The King is homosexual!' In the silence that followed, the voice of Minister of Finances Wigforss was heard saying: 'At his age . . . how vigorous . . . !?' After King Gustav's death in 1950 Haijby insisted on an investigation of the treatment to which he had been subjected. Such an investigation was made by the Chancellor of Justice, who found no reason to criticise the ways the authorities had dealt with the affair. Instead, Haijby was charged with blackmail, and in 1952 he was sentenced to eight years of hard labour. After his release on parole in 1956, he lived quietly until his death by suicide.

T. Erlander, *Memoirs III 1949–1954*, Stockholm, 1974; K. Haijby, *Patrik Kajson går igen*, Stockholm, 1947; K. Haijby, *Ett lysande följe*, Stockholm, 1951; M. Heuman, *Rättsaffärerna Kejne och Haijby*, Stockholm, 1978.

Jens Rydström

Haines, (Charles) William ('Billy') (1899–1973), American actor and interior designer. Born in Staunton, Virginia, son of the manager of the family tobacco factory, Haines was the eldest of five children and the self-annointed black sheep of the family. He showed an early predilection for fine clothes, furniture, dancing and practical jokes. At age 14 he ran away from home with 'a boyfriend' to Hopewell, Virginia, where the precocious and handsome six-footer worked at a Dupont factory by day and ran a 'dance hall' by night. Moving to New York City in 1916, Haines settled in Greenwich Village, where he became an active member of the neighbourhood's gay subculture, befriending many of its most colourful characters, including

Mitchell Foster, Larry Sullivan, Charlie Phelps (aka Charlie Spangles), a famous hermaphrodite performer, and his roommates, Jack Kelly and Archie Leach, later to meet success in Hollywood as designer Orry-Kelly and debonair leading man Cary Grant.

According to biographer William J. Mann, during Haines's early years in New York, he entered into beneficial relationships with both older men and women, from which he developed an eye for fine art and culture. 'A person could be forgiven for illiteracy', the high-school dropout would later quip, 'but never for a lack of good taste.' While working as a photographer's model, Haines won the Samuel Goldwyn 'New Faces' contest in 1921 and with co-winner Eleanor Boardman was offered a Hollywood film contract with Goldwyn studios. Haines arrived in Hollywood in 1922 and spent the next few years in a variety of undistinguished supporting roles. In 1925, his role in *Little Annie Rooney* with film legend Mary Pickford garnered attention. Later that year, as Jimmy Dugan in *Sally, Irene and Mary*, playing opposite lifelong pal Joan Crawford, his career took off. His portrayal of Tom Brown in *Brown of Harvard* (1926) and as Private 'Skeet' Burns in *Tell it to the Marines* (1927) made him the top male performer in MGM studio's roster of stars. By 1930 he was Hollywood's top-ranking box-office male star.

In a meteoric career that rose and fell in little more than a decade, Haines made more than 50 films, usually cast as a wisecracking but lovable juvenile playing opposite such female stars as Barbara La Marr, Boardman, Crawford and Marion Davies (*Show People*, 1928). Legend has it that Haines's career was cut short by his refusal to bow to Louis B. Mayer's demand that he give up his gay life. It is more probable that, losing his boyish good looks after age 30, Haines accepted the decline of his acting career with grace and had already directed his energies into a new career as an interior decorator.

Although he created the decor for only one film (*Craig's Wife*, 1935), Haines was overwhelmed with commissions to decorate homes of Hollywood notables. The crowning achievement of the design career of Haines Foster, later William Haines, Inc., was the 1968 commission to decorate Winfield House, the London residence of Walter Annenberg, American ambassador to Britain.

Unlike gay director George CUKOR, whose struggle to remain closeted was one of Hollywood's open secrets, Haines lived a completely uncloseted life and befriended more openly gay figures such as Cole PORTER and Clifton Webb. His relationship with Jimmie Shields, whom he met as a one-night stand in 1926, lasted for nearly 50 years. In 1936, the couple was the subject of scandal when Shields was accused of child abuse, but the allegations were never proved. Despite their reputation for outrageous campy behaviour and overcharged libidos well into middle age, Joan Crawford often referred to Haines and Shields as one of Hollywood's happiest married couples. Soon after Haines's death on 26 December 1973, Shields took an overdose of sleeping pills. 'Goodbye to all of you who have tried so hard to comfort me in my loss of William Haines, whom I have been with since 1926', Shields wrote in his suicide note, 'I now find it impossible to go it alone, I am much too lonely.'

W. J. Mann, *Wisecracker. The Life and Times of William Haines, Hollywood's First Openly Gay Star*, New York, 1998.

A. M. *Wentink*

Hall, Radclyffe (*c.* 1880–1943), British writer. Born in Hampshire, England around 1880 (dates vary) and named Marguerite Radclyffe-Hall, Radclyffe Hall was able to gain independence from the flamboyant demands of her divorced mother when she inherited a large sum of money at the age of 21. Though she wrote seven novels, five volumes of poetry and a collection of short stories, Radclyffe Hall – who preferred to use the first name John except in print – will probably forever be associated with her 1928 novel *The Well of Loneliness*, a lesbian 'classic' which has never been out of print and which has been translated into over a dozen languages. The novel was banned in England in 1928 after being declared obscene by a magistrate, Sir Chartres Biron, whose own name would have vanished into total obscurity if Virginia WOOLF had not satirised him, as an eavesdropper hiding behind a curtain, in her feminist essay *A Room of One's Own*, published the following year. The editor of the *Sunday Express* wrote that he would 'rather give a healthy girl or boy a phial of Prussic acid' than Hall's novel. Many English writers and critics, including E. M. FORSTER, Desmond MacCarthy, Vita SACKVILLE-WEST and Virginia Woolf – though not especially impressed with *The Well of Loneliness*'s artistic merits – were prepared to defend it against the charge of obscenity for its depiction of same-sex love; but no witnesses were permitted to testify at the trial.

The Well of Loneliness tells the story of Stephen Gordon, an upper-class Englishwoman drawn to other women and 'masculine' pursuits and dress. Stephen enlists in the women's ambulance unit when World War I erupts. She meets and falls in love with Mary Llewelyn, and the two return to the Gordon family estate and become lovers; but, fearing that Mary will come to resent her 'social isolation', Stephen eventually gives up Mary to her childhood friend Martin, who can provide her lover with social acceptance Stephen cannot. *The Well of Loneliness* depicts homosexuality as 'inversion', consistent with the views of nineteenth-century sexologists, such as Havelock ELLIS, who, upon Hall's request, wrote the novel's preface, assuring readers that the novel 'possesses a notable psychological and sociological significance'. It was Hall's stated intent to depict the 'invert' with sympathy; the ensuing virulent homophobic attacks against the novel are a testament to her success.

After being banned in England, the novel was published by Pegasus Press in Paris; attempts to ban it in the US failed.

More subtle than *The Well* in its treatment of lesbian themes, *The Unlit Lamp* (1924) is thought by many critics to be Hall's best novel. Her novel *Adam's Breed*, which chronicles the spiritual quest of an Italian man sickened by his culture's boundless consumption, especially for animal flesh, won the James Tait Black Memorial Prize and the Prix Fémina in 1926.

Hall's early mentor and lover Mabel Batten, called 'Ladye', encouraged her poetic career but also suggested that Hall write fiction. Shortly before Batten's death in 1915, Hall met Una, Lady Troubridge; they became lovers and were together for nearly 30 years. Two years after Hall's death from cancer in 1943, Troubridge published *The Life and Death of Radclyffe Hall*, an account of their long life together which suggests that *The Well of Loneliness* is not as autobiographical as many critics have insisted, for Troubridge presents Hall as more at peace with and accepting of her sexuality than her lesbian characters are of theirs.

M. Baker, *Our Three Selves: The Life of Radclyffe Hall*, London, 1985; S. Cline, *Radclyffe Hall: A Woman Called John*, London, 1997; C. Stillman Franks, *Beyond The Well of Loneliness: The Fiction of Radclyffe Hall*, Avebury, 1982; D. Souhami, *The Trials of Radclyffe Hall*, London, 1998.

Annette Oxindine

Hamilton, Alexander (*c.* 1754/5–1802), American politician. Hamilton served as George Washington's aide-de-camp during the American Revolutionary War and later in his first cabinet as Secretary of the Treasury. 'Washington's devotion to Hamilton was so marked', novelist Gertrude Atherton wrote, 'that their enemies spread the story that they were father and son.' However, none of the various dates claimed for Hamilton's birth coincided with Washington's 1751–1752 visit to the West Indies, where he was born. Hamilton's father had abandoned his mother, Rachel Levine, who died in 1768. As an orphan, Hamilton found a patron whose son Edward Stevens cherished 'those Vows of eternal Friendship' that the couple 'so often mutually exchanged'. On St Croix, Hamilton attracted a Presbyterian clergyman, who had fled a scandalous past in New Jersey and found a publisher for Hamilton's vivid description of a hurricane (in 1772). The minister raised money to send the boy to Princeton and later to Columbia University, where Stevens joined him.

In New York City Hamilton lived with 32-year-old 'bachelor' Hercules Mulligan, a haberdasher, who also worked as a spy for Washington while the British occupied New York City. Washington met Hamilton in Harlem. After a brief conversation, a biographer recounts how the general 'invited him to his marquee, and thus commenced that intercourse which has indissolubly linked their memories together.'

Hamilton became Washington's personal secretary and joined the general's 'family' of young male assistants. Hamilton served as aide from 1777 until 1781, pushed for the Constitution under which Washington was elected President in 1789, and then served in his cabinet. In their years together Washington and Hamilton had only one serious quarrel. Hamilton married Elizabeth Schuyler in 1780; Washington responded with coolness.

Hamilton was an adventurer who used relations to further his career. The Schuyler family possessed land and influence. Hamilton explained to his friend Henry Laurens, another aide, that his marriage would not change their love: 'as if after matrimony I was to be less devoted [to you] than I am now'. He explained that from a wife he needed what Laurens could not give him: 'I am a stranger in this country. I have no property there, only connections.'

Hamilton had dreams of military glory; he led troops in the final campaigns of the Revolutionary War and later against rebels in western Pennsylvania. He remained on intimate terms with General Frederick Steuben long after the war and may have supported Steuben's scheme to have Prince Henry of Prussia (himself a gay blade) become king of the United States. Hamilton's career came to a precipitous end when Aaron Burr shot him in a duel.

C. Shively, 'George Washington's Gay Mess', in W. Leyland (ed.) *Gay Roots: An Anthology of Gay History, Sex, Politics and Culture*, Vol. 2, San Francisco, 1993: 11–68.

Charley Shively

Hansen Fahlberg, Carl (Albert) (1870–1939), Danish author and police officer. Born out of wedlock, Carl Hansen was raised in poor circumstances by his long-widowed mother as an 'adopted' child. After his apprenticeship as a brazier, he travelled for four years as a journeyman through Germany, Austria, Italy, France and Switzerland. For more than a year he lived in Berlin and was introduced to its large homosexual subculture through a love affair with a male prostitute. In 1895, after doing military service, he became a constable in the Copenhagen Police Department. Under the pen name of 'Albert Hansen' he published an article in Magnus HIRSCHFELD's journal, *Jahrbuch für sexuelle Zwischenstufen* (1901), in which he undertook to prove that the fairy-tale author Hans Christian ANDERSEN had been a homosexual. His novel *Spild* (*Waste*, 1905) was widely acclaimed for its realistic and compassionate descriptions of the harsh living conditions in the proletarian districts of Copenhagen. In 1897–1903 he lived together with Hjalmar Sørensen. As a police officer Hansen was responsible for the introduction of the finger-printing method. In 1906 he was appointed police inspector and deputy commander of the Copenhagen CID. The same year he was implicated in a large homosexual scandal. After having been in custody for ten months, he suffered a nervous breakdown and was transferred to the psychiatric ward. Immediately after being released he mounted a ferocious attack on the judge in a series of newspaper articles. As a result, the key witness against him changed his testimony and thereby saved Hansen from being convicted for sodomy but not from being sentenced to two months of prison for gross indecency with minors.

In 1907 Hansen emigrated to the US, where he lived in Arkansas as a farmer until he was ruined in the Depression of 1929. He returned to Denmark in 1934. At a police parade the chief of police introduced him to younger colleagues as an early pioneer of criminal investigation and he received a small pension. In two autobiographical novels (published in 1937 and 1939), Hansen told the tale of his own childhood, of his years as a travelling journeyman, and of his time in Berlin – the first coming-out novels in Danish literature. He planned to write a third novel on his career as a police officer, which he had come to see as a kind of treason against his own class. In 1939 he took his own life.

A. Dreslov, H. C. Andersen og 'denne Albert Hansen', Copenhagen, 1977; C. Hansen Fahlberg, Et Barn blev kortfæstet, Copenhagen, 1937, and Nu flytter vi, sa' Nissen, Copenhagen, 1939; H. W. Kristensen, 'Carl Hansen Fahlberg. Politimand og landets første proletarforfatter', in Politihistorisk Selskabs Årsskrift, Copenhagen, 1982.

Wilhelm von Rosen

Harford, Lesbia (1891–1927), Australian poet. Lesbia Venner Keogh was born in Brighton, Melbourne, the eldest of four children. Convent-educated, she became one of the first female law graduates at the University of Melbourne. As an undergraduate, Harford fell in love with Katie Lush, a philosophy tutor at Ormond College. Her experience of desire between women in conservative Melbourne is encapsulated in the final stanza of one poem

from 1915: 'Would that I were Sappho, / Greece my land, not this! / There the noblest women, / When they loved, would kiss' ('I can't feel the sunshine'). Like Lush, Harford's significant male partners – Guido Baracchi and Pat Harford (whom she married in 1920) – were fellow labour radicals. Harford worked in clothing factories rather than exploiting class privilege. Born with a weak heart, she died of pneumonia. Her *Australian Dictionary of Biography* entry highlights Harford's socialism, but is silent on her lifelong relationship with Lush. As an example of an Australian woman giving public voice to lesbian desire between the wars, Harford's poetry retains importance.

C. Cuthbert, 'Lesbia Harford and Marie Pitt: Forgotten Poets', Hecate, 8, 1 (1982): 33–48; L. Harford, The Invaluable Mystery, Melbourne, 1987; J. Strauss, 'Stubborn Singers of their Full Song: Mary Gilmore and Lesbia Harford', in K. Ferres (ed.) The Time to Write: Australian Women Writers 1890–1930, Melbourne, 1993: 108–38.

Helen Driver

Harmodius and **Aristogiton** (sixth century BC), classical Greek political figures. Harmodius and Aristogiton were celebrated as the prime movers in the abolition of autocratic rule which prevailed in Athens during the latter half of the sixth century BC and as inaugurators of the era of democracy. Their names reverberated down the centuries, so that Plutarch, in the first century AD, could still retail an epigram to the effect that the best bronze was that of which the statues of Harmodius and Aristogiton were made. The two men were lovers, but the precise nature of the blend of political idealism and amorous intrigue in their exploit is variously reported, and difficult to determine.

Athens was ruled at the time by the sons of Pisistratus, the 'tyrant' (in Greek terms, an autocratic, but not necessarily oppressive ruler). Of the two sons, Hippias (the elder) exercised power, while Hipparchus was more given to love affairs and interest in the arts. According to Thucydides, Hipparchus was sexually attracted to Harmodius, who twice rebuffed his advances, whereupon Hipparchus humiliated the young man by disparaging his sister in public. Harmodius and his lover, Aristogiton, were incensed, and plotted to kill both Hippias and Hipparchus at the Panathenaic Festival of 514 BC. Believing, however, that others privy to the plot had betrayed their plans, they acted precipitately, and succeeded in killing only one of the brothers (Hipparchus). Harmodius died in the affray, while Aristogiton was taken captive and tortured before being put to death. Following the assassination, Hippias, now sole ruler, enforced his authority with increasing harshness, until in 510 BC he was expelled from Athens under the threat of an invading Spartan army. In 507 BC the foundations of democracy at Athens were laid by the constitutional reforms of Cleisthenes.

The fact that others besides Harmodius and Aristogiton were in the original plot to kill the tyrants suggests that there was a political as well as a personal motive for the attempt, and the most probable view is that the killing of Hipparchus set in train a process which resulted in the expulsion of Hippias (with Spartan help) and the founding of democracy.

What is beyond dispute is that the tyrant-slayers lived on as a potent symbol in the popular imagination – 'a supreme example of devotion to liberty at the price of life' (K. J. Dover). They were seen as liberators, celebrated in drinking songs as having brought *isonomia* (popular government) to Athens. Their descendants were given the right to free meals at the public expense. They were the first Athenians to have their statues erected in the *agora*, and when this statuary group (by Antenor) was carried off by the Persians as spoils of war (480–479 BC), a replacement (by Critius and Nesiotes) was set up in 477/6 BC. The latter substantially survives in a Roman marble copy.

The fourth century BC literary tradition contains many references to the noble example of the tyrannicides. Not only their devotion to liberty, but also their love was celebrated. The latter is recalled with approbation by the orators AESCHINES and Hyperides (one of the last defenders of liberty against Macedonian encroachment), and PLATO goes so far as to make Pausanias say (in the *Symposium*) that such love creates ambitions and strong bonds of affection which are intrinsically opposed to absolutist government – a principle exemplified in the actions of Harmodius and Aristogiton.

S. Brunnsåker, *The Tyrant-Slayers of Kritios and Nesiotes*, Stockholm, 2nd edn, 1971; R. Thomas, *Oral Tradition and Written Record in Classical Athens*, Cambridge, 1989: chap. 5; G. Vlastos, 'Isonomia', *American Journal of Philology* (1953): 337 ff.

Clifford Hindley

Hartley, L(eslie) P(oles) (1895–1972), British writer. 'The past is a foreign country: they do things differently there.' For many, this oft-cited and resonant opening of *The Go-Between* (1953) guarantees Leslie Poles Hartley a permanent place in the history of twentieth-century British fiction. Born in Whittlesea, Cambridgeshire, in 1895, the son of a Peterborough solicitor who also owned a successful brickworks, Hartley was educated at Harrow and Balliol College, Oxford, where his studies were interrupted by two years of service in World War I. At Oxford he met Lord David Cecil and Aldous Huxley, who gave him the introduction to the literary and social circles he desired. Over time he became acquainted with Lady Ottoline Morrell, Virginia WOOLF, Edith and Osbert SITWELL, Edith Wharton, E. M. FORSTER and Elizabeth Bowen. Regarded by some as an interloper, up from 'trade', he was able to rely on the loyalty of David Cecil – the platonic 'love of his life' according to Francis King – and the confidence of his old schoolfriend, C. H. B.

Kitchin, a minor novelist whose active embrace of homosexual relationships contrasted with Hartley's suppressed longings. Until his death in 1972, Hartley lived alone but for a household of servants, in London, Salisbury and at a home on the Avon, near Bath. Between the wars, Venice, the city of Baron Corvo (ROLFE), was a favoured and frequent destination.

Hartley began his career as a reviewer and went on to publish 17 novels and 5 collections of short stories, as well as *The Novelist's Responsibility* (1967), a compilation of lectures and essays. He was awarded the CBE in 1956 and named a Companion of Literature in 1972. The ghosts of Henry JAMES, Nathaniel Hawthorne, Marcel PROUST and E. M. FORSTER haunt his work, and his themes tend to reflect a life of emotional disguise and martyrdom. From *Simonetta Perkins* (1925) to *The Hireling* (1957), the 'unlit candle' of unexpressed love disfigures and destroys the lives of his protagonists. In Hartley's *Eustace and Hilda* trilogy (1944–1947), childhood is a prologue to a stunted maturity and eventual self-sacrifice. Young Leo Colston's unbidden sexual education in *The Go-Between* – the work of W. H. AUDEN's 'favourite novelist' – lays waste a life, while in *The Brickfield* (1964) and *The Betrayal* (1966), old age looks back upon childhood and a life once more punished by the loss of innocence. *The Harness Room* (1971) Hartley regarded as his only 'homosexual novel', and the relationship it depicts is characteristically framed by the roles of master and servant and doomed to tragic failure.

With the exception of his futurist fantasy, *Facial Justice* (1960), and fitful attempts to understand England's changing social climate after World War II, Hartley's instinctive gestures are retrospective. He remains an Edwardian survivor, wedded to privilege, clinging to the dream of a settled society. Two of his novels have been memorably adapted for the screen: *The Go-Between* in 1971 and *The Hireling* in 1973.

P. Bien, *L. P. Hartley*, University Park, Penn. 1963; E. T. Jones, *L. P. Hartley*, Boston, 1978; A. Mulkeen, *Wild Thyme, Winter Lightning: The Symbolic Novels of L. P. Hartley*, Detroit, 1974; A. Wright, *Foreign Country: The Life of L. P. Hartley*, London, 1996.

Roger Bowen

Hartley, Marsden (1877–1943) American painter. Born Edmund Hartley in Lewiston, Maine, Hartley adopted his stepmother's maiden surname as his first name. In 1912 he met Gertrude STEIN, who later championed his use of colour in his abstractions. In 1913, Hartley visited Berlin and Munich and met several members of the *Blaue Reiter* group. Even after the outbreak of World War I in August 1914 Hartley continued to live in Germany and only after the death of Karl von Freyburg did he return to the US. There has been considerable interest in his friendship with this young soldier, including numerous essays which identify them as lovers, although some have argued that Hartley's admiration was more poetic than physical. Hartley's *Portrait of a German Officer* (1914) includes von Freyburg's initials along with his own. Another *Portrait* (1914–1915) is one of twelve highly abstracted memorial paintings of von Freyburg, recognised only through stylised plumes, epaulettes and iron crosses. Hartley's heroic depiction of the German military was not well received in America and his interest in German military themes seemed to reach beyond any specific relationship.

Throughout his career, Hartley continued to explore his particular vision of the homosocial bond. Nearly 30 years later, in *Christ Held by Half-Naked Men* (1940–1941), an all-male *pietà* is recast with Nova Scotia fishermen. Stylistically distant from his earlier interest in abstraction, this work employs a crude realism closer to American Regionalism than modernist abstraction. American Regionalism as a style was usually associated with an interest in heroicising unadorned, plainspoken people. While Regionalism usually depicted cleansing acts of labour, contemplation or other wholesome activities, Hartley's late portraits present something of an enigma in that they suggest more than pious admiration. *Adelard the Drowned, Master of the 'Phantom'* (*c.* 1938–1939), portrays a sleepy-eyed fisherman, his bushy chest and square jaw nestled beneath his thickly sensuous brows. His moustache draws the viewer towards a delicate mouth in what must be seen as a profoundly moving memorial filled with both sensuality and longing, heightened by the placement of a small flower within an ample field of bristly hair.

P. McDonnell, *Marsden Hartley: American Modern*, Minneapolis, 1997; J. Weinberg, *Speaking for Vice: Homosexuality in the Art of Charles Demuth, Marsden Hartley, and the First American Avant-Garde*, New Haven, 1995.

Ken Gonzales-Day

Hartnell, Sir Norman (1901–1979), British fashion designer. Born in London to a middle-class family, as a child Hartnell was obsessed with actresses and the glamour of the stage. He studied architecture at Cambridge between 1921 and 1923, where he was a contemporary but not a friend of Cecil BEATON; the latter described him as 'horrid' when Hartnell was held up to him as an example of a good illustrator. At Cambridge, Hartnell designed dresses for all-male theatricals and was caricatured wearing a picture-dress. His early sketches are mannered, reminiscent of French illustrators such as Georges Lepape and ERTÉ. Leaving Cambridge without completing his degree, he worked for a court dressmaker, 'Madame Désirée', in 1923, before opening his own salon that same year. His Mayfair headquarters were chicly modern, with mirrored walls and mantlepieces. He showed in a Paris hotel in 1927, and achieved the acclaim of being appointed as dressmaker to the Royal Family in 1938. Hartnell's next salon in Bruton Street,

designed by Gerald Lacoste and Norris Wakefield in 1934, was influential in promoting the type of mirrored chic also deployed by decorators Elsie de Wolfe and Syrie Maugham. Featuring vast expanses of bevelled mirror panels and a silvered-glass mantlepiece, it was entirely carpeted and curtained in 'Hartnell green', a silvery-green; models emerged from a theatrical mirrored doorway; the white flowers were in the manner of Constance Spry. Hartnell's much-photographed private residences popularised the 'Vogue Regency' style which was more about Hollywood glamour than early nineteenth-century England.

Hartnell's fashion design is best remembered for the deployment of lavish spangled embroidery: he was 'more than partial to the jolly glitter of sequins', as he put it. His famous white wardrobe for Queen Elizabeth's state visit to France in 1938 used historicist references to the nineteenth-century crinoline which both softened and glamourised her image; ironically, his work was in turn popularised via the lens of Cecil Beaton. Hartnell received the Royal Warrant in 1940, and designed for the Utility scheme during World War II. He created the wedding dresses of the Princesses Elizabeth and Margaret and the 1953 Coronation gowns. Hartnell also designed for the theatre from the 1920s to the 1960s, including costumes for Mistinguett, Merle Oberon and Gertrude Lawrence. Rather like Beaton's infatuation with GARBO, Hartnell had a close relationship with the French actress Alice Delysia in the 1930s; her house on the Riviera was always filled with a collection of attractive young men.

Hartnell's private life is less well charted than that of many contemporaries, but his sense of camp irony can be gauged from the annual Christmas cards he sent to the society shoe-designer Edward Rayne: 'To the cobbler, from the little woman round the corner.' Hartnell's illustrative style was remarkably camp, rendering 1940s actresses as mannish mannequins and the

Royal Family as toothy starlets; the dust-jacket he designed for his autobiography, *Silver and Gold* (1955), featured swags of fringed drapery, pearls and gems more suitable for the wardrobe of a drag-queen than a princess. This is the great irony of Hartnell's career; in dressing the Royal Family in swaggering glamour, he unwittingly emphasised the more anachronistic aspects of their lifestyle in the increasingly casual post-war society.

Hartnell was commercially very successful, with ready-to-wear collections from 1942, and licensing arrangements with Saks Fifth Avenue in the 1940s. By 1939 he had a staff of about 400, producing around 2,000 couture dresses each year. As designer to royalty, Hartnell was very influential in Britain's former colonies such as Australia and Canada. In recent years he was perhaps best known for dressing the novelist Dame Barbara Cartland, to whom he had provided dresses since 1926. The House of Hartnell continues to dress Queen Elizabeth the Queen Mother. Knighted in 1977, he died in Windsor, Berkshire. Retrospectives of his work were exhibited in London and Brighton in 1985, and in Bath, 1985–1986.

Brighton Art Gallery and Bath City Council, *Norman Hartnell*, Brighton and Bath, 1985; N. Hartnell, *Silver and Gold*, London, 1955; C. McDowell, *A Hundred Years of Royal Style*, London, 1985.

Peter McNeil

Henri III de Valois (1551–1589), king of Poland and king of France. There is no monarch in France who embodies as much as does the last Valois king, Henri III (a descendant of fellow homosexual Lorenzo the Magnificent of Florence through his mother Catherine), the imagery of *pédérastie* (as the French put it). Henri III, thanks to the conjunction of Catholic fundamentalists and Huguenot pamphleteers in his own day, and to Dumas *père's* arch-romantic play, *Henri III et sa Cour* (1829), belongs to the *histoire noire* of French monarchy as retooled by history manual writers in the nineteenth century.

On the anti-Valois side, Catholics and Huguenots alike found him mainly repugnant for putting the interests of the French state, and of the sacredness of the royal blood line (a mystic notion specific to the French monarchy), above those of religious sectarianism, as witnessed by his securing the rights of Protestant Henri IV de Bourbon to his succession. Henri III represented what both the feudal nobility on the decline and the religious zealots on the ascent most abhorred: he was half a Médici (not noted for their respect for tradition) and, in the spirit of the Renaissance, albeit battered by the Wars of Religion, he relentlessly brought to its conclusion the 'process of civilisation' begun under his forebears Charles IX and François I, by modernising France. This meant a lesser reliance on feudal grandees ill-suited to state duties, an attention paid to new talents and social mobility at the service of the state, the development of the royal prerogatives to the detriment of customary laws, and keeping a critical eye on religious encroachment, papal and otherwise, over the monarchy. These trends prepared the way for the full development of the absolutist monarchy under Louis XIV.

For these very reasons he alienated the traditional supporters to the monarchy: the *parlement* of Paris, whose influence he tried to check; the high nobility, for whom he wished to substitute new men brought from the provinces; even the high clergy when the latter proved too compliant to Rome. Regarding the Protestants, he adopted a pragmatic attitude which enraged both the pro-Spanish Catholics and the ultra-Calvinists themselves: he simply asked them to respect the legitimacy of the Crown.

Such pragmatism, combined with political cunning, in which one ought to see the training he received both at the hands of his Médici mother and under the tutorship of an array of carefully chosen counsellors who were the top intellectuals of the day, was the direct cause for the emergence of the violent political indictment of the king as a 'male prostitute' (to quote Huguenot poet Agrippa d'Aubigné). Sex was used where other accusations failed.

Indeed, it is mainly at the hands of religious pamphleteers that Henri III was given the queer treatment. They wilfully read into his demeanour and politics the mark of the 'Beast'. His European ambitions (he was briefly King of Poland and tried to make his younger brother ruler of a buffer kingdom between the Holy Roman Empire and France), his Italianised speech that helped drain French itself (the 'royal tongue', as it was called) of its medieval provincialisms, his refined manners that were a harbinger of royal etiquette to come under Louis XIV, his passion for the arts in the true Renaissance spirit, all were stigmatised as signs of perversion both by feudal or parliamentary lords who saw a new kind of power emerge, and by bigots who saw in it the dreaded constitution of secularism.

Not that Henri III did not give his opponents ammunition. His infamous *mignons* (the word simply meant a 'favourite', an intimate counsellor one could rely on) were soon turned into *gitons* ('bumboys', an interesting case of the rediscovery of the Classics, PETRONIUS in this instance), which they probably were not. Some, like d'Epernon, were formidable men of war and politicians of the first rank. As Abbot Pierre de Brantôme (1540–1614) recalls in his erotic diaries, sexual acts were just that – they did not foster sexual identities. So, what about the *mignons* (the 'Forty-Five')? The king, in the midst of rebellion on several fronts, had to rely on close companions. He surrounded himself with young and provincial noblemen, untainted by court intrigues, a private militia who protected and advised him. To that effect he established the Order of the Holy Spirit in an attempt to inculcate in the nobility a new spirit of service; he held an Academy that heralded

the French Academy, scholars at the service of the king. Obviously, his enemies translated the Forty-Five as a Theban regiment, the Order (which soon outranked the Order of the Golden Fleece in prestige) as a black mass affair with sexual romps on the altar (the Duc d'Epernon was often portrayed as *le Diable*, the Devil himself), and the Academy as a horrid nest of humanist modernism.

Such gutter literature did cause Henri great harm at the time, and survived him (as in *L'Isle des Hermaphrodites*). Yet it must be noted that in the seventeenth century, although credence was given to his liking for young men while being also credited with having loved women, he remained as 'the king gifted with golden speech' – a master at public speaking, whose addresses quickly entered anthologies of rhetoric; in sum, an excellent monarch.

One had to wait for the Romantic search for exoticism in the past to see Henri III reappear in popular imagery as the paragon of duplicity (a trait associated with effeminacy), although Dumas *père* did correct in his *Quarante-Cinq* (1848) the critical portrait he had given of Henri III in 1829. It may well be, in his case, that the scandalous tincture of his first Romantic play (a great hit) was appropriate at the fall of the last Capetian (Charles X abdicated in 1830), but then quite out of place at the end of the reign of the placid and bourgeois Orléans king Louis-Philippe (1848) – who, by an ironical turn, was the descendant of another emblem of queer royalty, PHILIPPE, DUC D'ORLÉANS. Dumas was the first to rehabilitate Henri III, 'supremely royal'.

But damage has been caused to a king who had probably never in his life laid hands on anyone but his Queen and the Knights of the Holy Spirit when he first ordained them on the night of 31 December 1578. Henri IV de Bourbon, a rabid womaniser, knew this well, never took offence at being Henri III's successor and never sullied his memory. 'Henri III the

Queer' is, in sum, a cultural fabrication that evinces the enduring power of xenophobic and religious paradigms that often assimilate queerness and perversion in order to resist innovation, and find irrational channels for popular anger.

P.-J. Salazar, *Le projet d'Eloquence royale d'Amyot*, Paris, 1992; G. Poirier, *L'homosexualité dans l'imaginaire de la Renaissance*, Paris, 1996.

Philippe-Joseph Salazar

Herbert, Robert George Wyndham (1831–1905) and **Bramston, John** (1830–1921), British-Australian public servants. Robert Herbert's and John Bramston's lives were intertwined from the time they first met at Balliol College, Oxford University, in the early 1850s until Herbert's death in 1905. But whether they were lovers or just close friends is impossible to establish.

Herbert was the son of a barrister, grandson of the 1st Earl of Carnarvon and cousin and close associate of the 4th Earl. Bramston was from the middle classes but similarly educated. They shared rooms at Oxford in the 1850s and later in London, before spending six years living together, while leading public servants and politicians in Brisbane, Queensland, Australia. Herbert became Queensland's first Colonial Secretary (Premier) (1859–1866), while Bramston served as Clerk to the Executive Council. Later nominated to the Legislative Council (1864–1869), Bramston joined Herbert's government as Attorney-General for two months in 1865. They lived together on their Brisbane property 'Herston', a combination of their names. Herbert's letters home describe the happy domesticity of their lives.

After returning to England in 1866, they never again lived together, but they both worked in the Colonial Office from 1876 until the 1890s. After three years at another post, Herbert became Permanent Under-Secretary of the Colonial Office (1871–1892), and Agent-General for Tasmania (1893–1896). Herbert never married. Bramston married the Governor's niece during his second colonial tour of Queensland (1870–1872), and then moved to Hong Kong (1873–1876) before rejoining Herbert. Both remained strong advocates for Australia in the Colonial Office. Both received knighthoods and served as administrators of their Orders. What should we make of their relationship? Was it a romantic friendship that lasted 50 years or did it begin as a sexual relationship and mellow as they aged? Perhaps there is a clue in Herbert's 1864 explanation of why he had not married, written while he lived with Bramston at 'Herston': 'It does not seem to me reasonable to tell a man who is happy and content, to marry a woman who may turn out a great disappointment.'

B. Knox (ed.) *The Queensland Years of Robert Herbert, Premier: Letters and Papers*, St Lucia, 1977.

Clive Moore

Herod Atticus (Lucius Vibullius Hipparchus Tiberius Claudius Herodes Atticus) (*c.* 101–177), Roman official. Born a Roman citizen in Greece, Herod Atticus was a political figure (consul in 143) and successful orator and philosopher. He was a personal friend of the Emperor HADRIAN, and Emperor Antoninus Pius entrusted him with the education of Marcus Aurelius and Lucius Verus.

Herod Atticus was also one of the richest men of his time, and with his wealth he constructed various public buildings, including a stadium in Delphi, a theatre in Corinth and the Odeon bearing his name in Athens (which is still extant and even used for performances). In recompense, numerous statues were carved of him, such as one in the Louvre, from which it is possible to know exactly how he looked. He lived for many years in Rome, where traces of his huge estate, the 'Triopio', remain along the Appia Antica.

Herod had homosexual affairs which he made no attempt to hide. The most famous was the last one, and when his adolescent 'disciple' Polydeukes died in Athens (*c.* 173–174), Herod inaugurated a veritable personality cult of his friend, erecting statues (two fine copies of which are now in museums in Berlin and Palermo) and memorials to him proclaiming him a 'hero', in blatant imitation of Hadrian, who had posthumously proclamed his lover Antinous a god.

Polydeukes was not the only disciple whom Herod so honoured – he raised statues to at least two others who died while still young – but in this instance the theatrical ostentation of his mourning both scandalised and entertained his contemporaries. That the cult had an erotic basis is confirmed by the fact that Herod also erected maudlin devotional monuments to his wife, Regilla, when she died in Rome.

The lack of moderation in his passion for Polydeukes (more than its homosexual nature) earned Herod the mockery of rival philosophers, as recounted by Lucianus of Samosata in his *Life of Demonax*: he reports that the Cynic philosopher Demonax scorned Herod who, grieving for the loss of Polydeukes, kept a table covered with food and a coach and horses at the ready, as if he would return and climb in. Demonax added that PLATO was right to argue that a human has more than one soul, because it could not have been the same soul with which Herod had offered banquets to Regilla and Polydeukes as if they were still living, and wrote such fine speeches beforehand.

Giovanni Dall'Orto

Hilary the Englishman (*fl.* 1125), English poet. One of the most remarkable medieval singers of male homoerotic desire is Hilary the Englishman. Based on the evidence of his literary corpus, there is strong reason to believe that Hilary was born in England; however, the major part of his life was spent in France where he had gone to study under Abelard at Paris. Following

his training in Paris, Hilary went to Angers, eventually becoming a canon at Ronceray.

Hilary's importance to lesbian and gay history rests with his poetry, all of which is written in Latin. Fourteen of Hilary's poems survive in a single manuscript at the Bibliothèque Nationale in Paris; in addition to three biblical dramas, there are a number of lyrics which the nineteenth-century author of the *Dictionary of National Biography* entry on Hilary refers to as 'of a lighter and even licentious character'. No doubt the tantalising reference here is to the five extant amorous poems, four of which are addressed to boys (one other is to a woman).

Though the tradition of medieval homoerotic verse is much 'narrower' than the heteroerotic stream, the so-called renaissance which affected much of twelfth-century Western Europe created a cultural climate in which a relative flourishing of masculine same-gender literature occurred. As Stehling argues, because these representations of homoerotic longing appear only in Latin and never in the vernacular, male religious communities such as monasteries form the likeliest source for these comparatively erudite writings. Unlike the prose treatises of a roughly contemporary Englishman, AELRED OF RIEVAULX, however, Hilary's do not integrate the love of God with desire for other males. Hilary's homoerotic poems instead share with those of his near-contemporaries MARBOD OF RENNES and Baudri of Bourgueil an exclusive focus on the amorous feelings of a man for a boy; attraction for another grown male never enters their pictures.

Even after all the intervening centuries, the passionate intensity of Hilary's lyrics cannot fail to impress. In the poem titled 'To a Boy of Angers', he writes: 'I have thrown myself at your knees, / With my own knees bent, my hands joined; // As one of your suitors, / I use both tears and prayers.' This same text rehearses the image – familiar from heteroerotic texts –

of a lover whose desire leads him into a miserable state of love sickness: 'But now at last in a letter I confess my sickness, / And since I acknowledge it, I deserve health'. In 'To William of Anfonia', the speaker claims to 'burn with a malignant flame' of unrequited passion for this English lad; his emotions are so violent that his very being has been transformed: 'I no longer am what I used to be.'

Hilary's silent, hard-hearted youths never, though, offer respite from this pain. It is quite clear, too, that the lovers' yearned-for relief would be sexual. As the lover in the first of two poems called 'To an English Boy' asserts: 'You are completely handsome; there is no flaw in you – / Except this worthless decision to devote yourself to chastity'; along similar lines, in the second poem of the same name we read this jovial metaphor: 'I'll be the loot, you the robber – / To such a robber I surrender'.

Hilary's three poems to English boys signal their affiliation with ancient Greek pederastic ideals through inclusion of the myth of Jove and his handsome young cupbearer, GANYMEDE. William of Anfonia, for instance, is told that the king of the gods would 'become a bird for you / So that you might be joined with him forever'. Similarly, in the first 'English Boy' lyric, Hilary's speaker opines: 'Believe me, if the ancient times of Jove were to come again, / Ganymede would no longer be Jove's maid, / But you, ravished in the heavens, would give Jove / Pleasing cups by day, and even more pleasing kisses by night'. Hilary's fantasies of delightful nocturnal embracing on Mount Olympus is further confirmation of the thoroughly sensual orientation of his homoerotic vision.

As Stehling has shown, questions of gender representation and identity complicate the homoeroticism of poems by Hilary, Marbod, Baudri and other twelfth-century writers. Through their use of stock imagery and expressions of longing, many of these texts resemble heteroerotic addresses from a man to a woman; even the boys themselves are frequently feminised. In the first 'English Boy' poem, Hilary points to this proximity in ways that seem almost to prefigure Shakespeare's Sonnet 20: 'When nature created you, it wavered for a moment, / Deciding whether to bring you forth as a girl or a male'.

It seems unwise (as some have attempted) to dismiss the homoeroticism of Hilary's lyrics as merely dispassionate literary imitations of classical precedents. While more work remains to be done on the subject of the autobiographical dimension of these and other similar poems of the period, Boswell and Stehling make a convincing case for recognising their decidedly personal quality. Read in this light, Hilary's odes to love enrich our understanding of the plurality of living desires in the past as well as the present.

J. Boswell, *Christianity, Social Tolerance, and Homosexuality*, London, 1980: 239, 249–50, 372–4; W. Johansson and W. A. Percy, 'Homosexuality', in V. L. Bullough and J. A. Brundage (eds) *Handbook of Medieval Sexuality*, London, 1996: 155–89; Hilary the Englishman, 'Four Poems', in *Medieval Latin Poems of Male Love and Friendship*, trans. T. Stehling, New York, 1984: 68–75; T. Stehling, 'To Love a Medieval Boy', in S. Kellogg (ed.) *Essays on Gay Literature*, New York, 1985: 151–70.

Michael Morgan Holmes

Hiller, Kurt (1885–1972), German lawyer, publicist and activist. When Hiller died in 1972, he was the last of the leading men of the German homosexual movement of the pre-World War II era. During the final years of his life, Hiller wrote his memoirs, published as *Leben gegen die Zeit*. The title concisely demonstrates how he, as both a homosexual and a political activist, saw his life: as a fight against the maelstrom of history, against the strong forces in Germany that threatened humanism, individual freedom and rationalism.

Hiller grew up in a liberal intellectual milieu. He paid little attention to his

Jewish background because his family was completely assimilated. He studied law and wrote a dissertation in which he questioned the penalisation of homosexual intercourse, abortion, euthanasia, assisted suicide, incest and bestiality. Hiller firmly opposed any curtailment of individual freedom, as long as other people and society at large were not harmed by individual action. This was, in fact, the basic principle of his political activism. At the time of World War I, he was one of the main spokesmen of a group of young progressive intellectuals who gathered around the label 'Aktivismus' and who reacted in particular against the authoritarian structure and the irrational nationalism of Wilhelmine Germany.

In Weimar Germany, Hiller not only played a prominent role in the peace movement but also in the homosexual movement. Already before World War I, he was active in HIRSCHFELD's Wissenschaftlich-humanitäres Komitee and during the 1920s he was one of the driving forces behind attempts at reforming Germany's morals laws. Although Hiller cooperated with Hirschfeld, he did not support his biological theory of homosexuality, nor did he believe that the Zwischenstufentheorie could be used for political ends. He claimed that the primary motivation for homosexual emancipation should not be found in scientific evidence for homosexuality as being innate, but in the fundamental individual right to self-determination. In contrast to other leading figures in the German homosexual movement of those days, Hiller did not see a need for a scientific explanation or justification of homosexuality. To him, such a defensive attitude was merely a sign that homosexuals lacked pride and political awareness. Already in 1912, in Hirschfeld's Jahrbuch für sexuelle Zwischenstufen, Hiller wrote that homosexuals do not need to be satisfied with the compassion and understanding of those 'who pretend to be progressive', but that they have to stand up for their rights out of a sense of self-respect. Not homosexuals but their oppressors should offer their apologies, he felt. In formulating such views, Hiller was well ahead of his time.

Right after the Nazi take-over, Hiller was arrested, because in the famous Weltbühne he had sharply criticised the Nazi Party. During his nine months in concentration camps, he was seriously maltreated. After his release in 1934, he escaped from Germany and tried to continue his work as writer and political activist in Prague and later in London. His efforts to create a unified anti-fascist front on the left was frustrated by the communist politics dictated by Stalin. Only in 1955 did Hiller return to his native country for good. Paragraph 175, which made homosexual intercourse punishable by law and which was made even more rigid during the Third Reich, was still in effect in West Germany. One of Hiller's last activities involved the re-establishment of the Wissenschaftlich-humanitäres Komitee in 1962. This new committee, however, failed to generate much support. After the reformulation of Paragraph 175 in 1969, as a result of which homosexual intercourse was legally permitted, Hiller decided to disband the committee. Three years later he died.

K. Hiller, Leben gegen die Zeit. I Logos, II Eros, Reinbek bei Hamburg, 1972; H. Oosterhuis, 'Een modern homo-activist', in H. Hafkamp and M. van Lieshout (eds) Pijlen van naamloze liefde. Pioniers van de homo-emancipatie, Amsterdam, 1988: 180–4.

Harry Oosterhuis

Hirschfeld, Magnus (1868–1935), German sexologist and activist. Hirschfeld was born the son of a Jewish physician in Kolberg on the Pomeranian Baltic. In 1896, after training as a doctor, he moved to Berlin, where he began his activism on behalf of homosexual rights. In the aftermath of the Oscar WILDE trial, Hirschfeld argued in Sappho and Socrates (1896) for the legalisation of homosexuality. Drawing on the work of Karl Heinrich ULRICHS, Hirschfeld put forward a thoroughly medical explanation of what he called 'sexual intermediaries'. The desires of the 'Urning' and 'Urninden' – the male and female homosexual – are seen as the result of endocrinal anomalies during the development of the embryo. Most importantly, if homosexuality is less a matter of choice than biology, merely what Hirschfeld calls a 'developmental defect', then it should no longer be punished by law. Like Ulrichs, who described the male homosexual as having 'a woman's soul in a man's body', Hirschfeld regarded homosexuality as a form of 'psychological hermaphroditism'. The implication that all homosexual men are in some way effeminate was criticised by another advocate of homosexuality, Benedict FRIEDLÄNDER, who in his journal *Der Eigene* preferred to celebrate the manly and chivalric virtues of Hellenic pederasty.

Hirschfeld's growing fame as a scientific investigator of sexuality afforded some protection in his increasingly open advocacy of homosexual rights. In 1897, with Max Spohr and Edward Oberg, he formed the Wissenschaftlich-humanitäre Komitee (Scientific-Humanitarian Committee), which petitioned the German parliament for the legalisation of homosexuality. Although supported by many prominent individuals including Social Democrats August Bebel and Karl Kautsky, the Committee was unsuccessful on this and on many subsequent occasions over the next three decades. Hirschfeld worked tirelessly both within and outside the Committee, giving numerous talks on homosexuality to often enthusiastic audiences. In his medical practice he offered help and advice to countless individuals, carefully recording their stories for inclusion in his numerous studies of sexuality. Some of these appeared in his *Jahrbuch für sexuelle Zwischenstufen* (*Yearbook for Sexual Intermediaries*), published from 1899 until 1923. He also produced an im-

pressive series of books including *Berlins dritte Geschlecht* (*Berlin's Third Sex*, 1904) – a description of Berlin's flourishing gay life; a study of *Transvestites* (1910); and *Die Homosexualität des Mannes und des Weibes* (*Homosexuality in Men and Women*, 1914). As Charlotte Wolff emphasises in her authoritative study, Hirschfeld also devoted considerable attention to lesbians. He was an enthusiastic supporter of the women's movement, though he continued to insist on their inferior intellectual capacities. One of his proudest achievements was the foundation in Berlin of the Institute for Sexual Research in 1919, which became an important centre for the study of all aspects of sexuality. In the same year Hirschfeld appeared as a sexual therapist in what was probably the first sympathetic film about homosexuality, *Anders als die Andern* (*Different from the Others*).

Throughout his scientific and campaigning activities Hirschfeld displayed impressive determination and courage. He persisted even as the hopeful atmosphere of the 1890s – when new ideas about sexuality were in tune with the middle class moral reform movement – was engulfed by a series of scandals and calamities, from the suicide of business magnate Alfred KRUPP in 1902 and the homosexual spy scandal of 1906–1908 to the rise of Hitler's National Socialism. As both a homosexual and a Jew, Hirschfeld was the victim of frequent verbal and sometimes physical abuse. In the end he was forced to leave Germany and embarked, in 1930, on what became the extensive world tour documented in *Women East and West* (1935). He never returned to Germany. After a brief stay in Paris, Hirschfeld settled in Nice in the knowledge that his beloved Institute for Sexual Research would not survive. He died in 1935, mourned by his long-time lover Karl Giese as the 'gentle fanatic' of the homosexual rights movement.

M. Hirschfeld, *Women East and West:*

Impressions of a Sex Expert, London, 1935; J. Lauritsen and D. Thorstad, *The Early Homosexual Rights Movement: 1864–1935*, New York, 1974; J. D. Steakley, *The Homosexual Emancipation Movement in Germany*, Salem, New Hampshire, 1975; C. Wolff, *Magnus Hirschfeld, A Portrait of a Pioneer of Sexology*, London, 1986.

David West

Hitchin, Charles (c. 1675–1727), British law enforcement officer. In 1703 Hitchin married Elizabeth Wells of Hertfordshire. They lived on the north side of St Paul's Churchyard, London, where he practised his trade as a cabinet-maker. Elizabeth's father died in 1711, and Hitchin used her inheritance to buy the office of Under City-Marshall in 1712 for £700. This enabled him to regulate some 2,000 thieves, to blackmail them and others, to receive stolen goods and extract money from their owners for returning them, and to receive quarterly payments as protection money from brothels. Hitchin kept company with thieves at every tavern, brothel and eating-house in the City of London, and was accompanied on his evening walks by a gang of pickpocket boys. The notorious 'thief-taker' Jonathan Wild began his career as an assistant to Hitchin, but they separated on bad terms and attacked each other in a pamphlet war in 1718. One of Hitchin's men, William Field, gave evidence which resulted in Wild being hanged in 1725, and there is an illustration showing Hitchin riding immediately behind the cart that carried Wild to the gallows.

Though Hitchin was known as 'Madam' and 'Your Ladyship' in several molly houses, he once raided a molly house and arrested several men in drag; but after a few days in detention, they threatened to reveal his own sodomitical practices, and he arranged for their release. Hitchin was convicted of attempted sodomy in 1727, and sentenced to a £20 fine, six months' imprisonment, and to stand in the pillory near the Strand. When he was brought to the pillory in May,

many of his fellow thieves and fellow mollies barricaded the streets in order to impede an angry mob. The Drury Lane Ladies broke through a line of peace officers and pelted Hitchin with rocks and filth, the force of the missiles tearing his clothes off, and he fainted from exhaustion. He brought legal action against three men who had wounded him in the pillory. He was not immediately released after serving his six months, until he could raise money as security against his good behaviour, which he did by advertising his post for sale in the newspapers. He was discharged in November, but he had not recovered from his ordeal, and died that same month. His wife, in extreme poverty, petitioned the courts for relief.

Select Trials, London, 1734–1735; G. Howson, *Thief-Taker General: The Rise and Fall of Jonathan Wild*, London, 1970; R. Norton, *Mother Clap's Molly House*, London, 1992; J. Wild, *An Answer To A Late Insolent Libel . . . With a Diverting Scene of a Sodomitish Academy*, London, 1718.

Rictor Norton

Höch, Hannah (1889–1978), German artist. Höch, whose photomontages have been described as an 'exploration of the radical potential of feminine pleasure' (Lavin), was born Johanne Höch in Gotha, Thuringia. She was the first of five children.

The family was comfortably off, as Höch's father worked in insurance; her mother painted replicas of oil paintings. When her youngest sister was born in 1904, the 15-year-old Hannah had to leave the girls' high-school she had been attending to help care for the child at home. This suited her father's views on a woman's place and calling. She was 22 before she was able to enter art school; in 1912 she was enrolled at a college in Berlin's Charlottenburg, where she studied glass design with Harold Bengen. But with the outbreak of World War I in 1914 she returned to Gotha, working there for the Red Cross.

A year later she moved back to Berlin, this time to the college of the museum of arts and crafts, supporting herself financially by working as a designer in the handicrafts department of the publisher Ullstein. Back in Berlin, she met Raoul Hausmann, who was her lover for the next seven years, introducing her to the circles of the artistic avant-garde and, most importantly, to Dada. Höch and Hausmann were the principal instigators of avant-garde photomontage in Germany; Höch in particular specialised in exploring and deconstructing current media images of the 'New Woman' in the Weimar Republic. In 1919 they both took part in the first Berlin Dada exhibition, and in 1920 in the First International Dada-Fair.

In 1920 Höch left Hausmann and travelled to Italy with her sister, Grete, and the poet Regina Ullmann. She and Hausmann finally separated in 1922. On a trip to Holland four years later, she met the Dutch writer Til Brugman, whom Höch greatly admired. The two women became a couple, and lived together in The Hague for three years, and, after a move in 1929, for another six in Berlin. Despite this, Höch did not have a public image as lesbian; her own perception of her relationship was as a private affair. She and Brugmann collaborated on a volume called *Scheingehacktes* (*Apparently Hacked Up*, 1935), for which Brugman provided the text and Höch the illustrations. Höch later described Brugman as a dominant personality, like Hausmann; after their split she married a much younger man, Kurt Matthies, in 1938. They separated in 1942 and were divorced in 1944.

Despite being described as a 'cultural Bolschevik' by a Nazi commentator in 1937, Hannah Höch was able to survive the National Socialist period in Germany as an artist. After her divorce from Matthies she continued to live and work in Berlin until her death.

Berlinische Galerie, *Hannah Höch (1889–1978): Ihr Werk – Ihr Leben – Ihre Freunde*, Berlin, 1989; M. Lavin, *Cut with the Kitchen Knife: The Weimar Photomontages of Hannah Höch*, New Haven, 1993.

Sarah Colvin

Hopkins, Gerard Manley (1844–1889), British poet, cleric. Hopkins grew up near London in refined and pleasant circumstances. Always an exceptional student, he distinguished himself at Highgate School then, from 1863, at Balliol College, Oxford. There he became exposed to the liberal humanism of Matthew Arnold, the High Church movement of Edward Pusey and the sensual aestheticism of Walter PATER. By 1862 he had read THEOCRITUS's 'Thalusia' and 'Hylas', which celebrate the love of man and boy, and Hopkins was, at Oxford, sufficiently aware of the ancient Greek institution of *paederastia* that he was able, in an essay titled 'The Legend of the Rape of the Scout', to parody F. O. Müller's analysis of it. Judging from a paper that he wrote for his tutor, Pater, he was also aware of the homoerotic tenor of SHAKESPEARE's Sonnets. As an undergraduate Hopkins engaged in friendships that might safely be termed romantic, though they tended to be idealised and spiritualised. He developed a deep infatuation for Digby Dolben, the cousin of his close friend and later literary executor, Robert Bridges. It was with Dolben that Hopkins came closest to a physical relationship with another man. According to his diary, Hopkins was unable to keep himself from masturbating after meeting Dolben, and he generally struggled with feelings of self-loathing because he was often excited and aroused by strangers.

Arguably the most important influence on Hopkins as an undergraduate was the Oxford Movement, and in 1866, deeply moved by John (later Cardinal) NEWMAN's conversion, he became a Roman Catholic. This decision estranged him from both his family and a number of his acquaintants. As Kitchen points out, it is relevant to note that Victorians termed conversion to

Roman Catholicism 'perversion'. One friend who kept in contact with him was Pater, who remained amiable and even introduced Hopkins to the actively homosexual painter Simeon SOLOMON in 1868. In that same year, in what he called the 'Slaughter of the Innocents', Hopkins burned most of his poems, written after the Romantic manner of Keats.

One can thus only speculate about the erotic content of some of his early verse. It is clear from what he wrote later, however, that Hopkins supplemented the Christian tradition with the classical world-view that he was introduced to at university, which included the eroticisation of the male body. He was no Manichean; the body for him was just as worthy of redemption as the soul, and it is in this belief that one senses a connection to WHITMAN's celebration of the entire self, both spiritual and physical. Hopkins in fact went so far as to celebrate the physical beauty of Christ, in a sermon titled 'Christ Our Hero'.

After being ordained a Jesuit priest in 1877, Hopkins was encouraged by his superiors to write religious poetry. His first mature poem, 'The Wreck of the Deutschland' (1878), used language in such innovative ways that the Catholic magazine to which he submitted it 'dared not print it', as Hopkins put it. His work appears distinctly modern because his formal techniques were so innovative, particularly his purely accentual 'sprung rhythm' and his use of 'consonant chime', or layering of consonant and vowel sounds. Thematically, one finds suggestions of homoeroticism in some of his mature poems. 'The Bugler's First Communion' (1879) eroticises the robust type that Hopkins seemed to favour after Oxford, and 'Brothers' (1880) presents fraternal love in the mode of Greek *paederastia*. Richard Dellamora has read other Hopkins poems, such as 'Felix Randal' (1880) and 'To R. B.' (1889), in terms of homoeroticism as well.

Hopkins moved to Dublin in 1884 to take up a position as professor of classics at University College. There he wrote his 'terrible sonnets', that often, as in the case of 'I Wake and Feel the Fell of Dark, Not Day', treat despair in terms of sexuality and suggest a struggle with masturbation. Hopkins's most clearly homoerotic poem, written a year before his death, is the fragmentary 'Epithalamion'. The poem is ostensibly about marriage, but its opening scene (which he likely wrote while invigilating an examination) features a stranger watching boys bathing and a poetic voice revelling in the erotically charged moment. Hopkins likely became in some sense aware of the explicitly homoerotic nature of the poem because he later added both the title and an incomplete section that attempts to read the poem's sensuality in terms of heterosexual marriage. He later claimed that the poem was intended as an ode on the occasion of his brother Everard's marriage.

In a sense, his literary career did not begin until 29 years after his death, in 1918, when most of his poems appeared in print for the first time. Hopkins's lifelong conflicted relationship with his own sexuality is instructive and is particularly revealing about the struggles of a Catholic celibate with homoerotic inclinations.

R. Dellamora, ' "Spousal Love" in the Poetry of Gerard Manley Hopkins', in *Masculine Desire: The Sexual Politics of Victorian Aestheticism*, Chapel Hill, 1990; B. R. S. Fone, 'The Other Eden: Arcadia and the Homosexual Imagination', in S. Kellogg (ed.) *Essays on Gay Literature*, New York, 1985; P. Kitchen, *Gerard Manley Hopkins*, London, 1978.

George Piggford

Hössli, Heinrich (1784–1864), Swiss milliner, interior decorator and homosexual apologist and emancipationist. The first son of 14 children, Hössli was born in Glarus, where he grew up without formal schooling. In 1799, because of food shortages, he was sent to Berne, there learning the trade of hat-making which he practised in his home town. By the 1820s he was known as 'the leading ladies milliner of Glarus'; his success at this, combined with skilful interior decorating, earnt him the nickname *Modenhössli* (Fashion or Style Hössli). In 1811 he married Elisabeth Grebel from Zurich; unusually, she remained in Zurich, he at once returned to Glarus, and they lived apart for the rest of their lives. In the first two years of their marriage, they did see each other at least occasionally and had two sons; although Hössli played no part in their upbringing, he was on amicable terms with them. He retired from business in 1851 and wandered restlessly for the rest of his life.

In 1817 Hössli was profoundly shocked by the cruel execution in Berne of a 32-year-old legal adviser, Dr Franz Desgouttes, for the murder of his scribe, 22-year-old Daniel Hemmeler, with whom it emerged he was in love. Hössli declared that it was as if 'the scales had fallen from his eyes'; he 'could not be silent and remain a human being'. He felt it his terrible but pressing duty to inform the world of the true nature of love between men. He set about studying the subject but, lacking confidence in his abilities to write, approached in 1819 the most popular Swiss writer of the day, the German-born Heinrich Zschokke, a novelist who was involved in politics and had a reputation as an educator. Using the materials Hössli provided him, Zschokke wrote a short novel in the form of a dialogue that, starting with a fictionalised version of the Desgouttes case, canvassed the various forms of love, in particular that between men as practised in classical Greece. Though it contains much useful information on homosexuality, *Eros, oder über die Liebe* (1821) reached the conclusion that it would be frightful to offer Greek legislation on homoeroticism as an ideal. This reaffirmation of the status quo Hössli took as betrayal, and he determined to write the needed book himself. Fifteen years later appeared the first volume of *Eros; Die Männerliebe der Griechen; ihre Beziehungun zur Geschichte, Erzhiehung,* *Literatur and Gesetzgebung aller Zeiten* (*Eros; The Male Love of the Greeks: Its Relations to the History, Education, Literature and Legislation of All Ages*, 2 vols, 1836 and 1838). It immediately ran into trouble with the church authorities of Glarus, who banned its sale within the canton and prohibited further publication of the manuscript. Though he remained passionate about the cause, Hössli lost the will to continue with the book, and the projected third volume remained incomplete and unpublished at his death. The unsold volumes were destroyed in a fire in 1861 which reduced half the town of Glarus to ashes.

Eros; Die Männerliebe der Griechen compares the oppression of homosexuals to the persecution of witches, and burns with anger at the injustice of it. Hössli maintains the naturalness of male love and discusses the Greek conception of it and modern errors, pleading throughout for tolerance. The second volume reiterates the themes of the first and offers extracts from earlier writers, including notably an anthology of Greek, Roman, Arabic, Persian and Turkish pederastic poetry (the latter three fruits of German Romantic translation, unparalleled in English). Hössli's biographer, Ferdinand KARSCH-HAACK, who travelled to Switzerland in 1902 to examine surviving records and interview people who had known the milliner, correctly describes *Eros* as the most important work on male love since PLATO's *Symposium* and *Phaedrus*, but errs in judging it of equal merit to those Greek works. Though learned in its way and fired with righteous enthusiasm and an unshakable belief in the justice of the cause, it also everwhere reveals its author's lack of formal education. Its prose, if sometimes rising to eloquence, is generally clotted and ponderous, while the matter is poorly organised and repetitious and the argument weakly mounted and sustained. The book had few readers and almost no influence. When the next pioneer homosexual apologist, Karl Heinrich ULRICHS, learnt of it in 1866, it had been forgotten. Through Ulrichs the new German homosexual emancipation movement after 1896 knew of its existence, but not being reprinted then or since, it continued to be unread except for the extracts Karsch-Haack reprinted.

For understandable reasons, *Eros; Die Männerliebe der Griechen* does not actually reveal the author's sexual orientation, though it is impossible to believe that the vehemence of Hössli's commitment to the homosexual cause displayed in the book does not arise from personal involvement. The peculiar conduct of his marriage is consistent with homosexuality on his part; his overwrought reaction to the Desgouttes case suggests self-discovery or else self-acceptance. As it happens, his younger son Hansi was homosexual, and the son's surviving letters to his father (Hössli's side of the correspondence is lost) reveal that they discussed his son's homosexual love-affairs and homosexuality generally. To his father's expressed hope that he should have the good fortune to find a true friend for life, Hansi replied that it was difficult for him, and that the social disapprobation of male love militated against it. Hössli is reported to have been masculine in appearance without a touch of the feminine, but in his behaviour like a court lady; it was said that he possessed exactly the same temperament as his younger sister Barbara, extraordinarily lively, restless and unsettled.

F. Karsch-Haack, 'Quellenmateriel zur Beurteilung angeblicher und wirklicher Uranier. 4. Heinrich Hössli (1784–1864)', *Jahrbuch für sexuelle Zwischenstufen*, 1 (1903): 449–556; issued separately as *Der Putzmacher von Glarus, Heinrich Hössli*, Leipzig, 1903; reprinted in *Documents of the Homosexual Rights Movement in Germany*, New York, 1975; P. Derks, *Die Schande der heiligen Päderastie: Homosexualität und Öffentlichkeit in der deutschen Literatur, 1750–1850*, Berlin, 1990: 454–78.

Gary Simes

Houmark (Jens) Christian (1869–1950), Danish author and journalist. At age 15, Christian Houmark was the author of a play performed at a theatre in the provincial town of Ålborg. He attempted, without success, a career in the theatre, then became a journalist. His specialty was the long and penetrating interview in which his pointed characterisation often came close to perfidy; the fast change of words was lively and mannered. To be interviewed by Houmark was a mark of social distinction.

Houmark was an admirer and a close friend of the famed author Herman BANG, whom he succeeded as the one notorious and exemplary homosexual in Denmark. In 1910 he published *For Guds Aasyn (In the Eye of God)*, a tearful novel about an artistically inclined young man's chaste love for another young man. The word 'homosexual' does not appear. The moral was this: 'Do not ever seek happiness with someone to whom fate has not been as cruel as it has been to yourself. To seek it with anyone else is a crime against humanity.' Later in life Houmark became a 'queen' who expected his collegues to address him as 'countess' (since one of his love affairs had been with a count).

Shortly after Houmark's death in 1950 two autobiographies, mainly on his life as a homosexual, were published in accordance with his will. They are a protest against society's oppression of homosexuals. However, factual details, events and conversations related word-for-word are not trustworthy.

J. Houmark, *Timer, der blev til Dage*, Copenhagen, 1950, and *Naar jeg er død*, Copenhagen, 1950; J. Kistrup, 'Christian Houmark', *Dansk Biografisk Leksikon*, Vol. 6, Copenhagen, 1980: 585.

Wilhelm von Rosen

Housman, A(lfred) E(dward) (1859–1936), British poet and scholar. Known for little else but the collection of poems *The Shropshire Lad* (1896), Housman was a brilliant Latinist, from 1892 holding the Chair of Latin at University College London until he was appointed Professor of Latin at Cambridge University in 1911.

Educated at Bromsgrove School and Oxford, while at the latter he fell in love with Moses Jackson, a fellow student. The love was unrequited, and Housman nursed this sadness for the rest of his life. But it made him realise that he was homosexual. He worked for some years in the Civil Service, at the London Patent Office, all the while publishing academic papers in various scholarly journals. His academic appointments allowed him the freedom to pursue his research interest in a minor Latin poet, Manilius.

As for many Englishmen of his class and time, sexual freedom was only to be experienced in that exotic place, 'abroad'. He travelled widely in Europe, from Paris to Constantinople, indulging himself in those pleasures that his own country forbade. While on the Continent, he was also able to acquire a library of erotica such as would have been unavailable at home.

His self-enforced discretion meant that it has been only in recent years that details of his private life – including his sexual preferences, and their pleasuring – have become public knowledge. Probably his main emotional interest for much of his life was a young gondolier he met in Venice in 1900, and to whom he returned for many a golden summer. His brother Laurence was an early homosexual rights activist.

R. Graves, *A. E. Housman: The Scholar-Poet*, London, 1980.

Garry Wotherspoon

Howard, Brian (Christian de Claiborne) (1905–1958), British public figure. Howard was a flamboyant 'queen' and personality of the 1920s. As a precocious aesthete at Eton in the early 1920s, Howard founded, in 1922, the Eton Society of Arts, a discussion and exhibition group which included the writer Harold ACTON, future novelists Henry Yorke ('Henry Greene') and An-

thony Powell, future travel-writer Robert Byron and the painter Oliver MESSEL. The Society published an anthology of writing titled *Eton Candle* (1922), largely made up of contributions from Howard and Acton.

Howard's self-assurance and artistic convictions at Eton suggested to his contemporaries a brilliant future as an artist – a career which never materialised. After struggling through Eton and Oxford, Howard became a leading figure in the party circuit of the 'Bright Young People', and was a host of the perhaps most memorable of these functions, the 'Swimming Pool Party' (1928), as well as the creator of 'The Great Urban Dionysia' (1929), for which guests came dressed as characters from Greek mythology.

Howard spent the 1930s drifting around Europe, returning to Britain at the outbreak of World War II. He held positions in MI5 and the Royal Air Force during the war, after which he resumed his wanderings on the Continent with a boyfriend, Sam. In 1958, when Sam died by asphyxiation from a faulty gas heater, Howard killed himself by taking an overdose of sedatives.

It was Howard's flamboyant and 'out' personality which left its mark on his contemporaries. Anthony Blanche in Evelyn WAUGH's *Brideshead Revisited* owes something to him, and Ambrose Silk in Waugh's *Put Out More Flags* is a thinly disguised caricature of Howard. A parody of his talk and activities is to be found in Cyril Connolly's mock review ('Where Engels Fears to Tread') of a non-existent book (*From Oscar to Stalin: A Progress*, by 'Christian de Clavering') in Connolly's *The Condemned Playground* (London, 1946).

H. Carpenter, *The Brideshead Generation*, London, 1989; M. J. Lancaster (ed.) *Brian Howard: Portrait of a Failure*, London, 1968.

Jason Boyd

Hoyos y Vinent, Antonio de (1885–1940), Spanish writer. Hoyos y Vinent is a key representative of the often neglected homosexual culture that flourished in Spain during the first decades of the twentieth century. He modelled himself after the French decadent 'dandies' and became a popular, not always well liked, figure in Madrid's literary circles. His distinctive manner (he was a tall man with a somewhat grotesque face and hard of hearing) made him into something of a stock character who gets mentioned in several memoirs and accounts of the period (from Ramón Gómez de la Serna's *Nuevos retratos contemporáneos* to Pío Baroja's *Memorias* or, very significantly, Rafael Cansinos Assens's masterpiece of literary gossip *La novela de un literato*), often as if he were just a joke, more rarely as a pathetic figure to be pitied. He is also represented as a character in several literary works by leading authors such as Colombine and Pérez de Ayala, as well as Luis Antonio de Villena's recent *Divino* (1994).

Hoyos y Vinent was born in Madrid into an aristocratic family, and, being the older son, was entitled to inherit the title of Marquis. But his sexual extravagance, which he made no attempt to conceal, made him into something of a black sheep. He was interested in working-class rent boys and was often seen with them in literary salons and cafés. However, perhaps due to his social position, maybe because of his physique, he commanded some degree of awe and nobody dared to criticize him openly. If one is to believe personal accounts, homosexuality was a topic he referred to and defended lucidly, although his enemies would seldom stand to reason. His family became embarrassed by his reputation and mention of his existence was excised from family chronicles.

He wrote scores of pulpy, popular narratives, both novellas and short stories, which nowadays are notoriously difficult to find, as most were never reprinted. Although only a couple feature homosexuality in an explicit way, they reflect some of the topics of the homoerotic imagination

in Spain: portraits of low life and proletarian youths, boxers, bullfighters, sexy peasants discovered as they hide in the bushes, young innocent heiresses whose sensuality is aroused by male flesh enticingly described. The role of social repression, especially coming from institutionalised religion, often is brought to the fore, showing a keen awareness of the ideological slant of homophobia: homosexuality appears not as a mere 'perversion' but as dissent. In many of these narratives he introduces a character called Julito Calabrés, who often appears sauntering around social haunts and is depicted as an effete dandy: he is an alter-ego of the author. Although the artistic value of his writings is seldom defended, their originality and interest cannot be argued.

Hoyos y Vinent represents a strand of cultural life that was swept out with the arrival of Francoism: sensual, whimsical, often camp, and eminently popular. Accounts of this figure have normally avoided engaging with his politics (the exception is Villena). Hoyos was a card-carrying Communist, and one finds an interesting connection between his politics and his erotics, which has been silenced from the left: it is as if homosexuals had to be denied any legitimacy as anti-fascist dissidents. But the fact remains that many left-leaning Republican intellectuals could be rehabilitated by Francoism, provided they 'apologised' and agreed to conceal any other kind of dissidence; Hoyos did not. As a Communist and as a homosexual, he faced marginality and prison, and died shortly after the end of the Civil War, poor and ignored by his old acquaintances, hounded by his family and with no friends at all.

C. Alfonso García, 'El autorretrato de un héroe decadentista: Las narraciones de Hoyos y Vinent', in J. L. Caramés and S. González (eds) *Género y sexo en el discurso artístico*, Oviedo, 1994; L. A. de Villena, *Máscaras y formas del fin de siglo*, Madrid, 1988.

Alberto Mira

Huet, Pierre-Daniel (1630–1721), French man of letters. Huet – 'learned Europe's memory' as he was dubbed in the early years of the eighteenth century – offers a most remarkable insight into what could be the life of a homosexual of the French establishment in the age of Louis XIV.

Born in Caen (Normandy) into a family of recent converts to Roman Catholicism who had some pretensions to belonging to the lower nobility, Huet understood at an early age that, being fatherless, with two sisters for whom he would become legally responsible, the only career that was open to him, given his natural gifts for the humanities, was that of the Church.

His early years read like a manual of homosociality in strategising and networking. Gifted as he was, the adolescent Huet formed friendships with his Jesuit masters and more elderly Humanists, such as the Dupuy brothers, conveners of a *cabinet* (club), a model for the Académie française (1635). In his Latin *Memoirs* (1718) he actually takes great care at showing how infatuated with him one of his Jesuit tutors was (to the point of falling ill) and how precious to him was the company of older men for whom he deployed all his charms. He soon realised that he had both to conceal his *libertin* tendencies (*libertinage* blossomed at court, in the circles of PHILIPPE, DUC D'ORLÉANS and the VENDÔME brothers) and to assert his independence by manoeuvering between Church and State, the French court and the 'International of savants' (the 'Republic of Letters'), weaving networks of friends with whom he had passionate affairs, some platonic and some not. In his early twenties he was already the toast of humanist circles in Paris, a boy-wonder.

At 21, he pocketed some of his inheritance, and took himself, on horseback, to Holland and Sweden, where René Descartes had just died (1650). Huet narrates his many encounters, all literary, in Holland and, in veiled terms, a passionate affair with a certain Morus, later to become a pastor and minor Latin poet, an affair full of jealousy, bad nights, letters, recriminations and even a token young girl thrown in to delude the host family. They broke off in a tiff. Huet moved to Sweden (writing a wonderfully witty account) where Queen KRISTINA tried to force herself on him. He barely escaped his fate by punning in Greek to the literary-minded 'king' (such was her title) that he was one never to marry any woman. And she retorted, in Greek, she was herself one never to marry a man. As soon as he realised that the Minerva of the North would soon convert – and leave her library to Rome – he pilfered from her library an unknown commentary on St Matthew by the Church Father Origen, and cavalcaded back to France.

His career then took off, largely based upon the much awaited publication of his Latin *Commentary on Origen* (1668) and his careful usage of his now considerable network of friends and patrons. He even declined in 1663 the tutorship of young Karl-Gustav of Sweden, thus raising his stakes in France. His career was meteoric as a high official at the French court: given a pension by Louis XIV in 1663, he became first president of the Royal Academy of Physics (a forerunner of the Academy of Sciences), he landed the position of Under-Preceptor of Louis XIV's son, the *Grand Dauphin* (missing the top job, owing to lingering suspicions of *libertinage*), and for all intents and purposes he was the one who directed the education of Louis' heir; he entered the French Academy in 1674. Yet, a strategist always, he frequented the *préciosité* salons which operated at the margins of the court, sometime a meeting-point for the disgruntled feudal aristocracy. There he collaborated with *précieuse* Madame de La Fayette (1634–1693) in at least two of her novels, including it seems the ground-breaking *Princesse de Clèves* (1678), and with Jean Segrais (1624–1701) with whom he had an awful fight (the reasons for which are still not elucidated). One has simply to picture Huet, 'too beautiful for a man', in such circles to have an idea of a brilliant homosexual in action in a milieu that adumbrated modern *parisianisme*.

At 45 he fell seriously ill (in spite of his addiction to swimming, exercise, fresh air and good food), tormented by a 'secret illness' contracted in Holland (it may have been a fistula that never healed properly: Huet coyly notes, in Latin, that it had prevented him from riding comfortably ever since his first trip to the Low Countries). He then took holy orders and was given the most prestigious Soissons bishopric, a royal prebend the pope refused to confirm (that pope, in sharp contrast to his predecessors, had no time for sodomites who played royal preceptors to the Most Christian King, nor for humanists who were too well versed in canon law, as Huet was, in support of regalian rights over the papal ones). Laden with honours and rich stipends, he still found time to publish, at prime minister Colbert's request, the first economic analysis of the Dutch colonial empire – and he is credited with being the first to offer a history of the development of the novel in Europe (*Origin of Novels*, 1666).

By that time Huet was a leading, if not the leading, figure of Europe's old-style humanism. His violent attacks against Descartes gave him the reputation of a sharp-tongued satirist: he compared Descartes to a Lapp living off moss and teaching fellow Eskimos in a frozen philosophical cuckoo-land. All over Europe his friends rallied to publish his Latin or Greek poems, his essays, his *bons mots*. Numerous translations attest to his fame down to the late nineteenth century, at least among philologists. In terms of the history of gay literature, his annotations to the *Greek Anthology* – a collection of mainly pederastic verse – are still used today. Why he spent so much time on them is anyone's guess.

Aged, having lost his two dearest friends, the writer Gilles Ménage and the diplomat Ezéchiel Spanheim (to whom we owe a first-hand account of Louis XIV's court), he settled at the Jesuits' house in the Faubourg Saint-Jacques, Paris. He lived there for 20 years, often causing irritation to his reluctant hosts, who were to inherit his considerable and priceless library, in due course taken over by the Royal Library. The Jesuit house is now the Lycée Charlemagne, located near the Saint-Paul Métro station, in the middle of Paris's gay district. Huet is buried in Saint-Paul church, next to the Lycée, whose exuberant teenagers certainly lull him to eternal peace. There he held court, surrounded by younger men who seem to have helped him pass sweet old years, a seventeenth-century André GIDE, and like him an arbiter of literary tastes, a polymath, a man avid for honours, industrious and passionate.

As far as the humanist backdrop to his homosexuality is concerned, Huet perpetuates the tradition of a RABELAIS or MONTAIGNE, and, by his careful interlocking of amorous and official careers, he offers an example of a more modern sort of homosexual intellectual, at ease in a centralised and all-pervading French state, and whose later representatives would be Napoleonic CAMBACÉRÈS, the bourgeois Duc Decazes (so beautiful he got the premiership), the colonial proconsul in Morocco, Marshall Lyautey, and many a later Academician, such as Julien Green.

P.-D. Huet, *Mémoires* (1718), ed. Ph.-J. Salazar, Toulouse/Paris, 1993.

Philippe-Joseph Salazar

Hunter, Alberta (1895–1984), American blues singer and songwriter. Born in Memphis, Tennessee, to a poor family, Hunter started her singing career with King Oliver's Creole Jazz Band, emulating the styles of Al Jolson, Eddie Cantor and Sophie Tucker. As one of American's most popular blues singers in the 1920s, she projected an image of a tough woman who could take care of herself. Mostly she sang about anguished love affairs and these had a special resonance for gay audiences.

Hunter's 'Down Hearted Blues', as recorded by Bessie Smith, became the best-selling blues record of 1923. Throughout the 1920s and 1930s, some African-American entertainers pursued their careers in Europe, where they experienced less virulent racism and more hospitality than in the US. Women like Hunter, Josephine Baker, Adelaide Hall and Elisabeth Welch found that Europe offered more possibilities for work and acclaim, and they captured the continent with their songs, beauty, elegance and style.

In 1928 Hunter was featured with Paul Robeson in the London version of the musical *Show Boat* and later recalled: 'We went to Europe because we were recognised and given a chance. In Europe they had your name up in lights. People in the United States would not give us that chance.' In the 1930s she performed with the Jack Jackson Orchestra at London's Dorchester Hotel, and her admirers included Noel COWARD, Cole PORTER and the Prince of Wales. When she took part in a recording session with Jack Jackson at the Dorchester in 1934, Hunter included Coward's 'I Travel Alone' and Porter's 'Miss Otis Regrets'.

During World War II, Hunter toured extensively for the USO but by the mid-1950s offers of work were scarce. Retiring from show business, she turned to nursing and worked in a New York hospital for 20 years. In 1977 Hunter was forced to retire from nursing when it was discovered she had lied about her age, and had passed the mandatory retirement age of 70 (she was actually 82!). Horrified at the thought of retirement, she was persuaded to sing again, and became a sensation in New York at a Greenwich Village club called The Cookery. In 1979 she wrote and performed songs for the soundtrack of the film *Remember My Name* starring Geraldine Chaplin. Hunter died in New York at the age of 89. Says Frank C. Taylor and Gerard Cook in her biography: 'Alberta was a lesbian [but] she grew up in an era that did not permit discussion of sexuality, much less acceptance of homosexuality. The subject matter remained one she refused to discuss. But she went further. Alberta did everything to conceal this preference all her life. In her mind lesbianism tarnished the image of propriety and respectability she struggled so hard to achieve.'

F. C. Taylor with G. Cook, *Alberta – A Celebration in Blues*, New York, 1987.

Stephen Bourne

I

Ives, George (1867–1950), British writer. The illegitimate son of aristocratic parents, Ives was raised in privileged circumstances by his grandmother, and seems to have recognised and understood his sexual nature from boyhood. A good-looking young man, he early mixed in homosexual circles, had a brief affair with Lord Alfred DOUGLAS in 1893, and established a homosexual *ménage* at the Albany in Picadilly which WILDE took as the model for Algernon's domestic arrangements in *The Importance of Being Earnest*. Through his friendship with Edward CARPENTER and Oscar Wilde, which began in 1892, he became devoted to the cause of homosexual emancipation, and around 1893 was one of the founders of a secret homosexual brotherhood, the Order of Chaeronea, which with rituals and secret insignias was intended to provide mutual support for its members and to work for the cause. The name was taken from the Battle of Chaeronea (338 BC) in which the Sacred Band of Thebes, an élite force of three hundred young soldiers who were lovers, was slaughtered by the troops of Philip of Macedon. Despite innumerable references to the Order in Ives's voluminous unpublished diaries, its exact nature and activities remain unclear; the Order was, it seems, the first organised effort in Britain to further the cause of homosexuals, even if it did little of a public nature to this end. Members of the Order seem to have been among those who in 1913 founded the British Society for the Study of Sex-Psychology, the closest thing in the period to an open homosexual group.

Ives published two small volumes of verse, *Book of Chains* (1897) and *Eros' Throne* (1900), that contain poems cryptically or codedly celebrating homosexual love and lamenting the homosexual's sorry lot. Later he became interested in criminology, and *A History of Penal Methods: Criminals, Witches, Lunatics* (1914) – which is concerned with the penalisation of the socially marginalised – has a section dealing with the injustice of society's treatment of the homosexual and arguing for homosexual law reform. This topic is the principal gravamen of his booklet *The Continued Extension of the Criminal Law* (1922), in which he argues that the criminalisation of homosexual behaviour is an unjust and unjustifiable abridgement of the liberty of the Englishman. A later volume, *The Graeco-Roman View of Youth* (1926), deals more directly with homosexuality, though at a safe historical remove.

About 1905 Ives started to keep scapbooks of newspaper clippings that interested him, especially pertaining to homosexual matters, and these provided evidence for the *History of Penal Methods*. A selection from the 45 volumes was published by Paul Sieveking in 1980 under the title *Man Bites Man: The*

Scrapbook of an Edwardian Eccentric, George Ives. Throughout his life Ives kept a diary. Though he talks about homosexual emancipation, he is frequently evasive and cryptic and disguises identities. Even in this private journal he showed the caution and timidity that Wilde found so irritating in him. Like many other homosexuals, Ives was for his part appalled by the ostentatious folly of Wilde's behaviour in 1895, which set back the homosexual cause in England by a generation; notwithstanding, in the end he forgave Wilde and came to admire his courage in adversity.

J. Weeks, *Coming Out: Homosexual Politics in Britain, from the Nineteenth Century to the Present,* London, 1977: Chap. 10; J. Stokes, 'Wilde at Bay: The Diaries of George Ives', *English Literature in Transition 1880–1920,* 26 (1983): 175–86.

Gary Simes

Iwaszkiewicz, Jarosław (1894–1980), Polish writer. Born into the Polish minority living in Ukraine, Iwaszkiewicz studied law and music in Kiev from 1912, settling in Warsaw in 1918, where he belonged to Skamander, a group of lyrical poets which included other homosexuals, such as Jan LECHOŃ and Stanisław Baliński. In 1922, Iwaszkiewicz married Anna Lilpop, the daughter of a rich Warsaw industrialist, a marriage which resulted in two daughters. However, his marriage did not lead to a change in his life-style. A friend and cousin of the gay Polish composer Karol SZYMANOWSKI, Iwaszkiewicz wrote the libretto for his homoerotic opera *Król Roger,* premiered in Warsaw in 1926. Iwaszkiewicz joined the Ministry of Foreign Affairs, serving as a member of the Polish legations to Copenhagen and Brussels during 1932–1936. When Poland was occupied by Nazi Germany, he sheltered fugitives from the Nazis at the family home in Stawisko. Beginning in 1949, he cooperated with the new Communist government. For example, he was appointed chairman of the Polish Committee to Defend Peace and became a member of the Polish parliament. Iwaszkiewicz presided over the Union of Polish Writers (ZLP) three times; from 1955 he edited the important monthly literary periodical *Twórczość (Creation).* In 1970, he was awarded the International Lenin Prize.

His work is devoted to exploring the link between creativity and eroticism. His early poetic fable, *Ucieczka do Bagdadu (Escape from Baghdad,* 1923) already has a distinct homosexual accent. Many of his works have homoerotic plots. In *Panny w Wilka (Ladies from Wilko,* 1932), the protagonist Wiktor has an affair with his cousin Julcia, later acknowledged to be based on an affair the author had with a man (whom the novella transformed into a female). In later works, such as the novels *Czerwone tarcze (Red Shields,* 1934), *Młyn nad Utrat (The Mill over Utrata,* 1936) or the short stories *Nauczyciel (The Teacher)* and *Zygfryd (Siegried),* he was more open about homosexuality. Even in his most popular work, the family saga, *Sława i Chwała (Glory and Fame)* published in 1956–1962 and relating the fate of Poles between 1914 and 1945, homoeroticism appears.

Iwaszkiewicz also published many volumes of poetry, such as *Dionizje (Dionysios,* 1922) and *Mapa Pogody (Weather Map,* 1977), dramas, essays, journalism, translations and reminiscences. His autobiography, *Książka moich wspomnie (Book of my Memories,* 1957), recalls his fascination for the homoerotic. He translated into Polish the works of gay authors, such as RIMBAUD and GIDE. Iwaszkiewicz's life recalls the rich intellectual basis of Polish gay culture in the inter-war period as well as its continued existence in post-war Poland.

R. Przybylski, *Eros i Tanatos. Proza Jarosława Iwaszkiewicza 1916–1938,* Warsaw, 1970; G. Ritz, *Jarosław Iwaszkiewicz. Ein Grenzgänger* der Moderne, Bern, 1996; J. Rohozilski (ed.) *Jarosław Iwaszkiewicz. Materiały*, Warsaw, 1968; Andrzej Selerowicz, 'Odmieńcy: Jarosław Iwaszkiewicz 1894–1980', *Inaczej*, 4, 7 (37) (1993).

John Stanley

J

Jahnn, Hans Henny (1894–1959), German writer. Born in Stellingen, a suburb of Hamburg, he was the youngest son of a shipwright. At school he fell in love with a student who became his best gay friend, Gottlieb Harms. His parents were shocked, but he insisted that Harms was the man he really loved. At the beginning of World War I they decided to leave Germany in order to avoid military service. After several enlistment orders they fled to Norway, where Jahnn wrote his *Norwegian Diary*. He read many books about architecture and organ-building and was fascinated by mystical numerology. After the war they returned to Germany and lived in Hamburg and in a small village. In 1919 Jahnn published his first drama, *Pastor Ephraim Magnus*. Due to his studies in mythology and archaeology he founded a religious community named Ugrino, which was inspired by utopian concepts like Francis BACON's 'Nova Atlantis'. In 1923 he was employed to restore the organ of the St Jakobi Church in Hamburg. He developed a new approach and highlighted the significance of baroque organ music. In 1926 he married Ellinor Philips, a gymnastics teacher, although both thought that marriage was an old-fashioned institution; Harms married Philips's sister. When Harms, the man Jahnn loved more than anyone else, died in 1931 he designed his gravestone.

In the Nazi period Jahnn's second exile began. He knew that the homophobic attitude of Nazis would constitute a serious danger for gays. In August 1933 he moved to Zurich and later to the Danish island of Bornholm, where he lived on a farm and studied agriculture. He began to write *Das Holzschiff* and *Fluss ohne Ufer*. Although his books were not forbidden and not burnt in Nazi Germany, he had no opportunity of publishing because his bizarre style and his extraordinary topics were considered to be unusual and inappropriate. Therefore he was excluded from the national writers' guild. During his Danish exile he did not have any contacts with other political emigrants like Bertolt Brecht, who also lived in Denmark, because he feared that he could lose his citizenship and then he would never have the chance of being buried in the tomb of his beloved friend in Hamburg.

After the war Jahnn returned to Germany and founded the Free Academy of Arts. He was disappointed by the conservative and prudish climate in the 1950s and the beginning of the Cold War. Because of his pacifist attitude he participated in several activities and demonstrations against the nuclear armaments race and for the rights of animals. In 1959 he died of a heart attack and was buried near the grave of Harms.

Although his novels and dramas are regarded as unique in German literature, they have never been appreciated by the public. His strange lifestyle, his homo-sexual relationship and his unconventional opinions have become obstacles to a broader reception of his writings. His novels and dramas describe homosexuality and incest. Gay relationships are often embedded in a mythological setting and praise the dignity and uniqueness of nature. Homosexuality symbolises the unification of two men. In his novel *Perrudja*, whose narrative style was strongly influenced by James Joyce, he writes about a man, his mental development and his desires. In *Das Holzsschiff* he depicts the homoerotic dreams of a sailor and the symbolic importance of masculinity. Outsiders and outcasts are often the heroes and the protagonists of his writings. In his drama *Medea*, based on the famous tragedy of Euripides, Medea is an African woman with two illegitimate sons. One son has incestuous emotions towards his brother and confesses to him his deep affection. Although they try to overcome their destiny, they remain outsiders. This drama reflects the essential characteristics of Jahnn's writings: homosexuality, unconditional affection, incestuous inclinations, mythological settings and the connecting of love and death. The motto of Jahnn's life could be a sentence in his drama *Thomas Chatterton*: 'We want at least heresy for us. We want to be antagonists. We are the example for others who start with less courage.'

T. P. Freeman, *Structure and Symbolism in Hans Henny Jahnn's* Perrudja *in Microcosm: A Study of the Unity of the Novel*, Stanford, 1970; F. Krey, *Hans Henny Jahnn und die mann-männliche Liebe*, Frankfurt am Main, 1987; W. Popp (ed.) *Die Suche nach dem rechten Mann. Männerfreundschaft im literarischen Werk Hans Henny Jahnns*, Berlin, 1984; E. Wolffheim, *Hans Henny Jahnn*, Reinbek, 1989.

Gerald Pilz

James I and VI (1566–1625), king of Scotland (as James VI) from 1567, king of England (as James I) from 1603. He was called 'the wisest fool in Christendom' because his undoubted talents and intellect were not matched by political astuteness. Though he united the kingdoms of England and Scotland (bringing many benefits to Scotland) and brought peace to Europe, he had an acrimonious relationship with the English parliament, who disliked the Union and who objected to the expenditure of large sums upon the royal favourites

James's love for men aroused gossip from an early date. He fell in love with the French courtier Esmé Stuart, Seigneur d'Aubigny, at the age of 14, and raised him to a position of wealth and power. Later, contemporaries said that 'the King's best loved minion' was Alexander Lindsay, Lord Spynie, whom James appointed as his Vice-Chamberlain. Another minion of the early 1580s was Francis Stewart Hepburn, Earl of Bothwell, whom James nonchalantly kissed and embraced in public, causing great scandal. Perhaps his most devoted lover was Robert Carr, a handsome Scots lad who came to England in 1603 to run beside the royal coach as a page-boy. (Carr eventually became the Earl of Somerset but was disgraced when he married Lady Frances Howard in 1613 and became implicated in the murder of Sir Francis Overbury.)

James's most passionate and longest affair began in 1613 with George Villiers, who in ten years rose to become the Duke of Buckingham. Their relationship provoked censure in 1617 in the Privy Council, where Sir James Oglander said, 'I never yet saw any fond husband make so much or so great dalliance over his beautiful spouse as I have seen King James over his favourites, especially Buckingham.' James defended himself: 'I, James, am neither a god nor an angel, but a man like any other. Therefore I act like a man and confess to loving those dear to me more than other men. You may be sure that I love the Earl of Buckingham more than anyone else, and more than you who are here assembled. I wish to speak in my own be-half and not to have it thought to be a defect, for Jesus Christ did the same, and therefore I cannot be blamed. Christ had his John, and I have my George.'

Many love-letters survive from James to Buckingham, whom James addressed as 'sweet child and wife' and signed himself 'thy dear dad and husband'. Buckingham was a skilful politician, learned and witty, but also ambitious and haughty. He raised his entire family to positions of power and significantly contributed to England's national debt; many debate whether he reformed or increased the corruption at court. The arrogance with which king and favourite flaunted their relationship nearly provoked civil war, and parliament was dissolved so that James would not be forced to abdicate. James subsided into a state of depression after the death of Queen Anne in 1619 (he admired her greatly, though they had lived apart from 1606), and seemed to ignore everyone except Buckingham until his death. Buckingham was in turn assassinated by a disgruntled soldier wanting his back-pay in 1628, and bonfires were lit in London to celebrate his death.

A. Fraser, *King James*, London, 1974; R. Norton, *Mother Clap's Molly House*, London, 1992; F. Osborne, *Secret History of the Court of James the First*, Edinburgh, 1811; E. S. Turner, *The Court of St. James's*, New York, 1959.

Rictor Norton

James, Henry (1843–1916), American writer. Born in New York City, brother of William James (1842–1910) and Alice James (1848–1892), he wrote about his family in three volumes of autobiography: *A Small Boy and Others* (1913), *Notes of a Son and Brother* (1914), and *The Middle Years* (1917).

James is regarded as one of America's greatest writers, though he is equally among the greatest of British authors as well, having spent most of his life in England, where he wrote his finest work. Until recently, there had been little public speculation about his intimate life, especially since his major biographer, Leon Edel, doubted that James had any physical relationships; James never married, nor is it known that he had any lovers of either sex. However, it is well known that James entertained at Lamb House, his home in Rye, many young men who were homosexual, including Oscar WILDE's first lover, Robert Ross, and he cultivated the friendships of many other young men. E. M. FORSTER describes visiting Lamb House as a young novelist, intimating in his diary the homoerotic atmosphere of James's salon. When James was in his fifties, he formed a special friendship with a handsome young sculptor, Hendrik Andersen, who was far more ambitious than he was talented. James wrote letters to Andersen, remarkable, according to Edel, for the 'quantity of physical, tactile language employed'. James wrote, 'I hold you close', 'I feel, my dear boy, my arms around you', and 'I draw you close, I hold you long'. When Andersen's brother died in 1902, James asked Andersen to 'lean on me as on a brother and a lover'.

It is probable that James led an abstinent life, but it is equally probable that his erotic imagination was homosexual in character. Critics have long noted the absence of any clear libido in his heterosexual male characters, who are often introspective, sensitive and passive when confronting women and love. His villains, like Gilbert Osmond in *The Portrait of a Lady*, are frequently misogynistic and rarely convey passion of any sort. It is in his women characters that James could create fully passionate individuals. This imagining of the erotic life entirely in terms of women's lives is the primary internal evidence of James's homoeroticism. Recently, scholars have been much more forthright about speculations regarding James's sexuality, including Edel in the revision of his five-volume life of James, reissued abridged in one volume.

L. Edel, *Henry James: A Life*, 5 vols, Philadelphia, 1953–1972; one-volume abridgement, New York, 1985; R. W. B. Lewis, *The Jameses: A Family Narrative*, New York, 1991; F. Kaplan, *Henry James: The Imagination of Genius*, New York, 1994.

Seymour Kleinberg

Jansson, Eugène (1862–1915), Swedish painter. Described as the first Swedish gay painter, in 1905 Jansson was acknowledged as an artist with his monumental paintings of the Swedish capital in blue twilight or dawn, inspired by French Symbolists. After having earned this long-desired esteem from both the critics and the public, Jansson immediately abandoned for good the style that had created his success. He isolated himself for a few years to learn how to paint the male nude, which he always had aimed to do. In 1907 he exhibited *Naken yngling* (*Naked young man*), a full figure painting of his friend Knut Nyman (1887–1946), showing Nyman symbolically turning his back to Jansson's earlier paintings. This painting has been interpreted as saying that it is necessary to get close to and touch the naked body of the young man in order to understand Jansson's blue period. Jansson and Nyman became friends at the Naval bathhouse in Stockholm, where Jansson was a visitor. The two men shared a home in Jansson's studio until 1912. Jansson painted four monumental paintings with motifs from the same bath-house, and continued painting naked athletes until an attack of cerebral haemorrhage ended his life.

Greger Eman

Jean II le Bon (1319–1364), king of France. Jean became king of France in 1350. Like many sodomites in the Middle Ages or *ancien régime*, he was more of a bisexual than a homosexual in the modern sense of the word; he took a wife, Bonne de Luxembourg, and fathered ten children in eleven years. Yet the great love of his life

was Charles de La Cerda, a childhood friend. La Cerda was given various honours and appointed to the high position of *connétable* when Jean became king; he accompanied the king on all his official journeys to the provinces. La Cerda's rise at court excited the jealousy of the French barons, several of whom stabbed him to death in 1354. La Cerda's fate paralleled that of EDWARD II's Piers Gaveston in England and Juan II's Alvaro de Luna in Spain: the position of a royal favourite was a dangerous one.

Jean's grief on La Cerda's death was overt and public, producing episodes of fury and despair – the king's feelings, as was often true in the case of similar liaisons in early modern Europe, were well known. Jean himself was captured by the Black Prince in 1356 and taken to England, where he died.

J. Deviosse, *Jean Le Bon*, Paris, 1985.

Didier Godard

Jesus (*c.* 4 BC to 33 AD), founder of Christianity. Opinions have varied widely on how much can be known about the historical facts of Jesus's life. While nineteenth-century scholarship tended to the view that his life could be extensively reconstructed, others have taken the view that little can be confidently asserted beyond the bare fact of his existence, given the theological nature of the sources. This entry takes the more or less middle-of-the-road view that a core of historical fact can be established by the close analysis employed by historians in other contexts.

We know nothing about Jesus's own sexuality – the sources, for example, say neither that Jesus was married nor that he was unmarried – but in subsequent centuries Christianity was to be associated with a violently hostile attitude to homosexuality that has been taken as central to its beliefs, and the apparent silence of the historical Jesus on the subject has been an embarrassment to that view. In Roman-occupied Palestine, in which Jesus lived, homosexuality tended to be identified with gentile rather than Jewish culture, and the best argument that can be made for Jesus's espousal of what was to become the traditionally hostile Christian view of homosexuality turns on his use of the broad term 'porneia'. This would conventionally have included hostility to homosexuality. The problem with that argument (as well as its obvious circularity) is that it does not fit easily with the one occasion when Jesus is presented as coming into contact with the homosexuality of gentile culture.

This incident is related in two of the early accounts of Jesus's life: that attributed to Matthew (chapter 8) and that to Luke (chapter 7). As they recount the story, an officer in the Roman army – a 'centurion' – sought Jesus's help for his bond-servant, who was ill and in pain and (as Luke's account puts it) was precious to him. The climax of the story is Jesus's dramatic response to the expression the centurion used, and this has preserved the distinctively gentile context of the encounter, for (as the accounts explain) these were the words of a Roman soldier: 'Sir, I am not worthy to have you under my roof; just give the word and my bond-servant will be cured. For I am under authority myself, and have soldiers under me; and I say to one man: "Go", and he goes; to another: "Come here", and he comes; to my servant: "Do this", and he does it.'

The social outline of a homosexual relationship in Roman culture was often precisely the one we see here, between a master and his bond-servant. A pious Jew like Jesus – and those who were watching him – might have assumed easily that this was a homosexual relationship. This is not, of course, to say that it was or that Jesus assumed it to be so. The dramatic point in Jesus's response was that he looked past the question and responded on a plane radically different from the conventional moral judgement: 'When Jesus heard this he was astonished and said to those following him, "I tell you

solemnly, nowhere in Israel have I found faith like this".'

It was a radical response characteristic of a number of the incidents recounted about Jesus, in which Jesus looked beyond the conventional moral response to the reality before him; and their distinctiveness and coherence suggest that these incidents are part of that core of facts about Jesus that one can identify with some reasonable probability. It was a stance that was to prove deeply troubling to the authorities when applied to the social and religious injustices of Jesus's time, and it was part of the reason for Jesus's arrest and execution, an outcome that he seems to have foreseen was eventually inevitable. After his death, his followers held that Jesus returned from among the dead and still trace in their lives the influence of this extraordinary personality, but before such a claim the historian can only maintain a respectful silence.

M. Vasey, *Strangers and Friends: A New Exploration of Homosexuality and the Bible*, London, 1995.

Alan Bray

Jewett, Sarah Orne (1849–1909), American writer. Jewett was born in South Berwick, Maine. Daughter of a prosperous country doctor, she enjoyed a privileged childhood and remained financially secure throughout her life, a situation that allowed her to pursue her writing career as an independent woman.

Jewett enjoyed early critical success in her writing for her depiction of the 'Yankee' character and small-town New England life. Her novels and short stories exemplify the Regionalism literary movement of the period, in which realism is mixed with nostalgia for a simpler past.

Admired by literary contemporaries, including her *protégée* Willa Cather, Jewett has in recent years received renewed attention and critical praise for her examination of feminist and gender issues. Her most celebrated work, *The Country of the*

Pointed Firs (1896), is an episodic novel centring on relationships among a variety of women. Other works, such as the novel *A Country Doctor* (1884) and the short stories 'Martha's Lady' and 'Tom's Husband', remain surprisingly contemporary in their examination of the place of women in American society.

In her personal life, Jewett's relationship with her companion of 30 years, Annie Adams Fields, has come to personify the 'Boston marriage', a term popularised in Henry JAMES's novel *The Bostonians*, signifying a long-term attachment between two unmarried women. Jewett died in South Berwick, in the house in which she was born.

P. Blandford, *Sarah Orne Jewett – Her World and Her Work*, New York, 1994; M. Roman, *Sarah Orne Jewett: Reconstructing Gender*, Tuscaloosa, 1992; E. Silverthorne, *Sarah Orne Jewett – A Writer's Life*, New York, 1993.

David Garnes

João do Rio (pseudonym of Paulo Barreto) (1880–1921), Brazilian writer. Paulo Alberto Coelho Barreto, commonly known by one of his *noms de plume* as João do Rio (John from Rio), was born in Rio de Janeiro to a middle-class family. He gained literary prominence at age 23 through a series of journalistic reports about Afro-Brazilian and other non-Catholic religious practices in the nation's capital. His willingness to comb the city's hillside slums and visit poor and working-class suburbs in order to provide sensationalist accounts of the capital's *demi-mondes* also revolutionised Carioca journalism, and he is credited with being Brazil's first modern reporter. During his lifetime, he produced over 2,500 newspaper articles, short stories and essays on urban life.

At age 29, João do Rio won election to the Brazilian Academy of Letters. According to one biographer, Brazil's senior literary figure, Machado de Assis, and the eminent statesman Barão do Rio Branco had organized a faction to block João do Rio's election to the Academy on two occasions because of his questionable moral turpitude. After complex campaigning on his own behalf, however, João do Rio was admitted to the prestigious association with his third nomination. Emílio de Meneses, an important member of Rio de Janeiro's literary circles, allegedly composed a couplet that revealed some degree of public disdain for the sexual proclivities of the young author. Playing on the double meaning of *fresco* as an effeminate homosexual and as something cool, the verse went: 'Predicting the coming heat / The Academy, which worships the cold, / Not being able to buy fans / Opened its doors to João do Rio.'

This *belle époque* literary figure wrote eloquently about the art of *flânerie* in a collection of essays titled *A alma encantadora das ruas* (*The Streets' Enchanting Soul*), published in 1908. His journalistic interest in investigating the city's exotic and dangerous spots at all hours of the day and night produced imaginative vignettes of everyday life in turn-of-the-century Rio. João do Rio's decided sexual taste for men leads one to speculate about multiple meanings behind his celebratory prose in favour of the art of metropolitan strolling. Although little is known about the particulars of his erotic adventures, his nocturnal wanderings through Brazil's capital in search of innovative journalistic material may have also afforded him the opportunity to enjoy the sexual company of the sailors, soldiers and common people who were the subjects of his articles and essays. His literary rival, Lima Barreto, even parodied João do Rio's alleged sexual escapades in his 1909 novel *Recordações do escrivão Isaías Caminha* (*Memoirs of the Notary Public Isaías Caminha*). João do Rio becomes Raul de Gusmão, a 'talented lad' who is seen entering a cheap hotel with a naval gunman. In the story the rumour then spreads that the youth paid to have sex with the marine.

João do Rio dressed meticulously in

elegant attire complete with a hat, monocle and a walking cane. He embodied the cultural aspirations of the Brazilian élite who fastidiously imitated Europe's latest styles. He became an ardent admirer of Oscar WILDE and translated his play *Salomé* into Portuguese. In his essays, short stories and columns, João do Rio freely mimicked the latest continental literary ideas and fashions and recycled them in Brazil to an amused upper-class audience. While João do Rio played the part of the sophisticated Europeanised fop to exaggerated perfection in public, he remained discreet about the particulars of his private life in Brazil. Europe, it seems, provided a more favourable environment for unsanctioned licentious behaviour. One of the few times João do Rio explicitly revealed that he had experienced amorous emotions was in a personal letter describing a 1910 trip to the French Riviera.

Perhaps João do Rio's own concern for personal circumspection in Brazil explains why a known *fresco* who conformed to all of the stereotypes of the effeminate dandy managed to rise to the heights of Brazilian society. As long as João do Rio praised and reproduced the norms valued by Brazil's upper classes, he remained their darling. He was not immune, however, to public ridicule in cartoons that explicitly referred to his homoerotic desires. On one occasion, when he took an unpopular editorial stand regarding a dispute with Portugal, he received death threats and public attacks that highlighted the fact that he was a homosexual. Today João do Rio is mostly remembered for his vivid chronicles of everyday life in early twentieth-century Rio de Janeiro.

R. Magalhães Júnior, *A vida vertiginosa de João do Rio*, Rio de Janeiro, 1978; Jeffrey D. Needell, *A Tropical Belle Époque: Elite Culture and Society in Turn-of-the-Century Rio de Janeiro*, Cambridge, 1987; J. C. Rodrigues, *João do Rio: uma biografia*, Rio de Janeiro, 1996.

James N. Green

Jocelyn, Percy (1764–1843), Irish bishop. Third son of Robert, first Earl of Roden, he took his BA degree at Trinity College, Dublin, and was ordained in the (Anglican) Church of Ireland. He remained unmarried. After a series of comfortable church appointments, in 1809 he was appointed Bishop of Ferns and Leighlin and in 1820 Bishop of Clogher. In 1811 in Dublin he was accused by a servant of attempting to obtain sex. Jocelyn denied the accusation, charged the servant with criminal libel and won his case. On 19 July 1822 Jocelyn, on a visit to London, was detected at an alehouse in Westminster having sexual intercourse with a private soldier of the 1st Regiment of Guards. Although dressed as a clergyman, he refused to reveal his identity, although this was soon revealed. The news of the bishop's arrest caused an immediate sensation in London's clubs and coffee houses. On appearing in court the following day Jocelyn, who had wealthy friends, was released on bail; the soldier was kept in custody. When Jocelyn failed to appear in court the process was begun to deprive him of his ecclesiastical office. There is reason to believe that the government, rather than have a bishop found guilty of the crime of sodomy, was willing to let him escape. As expected, Jocelyn broke bail and fled to Scotland where he changed his name to Thomas Wilson and found private employment as a butler. He died in obscurity in Edinburgh.

Jocelyn was the most senior churchman in Britain to be involved in a public homosexual scandal in the nineteenth century. The fall of the Bishop of Clogher (the 'Bishop of Sodom') became a subject of satire and popular ribaldry.

W. T. Gibson, 'Homosexuality, Class and the Church in Nineteenth Century England: Two Case Studies', *Journal of Homosexuality*, 21, 4 (1991): 45–55; H. Montgomery Hyde, *The Strange Death of Lord Castlereagh*, London, 1959; H. Montgomery Hyde, *The Other Love*, London, 1972.

David Hilliard

Johanson, Klara [K.J.] (1875–1948), Swedish literary critic. Johanson was born in a small town in the southwest of Sweden into a family of shopkeepers. As an external candidate in 1894, she was the first woman in her home town to pass the final school examination at advanced level. Thereafter she studied humanities at Uppsala University, receiving a Master of Arts degree in 1897. During her years at the university, K.J. (as she referred to herself) was an active member of the Women Student Association. After completing her studies she moved to Stockholm, where she worked as a sub-editor at the journal of the Fredrika Bremer Association, *Dagny*, from 1898 to 1901. For the daily paper *Stockholms Dagblad* she wrote literary criticism and humorous stories, the latter under the pseudonym Huck Leber. In 1912 she withdrew from the paper to undertake other types of writing.

Together with her lover Ellen Kleman, she edited the letters of Fredrika Bremer in four volumes. She wrote essays and articles, translated from several languages and in 1907 edited the diary of a prostitute, a controversial book which attracted much attention. K.J.'s work is not translated into English, but in Swedish there is a selection of literary criticism, letters and diaries, memoirs from childhood, essays, humorous stories and student farces.

As a literary critic K.J. was creative in language and aesthetically sensitive, and she was also engaged in the ideas of her time and brought them forward for discussion. She often positioned herself against a pure woman/man dichotomy. Her world of ideas was influenced by German Romantic ideas as well as by the Austrian writer on sexual politics Rosa Mayreder. The attitude of K.J. was subjective, and she did not regard herself as a representative for anyone but herself. In her letters and diaries, we meet an independent and always reflective woman.

C. L. Anderson, 'Klara Johanson and American Literature', *Amerika och Norden* ed. Lars Åhnebrink (Publications of the Nordic Association for American Studies, 1 (1964): 113–33; H. Forsås-Scott, 'The Art of Klara Johanson', *Swedish Book Review* (1985): 27–30; M. Abenius, 'Klara Johanson', in *Kontakter*, 1944; J. Edfelt, *Klara Johanson*, 1984; G. Eman, *Nya himlar över en ny jord*, 1993; I. Svensson, *Klara Johanson som Kritiker*, 1997.

Ingrid Svensson

Jones, Captain Robert (*fl.* 1770–1780), British ice-skater. Jones was the man most responsible for popularising the art of ice-skating. His book *A Treatise on Skating* was first published in London in 1772, possibly in more than one edition; reissued with engravings in 1775; second edition in 1780, with a new song, 'The Skaters' March'; and many other editions, for example in 1797, 1823, 1825, 1855. (He also wrote *A New Treatise on Artificial Fireworks*, 1765, which was also frequently reprinted).

Skates manufactured to Jones's designs could be bought at Riccard's Manufactory in London. He was one of the first people to advocate the firm attachment of the skates to the shoes (by means of screws through the heels) rather than by means of straps and clips, in effect to make the skate integral (previously skaters had to keep re-tying the skates to their shoes, and they kept falling off). He wrote, 'An easy movement and graceful attitude are the sole objects of our attention.' Jones gives various instructions on how to achieve plain skating, graceful rolling and the spiral line, especially its most elegant attitude of a flying Mercury.

Though called Captain Jones, he was actually a lieutenant in the artillery corps of the army. In July 1772 he was convicted at the Old Bailey for sodomy upon Francis Henry Hay, aged 13. The newspapers debated his guilt or innocence, as he was a popular character; for example, he would go to masquerades dressed in the character of Punch. His famous *Treatise on Skating* was published during the course of his trial. He was sentenced to death, but on the day he was scheduled to be hanged, this was respited to imprisonment, and one month later he was granted a pardon by King George III on condition he go into exile. A newspaper reported in June 1773 that 'the famous Capt. Jones lives now in grandeur with a *lovely Ganymede* (his footboy) at Lyons, in the South of France'. There are many allusions to the scandal in contemporary satires and poetry.

The Malefactor's Register, London, 1779; R. Norton, *Mother Clap's Molly House*, London, 1992.

Rictor Norton

Jonsson, Tor (1916–1951), Norwegian poet. Jonsson grew up in a poor family in a small rural community in eastern Norway, and was very attached to his mother. After his mother's death, in June 1950, he moved to Oslo, where he committed suicide on New Year's Day, six months later.

His poems reveal a split personality. The poet admits that he is a man no one knows, because there is another living inside him, a man who never owned his proper words. Many of his poems express solitude and longing after someone, a friend to be near, maybe in an Arcadia, since only there does love grow: 'Never, never to speak out / about what you bear in your heart, / . . . / to live on lies in a crowd of people' (from 'Bunden til bålet', 'Bound to the fire').

Jonsson had at least one close friend, the poet Jan-Magnus Bruheim (1914–1988). They planned to build a cabin together in the mountains, a cabin Bruheim had to build alone. He called it Torbu ('Tor's cottage') after his friend. Bruheim's poem 'Venetape' ('Friend's loss') is a love poem written after the death of Tor Jonsson: 'I'm standing here in front closed, calling on you / from the solitary shore by the quiet lake / The cries break out of depth: Come back. / But friendship wakes no one up from death.'

Many of the themes and motifs in the poetry of Jonsson and Bruheim are closely related to the WHITMAN tradition, and to the works of another Norwegian poet, Åsmund Sveen (1910–1963). Already in his first collection of poems, *Andletet* (The Face, 1932), Sveen is much more explicit about his gay feelings: 'Now I know / I'm not like the others. / I'm different'. Several of Sveen's poems from the inter-war years have a homoerotic content, but his reputation as a poet has been overshadowed by the fact that he was a member of the Norwegian Nazi party during World War II. Of these three poets, Sveen is the only one who is officially known as gay.

J. O. Gatland, '"Å leva på lygn" – med Tor Jonsson', in J. G. Arntzen (ed.) *Med regnbuen som våpen. Festskrift til Karen-Christine Friele 1935–27. mai-1995*, Oslo, 1995; J. O. Gatland, *Mellom linjene. Homofile tema i norsk litteratur*, Oslo, 1990; J. O. Gatland, 'Mannens dikt om vennskap. Nokre nedslag i norsk litteratur', *Bokvennen*, 6, 2 (1997): 54–7.

Jan Olav Gatland

Julius II (Giuliano Della Ròvere) (1443–1513), pope from 1503 to 1513. Born into a humble family, he studied in a Franciscan friary in Perugia. His career took a different turn when his uncle, Francesco Della Ròvere (1414–1484), was elected pope, as SIXTUS IV. In 1471, the pope made him a cardinal and appointed him to diplomatic posts. After Giuliano Della Ròvere himself became pope, as Julius II, much of his activity was linked to a successful effort to establish control by the Papal States over a myriad of territories and fiefdoms which were nominally subject to it but were effectively independent. To this end, Julius II spent a good part of his pontificate, when he did not personally lead troops on the battlefield making and breaking military alliances. Such a state of affairs means that it is necessary to read with caution accounts about his homosexuality; it is not easy to know whether his numerous enemies accused him of sodomy in order to discredit him or whether, in doing so, they were attacking a weak point in their adversary's character.

Be that as it may, the fact remains that the accounts are in agreement that contemporaries thought Julius II to be a sodomite. The Venetian diarist Girolamo Priuli (late fifteenth/early sixteenth centuries) attested: 'He brought along with him his catamites, that is to say, some very handsome young men with whom he was publicly rumoured to have intercourse, and he was said to be the passive partner and to like this gomorrhean vice much, a thing really to abhor in anybody.' The Venetian historian Marino Sanudo (1466–1536) reported this sonnet, written in 1506 when the pope was about to conquer Bologna from the Bentivoglio family: 'Go back, holy father, to your St Peter's / and put the brake to your warm desire / because shooting to score and failing / dishonours more than staying still. / By spears made by flesh and glass / Bentivoglio will not be defeated / and you will not succeed, / although you always have somebody who pushes you from behind. / ... / So be content with / Corso, Trebbiano and Malvasia wine / and with very nice acts of sodomy; / you will be less blamed / in company of Squarcia and Curzio in your holy palace / keeping the bottle in your mouth, and the cock in your arse.'

Julius's reputation as a sodomite survived him (it was still repeated in lampoons in 1534); the accusation was used without reservation by Protestants in their polemics against 'papism'. Thus, for instance, the French Protestant Philippe de Mornay (1549–1623), while he accused all Italians of being sodomites, added specifically: 'This horror is ascribed to good Julius. We read in one text by our theologians in Paris about two gentlemen, whom Queen Anne, wife of King Louis XII, had entrusted to the cardinal of Nantes to take to Italy, and who had been raped by him.' These Protestant libels certainly lack credibility, just as do the Catholic libels which discussed Calvin's purported conviction for sodomy.

Julius II was the protector of the greatest artists of the Italian Renaissance, among them MICHELANGELO, who created his tomb in the basilica of San Pietro in Vincoli in Rome and the famous sculpted statue of Moses which stands in front of it.

P. de Morney, *Le Mystère d'iniquité, c'est à dire, l'histoire de la papauté*, Geneva, 1612; G. Priuli, *Diarii*, in *Rerum italicarum scriptores*, Vol. 24, Part 3, Bologna, 1938; M. Sanudo ('the younger'), *I diarii*, Venice, 1879–1902.

Giovanni Dall'Orto

Julius III (Giovanni Maria Ciocchi Del Monte) (1487–1555), pope from 1550 to 1555. Del Monte studied law in Perugia and Bologna, then took religious orders. He became archbishop of Siponto and, after holding various political offices in the Papal States, was made a cardinal in 1536. He was elected pope in 1550 because his political views seemed to guarantee that he would maintain an equidistance between the Holy Roman Empire and France; in reality, his policies were formed by the demands, and threats, of the Habsburgs. Julius III was nevertheless a man of culture and an art patron; he was a protector of MICHELANGELO and Palestrina and enlarged the Vatican Library and the University of Rome.

Julius III also caused what is possibly the worst homosexual scandal in the history of the papacy. Already when he was a cardinal, slanderous lampoons accused him of sodomy. The scandal erupted, however, only four months after he became pontiff, when he named as cardinal his 17-year-old lover, Innocenzo Del Monte (1532–1577), whom he already had adopted by his brother Baldovino. While still a cardinal, Julius had met Innocenzo, then called Santino, who was the 13-year-old son of one of his servants. The cardinal fell madly in love with the boy and used favours to secure the collusion of the boy's father. As a reward for this prostitution, the boy was given profitable ecclesiastical benefices at age 14, then was adopted by Baldovino Del Monte. Innocenzo's elevation to the cardinalate was the final reward for his obligingness.

Cardinals who were more sensitive to the need to reform the mores of the Church in order to combat the Protestant Reformation protested in vain against Innocenzo's nomination. Rumours also circulated around European courts; according to P. Messina, 'The Venetian ambassador Matteo Dandolo wrote that Del Monte "was a little scoundrel", and that the cardinal "took him [Innocenzo] into his bedroom and into his own bed as if he were his own son or grandson." . . . Onofrio Panvinio, with reference to the story, wrote that Julius III was "excessively given to intemperance in a life of luxuriousness and to his libido," . . . and, more explicitly, characterised him as *"puerorum amoribus implicitus"* [entangled in love for boys].' The list of such scandalised contemporary comments is long.

One more favourable, if mocking, rumour made the rounds in Rome, saying that Innocenzo had been made a cardinal as a reward for his being the keeper of the pope's monkey. For their part, the Protestants were convinced that Innocenzo's car-dinal's birretta had been a reward for the youth's sexual favours. The French poet Joachim du Bellay (1522?–1560) said in Sonnet CV of *Les Regrets*: 'Yet seeing a footman, a child, a beast, / a rascal, a poltroon made a cardinal / for having taken care of a monkey well, / a GANYMEDE wearing the red hat on his head / . . . these are miracles, my dear Morel, that take place in Rome alone'.

As if this were not enough, Innocenzo became one of the worst cardinals in the history of the Church. Left to his own devices at the age of 23, after Julius III's death, he was involved in a chain of heterosexual rapes, acts of violence and even murders. He always received light punishments, proof of the fact that those in positions of power are always indulgent to their own lot, even the most manifestly unworthy. The bodies of both Julius III and Innocenzo are buried in the Del Monte chapel in the church of San Pietro in Montorio in Rome.

J. du Bellay, *Les Regrets*, Paris, 1971; P. Messina, 'Del Monte, Innocenzo', *Dizionario biografico degli italiani*, Vol. 38, Rome, 1990: 131–41.

Giovanni Dall'Orto

K

Kains Jackson, Charles (Philip Castle)
(1857–1933), British poet. Kains Jackson
was dubbed (by Timothy d'Arch Smith)
one of the leaders of the 'Uranian' movement in his capacity as editor of the
monthly magazine *Artist and Journal of
Home Culture*. D'Arch Smith identified a
group of British writers at the end of the
nineteenth and beginning of the twentieth
centuries who were connected to each
other by varying degrees of acquaintance
and a common interest in (predominantly)
'boy-love', a phenomenon which he called
'Uranian'.

Kains Jackson became editor of the *Artist* in 1888. He discreetly solicited and surreptitiously printed works that had little to
do with the magazine's ostensible concern, the artistic profession, according to
d'Arch Smith: 'Quietly, infrequently, within its closely printed columns verse and
prose studies concerning boy-love were included, enclosed between more pedestrian
and timely reviews of exhibitions and
advertisements for oil-paints.' In this editorial role, he became acquainted with and
printed works by Lord Alfred DOUGLAS,
John Gambril Nicholson, Frederick ROLFE
('Baron Corvo') and John Addington
SYMONDS.

The last issue of the *Artist* that Kains
Jackson was to edit (April 1894) included
his 'The New Chivalry', an essay on the
social potential of boy-love. The argument, based on a mishmash of PLATO,
Thomas Malthus and Social Darwinism,
starts from the premise that 'for five centuries in England the necessity that the
race should increase and multiply has been
paramount, but these five centuries of assistance have now secured their result'.
Therefore, England has 'now moved into
conditions favourable to a real civilisation
and a high moral code', i.e. the 'New
Chivalry'. In contrast to the 'Old Chivalry'
(marriage founded on the imperative to
procreate), the 'New Chivalry' will be
based on more 'spiritual' considerations –
primarily beauty and intellect: 'A beautiful girl will be desired before a plain lad,
but a plain girl will not be considered in
the presence of a handsome boy. Where
boy and girl are of equal outward grace
the spiritual ideal will prevail over the
animal and the desire of influencing the
higher mind, the boy's, will prevail over
the old desire to add to the population.'

As d'Arch Smith notes, Kains Jackson's
conceptions that the 'New Chivalry' is a
solution to overpopulation, that males are
more compatible with other males than
with females, and that, as males are naturally superior to females, the union of two
males is therefore the highest and best
form of human relationships, 'appealed to
the more right-wing and reactionary' and
misogynistic 'Uranians', including, for example, Edwin Emmanuel BRADFORD,
author of *The New Chivalry and Other
Poems* (1918).

T. d'Arch Smith, *Love in Earnest: Some Notes on the Lives and Writings of English 'Uranian' Poets from 1889 to 1930*, London, 1970.

Jason Boyd

Käkikoski, Hilda Maria, formerly Sjöström (1864–1912), Finnish writer and member of parliament. Hilda Sjöström spent her tomboyish childhood in the countryside, but at the age of 14 she decided to move on her own to Helsinki, the capital of Finland, in order to attend a girls' school. There she cut her hair short and changed her Swedish name to the Finnish Käkikoski. She continued her studies and became a teacher of history and the Finnish language at the coeducational school in Helsinki. During these years, she fell in love with some of her fellow students and colleagues, who were, like herself, active members in the Finnish Women's Association (founded in 1884).

A vegetarian, and an eager gymnast and cyclist, her unconventional and self-assertive behaviour and mannish clothing intrigued her students. Following the example of Aleksandra Gripenberg, the 'master' of the rather conservative Finnish Women's Association, she became a writer for their magazine *Koti ja yhteiskunta* (*Home and Society*) and the vice-president of the Association. Gripenberg and Käkikoski are mentioned as 'the' women's rights advocates in the Finnish play *Juurakon Hulda* (1937) by Hella Wuolijoki. It is also possible that Fritz WETTERHOFF had these two women in mind when he informed Magnus HIRSCHFELD about 'the bearded leaders of the Finnish women's rights organisations with their broad shoulders and young female companions'.

While working as a teacher, Käkikoski lived for six years with a dear friend, the widowed Fanny Pajula, and the latter's son. After their separation in 1895, she wrote an unsent letter, where she speculated on 'the secret motive which the world cannot see' behind women's relationships. She thought of that as a selfish wish to enjoy the physical closeness and erotic feelings between friends which poisons women's friendships.

By 1905 Käkikoski had evolved into a charismatic speaker for women's suffrage. As a conservative representative she had received the highest number of votes in her district when in 1906 she was among the first 19 women to be elected for the new parliament of 200 seats.

Käkikoski had moved in with Hildi Ennola, a married friend, for whom she had feelings which she considered unsuitable. Having had an unfulfilled and painful affair with another collegue, Käkikoski began a correspondence with an American woman, Frances Weiss, whom she had met in a 'people's college' in Tärna, Sweden, in 1902. She also fell for a deaconess, Hanna Masalin, and was approached by politically active Helmi Kivalo. All these relationships continued until Käkikoski's death in 1912.

After Käkikoski's death, her friends from the Party and the Association decided to publish some of her journals, letters and writings (in two volumes, 1913, 1916). Although not all her 'childish' relationships were revealed, her feelings for women and her guilt about them could be reconstructed by a perceptive reader. The volumes became popular among women readers. This kind of openness about her relationships with women does not characterise a biography written by Esteri Karilas in 1934, where Käkikoski is described only in connection with the outstanding men of her time. Luckily the eloquent original sources are available in the literary archives of the Finnish Literature Society in Helsinki. Käkikoski is buried in Karjalohja, close to the grave of Hildi Ennola. A statue honouring her can be found in Porlammi.

T. Hainari (ed.) *Hilda Käkikoski kirjeittensä ja kirjoitelmiensa valossa*, Helsinki, 1913; T. Juvonen, *Sukupuoli ja halu Hilda Käkikosken kirjeenvaihdossa ja päiväkirjoissa*, Helsinki, 1995.

Tuula Juvonen

Karsch-Haack, Ferdinand (1853–1936), German entomologist and ethnologist. Born into a middle-class family – his father was a medical doctor working for the German administration in Münster, Westphalia – Karsch-Haack later moved to Berlin where he studied at the Friedrich Wilhelms University.

Karsch-Haack wrote his thesis on the gallwasp in 1877 and, considering this academic background, it is not surprising that one of his first articles on homosexuality in 1900 dealt with 'Pederasty and Tribady among Animals in Literature'. During the time that Karsch-Haack held the position of Curator at the Zoological Museum of Berlin University, he had many articles on homosexuality published in different journals, for example in the famous *Jahrbuch für sexuelle Zwischenstufen* (*Yearbook for Intermediate Stages of Sexuality*), edited by Magnus HIRSCHFELD. Unlike many others involved in the first homosexual movement in Germany, he always used his real name and not a pseudonym.

Best known of all his works are two huge volumes on same-sex behaviour in non-European cultures. In 1906 *Das gleichgeschlechtliche Leben der Kulturvölker – Ostasiaten: Chinesen, Japaner, Koreer* (*The Homosexual Life of the Civilised Peoples – East Asians: Chinese, Japanese, Koreans*) was published; it was intended to be the first volume of a trilogy dealing with non-European civilised peoples ('Kulturvölker'). Because of problems with his publisher, the volumes dealing with 'Semites, Hamites and Aryans' never appeared in print. But finally in 1911 *Das gleichgeschlechtliche Leben der Naturvölker* (*Homosexual Life in Primitive Cultures*) was published. Both works offered a surprising amount of information on the subject, considering that Karsch-Haack was a 'desk-bound ethnologist' who carried out little empirical research. His last work dealing with non-European countries was 'The Role of Homoeroticism in the Arab World' (1923),

which was, in both style and content, quite similar to his earlier works on homosexuality in East Asia but had a stronger focus on descriptions found in *belles lettres*.

As a result of his academic style – with tortuous sentences, some as long as one page – his essays did not appeal to a broader audience and it is not surprising that his 'life-style' magazine, called *Uranos*, published for a short period in 1921–1922, failed to attract many readers.

The most important feature of Karsch-Haack's writing was his strong cultural approach to homosexuality. For him, the development of sexual norms and behaviour was socially constructed and he maintained that for the independent observer as well as for the person engaging in homosexual acts it was hardly possible to perceive a difference between 'real' or 'pseudo' homosexuality, a differentiation which was very important for the typical medical ideas of that time. He ridiculed the medical approach where doctors and psychologists usually only came into contact with mentally disturbed 'Urnings' (homosexuals) and then considered these 'sick people' as typical examples of all homosexuals. Karsch-Haack was harshly criticised by many of his contemporaries for this unusual view of homosexuality: Iwan Bloch blamed Karsch-Haack for giving more or less descriptive pictures of homosexual behaviour and not looking for the genesis of it, and only Hirschfeld was enthusiastic about Karsch-Haack and described him as one of the most productive and valuable pioneers in the discipline of sexual science.

Karsch-Haack described many other possible reasons besides an innate drive for same-sex behaviour: 'lack of opportunity, greed for profit, indigence, misery, the attraction of beauty, temptation, goodwill, curiosity, the drive for adventure, the imitative instinct, moral laxity or indifference'. It is interesting that in Karsch-Haack's view, people who had been driven to homosexuality by external forces and not by an interior sexual drive would nevertheless in many cases remain homosexuals and then be indistinguishable from 'real' homosexuals. He cited as a proof for this the most high-ranking homosexual 'prostitutes' in classical China, the Sian-Kon (*Xianggong*), who were frequently kidnapped as young boys and then trained not only in sexual behaviour but also, like their female counterparts, in the arts, music and calligraphy.

Karsch-Haack was quite critical of Western civilisation and the Western 'scientific' approach which ignored the different values and attitudes in other highly developed societies; as early as 1906, he wrote, 'The Occident, misled by its worldly, ascetic Christian ideology, sees the Chinese, because of their broad-minded view of the world and their far-reaching tolerance in sexual matters, as the personification of immorality. The Chinese, however, have far more justification for seeing the Occidental, so-called Christian culture as the monstrous creation of an anti-culture, a damned and immoral degenerate culture whose most noteworthy efforts are aimed towards increasing the use of brutality and violence and the development of tools for mass murder.'

Karsch-Haack would seem to have had no real influence on his successors despite being quite progressive in his ideas. There are several possible explanations for this: Hitler's seizing of power in 1933, the destruction of Hirschfeld's Institute, the burning of the books and the ban on homosexuality led to the end of a scholarly tradition which had started so gloriously at the beginning of this century. Another quite simple reason for Karsch-Haack's lack of influence might have been the shift of emphasis from the German and French languages to English as the language of science; gender studies after 1970 were generally undertaken in English.

R. Bleys, *The Geography of Perversion: Male to Male Sexual Behaviour outside the West and*

Ethnographic Imagination, 1750–1918, London, 1995; J. Damm, 'Reminiszenz an Ferdinand Karsch-Haack. Der Blick auf fremde Kulturen als Mittel zur Toleranz in der eigenen Gesellschaft', in U. Ferdinand, A. Pretzel and A. Seeck (eds) *Verqueere Wissenschaft*, Münster, 1998.

Jens Damm

Kejne, Karl-Erik (1913–1960), Swedish cleric. A pastor in the Stockholm City Mission, Kejne accused a colleague of homosexual abuse, which led to a bitter feud, and to a spectacular moral panic, known in Sweden as the Kejne affair. In March 1950, the principal of a boys' home wrote a widely quoted article in *Dagens Nyheter* describing boy prostitution as a social plague. Shortly afterwards, other newspapers reported that Kejne was persecuted for his work against boy prostitution. Allegations were made that a high-ranking official protected Kejne's enemies and prevented his complaints from being dealt with. A parliamentary commission to investigate the accusations was set up. It was immediately accused of being infiltrated by homosexuals, upon which another commission had to investigate these latter accusations. Soon, the 'high-ranking official' was publicly identified as the Minister of Ecclesiastic Affairs, Nils Quensel. He was a bachelor who spent time and money on charity among poor young men in Stockholm. He also personally protected a couple of young workers, and rumour said that his relations with them were sexual. The Kejne commission did not find any evidence for this, but apparently there had been peculiar forms of interaction, such as spanking the boys. In the subsequent scandal, Quensel had to resign. The Kejne affair brought with it a campaign against the 'rot of justice' (*rättsrötan*) in society, with the main actors as disparate as the conservative Union of Swedish Mothers and the leftist author Vilhelm Moberg. Mass media created fears that an alleged network of powerful homosexuals had infiltrated the public sphere, protecting each other and threatening the security and just treatment of normal citizens. As opposed to the panics around homosexuality in many other countries, the one in Sweden was orchestrated largely by the political left, and the homophobic assaults were especially fierce in the anarcho-syndicalist newspaper *Arbetaren*.

T. Erlander, *Memoirs III 1949–1954*, Stockholm, 1974; M. Heuman, *Rättsaffärerna Kejne och Haijby*, Stockholm, 1978; G. Söderström, 'Affären Kejne', in *Sympatiens hemlighetsfulla makt. Stockholms homosexuella 1860–1960*, Stockholm, 1999.

Jens Rydström

Kertbeny, Károly Mária (1824–1882), Hungarian-Austrian writer. Kertbeny (also known by his Germanicised name Karl Maria Benkert) was a Vienna-born writer and journalist. In a letter to the sexologist Karl Heinrich ULRICHS, dated 6 May 1868, Kertbeny used the German equivalents of 'homosexual' and 'heterosexual' and is generally considered the inventor of these terms. Kertbeny coined 'homosexual' from the Greek *homo*, meaning 'same', and the Latin root for 'sexual'. Despite linguistic purists' objections to the combination, the term proved far more enduring than such other designations as 'similisexual', 'urning', 'uranian' and 'homophile', though it later lost popularity to 'gay' (or 'gay and lesbian') and, still later, in some circles, to 'queer'.

In 1869, while living in Berlin, Kertbeny anonymously published two pamphlets which criticised the anti-homosexual law codes of the North German confederation. His analysis, similar to that of Ulrichs, argued that sexual behaviour should be free of interference by the state and homosexual practices should be decriminalised; he thus campaigned for the removal of the infamous Paragraph 143 of the Prussian Penal Code, which was incorporated into the imperial German law code and survived for decades afterwards.

Kertbeny himself claimed not to be homosexual. He died in Budapest, supposedly from a syphilitic infection.

M. Herzer, 'Kertbeny and the Nameless Love', *Journal of Homosexuality*, 12 (1985): 1–25.

Robert Aldrich

Keynes, John Maynard (1883–1946), British economist and writer. Born in Cambridge, the son of John Neville Keynes, an esteemed economic scholar and Cambridge professor, and Florence Ada Brown, one of the first female graduates of Cambridge and the city's future mayor, Keynes was a product of privilege. He attended Eton, where he excelled in mathematics and the classics, receiving many academic prizes. Though frail and unathletic, he won the admiration of his peers and was elected to Pop, the school's élite governing body. Keynes entered King's College, Cambridge, in 1902, where, in short order, he excelled academically, socially and politically, being elected president of the University Union Society. At Cambridge, Keynes fell under the influence of economist Alfred Marshall, and soon gave up mathematics to pursue economics and politics. While at university, Keynes also befriended Lytton STRACHEY and was drawn into the Apostles, the élite club of free spirits, among whose members, mostly gay, were the guiding forces of Bloomsbury.

Keynes's first position after graduation from Cambridge in 1906 was in the India Office, during which time he wrote a definitive economic study of pre-World War I India. Returning to Cambridge in 1908, he taught economics there until 1915, when he was called into service in the Treasury office, the department responsible for the economic management of the war. Accompanying Lloyd George to the Versailles Peace Conference, Keynes was so appalled by the 'Cathaginian' nature of the reparations imposed on Germany that he resigned his position and wrote *The Economic Consequences of the Peace*

(1919), perhaps the most influential polemic in Western politics of the first quarter of the twentieth century.

Benefitting from his wise financial investments, Keynes was able to maintain a comfortable living far beyond the means of a Cambridge fellow. In 1925, after previously leading an exclusively homosexual life, he married Lydia Lopokova, a former DIAGHILEV ballerina, yet maintained close ties with Bloomsbury, despite opposition to his marriage among many members, including Leonard and Virginia WOOLF. His career as a journalist also flourished with assignments from the leftist *New Statesman*, *The Times* (London) and the *Manchester Guardian*. His permanent influence on twentieth-century economic thought was assured in the midst of the Depression, with the publication of *The General Theory of Employment, Interest and Money* (1935–1936). This monumental work asserted that economic depression could not be blamed on the unemployed but on the activities of business investors and governments. His endorsement of private investment, easy credit, low interest rates and the recommendation that governments run deficits in a slow economy influenced policies of most Western democracies in the second half of the twentieth century.

Limiting his activities following a severe heart attack in 1937, Keynes returned to Cambridge. During World War II he was recalled to a significant place in the international economic scene at the Bretton Woods Conference in 1944, which resulted in the setting up of the International Monetary Fund and the World Bank, and was instrumental in negotiating a multibillion dollar loan from the United States to Britain in 1945. On his appointment to the Court of the Bank of England, Keynes quipped, 'I am not sure which of us is being made an honest woman – the Old Lady [the familiar name for the Bank of England] or me.' Exhausted by the demands of his wartime activities, Keynes died in Firle, Sussex.

Prior to his marriage, Keynes engaged in several love affairs as well as casual sex with men. His most important relationships included Arthur Lee Hobhouse, the stunning fellow Trinity student over whom Keynes developed a fierce rivalry with Strachey; painter Duncan GRANT, his lover from 1908 to 1911, and lifelong friend; and writer Francis 'Frankie' Birrell, co-founder with David Garnett of the Bloomsbury-centered Cranium Club in the 1920s.

R. Skidelsky, *John Maynard Keynes: Hopes Betrayed, 1883–1920*, London, 1983 and *John Maynard Keynes: The Economist as Savior, 1920–37*, London, 1992.

A. M. Wentink

Kleist, Heinrich von (1777–1811), German writer. Kleist was a remarkably complex dramatist and author, whose ambiguous sexuality still sparks debate almost two centuries since his tragic suicide. He was the progeny of an illustrious Prussian military family, and oldest son of a Prussian captain and his second wife, neither of whom lived to see Kleist grow to full adulthood. Always displaying deeply patriotic convictions, he joined the Prussian army at age 15 and participated in military campaigns against French Revolutionary troops in the Rhineland. Modern biographical research suggests that Kleist probably had homosexual experiences during his military years. He developed lifelong, intense friendships with two of his fellow officers, Rühle von Lilienstern and Ernst von Pfuel. Kleist also experienced many deep friendships with women, but never physically consummated a heterosexual relationship. Kleist's dearest companion was his older half-sister, Ulrike, the family 'spinster', who preferred to wear men's clothing. He referred to her as his 'amphibic' sister, indecisive about life within the exclusive elements of manhood or womanhood. He professed to her that he wished she were a man so that he could utterly confide in her.

In 1799 Kleist left the army to take up

studies in the hopes of becoming a civil servant. Shortly thereafter he became engaged to Wilhelmine von Zenge, who eventually broke off the engagement when Kleist failed to rise in a career befitting her social station. While studying in Berlin in 1801, Kleist read Immanuel Kant's first *Critique*. He misinterpreted this philosophical treatise and pessimistically concluded that eternal truths did not exist, and that all of his life's endeavours were meaningless. This existential disillusionment shook Kleist's fragile psyche to its core, but also unlocked his writing talents. Only after this 'Kant crisis' did he realise his literary skills. His ensuing works treated provocative themes of ethical, moral and sexual ambivalences in a violent, chaotic world where perceived realities were mere delusions. During the last decade of his life, he wrote seven complete plays, one uncompleted, and eight novellas. He also edited two journals, *Berliner Abendblätter* and *Phöbus*, where many of his essays dealing with art and literature appeared.

Kleist, now considered one of Germany's greatest literary geniuses, was largely misunderstood during his lifetime. His gritty, skeptical realism resisted classification under either of the contemporary schools of German Classicism, extolling harmony and beauty, or Romanticism, emphasising folklore and fairy tales. His unconventional works were often considered too salacious or monstrous for the times. His last, and greatest play, the patriotic *Prinz Friedrich von Homburg* (1810), was severely criticised because of the title figure's 'unmanly' weeping fit when shown his own freshly dug grave. Kleist typically turned the tides on contemporary literary conventions by depicting males as the 'weaker sex'. His fiction heavily treated almost every variety of 'forbidden love', including interracial sex and lesbianism, possibly to obliquely express his own camouflaged homosexuality. A love-letter written to his friend Pfuel revealed most unambiguously his homosexual nature. In this letter, Kleist admit-

ted to Pfuel that he had often viewed his beautiful body while swimming 'with truly *girlish* feelings'. He also declared he would never marry, and entreated Pfuel to be wife, children and grandchildren to him instead. In 1803, while the two were staying in Paris, Kleist tried unsuccessfully to convince Pfuel to commit suicide with him. Eventually, in 1811, weary of critical defeats and financial hardships, the despondent Kleist found a willing partner in death, Henriette Vogel, a young officer's wife suffering from terminal illness, whom some erroneously maintain was Kleist's mistress. On 11 November 1811, Kleist shot Henriette, and then himself. A suicide note left for Ulrike said: 'There was no salvation for me on earth.'

Kleist was primarily a dramatist, but his blank-verse tragedies, however excellent, would appear very dated to modern readers. His novellas, however, published in two volumes of *Erzählungen* (*Tales*, 1810–1811), are starkly modern in style, theme and content. The most famous of these is *Die Verlobung in St. Domingo* (*The Betrothal in Santo Domingo*), which depicts the tragic romance of Gustav, a Swiss officer, and Toni, a half-caste quadroon who passed for white, set against the backdrop of a bloody 1803 slave revolt in the Caribbean. This work alone has inspired two operas and a film. Another novella, *Michael Kohlhaas*, provided material for E. L. Doctorow's 1975 novel *Ragtime*.

H. Detering, *Das offene Geheimnis: Zur literarischen Produktivität eines Tabus von Winckelmann bis zu Thomas Mann*, Göttingen, 1994; J. Maass, *Kleist: A Biography*, trans. R. Manheim, New York, 1983; H. D. Zimmermann, *Kleist, die Liebe und der Tod*, Frankfurt/Main, 1989.

Seán Henry

Kobylians'ka, Ol'ha (1863–1942), Ukrainian writer. Born in to a family of a minor civil servant in a small town in Bukovyna (Bucovina), a province in Austria-Hungary that is now divided between Ukraine and Romania, she was educated at home (unlike her brothers, who received full formal education). A voracious reader, she was fully bilingual in Ukranian and German, and her first attempts at writing were made in German, in the early 1880s; however, at the encouragement of her friends, she later switched to Ukranian. In 1891, after spending her early years in several small towns and villages in Bukovyna, she moved to Chernivtsi, the province's capital, where she lived for the rest of her life. There, influenced by several of her women friends who were prominent in the nascent women's rights movement in the Austrian-ruled part of Ukraine, she became a prominent advocate of women's emancipation and a leader of the Society of Ukranian Women in Bukovyna. At the same time, she was finally able to break into print with several of her works, may of them written earlier, such as *A Human Being* (written 1886, published 1894) and *Tsarevna* (written 1888–1893, published 1895). Along with such short stories as 'Nature' (written 1887, published 1895), they constituted an unprecedented event in Ukranian letters due both to their programmatic feminist standpoint (in a peculiar combination with Nietzschean overtones), the rejection of the populist fascination with the peasantry, and stylistic innovation, indebted to the German and Scandinavian writers of her time. Over the course of the decade, she continued producing short stories that brought forth strong, independent, educated female characters who also asserted their right for fulfilment of sexual needs (e.g. 'Nature' relates an educated women's sexual attraction to a robust young peasant man and contains the first description of a sexual act in Ukranian writing). Another story by her, 'Valse mélancolique' (1898), constituted a similarly pioneering treatment of same-sex love. The story, partly based on the author's own experiences, depicts an unconventional *ménage* of three women: a painter, a musician and

a scholar who is the story's narrator; all of them are strong-minded and passionate women in search of harmony and self-fulfilment. Though the characters' perfect union is shattered by the death of Sofia, the musician, the assertion of the very possibility of such a union was a statement unprecedented in its boldness.

Kobylians'ka's works were treated with unease by the leading Ukranian critics of the day, who had to acknowledge her stylistic brilliance but were uncomfortable with her subject matter, the only exception being Osyp Makovei, a writer of minor talent with whom Kobylians'ka had a relationship in the late 1890s and whose articles were basically paraphrases of Kobylians'ka's own thoughts about her work. The situation changed, however, with an 1899 article by the leading woman writer of the Russian-ruled part of Ukraine, Lesia Ukrainka (1871–1913). A poet and playwright, Ukrainka shared Kobylians'ka's stylistic and ideological concerns and advocated a new literature, modernist in form and feminist in spirit. The two writers eventually met in 1901, shortly after Kobylians'ka broke up with Makovei and Ukrainka lost her male lover to tuberculosis. Their meeting produced an intensely passionate union that, however, had to be realised though correspondence – they were prevented by circumstances and their poor health from living together – which lasted until Ukrainka's death. While over the years their letters eventually grew more restrained, the two remained deeply devoted to each other.

Soon after the publication of Ukrainka's article, Kobylians'ka finally found her way into the literary mainstream with the publication of her novel *The Land* (1902), a powerfully written indictment of the breakdown of traditional Ukranian rural life brought about by capitalism; this work won praise from all the major camps in Ukrainian letters. Her last important work, *On Sunday Morning She Gathered Herbs* (1909), is a symbolist novel based on the imagery from Ukrainian folk songs.

Kobylians'ka wrote little in the latter part of her life; however, her work was praised by the younger generation of Ukranian modernist writers who looked up to her as the major innovator in the style, tone and viewpoint of her fiction. She has been recognised as Ukraine's greatest woman prose writer, and in recent years new attention has been given to her writing and biography, in particular their lesbian aspect, thanks to the efforts of contemporary Ukranian feminist scholars.

S. Pavlychko, 'Modernism vs. Populism in Fin-de-Siècle Ukranian Literature: A Case of Gender Conflict', in P. Chester and S. Forrester (eds) *Engendering Slavic Literatures*, Bloomington, 1996: 83–103, and *Dyskurs modernizmu v ukrains'kii literaturi*, Kiev, 1997.

Vitaly Chernetsky

Kok, Martin (1850–1942), Danish author. Kok belonged to the first generation of homosexual men in Denmark. In the 1880s and 1890s he was the one notorious and publicly known homosexual who exemplified an otherwise hidden world of depravity and sexual perversity. In this role he was succeeded by the author Herman BANG, who eclipsed Kok through his literary talent and his ability to pose semi-publicly as a homosexual. In 1877 Kok and Joakim REINHARD became involved in the first publicised homosexual scandal in Copenhagen.

Kok published patriotic and nationalistic poetry and belonged politically to the Conservative Party. As such he was implicated in another homosexual scandal engineered in 1885 by the Social Democratic press. The homosexual element of the scandal was entirely fictitious. In 1893 Kok was arrested and spent three weeks in jail for gross indecency with a 16-year-old butcher's apprentice. This was not illegal and he was acquitted. While he was in jail a newspaper of the traditionalist agrarian left strongly hinted that Kok, when 8 years old, had been seduced by the now deceased author Hans Christian ANDERSEN,

'who all his life remained the finicky bachelor'. In a letter to Andersen's literary executor, Jonas Collin (the younger), Kok characterised the allegation as 'a mendacious fabrication'. Kok's denial was published. Although the alleged seduction is extremely implausible, it nevertheless became the starting point for the assumption that Andersen had been a homosexual.

W. von Rosen, *Månens Kulør. Studier i dansk bøssehistorie 1628–1912*, Copenhagen, 1993: 569–96, 610–13, 618–21.

Wilhelm von Rosen

Krafft-Ebing, Richard von (1840–1902), German-Austrian psychiatrist and sexologist, professor of psychiatry in Strasbourg (1871–1872), Graz (1872–1889), and Vienna (1889–1902). Although Krafft-Ebing, as one of the most prominent psychiatrists of his time in Central Europe, worked in many fields of psychiatry, he is remembered today as the author of *Psychopathia sexualis* and one of the founding fathers of scientific sexology. The first edition of his much-quoted book appeared in 1886 and it was soon followed by several new and expanded editions – 17 in German between 1886 and 1924 – and translations into several languages. By naming and classifying virtually all non-procreative sexuality, he was one of the first to synthesise medical knowledge of what was then labelled as sexual perversion. His interest in the broader aspects of sexual deviance emerged from his interest in forensic psychiatry, of which he was a pioneer and leading expert. *Psychopathia sexualis* was written for lawyers and doctors discussing sexual crimes in court. Krafft-Ebing's main thrust was that in many cases perversion was not a sin or a crime, but a disease. He stressed that many sexual disorders were inborn and his explanation of sexual deviance bore the stamp of degeneration theory.

From the 1880s, Krafft-Ebing published several articles on homosexuality, containing extensive case histories and autobiographies. *Psychopathia sexualis* was also illustrated with hundreds of case histories and autobiographical accounts, many of sadists, masochists, fetishists and especially of homosexuals. These were not only the stories of moral offenders, with whom he came into contact as an expert witness, and of patients hospitalised in one of the asylums or clinics where he was a medical superintendant; also represented were individuals who had contacted Krafft-Ebing of their own accord as private patients, or who corresponded with him because they had recognised themselves in published case histories. He encouraged them to contact him and they responded with letters and autobiographies. Many of Krafft-Ebing's aristocratic and bourgeois patients, who generally had contacted him of their own accord, were given ample opportunity to speak for themselves.

Homosexual men were eager to reveal their lives to Krafft-Ebing. Whereas he probably had expected them to be nervous and effeminate 'degenerates', they convincingly indicated that they enjoyed perfect health and that they were physically indistinguishable from their fellow men. Written by educated and often cosmopolitan men, some of the autobiographies were full of learned and literary references, philosophical and medical speculations as well as detailed self-analysis. The letters also vividly demonstrated a considerable degree of subjective suffering, not so much because of their writers' sexual orientation as such, but because of the social condemnation, the legal situation, the need to disguise their real nature, the fear of blackmail and of losing their social status. Several men stressed that their sexual behaviour could not be immoral or pathological, because they experienced their sexual desire as 'natural'.

There is no doubt that Krafft-Ebing's views were influenced by his patients and informants. After having published several autobiographies which showed the harmful effects of the German and Austrian

laws criminalising 'unnatural vice' (Paragraphs 175 and 129), he himself began to favour judicial reform. Krafft-Ebing lent his name to pleas for the abolition of Paragraph 175 and in *Psychopathia sexualis* he added that the book should contribute towards changing the law, thus putting an end to the errors and hardships of many centuries. When homosexuals began to organise protest movements at the close of the nineteenth century, they referred to Krafft-Ebing as a scientific authority who was on their side; and he indeed supported the homosexual rights movement which was founded in Berlin by HIRSCHFELD in 1897. After he signed Hirschfeld's petition advocating the abolition of Paragraph 175, he admitted in his last article on homosexuality, published in Hirschfeld's *Jahrbuch für sexuelle Zwischenstufen*, that the psychiatric conception of homosexuality had been one-sided and that there was truth in the views of many of his homosexual correspondents. Having referred earlier to the decline of Greece and Rome as warning examples from the past, he was now of the opinion that homosexuality was not incompatible with mental health or even with intellectual superiority. It was not a pathological phenomenon, but a biological and psychological condition that had to be accepted as a more or less deplorable but natural fate. Focusing less on sexual acts and more on abstract and psychological matters, he also attributed equal moral value to same-sex and heterosexual love.

Psychopathia sexualis was a best-seller, and it probably owed its success not only to its scientific merits, but also to its pornographic qualities. Several passages were only published in Latin translation because they were considered offensive. In addition to scientific expositions, there were extensive descriptions of sexual experiences and fantasies, of erotic temptations and amusements in big cities, examples from history and literature, fragments of semi-pornographic writings, candid advertisements and journalistic descriptions of events such as 'the Woman-haters' ball for Urnings in Berlin. By publishing letters and autobiographies and by quoting statements of his patients verbatim, Krafft-Ebing enabled voices to be heard that were usually silenced. Because he distinguished himself as an expert who had made a stand against traditional moral–religious and legal denunciations of sexual deviance, individuals approached him to find understanding, acceptance and support. Obviously, many homosexuals viewed Krafft-Ebing not simply as a doctor treating diseases; for many of his clients he must have been an ally, embodying an ideal of science as a means for improving their lot.

R. von Krafft-Ebing, *Psychopathia sexualis*, Stuttgart, 1886; Munich, 1984; R. Hauser, *Sexuality, Neurasthenia and the Law: Richard von Krafft-Ebing (1840–1902)*, London, 1992; H. Oosterhuis, 'Richard von Krafft-Ebing's "Step-Children of Nature"; Psychiatry and the Making of Homosexual Identity', in V. A. Rosario (ed.) *Science and Homosexualities*, New York, 1997: 67–88; H. Oosterhuis, *Step-children of Nature: Krafft-Ebing, Psychiatry and the Making of Sexual Identity*, Chicago, 2000.

Harry Oosterhuis

Kristina (1626–1689), queen of Sweden (1644–1654). Kristina is perhaps the best known women-loving woman in seventeenth-century Europe. She is generally portrayed as a lesbian in gay and feminist literature, but historians have often used any available homophobic strategy to explain away her cross-gender behaviour.

Kristina was the only child of King Gustaf II Adolf and Queen Maria Eleonora. Her father died when she was only 6 years old, and after that she was taken away from her mother, as Maria Eleonora was not considered capable of raising the future sovereign properly. Kristina was educated to be the ruler of one of the great powers in Europe at the time. She was trained in the same way as a prince would have been, both theoretically and physically. She learned to ride and shoot. She studied political science, economics, history, several languages and other subjects that a sovereign had to know. She also studied theology, natural science, philosophy and the arts. Kristina corresponded with many of the leading scholars of the time and was patron to several of them. She devoted almost all her spare time to her studies.

Kristina's father had died the death of a heroic warrior for Protestantism (people living in the countries that were ravaged by his troops, of course, took a very different view of the matter). Kristina brought the Thirty Years War to an end and she abandoned the religion for which her father had died. By converting to Catholicism she condemned herself to exile, abdicating in 1654. She left Sweden and settled in Rome, where she remained until the end of her life.

Kristina never married; she resolutely refused to do so in spite of the fact that her counsellors time after time reminded her of her duty to give Sweden an heir to the throne. One of her aphorisms reads: 'Matrimony is as good as incompatible with love.' One of the explanations for the contemporary rumours that Kristina sexually preferred women to men may be her critical opinion of marriage in general. But there are several other reasons that support the conclusion that she was involved in same-sex love affairs.

For example, the fact that she cross-dressed was widely noted. Her clothing was a mix between masculine and feminine styles and she wore men's shoes. Rumour had it that she might have been a hermaphrodite. And perhaps that was how she herself understood her sex. But then it must be underlined that in the seventeenth century the word 'hermaphrodite' meant something other than what it does today. In Kristina's time it was used for phenomena that we might call 'trans-', 'bi-', 'homosexual' or 'queer'.

In her autobiography – in which she addresses herself to God – Kristina writes about her own psychological and physical constitution: 'I thank You Lord for letting me be born a woman. The more so as You have shown me the grace of not letting any of the defects of my own sex be inherent in my soul, which You in mercy have made altogether male, just as the rest of my being.'

This passage has confused biographers and historians. Some of them have tried to prove that Kristina physically was a mixture of a man and a woman, and in 1965 this led to an investigation of her mortal remains. The findings were that she had a normal female body.

Kristina's transgressions had to do with gender. She walked, sat, talked, moved and gesticulated in a way that her contemporaries described as masculine. She preferred men's company to women's – unless the women were very beautiful, in which case she courted them.

Kristina's manners fitted men's roles better than women's, and during her time in Rome this often gave rise to the pope's dissatisfaction. Her free social manners were incompatible with the image of her that the Vatican tried to propagate, that of a pious virgin queen from the North who left her country to devote her life to her Saviour.

The passion of Kristina's youth was a woman, Ebba Sparre, the beauty of the court. Kristina spent most of her spare time – including the nights – with 'la belle comtesse' – often calling attention to her beauty. She even introduced her to the English ambassador Whitelocke as her 'bed-fellow', asking him if he found Sparre's reason as striking as her beauty. When Kristina left Sweden she wrote passionate love-letters to Sparre, in which she told her that she would always love her – and she did. Sparre died a few years after Kristina's exile; shortly before, Kristina had tried to persuade Sparre to meet her in Hamburg.

However, Kristina made advances to other women as well. There are several statements which bear witness to her erotic interest in women. Elector Edvard of Bavaria wrote in a letter about Kristina: 'She dearly loves beautiful women. In Lyon she met one who very much pleased her. She kissed her everywhere: on the throat, the eyes, the forehead, very passionately and she even wanted to kiss the tongue in her mouth and to sleep with her, which the woman however did not want to do.'

Many panegyrics have been written on Queen Kristina, often produced by the Catholic Church. But she has also been accused of all kinds of excesses, sexual and others. She has been described as frigid and as man-mad, as asexual and as polymorphously perverse, as a lesbian and as a hermaphrodite.

Many powerful women in history have been demonised in similar ways. Probably this is a strategy to explain away the fact that they were women and that they were powerful. Femininity and power are not supposed to go well together. In Kristina's case it is also used to make excuses for her refusal to get married.

For most people today, the image of Queen Kristina is probably influenced by the way Greta GARBO acted her part in a film in 1933. Garbo was happy to accept this particular role, but very disappointed when she read the hetero-normalising script that transformed the exceptional Kristina into a woman who gives everything away for the love of a man. The plot is thoroughly fictive: Kristina would never have done anything like that. Garbo, however, did her best to give her audience something of the historical figure that she herself had found so fascinating. The passionate way she kisses Sparre definitely undermines heteronormativity.

Christina, *Självbiografi och aforismer*, Stockholm, 1957; Christina, *Brev från sex decennier*, Stockholm, 1966; S. Åkerman, *Queen Christina of Sweden and Her Circle: The Transformation of a Seventeenth-Century Philosophical Libertine*, New York, 1991.

Eva Borgström

Krupp, Friedrich (1854–1902), German businessman. Head of his family's steel and armaments firm, Krupp was reputedly the wealthiest man in *fin de siècle* Germany, and was married and the father of two children. From 1898, Krupp began to spend his holidays on the Italian island of Capri, which then and afterwards attracted a number of northern European homosexual men and lesbians, including the artist Christian Wilhelm Allers, the French poet Jacques d'ADELSWÄRD-FERSEN, the painter Romaine BROOKS and her friend Renée VIVIEN, the travel-writer Norman DOUGLAS and fellow novelist Compton MACKENZIE. The visitors enjoyed the idyllic climate and scenery, and the men often made friends with local youths.

Krupp built a house on Capri and spent four seasons there, often in the company of German friends rumoured to be homosexual. He pursued his interest in natural history, rebuilt the island's premier hotel and dispensed patronage to local artists. In return, the Capri city council bestowed honorary citizenship on him in 1900. Krupp enjoyed a number of sexual liaisons with young men, his closest attachment to an 18-year-old barber and amateur musician.

The Capresi seemed untroubled by Krupp's activities with the exception of a schoolmaster who held a personal grudge against the German. He provided details of Krupp's sexual contacts to a Neapolitan newspaper, which tried to blackmail Krupp by threatening to expose him; Krupp refused, and an article was published. Left-wing newspapers in Italy and Germany (including the German Socialist Party's newspaper) picked up the reports about the corruption of youth by Germany's leading capitalist. Krupp sued the socialist newspaper for libel, but the Italian government forbade him from

returning to Capri. Krupp then unexpectedly died, perhaps from a heart condition made worse by the stress or more likely by taking his own life. He left several benefactions to individual Capresi (especially to his barber friend) and bequeathed his house to the people of the island.

R. Aldrich, *The Seduction of the Mediterreanean: Writing, Art and Homosexual Fantasy*, London, 1993; J. Money, *Capri, Island of Pleasure*, London, 1986.

Robert Aldrich

Kupffer, Elisár von (1872–1942), German poet and painter. This aesthete of Baltic aristocratic ancestry gained popularity in homosexual circles around the turn of the century with his anthology of homoerotic literature from Antiquity to his own time, *Lieblingminne und Freundesliebe in der Weltliteratur* (1900). Although he primarily included poetry and prose from well known, respected authors, Kupffer encountered a great deal of resistance to his project in Wilhelmine Germany. Influential friends were able to prevent the first edition of the work from being confiscated, but the second edition fell prey to the censor. With his anthology Kupffer hoped to counterbalance the biomedical and psychiatric explanations of homosexuality, namely those of the influential Richard von KRAFFT-EBING and Magnus HIRSCHFELD. In fact, he rejected the terms 'homosexuality' or 'uranism' because to him these reinforced the stigma of sickly deviation and the effeminacy of men. Instead, he introduced the words *Lieblingminne* and *Freundesliebe* to indicate that same-sex love should be viewed not as a biomedical issue, but as a cultural and historical one.

Kupffer's highly polemical introduction to the anthology was published in Adolf BRAND's *Der Eigene* and with this essay about the 'ethical-political meaning' of homoeroticism Kupffer set the tone for other members of the Gemeinschaft der Eigenen. His intention was not to explain and justify an inborn homosexual disposition, but to refer to various cultural forms of male love by using literary sources from classical Greece, the Renaissance and the German Romantic movement. With this, he tried to demonstrate that a good deal of homoeroticism lay hidden under the denominator of friendship and that male bonding had always been of great cultural and political significance. According to Kupffer, Greek boy-love, pedagogical eros and the cult of romantic friendship were discredited by the medical meddling with same-sex love.

In his anthology, Kupffer glorified masculinity and depicted effeminate homosexual men as decadent monsters. However, later he and his friend, the philosopher Eduard von Mayer, elevated androgyny as the state of human perfection. In his paintings Kupffer did not portray stout, brawny, blond Aryan heroes, but plump feminine boys. Together with Mayer, Kupffer contrived an esoteric doctrine called Klarismus, for which they built the Sanctuarium Artis Elisarion near Locarno in Switzerland. The centre of this building, designed as temple and museum in one, was a round room, the walls of which were covered with a monumental painting by Kupffer. Eigthy-four strikingly similar naked ephebic youths with faraway expressions – self-images of the narcissistic young Kupffer himself – were portrayed in various positions. Homoerotic aesthetics would enable people to release themselves from the ugliness of mundane reality, Kupffer and Mayer believed. Eros could bring people together, forge unity between feeling and reason, and thus restore human integrity. Despite their countless publications – a 'klaristische' publishing house was even established – Kupffer and Mayer failed to win a substantial following for their esoteric visions. After Kupffer's death, his Sanctuarium became no more than an artistic curiosity. After Mayer's death in 1960 it became dilapidated, signifying that the era of wealthy aesthetes who projected their homosexual desire in fantasy castles was basically over by then.

M. Keilson-Lauritz, 'Vorwort', in E. von Kupffer, *Lieblingminne und Freundesliebe in der Weltliteratur. Eine Sammlung mit einer ethisch-politischen Einleitung*, Berlin, 1995; H. Ekkehard, *Elisár von Kupffer (1872–1942)*, Basel, 1979.

Harry Oosterhuis

Kuzmin, Mikhail (Alekseevich) (1872–1936), Russian poet, writer and composer. Born into a wealthy noble family in Yaroslavl, in 1884 his family moved to St Petersburg, where he spent most of his life. He studied music and composition at the St Petersburg conservatory, and Italian and German literatures independently on the advice of his friend Georgy Chicherin (a future Bolshevik and People's Commissar for Foreign Affairs). In 1893 Kuzmin fell in love with a certain 'Prince George', a military officer four years his senior. They became lovers and travelled together to Turkey, Egypt and Greece. On the way back, Kuzmin's companion died suddenly from heart disease in Vienna. Afterwards Kuzmin did not have long-term romantic attachments for several years, at times committing himself to 'chastity' as advocated by Chicherin, who also was gay. Russian Orthodox by birth, in the 1890s Kuzmin went through phases of intense attraction to Catholicism and to the Old Belief (a Russian Christian schism, condemned by the Orthodox Church). His later poetry prominently includes motifs of early Christianity, Byzantium, eighteenth-century France and the Italian Renaissance, as well as Russian religious themes often coloured by a sectarian sensibility. A religious person throughout most of his life, Kuzmin admitted at the end that he had lost his faith.

In the early years of the twentieth century, the focus of Kuzmin's artistic activity gradually shifted from composing music to writing poetry. Kuzmin entered the St Petersburg élite artistic circles around 1906. Through his gay friends in the

Evenings for Contemporary Music, an informal society devoted to modern music, he became known among the capital's literati as a promising poet and the author of a novel which advocated homosexual love between men. This novel, *Wings*, caused a sensation when it was published in November 1906 in a special issue of the main Symbolist literary journal *Libra*. Written in 1904–1906, *Wings* tells a coming-of-age story in the tradition of the *Bildungsroman*. The novel's protagonist, Vania (Ivan) Smurov, discovers his homosexuality and comes to terms with it, overcoming doubts and hesitation. Although Kuzmin's advocacy of homosexual love in *Wings* had aesthetic, theological and philosophical components, *Wings* also describes in some detail St Petersburg gay life of the day, in which Kuzmin had become an active participant. His lovers varied from prominent young artists (Sergei Sudeikin, Konstantin Somov) to part-time hustlers and bath-house employees (young men from the lower classes, whose responsibilities included having paid sex with their wealthy customers). Kuzmin's unapologetic depiction in *Wings* of the institutions of commercial gay sex, such as bath-houses, brought him extra notoriety as newspapers published caricatures of him in the company of bath-house boys, and commented on the spread of 'sexual degeneration'. Branded a 'Russian Oscar WILDE' by the popular press, Kuzmin had mixed feelings about this reputation: he enjoyed being famous, but resented the overtones of Dionysian tragic revolt and redemptive suffering which were inseparable from Wilde's reputation in Russia.

As the financial circumstances of his family deteriorated, Kuzmin had to make a living off his writing; he was very prolific and created both masterpieces (mostly poetry) and hastily crafted works (especially in prose). Starting with 'The Alexandria Songs', a lyrical cycle published in *Libra* in 1906, and his first verse collection, *Nets* (1908), Kuzmin's poetry received wide recognition and popularity. He performed some of his poems to his own music, accompanying himself on the piano. In the years following his poetic début, he acquired numerous friendships in the literary and artistic mileu of the Russian 'Silver Age'. Kuzmin participated in many collective theatrical and artistic projects (including the homoerotic Hafiz society, which gathered in the apartment of the poet Viacheslav Ivanov, who was cultivating a mystically conceived bisexuality in 1906–1907). From 1906 to 1913, Kuzmin had numerous love affairs, some tragic, some quotidian, their main common feature being the inspiration they gave him for very fine and distinctly homoerotic love poetry. Kuzmin never fully belonged to any organised literary movement, but he managed to exercise influence on, and to earn the highest respect from, various modernist camps.

In early 1913 Kuzmin (who was usually attracted to younger men) met an 18-year-old budding writer, Yury Yurkun (a Russified version of his Lithuanian name, Joseph Yurkunas), who became Kuzmin's companion and literary protégé for the rest of his life. Because of his fear that Yurkun would be conscripted into the army, the apolitical Kuzmin condoned the Bolshevik coup in October 1917, which promised to end the Russian participation in World War I. Yurkun was nevertheless drafted by the Bolsheviks themselves, although he managed to desert quickly, and his desertion went unpunished in the general chaos of the post-revolutionary years. During the years of War Communism (1918–1921), Kuzmin and Yurkun stayed in St Petersburg (renamed Petrograd). Kuzmin quickly lost his sympathy for the new regime, appalled by its cruelty, suppression of civil liberties and utter disregard for 'bourgeois' culture. The publishing industry, along with the rest of the economy, had disintegrated, and Kuzmin lost almost all means to support himself and Yurkun. Kuzmin turned in these years from a dandy and aesthete into a sickly and untidy old man, always on the verge of starvation. (Malnutrition contributed to the death in 1921 of Aleksandr Blok, Kuzmin's close friend, whom he called Russia's 'first poet'. Nikolai Gumilev, another friend of Kuzmin and a major poet, was shot by the Bolsheviks' political police.) The New Economic Policy introduced in 1921 temporarily restored some elements of a market economy; and until his death Kuzmin worked very hard as a theatre critic, librettist and translator, but for only a meagre income. Yurkun was briefly arrested in 1918. In 1931 secret police searched Kuzmin's apartment, confiscated Yurkun's manuscripts and forced Yurkun to sign an agreement to cooperate. It took Kuzmin's old literary connections to free his companion from this obligation. In hopes that the Bolshevik nightmare would go away, and unable to imagine living abroad, Kuzmin never emigrated. Instead, he steadily carved a niche for himself in the oppressive Soviet cultural environment. The communal apartment, which he and Yurkun shared with Yurkun's mother and several other renters, became one of the few centres of unofficial literary life in Leningrad. His eleventh and last volume of poetry, *The Trout Breaks the Ice*, was published in 1929. This book, considered by many his best, contains some of the most beautiful, complex, dramatic and gay Russian poetry.

Starting with *Wings*, Kuzmin became the symbol of Russian gay culture. His last public poetry reading in 1928 was characterised by a contemporary as 'the last rally of Leningrad homosexuals'. After 1934,

when Stalin recriminalised homosexuality (it had disappeared from the criminal code after the revolution), such gatherings would be unthinkable.

Kuzmin died from pneumonia in 1936. Two years later, Yurkun was arrested and executed in the course of massive political purges. Throughout most of his life, Kuzmin had kept a diary. After it was sold in 1933 to the State Literary Museum, the diary was studied for several years by the secret police, which is rumoured to have used it when it made arrests in the late 1930s. This voluminous work, up to this day published only in parts, is known to scholars as one of the most important sources on twentieth-century Russian cultural history and as one of Kuzmin's masterpieces. Only a small selection of Kuzmin's poems was reprinted in anthologies published in the Soviet Union. Kuzmin scholarship, however, existed both in the Soviet Union and the West; this field of Russian literary studies habitually attracted an unusually high proportion of gay scholars. Since the collapse of the Soviet Union, Kuzmin's legacy has been canonised, studied and published widely in Russia. In a tribute to the poet, one of the first gay advocacy groups in postcommunist Russia assumed the name Wings.

J. Malmstad and N. Bogomolov, *Mikhail Kuzmin: A Life in Art*, Cambridge, Mass., 1999; M. Kuzmin, *Dnevnik 1934 goda*, ed. G. Morev, St Petersburg, 1998.

Evgenii Bershtein

L

Labouchere, Henry (Du Pre) (1831–1912), British politician. Labouchere was proprietor of the journal *Truth* and the maverick 'Liberal-Radical' Member of Parliament who authored the infamous 'Labouchere Amendment' of the Criminal Law Amendment Act of 1885, which was to broadly criminalise the lives of homosexual men in Great Britain until the passing of the Sexual Offenses Act of 1967.

The agitations of social-purity campaigners in the 1880s over the supposed 'monumental traffic' of young British girls sold into sexual slavery on the Continent had forced the government to move precipitously to draft the Criminal Law Amendment Bill (titled 'An Act to make further provision for the Protection of Women and Girls, the suppression of brothels, and other purposes'). Late in the night of 6 August 1885, in a sparsely attended sitting of the House of Commons, whose members were impatient to have the bill passed so they could address themselves to the coming General Election, Labouchere rose to move that the following amendment be included in the bill: 'Any male person who, in public or private, commits, or is a party to the commission of, or procures or attempts to procure the commission by any male person of, any act of gross indecency with another male person, shall be guilty of a misdemeanor, and being convicted thereof, shall be liable, at the discretion of the court, to be imprisoned for any term not exceeding one year with or without hard labour.' Labouchere's only comment was that at present the law only penalised 'an assault of the kind here dealt with' if one of the parties was under the age of 13, and that his amendment was designed 'to make the law applicable to any person, whether under the age of thirteen, or over that age'. (This statement was grossly inaccurate.)

However, the Attorney-General, Sir Henry James, accepted the amendment on behalf of the government, but moved that the maximum penalty be increased to two years instead of one. This was accepted, and without any further debate, the 'Labouchere Amendment', under the title 'Outrages on public decency', was incorporated into the bill as Section 11. The next night, 7 August, the bill went through its third reading and was passed, becoming law on 1 January 1886.

F. B. Smith convincingly reveals that Labouchere's intention throughout the debate in the House was to defeat the Criminal Law Amendment Bill, which he opposed, by means of 'sheer ratty obstructiveness' – a technique that he was fond of using throughout his parliamentary career. Labouchere made a number of unsuccessful attempts to include clauses in the bill that were intended, due to their impracticality or absurdity, to defeat it, or at least to send it to a

Parliamentary Select Committee for drastic revision. That Labouchere stated that his amendment's intent was to criminalise gross indecency between males 'over thirteen' suggests that he was trying to make evident, given that the bill had been thrown together in response to the hysteria over juvenile prostitution, the bill's central flaw: was its purpose to criminalise sexual acts on the basis of age, or to criminalise, in its entirety, a type of behaviour (prostitution, homosexuality), regardless of age?

In May 1885, he had responded to the agitation for the passing of the Criminal Law Amendment Bill by ridiculing it as 'a measure which must surely have originated with Arcadians'. He saw it as hopelessly idealistic, impractical, unnecessary and discriminatory to the working and agricultural classes, where women often married young. Ironically, given that the 'Labouchere Amendment' later became known as 'The Blackmailer's Charter', he warned that the bill 'would be more correctly described as a measure for facilitating every sort of extortion and blackmail'.

It is important to note that the law predating the 1885 Criminal Amendment Act, the 1861 Offences Against the Person Act, already criminalised all sexual acts between males. The 1861 Act had changed the penalty of the existing crime of sodomy from death to life imprisonment, and added the crimes of 'attempted sodomy' (covering every homosexual sexual act apart from sodomy), 'assault with intent to commit sodomy' and 'indecent assault on a male person by a male person' (covering any sexual act committed with a male under 16 by a male over 16).

The Labouchere Amendment, while redundant as regards the criminalisation of sexual acts between males, shifted the legal prosecution of homosexuality from specific sexual acts to general social behaviour indicative of 'gross indecency'. This shift is revealed in, for example, the conviction of Oscar WILDE on the 'evidence' that he was acquainted with men who were grooms and valets. (Likewise,

the evidence of the gross indecency of his co-defendant, Alfred Taylor, was seen in his habit of keeping his rooms curtained, burning incense and owning a dress.) Similar was the conviction of Rupert Croft-Cooke on the basis that he had, in defiance of social convention, invited two naval men to stay at his house, and of co-defendants Lord Montagu of Beaulieu, Michael Pitt-Rivers and Peter Wildeblood on the basis of their suspicious acquaintanceship with two men who were lowly members of the Royal Air Force. As such, Labouchere's Amendment went beyond the criminalisation of sexual acts and made the unconventionality of the social patterns of homosexual life the basis of successful convictions.

P. Higgins, *Heterosexual Dictatorship*, London, 1996; F. B. Smith, 'Labouchere's Amendment to the Criminal Law Amendment Bill', *Historical Studies*, 17 (1976): 165–75.

Jason Boyd

Lagerlöf, Selma (1858–1940), Swedish writer. In 1909 Lagerlöf was the first woman to win the Nobel prize for literature. She grew up at Mårbacka, a small manor in Värmland. She attended the Royal Teacher's College for Women in Stockholm, where she came into contact with new ideas and women who became her lifelong friends. Initially she studied against her father's will. He died shortly after she had graduated and the family had to sell the farm. Before Lagerlöf could make a living from her pen, she was a teacher for ten years.

During her years in college, Lagerlöf had made herself popular by writing verse for special occasions. She had several sonnets published in the feminist periodical *Dagny*. Sophie Adlersparre, the prime mover of the early bourgeois feminist movement, encouraged and helped Lagerlöf with her first novel, *The Story of Gösta Berling* (1891), a bold breakthrough with a new type of prose–poetry. Lagerlöf had confidence in her own genius as a writer even before she had made herself a name as one. The reactions of leading male critics on her début made her change her style of writing. Her subsequent work was more traditional in form but did contain deep psychological insights. Lagerlöf's texts, if read on the surface, can be understood as conforming to dominant moral values, but they are written in a double voice and do often contain a revaluation of patriarchal values. Conflicts concerning female creativity and desire could be written into male characters. She won her greatest acclaim with two books characterised by their national romanticism: *Jerusalem* (1901–1902) and *The Wonderful Adventures of Nils Holgersson* (1906–1907).

All her life Lagerlöf had close emotional ties to other women. The intellectual networks which supported and stimulated her were all female, including teachers working for pedagogical reform and feminists working for suffrage. Particularly important were her friends in Denmark during her years as a teacher in Landskrona (1885–1895).

The over 2,500 letters that Lagerlöf wrote to her most intimate friends were sealed until 50 years after her death; they reveal a woman full of passion. In 1894 she met the widowed author Sophie Elkan and fell in love. Her first letters give evidence as to her negotiations in connection with her sexual identity. Lagerlöf's feelings evidently were both of a spiritual and a physical nature, but Elkan seemed reluctant to live out the physical side of the relationship that lasted until her death in 1921. Elkan introduced Lagerlöf to new circles and together they travelled extensively throughout Europe. In 1902 Lagerlöf met Valborg Olander, a teacher who aimed at pedagogical reform and who was active in the suffrage movement. Although they never lived together, the relationship they formed lasted throughout Lagerlöf's life. In Olander Lagerlöf found a loving and supporting companion.

When Lagerlöf won the Nobel prize she bought back her childhood home: Mårbacka is now, according to her will, a museum. It is open to the public and a living memory of Lagerlöf's life and work. But the importance of her relationships with women is still not acknowledged by all who treasure her memory.

H. Forsås-Scott, *Swedish Women's Writing 1850–1995*, London, 1997.

Lisbeth Stenberg

Larsen, Nella (1891–1964), Caribbean-American writer. Larsen is a North American novelist associated with the movement now known as the 'Harlem Renaissance', which has been credited with the burgeoning or 'coming out' of black arts and writing as a distinctly racial force. Larsen wrote two important novellas, *Quicksand* (1928) and *Passing* (1929), which thematise the problematic categorisation of racial, sexual and gendered identity in early twentieth-century North America. The racially ambiguous 'tragic mulatto' is central to both novels and through this figure Larsen explores the visibility of intertwined racial and sexual orientations. The theme of passing as white in Larsen's *Passing* presents the light-skinned mulatto as a crossing figure who transgresses racial boundaries through her movement between black and white communities. The racial passing novel, like other versions of passing such as passing as a man or passing as heterosexual, engages with questions of classification and identification in relation to such categories as race, sex and gender.

Passing has recently been the subject of critical debate concerning its homosexual content. Larsen's biographer, Thadious Davis, rejects lesbian readings of Larsen's novella, although she writes that 'Larsen frequently associated with a literary and theater crowd that included lesbians, homosexuals, and bisexuals who were open in their sexual preferences.' Deborah McDowell's introduction to the reissued edition of *Passing* and *Quicksand* in 1986 uncovered the possibility of a lesbian subtext in *Passing*. McDowell writes that 'Larsen envelops the subplot of Irene's developing of unnamed and unacknowledged desire for Clare in the safe and familiar plot of racial passing.' More recently, queer theorist Judith Butler has explored the possibility of a queer identity in the novella through a reading of the intersecting vectors of race, gender and sexuality.

As *Passing* demonstrates, the act of passing as white was often written about in tandem with the theme of passing as heterosexual. Both themes can be found in James Weldon Johnson's *The Autobiography of an Ex-Colored Man* (1912) and in Carl VAN VECHTEN's *Nigger Heaven* (1926). The thematic crossover of these two practices in early twentieth-century North American fiction demonstrates the way in which race and sex were often conflated in readings and writings of black Americans. Van Vechten's sensational and very popular novel *Nigger Heaven* sexualises and exoticises the black community in Harlem. Like Larsen's *Passing*, *Nigger Heaven* depicts the nightclubs in Harlem which allowed interracial mixing and became meeting places for gays and lesbians. A friend and mentor of Larsen, Van Vechten appears as a character in *Passing* and was influential in introducing her and other black writers to publishers in the 1920s. Larsen's novels reflect an ambivalence about the centrality of Harlem as a racialised and sexualised literary and geographical topos. Her novels reveal the tensions that surrounded white patronage and black performances during the period and that permeated the aesthetic climate of the Harlem or 'Negro' Renaissance.

Larsen's fiction critiques the racialised and sexualised hierarchies that structured the cultural production of literature, art and music in the early twentieth century. At the same time, her self-production as a foreigner detached from American 'Negro' origins and her characterisation of passing women suggest that she did not wholly identify with either black or white identity. The child of a first-generation Danish immigrant and a West Indian man, Larsen never knew her father and was alienated from her mother in her early teens. Her professional career as a writer began when she moved to Harlem with her husband, Elmer Imes, a scientist, in the early 1920s. Larsen's unstable marriage ended in divorce in 1933. Like the practice of passing in her texts, Larsen's career is characterised by authorial masquerades and self-invention; for instance, she fabricated biographical details related to her Danish ethnicity and used a male pseudonym in her early writing. After a plagiarism scandal, Larsen left writing and returned to nursing.

J. Butler, *Bodies that Matter*, New York, 1994; T. M. Davis, *Nella Larsen, Novelist of the Harlem Renaissance: A Woman's Life Unveiled*, Baton Rouge, 1994; N. Larsen, *Quicksand and Passing*, ed. D. E. McDowell, New Brunswick, 1986.

Monique Rooney

Last, Joseph C. F. (1898–1972), Dutch writer. Jef Last has a lasting fame as the main socialist writer in Dutch. His own great times were the 1930s, when he joined André GIDE on his voyage to the Soviet Union and fought as an officer for the Spanish Republic against Franco. Not only an activist and a soldier, he was a prolific writer of novels, poetry and essays. He published about 60 books of his own and 20 translations from French, English, Russian, Spanish, Chinese and Japanese. In 1923 he married Ida ter Haar and had three daughters. Notwithstanding his same-sex interests, the marriage continued until Last's death.

Last's life was more colourful than his literary career. He became a socialist when he saw the poverty of the English lower classes. Leaving his safe place as a student of Chinese in Leyden, he became a sailor and worked in factories in the United States. In 1929 he left the socialists for the

Revolutionary Socialist Party and from 1933 until 1938 he was a communist. In the spring of 1936 Gide asked Last to help him as a translator on his voyage to the Soviet Union. Last had lived for nine months in Moscow as a liaison officer between the Dutch and Russian Communist Parties and spoke Russian. The trip made Last critical of Communism, but according to him Gide went too far in his reproaches and thus supported the rising fascist powers in Europe. To combat fascism, he himself went to Spain and fought in the Spanish Army in 1936–1937, refusing to join the Communist International Brigades. After he left the party, Last was attacked fiercely by the Communists, who used the gay angle to discredit both him and Gide. In World War II, he participated in the leftist resistance. After the war, he took part from the beginning in the homophile movement COC. In the 1960s he was a candidate for the Amsterdam city council for 'provo', the libertarian-anarchist movement of the sexual revolution.

His best books have a gay content, especially *Zuiderzee* (1934) and *Huis zonder venster* (*House Without Windows*, 1935). The first novel describes the decline of a fishing village after a dam has closed it off from the sea. The two main characters, two young masculine fishermen, have a homoerotic relationship that remains unfulfilled and ends tragically. The second novel, set in Morocco, has a fine portrait of a decadent homosexual whose life of Arab pleasures ends fatally in murder. In these novels, Last explores opposite gay stereotypes, but both have the same dramatic finale fitting the times. After the war, Last travelled much in the Far East. He regularly contributed to the gay press and in 1966 published his memoirs, *Mijn vriend André Gide*, as a tribute to his great libertarian example.

Niko van de Pavert, *Jef Last, tussen de partij en zichzelf*, Nijmegen, 1982.

Gert Hekma

Latini, Brunetto (*c.* 1220–1295?), Italian author and poet. The son of a judge, Latini was born in Florence, where he took up political activity and held various important posts, becoming chancellor and notary of the *comune* (municipality). Because of internal political disputes in Florence, he spent a long period of exile in France, returning in 1266. Latini's literary fame derives largely from *Li Livres dou trésor*, one of the first 'encyclopedias' (which he wrote in French), and to a long didactic poem, 'Il tesoretto' (written in the Tuscan vernacular).

Yet after his death Latini was less remembered for his literary works than for the fact that Dante Alighieri (1265–1321), the 'father of the Italian language', made him the key figure in the circle of sodomites in hell, in Canto XV of *The Divine Comedy*. Dante treated Latini with such deference – paying tribute to him as his intellectual mentor – that generations of commentators on *The Divine Comedy* have been scandalised. How was it possible that a person guilty of the filthiest of all sins could otherwise be treated with such care as implied in the 'Inferno'?

The answer, as the *Enciclopedia dantesca* correctly emphasises, is that Dante was the product of an age in which sodomy was a most grave sin in terms of religious morality, but less grave in the eyes of lay morality. It was only during the last years of Dante's life that secular morality changed to such a point that the Italian communes adopted the first laws which punished sodomy with death. The two-sided nature of Dante's judgement on Latini – condemning him to hell but also honouring him – was thus the expression of the doubled-edged views of the society in which he lived: attitudes which would undergo a total change in the course of only a few decades. This explains why, only a few years after Dante's death, his position on sodomy was incomprehensible to commentators and remained so until very recent times.

This explains, as well, why the question

of Latini's homosexuality has been discussed so frequently in the last century and a half and why Dante's medieval view – that the sodomite, though a contemptible sinner, could also be an admirable person – was unacceptable (given the homophobia of modern scholars). Some, among them Kay and Pézard, even managed to deny that the sodomites of the 'Inferno' were truly sodomites. In order to deny Latini's sexuality, they insisted that he was married – but so were most homosexuals of his time – and that in *Li livres dou trésor* he repeatedly condemned sodomy – but it would have been unthinkable to do otherwise in a moralistic work.

Such arguments lost credibility, however, when Silvio Avalle D'Arco rediscovered and published a love poem, 'S'eo son distretto inamoratamente' ('If I am pressed by love'), which Latini wrote to a man, Bondie Dietaiuti. The poem had long been known, but until Avalle's study, writers had purported that it was written for a woman, and censored the fact that Dietaiuti had written a verse response to Latini, 'Amor, quando mi membra' ('Love, when I remember'). Notwithstanding this indubitable proof, Latini's homosexuality continues to be a source of great embarrassment for a majority of Dante scholars, and the debate, incredibly, continues today.

S. Avalle D'Arco, *Ai luoghi di delizia pieni*, Milan, 1976; G. Dall'Orto, 'L'omosessualità nella poesia volgare italiana fino al tempo di Dante', *Sodoma*, 3 (Spring/Summer 1986): 13–35; *Enciclopedia dantesca*, Rome, 1976: Vol. 5, pp. 285–7; M. Goodich, *The Unmentionable Vice*, Santa Barbara, 1979; R. Kay, *Dante's Swift and Strong: Essays on 'Inferno' XV*, Lawrence, 1978; A. Pézard, *Dante sous la pluie de feu*, Paris, 1950.

Giovanni Dall'Orto

Lawrence, D(avid) H(erbert) (1885–1930), British novelist, poet, playwright, painter. Born into the mining community of Eastwood, Nottinghamshire, Lawrence grew up in considerable poverty and suffered from childhood illnesses that eventually developed into tuberculosis. With the help of a scholarship, he attended Nottingham high school for three years, but at 15 was forced to give up his education and take a job as a clerk in a surgical goods factory. In 1906, having worked to save some money, he took up a scholarship at Nottingham University College to study for a teaching certificate.

Lawrence was writing poetry and short fiction during this period, and his first novel, *The White Peacock*, appeared in 1911; it was followed soon after by *The Trespasser* (1912). These novels serve as early explorations into the relations between the sexes and conventional gender codes which Lawrence would probe and examine throughout his literary career. *Sons and Lovers* (1913) is a faithful autobiographical account of the close bond he had with his mother and the tempestuous relationship between his mother and father. His next novel, *The Rainbow* (1915), was seized by the police and declared obscene; his frank depiction of a lesbian relationship between two of the characters rendered the novel unlawful, and Lawrence had to surrender all remaining copies to the magistrate. The theme of lesbianism is also present in *The Fox* (1923), a novel about a tormented love triangle wherein a man threatens the love of two women.

Lawrence's interest in male homosexuality first found its way into print with the publication of 'The Prussian Officer' (1914), a short story about an abusive homoerotic relationship between a military officer and his orderly. *Women in Love* (1916) continues this homoerotic theme by representing a misunderstood and failed relationship between the two male protagonists. *Aaron's Rod* (1922), a novel that Lawrence had begun in 1918, may be read as a *roman à clef* which celebrates Lawrence's unrequited love for John Middleton Murry. In 1926 Lawrence published *The Plumed Serpent*, a novel of ritual and romance set in Mexico, which delves into Lawrence's desire for romantic male friendship. Homoeroticism also influenced his last novel, *Lady Chatterley's Lover* (1928), in so far as the male protagonist was based on a character (Scudder) in E. M. FORSTER's gay novel, *Maurice*.

Although he met Frieda Weekley (née von Richthofen) in 1912 and lived with her until his death, Lawrence pursued loving relationships with a number of men. After his disappointment with Murry – who dismissed Lawrence's declarations of love – Lawrence became emotionally attached to William Henry Hocking. He was physically attracted to Hocking and Lawrence wrote that he admired Hocking's 'high sensuous development', his 'virility' and his 'manly independence'. Hocking was led to believe that 'Lawrence was homosexual', but their relationship never developed beyond a close friendship.

Other contemporaries and friends of Lawrence included Forster and Edward CARPENTER, both of whom wrote openly about homosexuality and inspired Lawrence's textual examinations of male–male love. Lawrence also interacted with the homosexual men and women in the Bloomsbury group, and was a great admirer of Walt WHITMAN's homoerotic poetry. As well as writing many other novels and collections of poetry, his nonfictional works include *Twilight in Italy* (1916), *Sea and Sardinia* (1921), *Etruscan Places* (1932), *Fantasia of the Unconscious* (1922), *Apocalypse* (1931) and *Studies in Classic American Literature* (1923).

B. Maddox, *D. H. Lawrence: The Story of a Marriage*, New York, 1995; J. Meyers, *D. H. Lawrence: A Biography*, New York, 1992.

Justin D. Edwards

Lawrence, T(homas) E(dward) (1888–1935), British military figure and writer. Known as Lawrence of Arabia, Lawrence was a hero of World War I, a best-selling author and a popular legend even during his lifetime, which was cut short by his death in a motorcycle accident.

Lawrence was born to a prosperous family – though as an illegitimate child, since his father had eloped with his mother although he was already married – in Wales and educated at Oxford University. From 1910 to 1913, he participated in an archaeological dig at Carchemish in Syria. At the beginning of the war, he joined the British Intelligence Service in Cairo but was soon sent to Mesopotamia. Colonel Lawrence, working to advance British war aims, then spurred on the arduous but successful Arab Revolt against the Turks and triumphantly entered Damascus in October 1918. Returning to Britain, he wrote his memoirs, *Seven Pillars of Wisdom*, although a full version of the book was only commercially published after his death. In the early 1920s, Lawrence worked as an adviser on Arab affairs to the Colonial Office, then briefly served in the Tank Corps, before spending 12 years in the Royal Air Force.

Lawrence admitted having no attraction to women and shied away from sexual contacts. In Syria in 1911, he formed a close friendship with a handsome 14-year-old Arab, nicknamed Dahoum, a donkey-boy, with whom he shared his quarters. Eyebrows were raised when Lawrence sculpted a figure of a naked Dahoum and mounted it on his roof. Dahoum accompanied Lawrence to Britain in 1913 and to the Sinai the following year. It is possible that Lawrence's reconnaissance behind enemy lines in 1917 was partly an effort to see his friend. The young man died of typhus behind Turkish lines. Lawrence was distraught at his death, and the poem which introduces *Seven Pillars of Wisdom* is dedicated 'To S.A.', who has been identified as Dahoum (whose real name was Selim Ahmad). The poem, in declaring, 'I loved you, so I drew these tides of men into my hands / and wrote my will across the sky in stars / To earn you Freedom . . .', links Lawrence's emotional bond to the youth with his efforts on behalf of the

Arabs. He wrote to the poet Robert Graves that Dahoum was the great love of his life, although it is unknown whether they had a physical relationship.

Seven Pillars of Wisdom opens with a mystical reflection on the effects of Arabia on Lawrence and includes, on only the second page, a scene of young Arab men engaged in sexual play in the desert. A later chapter recounts Lawrence's capture, while he was travelling incognito to spy on the Turkish position in Deraa, in 1917. The Turkish *bey* tried to persuade Lawrence to have sex with him; when he refused, soldiers beat and, although it is not explicitly stated, probably raped Lawrence; he confessed that he had felt 'a delicious warmth, probably sexual' during the attack. On a number of occasions in the later 1920s and 1930s, in Britain, Lawrence had himself violently beaten by a Scotsman hired for the purpose in a curious masquerade in which Lawrence pretended that he was being punished for some misdemeanour at the instigation of an uncle. Biographers have connected this fetishism with his experiences in Deraa as evidence of homosexual masochism. That behaviour, and the attachment to Dahoum, show two sides to the troubled sexuality of one of Britain's greatest imperial figures.

J. E. Mack, *A Prince of Our Disorder: The Life of T. E. Lawrence*, London, 1976; M. Asher, *Lawrence: The Uncrowned King of Arabia*, London, 1998.

Robert Aldrich

Leadbeater, Charles Webster (1854–1934), British spiritualist and writer. Leadbeater was born in Stockport, in the County of Chester, in 1854, to lower-middle-class parents. He took orders in the Church of England, and became curate in a small village parish, eventually turning to High Anglicanism for spiritual and aesthetic satisfaction. He also began to dabble in occultism.

Joining the London Lodge of the Theosophist Society, he met the society's founder, Helena Blavatsky, and in 1884 resigned his parish and travelled with her to India. Seven years later, on Blavatsky's death, he became close to her successor, Annie Besant, with whom he worked to expand the movement over the following decades. His interest in the occult did not preclude his Christianity: while in Sydney, in 1916, he founded the Liberal Catholic Church, with himself as Bishop.

Over the years, there had been occasional scandals over Leadbeater's interest in young boys, as in the case of Krishnamurti, an attractive young Brahmin whom Leadbeater 'acquired' in 1909, proclaiming him to be the future world saviour. A court battle with the boy's father ensued, giving unwanted publicity to the movement – and to Leadbeater. In Sydney, in 1922, another of these scandals burst. The bishop was charged with indecencies against minors. His case made headlines throughout Australia, when police investigations revealed that it had been his practice to have a boy with him, even in bed or bath, ostensibly to monitor the aging bishop's health. Sydney could talk of little else than the 'swish bish'. Even though the charges were eventually dismissed, Leadbeater never lived down the scandal.

At a time when few people even knew about – certainly did not understand – homosexuality, he was, for most Australians, the very public face of a homosexual scandal. He died in Perth, Western Australia, in his eighty-seventh year.

G. Tillett, *The Elder Brother: A Biography of Charles Webster Leadbeater*, London, 1982.

Garry Wotherspoon

Lechoń, Jan (Leszek Józef Serafimowicz) (1899–1956), Polish writer. The second of three boys born into the middling gentry intelligentsia of Warsaw, Lechoń débuted as a poetic *Wunderkind* at the age of 13. By 1916, when he began studying philology at the University of Warsaw, he was already the author of two collections of poetry and a one-act play that had been performed by some of Warsaw's leading actors. During his university years, Lechoń collaborated with the journal *Pro arte et studio*, the germ of inter-war Poland's most renowned poetic group, Skamander (which included, among others, Jarosław IWASZKIEWICZ), whose immensely popular artistic cabaret 'Pod Picadorem' he helped found in 1918. In 1920, Lechoń published *Karmazynowy poemat* (*The Scarlet Poem*), a slim collection of poetry celebrating Poland's independence and some of its most resonant national myths. At once provocative and unabashedly patriotic, accessible but also meticulously wrought and self-conscious, the volume was enthusiastically received. Together with Lechoń's activities as a critic and satirist, the book's success gained the socially ambitious writer entry into Poland's cultural and ruling élites. Fame, however, exacted its price on the emotionally unstable youth, contributing to a nervous breakdown and an attempted suicide. Reflections of these experiences can be found in *Srebrne i czarne* (*Silver and Black*, 1924), a collection of no less studied (and no less popular) poems about love and death, but also his last until the outbreak of World War II. While ostensibly informed by an ill-fated attachment to a woman, the volume's darkly passionate love lyrics contain unmistakable intimations of homoerotic desire, although as their author was to boast later, 'No one will ever learn anything about my life from my poems.' However this may be, there is evidence that a troubled homosexual affair influenced Lechoń's decision to abandon his beloved Warsaw in 1930.

Thanks to his connections with the Piłsudski government, which he ardently supported, Lechoń managed to land himself a position as an unofficial cultural attaché with the Polish embassy in Paris, where he remained until 1939. As an habitué of some of the most prominent salons of inter-war France, he came into contact with such cultural luminaries as Marie Sert, André GIDE, Paul Claudel,

Jean COCTEAU and Jules Romain. His correspondence from the period is full of social, artistic and political gossip, but also reveals a vain, delusional man haunted by loneliness and creative impotence.

The outbreak of the war forced Lechoń to flee Paris. Together with some of his fellow Skamanderites, he made his way to Portugal, Brazil and finally New York City, where he settled in 1941. The Nazi occupation of Poland as well as the resistance of its inhabitants broke Lechoń's long poetic silence. During the course of the war, he wrote a number of patriotic poems (published in separate volumes in 1942 and 1945) in which he attempted to give voice to collective emotions, self-consciously assuming the stance of a national bard. At the same time, he contributed to the propaganda effort of the Polish government-in-exile in London, with whose anti-communist cultural institutions he would be connected for the remainder of his life.

With the end of the war, Lechoń again became consumed by what he perceived to be his creative impotence and failure to live up to expectations, although the finely chiselled poems he wrote between 1950 and 1953 (published as part of his *Collected Poems* in 1954) include some of his most powerful ones, suffused with nostalgia and premonitions of death. Perhaps as a form of compensation for his growing marginalisation as an *émigré* poet, Lechoń set about recreating, and mythologising, his pre-war reputation – the 'Lechoń legend' – within the Polish *émigré* ghetto of New York. His public activity as *littérateur*, lecturer, regular contributor to Radio Free Europe and charmingly eccentric guest in *émigré* salons was, however, conditioned by a profound personal crisis.

Upon the suggestion of a psychiatrist, Lechoń began keeping a diary (1949–1956), arguably his most fascinating literary creation. Amidst recondite autobiographical reminiscences, provocatively old-fashioned pronouncements on culture, and pathetic struggles with creative paralysis, the diary is also a document of Lechoń's attempt to come to terms with what, in reference to PROUST, he calls 'at once the entire tragedy and demonism of homosexuality'. Since he was writing with an eye towards a reading public, his pointed (and often self-hating) appreciations of WILDE, Gide, Cocteau, Genet, Capote, Vidal and Tennessee Williams, but more intimately, his veiled yet insistent references to a 'beloved person' (Aubrey Johnson) as well as to various '*peccati di carne*', 'demons and incubi', 'Anacreonts', '*lapins*' and '*ce qu'il ne fallait pas*', may be read as a desperate effort to signal his sexual orientation. Oppressed by a sense of *émigré* obsolescence and poetic sterility, unable to resolve the conflict between his programmatically traditionalist Polish public persona and the anxieties of an aging, impecunious homosexual in an America beset by McCarthyism, Lechoń jumped to his death from a Manhattan hotel window on 8 June 1956. As he wrote in one of his last poems, 'For one who's kept his silence as much as I have, O Erinyes, / There is no silence that can be frightening anymore.'

The 'legend' of Jan Lechoń notwithstanding, his stature as one of Poland's outstanding twentieth-century poets remains secure. The publication of his *Diary* (1967–1973) only enhanced his reputation, although it has been inflated, to some extent, by both his aura as an *émigré* and his cultural conservatism. Yet by the same token, Lechoń's homosexuality remains a delicate topic, subject as it is to the peculiar taboos with which Polish society continues to surround its national icons.

K. Adamczyk, *Dziennik jako wyzwanie. Lechoń, Gombrowicz, Herling-Grudziński*, Cracow, 1994; R. Koropeckyj, 'Konstrukcje homoseksualizmu w *Dzienniku* Jana Lechonia (Próba innej lektury)', *Teksty Drugie*, 4 (1996): 154–68; J. Marx, *Skamandryci*, Warsaw, 1993; W. Wyskiel, *Kręgi Wygnania. Jan Lechoń na obczyźnie*, Cracow, n.d.

Roman Koropeckyj

Leduc, Violette (1907–1972), French writer. Leduc was born in Arras, the illegitimate daughter of a servant and the son of the house where she worked. She was variously brought up by her mother and grandmother until the latter's death in 1916. After her mother's marriage in 1920 she was packed off to boarding school, her sense of displacement being heightened by the birth of her half-brother in 1923. At school she had two lesbian relationships. The second, with a teacher, led to her expulsion in 1926, though the relationship was to continue for eight more years. Joining her family, now in Paris, she worked for the publishing house Plon from 1927 to 1934 but was forced by illness to quit. In an attempt to keep herself by freelance work, she then started writing articles on a variety of topics for women's magazines.

In 1939 she married an old friend, Gabriel Mercier, but the marriage seems to have been designed to torture them both, and it lasted only briefly. Her sexual and emotional desires were becoming more and more fixated on impossible objects, notably the notoriously predatory homosexual Maurice SACHS, whom she had met in 1934. During the Occupation she took refuge with Sachs in the Normandy village of Anceins, where the two of them ran a profitable black-market racket in fresh foods, a 'career' which Leduc continued when Sachs disappeared on a trip to Paris. It was in Normandy that she began her first attempt at serious writing, a draft of *L'Asphyxie* (*Asphyxia*). Immediately after the war, Leduc was introduced to Simone de Beauvoir, who was to be the driving force behind her career for the rest of her life. Thanks to de Beauvoir's influence she was able to publish *L'Asphyxie* in 1945, *L'Affamée* (*The Starving Woman*) in 1948 and a censored version of *Ravages* in 1955. But the limitations of her relationship with her mentor, and with another implausible target for her affections, Jacques Guérin, a wealthy homosexual businessman, led to mental collapse and 'treatment' in a clinic (1957). Thereafter the threat of mental illness was never far from her, her fixation on impossible objects rapidly manifesting itself again in the form of a passion for Jean Genet. She published *La Vieille Fille et la mort* (*The Old Woman and Death*) in 1958 and *Trésors à prendre* (*Treasures for the Taking*) in 1960, but it was only with her 'autobiography' *La Bâtarde* (*The Bastard*, 1964) that she achieved critical recognition and public success. She followed with two more volumes in the same mode, *La Folie en tête* (*Madness to the Fore*, 1970) and the posthumously published *Chasse à l'amour* (*The Pursuit of Love*, 1973). In the late 1960s she was taken up by Parisian society, wrote for *Vogue*, was photographed by Cartier-Bresson and made a brief appearance in an avant-garde film. But eventually, rightly suspicious of the fashionable world, she withdrew to the south of France, where she settled down to write. She died of cancer.

Leduc's lesbian experiences have to be seen in the wider context of her complex personality. There is no doubt of the strength of her physical passion for women, as evidenced in *Thérèse et Isabelle* (1966), the text constructed from the passages which her publishers had cut from *Ravages* in 1955. But there is equally no doubt of her awareness of the erotic potential of the male body, her descriptions of which rival those of COLETTE. At one level, what dictates her sexual responses is a panerotic sensitivity to all aspects of sensuality; at another, it is her overpowering sense of marginalisation in all aspects of life.

I. de Courtivron, *Violette Leduc*, Boston, 1985.
                                    Christopher Robinson

Lee, Vernon (1856–1935), British writer. Vernon Lee was born Violet Paget near Boulogne, France. She spent much of her youth travelling in Germany, later moving with her family to Italy, where she lived most of her life.

Lee began to publish during early ado-

lescence, although it was not until 1878 that she felt that a masculine pseudonym would guarantee her writing more attention and respect. In spite of this attempt, her identity was quite well known in literary and artistic circles, and she was widely respected for her breadth of knowledge and keen intellectual powers. Lee's circle included a host of famous male writers, yet she tended to prefer the close friendships of women. Mary Robinson was Lee's main companion for almost seven years. After the disappointment of her separation from Robinson, Lee's hopes were revived by Clementina (Kit) Anstruther-Thomson (1857–1921), with whom she nurtured both a business and personal relationship for ten years.

Lee published, in a variety of languages, over 45 works, including fiction, travel writings such as *Genus Loci* (1899) and *The Sentimental Traveller* (1908), and aesthetic theory. Her *Studies of the Eighteenth Century in Italy* (1880) brought her almost instant recognition in London. Later historical novels such as *Ottilie* (1883) and *Penelope Brandling* (1903) were also well received. A satirical novel, *Miss Brown* (1884), is a scathing parody of male aesthetic writers such as Henry JAMES, a theme taken up again in her 1896 short story, 'Lady Tal'. Lee also published collections of short stories, such as *Hauntings* (1890), which includes 'Oke of Okehurst', an interesting combination of aestheticism, androgyny and the supernatural. Her works on aesthetics were inspired by studies and conversations with Anstruther-Thomson, who co-authored *The Beautiful* (1913). These works received some critical praise, although more informed psychological studies on aesthetics soon eclipsed their scientific value. During their work on aesthetics, Lee and Anstruther-Thomson developed a theory of 'empathy' to describe human reactions to beautiful works of art.

Literary scholarship on Lee has recently been aided by studies of the pair's extensive correspondence, which, according to

Mannocchi, provides a 'unique record of the romantic friendship and intellectual collaboration between two women'. Even when their romantic relationship ended, the women remained good friends until Anstruther-Thomson's death. Their letters strikingly combine scholarly and literary work with intimate expressions of love. A number of 'New Women' at the turn of the century developed significant emotional and intellectual relationships with other women, including Edith Somerville and Violet Martin ('Martin Ross') and Katherine Bradley and Edith Cooper, together known as 'Michael FIELD'.

In her introduction to Anstruther-Thomson's *Art and Man*, published three years after her death, Lee speaks honestly of her love for her friend, 'love in the truest classical tradition, a tradition that exalted love of both the beauty of body and the beauty of mind'. While Lee provided the expertise necessary to express her appreciation of beauty, Anstruther-Thomson provided Lee with the inspiration to continue writing along aesthetic lines. Lee was impressed by her friend's intuitive understanding of art, while Anstruther-Thomson learned much from the psychological framework Lee offered. Through their work, they desired to teach the less privileged in society how to appreciate art. By combining the personal with the theoretical, the pair collaborated to make a unique contribution to psychological aesthetics.

After a nervous breakdown caused by false accusations of plagiarism and by the disappointment of her work going largely unappreciated, Anstruther-Thomson began to doubt the value of the collaboration, and to slowly separate her life from Lee. Although Lee attempted to retrieve this inspiration through collaborative work with other friends, none proved as meaningful or fruitful as her years with Anstruther-Thomson.

P. Gunn, *Vernon Lee: Violet Paget, 1856–1935*,

London, 1964; P. F. Mannocchi, 'Vernon Lee and Kit Anstruther-Thomson: A Study of Love and Collaboration Between Romantic Friends', *Women's Studies*, 12, 2 (1986): 129–48.

Erin E. MacDonald

Lempicka, Tamara de (1898?–1980), Polish artist. The exact date of Lempicka's birth is not known, but she was born in or near Warsaw, and before she was 20 had married Tadeusz Lempicki and lived in St Petersburg: they moved to Paris in 1917. After her daughter Kizette was born, she studied painting with Maurice Denis and André Lhote.

Her paintings combined the space of synthetic Cubism and mannerist formal distortions, particularly that of PONTORMO, with the stylised poses and extravagant posturing of the fashionable élite. She was bisexual and her affairs with men and women were carried out in ways that were scandalous and transgressive. Similarly she used formal and narrative elements in her portraits and nude studies to produce overpowering effects of desire and seduction. In her *Self-Portrait* of 1932, seated behind the wheel of a car, she is the woman of independence. In 1934 she remarried a rich Hungarian aristocrat and at the outbreak of war went to live in America. She was given a retrospective in Paris in 1972.

T. Loughlin, 'Tamara de Lempicka's Women', *Art Criticism*, 13, 1 (1998): 97–106.

Elizabeth Ashburn

Leo X (Giovanni de' Médici) (1475–1521), pope from 1513 to 1521. The son of Lorenzo the Magnificent, Giovanni de' Médici was destined for an ecclesiastical career, and, at the age of only 13, was secretly made a cardinal. He received a refined humanistic education and was even tutored by Marsilio FICINO and Angelo Poliziano; from 1489 to 1491 he studied theology and canon law in Pisa. In 1492, he finally donned the insignia of a cardinal and began participating in church activities. He was in Florence two years later when the Médici dynasty was deposed and a republic proclaimed; Giovanni was able to flee and, after a sojourn abroad, moved into a palace in Rome (now the Palazzo Madama) in 1500. Here he took part in the various political activities of the Papal States until he led troops allied with the pope into Florence in 1512 and oversaw the re-establishment of his family's dynasty. On the death of JULIUS II, Giovanni de' Médici was elected pope without contest. His papacy, dominated by political events and the wars which ravaged Italy at the time, witnessed the Protestant rebellion of Martin Luther – whom Leo condemned in 1520 – though the pope failed to foresee its import. Leo died so suddenly that rumours of his being poisoned spread, rumours which an autopsy did not substantiate. He was a humanist pontiff who was a patron of culture and protector of artists – a famous portrait of him by Raphael can be seen in the Pitti museum in Florence. Contemporaries, however, judged his interest in wordly social activities rather excessive.

Various indications point to Leo's homosexuality. The principal evidence is the account of the historian Francesco Guicciardini (1483–1540), who, just a few years after Leo's death, wrote in 1525: 'At the beginning of his pontificate most people deemed him very chaste; however, he was afterwards discovered to be exceedingly devoted – and every day with less and less shame – to that kind of pleasure that for honour's sake may not be named.' Addressing this accusation, a modern biographer, Falconi, stated: 'From the conciseness of this charge, it is obvious that Guicciardini knew he was not telling something generally unheard of.' Indeed the accusation of sodomy often reappeared in libellous tracts, one of which, written after his death, named Count Ludovico Rangone and Galeotto Malatesta as his lovers.

Falconi finds particularly significant the story of Marc'Antonio Flaminio (1498–

1550): 'He was taken to Rome in 1514 by his father Gian Antonio, a noted Venetian man of letters, when he was barely sixteen years of age. The purpose of the trip was to present to the new pope a poem urging him to wage war against the Turks.' The youth pleased Leo so well that he offered to take him under his protection and to pay the best tutors for his lessons. However, Gian Antonio declined the offer, and the boy returned home, though he later managed to change his father's mind. Gian Antonio, in 1515, ordered his son to go to Bologna to study philosophy, at which point the pope intervened and had his secretary, Beroaldo, offer to take the youth into the papal secretariat. Thus the doors to a career, to which many better educated and more powerful men aspired, effortlessly opened to a 17-year-old youth. Yet Gian Antonio again forced his son to decline the proposition. The story has led Falconi, not without reason, to imagine that Gian Antonio suspected (or even knew about) the pope's ulterior motives.

The existence of other unpublished documents suggests that the question of Leo's homosexuality may in future be discussed on the basis of firmer evidence.

G. A. Cesareo, *Pasquino e pasquinate nella Roma di Leone X*, Rome, 1938, especially pp. 74–5 and 88; C. Falconi, *Leone X*, Milan, 1987: 455–61.

                                    Giovanni Dall'Orto

Leonardo da Vinci (1452–1519), Italian artist and scientist. The illegitimate son of a Florentine notary and a rural woman, Leonardo was reared and educated in his father's home. In 1476 he was apprenticed to the studio of the painter Andrea del Verrocchio, and two years later earned his first commission. In 1482 he moved to Milan, where he remained until 1499, when he returned to Florence. The next year he entered the service of the French king, remaining in France until he returned to Florence once again from 1506 to 1507, followed by five years in Milan.

Failing to win employment in Rome, from 1516 until his death Leonardo lived in France with his disciple and heir, Francesco Melzi (1491–1568); the two had lived together since 1509.

Leonardo is the most celebrated Renaissance intellectual because of his multiple interests, from military architecture to anatomy, geometry to hydraulics, physics to engineering. Although during his lifetime patrons hired him for a variety of work – from planning fortresses and canals to designing costumes for balls – today he is best known as one of the most important painters in Western art.

Leonardo's great fame has attracted attention to his private life, bringing to light the question of his sexuality; there is considerable circumstantial evidence of homosexual affairs. The first is a denunciation for sodomy, dated 9 April 1476, in which the 23-year-old Leonardo, then living in Florence, was accused along with others of having sodomised a young prostitute, 17-year-old Jacopo Saltarelli. Contrary to what is commonly asserted, Leonardo was not acquitted of the crime; instead, he was freed on technical grounds: the accusation was anonymous and Florentine law permitted only confidential, but not anonymous, accusations. The case was thus closed without a verdict on 7 June 1476.

A second piece of evidence is an imaginary dialogue between Fidia and Leonardo that a painter who worked in Milan, Giampaolo Lomazzo (1538–1600), wrote around 1563. Lomazzo, who had collected information from those who frequented Leonardo in Milan for his own writings on art, put into Leonardo's mouth an incredible defence of love between men: 'Leonardo: "Among painters [who] gained fame were my pupil, Antonio Boltraffio, together with Salai, whom I loved through his life more than anyone else, although I loved several [male] persons." Fidia: "Did you play the 'rear-game' that Florentines like so much?" Leonardo: "Several times! Just consider that he was a very handsome

lad, especially at 15." Fidia: "Are you not ashamed in saying this?" Leonardo: "Ashamed? Among virtuous men, there is nothing more praiseworthy than this . . . You should know that masculine love only stems from virtue bonding men together, with various types of affection in friendship, so that from a tender age, they enter the virile age being closer friends".' Furthermore, Lomazzo charged that Leonardo kept Salai with him only because he was his 'GANYMEDE'.

Third, rumours circulated about the relationships between Leonardo and 'Salai' (Devil), Gian Giacomo Caprotti (*c.* 1480–1524), the disciple whom Leonardo 'treated as a son' and who, in 1494, followed him in his peregrinations around Italy. The most direct insinuation about a sexual relationship between the two is found in the 'Codice Atlantico' contained in Leonardo's drawings; on the recto of several sheets (132–3), scribbled by an assistant, appear two erect penises (with legs and tails) walking towards an arse on which is written 'Salaj'. Leonardo's passion for Salai was justified neither by his artistic ability, since he was a mediocre painter, nor by his human virtues, since as soon as the youth set foot in his house Leonardo characterised him as a 'lying stubborn greedy thief'. In 1497, when he was 17, an embittered Leonardo noted, 'Salai is stealing money.'

A modern scholar, Wasserman, while not daring to admit that Leonardo liked Salai for his beauty, conceded: 'He was bewitching and handsome, as Vasari said, "he was endowed with grace and beauty, and had beautiful thick and curly hair". His positive qualities, beyond being obliging, were enough to keep Leonardo's affections.'

A fourth piece of evidence to consider are Leonardo's erotic drawings, which clearly refute the artist's supposedly 'asexual' and puritanical character. In one note, Leonardo himself speaks in Neoplatonic terms of the union of the 'lover' and the 'beloved' (in both cases, using the masculine gender): 'The lover moves towards the beloved as Subject does with Form, as sense does with the perceived thing, and they unite and become one. . . . When the lover reaches the beloved, there he rests.'

Finally, mention could be made of the mysterious imprisonment to which Leonardo was subjected in Florence, about which nothing is known except that Leonardo, in a note, attributed it enigmatically to having wanted to paint Jesus as a *putto* (boy).

In 1910, Freud published a famous psychoanalysis of Leonardo; yet this work is based entirely on an error of translation. Freud mistook the 'kite' which appeared in one of Leonardo's dreams for a 'vulture', and based his analysis on this symbol of a bird of prey.

G. Dall'Orto, 'Leonardo e i ragazzi', *Babilonia*, 164 (March 1998): 74–6; G. Fumagalli, *Eros di Leonardo*, Milan, 1952; M. Schapiro, 'Leonardo and Freud: An Art Historical Study', *Journal of the History of Ideas*, 17 (1956): 147–78; J. Wasserman, 'Caprotti, Gian Giacomo', in *Dizionario biografico degli italiani*, Rome, 1976.
Giovanni Dall'Orto

Leopardi, Giàcomo (1798–1837), Italian poet and writer. Leopardi was born in Recanati, the son of Count Monaldo Leopardi, an intellectual who belonged to the most reactionary wing of the nobility in the Papal States. The young Leopardi took advantage of his father's well endowed library, and from an early age distinguished himself as a classical scholar and a student of modern languages. He lived in various Italian cities (Florence, Rome, Bologna, Milan, Naples), working for different publishers. A victim of physical deformities and chronic ailments from early childhood – illnesses which periodically jeopardised his work engagements – he could never acquire the complete independence from his family for which he longed; this compelled him to compromise with his learned but reactionary father. Unhappiness deriving from these circumstances (and, one might add, from his unrequited homosexual attachments) contributed to his being labelled the 'poet of pessimism'.

Classical in his education, Leopardi was a Romantic in his sensibility. His 'patriotic' ideals, as expressed in the poem 'All'Italia' (1821), made him popular among Italian nationalist readers and, after the unification of Italy in 1860, secured him a role as 'national poet'. During his early life, however, his sentiments had made him suspect to authorities who, immediately after the Congress of Vienna in 1815, were particularly hostile to any political changes. Among his verse and prose works are *Canzoni* (1824), *Versi* (1826), *Operette morali* (1827) and *Canti* (1831). He died, aged only 39, in Naples, where he had moved looking for a milder climate. His tomb, classified as an Italian national monument, is located in the Parco Virgiliano in Naples.

Soon after his death, Leopardi became a sort of national icon, about whom it was possible to write only in positive terms. He is still considered amongst the two or three greatest nineteenth-century Italian poets. Such a status made it unthinkable to circulate information relating to his homosexuality and, two hundred years after his birth, the family of Count Leopardi still keeps secret some of his papers, denying access even to researchers.

Various hints about his sexuality were nevertheless made by the Neapolitan writer Antonio Ranieri (1806–1888), Leopardi's close friend in his later life. Leopardi met Ranieri, when the latter was a 21-year-old student, in Florence in 1827. Three years later they were seeing each other regularly, and they spent five months together in Rome in 1831–1832. Ranieri in 1832 returned to Naples, as he was on the verge of bankruptcy. Leopardi wrote frequent love-letters to him from Florence. In the letters appear such declarations as: 'Ranieri mine, you will never abandon me, nor grow cold in your love for me. . . . Whatever decision you take, please arrange things in such a way that we can live for each other, or at least that I live for you, my only and last hope. Farewell, my soul. I embrace you on this heart of mine, which in any possible and impossible circumstances will remain eternally yours.'

Such a remarkable friendship did not go unnoticed, as evidenced in another letter, of 5 January 1833, which referred to the derisory comments which it had evoked: 'Poor Ranieri mine! If human beings laugh at you because of me, at least the idea that they laugh at me because of you gives comfort to me, since as far as you are concerned, I always behaved and will behave worse than a child. Yet the world always laughs at those things that, if it did not laugh, it would be forced to admire, and always blames, like the fox, what it envies.'

When these and similar love-letters written by Leopardi were published – after Ranieri tried unsuccessfully to stop their publication – Ranieri wrote a memoir for the press about his friendship with the poet. Here he took it upon himself to repeat gossip (some of it in bad taste) and coded allusions to Leopardi's sexual tastes. A propos of the infamous letters, he wrote: 'I confess I never intended to allow him to take with me that liberty which, I am told, can be read in some of his letters. And I say "I am told" because, since they were first published, I have thrice tried to read them and thrice have I caught a fever.'

Scholars have nevertheless indignantly dismissed the value of these letters as evidence of Leopardi's homosexuality. They insist that in the Romantic period it was 'normal' for persons of the same sex to write such love-letters to each other. (But was it? Even Ranieri himself admitted that Leopardi's letters went far beyond the conventions of the time, to such a point that the letters, even 60 years later, made him feverish – no matter whether the fever was real or simulated.) As if this were not enough, Ranieri found it necessary to recount his friend's 'little night visits', his practice of inviting unknown persons to his house; when they arrived, Ranieri had

to leave the room in which Leopardi received his 'acquaintances'.

Is there reason to believe that Leopardi and Ranieri had a (sexual) relationship? Such facts as those already mentioned do not provide proof; if there can be little doubt about Leopardi's infatuation with Ranieri, the motives of Ranieri – about whose aggressive heterosexuality there is ample evidence – do not seem likewise noble. Historians such as Moroncini have shown that in the last years of their 'friendship', Ranieri lived with Leopardi because the poet supported him. Furthermore, Ranieri complains in his memoirs that Leopardi vexed him with endless 'love soliloquies' in circumstances 'the detail of which it is not very decorous to give'. Critics have always explained away this complaint by saying that Leopardi spoke to poor Ranieri about his hopeless and unrequited heterosexual loves. Yet one piece of evidence, which is normally (and intentionally) neglected was collected among those who had known Leopardi when he lived in Florence. In Tuscany, Leopardi wrote verses about a woman, Fanny Targioni-Tozzetti (called 'Aspasia' in the verses), whom Ranieri also loved. According to this piece of evidence, he was so in love with her that he became frenzied about love whenever he saw her younger and handsome brother – the official interpretation has it that this is because in her brother's features, he recognised 'Aspasia'. Moreover, the account adds that in his frenzy of love, Leopardi went so far as to direct his sentiments towards Ranieri.

As can be seen, notwithstanding an almost two-hundred-year censorship which made homosexuality a taboo topic in literary debate through both homophobia and puritanical 'defence' of Italian 'national treasures', evidence still exists to put the record right, if not exactly straight.

G. Dall'Orto, 'Sempre caro mi fu . . . ', *Babilonia*, 141 (February 1996): 68–70; G. Leopardi, *Lettere*, Florence, 1958: letters 481 ff. from

1832–1833; F. Moroncini, 'Il retroscena e il supplemento del libro del Ranieri sul "sodalizio", *Nuova antologia*, 356 (1933): 384–416; A. Ranieri, *Sette anni di sodalizio con Giàcomo Leopardi*, Milano, 1979, especially pp. 38–9, 55–6, 73 and introduction by Alberto Arbasino.

Giovanni Dall'Orto

Leyendecker, J(oseph) C(hristian) (1874–1951), German-American painter. Although overshadowed by the better-remembered Norman Rockwell, Leyendecker was the most influential commercial artist of early twentieth-century America; in fact Rockwell idolised Leyendecker, now credited as formative for Rockwell's early style.

The son of German immigrants, he was raised in Chicago where he trained at the school of the Art Institute of Chicago and later at the Académie Julian, Paris. From the late 1890s to 1951 he had a successful career illustrating American books, magazines and commercial advertising. His work appeared on covers of the most widely read American magazines of the day including *Collier's* and *The Century*, with 322 covers for *The Saturday Evening Post* (1899–1943). He produced patriotic posters during both world wars. Leyendecker also provided advertising images for Karo Corn Syrup, Kellogg's Corn Flakes, Pierce–Arrow Automobiles, B. Kuppenheimer Clothiers, Interwoven Socks, S. T. Copoer Underwear (now Jockey International) and most notably for the Cluett, Peabody and Co., Inc.'s famous 'Arrow Collar Man' campaign (c. 1905–1931).

It is impossible to overestimate the cultural currency of the Arrow Collar Man. He inspired songs, jokes, satires, Broadway musicals, even F. Scott Fitzgerald. The clean-shaven and square-jawed Arrow Collar Man epitomised early twentieth-century American ideals of restrained, self-contained, and above all physical, masculinity. Fan mail for the Arrow Collar Man rivalled that of Hollywood movie star Rudolph VALENTINO. Leyendecker's imagery walked a careful line of acceptable male-looking, inciting desire among male consumers for men's fashions while containing the threat of sexual desire implicit in their looking at male models. None other than Giorgio Armani would appropriate Leyendecker's compositional style for a men's couture campaign in 1980.

While product sales attest to the success of Leyendecker's imagery, there remains a surprising degree of homoeroticism in his work. The artist doted lovingly on the physique of athletic male bodies and fantastic physical specimens with broad shoulders, narrow waists, muscular buttocks and strong legs. More than a few images featuring inter-male admiration smoulder with desire, while phallic canes, swords, riding crops, golf clubs and flagpoles suggest, at least to certain viewers, relations not overtly consummated. It remains to be determined whether the homoeroticism of Leyendecker's work was subtextual and only available to a knowing few, or whether it was central to the commercial desires of all male consumers.

The ironic height of Leyendecker's coded imagery must be that one of the artist's models for the Arrow Collar Man was Charles Beach, his assistant, business manager and live-in companion for 50 years (1901–1951). Although Leyendecker retained the original paintings of his work, upon his death they were sold for a pittance at a lawn sale and are now difficult to locate. Significant collections are held by the Haggin Museum (in Stockton, California) and Illustration House (New York).

G. Kriss, 'The Father of the New Year's Baby', *New York Times*, 27 December 1998; R. Martin, 'J. C. Leyendecker and the Homoerotic Invention of Men's Fashion Icons, 1910–1930', *Prospects*, 21 (1996): 453–71; R. Martin, 'Gay Blades: Homoerotic Content in J. C. Leyendecker's Gillette Advertising Images', *Journal of American Culture*, 18 (Summer 1995): 75–

82; M. Schau, *J. C. Leyendecker*, New York, 1974.

Michael J. Murphy

Lifar, Serge (1905–1986), Russian dancer and choreographer. Born in Kiev, one of the most controversial figures of twentieth-century ballet, Lifar was praised in his youth for his physical beauty and riveting stage presence and later recognised as a capable, prolific and innovative choreographer.

The son of a Russian civil servant, he first studied piano at the Kiev Conservatory of Music. In 1921, at age 16, he started dance training at Bronislava Nijinska's Kiev studio. When Nijinska rejoined DIAGHILEV's Ballets Russes and called for a number of her students to work with her, among them was Lifar, who joined the company in 1923. 'A stranger to the pleasures of the bed' and a 'poor lover' by his own later admission, Lifar nevertheless recognised that he was 'sought after by people of both sexes' and eventually set out to take the place not only of Anton Dolin, Diaghilev's interim favourite, but Diaghilev's long-time secretary, librettist and confidant, Boris Kochno, as well. He eventually succeeded in replacing the highly independent Dolin, who had other career goals and would soon leave the Ballets Russes. But he was no match for the urbane and intellectual Kochno, with whom he shared a rivalry that survived Diaghilev's death. As with Léonide Massine, Diaghilev overlooked the flaws in Lifar's technique and, assisted by the choreographic innovations of George Balanchine, capitalised on his physical perfection, exuberant energy, expressive talents and a desire to work.

Promoted to the rank of soloist in 1924, Lifar was living with Diaghilev by 1925. Despite a stormy relationship, he went to lengths to please his lover, including agreeing to rhinoplasty. At Diaghilev's behest, Lifar read ponderous tomes and studied relentlessly. Under the tutelage of Cecchetti, Egorova and Nicholas Legat, his technique improved remarkably. Owing to an acquired glamour as well as his hard-won virtuosity, Lifar became the *premier danseur* in the company's final, most modern, years. Between 1923–1929, he created roles in milestone works by Nijinska *(Les Facheux, Le Train Bleu)*, Massine *(Les Matelots, Pas d'Acier, Ode)* and George Balanchine *(La Chatte, Apollon Musagètes/Apollo, Le Fils Prodigue/ Prodigal Son, Le Bal)*.

Being, in Richard Buckle's words, as 'ambitious as it is possible to be', Lifar saw himself not only as Diaghilev's last lover and protégé (although Igor Markhevitch had already replaced him in Diaghilev's affections), but as his artistic heir as well. But when he intended to take over the Ballets Russes after his mentor's death in August 1929, the dancers refused to work for Lifar rather than Kochno, and the company folded. That same year, Lifar took advantage of an offer to choreograph the *Creatures of Prometheus* for the Paris Opera, replacing the original choreographer, Balanchine, who had fallen ill. After a brief interlude as star dancer of *Corchoran's 1930 Revue* in London, appearing in Balanchine's and his own ballet, he returned to Paris.

Based largely on the success of his performance in *Prometheus*, Lifar was offered the artistic directorship of the Paris Opera and immediately embarked on a mission to resurrect the former glory of the venerable institution, which had been in serious artistic decline since the mid-nineteenth century. Between 1931 and 1944, he reigned as the driving force of the Opera as *premier danseur étoile*, choreographer and ballet director. After the Allied liberation of Paris in 1944, Lifar was labelled a Nazi sympathiser and dismissed from the Opera. The validity of the charges remains unresolved. Followed by a number of loyal dancers, he formed the Nouveau Ballet de Monte Carlo, serving as *premier danseur* and choreographer. Due to public demand, Lifar was recalled to the Paris Opera as ballet master in 1947 but did not dance again until 1949. In 1948, scandal followed Lifar to the United States, where he was greeted with protests and booed as a collaborator when he appeared with the Paris Opera dancers in New York. Limited by administrative restrictions, Lifar never regained his former artistic freedom and again left the Paris Opera in 1958.

Throughout his career, he choreographed hundreds of ballets, frequently in collaboration with leading modern composers and designers. Many of his works are now negligible, but his choreography was frequently daring for its time if not brilliant. Among his most significant works are *Icare/Icarus* (1935), *Suite en Blanc* (1943) and *Mirages* (1944), as well as revisions and recensions of ballets by Fokine, NIJINSKY and Massine, and stagings of nineteenth-century classics including *Giselle* (he was considered one of the century's great Albrechts) and *Sylvia* (1941).

His talent as an evocative performer spilled over into his choreography, which emphasised the individual dancer's technical and expressive gifts. Among the French dancers whose talents he promoted were Janine Charrat, Roland Petit, Zizi Jeanmaire, Colette Marchand, Yvette Chauviré and Michel Renault. Although few of his works made a lasting impact internationally, his place in dance history is assured for having overseen the renascence of French ballet, earning him the esteem of the French public as a cultural icon. Lifar was also the founder of the Institut Chorégraphique de l'Opéra (1947) and revived the Académie de Danse, originally founded by Louis XIV in 1661.

A prolific writer, Lifar published more than 25 books on dance including histories, criticism, choreographic treatises and biographies of Diaghilev, the nineteenth-century ballerina Carlotta Grisi and Auguste Vestris, the eighteenth-century 'God of the dance', to whom Lifar frequently compared himself, as well as a preening autobiography, *Ma Vie* (1965). In that book, Lifar vows that his only love was his art: 'My partners [apparently both men and women] showed themselves rather jealous of this stage pleasure which dominated me more than anything else and which they guessed stole me away surreptitiously from them.' In this, he was not unlike the otherwise inimitable Nijinsky.

R. Buckle, *Diaghilev*, New York, 1979, and *In the Wake of Diaghilev*, New York, 1982; L. Garafola, *Diaghilev's Ballets Russes*, New York, 1989; J. Gruen, 'Serge Lifar', in *The Private World of Ballet*, New York, 1975.

A. M. Wentink

Linck, Catharina Margaretha (c. 1694–1721), German lesbian. Linck was one of a small number of women in German history who are known to have been punished for the crime of homosexuality. In 1721, she was executed for attempting to pass as a man and for marrying another woman. Her trial took place in Halberstadt in Germany when she was about 27, making her approximate birth date 1694. At the time of the trial, Linck was calling herself Anastasius Lagrantinus Rosenstengel, and was married to a younger woman, Catharina Mühlhahn.

It seems that Linck/Rosenstengel had been dressing as and passing for a man since adolescence. In her early youth she became a soldier in the service of Hanover, but deserted from the army in 1708; when she was caught, she managed to escape the punishment of hanging usually meted out to deserters by revealing herself as a woman. She later found employment as a dyer and cloth maker, and in 1717 married Mühlhahn – who claimed not to have known at that time that her partner was not a man. The marriage was not entirely harmonious: at the trial it was claimed that Linck beat Mühlhahn, and stole and sold household objects for money that she spent on drinking and gambling. Her downfall came when, in a state of inebriation, she attempted to force sexual attentions on a sick Mühlhahn and got into a quarrel with her wife. Mühlhahn's mother, who was present, apparently accused her of being a woman rather than a man, and tore open her trousers to prove it. The court case ensued.

In the course of the court's proceedings, a leather penis and another leather object like a horn, which Linck was alleged to have used for urinating, were produced as evidence against her. These played a key role in deciding her fate. Until 1794 a Prussian Code dictated that those found guilty of 'unnatural acts' were to be burned at the stake, but the factor that defined deeds worthy of capital punishment was sodomy or penetration. The lawyers who dealt with Linck's case were unsure whether lesbianism entailed the death sentence, noting that the Bible does not prescribe on this subject as it does on male homosexuality, and they suggested flogging or imprisonment as possible alternatives. But Linck, whose assumed name 'Rosenstengel' (rose-stem) is both feminine and phallic in its connotations, was finally sentenced to beheading on the grounds that she had penetrated Mühlhahn's mouth and vagina with her leather penis, allegations treated in extensive and sometimes repetitive detail in the trial records. Mühlhahn was sentenced to be imprisoned and then banished for her part in the affair. The mandatory death sentence was not relaxed until 1837, when it was commuted to imprisonment, and in 1851 a new code rendered only men punishable, and women by implication incapable of homosexual activity.

B. Eriksson (trans.), 'A Lesbian Execution in Germany, 1721: The Trial Records', in S. J. Licata and R. P. Petersen (eds) *The Gay Past: A Collection of Historical Essays*, New York, 1985 (1981); L. Faderman and B. Eriksson, *Lesbians in Germany: 1890's–1920's*, Tallahassee, 1990 (1980).

Sarah Colvin

Lister, Anne (1791–1840), British gentlewoman landowner. Lister was born in Yorkshire, England, to a moderately wealthy family and was one of six children. Three of the sons died in childhood and the fourth died in 1813. Lister was rather masculine in appearance, and she had an unfeminine interest in education. In 1805 she was sent to the Manor School in York, where she acquired a reputation as a tomboy. Her first romantic relationship was with Eliza Raine, a girl with whom she shared a bedroom at the school. It was a physical relationship, and very passionate, but she also flirted with other girls.

It had been decided as early as 1814 that Lister would inherit one of the family properties and her sister the other. Accordingly, in 1815 she arrived in Halifax to live at Shibden Hall, the property of her uncle James, where she was to learn about the property and its administration in preparation for her eventual ownership of it. Lister was an ambitious woman who sought to escape her low gentry origins and move into the life of the wealthier classes. Through school contacts, she became friends with some of the wealthy families of York, in particular the Norcliffes. They were large landowners, well travelled and cosmopolitan. Her main interest in the family, however, was their daughter Isabella.

Anne met Isabella Norcliffe when she was 19 and Norcliffe was 25. They began an affair, but Norcliffe was soon passed over for Mariana Belcombe. The relationship between Lister and Belcombe was not without difficulties. Belcombe was shortly to be married to a middle-aged landowner. Lister felt betrayed, but they continued to see each other and to sleep together. But the husband discovered one of Lister's passionate letters to Belcombe and forbade her to come to the house, intercepting all the mail. In addition to the problems with Belcombe's husband, Lister began to suspect in 1821 that she had contracted a venereal disease. It seemed that Belcombe had contracted it from her husband and then passed it on to Lister. Lister was still sleeping with Norcliffe occasionally, however, and had passed it on to her.

Lister abstained from sexual activity while she attempted to cure herself. Belcombe became concerned about the implications for her new respectability of being discovered in a lesbian relationship. Lister appeared somewhat masculine and was insufficiently stylish in dress, and in 1823 Belcombe began to distance herself from Lister. Her response was to indulge her long-held wish for a visit to Paris. She left Belcombe.

In 1826, Lister gained ownership of Shibden Hall and the resources of its estate, which included coal. Coal was, at this time, becoming an increasingly important fuel, and Lister was quick to capitalise on it. She was a shrewd businesswoman, managing the estate well. She also was politically conservative, remaining staunchly loyal to king and country and largely opposed to the political advancement of women. Despite her conservatism, she was an example to women of the possibilities of education, which she prized. In the 1830s, she entered a business and sexual partnership with Anne Walker, a neighbouring landowner. Walker was uneasy about sexual intimacy, and the relationship focused primarily on their shared interests in business and travel. The two Annes travelled through Europe and eventually to Russia. Lister died in the Caucasus in 1840 and Walker went insane upon her return to England.

Lister's lengthy journals for the period 1817–1840, which have been transcribed from code by Helena Whitbread, offer a unique insight into the world of a nineteenth-century lesbian woman. Lister continued throughout her life to have passionate physical relationships with women. She was unusually explicit about her love-making in the coded portions of her journals, even referring to orgasm, which she called a 'kiss'. Some of her relationships were lengthy ones, but she was also essentially non-monogamous, often having at least two relationships simultaneously or at least flirting outside of her relationships.

It is the frankness of her diaries and the wide range of her sexual relationships which make Lister an important figure in lesbian history. Lillian Faderman and others have argued that 'lesbian' women of Lister's period and class probably did not engage in a genital sexuality, but Lister's journals suggest otherwise. Moreover, Lister's diaries reveal that she was fully conscious of her sexuality, writing in 1821, 'I love and only love the fairer sex and thus, beloved by them in turn my heart revolts from any love but theirs.' While Lister did not use the word 'lesbian' to describe herself, her relationships and her struggle for an identity based on her sexuality are consistent with many of the attributes of the modern lesbian identity. She was acutely aware of social attitudes towards 'Sapphists', however, as indicated by the code she developed during her first affair and used extensively in letters and diaries during her affair with Belcombe to disguise the nature of their relationship. Lister's explicitness about and ambivalence towards her 'oddity', as she called it, provide the historian with a unique perspective on the experience of lesbians in early nineteenth-century England.

A. Clark, 'Anne Lister's Construction of Lesbian Identity', *Journal of the History of Sexuality*, 7, 1 (1996): 23–50; J. Liddington, *Female Fortune: Land, Gender and Authority: The Anne Lister Diaries and Other Writings, 1833–1836*, London, 1998; H. Whitbread (ed.) *I Know My Own Heart: The Diaries of Anne Lister 1791–1840*, London, 1988.

                                                    Karen Duder

Lorca, Federico García (1898–1936), Spanish poet and playwright. The debates on and around Federico García Lorca's sexual orientation still rage in the somewhat rusty world of the Spanish literary establishment. Many critics and scholars still suggest it is an issue that lacks any relevance whatsoever for an understanding of the artist's work and life and *therefore* (although the link is less clear than it pretends to be) it should not be discussed. For others, it is just a matter of gossip. Another faction, perhaps more generous, admits its importance, but then gets into the kind of analysis that renders homosexuality an absolute 'other' and prevents readers from understanding the positive role it may have had in the poet's work. Research on the subject has been made difficult both by García Lorca's family and critics, who often use positions of power (editorial columns in literary supplements, for instance) to downplay the issue of sexual identity and question the work of anybody who dares to suggest it might indeed be important. Biographically, there is little doubt about it, but even so, homosexuality has to be silenced and misread as if something very important was at stake. It seems that this is indeed the case.

In the past decade or so, Lorca has become something of a national poet, the centre of the Spanish poetic canon in the twentieth century. Celebrations of the poet's centenary in 1998 cemented his status against other members of the same generation, such as Nobel prize winner Vicente Aleixandre and Luis Cernuda. To place homosexuality anywhere near the centre of Lorca's artistic background and concerns is to attach a cultural importance to it that few critics would like to accept explicitly. Moreover, there is the issue of reputations and individual involvement: Lorca had very many friends and acquaintances, and in time many of them have claimed a portion of the sacred writer; obviously the poet's sexual orientation, which may or may not have bothered them at the time, becomes an embarrassment when retelling the story and has to be swept under the carpet. Lorca is hardly the issue here: individuals who met him and find homosexuality problematic are.

Lorca was the son of a wealthy Andalusian landowner. He was born in a small village in the province of Granada, but soon moved to the capital, where he spent most of his childhood and adolescence.

He never seems to have been a bright student, and at school relationships with his peers appear to have been difficult. He was often made fun of, and the issue of effeminacy was one of the reasons. He loved the mythical Granada that had belonged to the Islamic empire: a town where sensuality and intellectual pursuits, art and pleasure, coexisted; but he was clearly uncomfortable with the town he inhabited, with its bourgeois inhabitants, with its moral intolerance. In 1918 he moved to Madrid to pursue his education at the liberal Residencia de Estudiantes. Accounts of this period regarding Lorca's sexuality vary. This is the time when Lorca emerged as a popular character, a successful performer with whom everybody wanted to be friends. He became good friends with intellectual and artistic luminaries such as the film-maker Luis Buñuel and the painter Salvador Dalí. Between Lorca and the latter there seems to have developed a warm (one hesitates to say 'passionate') friendship. They were very close for years and then Dalí reacted almost violently against his and Lorca's feelings. The poet felt betrayed by this and the shadow of Dalí is ever-present in his work from that moment. Buñuel's reaction when learning of his friend's sexual orientation was even harsher.

By the mid-1920s Lorca was an up-and-coming poet with very little published work but well integrated into the artistic milieu. In 1925, he met Emilio Aladrén, a bisexual sculptor who would use Lorca's friendship for personal advancement. It is hard to know exactly what Lorca's feelings were; if he was in love, it was a somewhat immature relationship that ended badly. But the experience seems to have given him a new insight into the workings of sexual attraction, which would be reflected in his work and would provide a new perspective on love, specifically on homosexual love, as a particular kind of emotion subjected to social restrictions.

Partly to overcome his romantic failure, Lorca travelled to the US in 1929. By then some of his books had already come out, but he was yet to make his mark as a playwright. New York was one of the key experiences in his artistic carreer. He certainly felt isolated and melancholy, but it was also there that, away from prying eyes, he seems to have explored his own sexuality, and the person who returned to Spain was much more mature, more inclined to deal with it in poetic terms. After a short period in Cuba, he returned to Spain in 1931, where he embarked on an astonishingly fertile period both artistically and personally. Images of a troubled and nevertheless enticing sexuality abound in his work of this time, and homosexuality appears explicitly, represented both in *Poet in New York*, a book of poems, and in one of his key plays, *The Public*, conceived during his trip to America. The former includes the piece 'Ode to Walt WHITMAN', a somewhat troubled embracing of the older poet's supposedly free and innocent sexuality, that is opposed to preying versions of homosexuality he witnessed or experienced in New York. *The Public* is probably the most important European play on homosexuality written in the 1930s and also among the most formally inventive. Sexuality in general and homosexuality in particular are dissected as a set of masks and feelings difficult to express, but the play clearly argues their expression. It is this pro-homosexual stance that may have prevented the play from being performed.

Lorca attempted at least two more plays in which homosexuality featured centrally: *La destrucción de sodoma* (*The Destruction of Sodom*) and *La bola negra* (*The Black Spot*), but neither has survived. Homoeroticism and emotional staleness due to the impossibility of expressing his own feelings are also present in *Let Five Years Pass*, one of his most avant-garde works. Publication of other more or less explicitly homosexual works has been made difficult by the family: the *Sonetos del amor oscuro* (*Sonnets of Dark Love*) had to be published illegally amid strong opposition from the family and other critics close to their interests. Finally there have been well intentioned but rather simplistic attempts to link the long-suffering, socially repressed women characters in Lorca's major plays (*Yerma, Blood Wedding, The House of Bernarda Alba*) to the poet's personality in a re-enactment of the Proustian 'Albertine strategy', but such an approach is often misguided. The fact remains that we do not know enough about the way Lorca chose to articulate his sexuality in writing, and that a more complex view of it, possibly informed by theoretical work around it, has yet to be achieved. Lorca's last years seem to have been relatively happy: he was now famous and he found a new love in his secretary, Rodríguez Rapún. The circumstances of Lorca's death are less murky now than they used to be: he was killed by intemperate fascists impatient with his political allegiances and sexual orientation, maybe with an element of revenge for some of the poet's statements. Yet some points remain unclear: the role of homophobia in the circumstances that led to the murder and the possibility of a political plot remain in the air.

D. Eisenberg, 'Reaction to the Publication of the *Sonetos del amor oscuro*', *Bulletin of Hispanic Studies*, 65 (1988); I. Gibson, *Federico García Lorca: A Life*, London, 1989; A. Sahuquillo, *García Lorca y la cultura de la homosexualidad masculina: Lorca, Cernuda, Dalí, Gil-Albert, Prados y la voz silenciada del amor homosexual*, Alicante, 1991.

Alberto Mira

Lorrain, Jean (1855–1906), French writer. Born Paul Duval, into a comfortable middle-class family in Fécamp (Normandy), he was a dreamy, sensitive child very attached to his mother. Dispatched to study law in Paris, he soon abandoned an uncongenial course and took up a literary career under the pseudonym Jean Lorrain. He began with collections of poetry whose very titles – *Le Sang des Dieux* (*The*

Blood of the Gods, 1882), *La Forêt bleue* (*The Blue Forest*, 1883) – indicate their allegiance to the still fashionable Parnassian mode but already include an admixture of a decadence which was not merely a literary manner. *Le Sang des Dieux*, for example, includes a cycle titled 'Ephèbes' which contains references to androgyny, criminal passion, 'misunderstood love' and 'bizarre love' whilst invoking such classical symbols of pederasty as GANYMEDE and ANTINOUS, and the sonnet 'Prince héritier' in the collection *Modernités* (1885) openly refers to sodomy between an aristocrat and stable boys. Lorrain rapidly moved on to try his hand at novels and plays, but he first really began to make a name for himself as a columnist in the Parisian press, particularly for *L'Evénement* (1887–1890), *L'Echo de Paris* (1890–1895) and *Le Journal* (1895–1905), where his contributions became notorious for their barbed wit and a certain pessimistic moralism. His fascination with decadence was reflected from an early age in his own lifestyle, where drugs, his avowed homosexuality and frequenting of the criminal fringe played central roles. As a consequence he was often involved in controversy or the cause of public outrage. In 1892, for example, he was convicted of an 'offence against public morals' and fined 3,000 francs for publishing a story with lesbian implications in *L'Echo de Paris*; in 1903 a painter, Jeanne Jacquemin, recognising herself in one of Lorrain's 'Pall Mall' columns in *Le Journal*, sued for libel, the case this time costing him 25,000 francs. Perhaps the sheer franticness of his career explains the fact that it was only relatively late on that he wrote his major novels, *Monsieur de Bougrelon* (1897), *Monsieur de Phocas* (1901) and *Le Vice errant* (*Vice Abroad*, 1902), all of which stage a larger-than-life central character steeped in vice and, in the latter two cases, confirmedly homosexual. Though these heroes are portrayed as following a path to destruction, it is certainly true that by airing previously forbidden topics Lorrain

helped to prepare public opinion for the less bizarre accounts of homoeroticism shortly to appear in the works of GIDE and PROUST. Nor are thematic issues the only ways in which Lorrain's sexuality affected his writing. His best work consciously refuses boundaries and categorisation, moving between the conventions of the documentary account of contemporary mores, the romance of high society and the Gothic tale. It was perhaps fitting that, though he had retired to the Côte d'Azur, it was in Paris that Lorrain eventually died, as a result of medical complications connected with his drug-taking.

P. Jullian, *Jean Lorrain ou le Satiricon 1900*, Paris, 1974; P. Winn, *Sexualités décadentes chez Jean Lorrain*, Amsterdam, 1997.

Christopher Robinson

Lot, Biblical figure. Lot is a central figure in the story of Sodom and Gomorrah, which has been the excuse for centuries of Christian persecution of gay men, and continues to be so. According to the Book of Genesis, the first book of the Jewish and Christian scriptures, Lot was the nephew of Abraham, the founder of the Hebrew nation. When Abraham and Lot travelled north from Egypt, Lot settled in the Jordan Valley while Abraham went on to Canaan. Lot settled in the city of Sodom, near the Dead Sea.

In Genesis 18 and 19, God consults Abraham about the alleged sinfulness of Sodom and another city, Gomorrah. Abraham, who is no fool, asks God, 'Wilt thou also destroy the righteous with the wicked?' God avoids the question and says he will not destroy the cities if he can find 100 innocent people in them. Abraham plea-bargains with him, and God finally agrees that he will spare Sodom and Gomorrah if that many innocent people can be found.

God then sends two angels to Sodom to investigate. They stay at Lot's house. The men of Sodom come to the house and demand that the angels be produced, 'that we may know them'. Lot refuses, but sportingly offers them his two virgin daughters instead. The men refuse and try to break into the house, but the angels strike them all blind. The angels then tell Lot that God is going to destroy the city, and urge him to leave with his family. He does so, and God then destroys Sodom and Gomorrah and the whole region with burning sulphur. Lot's wife, however, looks back as they flee, so God kills her too by turning her into a pillar of salt.

Christians have come to believe that the sin for which Sodom and Gomorrah were destroyed was homosexuality. Modern translations of the Bible deliberately perpetuate this belief. The passage which in the King James Bible read: 'And they called unto Lot, and said unto him, Where are the men which came in to thee this night? bring them out unto us, that we may know them', has more recently been rendered as: 'They called out to Lot and asked, "Where are the men who came to stay with you tonight? Bring them out to us!" They wanted to have sex with them.' (*Good News Bible*, 1976).

In fact, the story as presented gives no evidence at all that the inhabitants of the cities practised homosexuality, or if they did that they practised it more than anyone else in ancient Israel. It seems strange that thousands should die for this alleged sin, while Lot, who offers his virgin daughters to be raped, should be exonerated.

More crucially, even the meaning of the passage quoted above has been disputed. John Boswell, in *Christianity, Social Tolerance, and Homosexuality* (1980), points out that the Hebrew verb 'to know' is frequently used in the Bible in a non-sexual context, and only rarely in the sense of 'to have sex with'. He also points out that nowhere in the Bible is it explicitly stated that the sin of Sodom was homosexuality. He quotes Jesus as suggesting that the sin of Sodom was in fact inhospitality. He suggests that it was several centuries into the Christian era before the story of Sodom was seized on as a pretext for Christian homophobia.

However that may be, the story has had potent consequences for gay men for the past 2,000 years. 'Sodomy' became the standard religious and legal term for homosexuality, though American 'sodomy statutes' came to include other illegal practices as well, such as heterosexual oral and anal sex. Christian and Jewish fundamentalists continue to quote the story along with other Biblical texts as a rationale for persecution and discrimination against gay men. Fortunately, however, some mainstream Christian denominations no longer accept the Old Testament as literal truth, and no longer seek to excuse homophobia on these grounds.

Adam Carr

Loti, Pierre (1850–1923), French writer. Loti was born Louis-Marie-Julien Viaud, the son of a Protestant mother and a Catholic father who worked for the municipal administration of Rochefort. Both his mother's and father's families had ties to the navy, and in 1866 Loti followed in his brother's footsteps by setting off to sea. Loti's many years of travelling with the navy took him all around the world: to Tahiti, Turkey, Africa, the Americas and Japan. He drew upon his adventures – especially his amorous ones – to write stories of intrigue and romance that became wildly popular with French readers. Novels such as *Aziyadé* (1879), *Le Marriage de Loti* (1880) and *Madame Chrysanthème* (1885) familiarised readers with the customs and lifestyles of cultures across the world. Loti's success as a writer earned him the the Legion of Honor in 1887 and election to the Académie Française in 1892. In his work, Loti attempted to demonstrate the value of indigenous cultures, and often portrayed the introduction of European 'civilisation' in a negative light. Loti was especially fond of Turkey, the site of a love affair that marked him forever. He returned again and again to Turkey throughout his life, and became its staunchest defender in the years leading to World War I when conflict in the Balkans threatened the integrity of the Ottoman Empire. Loti even transformed his home in Rochefort into a shrine to Istanbul and his lost love, transforming entire rooms with the installation of Turkish furniture and decorations, including Muslim prayer rugs.

Loti was an enigmatic figure during his lifetime, and has remained so for critics even today. He loved secrecy and intrigue as much as he loved pretending to be someone he was not. On becoming famous, he was known for his elaborate theme-based costume parties and for travelling in Parisian society, in make-up and elevated heels, in the company of a group of handsome young sailors. Loti seemed to have formed relationships with both men and women, although the exact details of these relationships are hard to determine, since Loti claimed that his fiction was based on his experiences, but regularly altered names and personalities. His private journals are often just as mystifying; he wrote some sections of them in code and destroyed others. Nonetheless, it seems that Loti's first significant relationship was with a fellow sailor, Joseph Bernard. The two were inseparable for many years, travelling to Tahiti and Senegal together, sharing their finances and acting in many ways as a married couple. During his time with Bernard, however, Loti may have had at least two love affairs with women. The second, in Senegal, ended in 1874, the same year that he and Bernard broke off their relationship. Loti suffered a nervous breakdown as a result of his romantic troubles, but recovered when sent to Turkey, where he may have had relationships with both a woman and a man. In 1886, in part to stem gossip that was circulating about him, his family convinced him to marry. He spent little time with his wife, and in his later life set up a second household in the same city with a Basque woman who had become his lover and her

children. Loti, for all of his eccentricities and love for secrecy, seems to have been a well-liked and well-respected writer during his lifetime.

L. Blanch, *Pierre Loti: Portrait of an Escapist*, London, 1983; A. Quella-Villéger, *Pierre Loti l'incompris*, Paris, 1986.

Victoria Thompson

Louis XVIII (1755–1824), king of France. Born in Versailles, the future king first carried the title of Comte de Provence; he became pretender to the throne after the death of Louis XVI and his nephew. During the Revolution, he fled France in 1791 with a friend, the Comte d'Avaray – a dramatic episode in which he seems to have most appreciated being in close and permanent contact with his companion. Louis' exile lasted more than 20 years. Until 1809, d'Avaray was the king's official favourite and was called 'the king's friend'. He was succeeded in this role by the Comte de Blacas, a handsome 38-year-old Provençal. When Louis returned permanently to France as king after Napoleon's downfall in 1815, he was forced to separate from Blacas under pressure from the European allied powers.

Louis replaced him by a 31-year-old, Elie Decazes, a tall, handsome, well built and intelligent man who was prefect of police when he first met the king; Decazes provided chaste affection to the aged, obese and ill sovereign, and was the great love of his life. Thanks to his fine figure, and to his undoubted talents, Decazes became a minister, pursuing liberal policies to the great discomfort of the reactionary ultra-royalists. In the best conspiratorial traditions of the old regime, they hoped to bring about his fall by creating a rival, and brought Blacas back to Paris. The king was moved to see his old favourite, but remained faithful to his current companion. Decazes's rise continued, as he became Minister of the Interior in 1818, then President of the Council (prime minister) in 1819. However, after the assassination of the Duc de Berry, Louis had to choose – like his ancestor Louis XIII – between his favourite and the demands of the state, and he sent Decazes away. 'From this moment, I wiped myself out', the king said, and he progressively took less interest in politics, leaving the ultra-royalists in control until his death.

In re-establishing the monarchy after what he considered the 'parenthesis' of the Revolution, Louis had wanted to return to the traditions of the old regime – he was at least able to do so in his emotional life. He was the last French head of state officially and publicly to have 'favourites' and to give them a political role.

E. Lever, *Louis XVIII*, Paris, 1988; Duc de Castries, *Louis XVIII*, Paris, 1969.

Didier Godard

Louÿs, Pierre-Félix (1870–1925), French writer. Louÿs's dissipated lifestyle can perhaps be traced back to the death from tuberculoisis, when he was a young man, of his mother and brother. Louÿs was convinced that he too would die at a young age, a belief reinforced by periodic illness. This belief led him to focus his energy on the present moment; he devoted himself to pleasure and to art, squandering his resources and dying penniless and in the midst of an attack of dementia.

Louÿs is perhaps best remembered today as the author of erotic poetry and prose that celebrated lesbian love. Works such as *Les Chansons de Bilitis* (1894) and *Aphrodite* (1896) became enormous successes during Louÿs's lifetime, in part because of their lesbian themes. Louÿs, however, was disappointed at the public reaction to his work; rather than scandalise and titillate, he claimed that he sought to dismantle the prejudices against the free expression of sexual love that made bourgeois morality such an oppressive institution.

Though Louÿs advocated a more open view towards sexuality and painted a highly sympathetic picture of lesbian love,

his attitude towards male homosexuality was more ambiguous. Louÿs, a lover of Greek culture who believed in the value of the inner life and in the pursuit of beauty through art, was part of both the Parnassian and Symbolist literary movements in *fin de siècle* Paris. As such, his circle included many well known homosexual writers of the period, such as Marcel PROUST, André GIDE (a close friend since high school) and Oscar WILDE (who had dedicated his *Salomé* to Louÿs). However, although in his Greek translations he had treated male homosexuality in a sympathetic manner, Louÿs repeatedly expressed concern that others might assume he was homosexual. He broke off relations with Wilde once he learned of the nature of his relationship with Lord Alfred DOUGLAS, and worried during Wilde's trial that his own association with the English writer might lead people to doubt his own inclinations. Similar fears may have contributed to Louÿs's break with Gide. Although most critics have explained this by reference to different outlooks on life and literature as well as different personalities, the correspondence of the two men also reveals that Louÿs was growing increasingly intolerant of Gide's continued use of terms that others might misinterpret (the two sometimes referred to each other as 'husband' and 'wife' in their correspondence). Before the break, however, Louÿs had encouraged Gide's literary efforts, as he had those of other young men whom he believed had talent, including Paul Valéry, a close friend for many years.

Louÿs was notorious during his lifetime for his many affairs. His inconstancy in love and his continuous financial difficulties undermined his first marriage, to Louise de Hérédia, which ended in divorce in 1913. A second marriage, to Aline Steenackers, took place in 1923, two years before the writer's death and during a prolonged bout of dementia. The poetry he wrote during his final years reveals his sense of disappointment at a life of broken friendships, drug abuse and betrayals in love.

G. Millan, *Pierre Louÿs: ou, le culte de l'amitié*, Aix-en-Provence, 1979; J.-P. Goujon, *Pierre Louÿs: une vie secrète, 1870–1925*, Paris, 1988.

Victoria Thompson

Lowell, Amy (1874–1925), American poet. Lowell was born in Brookline, Massachusetts, where she lived throughout her childhood and adult life in the family home, even after her parents' deaths, sharing it for many years with her lover and partner, Ada Dwyer Russell.

The Lowell family was a respected upper-class family in New England, noted for leadership in the arts, law, education and social affairs. Lowell received commendations for her writing from an early age, and her childhood and youth were filled with the benefits which class and privilege offer: excellent private schooling, lessons in the arts, visits to museums, theatre performances and travel to Europe. She also educated herself in her father's library and in the Boston Atheneum, in particular discovering poetry and the work of Keats. Her father complimented her poetry writing and other talents, but the family did not openly encourage her to have a public career.

In 1891 she formally made her début in Boston society and spent several years engaged in social pursuits. During 1897–1898 she travelled to Egypt, prompting an exploration into non-Western cultures, and upon her return to Boston her life took a more serious turn and she began to devote herself to writing poetry.

Lowell's poetry was a moving voice within the Imagist movement. Symbolism had dominated English poetry during the 1890s, and Lowell was one of the poets who moved poetic style into bolder forms using a very emotional free verse, more literal descriptions, Orientalism, prose poetry and coded use of homoerotic images of women. She said all poetry consists only of vision and words, and felt strongly that it was meant to be a primarily oral tradition.

Her first poetry was published in 1910, and her first volume, *A Dome of Many-Coloured Glass* (1912), was followed by *Sword Blades and Poppy Seeds* (1914), *A Critical Fable* (1922) and dramatic monologues, such as the widely anthologised poem 'Patterns'. She lectured widely, read poetry and wrote criticism throughout her career.

She was also noted for her strong, independent, dramatic and courageous personality. Among her peers she was unusual for transgressing conventions, smoking cigars and forming a 'Boston Marriage' with Ada Dwyer Russell. She died after a stroke at her home.

S. Foster Damon, *Amy Lowell: A Chronicle*, Boston, 1935; L. Faderman, *Surpassing the Love of Men*, New York, 1981; C. Summers (ed.) *The Gay and Lesbian Literary Heritage*, New York, 1995.

Sarah Holmes

Ludwig II (1845–1886), king of Bavaria (1864–1886). Heir to the Wittelsbach dynasty which ruled Bavaria, Ludwig succeeded his father to the throne in 1864. More interested in art and music than in statecraft, he immediately established contact with Richard Wagner, writing that he was the 'most ardent admirer' of the composer. Wagner replied 'in utmost rapture' and soon visited the young king. Thus began a long friendship and artistic patronage – Ludwig gave Wagner an annual stipend, commissioned the *Ring* cycle of operas and later built the theatre in Bayreuth where the operas continue to be performed. The relationship between king and composer was exceptionally intimate. Wagner wrote before one visit, 'I fly to him as to a lover. . . . It is a beautiful relationship'; while Wagner was a guest, the king had a note taken to him, reading 'I am in your angelic arms'. The German language of the period, and the overwrought Romantic sentiments still popular in the late nineteenth century, explain the feverish nature of their correspondence, and Wilfrid Blunt denies that Ludwig and

Wagner had a physical relationship. Ludwig himself admitted to a woman friend: 'I hear there are still the most curious rumours about my relationship with Wagner.' Courtiers seemed more worried about the money Ludwig lavished on Wagner and the possible political influence of the composer.

Ludwig, although considered keenly intelligent, was inattentive to state matters. In 1866, he sided with Austria-Hungary in a failed war against Prussia; four years later, the Prussian chancellor, Bismarck, got him to sign a letter inviting the Prussian king to become emperor of a united Germany. Ludwig, however, was much concerned with building palaces – the Romanesque–Byzantine–Gothic pastiche of Neuschwanstein, rococo Lindenhof, and Herrenchiemsee, modelled on Versailles. Ludwig had unbounded admiration for the French *ancien régime*, perhaps imagining himself a new Sun King. He was also fascinated by the Middle Ages and the Orient.

Ludwig wrote in his posthumously published diaries about struggles with his homosexuality. Once engaged, he repeatedly postponed then cancelled his wedding. He had a number of liaisons with courtiers and equerries, such as Prince Paul von Thurn und Taxis and Richard Hornig – Hornig remained in his service for 20 years, though Ludwig never forgave him for marrying. He also organised nocturnal picnics where stable-boys and troopers danced naked; when he spotted particularly handsome soldiers in parades, Ludwig sometimes appointed them to his personal staff on the spot. His last significant obsession was a Hungarian actor, Josef Kainz, whom he showered with gifts and took on holiday to Switzerland.

The king's behaviour became increasingly erratic, and neglect of state affairs more obvious. Ministers became convinced that he was unbalanced. In 1886 government leaders had Ludwig declared insane, appointed his uncle as regent and took the king to a palace on Lake Starnberg. The following day, Ludwig went for a walk with Berhard von Gudden, the leading alienist in Germany. The bodies of both men were found floating in the lake later that day. It remains uncertain whether the deaths were suicides, murders or heart attacks.

Ludwig achieved fame in life and death as 'the mad king of Bavaria', although biographers disagree about the nature (or even reality) of his mental illness. The Empress of Austria (to whose younger sister Ludwig had been engaged) remarked: 'The King was not mad; he was just an eccentric living in a world of dreams.' Historians might well speculate about the role of homosexuality in Ludwig's fantasies and behaviour, as well as in his eventual downfall and death.

W. Blunt, *The Dream King: Ludwig II of Bavaria*, London, 1970.

Robert Aldrich

Lully, Jean-Baptiste (1632–1687), Italian-French composer. Born Giovanni Battista Lulli in Florence, Lully was only 14 when he was noticed by a French aristocrat looking for a domestic servant for 'Grande Mademoiselle', the niece of King Louis XIII. During his years in her employ, Lully perfected his musical and dancing talents. The young Louis XIV remarked on the genius of the Italian – hardly older than the new French king – and accorded him musical and social favours. In 1661, Lully was naturalised as a French subject and named Master of the King's Music. He composed the music for royal ballets and for Molière's comedies and directed the Academy of Music. Lully was also one of the creators of French opera, with works such as *Atys*, *Armide* and *Acis et Galatée*.

Throughout his life, Lully contracted various, often notorious, homosexual liaisons. In his early years in Paris, he frequented several atheist libertines and sodomites, including SAINT-PAVIN and d'Assoucy. The latter had been one of Lully's music teachers and when he was arrested and imprisoned, the Master of the King's Music brought musicians to play under the window of his cell.

Lully kept a series of 'music pages' at his home, young men who were ostensibly his pupils. The best known was a certain Brunet, 'handsome as Cupid', according to contemporaries. Lully and Brunet's affair created a stir at court, and Lully had to promise not to see the youth again. There was no other sanction against his conduct, as Louis XIV wanted to avoid public scandals; otherwise he accepted the homosexuality of Lully and several generals, cardinals and others in his court.

R. de Candé, *Dictionnaire des musiciens*, Paris, 1964; E. Haymann, *Lulli*, Paris, 1991.

Didier Godard

Lynes, George Platt (1907–1955), American photographer. Born in East Orange, New Jersey, Lynes was educated privately. In the summer of 1925 he made the first of several visits to Paris, where he met Gertrude STEIN, Jean COCTEAU, André GIDE, Pavel TCHELITCHEV, Glenway Westcott and Monroe Wheeler, who all remained lifelong friends. The gift of a camera in 1927 encouraged Lynes to teach himself photography and he exhibited a number of portraits at Park Place Book Shop the following year. A friendship with Julian Levy, a New York dealer in Surrealist art, led to Lynes's first significant exhibition at Levy's gallery in 1932. Following the publication of his celebrity portraits in *Vogue* and *Harper's Bazaar*, and needing to support himself after his father's death, Lynes opened a successful studio in New York. Throughout the 1930s he continued to produce commercial portrait and fashion photography and in 1934 was invited by Lincoln Kirstein and George Balanchine to photograph the dancers and productions of the newly founded American Ballet (which later became the New York City Ballet). The association continued until Lynes's death and gave rise to a notable body of dance photography.

In addition to his commercial and portrait work, Lynes produced photographs which combined Surrealism (Man Ray being an early influence) with other modernist styles such as Cubism and Expressionism, and his photograph *The Sleepwalker* was included in the Museum of Modern Art's 1936 exhibition, 'Fantastic Art: Dada and Surrealism'. Beginning in the early 1930s, Lynes produced highly stylised photographs of male nudes (either singly or in pairs or trios) often posed in the studio as enigmatic tableaux or with unconventional props. Rejecting the soft-focus tonal aesthetic and natural light of Pictorialist photography (typified by Fred Holland DAY), Lynes employed carefully staged theatrical lighting that gave a sharp clarity and strong plasticity to his subjects by dramatically juxtaposing deep shadows with intense, almost clinical, spot illumination.

Although Lynes also photographed female nudes, the male nude remained his principal subject in a series of photographs, produced between 1936 and 1939, depicting Greek mythological figures, for example *Birth of Dionysus*, *Pan*, *Orpheus and Eros*, and *Endymion and Selene*, which prefigure the self-consciously camp aesthetic of photographers such as Pierre et Gilles some 50 years later. Though the cloak of mythology partly legitimised the depiction of the male nude, Lynes never published his homoerotic photographs, in order to protect his commercial reputation, but instead circulated them amongst his friends. However, he regarded his private work to be far more important than his fashion photographs and commercial portraiture, and neglect of his professional career led to the eventual bankruptcy of his studio. Lynes was also closely associated with, and photographed, a number of gay artists such as Marsden HARTLEY, Paul Cadmus and Jared French, and several of his portraits, for example of the English novelists Christopher Isherwood (1940) and Somerset Maugham (1941) and of Hartley (1943) make clear the sitters' sexuality by posing them with a young man.

In 1941 Lynes had a major one-man show at the Pierre Matisse Gallery in New York, but in 1942, disillusioned with his career and prompted perhaps by the death that year of his lover George Tichenor in the war, he moved to Los Angeles to head the Hollywood studio of *Vogue*, only to return to New York, even more disillusioned, in 1948. While living in Hollywood, Lynes used his house as the setting for a number of wistful, even melancholic, photographs of silhouetted male nudes posed in shadowy rooms. The photographs from the late 1940s also mark a shift towards a pared-down style which employed minimal, if any, use of props, relying instead on just pose and lighting.

Unable to revive his career in New York, Lynes declared bankruptcy in 1951 and was supported by friends and occasional work. In his final years he published male nudes in the Swiss magazine *Der Kreis* (*The Circle*) under his own name, the pseudonym Roberto Rolf and 'In Memory of a Great Master of Photography', and two hundred of his photographs were bought by the sex researcher Alfred Kinsey and remain in the collection of the Kinsey Institute. Diagnosed terminally ill with lung cancer in May 1955, Lynes destroyed many of his negatives and prints, including his fashion photographs and his nudes, and died that year in New York.

J. Crump, *George Platt Lynes: Photographs from the Kinsey Institute*, Boston, 1993; J. Woody (ed.) *George Platt Lynes: Photographs, 1931–1955*, Pasadena, 1981, and *George Platt Lynes: Portraits*, Santa Fe, 1994.

David L. Phillips

M

McAlmon, Robert (1896–1956), American writer, publisher. Born in Clifton, Kansas, McAlmon's life typifies what has been described as 'the lost generation'. A homosexual American expatriate, he moved to London and then to Paris from New York in 1921. While in London, McAlmon entered into a marriage of convenience with Annie Winifred Ellerman (better known as Bryher), the daughter of the English shipping magnate Sir John Ellerman. After this marriage broke up, McAlmon received a large alimony settlement which enabled him to contribute to the advancement of modernist writing by publishing work that had not been fully appreciated or recognised. He then formed the small press known as Contact Editions, which first published modernist classics such as Hemingway's *Three Stories and Ten Poems* (1923), William Carlos Williams's *Spring and All* (1923), Gertrude STEIN's *The Making of Americans* (1925) and, among other experimental writing, Djuna BARNES's *The Ladies Almanack* (1928).

Although he was never open about his homosexuality, McAlmon frequently wrote about same-sex desire. McAlmon's *The Village* (1924) is an episodic and plotless novel which chronicles the relationship of two village boys; one takes their intense bond seriously, while the other dismisses it as he grows up and settles into a heterosexual life. His collection of short stories, *The Distinguished Air* (1925), includes 'Miss Knight', 'Distinguished Air' and 'The Lodging House'. Set in post-World War I Berlin (a decade before Christopher Isherwood arrived), these stories follow American characters as they search for drugs and young boys in decadent nightclubs. Homosexual themes are also explored in *A Hasty Bunch*, a collection of stories that McAlmon published in 1922; the story 'A Boy's Discovery', for instance, describes the rough and passionate relationship of two 9-year-old boys. As well as publishing other novels and short stories, McAlmon's most famous work is the autobiographical *Being Geniuses Together* (1938). His poems in free verse were published in *Explorations* (1921), *The Portrait of a Generation* (1926), *North America, Continent of Conjecture* (1929) and *Not Alone Lost* (1937).

One of McAlmon's more passionate relationships was with the Canadian writer John GLASSCO. Between 1927 and 1929, the two men lived in Paris and travelled together throughout Europe. But because McAlmon never admitted his homosexuality publicly, he left his relationship with Glassco out of his memoir *Being Geniuses Together*. However, Glassco, in a section of the manuscript that was expunged from the published text of his *Memoirs of Montparnasse* (1970), records his overtly sexual relationship with McAlmon.

J. Glassco, *Memoirs of Montparnasse*, Oxford, 1970.

Justin D. Edwards

Macdonald, Sir Hector Archibald (1853–1903), British soldier. Macdonald was born the son of a Scottish crofter and worked as an apprentice draper before enlisting in the army at the age of 17; he rose rapidly through the ranks and ultimately became a major-general. Macdonald first saw action, and was commissioned as an officer, in the Second Afghan War in the late 1870s, then distinguished himself in the Battle of Majuba Hill in South Africa in 1881. After postings in Britain and Ireland, he was sent to Egypt in 1884. There he recruited and trained a battalion of Sudanese soldiers, whom he led into several victorious battles, including one of the most legendary in British imperial history, Omdurman. Macdonald was generally considered the real hero in the defeat of the Mahdist troops, reconquering the Sudan for the British and avenging the killing of General George Gordon in 1885. Macdonald returned home to a triumphant welcome, but soon left to take part in the Boer War. He suffered a relatively minor wound in South Africa, and was somewhat sidelined from command by his superiors (particularly Kitchener), but received a knighthood for his work. In 1902, the army sent Macdonald to India to take up a regional command, but he was there only briefly before being moved to Ceylon (Sri Lanka) as Commanding Officer of British forces.

Macdonald, a highly disciplined and demanding officer, immediately offended his subalterns with criticism of the lack of professionalism of both the army and the militia. Neither the snobbish British expatriates nor the governor, Sir Joseph West Ridgeway, took to the rough-hewn commander of Scottish peasant background, despite his great reputation. After only 11 months, West Ridgeway summoned Macdonald to tell him that he must return to England to answer to 'grave, very grave charges'. Although details remain unclear, Macdonald was alleged to have committed sexual improprieties with four Ceylonese youths or (in a different version) to have exposed himself in a train carriage with 70 schoolboys. In London, Lord Roberts, the Chief of the Imperial General Staff (who had given Macdonald his officer's commission in India), ordered him to return to Ceylon to face a court-martial. *En route*, Macdonald committed suicide in a Paris hotel room.

Macdonald had secretly married in 1884 and fathered a son, although he saw his wife on only four brief occasions in 19 years and never revealed his marriage to his military superiors. Rumours circulated about a supposed affair with a male Boer prisoner in a concentration camp over which Macdonald had authority in South Africa in 1900, and about unspecified irregular sexual activities in India in 1902. There were also rumours about his friendship with a Burgher (mixed-race) Ceylonese family, especially with the two sons whom some said were his catamites. Macdonald did have close friendships with a number of youths in Britain, often as part of his efforts to encourage imperial vocations. Nevertheless, there is no firm evidence concerning homosexual activities, and the Scottish verdict of 'not proven' seems appropriate concerning Macdonald's homosexuality.

Despite his massive public popularity, Macdonald had encountered hostility in his career because of a modest background that separated him from the aristocratic military élite, clashes with several superior officers such as Kitchener (himself considered of ambivalent sexuality), criticism of some military policy and unpopular support for conscription, failure to curry favour with expatriates, and fraternisation with 'natives'. Such behaviour worked against him, and a cleric commented that 'had he been the son of a duke, an easier way of escape would have been made for him' in order to avoid a court-martial, perhaps simply by his being transferred to a different posting. Whether 'Fighting Mac' took his life because the allegations of sexual conduct were warranted, or because he realised that a court-martial, whatever the verdict, would end his military career, will never be known. Coming only several years after the conviction of Oscar WILDE, even charges of homosexual behaviour were especially fateful to the reputation of a respectable public figure, leaving suicide, for some, the only honourable option.

T. Royle, *Death Before Dishonour: The True Story of Fighting Mac*, Edinburgh, 1982; K. I. E. MacLeod, *The Ranker: The Story of Sir Hector Macdonald's Death*, Cortland, NY, 1976.

Robert Aldrich

Macedo, Francisco Ferraz de (1845–1907), Portuguese-Brazilian doctor, anthropologist and criminologist. Macedo was born in Águeda, Portugal but emigrated to Brazil as a child with his parents. Although from a poor background, he managed to qualify first as a pharmacist and then as a doctor, becoming rich from private practice. Returning to Portugal in 1881, he dedicated himself to anthropology as it was then understood, and in particular to anthropometry, the scientific measurement and classification of skeletons and skulls. For this purpose he built up a large collection of bones obtained from the common grave in Lisbon. He had wide scientific and literary interests, engaging passionately in the debates of the period. Among his contemporaries he had a reputation for rigorous scientific observation and confused theorising. He also helped to popularise the notions of criminology, co-editing a publication entitled *Galeria de Criminosos Célebres* (*Gallery of Celebrated Criminals*) which appeared in seven volumes from 1896 to 1908. His last days were marked by misfortune as his wife and children died before him and he lost his property in Brazil. He died in Lisbon.

Macedo was the first medical person to write about homosexuality in Brazil. His doctoral thesis, which was published in 1873 with the title *Da Prostituição em Geral, e em Particular em Relação á Cidade do Rio de Janeiro: Prophylaxia da Syphilis* (*About Prostitution in General, and in Particular in Relation to Rio de Janeiro: Prevention of Syphilis*), was a detailed statistical survey of the prevalence of prostitution in the Brazilian capital. Although mainly concerned with female prostitution following the model of Parent-Duchatelet's work in Paris, Ferraz de Macedo devoted one chapter to homosexuality and gave a quite detailed description of gay life at the time.

Macedo began the chapter by writing about women, noting the prevalence of anal intercourse, lesbianism and masturbation among female prostitutes. Then, under the heading 'Sodomy or Masculine Prostitution', he noted that adepts of sexual relations between men could be found in all classes and age groups, but were concentrated in certain districts of the city, which he listed. In nearly all districts there were special houses which rented rooms by the hour for sexual purposes.

Macedo went on to classify his subjects into active and passive sodomites. Many passive sodomites lived in indolence or from prostitution while active sodomites were drawn from the ranks of soldiers, who did it for lack of time or financial means, as well as craftsmen and shop-workers, who were motivated by fear of syphilis or a wish to avoid the expense of female prostitutes. Passive male prostitutes could be recognised by the way they walked and their effeminate manner of talking as well as the places and company they were seen in, especially theatre entrances, billiard rooms, bars, cafés and public squares. He described a typical example as aged between 12 and 20, wearing varnished boots, tight trousers, a short, elegant coat, embroidered shirt, red or blue silk handkerchief, a tall white beaver hat, curled perfumed hair, a walking stick, pince-nez, gold watch and chain, kid gloves and a Havana cigar. At the other extreme were hungry, syphilitic children wearing ragged or patched clothes, smoking and swearing, who would perform indecent acts for a pittance.

Macedo noted that passive sodomites loved walking in crowded public places, while it was impossible to recognise active sodomites except when they were seen in the company of notorious passives. Some sodomites were given exclusively to same-sex relations and had an aversion for women while others did have intercourse with women. He described how sodomites made contact, with a few words or a simple nod of the head for prostitutes, or by asking for a light for their cigarette and then offering an invitation to the theatre, a meal or a stroll in the case of others.

Macedo blamed the spread of sodomy and masturbation among boys from better-off families on boarding schools, and among soldiers on lack of money. In his conclusion, however, despite making a vague reference to the need for police and legislative action, he pinned his hope on education since he thought that sodomy was mainly restricted to the illiterate and unemployed and he could not believe that it held any attraction for the better-educated. He also urged that idle men and boys who congregated in places of entertainment should be forced to work. This was in line with the book's call for the official regulation of prostitution.

The chapter is notable for its detailed observation of local customs, its pragmatic approach and lack of theorising and, despite its condemnation of homosexuality, a relatively moderate attitude. Thirty years later, back in Portugal, Macedo returned to the subject of sodomy in an article published in 1902 in the *Galeria de Criminosos Célebres* and as a pamphlet with the title *Os Devassos, Concupiscentes e Sodomitas: Patologia e Crimes* (*Debauchees, Lustful Men and Sodomites: Pathology and Crimes*). Although he reprinted most of his earlier chapter in this article (without indicating

that it referred to Rio rather than Lisbon), Macedo adopted a much more strident tone. The article was marked by an insistent, violent, almost hysterical condemnation of general licentiousness and homosexuality. It contained no observations about homosexual life in Portugal, despite a number of well-publicised scandals in the 1880s which would have provided ample material. Instead it indulged in a confused theorising based on a hotchpotch of ideas drawn from contemporary scientific theories about morphology, insanity and cells, and couched in medical phraseology. Its sense of moral outrage was underscored by references to degeneration theory, with its emphasis on hereditary defects. The article concluded with an appeal to eugenics, arguing that society should prevent such debauchees from reproducing.

This article was not the first medical work on homosexuality to be published in Portugal. Adelino Silva's *A Inversão Sexual* (*Sexual Inversion*) appeared in 1896, employing a more up-to-date scientific discourse, with terms such as 'uranist' and 'homosexual', and including a brief description of homosexual behaviour in Lisbon and Oporto. Although Macedo used the already dated term 'sodomite', his work is better known, perhaps because of its picturesque title, and the copy of the pamphlet in the National Library in Lisbon is well-thumbed. It is, however, a poor sequel to his earlier work.

Grande Enciclopédia Portuguesa e Brasileira, vol. 11: 152–4; L. C. Soares, *Rameiras, Ilhoas, Polacas . . . A Prostituição no Rio de Janeiro do Século XIX*, São Paulo, 1992.

Robert Howes

McKay, Claude (1889–1948), Jamaican-American writer. Born into a poor family in Sunny Ville (Clarendon Parish), Jamaica, McKay, at a young age, became interested in the Caribbean and West African folk stories that were told to him by his father. His first book of poetry, *Songs* of Jamaica (1912), draws from this folk tradition by celebrating the stories and lives of Jamaican peasants. Although he worked at odd jobs – doing everything from working as a cabinetmaker to taking a job as a police constable – he continued to write poetry, and after the publication of his second book, Constab Ballads (1912), he became the first black to receive the medal of the Jamaican Institute of Arts and Sciences. McKay used the prize money to move to the United States and, after dropping out of the agricultural science programme at Kansas State College, he moved to Harlem to resume writing. It was not long thereafter that he became the first major poet of the Harlem Renaissance.

In 1922, he published his most important collection of poetry, Harlem Shadows, which, in the opinion of some critics, virtually inaugurated the Harlem Renaissance. In this collection, McKay empathises with the sufferings of the working-class blacks and the victims of racial oppression; in fact, his most famous poem, 'If We Must Die', was written in response to the 1919 riots of working-class blacks in northern American cities. His next literary achievement was the novel Home to Harlem (1928), which was the first novel by an African-American to become a bestseller. This novel depicts the nightlife of 1920s Harlem, and it seems to have satisfied a consuming curiosity on the part of Americans for information about life in Harlem. In fact, many critics read the novel as existing mainly for the purpose of taking the reader on a tour of the black neighbourhood. Along the way, the narrator moves through Harlem's clubs, many of which include 'skirt men', 'pansies', 'dark dandies', 'faggotty men' and 'bulldykers'. The scenes in some of these clubs also include drag shows and characters who exhibit fluid gender identities; many of these men and women are representative of the lesbian and gay subculture that developed in 1920s Harlem. This novel, like

Carl van VECHTEN's Nigger Heaven (1926), was despised by black intellectuals such as W. E. B. Du Bois, who claimed that McKay's depictions of African-American life (and sexuality) made him feel 'dirty'. McKay's next novels, Banjo (1929), set in Europe, and Banana Bottom (1933), set in Jamaica, do not include any overt homosexual themes.

McKay did not hide his sexual desires for both men and women, but little is known about his relationships. Some scholars speculate that during his tenure on The Liberator, a leftist magazine based in Greenwich Village, he may have had affairs with Waldo Frank and Edward Arlington Robinson. Other scholars claim that while living in Paris in 1929 McKay had a sexual relationship with the Canadian writer John GLASSCO. But details about his affairs remain sketchy.

McKay's other collections of verse include Songs of Jamica (1912) and Spring in New Hampshire (1920). His collection of short stories, Gingertown (1932), investigates (among other things) issues of sexuality. And his nonfiction, A Long Way from Home (1937) and Harlem: Negro Metropolis (1940), is interesting and insightful.

W. F. Cooper, Claude McKay: Rebel Sojourner in the Harlem Renaissance, Baton Rouge, 1987; J. R. Giles, Claude McKay, Boston, 1989; A. L. McLeod, Claude McKay: Centennial Studies, New York, 1992.

Justin D. Edwards

Mackay, John Henry (1864–1933), Scottish-German writer. Born in Scotland, Mackay was only 2 years old when his father died and his mother returned to her family in northern Germany. He grew up in a small town, but spent the rest of his life in larger cities. His year abroad in London opened his eyes to 'the social question' and his almost 40 years in Berlin left an indelible imprint of metropolitan life, in all its variety, on his works.

Mackay gained fame in the late

nineteenth century with his successful volume of verse, *Sturm* (*Storm*, 1888) and his biography of the anarchist philosopher Max Stirner. His own fiction and poetry over the next decades propounded his belief in a philosophy of 'individualist anarchism'. He also was deeply involved in the struggle for homosexual rights during this era. He sympathised with men like Benedict FRIEDLÄNDER and Adolf BRAND who shared his antagonism to Magnus HIRSCHFELD's stress on the effeminate qualities of male homosexuals. Although he, too, loved teenaged males, he did not share Friedländer and Brand's belief that male–male love was superior to heterosexual love. Arguing from his individualist philosophy, Mackay believed that any love is right and true if it does not infringe on another's freedom.

From that ethic, but within the social context of anti-homosexual sentiment and legislation in Germany at that time, Mackay wrote a series of six works between 1905 and 1909 which he titled *Die Bücher der namenlosen Liebe* (*Books of the Nameless Love*). In view of German censorship laws, Mackay wisely used a pseudonym, 'Sagitta', and published the books abroad in one volume in 1913. The six works employ various genres (prose polemics, poetry, a one-act play and a novella) as they detail the path which a homosexual must travel in order to gain self-acceptance. Mackay hoped his works would inspire homosexual men to stand up for their love, an act that could lead to social and legal change. Instead, several of the *Bücher* were declared obscene and then confiscated, and having to sell them by subscription severely limited his readership.

Mackay reissued the complete *Bücher* in 1924, but still did not realise his dream of rallying his readers into action against anti-homosexual discrimination. Nevertheless, he made one final effort to create a fictional vision which might inspire his fellow homosexuals. *Der Puppenjunge: Die Geschichte einer namenlosen Liebe aus der Friedrichstrasse* (*The Hustler*, 1926)

stands as his most valiant and most artistically successful effort in his struggle.

This novel presents in fictionalised form and in a different situation the battle which Mackay waged with the authorities and which he lost. Hermann Graff falls in love with a 16-year-old prostitute, Günther Nielsen. Their relationship goes through many stages, but finally reaches the point where both can freely express the love they feel for each other. Günther's inherently trusting and essentially good nature is ruined by circumstances and by the bad influence of the friends he finds in Berlin's underworld. Hermann starts him on the way back to that original state, but society intervenes and ends the barely begun process.

As a work of fiction which opposes social and legal condemnation of such love, this novel affords its readers hope whereas the previous volume left them with only despair. These characters band together, creating a feeling of solidarity which enables them to resist the oppression society exerts upon them. Although Mackay never achieved the goal he set for his work as 'Sagitta', he hoped that a future time would see its success. In his will, he stated that any future publications of these works should also bear his true name. Since the early 1980s, thanks in large part to the critic and translator Hubert Kennedy, gay readers have discovered John Henry Mackay for their own time.

H. Kennedy, *Anarchist der Liebe: John Henry Mackay als Sagitta*, trans. A. Carstens, Berlin, 1988; T. A. Riley, *Germany's Post-Anarchist John Henry Mackay: A Contribution to the History of German Literature at the Turn of the Century, 1880–1920*, New York, 1972; K. H. Z. Solneman [Kurt Helmut Zube], *Der Bahnbrecher John Henry Mackay: Sein Leben und sein Werk*, Freiburg/Br., 1979.

James W. Jones

Mackenzie, Sir Edward (Montague) Compton (1883–1972), British writer. Son of well known actor/manager Edward

Compton and American actress Virginia Bateman, Mackenzie was born on theatrical tour at West Hartlepool, England. His sister also became an actress. One of the most prolific twentieth-century British writers, Mackenzie wrote more than 100 novels, plays, biographies and multi-volume autobiographical works, including the World War I reminiscences *Greece in My Life* (five volumes) and his ten-volume autobiography, *My Life and Times*. His early satirical works were highly successful, drawing praise from J. M. BARRIE, W. B. Yeats, Ford Madox Ford, Henry JAMES and F. Scott Fitzgerald.

Mackenzie attended Magdalen College, Oxford, where he founded a literary magazine and took a degree in modern history in 1904. After a brief flirtation with the stage, he turned to writing and, at 28, published his first novel, *The Passionate Elopement* (1911). Humour and satire characterized his early novels *Carnival* (1912) and *Sinister Street* (1913–1914), the latter a tale of Oxford, which Ford Madox Ford praised as 'a work of real genius' and which had a profound effect on its generation. During World War I, Mackenzie was commissioned into the Royal Marines, served in Australia and spent three years as a Secret Service agent in Greece. His memories of those years were recorded in *Greek Memories* (1932), for which he was accused of revealing too much about the secret service. He used his subsequent castigation, surveillance and trial under the Official Secrets Act for having exposed too much about British Intelligence, as fodder for his satirical novel *Water on the Brain* (1932).

Married three times, Mackenzie was apparently heterosexual but nevertheless wrote sympathetically on gay themes. In the 1920s, he wrote novels significant for their sympathetic treatment of lesbian characters in *Vestal Fire* (1927) and *Extraordinary Women* (1928), and in 1956 he produced a portrait of the lives of two gay men in *Thin Ice*.

A man of vast and varied interests and causes, Mackenzie wrote on topics ranging from Roman Catholicism to cats. An ardent Scottish nationalist, he lived in Scotland after 1928 and helped form the Scottish National Party. He served as rector of Glasgow University (1931–1934), as literary critic for the *Daily Mail* (1931–1935), as an early radio broadcaster and as founder-editor of *Gramaphone Magazine* (1923–1962). Mackenzie was named OBE in 1919 and knighted in 1952.

K. Young, *Compton Mackenzie* London, 1968.
                                            A. M. Wentink

Maecenas, Gaius (69/68–8 BC), Roman statesman and patron of literature. Gaius Maecenas was the descendant of an Etruscan family and belonged to the 'bourgeois' class of Roman knights. He was a friend and counsellor of Octavian (later Augustus) and was entrusted by him with the administration of Rome while Octavian fought with Pompey the Younger (38–36 BC). After the civil wars ended with Octavian's victory, Maecenas retired to private life while remaining an influential adviser during Augustus's reign.

Gaius Maecenas used his enormous wealth to create an artistic coterie of poets and writers of the first order, among them VIRGIL (70–19 BC), Horace and Propertius, all of whom he patronised and financed. The aim of his circle was twofold: to encourage the arts – Maecenas himself was a poet and refined connoisseur – and to orchestrate political propaganda in favour of Augustus; it succeeded in both goals. For this activity, Gaius Maecenas became such a symbol that a *maecenas* came to mean any intelligent and refined patron of the arts and artists.

Maecenas's love for his own sex was common knowledge in his time and in his own set, but it is today generally silenced. His best documented love was for a young pantomime actor and freed slave, Bathyllus; their relationship is discussed by Lucius Cornutus (*Commentary to Persius' 'Satirae'*, V. 123), Tacitus (*Annals*, I. 54) and Dio Cassius (*Roman History*, LV. 17), while Horace (*Epodon liber*, XIV. 10–15) even drew a parallel between his hetero-sexual love for Phrines and that of Ana-creon for another Bathyllus, as a coded homage to Maecenas's love. Maecenas's homosexual preferences were so notorious that after his death, an anonymous poet writing under the name of Virgil – although it could not be the famous Virgil, who died 11 years before Maecenas – wrote *Elegiae in Mecenatem* to defend his memory. In the first elegy (reprinted in *Minor Latin Poets*) he hints at the re-proaches of lax mores against Maecenas; he then says that any relaxation of stand-ards only came as a repose from hard-fought battles; finally, he adds that even Jove rested after his labours and kid-napped GANYMEDE to have him pour ambrosia for the besotted god. The accus-ation of Maeceneas's 'softness' was also taken up by Seneca (*Quaestiones natu-rales*, VII. 31).

With such a reputation in mind, one is not suprised to find a celebrated legend about Maecenas circulating in the Renais-sance: Maecenas was supposed to have given to VIRGIL a slave, Alexis, of whom he was enamoured. Virgil's love for Alexis was thus celebrated in his famous, and most homosexual, second eclogue. (In reality, classical sources indicate that Asin-ius Pollio, rather than Maecenas, gave the slave to Virgil.) References to this legend appear in Francesco BERNI's 'Capitolo di un ragazzo' ('A Chapter to obtain a boy') and Platino Plato's elegy 'Ad Mecenatem pro puero ducali' ('To Maecenas, to ob-tain a boy from the duke'), both written in order to obtain a page from their protector.

J. Wight Duff and A. M. Duff (eds) *Minor Latin Poets*, Cambridge, Mass., 1982.

Giovanni Dall'Orto

Magnus Eriksson (1316–1374), king of Sweden 1319–1364, of Norway 1319–1355, of Scania 1332–1360. Magnus was married to Countess Blanche of Namur in 1335, crowned in Stockholm in July 1336, excommunicated by Pope Innocent VI in 1358, and held a prisoner in Stockholm castle from 1365 to 1371. One of the most remarkable Swedish rulers, Magnus abolished thraldom in 1335, established national legislation, organised communi-cations and bought the province of Scania from Denmark in 1343 for 49,000 silver marks. Birgitta Birgersdotter (St Bridget) first supported Magnus, but later turned against him. The enormous Scanian ran-som forced Magnus to borrow from the church and nobility, increase taxes and confiscate noblemen's land. Magnus' debt to the Holy See provoked his excommuni-cation in 1358.

Leading families were vexed by the ad-vancement of Magnus' favourite, Bengt Algotsson, whom he made Duke of Fin-land and Halland and Stateholder of Scania. Duke Bengt was fiercely hated by the nobility and was slain in Scania in 1360. In a revelation written by Bridget in Rome in 1361, the Virgin Mary expresses her disappointment with Magnus's rule and exhorts Swedish noblemen to tell him: 'You have the foulest reputation that a Christian man can have, that you have had intercourse [*naturabland*] with men. We think it may be true, because you love men more than God or your own soul or your own wife.' Furthermore, Mary accuses Magnus of defying his excommunication by going to mass, 'robbing land and goods', and betraying the faithful Scani-ans. These accusations were repeated and spread by St Bridget's allies after Magnus's imprisonment in 1365. He remained a prisoner until peace was settled with his successor in 1371. Magnus spent his re-maining years with his son Haakon, king of Norway, until he drowned in a storm off the Norwegian coast.

Magnus's posthumous reputation was sombre. In *Libellus de Magno Erici rege* (fourteenth century), Bridget's accusations were repeated, and they were further elab-orated in a rhyme chronicle, *Förbindel-*

sedikten (fifteenth century). Johannes Magnus, the last Catholic archbishop of Sweden, thought Magnus worse than Caligula, Domitianus and Nero. After the Reformation, however, some positive judgements were passed. A king with such disastrous relations to the Vatican, it was said, could not be all bad. The tendency in contemporary history is to interpret Bridget's accusations as the stereotypical canon of evil characteristics that would be associated with a *rex iniquus*, and to emphasise Magnus's ability as a ruler. Duke Bengt's birthright has also been a bone of contention. If he were of humble origins, his advancement would be the more exceptional. Magnus's ancient nickname, Magnus Smek (literally, Magnus Caress), is explained in two ways. Those who wish to emphasise his possible perversion explain it as connected with his sexual practices, while those who want to downplay this possibility link it to his failure as a warlord.

J. Liliequist, 'State Policy, Popular Discourse, and the Silence on Homosexual Acts in Early Modern Sweden', *Journal of Homosexuality*, 35, 3/4 (1998); M. Nordberg, *I kung Magnus tid. Norden under Magnus Eriksson 1317–1374*, Stockholm, 1995.

Jens Rydström

Malmberg, Aino Emma Wilhelmiina (1865–1933), Finnish writer. The daughter of a Lutheran clergyman from the Finnish countryside, Malmberg studied English and humanities at the University of Helsinki as one of the first female university students in Finland. After graduation she worked as a college teacher, literary translator and, having moved to Britain in 1909, as a public lecturer and journalist. Malmberg had worked in the illegal movement promoting Finland's independence from Russia and, after having been arrested but released by the Russian police, she went into self-exile to London, where she continued her work for Finland's freedom. She gave public lectures on Finland's be-

half in Britain, and also travelled widely and gave lectures in the United States, including Hawaii.

Malmberg also published one novel and two collections of short stories. One of her short stories, 'Ystävyyttä' ('Friendship'), published in 1903, is a description of a spinster teacher couple. This couple consisted of a masculine and a feminine woman, which was typified later in the North American context as 'butch' and 'femme'. The sexologists of the late nineteenth century had often described this kind of female couple, as did many writers of *belles lettres*.

The Swedish author August STRINDBERG and many of his French male colleagues had published descriptions of 'lesbians', which are similar to Malmberg's depiction of the female couple. What is exceptional about Malmberg's short story is that this representation of a lesbian couple is written by a woman and so early. Malmberg's text is very playful and full of irony.

Malmberg married early, during her second year of study, which was exceptional in her time. The convention of the time required her to stay at home, at least after having given birth to a child one year later, but she continued her studies. After graduation, her career as a working academic mother continued, even though she had given birth to three children. Many of her choices in life were exceptional, and caused resentment. In 1909 she divorced her husband.

When Finland gained independence in 1917, the Finnish League of Women proposed Malmberg as Finland's ambassador to the United States. The time was not right for a woman ambassador in Finland, although the Ministry of Foreign Affairs unofficially paid her a minor reward in the 1920s for her activities in London. She had established very good connections with British high-level politicians and other important figures, and often succeeded much better than the official (male) diplomats, who used her connections.

In New York, where Malmberg lived in 1912–1913, 1915 and again in 1917–1918, she shared a flat with Rose Strunsky, a member of the Heterodoxy Club, a radical feminist club based in Greenwich Village, where Malmberg is known to have lectured. Strunsky and Malmberg had met in Finland in 1907 and remained close friends throughout the rest of their lives. Whenever Strunsky visited London for longer periods, she always stayed in Malmberg's flat.

The Malmberg collection in the Finnish National Archives contains much material about her political career and correspondence with authors whose books she translated into Finnish (e.g. Rudyard Kipling and George Bernard Shaw). But there are no diaries and very few personal letters from female friends, even though it is known from other sources that she had extensive correspondence with several of them. From the 25-year-long correspondence with Strunsky, there is only a single letter in the archives. Due to the lack of personal material, it is not possible to say anything about Malmberg's intimate relationships, whether with men or with women.

J. Schwarz, *Radical Feminists of Heterodoxy: Greenwich Village 1912–1940*, Norwich, 1986.

Kati Mustola

Mammen, Jeanne (1890–1976), German artist. Mammen was born in Berlin and spent the major part of her life there. She went to Paris as a child and studied art at the Académie Julian as well as in Brussels and Rome, and is best known for her graphics and painting during the 'Golden Twenties'. She was associated with the Neue Sachlichkeit (New Objectivity) and her graphic work for women's magazines such as *Die Dame* addressed the changing roles for women, particularly the *neue Frau* (New Woman). Her satirical work confronted the stereotypical image of the New Woman and explored the negative experiences of this period, including drug and alcohol abuse, prostitution, boredom and the poverty of many relationships.

In her fashion illustrations she showed the bobbed hair, boyish clothes and androgynous suits of the 'flappers'. In works such as *Masked Ball* (1932), Mammen documented the way that these conventions were exploited by fashionable urban lesbians to produce images of empowered women consciously using masquerade to challenge gender boundaries. She produced many studies of *Eldorado*, the underground nightlife of the lesbian and gay scene.

Between 1931 and 1932 she was commissioned to produce ten lithographs on lesbian love for Pierre LOUŸS's book *The Songs of Bilitis*, but the Nazis banned its publication and continued to harass her throughout the war. However, she continued to make art and after her death in 1976 the Jeanne Mammen Gesellschaft was set up in her Berlin studio.

Exhibition Catalogue, *Three Berlin Artists of the Wiemar Era: Hannah Höch, Käthe Kollwitz, Jeanne Mammen*, Des Moines, 1994; K. Sykora, 'Jeanne Mammen', *Women's Art Journal*, 9, 2 (1988–1989), 28–31.

Elizabeth Ashburn

Mann, Erika (1905–1969), German-Swiss-American journalist, travel writer, actor. Mann was the oldest of the six children of Katia and Thomas MANN, educated at the *Luisengymnasium* in Munich. After passing her school-leaving exams in 1924 she moved to Berlin to train as an actor. In the course of the next eight years she performed at theatres all over Germany, including Berlin, Bremen, Frankfurt, Hamburg and Munich.

Her most lasting close relationship was with her nearest sibling, Klaus MANN, who had been born a year after her, although the pair were frequently referred to as 'the twins'. Klaus was openly homosexual and a writer: in 1925 Erika and another 'famous daughter', Pamela Wedekind, played the lesbian title couple in his play *Anja und Ester* (*Anja and Ester*). The play was rubbished by the critics, but still stirred up a scandal, not least because of the two high-profile families involved.

The Hamburg production of *Anja and Ester* was directed by Gustaf Gründgens. Gründgens and Mann were married in 1926, and divorced in 1929. In the meantime, in 1927–1928, she set off on a round-the-world tour with her brother Klaus, and together they wrote the book of their journey, called *Rundherum: Ein heiteres Reisebuch* (*All the Way Round: A Light-Hearted Travel Book*, 1929). Soon after, they co-authored another travel book, the *Buch von der Riviera: Was nicht im Baedeker steht* (*The Book of the Riviera: Things You Won't Find in Baedeker's*, 1931, reprinted in 1989).

In 1932, in response to the alarming rise of National Socialism in Germany, Erika Mann founded a political cabaret, the Pfeffermühlentheater (Pepper Mill Theatre), in Berlin. Her collaborators in the project were the actress Therese Giehse, her lover, the composer Magnus Henning and Klaus Mann. The premiere on 1 January 1933 was a resounding success; but when the Nazis took power on 30 January further performances were rendered impossible. In March 1933 the Pfeffermühle moved into exile in Zurich. However, touring even in the countries around Germany grew increasingly difficult, and eventually the group abandoned Europe, attempting unsuccessfully to relaunch themselves in New York in January 1937. Giehse and Henning travelled back to Europe, but Mann decided to stay in the US, where she lectured on the National Socialist regime and attempted to expose its intentions and practices in books such as her *School for Barbarians: Education under the Nazis* (1938).

During the Spanish Civil War Erika and Klaus again set off together, this time to report on the situation in Spain. In 1940–1941 she lived briefly in London, working with the BBC, and acquired British citizenship through her arranged marriage to W. H. AUDEN. Her attempts to acquire US citizenship were thwarted, as in the McCarthy era she was considered politically suspicious; she eventually returned to Switzerland with her parents in 1952, settling in Kilchberg on Lake Zurich. There she worked with her father, Thomas Mann, as a translator of his lectures, wrote the screenplay for films of his novels and edited a collection of his letters for publication after his death in 1955.

Klaus Mann committed suicide in 1949, and Erika honoured his life in *Klaus Mann zum Gedächtnis* (*In Memory of Klaus Mann*, 1950). She died after an operation to remove a brain tumour on 27 August 1969. Her other writings include *Escape to Life* (1939) and *The Other Germany* (1940, both with Klaus Mann), *The Lights Go Down* (1940), and *Das letzte Jahr: Bericht über meinen Vater* (*The Final Year: An Account of my Father*, 1956).

I. von der Lühe, *Erika Mann: Eine Biographie*, Frankfurt a. M., 1993; C. Schöppmann (ed.) *Im Fluchtgepäck die Sprache: Deutschsprachige Schriftstellerinnen im Exil*, Berlin, 1991; R. Wall, *Lexikon deutschsprachiger Schriftstellerinnen im Exil 1933 bis 1945*, Freiburg i. Br., 1995.

Sarah Colvin

Mann, Klaus (1906–1949), German writer. Born the second of Thomas MANN's six children, Klaus Mann both used his father's reputation and suffered under it throughout his literary career. Schooled at home in Munich and in independently run, alternative schools, he never completed his formal education nor did he attend university. None of this held him back from becoming the representative author of the young generation that enjoyed the freedoms and excesses which Weimar democracy offered between 1919 and 1933.

Mann wrote quickly and easily. In his début year, 1925, he published a play, a novel and a collection of stories. Many (including at times he himself), criticise his fiction as being rather superficial in characterisation and clichéd in plot development, but most agree that he found a style that both revealed and spoke to his times. He lived through the most tumultuous years in German history and left Germany only weeks after the Nazis had come to power. He spent the rest of his life as an emigrant, at home everywhere and nowhere: during his lifetime he changed citizenship three times (German, Czech, American) and wrote in German and in English. An outgoing, but also rather hectic personality, he made acquaintances easily, had many amorous and sexual affairs, but never formed a long-lasting love relationship.

For most of his life, Mann was quite open about his homosexuality and never seems to have suffered pangs of guilt about it. He went into the closet in order to enlist in the US Army in 1943, and his autobiography, *The Turning Point* (1942), one of his most well known works, says nothing very openly about his love for men (although one does not need to read too deeply between the lines to find it). What role this played in his increasing alienation from the post-war world for which he had had such utopian hopes remains unclear. It is certain that his addiction to drugs (a long-time problem) and difficulty with his writing led to his suicide in Cannes in May 1949.

Gay and lesbian characters figure significantly in many of his plays and stories. *Anja und Esther* (*Anja and Esther*, 1925) put lesbian and gay relationships on the stage; *Treffpunkt im Unendlichen* (*Meeting Point in Infinity*, 1932) is one of several novels in which homosexual characters experience unrequited love or lead failed lives marked by alienation, drug addiction and other metropolitan woes. In his three works on men from the homosexual pantheon, however, his novels achieve greater artistic success even though none of these figures finds lasting happiness: *Alexander* (1932), concerning ALEXANDER the

Great: *Symphonie Pathétique* (1935), concerning TCHAIKOVSKY; and *Vergittertes Fenster* (*Barred Window*, 1937), concerning the Bavarian King LUDWIG II.

Perhaps Mann's most famous novel is *Mephisto* (1936). It follows the career of Hendrik Höfgen as he climbs the artistic hierarchy in Nazi Germany, selling out to the new order in order to save his skin and make himself a star on the Berlin stage. Based on the actor Gustaf Gründgens, who had been a friend of Mann's (and for a short time even his brother-in-law), the novel was banned for decades in West Germany because Gründgens was still a star and claimed that the book libelled him.

Although Mann produced a large body of fiction in the years 1925 to 1939, he seems to have found a true calling as essayist and editor from 1933 onwards. He devoted himself to the anti-fascist cause and co-founded two significant literary journals: *Die Sammlung* (*The Collection*, 1933–1935) and *Decision* (1941–1942). His essay on the homophobic attacks used by the left to discredit the Nazis, 'Homosexualität und Faschismus' ('Homosexuality and Fascism,' 1934), is often cited as a central gay text of the early 1930s. Mann wrote a major treatise on his French mentor, *André Gide and the Crisis of Modern Thought* (1943), as well as significant essays on other gay authors such as Walt WHITMAN and Jean COCTEAU.

Mann defended the 'other Germany' in exile and planned for its rebirth after the defeat of the Nazis. As an American soldier, he returned to his homeland in May 1945. He found very little to hope for; it seemed to him that the 12 years of National Socialism had changed Germans too deeply.

His unlived dreams of German democracy and European unity, along with his difficulty in writing and his addiction to drugs, certainly contributed to his desire to end his life. Mann was rediscovered by German gay critics and editors in the 1980s. As his works, diaries and letters have become available again, a fuller picture and deeper appreciation of Mann as in important figure in the history of both German letters and gay literature have developed.

G. Härle, *Männerweiblichkeit: Zur Homosexualität bei Klaus und Thomas Mann*, Frankfurt am Main, 1988; F. Kroll (ed.) *Klaus-Mann-Schriftenreihe*, vols. 1–5, Wiesbaden, 1976–1986; S. Zynda, *Sexualität bei Klaus Mann*, Bonn, 1986.

James W. Jones

Mann, Thomas (1875–1955), German writer. A man of complexities and contradictions, this perhaps greatest German writer of the twentieth century created both a literature and a life that alternately masked and revealed homosexual desire. The contradictions were clear from an early age. His father, a widely respected businessman and political figure in the North German port of Lübeck, expected his son to follow the path he had taken towards upper-middle-class success and respectability. Thomas had no interest in the world of his father, preferring the realm of the arts that his mother opened for him. Yet both his literature and his life can be seen as attempts to bridge the seemingly opposing identities of solid citizen and artist.

As a schoolboy, Mann experienced intense infatuations for two of his classmates, Armin Martens and Willri Timpe. They seem to have responded with, at best, an embrace and, at worst, bewilderment. These disappointments in youth set a pattern Mann would follow his entire life: experiencing love for another male from afar, finding pleasure and to some extent even fulfilment in being the lover, never the beloved, and then transforming that experience into literary art.

The love for Armin Martens served as the inspiration for Tonio Kröger's love for his best friend Hans Hansen in Mann's 1903 novella *Tonio Kröger*. There we read of the title character's longing for 'the blond-haired and the blue-eyed', untroubled by doubts as to whether they fit in or sorrow from unanswered yearning. A moment from Thomas's relationship with Timpe became a key scene in Mann's 1924 novel *Der Zauberberg* (*The Magic Mountain*). When the main character, Hans Castorp, borrows a pencil from a young schoolmate, the description infuses the exchange of the pencil with homosexual symbolism.

Mann felt 'that central experience of my heart when I was twenty-five' for Paul Ehrenberg, an artist who was two years younger than Mann. Decades later, Mann described his feelings during this four-year relationship as 'passionate love' and 'ecstatic happiness' followed by periods of 'self-disgust'. Whether that tumult of emotion, a response to society's rejection of homosexual love, led him to marriage because he lacked the courage to live out his desire or because he wanted to escape those feelings cannot be known definitively. We do know that he suddenly and ardently pursued Katia Pringsheim in 1904; they married the next year. That he genuinely loved her should not be doubted, but he himself noted in his diaries that he never felt for anyone the passion he had for Ehrenberg.

Their marriage provided him with the haven and stability from which he could continue to explore his favourite themes and desires. A 1911 family trip to Venice resulted in what is Mann's best-known work of 'gay literature', the 1912 novella *Der Tod in Venedig* (*Death in Venice*). The author, already the father of several children, became entranced by a 10-year-old Polish boy, Wladyslaw Moes, who served as the inspiration for the story's tale of a middle-aged German author, Gustav Aschenbach, who falls in love from afar with a beautiful Polish boy, Tadzio. The novella contains Mann's most poignant expression of that desire which could lead to the height of artistic achievement but never to an actual relationship between two males.

Although Mann was never a very good student, he became renowned for his erudition, which expressed itself not only in his lengthy novels but also in the many lectures he gave throughout Europe and the United States on the great figures of German cultural history (Goethe, Schiller, NIETZSCHE, FREUD.) He also found inspiration in men who now, like Mann himself, are counted among the pantheon of gay literature: Walt WHITMAN, André GIDE, Gore Vidal. In his fifties, he published important essays on marriage (1925) and the German poet August von PLATEN (1930). He defined marriage as a positive, society-building force in contrast to the creative, but ultimately socially destructive role he allotted to homosexuality. Platen's reputation had diminished, in part due to revelations of homosexual desire in his published diaries, but Mann read his poetry as great precisely because of that desire. Mann reached perhaps the peak of his life as 'representative' of 'German culture' when he was awarded the Nobel prize for literature in 1929.

In between those essays, Mann fell in love for the last time. The object of his affection was Klaus Heuser, the 17-year-old son of Mann's acquaintance Werner Heuser, an art historian. Although it did not last long, it marked for Mann a 'more mature, more controlled, happier' relationship than the one with Ehrenberg had been. Mann experienced a final moment of passionate desire for Franz Westermeier, a young man who waited on him during a stay at a Zurich hotel in 1950. While Heuser responded to Mann's affection, Westermeier seems to have been rather oblivious to the nature of the elderly man's feelings.

In his later novels, Mann also made use of these loves and attractions. His love for Paul Ehrenberg became transformed in *Doktor Faustus* (1947) into the relationship between the protagonist Adrian Leverkühn and his admirer Rudi Schwerdtfeger. The attraction to Franz Westermeier inspired passages in the final novel, *Die*

Bekenntnisse des Hochstaplers Felix Krull (*Confessions of Felix Krull, Confidence Man*, 1954).

The publication of his diaries in recent years has led to a more complete picture of Mann in terms of his homosexuality. Earlier, critics often tried to explain away the same-sex desire in his works, usually by claiming it was not really about 'sex' but was at most Platonic love. In addition, the image was created of the author being far removed from everyday life and even from his own family. Both views have had to be thoroughly revised. We now know, despite Mann's destruction of the diaries he kept up to 1918, of his life-long desires for other males and their importance for his life's work. We also know that he had several close friends who were homosexual and who helped shape his ideas on such varied topics as democracy and Friedrich Nietzsche. Nor did Mann always hide his desire. Katia knew full well of his infatuation in Venice and his eldest daughter, Erika, had to call him to task when his staring after the Zurich waiter became too blatant.

Complexities and contradictions marked his personal life as well as his fiction. His marriage lasted a half century and produced six children. The three eldest (Erika, Klaus, Golo) were all homosexual. He and Katia created a seemingly stable home-life and then were forced to recreate it over and over as they moved their family, including relatives, away from the Nazis, to Switzerland and then the United States. Both Thomas and Katia Mann took American citizenship in 1944 and fully intended to maintain their residence in the Los Angeles area for the rest of their lives, but the increasingly anti-communist, xenophobic mood of America in the late 1940s drove them, even though not communist, back to Kilchberg, Switzerland, where Mann died on 11 August 1955.

K. W. Böhm, *Zwischen Selbstzucht und Verlangen: Thomas Mann und das Stigma Homosexualität*, Würzburg, 1991; A. Heilbut, *Thomas*

Mann: Eros and Literature, New York, 1996; C. Koelb (ed. and trans.) *Thomas Mann: Death in Venice: A New Translation, Backgrounds and Contexts, Criticism*, New York, 1994.

James W. Jones

Marbod of Rennes (1035–1123), French cleric and poet. Born in Angers, Marbod was master of the cathedral school in Angers, then bishop of Rennes. Several of his poems speak of handsome boys and homosexual desire but reject physical relations. A poem speaking of 'the remarkable boy whose beauty sets me on fire' (translated by Thomas Stehling) is nevertheless titled 'An Argument Against Sexual Love' and another is 'An Argument Against Copulation Between People of Only One Sex'. John Boswell says that it is 'clear that the bishop did have a lover, to whom he sent an urgent demand to return from a distant city where he was on business if he wished Marbod to remain faithful to him, since strenuous efforts were being made to woo him away'.

Marbod's verses, like those of Baudri of Bourgueil (one of his students) and Hildebert of Lavardin (to whom Marbod dedicated a work), exemplify a tradition of medieval poetry which celebrated same-sex friendship while generally denouncing the wickedness of sexual relations.

T. Stehling (trans.) *Medieval Latin Poems of Male Love and Friendship*, New York, 1984; J. Boswell, *Christianity, Social Tolerance, and Homosexuality*, Chicago, 1980.

Robert Aldrich

Marées, Hans von (1837–1887), German painter. Born into a comfortable family in Dessau, Marées studied in Berlin and lived in Munich before moving, in 1864, to Italy, where he spent most of the rest of his life. In Rome, he met a German sculptor and architect, Adolf Hildebrand, ten years his junior. Thus began an eight-year romantic friendship, as Marées followed his protégé back to Germany and then they returned to live together to Italy; the relationship ended when Hildebrand fell in love with a woman.

Marées and Hildebrand worked together on the decorations of the Stazione Zoologica in Naples. The panels Marées painted show brawny semi-nude rowers, and handsome naked youths and men in an orange grove (a favourite subject of Marées), as well as German expatriates in a café. Generally interpreted as representing the union of Germany and Italy, the paintings symbolise the pilgrimage of northern artists to the cultural shrines of the Mediterranean. The sensual and sexual attractions of the south are also evident in the arcadian images. Several other works by Marées also include homoerotic allusions, notably a painting of *The Rape of Ganymede*.

Many artists from northern Europe, trained in the classics and aspiring to a neo-classical standard of academic beauty in their art, sought inspiration in Italy during the nineteenth century. Some, such as the Germans Friedrich Overbeck and Franz Pforr, who influenced Marées, were also linked by intimate friendship. Others found companions among the Italian youths in a society where sexual mores, and law codes, differed from those of the countries the Germans, Englishmen and Scandinavians left.

Marées himself died in Italy; Hildebrand later designed a museum constructed in his memory in Munich.

R. Aldrich, *The Seduction of the Mediterranean: Writing, Art and Homosexual Fantasy*, London, 1993; C. Lenz (ed.) *Hans von Marées*, Munich, 1987.

Robert Aldrich

Margherita d'Austria (or 'di Parma') (1522–1586), Italian noblewoman. The illegitimate daughter of the Holy Roman Emperor Charles V, Margherita was born in Oudenaarde and grew up in Brussels under the care of her aunt Margaret of Habsburg; from Belgium, she took her taste for Flemish art to the court of

Parma. She was first married, in 1536, to Duke Alessandro de' Médici; soon widowed, two years later she wed Ottavio Farnese, the nephew of Pope Paul III (Alessandro Farnese), who at 14 was two years younger than Margherita. Already during her first marriage, rumours of Margherita's aversion for men spread through Florence, and she wanted nothing to do with her second husband, whose approaches she rejected, in whose face she literally slammed her door, and whom she refused to see. The scandal quickly made the rounds of the Italian and other European courts and, until 1540, there was talk of the marriage being annulled since it had not yet been 'consummated'. Margherita explained her refusal to have sexual relations with her husband by saying that the Emperor had not ordered her to do so, nor had she promised it, having agreed only to share a bed with her husband. Ottavio rapidly became the butt of unkind ridicule; Pasquino, for instance, made up jokes about possible sexual combinations for the couple, including the scenario of Pope Paul entering their bedchamber to sodomise both of them.

Margherita's love for a noble lady of Siena, Laudomia Forteguerri, was remarked upon by her contemporaries. Agnolo Firenzuola, in his 'Dialogue on the Beauty of Women', explicitly referred to the relationship as an example of 'chaste and pure' love between women, but Pierre de Bourdelle did not hesitate to speak of the 'dissolute and lascivious' passion between Margherita and Laudomia. Margherita has a robust figure, wore 'masculine' fashion and liked hunting; Laudomia had participated actively in the defence of Siena when the city was besieged by the grand duke of Tuscany.

In 1543, for the sake of the dynasty, Margherita gave in to pressure and was officially reconciled with her husband; two years later she gave birth to twins, Alessandro and Carlo (the latter of whom died prematurely in 1549). Her social duties fulfilled, she afterwards again reduced contacts with her husband to a minimum and lived on various domains in the Abruzzi; for example, the city of Leonessa already by 1537 had become her personal fief. However, she did not withdraw from public life: in 1558 she began building the Farnese palace in Piacenzo, and the following year she was named regent of The Netherlands; in 1567 she became protector of the Aquila and in 1580 she once again served in the Low Countries. Only two years later did she retire to private life and settled in Ortona, a city in the Abruzzi which she purchased for 54,000 ducats. She devoted herself to wine-growing, and her wines were esteemed by all the principal European courts. One of the wines produced in Ortona is still called 'Farnese' in her honour, and all of the numerous places where she lived retain traces of 'Madama' Margherita, such as the Villa Madama, today the seat of the Italian Ministry of Foreign Affairs in Rome. The town of Castel Madama in the Roman hinterland, where Margherita made lengthy visits to the Castello Orisno, each July hosts the 'Madama Margherita' *palio* (horse race). Margherita died in 1586 and was buried, as she had requested, in Piacenza.

P. de Bourdeille (*seigneur* de Brantome), *Le Dame galanti*, Milan, 1982; A. Firenzuola, *Opere scelte*, Turin, 1957; R. Levevfre, '*Madonna' Margarita d'Austria*, Rome, 1986.

Maria Di Rienzo

Marlowe, Christopher (1564–1593), English dramatist and poet. Marlowe was born the son of a Canterbury shoemaker, but the openness of the English universities of the time took the young Marlowe to Corpus Christi College, Cambridge, where he may have written his first play, *Dido, Queen of Carthage*. This did not, however, bring him the employment in a noble household that his humanist education had prepared him for, and he appears to have been employed in the obscure underworld of government spies. He was also delated to the authorities as a dangerous character and was to die in a tavern brawl.

His plays and poems appear to have been as disturbing to his own time as they have proved to be since, and homosexuality figures centrally in them. *Dido* opens with the provocative spectacle of the god Jupiter dandling his catamite GANYMEDE on his knee, and in Marlowe's poem *Hero and Leander*, the passion of Neptune for the naked Leander swimming the Hellespont is as sensual (and as comic). Marlowe's play *Edward II* is the most revealing view left by the sixteenth century of the place homosexuality occupied in the England of his time. The subject of the play is the fall and eventual murder of the fourteenth-century English king EDWARD II, the first beginning of which was his passion for his lover Piers Gaveston. The plot has an historical basis, but the conventions of the play are those of Marlowe's own time rather than the fourteenth century, and it is these that the play illumines. The critics who have written of the apparently openly 'homosexual' nature of the play have not, though, grasped the extent to which the intense emotion, the passionate language and the embraces we see between these two men had parallels in the conventions of friendship between men in Marlowe's England, where homoeroticism, jokingly suggested (and as lightly denied), was the stuff of everyday life. Shakespeare's Sonnets are only the most enduring product of that easy homoeroticism.

The radical difference to be seen in Marlowe's *Edward II* is that there, such gestures are given a weight Marlowe's contemporaries were rarely prepared to accord them, most shockingly in the hideous sodomitical murder of Edward at the end of the play. Yet Edward's murder is at the hands of a man called Lightborne, whose name is an anglicised version of Lucifer, the father of all lies. In *Edward II* Marlowe describes what could be a sodomitical relationship, but places it within the conventions of the masculine friendship of his time, in a tension that he never allows to be resolved.

Marlowe's oblique view of homosexuality has been explained in biographical terms, on the basis of an apparently outspoken defence of homosexuality attributed to Marlowe by a certain Richard Baines that reached the eyes of the authorities at the time of Marlowe's death. The problem with this explanation is that this was a charge that others similarly on the edge of society were also ready to make. The radical religious reformer Henry Barrow (who was executed in 1593) also claimed that the conventions of masculine friendship were a cover for sodomy; and Philip Stubbes, the enemy of the theatres, made the same charge against the theatres' transvestite conventions. Such claims turned to their own use the weight that was attached in Marlowe's England to the vaguely defined sin of 'sodomy': that it represented a potential for chaos and disorder that was easily associated with disorder in other spheres also. It was because radicals like Philip Stubbes or Henry Barrow were the enemies of the theatres or the established order that they were ready to see in them the sodomy that others were reluctant to name.

It was a dangerous claim, for those who made it and for those it was directed against; but when its intended object was sufficiently vulnerable it could all too easily take hold. It was this largely unspoken uncertainty in the conventions of masculine friendship that Marlowe's *Edward II* held up so frighteningly to its audience. SHAKESPEARE's Sonnets are a brilliant testimony to the extent to which the masculine friendship of his time, that flower-strewn world of Renaissance friendship between men, could be protected from a charge of sodomy; Christopher Marlowe's *Edward II* is a reminder of how vulnerable that protection was.

J. Goldberg, *Sodometries*, Stanford, 1992; A. Bray, 'Homosexuality and the Signs of Male

Friendship in Elizabethan England', *History Workshop Journal*, 29 (Spring 1990): 1–19.

Alan Bray

Martial (Marcus Valerius Martialis) (*c.* 39–41 to *c.* 104), Latin epigrammatist. Martial was born in the ancient Spanish town of Bilbilis (near modern Calatayud) of parents wealthy enough to afford for their son the standard Roman grammatical and rhetorical education, which included Greek. Like talented or ambitious provincials at all times, he moved to the metropolis, Rome, in 64, where he lived and prospered as a poet, first under the patronage of the Senecas and then other wealthy benefactors; he acquired an estate at Nomentum, presumably a gift, and later a townhouse, and was made an honorary military tribune, a position that entailed wealth. He first came to prominence in 80 with a book of epigrams known as *Liber de spectaculis*, marking the 100 days of 'games' the Emperor Titus held to open the still-incomplete Colosseum and to glorify the Flavian dynasty. *Xenia* and *Apophoreta* (now Books XIII and XIV) followed in 84 or 85, collections of distichs, the first commemorating gifts (*xenia*) of food and drink and the second other presents given to parting guests (*apophoreta*). Between 85 and 101 he issued 12 further books of epigrams, becoming a leading poet of his day. His flattery of DOMITIAN, which reached its zenith in Book X, brought him imperial favour. As it happened, Domitian was assassinated in 96, necessitating a revision of Book X in 98. Martial did not fit into the new, more austere order and judged it politic to retire to his birthplace in Spain, where he lived on a pleasant and productive estate provided by a wealthy patroness, Marcella. Whatever the pleasures and benefits of prosperous rural retirement, he missed the bustle and cut and thrust of life in Rome. His death, around 104, is reported in a letter of his friend, the younger Pliny.

Possessed of immense technical competence and intimate familiarity with the Graeco-Roman literary tradition, Martial was mordant and bitchy, and relentlessly exposed the foibles and failings of his contemporaries. The account of the sexual doings and habits of Flavian Rome that his verses provide is the most detailed, the most nuanced of any period in history before our own. It is these poems that gained the poet his reputation for obscenity (hence, after greatly influencing the development of English poetry in the seventeenth century, the decline in his critical esteem from the eighteenth century until the 1980s). Martial had other moods and wrote other kinds of epigrams. Apart from the poems of flattery, which were the price of the patronage that sustained him, there are epigrams describing the good life, celebrating friends and friendship, and giving thanks for recovery from illness. Others examine patronage and gift-giving and discuss the book trade. There are, too, poems of a more personally revealing nature, moving epitaphs for favourite boys, and accounts of the qualities he looks for or appreciates in a boyfriend.

Poems such as these last leave us in little doubt that his primary sexual orientation was homosexual; he responded to male beauty, and desired the affectionate company and attentions of and sex with younger men, though he speaks of occasional encounters with women. It seems highly unlikely that he was married, despite a few references to a wife. In the circles in which he moved, it did not matter, for men, whether one preferred one's own sex or the other or both, and he makes it known that he preferred his own.

J. P. Sullivan, *Martial, the Unexpected Classic: A Literary and Historical Study*, Cambridge, 1991, and *The Classical Heritage: Martial*, New York, 1993.

Gary Simes

Martin du Gard, Roger (1881–1958), French writer. Martin du Gard must be one of the least known French winners of the Nobel prize for literature (1937). His bisexuality is a fact even less well known, not least because the main source of information for his life, the *Souvenirs auto-biographiques et littéraires* which he compiled for the first volume of the collected edition of his work (1955), gives no hint of it. The works on which his reputation was established, his documentary novel about the Dreyfus Affair, *Jean Barois* (1911), and his novel cycle *Les Thibault* (1922–1940), are concerned with the ways in which the broader movements of history and the destiny of individuals interlock. Although there are a few timid references to homosexuality in *Les Thibault*, the part reserved in such works for any kind of sexuality is quite small.

Martin du Gard was a close friend of André GIDE, sharing some of his sexual interests but much more cautious about revealing such interests even in the apparently tolerant atmosphere of Paris in the 1920s. Martin du Gard, like Gide a married man (since 1906) though rather more happily so, firmly advised Gide against public confession of his sexual orientation and suppressed all autobiographical reference to his own. None the less he was the author of a play, *Un Taciturne* (1931), which centres on the impossible passion of an older man for a young male protégé. Despite the fact that the hero commits suicide without ever declaring himself, the play raised much critical and public outrage, a factor which appeared to justify Martin du Gard's own timidity. In the 1940s and 1950s, while working on *Mémoires du lieutenant-colonel Maumort*, he compiled a substantial dossier on homosexual issues with the intention of showing that it was a natural condition. Yet even then, he felt that this precluded the publication of the novel during his lifetime; at most he envisaged a private publication of selected chapters relating to sexual education. The key section, the narration of the relationship between a young junior army officer, Xavier de Balcourt, and a 17½-year-old baker's boy, is a classic tale of ill-fated passion – the boy is drowned while trying to swim across a river to see his lover – and has no ostensible biographical applications. But the lyricism with which adolescent male bodies are invoked is itself revealing enough. Martin du Gard decreed that the novel, which in fact was never finished, should only appear posthumously; it was first published in 1983.

D. Boak, *Roger Martin du Gard*, Oxford, 1963; C. Robinson, *Scandal in the Ink*, London, 1995.
Christopher Robinson

Massimi (or Massimo), **Pacifico** (also known as Pacifico d'Ascoli) (1400–*c*. 1500), Italian writer. It would be pointless to search for references to Massimi in the history of Italian literature, not only because he wrote in Latin, but particularly because his most important work, the *Hecatelegium*, published in 1489, was of such frankness concerning homosexuality that it may be considered unique. What other Renaissance poet dared to admit openly that he had practiced passive sodomy? Massimi's uncompromising verses condemned him to ostracism by literary historians.

According to the study by Carmelo Calì (the only available source), Massimi was born in Ascoli to a noble and wealthy family which had been exiled for political reasons. He led an adventurous life, though never succeeding in obtaining the permanent position at court to which he aspired. Returning from exile in 1426, Massimi married and fathered three children. Again exiled from 1445 to 1448, he served in the army of the king of Naples. In 1452 he was able to return to Ascoli, where he remained for six years, only to be exiled anew for political sedition; his estate was also confiscated. By 1459, having abandoned his wife (the object of violent poems), he was a law student in Perugia, where he also gained a reputation as a Latin poet and secured employment. In 1476, he was invited to Rome by Pope SIXTUS IV but, failing to obtain employment, moved to Lucca, where he taught poetry, rhetoric, Greek and Latin. In 1489, Massimi went to Florence, where he was able to get his book published and earned his living as private tutor; later he moved to Fano, where he died. His epitaph says that he worked as a lawyer and reached the age of 80, though he may have been almost a centenarian at his death.

Massimi applied to Latin poetry the taste for erotic *double entendre* which is found in Italian fifteenth-century verse; so deft was he that when an expurgated edition of the *Hecatelegium* was published in 1691 in Parma, a number of cases of *double entendre* escaped the censors. Homosexual themes also appear in some 20 unpublished epigrams and verse letters (now held by the national library in Venice). Massimi was notorious as a sodomite during his own life, admitting that when he walked in the streets, boys touched their ear in a gesture – still used today – to indicate a 'poof'. In a 1501 letter, Machiavelli listed Massimi among poets who would have been burned at the stake as sodomites in Rome were it not for the protection of powerful cardinals.

Only the least compromising verses of the *Hecatelegium* were reprinted; the only complete edition, published in Paris in 1885, was limited to 150 copies. An edition by Juliette Desjardins and the partial translations included in James Wilhelm's anthology nevertheless have allowed readers to discover a poet whose homosexual work is both extraordinarily explicit and extraordinarily rich in information about the private and social life of a Renaissance sodomite.

C. Calì, *Pacifico Massimi e l'*Hecatelegium, Catania, 1896; P. Massimo d'Ascoli, *Hecatelegium*, ed. J. Desjardins, Grenoble, 1986; J. Wilhelm (ed.) *Gay and Lesbian Poetry: An Anthology from Sappho to Michelangelo*, New York, 1995: 290–302.

Giovanni Dall'Orto

Mathebula, Nongoloza (Jan Note) (1867–

1948), South African gang leader. Nongoloza was the founder and leader of the Regiment of the Hills – a network of gangsters who operated on the peripheries of Johannesburg during the 1890s. In 1912, after spending extensive periods in prison, Nongoloza gave testimony to Jacob de Villiers Roos, the Director of Prisons in the Transvaal province of South Africa. Through this testimony he revealed the workings of his gang. He maintained that 'even when we were free on the hills south of Johannesburg some of us had women and others had young men for sexual purposes'. The gang was renamed the Ninevites in the mid-1890s and, as 'King of the Ninevites', Note issued a decree that forbade physical contact with women. He introduced a system whereby the men of his regiment took boy-wives from amongst their ranks. This practice meant that the Ninevites became closely associated with homosexuality. The reputation was extended to the prison system, where the rituals associated with same-sex unions were replicated by the Ninevites during the long spells that the gang members spent in South African gaols. The contemporary '28 Gang', whose influence remains strong in South African prisons, is modelled closely on the Ninevites. The slang word 'Nongoloz', used to this day, loosely translates as 'sodomite'.

C. Van Onselen, *The Small Matter of a Horse: The Life of 'Nongoloza' Mathebula, 1867–1948*, Johannesburg, 1984; A. Achmat, 'Apostles of Civilised Vice: Immoral Practices and Unnatural Vice in South African Prisons and Compounds, 1890–1920', *Social Dynamics*, 19 (1993): 92–110.

Graeme Reid

Mayne, Xavier (pseudonym of Edward Irenaeus Prime-Stevenson) (1868–1942), American writer. Xavier Mayne was the first American author to write an openly gay novel. He was the youngest of five children born in New Jersey to a Presbyterian minister and a schoolmistress. He was educated in the classics and passed the State Bar, but evidently never practised law. Instead he became a writer of fiction, poetry and music criticism. During the 1880s and 1890s, he served as literary reviewer and music critic for prominent publications like *Harper's* and the New York *Independent*. At age 19, he began publishing popular 'boy's books' such as *White Cockades* (1887) and *Left to Themselves* (1891), both of which extol intense, homoerotically tinged friendships between adolescent males. As a notable author, Prime-Stevenson's name was included in the first edition of *Who's Who in America* (1899–1900).

In 1901 Prime-Stevenson emigrated to Europe and began addressing homosexuality directly in his writings, albeit in the guise of 'Xavier Mayne'. In 1906 his novel *Imre: A Memorandum* was privately printed in Naples. *Imre* was the first novel by an American to deal with homosexuality positively and openly, and not as some unspeakable secret leading to an inevitable suicide. The story recounts a budding romance in Budapest between two masculine men: the narrator Oswald, a cultivated Englishman 'past thirty', and Imre von N . . . , a blond Hungarian lieutenant of 25. The pair first meet in an outdoor café and fall into a discussion of their common musical and literary interests. What follows is an early prototype for what would much later become the standard plot for 'coming out' literature. Psychological tensions build as their friendship mutually deepens and sexual preferences are speculated about. The pair eventually come out to each other and unite in 'the friendship which is love, the love which is friendship' at the story's unprecedented happy conclusion. The tone of the work is quite cerebral, with numerous poetic citations from August von PLATEN and BYRON. Modern readers may find the plot contrived and the flowery prose quite unnatural in this gem of art nouveau literature, but *Imre* functions as a veritable time capsule of the *fin de siècle*,

giving insights into the artistic, musical and literary tastes of cultivated gay men a century ago, as well as describing the social persecutions they endured.

Imre apparently evolved from a case history recorded later in Mayne's ponderous sexological treatise *The Intersexes: A History of Similisexualism as a Problem in Social Life* (1908), also privately printed in Naples. It was an impassioned defence of homosexuality from a scientific, legal, historical and personal perspective. A unique contribution to homosexual studies, it offered English translations of hitherto untranslated European research, chiefly the findings of Karl Heinrich ULRICHS, Magnus HIRSCHFELD and Richard von KRAFFT-EBING. Although a valuable document, *Intersexes* has been criticised for its length, sloppy editing and outdated theoretical debates. It offered nothing new scientifically, although Mayne clearly disagreed with Ulrichs's original theory that 'Uranians' (gay males) were almost always accompanied by feminine attributes. Showing that he was not immune to the prejudices of the times, Mayne stressed the masculine element in gay relationships and shunned 'passive sodomists' whom he misogynously described as 'womanish' degenerates. He also revealed himself to be still very much trapped in the prudery of the nineteenth century, when bodily relationships had been de-emphasised. He chastely disavowed the need for anal intercourse or 'buccal onanism' (oral sex) during man-to-man lovemaking, stressing that a mere physical embrace, even partially clothed, was frequently sufficient to achieve orgasm.

Prime-Stevenson published a collection of short stories under his true name titled *Her Enemy, Some Friends, and Other Personages* (1913), many of which were poignant accounts of gay love among the upper class. One of these stories, 'Out in the Sun', provides a detailed inventory of a gay man's library and shows which books were coded lavender a century ago. Prime-Stevenson's literary production dwindled in later life and he died of a heart attack in Lausanne, Switzerland. His obituary in the *New York Times* credited him as an author and music critic, but predictably made no reference to his homosexual contributions. Fortunately, his legacy as 'Xavier Mayne' has been preserved in reprinted editions from Arno Press.

N. I. Garde, 'The First Native American *Gay* Novel', *One Institute Quarterly: Homophile Studies*, Spring 1960: 185–90 N. I. Garde, 'The Mysterious Father of American Homophile Literature', *One Institute Quarterly: Homophile Studies*, Fall 1958: 94–8; J. Gifford, *Daynesford's Library: American Homosexual Writing, 1900–1913*, Amherst, 1995; M. J. Livesey, *From This Moment On: The Homosexual Origins of the Gay Novel in America*, Ph.D. thesis, University of Wisconsin, 1997.

Seán Henry

Mead, Margaret (1901–1978), American anthropologist. From the 1928 publication of her first field observations in *Coming of Age in Samoa*, Mead was widely known for using accounts of 'primitive' cultures to show alternatives to American assumptions – particularly about the 'naturalness' of race, gender and sex stratification, and about the universality of child-rearing practices. She was a student at Columbia University of Franz Boas (1858–1942), who was the major institutionaliser of anthropology in North America and was also an implacable critic of racial explanations of cultural phenomena. Mead popularised cultural relativism from the American Museum of Natural History in New York City, where she spent her entire career.

Married three times, Mead maintained a very close working and sexual relationship with Boas's chosen successor, Ruth BENEDICT (1887–1948). After Benedict's death and Mead's final divorce, her primary working and emotional relationships were with other women, although men were also included in the quasi-family she fostered. Posthumous confirmation of her

bisexuality by her daughter, Mary Catherine Bateson, has left open questions about sexual relations with other, still-living women. During her lifetime, Mead never publicly acknowledged having sexual relations with women. Indeed, although she wrote two books about Benedict, Mead's many autobiographical writings emphasised her roles as daughter, wife and mother.

In her early work, especially *Sex and Temperament* (1935), Mead fostered the impression that gender was infinitely malleable. But in her 1949 book *Male and Female*, she explicitly recognised considerable biological constraints on cultural patterning of gender differences and both the range and expression of individual psychologies.

A pioneer in team ethnography and in the use of photography, Mead was very concerned with enhancing the objectivity of reports of behaviour in various cultures. At the same time Mead proclaimed analyses of American culture based mostly or entirely on her intuitions as a native. As is generally the case with popularisers, her reputation outside her profession of anthropology was greater than within it. Even recent revelations as to the accuracy of some of her early observations have failed to dent this reputation.

M. C. Bateson, *Through a Daughter's Eyes*, New York, 1984; S. Long and J. Borneman, 'Power, Objectivity, and the Other: The Creation of Sexual Species in Modernist Discourses', *Dialectical Anthropology*, 15 (1990): 285–314; M. Mead, *Blackberry Winter*, New York, 1972.

Stephen O. Murray

Medici, Ferdinando II de' (1610–1670), fifth grand-duke of Tuscany. No great events of note marked Ferdinando II's reign, and he has gone down in history as a weak and incompetent ruler. Yet he practised the only possible political strategy at a time when a regional state such as Tuscany had become too small to face up to the great nation-states which were dividing both power in Europe and domination over Italy: a policy of 'equidistance' as Tuscany shifted between Spain, France and the Holy Roman Empire. A period which historians have prejudicially characterised as one without major developments was, in reality, one without war, though an epoch culturally suffocated by the Counter-Reformation.

From a sexual point of view, the sovereign did his duty: in 1635 he married his cousin Vittoria Della Ròvere and produced two sons who survived him. Otherwise, his preferences ran towards men, and were well known at the time. Luigi Gualtieri recorded a number of different anecdotes relating to his sexual behaviour. For instance, on one winter's evening, his mother brought to Ferdinando a list of sodomites whom she thought ought to be punished by the state; Ferdinando objected that the list was incomplete, and wrote his own name on it. When his mother insisted that the sodomites should be burned at the stake, he threw the list into the fireplace and said, 'They are hereby burned just as you condemned them.'

Marital relations with his wife were interrupted when she once entered Ferdinando's bedroom unannounced and found him making love to his page, Bruto Della Molara. When Vittoria tried to punish him by sulking, he reacted by breaking off all sexual relations with her (a state of affairs which lasted for 18 years). When she tried to intimidate him by asking the priest of the church of San Lorenzo (where Ferdinando attended mass) to preach a fiery sermon denouncing sodomy, according to gossip reported by Gualtieri, the grandduke ordered Bruto to take a gift to the priest in order to seduce him. Bruto acquitted himself of the task and the priest called on Ferdinando to thank him for the gift, whereupon the grand-duke told the priest he knew about Bruto's feat. The terrified Jesuit fled Florence, victim to one of the first cases of 'outing' in history.

It is noteworthy that Ferdinando and Bruto had a long-lasting relationship to such an extent that Bruto left his service as page only at the age of 36.

H. Acton, *The Last Medici*, London, 1938 and 1958; G. Dall'Orto, 'I Médici visti da dietro', *Babilonia*, 100 (May 1992): 65–7; [L. Gualtieri], *Storia della nobile e reale famiglia de' Medici*, published as L. Ombrosi, *Vita dei Médici sodomiti*, Milan, 1965, and translated by H. Acton, *The Last of the Medici*, Florence, 1930.

Giovanni Dall'Orto

Medici, Giovanni Gastone (Gian Gastone) de' (1671–1737), grandson of Ferdinando II de' Médici and last sovereign ruler of the Médici dynasty (reigned 1723–1737).

As the second son of the grand-duke, Gian Gastone was not expected to inherit the throne until, in 1713, his elder brother Ferdinando died without heirs. Until then Gian Gastone had just profited from his brother's great patronage of music to develop relationships – not limited to artistic ones – with musicians such as Baldassarre Galuppi ('Il Buranello', 1706–1785) and singers like the celebrated castrato Gaetano Majorano ('Il Caffarelli', 1710–1783). For dynastic reasons, in 1697, Gian Gastone had been married to a Germano-Bohemian princess, but they produced no offspring.

Already by 1699 he had scandalously begun to spend much of his time away from his wife, in Prague, where his lackey Giuliano Dami procured ever-changing lovers for him from among the city's students and servants. Dami, himself a homosexual, was born in 1683, the son of peasants. Gian Gastone had noticed him because of his exceptional beauty, which had already attracted Marquess Ferdinando Capponi, who agreed to 'cede' Dami to Gian Gastone.

In 1705, Gian Gastone left his wife and returned to Florence, where he acceded to the throne on the death of his father, Cosimo III, in 1723. Without heirs, however, he witnessed the European powers dividing his realm even during his own lifetime.

During the first part of his rule, he demonstrated a capacity to make audacious political changes; for example, to abolish public executions, to disband the political police and to expel the Jesuits from the Tuscan state. But seeing his throne disputed among foreign powers, he grew discouraged, lost his initiative and spent his remaining years pursuing his own interests, abandoning himself to his eccentricities, especially sexual ones, and occupying himself little if at all with the tasks of government. Dami served as his accomplice and factotum during these years, amassing a considerable fortune in doing so.

Dami was on a constant quest for new lovers for Gian Gastone. Those who particularly pleased him, nicknamed *ruspanti* (from the name of a coin, the *ruspo*), were awarded an annuity; at the grand-duke's death, they numbered 350 people (including four women). Luigi Gualtieri (whose work Harold ACTON draws on, though with much prudishness) recounts an impressive number of anecdotes about Gian Gastone's homosexual proclivities. He mentions Gian Gastone's penchant for 'scat' and for 'verbal abuse' – while having sexual relations, he liked to have himself called not '*Altezza Reale*' ('Royal Highness') but '*Altezza Realona*' ('Fat Queen').

On the death of Gian Gastone, the grand-duchy of Tuscany fell under the control of the Lorena branch of the Habsburg dynasty. Trying to present themselves as a dynasty which governed better than their predecessors, the Lorena did everything possible to show the last Médici sovereign in a bad light. Treated as a person of disgraceful reputation, Gian Gastone was buried behind an altar in a hidden corner of the crypt housing the Medici tombs in the church of San Lorenzo in Florence, thus depriving the final Medici ruler of a monumental sepulchre in the grand upstairs chapel. A bust of him stands beside the upper entrance to the Uffizi Museum in Florence.

H. Acton, *The Last Medici*, London, 1932 and

1958; A. Bruschi, *Gian Gastone: Un trono di solitudine nella caligine di un crepuscolo*, Florence, 1995; G. Dall'Orto, 'I Medici visti da dietro', *Babilonia*, 100 (May 1992): 65–7; [Luigi Gualtieri], *Storia della nobile e reale famiglia de' Médici*, published as L. Ombrosi, *Vita dei Médici sodomiti*, Milan, 1965; D. Fernandez, *Le Dernier des Médicis*, Paris, 1994.

Giovanni Dall'Orto

Meleager (first century BC), Hellenistic poet and philosopher. Meleager was a native of Gadara in Syria, one of those eastern territories which adopted Greek language and culture following the conquests of ALEXANDER of Macedon. Meleager was trilingual, speaking Greek, Syrian and Phoenician. He flourished about 100 BC, living most of his life in Tyre but retiring to the island of Cos in his old age. His philosophical (Cynic) discourses are lost, but he is chiefly remembered for his amatory epigrams – short poems written in a metre of elegiac couplets and addressed to a variety of lovers, both male and female.

Meleager was, it seems, the first person to compile a collection of poems by various poets. Known as the *Garland of Meleager*, its preface identified each poet with a flower – hence the term 'anthology' (literally, 'flower-gathering'). The *Garland* has not been preserved in its entirety, but substantial extracts (including Meleager's own poems) are found in a much later (and larger) collection known as the Greek Anthology.

Meleager's desire was directed towards men and women in almost equal measure. The epigrams addressed to young men are included in a separate book (12) of the Greek Anthology known as STRATO's *Musa Puerilis* (*Muse of boy-love*). Strato of Sardis, the compiler of this section, lived during the reign of the Emperor HADRIAN. He himself wrote love poems, exclusively about boys. He included many of his own epigrams in the collection, as well as pederastic verse by others, such as Asclepiades of Samos (flourished 300–270 BC), chief developer of the genre, and

Rhianus of Crete (born around 275 BC), though the latter was better known in antiquity as a Homeric scholar and writer of epic poetry.

The writers of epigram aimed at elegance and (often witty) refinement of expression. Meleager has frequent recourse to mythology and conceit (in the Elizabethan sense). He worries that Zeus will seize his 'GANYMEDE' (12. 65); Myiscus (one of his boys) is 'a sun whose blaze extinguishes the stars' (12. 59). The coupling of such a style with addresses to so many lovers has prompted the charge that literary artifice has eclipsed feeling. But in a significant minority of poems Meleager seems to touch a sincere vein of romantic emotion. He speaks of separation from one lover as being robbed of 'half my soul' (12. 52). Of another he declares: 'If I gaze upon Theron, I see all things. But if I behold all things, yet see him not, then again I see nothing' (12. 60). Strato, on the other hand, often deals directly with physical desire and sexual activity. Thus, on seeing Cyris: 'You have brought your gorgeous loins to rest against the wall, Cyris. Why make a pass at the stone? It can do nothing' (12. 213). Along with more conventional epigrams hymning beauty in boys, Strato can with equal elegance and directness compare the shape of their cocks (12. 3, see also 12. 207) or praise french kissing (12. 183), or the pleasure of a threesome in bed (12. 210).

A selection of poems from the Greek Anthology is available in translation in *The Penguin Book of Homosexual Verse*, edited by Stephen Coote (1983).

D. H. Garrison, *Mild Frenzy: A Reading of the Hellenistic Love Epigram*, Wiesbaden, 1978.
Clifford Hindley

Melville, Herman (1819–1891), American novelist. Forgotten during his lifetime and for decades after his death, Herman Melville is today regarded as one of the major American writers of the nineteenth century. In more recent years, Melville's work has been the subject of several critical studies that argue convincingly for a gay subtext in much of his work.

Melville was born into an upper-middle-class family in New York City. The failure of his father's import business and his untimely death when Melville was 13 were followed by years of difficulty for the family, and at the age of 20 Melville signed on as a cabin boy on a transatlantic merchant ship. He subsequently joined the crew of a whaler and later enlisted in the United States Navy, experiencing during the period 1841–1844 a series of exotic adventures in the South Pacific.

After his return to New York, Melville wrote several critically and commercially successful novels: *Typee* (1846), *Omoo* (1847), *Mardi* (1849), *Redburn* (1849), and *White Jacket* (1850). Married in 1847 and eventually the father of four, Melville moved his family to the Berkshire hills of Western Massachusetts in 1850. It is there that he wrote his masterpiece, *Moby Dick* (1851).

Melville's sprawling, symbolic epic was not well received, and he never again achieved the popular success of his earlier novels. Another work of fiction, *Pierre* (1852), and a long poem, *Clarel* (1876), figure among his other major writings, along with the short novel *Billy Budd*, not published until 1924 and now considered second to *Moby Dick* in his *œuvre*. Melville eventually worked for 19 years as a federal customs inspector for the port of New York City, where he eventually died.

Melville began to receive increased critical attention in the 1920s, and several psychoanalytic studies of his life appeared in the post-World War II years. Although there has been much conjecture regarding the precise nature of his relationship with the novelist Nathaniel Hawthorne (their close friendship suffered an abrupt, unexplained rupture in 1852), Melville's writings provide the best case for including him in the gay literary canon.

Homoerotic overtones in the early seafaring novels are unmistakable, from extended descriptions of the male beauty of the South Sea islanders to romanticised depictions of sailor friends and comrades on board ship. In *Moby Dick*, male bonding is notable in the 'marriage bed' episode involving Ishmael and Queequeg, as well as in the intensely erotic and metaphoric 'Squeeze of the Hand' chapter describing the camaraderie of sailors extracting spermaceti from a dead whale.

Billy Budd, written at the very end of Melville's life, is both the most explicit and sombre of his writings in terms of gay content. Billy, innocent and handsome, is destroyed by the evil and sexually repressed master-at-arms Claggert in a harsh and unforgiving world far removed from the simpler, idyllic paradise described in the earlier South Sea novels.

N. Arvin, *Herman Melville: A Critical Biography*, New York, 1950; R. Chase, *Herman Melville: A Critical Study*, New York, 1949; E. Haviland Miller, *Melville*, New York, 1975; E. Kosofsky Sedgwick, *Epistemology of the Closet*, Berkeley, 1990.

David Garnes

Messel, Oliver (1904–1978), British stage-designer, artist. Born in England to a wealthy banking family, Messel studied at Eton College, where Harold ACTON and Brian HOWARD were part of his group, and then at the Slade School of Fine Art, London. His youthful art was influenced by the style and subjects of the artist Glyn Philpot, whose paintings of Negro men are strongly homoerotic. In 1925 Messel designed masks for Serge DIAGHILEV's ballet *Zéphyr et Flore*; in the late 1920s he provided sets and costumes for C. B. Cochran's revues. The famous white bedroom set for *Helen!* (1932) was a paradigm of inter-war camp and influenced high-style interior design. Like Cecil BEATON, whom at one stage he lived opposite in London, and Stephen Tennant, his work utilised baroque and rococo references in order to conjure escapist fantasy. He designed sets for theatre, ballet and opera in

England and the US, as well as working for Hollywood, designing the films *Romeo and Juliet* (1936), *Caesar and Cleopatra* (1946) and *Suddenly Last Summer* (1960). For a time he was the highest paid set-designer in the world. In the 1950s he designed textiles for Seker silk fabrics, furniture, parties and interiors; his designs for royal boxes at Convent Garden and the exterior of the Dorchester Hotel, London, for the Coronation (1953) made very prominent the camp swagger which had characterised the work of Rex Whistler and Beaton. These men placed a queer aesthetic at the heart of the British establishment. Messel's famous design for the suite of the Dorchester Hotel (1953) was restored in 1981. He had close relationships with men including Peter Glenville, and his companion and administrator of 30 years, Vagn Riis-Hansen. From 1967 Messel lived in Barbados, designing beautiful and simple villas which synthesised the European eighteenth century with local traditions. These included a house in Mustique, Les Jolies Eaux, for Princess Margaret, at that time his niece by marriage. Messel died in Barbados and was buried at his childhood home, Nymans, Sussex.

C. Castle, *Oliver Messel: A Biography*, London, 1986.

Peter McNeil

Mew, Charlotte Mary (1869–1928), British writer. As her poems and short stories suggest, Mew's life was frequented by loss, rejection and isolation. Born in London, she was one of seven siblings; three died while still children and two went insane later in life. Mew lived most of her adult life with her remaining sister. The poet is reported to have told a friend that, due to a fear of hereditary insanity, the two had resolved never to have children. Mew attended the Gower Street School for Girls, where she studied art, music and English literature. She became strongly attached to the headmistress, Lucy Harrison, whose own greatest bond in life was with another instructor, Amy Greener. Mew then attended lectures at University College London. In 1894, her short story 'Passed' was published in the *Yellow Book*. As part of the aestheticist community surrounding the journal, Mew came into contact with authors such as Max Beerbohm, George Moore, Arthur Symons and Henry JAMES. Despite this début in perhaps the best known arts journal of the decade, Mew's literary career failed to blossom, as did her experiences with love.

In 1898, Mew fell in love with Ella D'Arcy, a writer and the assistant literary editor of the *Yellow Book*. D'Arcy, however, did not reciprocate the affection. Nine years later, Mew fell in love with May Sinclair, a well known novelist who was active in the suffrage movement. Sinclair was friendly with Mew and helped with her career. Her presentation of Mew's work to Ezra Pound led to the publication of the poem 'The Fête' in the *Egoist*. Nevertheless, Sinclair did not return Mew's affections, and may have even unsympathetically informed others of the poet's lesbianism. Mew did find a strong degree of same-sex friendship, however, from Alida Klemantaski, who married the publisher Harold Monro. Mew's first and most famous collection of poetry, *The Farmer's Bride* (1916), was published by the Poetry Bookshop, run by the Monros. The heroine of the title poem, which had first appeared four years earlier in the *Nation*, suggests the suffragist heroine of Thomas Hardy's novel *Jude the Obscure*. While the collection was not a major financial success, the book familiarised a number of prominent members of the literary community with her work, including Hardy, Robert Bridges, H. D. (Hilda DOOLITTLE) and Siegfried SASSOON. Mew's creative production diminished at this time, although a second edition of *The Farmer's Bride* appeared in 1921 with added poems. Her sister died of cancer in 1927 and Mew committed suicide the next year. A year later, Alida Monro published

a second collection of Mew's poems, *The Rambling Sailor*.

Uninterested in finding solace with men and unable to find any from women, Mew's writing reflects her sense of isolation and misunderstanding. In an essay on Emily Brontë, she discusses Brontë's 'passion untouched by mortality' and her 'ever-unsatisfied desire', and her own writing echoes the uncommon, unfulfilled passions that she found in this earlier work. Many of her stories, such as 'Some Ways of Love' and 'An Open Door', present heroines who are, for various reasons, unable to fulfil traditional heterosexual relations, although no positive alternative is offered. Mew's poetry combines dramatic monologue with clean, modernist symbolism simultaneously to challenge patriarchal hierarchies (including that of Christianity) and to articulate her sense of isolation. Many of the stories and poems build around a central image of the grave as a site of oppression, repression, or even liberation from not only contemporary social norms but also the moral code of the afterlife. Mew remained inconsistent in her religious faith throughout her life. Although never overtly lesbian, her often formally experimental poetry is strongly woman-centred and offers many sympathetic, pseudo-erotic descriptions of isolated, misunderstood and alienated women. Mew's writing poignantly depicts the conflict between her private passions and the broader social context which hindered their realisation.

P. Fitzgerald, *Charlotte Mew and Her Friends*, London, 1984; C. Mew, *Collected Poems and Prose*, ed. V. Warner, Manchester, 1981.

Dennis Denisoff

Michelangelo (Buonarroti) (1475–1564), Italian sculptor, painter, architect and poet. The most important artist of the Italian High Renaissance, whose output spanned over seven decades, and a key figure within European art history, the 'divine' Michelangelo became the archetype of the artist as tragic and transcendent genius and was viewed by some contemporaries (such as his first biographer, Giorgio Vasari) not only as the culmination of artistic perfection but as a figure 'beyond human experience'.

Michelangelo was born in Caprese (near Arezzo), where his father Lodovico Buonarroti, a minor member of the Florentine bourgeoisie, was a temporary magistrate; his mother died when he was 6 – this early loss echoing in subsequent images of the Madonna. In 1488 he became an apprentice painter in the Florentine studio of Domenico Ghirlandaio, and the following year he joined a group of young sculptors working under Bertoldo di Giovanni in the Médici garden museum at San Marco despite opposition from his father, who regarded sculpture as a manual trade. Precociously talented, Michelangelo later encouraged the view, through his pupil and official biographer Ascanio Condivi, that he was not beholden to any training but was instead a fully self-sufficient and untutored talent. His copy of an antique faun's head brought Michelangelo to the attention of Lorenzo the Magnificent, who made the young sculptor a member of his household, thereby also reconciling Lodovico to his son's chosen career. Michelangelo's maturation as a sculptor was signalled by two works: the Pietà (1497–1500), a work of technical virtuosity, restrained pathos and graceful elegance, and the David (1501–1504), a sculpture of concentrated formal dynamism and the first example of his abiding interest in the heroic male nude. This interest was complemented in drawings and paintings from this period, notably the highly influential preparatory cartoon (lost in the sixteenth century but known through copies) for a fresco (that did not eventuate) of the Battle of Cascina (1505–1507) in the Palazzo Vecchio in Florence, which depicted a complex scene of male nudes in a variety of difficult poses, and the panel painting, The Holy Family (or Doni Tondo, 1503–1504), which includes a group of male nudes including two who have been interpreted (not entirely convincingly) as homosexual lovers.

In 1505 Michelangelo was summoned to Rome by Pope JULIUS II to begin work on a massively ambitious tomb for St Peter's. Intermittent work on what Condivi described as 'the tragedy of the tomb' continued for over 40 years but, despite completion of some of the figures (including the various Slaves and Moses), the project was never realised. In 1506 Michelangelo began preparatory drawings for a fresco on the vault of the Sistine Chapel in the Vatican, a project that occupied him from 1508 to 1512. The radical stylistic innovations of the ceiling fresco, especially the rendition of the later figures, introduced an entirely new visual language into Renaissance painting (prefiguring both Mannerism and the Baroque), and prompted Vasari to comment that the ceiling 'has proved a veritable beacon to our art . . . restoring light to a world that for centuries had been plunged into darkness . . . painters no longer need to seek new inventions'. Michelangelo painted further frescos in the Vatican – the sombre and compositionally complex Last Judgement (1536–1541), which was not universally well received (the nudity in particular upsetting Counter-Reformation sensibilities), and the Pauline Chapel frescos (1542–1550) of the Conversion of Saul and the Crucifixion of St Peter. Aside from intermittent work on the Julius tomb, later sculptural projects included the Medici funerary chapel in San Lorenzo in Florence (1519–1534), which contains Michelangelo's only two sculptured female nudes (Dawn and Night), whose lack of sensuality or erotic energy clearly contrasts with his male nudes, and the intensely withdrawn and ascetic Rondanini Pietà (1556–1564, unfinished). In his later years Michelangelo was increasingly occupied with architectural commissions, including work on the San Lorenzo Sacristy and the Biblioteca Laurenziana in Florence (1524–1562), the redesign of the

Campidoglio on the Capitoline Hill in Rome and, of greatest significance, his designs for the Basilica of St Peter's.

Despite occasional instances of gossip and innuendo (e.g. Pietro Aretino's suggestions of pederasty), there is no clear evidence of Michelangelo's homosexuality or, at least, none indicating overt sexual activity. Indeed, Condivi claimed that Michelangelo was chaste. None the less, the physical beauty of many of his monumental male nudes, such as the *David*, the *Creation of Adam* and the decorative male nudes (*Ignudi*) on the Sistine ceiling, gives a clear indication as to where Michelangelo's erotic interests lay. In addition, in 1532 Michelangelo met and fell in love with a young Roman nobleman, Tommaso de' Cavalieri, described by the humanist Benedetto VARCHI as possessing 'not only incomparable physical beauty, but so much elegance in manners, such excellent intelligence, and such graceful behaviour'. Tommaso married in 1538 and had two sons, but Michelangelo remained devoted for the rest of his life, dedicating numerous poems and several presentation drawings to him (e.g. *The Rape of Ganymede*, 1532). However, when Michelangelo's nephew and namesake eventually published over one hundred poems in 1623, any suggestion of homosexuality was effaced by altering the gender of the poems' subjects and addressees. John Addington SYMONDS's translation of a selection of the poems, together with his biography of the artist, sought to redress this suppression of Michelangelo's homosexuality which, even if largely unknowable, was none the less a key aspect of his art.

Increasingly recognised as a notable literary achievement in their own right (despite their density of language and often complex construction), Michelangelo's poems also provide useful insights into his beliefs and aesthetic precepts such as the broadly Neoplatonic notion that physical beauty could be a conduit to transcendent spiritual beauty, for example 'beauty . . . moves and carries every healthy mind to

heaven'. However, while Neoplatonism was part of the culture of the Medici circle, and of Michelangelo himself, and may also have fostered an emergent homosexual identity (see Saslow), claims that Michelangelo's art illustrates a fully developed Neoplatonic system (see Tolnay) have been downplayed in recent scholarship. Neoplatonic influences upon Michelangelo should also be placed within a broader framework of Christian belief affecting his art, particularly from the late 1530s; indeed, the contrasting moral codes of Neoplatonism and Catholicism may partly account for Michelangelo's ambivalent sexual feelings. In his later years Michelangelo also witnessed the emergence of the austere spirituality of the Counter-Reformation, especially in Rome, where he had settled permanently in 1534. His Christian faith was reinforced by his friendship with Vittoria Colonna, the Marchesa di Pescara, whom he met in 1536 and with whom he remained in close contact until her death in 1547. Her dedication to Catholicism strongly influenced his own devout religiosity as expressed, for example, in his sacred poetry that gave voice to a growing preoccupation with death and salvation.

In 1563 Michelangelo was elected an academician of the Florentine Accademia del Disegno and, despite his old age, he continued to work on a number of projects (principally architectural) until his death in Rome.

H. Hibbard, *Michelangelo*, London, 1979; Michelangelo, *Michelangelo: The Poems*, ed. and trans. C. Ryan, London, 1996; J. Saslow, *Ganymede in the Renaissance*, New Haven, 1986; J. A. Symonds, *The Life of Michelangelo Buonarotti*, 2 vols, London, 1893; C. de Tolnay, *Michelangelo*, 5 vols, Princeton, 1943–1960; C. de Tolnay, *The Art and Thought of Michelangelo*, New York, 1964.

David L. Phillips

Mieli, Aldo (1879–1950), Italian scholar and activist. Mieli was born in Livorno,

Italy and died in the town of Florida, near Buenos Aires, Argentina. He came from a wealthy Jewish family and received a degree in chemistry from the University of Pisa. After graduation, he lived for a time in Leipzig, Germany. On his return to Italy, he began collaborating with various academic journals and, in 1908, took up a lecturership at the University of Rome. He held socialist and pacifist ideas, arriving at a belief in socialism as a sort of 'extremist' positivism; in a simple fashion, he was confident in the power of reason and science to resolve the world's problems. This belief remained the basis of Mieli's values throughout a career as a disseminator of science and a polemicist marked by unfettered enthusiasm, even during the darkest moments of his life. It was also his major handicap, as his unbounded optimism verged on naïvety. In the years after 1908, Mieli created, worked on and himself generally financed numerous journals dedicated to science and the history of science. For instance, on his initiative was created what is now the *Archives internationales d'histoire des sciences*, still among the most authoritative international journals of the history of science.

In 1916, Mieli first addressed himself to the question of sexuality and published *Il libro dell'amore: Prefazione (The Book of Love: Preface)*, 16 pages of aphorisms and reflections. Five years later, he made his greatest contribution to sexual liberation in Italy by founding the journal *Rassegna di studi sessuali*, which he edited until 1928 and in which were discussed issues such as divorce, the closing of brothels, sex education for the young, and homosexuality. Most of the public figures interested in sexual liberation and sexual issues in Italy contributed to Mieli's journal. Particular attention was given to the question of homosexuality, and the journal translated articles and published reviews of many of the books of those active in Magnus HIRSCHFELD's Scientific-Humanitarian Committee. Mieli also took part in the international meetings of Hirschfeld's

Committee, as shown by the photographs of the conferences published in the *Rassegna*.

From a scientific point of view, Mieli was convinced that homosexuality was biologically innate; perhaps, he believed, with hormonal causes. He was nevertheless equally convinced of the 'normality' of homosexuals, to the point of being irritated with the idea of Hirschfeld, whom he otherwise much admired, that homosexuality was an 'intermediate' sexual state.

The foundation of the *Rassegna* was accompanied by the setting-up of a *Società Italiana per lo studio delle questioni sessuali*, of which it was the official organ. Especially noteworthy was the publication by the *Rassegna*, in 1922, within an article about the German homosexual movement, of a veritable proclamation inciting Italian homosexuals to unite and assert their rights. The author was Numa Praetorius (the pseudonym of Eugen Wilhelm), one of the members of Hirschfeld's Committee. However, Wilhelm's call sounded at an inopportune moment – 1922 was the year of Mussolini's *coup d'état* and takeover of the government.

For several years, until Fascism succeeded in taking control of all corners of Italian society, Mieli was able, despite increasing difficulties, to pursue his campaign. But in 1928, when the publishing company which he had set up had to be closed, Mieli realised that time was running out and he fled to France. The decision to leave Italy at the time was a good one. Carola Susani has located in the national archives in Rome an unpublished dossier which the Fascist political police had compiled on Mieli; in addition to labelling him a 'passive pederast', it also said that he was a 'dangerous socialist – to be arrested' if he returned to Italy.

Mieli arrived in Paris with Angelo Pisani (born in 1899), his lover, assistant and secretary. He also brought with him his library, rich in valuable ancient scientific works, which (in return for a pension) he gave to the Centre de Synthèse; he also became an associate of the Centre as an historian of science. He seems to have given up his homosexual activism, though when Hirschfeld died, Mieli wrote a fine and explicit obituary for the German scientist and reformer. In 1939, faced with the danger of a German attack on France, Mieli – who would have suffered as a Jew, socialist and homosexual – logically decided to flee once again. Profitting from the summer vacation, he clandestinely packed most of his library (some four metric tonnes of books) and, much to the anger of the Centre de Synthèse, took it with him when he left for Argentina. There he gave the library to the Faculty of Letters and Philosophy at the University of Buenos Aires (where the collection remains), in return for an annuity of 500 pesos a month, a sum which became vital to him in his last years. At his death, Mieli was still working on a project which had preoccupied him all during his life, an international history of science; the work was finished and posthumously published by his devoted colleague José Babini.

It is difficult to draw up a balance-sheet about the activities of a person who was sincere and courageous, but who had the misfortune to undertake his campaign at a time when Fascism and anti-Semitism doomed it to failure. Mieli himself, in 'Digressions autobiographiques', written near the end of his life, provided his own summing-up: '[In my life] I took part, with love, in both serious and purely recreational meetings of workers and peasants, whom I considered my true brothers, and I sometimes helped them in their struggle against capitalism. I believe that at various moments a good number of workers and peasants placed their sincere and cordial confidence in me. Fascism destroyed every movement of salvation in Italy and set up a real reign of hatred. However, one cannot doubt that in a few souls I awoke a feeling of human solidarity. I have fought for years, with my pen and by my actions, in favour of a better understanding of sex-

ual life, to contradict deeply rooted opinions, to proclaim the reign of love – physical and spiritual. I am certain of having obtained some successes, of having convinced a few sceptical people, of having given consolation and strength to a few despairing souls. Yet, in appearance if not if reality, all of my efforts resulted in failure when another type of morality, that of force, high-handedness and superstition, began to dominate peoples which it reduced to slavery.'

Mieli's words were bitter, but he at least had the comfort of seeing the defeat of these forces of hatred which had rendered his efforts in vain, and to see the growing esteem in which his life's work was held. But, at the same time, his words were proud utterances of one who had nothing to regret about what he had done in his life and who would, if necessary, do it all again.

J. Babini, 'Para una bibliografía de Aldo Mieli', *Physis*, 21 (1979): 357–424; G. Dall'Orto, 'Un pioniere gay: Aldo Mieli', *Babilonia*, 57 (June 1988): 52–4; A. Mieli, 'Digressions autobiographiques', *Archives internationales d'histoire des sciences*, 27 (1948): 494–505; A. Mieli, *Il libro dell'amore*, Florence, 1916; C. Pogliano, 'Aldo Mieli, storico della scienza', *Belfagor*, 38 (1983): 537–57; P. Sergescu, 'Aldo Mieli', *Actes du VIe congrès international d'histoire des sciences (1950)*, Paris, 1955: 79–95; C. Susani, 'Una critica della norma nell'Italia del Fascismo', in E. Venturelli (ed.) *Le parole e la storia: Ricerche su omosessualità e cultura*, Bologna, 1991: 110–19.

                                     Giovanni Dall'Orto

Mistral, Gabriela (1898–1957), Chilean poet and teacher. Mistral's importance as a public figure clearly reaches beyond her writing. Born Lucila Godoy Alcayaga and brought up in near poverty, she reinvented herself as Gabriela Mistral when she became a schoolteacher. She started writing poetry in her twenties and these early poems, especially the ones dealing with her feelings for a man who died, impressed the critics. In her twenties she became a public figure not only as a poet, but also as a schoolteacher and a reformer in educational issues. This role would be the key to her own freedom, In 1922 she left for Mexico, where she played an important part in the educational reform that took place after the Revolution. From 1925 she travelled widely in Europe and Latin America, reinforcing her role as 'cultural ambassador' as well as dealing with political issues in a series of newspaper articles of some resonance. Her most famous books are *Tala* and *Lagar*. It is possible to read a lesbian voice articulated in the former.

In her own lifetime, she became a legend of international status, a matriarchial symbol for generations of Latin American people. Mistral joins the ranks of other such matriarchal figures, fascinating and deserving attention, but whose sexual politics are, at the very least, problematic. Like Eva Perón, Gabriela Mistral has been presented both as a feminist icon and as a reactionary character. On the one hand, such women clearly stood up to patriarchal structures and managed to reach positions traditionally ascribed to men. Mistral lived in Europe and several Latin American countries for a long time. She was an independent woman who escaped some of the duties society forces on women, such as childbearing. On the other hand, one cannot leave aside the fact that her personal freedom was achieved only after paying a price; childless, she would become 'the mother of all', and the absence of visible masculine attachments contributed to the image of a virginal schoolteacher who poured herself into other people. In her poetry, she seems to have accepted this role and worked to establish herself as an apostle for liberation.

Mistral's story becomes even more complex when one starts to lend credibility to rumours of conscious lesbian desire. Her virginal life has often been accepted unproblematically by commentators: it fitted the myth so easily that, had

she actually maintained emotional liaisons with men, one suspects that these would have been downplayed. At most, in order to give the goddess a human side, an ambiguous relationship in youth is almost brandished by apologists as an alibi. We are told she loved this man so much that she kept his memory alive and was unable to love anybody else: thus she paid her debt to patriarchalism. In this context, the idea that it might all have been only a mask would put her figure under a different light. In fact, Mistral may have used all this paraphernalia, her writings included, as a disguise of her real feelings. Her lesbianism was an open secret nobody talked about and yet nobody could really deny. A number of short stories where lesbianism is more than a possibility present thinly veiled portraits of Mistral. Only the noise created by the international legend kept it in the dark for so long. Still, one risks aggressive reactions from specialists as soon as the issue is raised: there has never been any proof of lesbian desire or liaisons, either biographical or literary, they claim, re-enacting a claim for what feminists used to call 'the smoking dildo', that undeniable piece of 'evidence' heterosexist critics always seem to need in order to give up on their claims that their subject was nothing but a complete, healthy heterosexual. It is true that most of the evidence is marginal or, at best, anecdotal. But similar rumours have been expressed about other members of Mistral's intellectual circle, such as Lydia Cabrera and Teresa de la Parra. Her strong attachment to these women and her mistrust of male friendship is also clear. Even if Mistral did not conform to any lesbian identity, it seems clear that she strongly rejected, on a personal level, the female identity patriarchalism was forcing on her, and her performance as 'The Schoolteacher of America' may well have been regarded as a way to escape, on an individual level, such pressures. Being a cultural ambassador, she could live abroad, decide on the people she lived with and, most importantly, she was allowed to use her intellect in her work. Gabriela Mistral was the first Latin American to win the Nobel prize (in 1945).

L. Fiol-Matta, 'The Schoolteacher of America: Gender, Sexuality, and Nation in Gabriela Mistral', in E. L. Bergmann and P. J. Smith (eds) ¿Entiendes? Queer Readings, Hispanic Writings, Durham, 1995.

Alberto Mira

Molina, Miguel de (1908–1993), Spanish entertainer. During the years of the Spanish Republic, no performer could compare to Miguel de Molina. He had a unmistakably personal style that combined Andalusian dancing, deep emotionalism in his voice, spectacular costumes and a narcissistic stage persona that made him extremely popular among audiences. His self-made shirts became legendary, and some of the songs he made popular ('La bien pagá', 'Ojos verdes') became extremely well known and are now a part of the country's musical history.

Molina came from a background of extreme poverty, and in his autobiography tells of his difficult childhood in which he had to hustle for a living. He left home in his teens and found occasional work in brothels, where he sometimes entertained both the prostitutes and the clients with songs. Even though his homosexuality is openly acknowledged, he is notoriously coy about any affairs at this time, the exception being a youth he met on a short trip to Africa: a night of love is fondly remembered. Back in Spain, he made some money organising parties for wealthy people in Granada and Seville, before going to Madrid to try his luck in show business. His first vocation was dance, and he was cast in a production of Manuel de Falla's ballet *El amor brujo*. Soon he developed his own act, in which he combined cabaret and flamenco. He was also a wonderful comic interpreter, and his sense of humour was very close to what today would be recognised as 'low camp'. In the period between 1936 and 1942 he toured the country with Amalia Isaura, and spent most of the Civil War on Republican ground. This, together with his homosexuality and his sympathies for the left (although he would afterwards claim this was not a political position, but a sense of kinship with the poor), would have disastrous consequences for his career.

After the war he was exploited by an impresario who took advantage of his vulnerability, and when he decided to go independent again, he was prohibited from performing. He left the country for Argentina, where he was hugely successful. He never seems to have been very happy in his love-life: in his memoirs he appears as someone always taken advantage of, who never had a lasting and fulfilling relationship. But he is a very unreliable narrator, often anxious to appear as an innocent victim of circumstances. Behind his story it is easy to read another one, about an egotist who demanded more love than he could give, someone who would compromise his integrity to achieve fame and fortune and who seems to be imprisoned in the star personality he had created. Exile was not easy, and the Argentinian government soon threatened him with expulsion. In his own version, it was the direct intervention of Eva Perón that helped him to stay and continue with his career. His support for the Perón government, which he claimed had nothing to do with politics, made him a despised figure in later years. Homophobia also seems to have been the cause of the neglect he then experienced; unable to withstand the pressure on him, he withdrew from artistic life in 1960. He had earned enough money not to die in poverty, but he did feel rejected in his later years.

The case of Molina illustrates how much more difficult things are for open homosexuals in most professions: sexual orientation is always held against gay people as something that somehow makes them less deserving of praise. Whereas many other personalities who had faced persecution under Francoism were being 'rediscovered' and promoted in the early 1980s, Molina was overlooked and recognition came too late. By then he was a bitter old man, who had been living alone for too long and who felt unfairly treated by his own country. His life inspired two musical films by gay film director Jaime Chávarri: *Las cosas del querer* (1989) and *Las cosas del querer 2* (1995).

M. de Molina, *Botín de Guerra*, Barcelona, 1998.

Alberto Mira

Montaigne, Michel Eyquem de (1533–1592), French writer and statesman. Born at Montaigne near Bordeaux, Montaigne belonged to a new but well established family from the merchant class, from Gascon and Aragonese descent as was often the case in Aquitaine. He received a humanist education, in the course of which he was taught by Marc-Antoine MURET, and, in the midst of the unfolding Wars of Religion, revealed himself a skilled negotiatior between the 'three Henris' – King HENRI III of France, King Henri of Navarre, the leader of the 'United Protestant Provinces' (that is, of the Huguenot party) (and later King Henri IV of France – the first of the Bourbon dynasty), and Duc Henri de Guise, leader of the Ultra-Catholics, the *Ligue*. A *politique*, as the word went at the time, he believed in conflict resolution and, due to his scepticism, a philosophical trend he actually set in motion which would later have an important impact on seventeenth-century French culture, in the utter relativity of political opinions. A Catholic among Protestants, a 'new man' among the old landed nobility, a humanist (trained by the very best, including Gouvéa and Buchanan) among uncouth Gascons and illiterate 'fishmongers' – an epithet thrown at him by his neighbour, the illustrious humanist Jules-César Scaliger – Montaigne served his country and the city of Bordeaux well. As mayor of Bordeaux, a key French city, he played a crucial role; a mayor was a real power in the realm in terms of prestige, independence and authority.

Yet the main thread of his life is not his public activity but his famous and brilliant book, *Les Essais* (1580–1588), translated by John Florio – a fellow homosexual – for the court of Prince Henry of Wales (1603), and quoted by SHAKESPEARE in *The Tempest*. His book is a series of essays on the 'business of living' in hard times, and a most original affirmation of the individual's prerogative to reclaim one's autonomy in the midst of conflicts. It became an immediate European success.

However, the emotional core of the *Essais* is the famous Chapter I. 27, *De l'amitié* ('On Friendship'). Montaigne worked at this essay from edition to edition and it is in the posthumous edition of 1595 (the 1588 version he was annotating as he died) that one finds, at last perfected, a much quoted formula: 'Parce que c'était lui', firmly written, with, more hesitantly in lighter ink, the coda, 'Parce que c'était moi' ('Because is was him, because it was me'). The 1580 text had simply read: 'If you were to pressure me to tell you why I loved him, I would not be able to explain it'. The job was done on his death bed. 'Him' was his friend Etienne de La Boétie (1530–1563).

They met sometime between 1557 and 1559 at public festivities. Until La Boétie's death (of the plague), they lived a ravished friendship, nurtured by poems in Latin and not too frequent encounters. Montaigne talks of four wonderful years of *sainte couture* (a sacred bond) between these two young men, La Boétie having already reached fame for his political discourses, among which was his *Discours de la servitude volontaire* written at the age of 18 (published in 1576). The *Discours* was the first to explain the principle of civil disobedience and is a classic in political science. The fiery La Boétie and the reserved Montaigne loved each other for four years. Montaigne thought he never recovered from La Boétie's death.

Aimer is the key word: in all such cases

(like the love between fellow humanist Blaise de Vigenère (1523–1596), close to HENRI III, and financier Giovanni Andreossi) *aimer* is reserved for male 'friendship' as we would now paraphrase it. At the time *aimer*, especially among humanists, meant just that, 'to love a male friend'. The word was hardly used in what we now call heterosexual relations. Vigenère, who dedicated his momentous *Trois Dialogues de l'amitié* (1579) to Henri III, is clear on that point: *aimer* is reserved to that bond between men, whereas *volupté* (read 'sexual satisfaction') is reserved to relations between men and women. It has even been proposed that the *Essais* were composed by Montaigne to celebrate and commemorate La Boétie's death, as if, after those four years of 'sacred bond' (*couture* actually means 'stitching together two pieces of cloth'), Montaigne was left alone, with only his book as solace.

Whether or not Montaigne and La Boétie did have sex is not the point. If they did, it is unlikely they would write about it, not out of shame but because it meant nothing to humanists engaged in public affairs to mention sex. 'Sex' was not a social or mental category as it is now. Carrying no identity load, 'sex' was merely sexual acts. What had sense was *aimer*, and *aimer* was a masculine matter alone (with the exception of some literary 'loves', modelled on the Italian sonnetists, 'literary affairs' indeed).

Yet, if one wishes to track Montaigne's sexuality, the journal he kept during a voyage on horseback to Italy in 1580–1581 is tantalising enough. Accompanied by a group of near-adolescent noblemen, he travelled (at 47, an old man by the standards of the time) to Italy with a mysterious young secretary, who seems to have penned the diary, and disappeared in the streets of Rome on 15 February 1581. Much has been said about their relationship, the choice of entourage and Montaigne's amused notes on Italian life and anecdotes. In the Tyrol, he started chatting

up, in Latin, a student, a gorgeous young man – who turned out to be, to his disappointment, a girl. (Note: Who is writing down the anecdote, Montaigne or the companion-secretary?) And, listing museum marvels (Montaigne invented Italian gay tourism, by the way, if not altogether the 'grand tour' of the young English aristocrats), he mentions the *Adonis*, the Belvedere *Antinous*, the *Laocoön*, MICHELANGELO's *Moses*, icons of male beauty, and 'some beautiful woman thrown at the feet of Paul III' (Giulio Farnese). One is left more than wondering when he takes care to make an entry on male marriage rites performed at the Porta Latina in the Portuguese community. Was he (or his companion) lifting the veil?

Montaigne criticism is still reluctant to accept even his friendship with La Boétie, so strong is the positivist yoke of hetero-centred criticism. Yet Essay I. 27 remains a touchstone for any investigation of homosexuality in the early modern period.

M. de Montaigne, *The Essays* (numerous editions); M. Screech, *Montaigne and Melancholy*, London, 1983; P.-J. Salazar, 'Herculean Lovers. Towards a History of Men's Friendship in the 17th Century', *Thamyris*, 4, 2 (1997): 249–66.

Philippe-Joseph Salazar

Montesquiou-Fezensac, Count Robert de (1855–1921), French writer and aesthete. Montesquiou was, in the words of his biographer Philippe Jullian, 'one of the few dandies France has ever produced'. A poet, novelist and critic, he was best known as a handsome, wealthy and cultured man-about-town in the sparkling cultural life of the Belle Epoque.

Born in Paris, Montesquiou traced his gilded lineage back to the tenth century and claimed d'Artagnan as one of his ancestors. He spent his childhood, and indeed the rest of his life, in the privileged milieu of aristocrats in the most fashionable neighbourhoods of Paris and in provincial châteaux. Educated first at a public *lycée* then at a private Jesuit school, Montesquiou was never obliged to work for a living. He published a number of volumes of poetry, including *Les Chauves-Souris* (*The Bats*), *Les Hortensias Bleus* (*Blue Hortensias*), *Les Paons* (*Peacocks*), *Les Perles Rouges* (*Red Pearls*) – the titles give some indication of verses which, as Jullian says, are 'heavily burdened with symbolist preciosities' – a novel, *La Petite Mademoiselle* (*The Little Lady*), with himself as an English governess, and criticism. Though now almost forgotten, his works earned him election to the prestigious French Academy.

Montesquiou met and entertained almost everyone who was anyone in late nineteenth- and early twentieth-century France. Early acquaintances included the poets Stéphane Mallarmé and Paul VERLAINE, the painters Jacques-Emile Blanche and Gustave Moreau and the composer Gabriel Fauré. He promoted the Art Nouveau glass-workers Gallé and Lalique, and patronised DIAGHILEV's Ballets Russes. He was a close and perhaps intimate friend of James McNeil Whistler and an admirer of Aubrey Beardsley. He had a brief (probably non-sexual) affair with the actress Sarah Bernhardt. He numbered among his other friends the writer COLETTE and various members of the lesbian circle gathered around Natalie Clifford BARNEY and Renée VIVIEN. He met WILDE (whom he did not like), knew LOTI, GIDE and COCTEAU, and in 1893 made the acquaintance of Marcel PROUST.

Proust drew on Montesquiou for the homosexual Baron de Charlus in *Remembrances of Things Past*, a work Montesquiou admired; he wrote, on the publication of *Cities of the Plain*, 'For the first time someone dares, you dare to take as a straight subject … the vice of TIBERIUS and of the shepherd Corydon'. Montesquiou had himself already appeared in Joris-Karl Huysman's *A Rebours* (*Against the Grain*), transformed into the decadent aristocrat des Esseintes. He also appeared in novels by Edmond Rostand and Jean LORRAIN – portraits which he found less congenial – and probably contributed to Wilde's *The Picture of Dorian Gray*.

Montesquiou was renowned for behaviour which might now be termed 'camp' (though he loathed vulgarity and avoided scandal). His houses were filled with Japanese lanterns and kimonos, bearskins, Louis XV dresses, Spanish chasubles and Oriental tapestries, and he kept a lock of BYRON's hair. At costume balls, he sometimes dressed as Louis XIV or a Renaissance courtier. On occasion he crossed the Channel to shop for outfits in Bond Street and Saville Row. His parties, including those in the various mansions in which he lived, one called the Pavilion of the Muses, another the Pink Palace, were famous, and his guest lists included the cream of Paris society – though one *soirée*, specially designed to commemorate Verlaine, fizzled (to Montesquiou's humiliation) when an acquaintance jokingly inserted a notice in a newspaper saying that the *fête* had been cancelled on the very day it was to be held.

In 1885 Montesquiou met a handsome young Peruvian, Gabriel Yturri, who that evening wrote to him: 'I am devoted to you, body and soul, for life. I will give everything I possess to spare you a moment of sadness.' Yturri became Montesquiou's secretary, and they remained together for 20 years, until Yturri died of diabetes in 1905. His last words were addressed to Montesquiou: 'I thank you for having made known to me those beautiful things which have so much charmed me.' When Montesquiou died, he had himself buried next to Yturri in the cemetery in Versailles. Montesquiou left his estate to a man who had become his secretary and companion after Yturri's death.

P. Jullian, *Robert de Montesquiou*, London, 1967; P. Chaleyssin, *Robert de Montesquiou: Mécène et dandy*, Paris, 1992; J. Huas, *L'Homosexualité au temps de Proust*, Dinard, 1992.

Robert Aldrich

Montherlant, Henry de (1896–1972), French writer. Montherlant was born in Paris from an old, aristocratic Roman Catholic family. His father, who was wholly engrossed in horses and *objets d'art*, left the boy's upbringing to his mother and maternal grandmother. After early studies at the fashionable Lycée Janson-de-Sailly, he completed his schooling at the Collège Sainte-Croix de Neuilly, where, as his long-withheld autobiographical novel *Les Garçons* (*The Boys*) shows, his emotional and sexual interest in other boys flowered freely. His educational career was in other respects less than brilliant: he had trouble passing the *baccalauréat* and he later failed his first-year law examinations at the Institut Catholique. His two great adolescent passions were writing and bullfighting: he took up the latter sport seriously (to him it was the apotheosis of masculinity) and killed his first bull at Burgos in 1911. Irked by the fact that he was not called up until 1914, he asked to be transferred immediately to active service and was posted to the 360th infantry regiment. He was three times mentioned in dispatches and was badly wounded in 1918. Male adolescence, sport and masculinity (as exhibited in bullfighting and on the battlefield) rapidly established themselves as the central preoccupations of his post-war writings. Between 1920 and 1935 his sense of marginality expressed itself in a constant physical displacement, as he travelled around Italy, Spain and North Africa. During this period he constantly reiterates the need to be free of all ties in order to be open to all the possibilities of personal development, a credo which he expanded into a need to embody all moral attitudes within himself, however apparently opposed, since 'everything is true' (preface to *Aux Fontaines du Désir* [*At the Springs of Desire*], 1927). Throughout the novels and plays for which he is best known, from *Les Célibataires* of 1934 to *Le Maître de Santiago* of 1947, this credo is reflected in a series of thoroughly unpleasant, egotistically self-indulgent characters.

Yet there was another side to Montherlant, as evinced by his work with the Swiss Red Cross, between 1942 and 1945, for French child war victims. There is in fact an idealist Montherlant, but it is reflected in two works which he himself held back from the public gaze: the play *La Ville dont le prince est un enfant* (*The City whose Prince is a Child*), which he published in 1951 but refused to allow the Comédie-Française to perform, and the novel *Les Garçons*, which he published only in 1969 and which includes another account of the events covered by the play and in some sense provides it with a context. These works reveal that the Montherlant paradise from which his life was an enforced exile was the world of male adolescence. Montherlant was a pederast in the strict sense; he liked adolescent boys and he hated the conventional family structure which locked them away from what he regarded as proper male influence. His schoolboys live in a world of antique heroic values. What he wants is to enrol them into a cult of conventional masculinity which has the same overtones of suppressed homoeroticism as does much 1930s fiction of adult masculinity (e.g. Hemingway). Yet at the same time what he treasures in them is an androgynous beauty, which fades with their passage to manhood and for which he has his own uses. Although he himself said little of the latter, his friend Roger Peyrefitte has been much more indiscreet, describing in his *Propos secrets* and *Nouveaux propos secrets* various incidents involving the two of them, of boy hunting, tangles with the police and other complications. Clearly, right to the end he sustained his belief in the credo that he should be morally above all restraints. At the same time he was obsessed by the need for a public face of propriety, and was rewarded for his efforts by election to the Académie Française in 1960.

P. Sipriot, *Montherlant sans masque*, Vol. 1,

L'Enfant prodigue, Paris, 1982; Vol. 2, *Ecris avec ton sang*, Paris, 1990.

Christopher Robinson

Moonlite, Captain (Andrew George Scott) (1842–1880), Australian outlaw. In Australia, 'bushrangers' have the iconic status afforded Robin Hood in England and some of the gunslinger cowboys in the US: anti-heroes and outsiders, they nevertheless provided 'masculine' heroes for a frontier society with little in the way of major figures from its relatively brief Anglo-European past.

Born in County Down, Ireland, and educated there and later in London, Scott was the archetypal nineteenth-century adventurer. His first travels took him, in 1860, to Italy, where he fought for Garibaldi's redshirts against the country's Bourbon rulers. Then, migrating to New Zealand, he took part in the Maori Wars, receiving, however, a dishonourable discharge because of shady financial dealings. Taking ship to the US, he joined the Union Army under Sherman, and made a small fortune, dealing in army goods and cotton. In 1865 he took his discharge, and moved to San Francisco, but reappeared in Sydney two years later, with probably forged letters of introduction, which permitted him to move in the best society.

Scott then became a lay reader in the Anglican Church, locating at Egerton, a small but affluent mining town in the Victorian gold fields. It was here that the masked figure of Captain Moonlite first appeared, robbing a local bank agent. Scott soon became a suspect, and was eventually tried for the crime. His striking appearance, his colourful past, and a successful but brief escape from custody all added to his reputation, making him something of a public figure. He was, however, convicted and sentenced to ten years jail.

Released in 1879, Scott had difficulty earning a living, his notoriety ensuring that he was constantly harassed by police. So, with a group of young companions, he decided to move overland to New South Wales, seeking work at various cattle stations. Some months later, on the verge of starvation, they held up one of these, and the inevitable shoot-out with police occurred. Several of Scott's gang were killed, including one James Nesbit, Scott's closest companion, whom he had met while in jail. For his part in the hold-up (in which a policeman had been killed), Scott received the death sentence.

While in jail, awaiting his hanging, Scott wrote many letters to friends, in which he spelt out, in terms amazingly explicit for the Victorian era, his love for Nesbit: 'We were one in heart and soul, he died in my arms and I long to join him where there shall be no more parting.' Scott (who wore a ring made of Nesbit's hair) also spelt out his desired burial arrangements: to share the same grave as Nesbit, with an inscription declaring their love on their joint tombstone.

From a late twentieth-century perspective, his letters – articulating as they do in extravagant and glowing terms what was clearly 'the love that dare not speak its name' – are potent documents. They have a special relevance for a society like Australia, where the homosocial and homosexual dimensions of the phenomenon of 'mateship' have yet to be fully explored.

G. Calderwood, *Captain Moonlite: Bushranger*, Melbourne, 1971; S. J. Williams, *The Moonlite Papers*, Vol. 1, Woden, 1988; G. Wotherspoon, 'Moonlight and . . . Romance? The death-cell letters of Captain Moonlite and some of their implications', *Journal of the Royal Australian Historical Society*, 78, 3 and 4 (1992): 76–91.

Garry Wotherspoon

Muret, Marc-Antoine (1526–1585), French humanist. Muret was born in the village of the same name in the Limousin region, and at a relatively young age, in 1544, became a schoolteacher; among his students in Bordeaux, where he lived in 1547–1548, was MONTAIGNE. His life took a different turn in 1553, when he fled Paris, where he had been well regarded, after being arrested for sodomy and heresy; documents suggest that he was saved only by the intervention of powerful friends. As soon as possible, Muret moved to Toulouse, where he studied and taught law, but his stay there was brief. In 1554, he fled again to avoid another trial for sodomy and heresy. Along with his lover Memmius Frémiot (who had also fled), Muret was condemned to death *in absentia* and his effigy was burned at the stake.

Taking refuge in Venice, Muret taught and worked with the great humanist publisher Aldo Manuzio in the publication of Latin classics. In early 1558, he left Venice; according to his friend the humanist Joseph Joost Scaliger (1540–1609): 'Muret fled from Toulouse, went to Venice, but having tried to sodomise the sons of some of the most distinguished noblemen, he then fled to Rome. . . . He was a learned man, but in Venice they could not stand him because of his pederasty.' Scaliger, however, exaggerates; Muret's biographer, Dejob, emphasises that he was never put on trial in Venice. Nevertheless, private letters suggest that it was rumours about his homosexuality that led him to leave the city.

Muret now took a teaching post in Padua, the seat of a prestigious university, but in 1558 the continuing rumours about his private life led to the loss of his students and obliged him to return to Venice. This catastrophe was the last he had to endure. Thanks to a recommendation from Cardinal Ippolito d'Este, Muret was able to move to Ferrara, then to Rome in 1563, when he obtained a university position teaching moral philosophy, law and rhetoric: this he kept until 1584. In Rome, Muret earned esteem and wealth. In 1572, in return for his cultural contributions, the pope made him a Roman citizen. In 1576, Muret was ordained to the priesthood.

Muret's numerous works include Latin poetry, commentaries on Latin classics, studies of philology (*Variae lectiones*, 1559–1600) and rhetoric, ceremonial orations and other writings. His work continued to have a high reputation among later generations, but his decision to become a priest led Protestants to write openly about his homosexuality, whilst Catholics did everything possible to hide it. Dejob, indeed, mentions the existence of a seventeenth-century *Apologia pro Mureto criminis sodomiae postulato* written by one J. Voigt to defend Muret against rumours of sodomy. In fact, the names of at least two of Muret's lovers are known: Frémiot and Daniel Schleicher, one of his students, whom he called his 'son who is dearer than anything', and to whom he wrote a Latin love ode.

C. Dejob, *Marc-Antoine Muret, un professeur français en Italie dans la seconde moitié du XVIe siècle*, Paris, 1881, and Geneva, 1970; G. Ménage, *Anti-Baillet*, The Hague, 1688: chapter 83; G. V. Rossi (Janus Nicias Erythraeus), *Pinacotheca virorum illustrium*, Colonia Agrippinae, 1645–1648; J. J. Scaliger, 'Scaligeriana II', in *Scaligeriana, thuana, perroniana, pithoeana et colemesiana*, Amsterdam, 1750: Vol. 2, pp. 257 and 465.

Giovanni Dall'Orto

N

Nehemiah (son of Hacaliah) (fifth century BC), Biblical figure. Nehemiah was the writer of memoirs contained in the book called by his name in the Writings section of Hebrew Scripture. Nehemiah's story begins when, as a Jew in exile, he is cupbearer at the Persian court at Shushan to King Artaxerxes I Longimanus (446 BC). In favour with the king, he received permission to return to Judah, where as governor he supervised the rebuilding of the walls of Jerusalem, and undertook a number of social reforms. He returned to Babylon around 434 BC, but 'after some time' again received permission to return to Jerusalem. The date of his death is unknown. Certainly he was no longer governor by 407 BC.

Although not all scholars are agreed, there is textual and other evidence that Nehemiah was a eunuch. He certainly seems to have been regarded as such in later Judaism – a usually reliable text of the Septuagint, the Greek version of the Hebrew Bible, describes him as a *eunochos* (eunuch), rather than an *oinochoos*. Further, he served in the presence of both the king and queen, which increases the probability of his having been castrated.

According to Jewish law, 'no one whose testicles are crushed or whose penis is cut off shall be admitted to the assembly of the Lord'. Thus Nehemiah could not enter certain areas of the temple. His enemy Shemaiah attempted to trick him into doing so. Without children to remember him for posterity, Nehemiah prayed repeatedly: 'Remember for my good, O my God, all that I have done for this people.'

Later tradition relaxed the Deuteronomic prohibition and pledged posterity for eunuchs in the divine memory that never forgets. Nehemiah's service to his people and nation – despite prejudice and social and religious disadvantage – did indeed make a difference to the accommodation, if not yet the affirmation, of a denigrated sexual minority.

Deuteronomy 23: 1; Nehemiah 5: 19, 13: 14, 22, 31; Isaiah 56: 3–5.

David J. Bromell

Nero (Nero Claudius Caesar) (37–68), Roman emperor. Through his mother Agrippina a great-great-grandson of Augustus and through his father Gnaeus Domitius Ahenobarbus a great-grandson of Mark Antony and Octavia, the sister of Augustus, Nero was the last emperor of the dynasty founded by Augustus.

Nero succeeded the emperor Claudius in 54, thanks to his mother, who had married her uncle the emperor in 49, and ruled Rome until he committed suicide when faced with revolution in the army in Spain, which spread to Germany and eventually involved the whole empire. During his reign occurred the most famous of the fires which periodically ravaged Rome, the

Great Fire of AD 64, responsibility for which was blamed on a new religious sect, the Christians. Nero's ferocity in punishing these Christians was to ensure his survival in popular memory as the archetypal cruel tyrant, an image which only partially reflects the complexity of this man's character. His interests lay more in cultural than military pursuits, and while his literary efforts have not survived, the decorative effects of the new palace, the Golden House (*Domus Aurea*) he built after the Great Fire, inspired Renaissance artists when it was rediscovered in 1494. Apart from his three marriages (to Octavia, daughter of Claudius, then Poppaea Sabina and finally Statilia Messalina), Nero is reported to have been infatuated with a freedwoman, Acte, and to have enjoyed an incestuous relationship with his mother.

SUETONIUS also relates ('Nero', 28–9) how Nero enjoyed sexual relationships with men, even to the extent of castrating one Sporus, marrying him and treating him as a wife. Moreover, Nero is alleged to have taken the passive role with Doryphorus. Such stories of sexual appetite were intended as indicators of his depravity and tyranny, along with the numerous executions he ordered, including that of his onetime tutor and adviser, the philosopher Seneca. Despite his unpopularity with the Senate and more traditional elements in Roman society, the fact that after his death there were several people who claimed to be Nero suggests that he had enjoyed a measure of popularity among ordinary people, who were no doubt impressed by his generosity and the general improvements he made in Rome during the rebuilding following the fire. As Nero was away at Anzio when the fire broke out, it is unlikely that he ever fiddled while Rome burned; on the contrary he returned to the city to oversee relief operations. What the Nero tradition demonstrates is the power of hostile sources to shape popular belief.

Suetonius, 'Nero', in *Lives of the Caesars and Extracts from Lives of Illustrious Men*, trans. J. C. Rolfe, 2 vols, London, 1914; Suetonius, *The Twelve Caesars*, trans. R. Graves, Harmondsworth, 1957; Tacitus, *The Annals of Imperial Rome*, trans. M. Grant, Harmondsworth, 1971; M. Grant, *Nero*, London, 1969; M. Griffin, *Nero: The End of a Dynasty*, London, 1984; B. Warmington, *Nero: Reality and Legend*, London, 1981.

Roger Pitcher

Newcastle, Margaret Cavendish, Duchess of (1623–1673), British writer. Born into a prosperous gentry family in Essex, Margaret became a Maid of Honour to Queen Henrietta Maria in 1643 and travelled with her into Parisian exile in 1644. There she met and married, in 1645, the widowed courtier William Cavendish, Marquis (later Duke) of Newcastle, 30 years her senior, a well known patron of, and participant in, the arts and one of Charles I's chief military commanders. The Newcastles lived lavishly on credit in Antwerp, a centre for exiled Royalists, until the Restoration, after which they virtually retired to Newcastle's estate in Nottinghamshire.

Cavendish had no children and devoted herself, with her husband's support, to the solitary practice of writing: 'I delight myself with myself', she said in *Sociable Letters* (1664). But the private, autoerotic pleasures of Cavendish's writing are complexly linked to an even more unusual desire for publication, each book issued under the authorising dignity of her married name. Still more strikingly, and despite her lack of formal training, Cavendish associated herself with the especially masculinised and secular genres of philosophy and the new science, in titles such as *Philosophical and Physical Opinions* (1655) and *Observations Upon Experimental Philosophy* (1666), arguing ingeniously that women's exclusion from the privileges of education, 'kept like birds to hop up and down in our houses', particularly suited them to original speculation and experimental method. The audacity and sheer copiousness of Cavendish's writing, in combination with the deliberate eccentricity of her manners and dress, made her an infamous figure in her own time. After witnessing one of her rare London appearances, Pepys wrote in his diary: 'The whole story of this Lady is a romance, and all she doth is romantic', while Dorothy Osborne complained in a letter, 'there are many soberer people in Bedlam'. Even Virginia WOOLF, in *A Room of One's Own*, called her 'a vision of loneliness and riot ... as if some giant cucumber had spread itself over all the roses and carnations and choked them to death'. For a new generation of feminist scholars, Cavendish's appeal lies precisely in her hermaphroditic self-fashioning and her lifelong engagement with sex and representation, writing and power.

Cavendish occupies a significant place in the history of English women's writing as the author of more than a dozen substantial and lavishly printed books between 1653 and 1668, spanning poetry, fiction, natural philosophy, drama, familiar letters, essays, autobiography and biography. Amongst seventeenth-century women only Aphra BEHN can compare with the range and quantity of Cavendish's œuvre. Cavendish's texts enact the cultivation of fame through spectacularised female authorship and personal 'singularity', constantly engaging the nexus of sex, gender and rank to stage a discourse of power and knowledge centred upon the transgressive potential of the heroically chaste, ambitious and intelligent woman. The question of female sexuality is thoroughly mediated in Cavendish's work by the fetishisation of chastity as the prerequisite for advantageous marriage, while advantageous marriage is itself figured as the prerequisite for women's greatest access to power, pleasure and knowledge. In her fiction, and in plays such as *The Presence* (1668) and *The Convent of Pleasure* (1668), Cavendish frequently thematises the need to counter the threat of powerful affect between women; her overt defence of the imperatives of heterosexual con-

jugality suggests its vulnerability. In the prose fiction 'Assaulted and Pursued Chastity' (*Nature's Pictures*, 1656), the unmarried Queen of Amity not only falls in love with Travellia, the cross-dressed heroine of 'masculine and courageous spirit', but her passion continues unabated after the truth of Travellia's gender is revealed. Only divine intervention cures the Queen by transferring her passion to a proper object, the King of Amour: 'Since I cannot marry her, and so make her my husband, I will keep her if I can, and so make her my friend.' Similarly, the extreme 'amity' between two married women, the Empress and her scribe, 'Margaret Newcastle', in *The Blazing World* (1666), is the subject of a teasingly self-conscious negotiation: 'Husbands have reason to be jealous of Platonick Lovers, for they are very dangerous, as being not onely very intimate and close, but subtil and insinuating.'

In Cavendish's writing, the most beneficial alliance is the one which transforms a female commoner into either a Duchess or a Queen, thus replicating or improving the example of her own marriage (a marriage that had been opposed by Henrietta Maria as too exalted for her Maid of Honour). The unique status of the sovereign woman, especially the romance plot of a 'maid' who becomes a Queen or Empress through her own merit, particularly galvanised Cavendish as a figure for the utopian supervention of gender ideology and the magnetic attraction of power. In the prefatory address 'To the Reader' in *The Blazing World*, Cavendish confesses that she is 'as ambitious as ever any of my sex was': 'Though I cannot be Henry the Fifth, or Charles the Second, yet I endeavour to be Margaret the First.' After a long gap, most of Cavendish's works are now in print again in modern or facsimile editions.

The Blazing World and Other Writings by Margaret Cavendish, ed. K. Lilley, London, 1994; *The Plays of Margaret Cavendish*, ed. A.

Shaver, Baltimore, 1999; A. Battigelli, *Margaret Cavendish and the Exiles of the Mind*, Lexington, 1998.

Kate Lilley

Newman, John Henry (1801–1890), Anglican clergyman, Roman Catholic cardinal and theologian. Born in London into a middle-class family whose fortunes were declining, he was educated at Ealing School, from where he went to Trinity College at Oxford University. He graduated BA in 1820. Although he failed to achieve the brilliant degree that everyone expected, his intellectual ability was widely recognised and in 1822 he was elected a fellow of Oriel College. In 1825 he was ordained priest in the Church of England and in 1828 was appointed vicar of the University Church of St Mary the Virgin in Oxford. From 1833 he was one of the leaders of the Oxford Movement, which asserted the essentially Catholic nature of the Church of England. In 1842 he retired from St Mary's to the village of Littlemore, where he lived in a quasi-monastic community with a number of young men who had gathered around him. In 1845 he was received into the Roman Catholic Church, as 'the one true Fold of the Redeemer', and two years later was ordained a Catholic priest. Attracted by the rule of the Oratorians, a religious congregation founded in Rome in the sixteenth century, on his return to England in 1848 he set up the Oratory in Birmingham. Apart from four years as rector of the Catholic University in Dublin in 1854–1858, he lived in Birmingham for the remainder of his long life. In 1879 he was made Cardinal by Pope Leo XIII. Newman wrote many major works of theology, philosophy and apologetics. He is widely regarded as among the greatest of modern English theologians. Within the Roman Catholic Church the cause for his canonisation as a saint was introduced in 1958.

The sexuality of Newman and his circle has long been a subject for conjecture. Much of the evidence is ambiguous. Charles Kingsley's famous attack on Newman in 1864, which spurred Newman to write his *Apologia Pro Vita Sua*, contains much sexualised language: it may be interpreted as a conflict over meanings of masculinity. Others wrote of Newman's lack of virility and his 'characteristically feminine nature'. The idea that the Oxford Movement contained a significant stream of homoeroticism was popularised by Geoffrey Faber in *Oxford Apostles* (1933), in which he portrayed Newman as a sublimated homosexual with feminine characteristics. Certainly the Oxford Movement attracted a number of fervent young men and produced some intense masculine friendships, though in the self-contained male world of Oxford University this was hardly surprising. Newman did not shun friendships with women, but these were invariably at a distance. There is no evidence that he was ever drawn to a heterosexual union. From the age of 15 he was convinced that it was the will of God that he should lead a single life. In Oxford he taught that celibacy, for the priesthood, was 'a high state of life, to which the multitude of men cannot aspire'. His deepest emotional relationships were with younger men who were his disciples. The most significant of these were the flamboyant Richard Hurrell Froude, who died in 1836, and Ambrose St John, who lived with Newman from 1843. He followed Newman into the Roman Catholic Church and became a member of the Birmingham Oratory, where he lived until his death in 1875. Newman was profoundly affected by the loss of these intimate friends. At his own request, he was buried in the same grave as St John. Among gay Roman Catholics he is a hero figure.

G. Faber, *Oxford Apostles: A Character Study of the Oxford Movement*, London, 1933; S. Gilley, *Newman and his Age*, London, 1990; D. Hilliard, 'UnEnglish and Unmanly: Anglo-Catholicism and Homosexuality', *Victorian Studies*, 25, 2 (1982): 181–210; I. Ker, *John Henry Newman: A Biography*, Oxford,

1988; J. H. Rigg, *Oxford High Anglicanism and its Chief Leaders*, London, 1895; M. Trevor, *Newman: The Pillar of the Cloud* and *Newman: Light in Winter*, London, 1962.

David Hilliard

Nichols, Beverley (1898–1983), British writer. Nichols wrote novels, plays and musical revues, children's books and a book of poems. He also published books on subjects ranging from religion to gardening, celebrity interviews and autobiographies.

The material for Nichols's six novels was largely autobiographical. *Prelude* (1920) was drawn from his schoolboy days, *Patchwork* (1921) from his undergraduate days, *Evensong* (1932) from his friendship with opera diva Nellie Melba, *Revue* (1939) from the problems in staging his musical revue 'Floodlight' (1936). In *Self* (1922), Nichols used his own sex life and mores in creating the female protagonist – a 1920s Becky Sharp.

His fourth novel, *Crazy Pavements* (1927), is a rewriting of WILDE's *The Picture of Dorian Gray*. The naïve Brian Elme is corrupted by two decadent aristocrats, but unlike Dorian Gray, manages to revert back to his initial innocence before being completely demoralised. Nichols remarked to his biographer that *Crazy Pavements* 'had caused him problems because . . . it was really a homosexual story doctored for general consumption. . . . Today I could write it as it actually was, but, in those days, it was out of the question.'

Nichols's six volumes of autobiography are factually unreliable. This is especially true for his melodramatic demonisation of his alcoholic father – *Father Figure* (1972). This memoir contains the much-cited incident concerning Nichols's father's enraged and violent reaction upon finding him reading *The Picture of Dorian Gray*, which signified, for Nichols's father, his son's possible homosexuality. Connors's biography corrects these fabulations and provides a frank portrait of Nichols's rela-tionships and promiscuous sex life, including his penchant for rough trade and masochistic sex.

What is of interest in Nichols's life as an author is the complex relationship between his insatiable desire for celebrity (he was and always wanted to be, in one reviewer's words, 'the author of the moment with the book of the moment') and his use of his life as a basis for a great deal of his work. His homosexuality problematised the ways in which he could use this material without alienating his readers. Novels like *Crazy Pavements* testify to the fine line Nichols walked between writing about homosexuality and what would be conventionally acceptable. It is this desire to include rather than omit homosexuality that makes his work particularly interesting.

B. Connors, *Beverley Nichols: A Life*, London, 1991.

Jason Boyd

Nicolson, Sir Harold (George) (1886–1968), British diplomat and writer. Nicolson was born in Teheran, Persia (Iran), the third son of British diplomat Sir Arthur Nicolson, later Lord Carnock, and Catherine Rowan Hamilton. Following a childhood spent in Europe, Turkey and Russia, Nicolson enrolled at Balliol College, Oxford, graduating in 1909. Over the next 20 years, he served in the Foreign Office in Persia, Hungary, Bulgaria and Morocco. He made significant contributions to the drafting of the Balfour Declaration during World War I and his participation on the British delegation to the Paris Peace Conference served as the basis for his *Peacemaking, 1919* (1933). Later works on diplomacy include *Diplomacy* (1939), *The Congress of Vienna* (1946) and *The Evolution of the Diplomatic Method* (1954). In 1929, he resigned his diplomatic post in Berlin to pursue a writing career in fiction, nonfiction and journalism. Between 1935 and 1945, he served in the House of Commons as a member of the National

Labour Party. His broadcasts for the BBC, begun in the 1930s, continued throughout his life, and he served on its Board of Governors. Among his 125 published works are travel books, fiction and biographies of subjects of gay interest including VERLAINE, BYRON, Swinburne and Baudelaire, as well as portraits of TENNYSON, Lord Curzon, his father (Portrait of a Diplomatist, 1930), Dwight Morrow and the official biography of King George V (1952), for which he was knighted in 1953.

In 1913, Nicolson married the poet and novelist Victoria (Vita) SACKVILLE-WEST, entering into one of the most legendary gay/lesbian marriages of the twentieth century. Throughout their long marriage the couple coexisted within a seemingly conventional union, which produced two sons, Benedict and Nigel. Yet they led separate intimate lives: Nicolson in a series of passing relationships with younger men, Sackville-West in deep attachments to Violet Keppel TREFUSIS (recalled in her unpublished autobiographical novel Challenge), and author Virginia WOOLF, with whom she conducted a correspondence comprising one of the century's most significant records of lesbian love. Despite these separate lives, the unconventional Nicolson–Sackville-West marriage, sensitively chronicled by their son Nigel in Portrait of a Marriage (1973), was a profound friendship that proved conducive to their writing careers as well as to the creation of one of the world's most extraordinary formal gardens at their home at Sissinghurst Castle, Kent. The couple remained together until Sackville-West's death in 1962. Harold Nicolson died at Sissinghurst six years later.

Diaries and Letters by Harold Nicolson, ed. N. Nicolson, New York, 1966; N. Nicolson, Portrait of a Marriage, New York, 1973.

A. M. Wentink

Nietzsche, Friedrich (1844–1900), German philosopher. Nietzsche was born in Roecken, a village in Saxony. His father had studied theology and was a Protestant clergyman, though he never became accustomed to the restricted life of a small village. After his father's death, Nietzsche received a scholarship to attend the famous boarding school of Schulpforta near Naumburg. There he met his first friends and discovered that he might have homoerotic desires. He fell in love with one of the students and wrote several poems about his relationship. He read poets like August von PLATEN and Lord BYRON, whose adventurous life he admired.

In 1864 Nietzsche finished secondary school and enrolled in philosophy and classical philology at the university in Bonn. He also became a member of the Franconia fraternity, where he had several homoerotic experiences with other students. In 1865 he decided to study at the university in Leipzig. There he found another friend, Erwin Rohde, to whom he confessed his love. They shared a deep fascination for Greek poetry and philosophy. The philologist Ritschl recognised Nietzsche's extraordinary talent and encouraged him. In 1869 he became a professor of Greek and Latin philology in Basel, where the students appreciated his remarkable enthusiasm for antiquities and noticed his love for Greek sculptures and men. He was also strongly influenced by Arthur SCHOPENHAUER's philosophy and his critical approach to the work of other scholars and the philosophers.

In 1872 Nietzsche published a book, Die Geburt der Tragödie aus dem Geiste der Musik (The Birth of Tragedy out of the Spirit of Music), that emphasised the forgotten irrational and emotional aspects of Greek culture. Whereas the conventional interpretations concentrated on the rational arguments of Greek philosophy, he stressed the significance of the irrational aspects in mythology and the mysteries, and of Dionysos as a leading voice in Greek culture. The treatise caused a scandal, and many philologists rejected his position.

Even more disastrous was his reverence

for Richard Wagner, the famous opera composer. Although Nietzsche admired his music, Wagner hated homosexual men and did not hesitate to spread rumours about Nietzsche's homosexuality. The topic was fashionable because many people assumed that LUDWIG II, the king of Bavaria, was a homosexual man, too, and Bavaria was the only kingdom in Germany without anti-sodomy laws. When Nietzsche heard of these rumours he ended his friendship with Wagner.

In Basel he felt more and more uncomfortable and lonesome. He was not able to stand the hostile atmosphere and became depressive. In 1879 he was allowed to leave the university and received a modest pension. In the following years he spent his life together with his Jewish friend Paul Ree, in Switzerland and in Italy. This country was considered a paradise for homosexual men in the nineteenth century, and other gay poets and writers such as Platen, Hans Christian ANDERSEN and André GIDE described the hospitality of Italy and especially the island of Capri. At this time Nietzsche published some of his most important philosophical books, *Also sprach Zarathustra* and *Jenseits von Gut und Böse*. His philosophy condemned Christian values, which he called the morals of slaves, proclaimed that God is dead and praised the joy of life in the Renaissance as embodied by unscrupulous people like Cesare Borgia.

In 1888 Nietzsche fell ill, and his insanity became more and more obvious as he lost his clear thinking and his identity. His homophobic sister Elisabeth cared for him in order to share his glory and his fame, and tried to censor his books and his letters by destroying compromising writings. Physicians found out that Nietzsche had contracted syphilis and that he had reached the final stage, which was characterised by a serious mental disorder. After many years of deep insanity, Nietzsche died in Weimar.

V. Gerhardt, *Friedrich Nietzsche*, Munich,

1992; J. Koehler, *Zarathustras Geheimnis*, Nördlingen, 1989; W. Nigg, *Friedrich Nietzsche*, Zurich, 1994.

Gerald Pilz

Nijinsky, Vaslav (1888/9–1950), Russian dancer and choreographer. Born Vaslav Fomich Nizhinsky (Nijinsky) in Kiev, he was the son of Polish dancers who were his first teachers. At age 10, he entered the Imperial Theatre School, St Petersburg, and was soon recognised as a talented if distant and introverted student. Despite illnesses, his promise was unquestionable and, in 1906, while still a student, he made his début with the Imperial Ballet at the Maryinsky Theatre. Immediately upon graduation in 1907, he entered the Maryinsky as a *choryphe* (a rank between *corps de ballet* and soloist) and partnered the *prima ballerina assoluta* Mathilde Kschessinka. His rise was meteoric, but already he showed signs of unconventional behaviour.

That same year Nijinsky was introduced by a fellow dancer to Prince Pavel Lvov and became his lover. Perhaps because Nijinsky lacked his onstage eloquence in social intercourse offstage or because, as Richard Buckle reports, Nijinsky 'was small in a part where size is usually admired', the affair was short-lived. Lvov introduced Nijinsky to potential admirers including, in late 1908, the impresario Serge DIAGHILEV. According to his diary, Nijinsky 'loved' Lvov, but seeing an opportunity to promote his career, entered into an affair with Diaghilev. He became a principal dancer of Diaghilev's company in its historic 1909 and 1910 Paris seasons which introduced Russian ballet to the West. In 1911, the frequently obstinate artist refused to change his 're-vealing' costume in a performance of *Giselle*, and was dismissed by the Maryinsky, thereby terminating his remaining two-year obligation to the Imperial Ballet. Having secured the exclusive claim on Nijinsky's talent, Diaghilev was able to transform his formerly 'pickup' company of Russian dancers into the permanent institution of the Ballets Russes. Nijinksy's phenomenal rise and acclaim as 'le Dieu de la Danse' among audiences and with the social and aristocratic élite of Western Europe all but eclipsed other male dancers in the company. The undercurrent of rivalry and eventual animosity among his peers, all but incomprehensible to the naïve Nijinsky, most probably was encouraged by Diaghilev to intensify the young dancer's dependency.

Fokine's pioneering anti-classical ballets, created in collaboration with artists Léon Bakst and Alexandre Benois and the composer Igor Stravinsky, fueled the reputation of the Ballets Russes as a crucible of modern art. *Chopiniana* (later *Les Sylphides*, 1908/9), *Egyptian Nights* (later *Cléopatre*, 1908); *Schéhérézade*, *Les Orientales* (1910), *Le Carnaval* (1910/11), *Le Spectre de la Rose*, *Narcisse*, *Petrushka* (1911), *Le Dieu Bleu* and *Daphnis et Chloé* (1912) served as vehicles for Nijinsky's virtuosity and poetic acting. Nijinsky's intimacy with Diaghilev, with whom he lived openly in a notorious relationship, the impresario's patronage of Nijinsky's choreography and his dislike of Mikhail Fokine's interpretation of *Daphnis and Chloé* caused a rift in the Ballets Russes and Fokine's abrupt departure in 1912.

Now the official Ballets Russes choreographer, Nijinsky created three ballets for Diaghilev in two years: *L'Après-Midi d'un Faune* (1912), *Le Sacre du Printemps* (1913) and *Jeux* (1913). His choreography was at once radically experimental, idiosyncratic and scandalous and his iconoclastic works rarely understood and too 'modern' even for the Ballets Russes. With decor by Bakst and Nicholas Roerich, and scores by, among others, Debussy, Stravinsky and Richard Strauss, he created frieze-like stylisation and autoeroticism in *Faune*, barbaric stomping and convulsions in *Sacre* (causing a riot at its Paris premiere), bisexual (originally intended as homosexual) innuendo in *Jeux* and improvisational chaos in Strauss's *Tyl Eulenspiegel*.

Nijinsky's impulsive marriage to Romola de Pulszky on the Ballets Russes tour to South America in 1913 devastated Diaghilev, who dismissed Nijinsky from the company. In early 1914, Nijinsky was asked to form a London-based company. Lacking conventional communication skills, let alone business and administrative acuity, the dancer fell ill and the company folded in less than a month. Nijinsky and his family were then detained in Hungary as prisoners of war. To ensure star power for the Ballets Russes' New York engagement, Diaghilev was induced to rehire Nijinsky. The Metropolitan Opera Board subsequently hired Nijinsky as artistic director for a second chaotic American tour. Yet the Ballets Russes had become a hostile environment for Nijinsky; Diaghilev, with whom he constantly quarrelled about money, had taken a new lover/protégé, Léonide Massine, and many dancers were openly antagonistic.

After a brief tour of Spain and South America in 1917, Nijinsky settled in Switzerland to wait out World War I. His last appearance was a mystical anti-war statement danced for a private audience in 1919. Thereafter, he receded into schizophrenia and delusion. The diaries in which the artist vacillates between the euphoria of being one with God and the horror of uncontrollable madness comprise one of history's great artistic and sexual confessional documents; an unexpurgated version was only published in 1995. Nijinsky was shuttled between various private homes and institutions for the rest of his life and cared for by his wife.

As a creator, Nijinsky revealed traces of a rare and revolutionary choreographic genius that, because of a tragic inability to articulate his own theories or successfully notate his dances, will never completely be understood. The embodiment of the exotic and sensual art of the first decade of the Ballets Russes, Nijinsky the dancer has been enshrined as a symbol of the full range of sexual identities from androgyny to homoeroticism.

R. Buckle, *Nijinsky*, London, 1971; L. Kirstein, *Nijinsky Dancing*, New York, 1995; P. Ostwald, *Vaslav Nijinsky: A Leap into Madness*, London, 1991; K. Kopelson, *The Queer Afterlife of Vaslav Nijinsky*, London, 1997.

A. M. Wentink

Novello, Ivor (1893–1951), British actor, dramatist and composer. Novello's real name was David Ivor Davies; he changed his name by deed poll in 1927. He was brought up in the Welsh city of Cardiff in a musical family. His mother, Clara Novello Davies ('Madame Clara'), was a well known musician, singer and teacher who later taught singing in London and New York; until her death in 1943 she was a close companion of her son. Novello was educated privately, then won a choral scholarship to Magdalen College School, Oxford, where he sang soprano in the chapel choir. As a youth he began to compose songs and was drawn to the theatre, so moved to London. From 1913 he lived with his mother in a flat on the roof of the Strand Theatre in Aldwych. This remained his London residence until his death.

During World War I Novello served without distinction, mainly doing clerical work, in the Royal Naval Air Service, and continued to write many songs. His greatest success was 'Keep the Home Fires Burning' (1914), which became one of the most popular songs of the war and brought him both fame and a substantial income from royalties. After the war he acted in many silent films. In 1922–1923 he went to the United States to work with the director D. W. Griffith, and in 1930–1931 he spent nine months acting in sound films for MGM in Hollywood. However, Novello preferred the live theatre. He returned to London, where he quickly established his reputation as a successful dramatist and actor-manager. From the 1920s until his death Novello was a dominant figure on the English stage, his principal rival being Noel COWARD. Novello wrote 15 plays and appeared in 21. From 1935 he wrote and composed lavishly staged and sentimental musical plays. The best known of these were *The Dancing Years* (1939) and *King's Rhapsody* (1949), both of which were turned into films. *Perchance to Dream* (1945) included the famous song 'We'll Gather Lilacs'.

In appearance, by the canons of male beauty of the 1920s, 'Ivor' (as everybody called him) was strikingly handsome, with a shock of raven-black hair, pale skin, expressive eyes and a charming smile. He had a remarkable stage presence. His plays were always successful when he acted in them. As a male sex symbol, with a touch of class, he attracted a huge (mainly female) following. The popular press often linked him romantically with prominent female actors such as Gladys Cooper, but in the theatre world it was generally known that he was 'not the marrying kind'. In 1944, during World War II, he was imprisoned for a month for the offence of evading the wartime petrol restrictions. The harsh punishment was imposed by a judge who loathed homosexuals.

Novello had many male lovers and employed a high proportion of gay actors in his plays. In his own circle he referred to *The Dancing Years* as 'The Prancing Queers'. His partner Robert (Bobbie) Andrews, an actor with whom he had lived since 1917 at their country house, survived him. Novello exemplified the homosexual man for whom the theatre was a dream world of colour, emotion and glamour, and the popular actor whose sexual life had to be concealed from his fans.

J. Harding, *Ivor Novello*, London, 1987; W. Macqueen Pope, *Ivor: The Story of an Achievement: A Biography of Ivor Novello*, London, 1951; R. Rose, *Perchance to Dream: The World of Ivor Novello*, London, 1974; S. Wilson, *Ivor*, London, 1975.

David Hilliard

Novo, Salvador (1904–1974), Mexican poet. Novo was a member of the avant-garde group Contemporáneos. As a poet he started his career at an early age; *Poemas de adolescencia* (1918–1920) is his first book. *Nuevo amor* (*New Love*, 1933) is considered one of the best collections of poetry ever written in Spanish. The *Romance de Angelillo y Adela* (*Ballad of Angelillo and Adela*, 1934) chronicles a love affair he had with the poet Federico García LORCA. *Poemas proletarios* (*Proletariat Poems*, 1934) are written in an anti-heroic mode; they do not vindicate the virile values of the revolution. In *Never Ever* (1934), 'VIII' is an erotic poem like the ones in *Nuevo amor*. *Sátira. El libro ca . . .* (Satire. The son of a . . . book, 1955) represents the triumph of the baroque in Novo's poetry – the æsthetics of meanness. He was a member of the influential group of Teatro Ulises, also a translator of foreign plays, a stage director, the deputy of theatre under Carlos Chávez, and founder of the Theatre-Restaurant La Capilla. The play *Cuauhtémoc* (1962) tells the story of Mexico's conquest. The play *El tercer Fausto* (*The Third Faust*, 1934) is an openly gay drama: Alberto sells his soul to the devil to become a woman in order to conquer the love of Armando. Once Alberto becomes Ella (She), Alberto finds out that Armando was already in love with him. Novo also wrote, among other plays, *La guerra de las gordas* (*The War of the Fatties*, 1963).

El joven (*The Young Man*, 1923) is a short story of outstanding quality, a Proustian exercise in which a young man wanders around in the brand new metropolis that is becoming the Mexico City of the 1920s. *Nueva grandeza mexicana* (*New Mexican Grandeur*, 1943) is a modern chronicle of Mexico City. It has been very influential because of its depiction of Mexican popular culture. *Cocina mexicana o historia gastronómica de la ciudad de México* (*Mexican Cuisine of Mexico City*, 1967) is a history of Mexican food. 'Memoirs', the erotic memoirs of Novo, present in explicit detail the underground gay life of Mexico City. *Continente vacío* (*Empty Continent*, 1935) is a key book to

understand the *desencanto* after the period of Panamerican ideas of Ibero-American leaders like Vasconcelos. Nine volumes under the generic title of *Vida en México* (*Life in Mexico*) collect their newspaper articles. Novo became the best paid op-ed writer in Mexico; he was also a pioneer in radio and television. *Letras vencidas* (*Defeated words*, 1962) is a collection of articles. As the title indicates, they present a moment of pessimism, despite the fact that at the same moment he was at the peak of his fame and recognition. Novo was official chronicler of Mexico City and a member of the Mexican Academy of Letters. He also wrote the script of *El signo de la muerte* (*The Sign of Death*, 1936), one of the first movies by Cantinflas. Novo always remained out of the closet and tried to influence and educate Mexican public opinion about the naturalness of homosexuality, using studies about sexuality published in the United States.

Salvador A. Oropesa

Nugent, (Richard) Bruce (1906–1987), American writer and artist. Born in Washington, DC, Nugent was raised by middle-class parents, whom he described as both Bohemian and respectable members of the city's black bourgeoisie. Nugent early confirmed to his mother his sexual interest in men after his younger brother reported seeing him kiss a male friend; his father, however, never directly discussed the matter with him, though Nugent felt he had some suspicions. Following his father's death, the family moved to New York when Nugent was 13. He returned briefly to Washington in 1924 after declaring himself an artist and losing his mother's financial support. During that year, he met a number of influential writers and critics, among them the poet Langston Hughes and Howard University professor Alain Locke, whose anthology *The New Negro* (1925), a signal text of the Harlem Renaissance, included Nugent's short story 'Sahdji'.

Accompanied by Hughes, Nugent returned to New York City the following year. There he helped found the Dark Tower, a Harlem salon for black writers and artists. He also contributed stories and artwork to a number of publications in which he freely explored homoeroticism, feminine sexuality and the conundrums of gender-based desire. His cover for the March 1926 issue of the National Urban League's magazine *Opportunity* featured a man in drag. That same year, in addition to illustrations, Nugent contributed 'Smoke, Lilies, and Jade' to the only published issue of the literary quarterly *Fire!!* This elliptical, loosely autobiographical story was the first portrayal of male homosexual desire in African-American fiction. Though focused on his affair with a man he calls Beauty, the protagonist Alex expresses an equal sexual interest in women, and he realises at the end of the story that 'one *can* love two at the same time'.

Though always comfortable with and forthright about his sexual interests, Nugent used the pseudonym Richard Bruce and the initials RNB for his 'gay-themed' work out of deference to his mother's wishes that he protect the family name. In 1952, he married Grace Elizabeth Marr. The marriage lasted until his wife's death in 1969, but Nugent continued to have sexual relationships with men during that time. Nugent spent the latter years of his life in Hoboken, New Jersey, across the river from Manhattan, where he continued to live as a Bohemian artist supported by social security and the goodwill of others.

As the Harlem Renaissance undergoes its own renaissance, Nugent has become the focus of new attentions. His unreserved candour about his sexuality during the 1920s set him apart from his gay and bisexual contemporaries and has made him a particularly important icon in recent African-American queer literary and historical work. The British filmmaker Isaac Julien used excerpts from 'Smoke, Lilies, and Jade' as part of the soundtrack of *Looking for Langston* (1989), a meditation on Hughes, the Harlem Renaissance and male homosexual desire. Though he is a minor figure in the official canon of the Harlem Renaissance, Nugent's queerness makes more legible the significant if subtly coded queerness of that larger cultural movement.

D. Levering Lewis, *When Harlem Was in Vogue*, New York, 1981; E. Garber, 'Richard Bruce Nugent', in *Afro-American Writers from the Harlem Renaissance to 1940: Dictionary of Literary Biography*, Detroit, 1987: Vol. 51, pp. 213–21; C. M. Smith, 'Bruce Nugent: Bohemian of the Harlem Renaissance', in J. Beam (ed.) *In the Life: A Black Gay Anthology*, Boston, 1986: 209–20.

Scott Bravmann

O

Ohlfsen, Dora (Dorothea Ohlfsen-Bagge) (1867–1948), Australian sculptor. Ohlfsen was born in Ballarat, Victoria. Her father was Norwegian and her mother Australian. She travelled to Germany in 1883 to continue her piano studies; however, when she contracted neuritis, she began teaching music in Germany and later in Russia. She lived in St Petersburg with a Madame Kerbitz and took up painting; she sold one of her works to the Tsarina. Her extensive knowledge of languages gained her employment with the American ambassador and allowed her to write on music, theatre, drama and art for Russian and American newspapers. After travelling through various Baltic countries, she settled in Rome to study sculpture at the French Academy and with the French engraver, Pierre Dautel. She produced many medallions using academic portraits and Symbolist compositions.

During World War I she became a Red Cross nurse in Italy. In order to aid Australian soldiers she designed, and paid for, the *Anzac Medallion* which was sold to raise funds in London in 1916. The Fascist government were patrons of her work and she produced a large relief portrait medallion of Mussolini and a war memorial, *Sacrifice*, at Formia, in 1924–1926. Ohlfsen was commissioned by Mussolini to design this memorial because her art studies had been solely in Italy and she had nursed Italian soldiers during the war. This is the only work of its kind in Italy to be made by a woman or a foreigner.

Ohlfsen returned to Australia in 1912 and again in 1921–1922, when she made medallions of notables such as Sir James Fairfax, Billy Hughes and Nellie Stewart. Her work is represented in the Art Gallery of New South Wales, the British Museum and Petit Palais, Paris. In 1948 she and her companion, the Russian Baroness Hélène de Kuegelgen, were found gassed in her studio in Rome.

J. Kerr (ed.) *Heritage: The National Women's Art Book*, Sydney, 1995.

Elizabeth Ashburn

Ottesen-Jensen, Elise (1886–1973), known as 'Ottar', Swedish sex educator and reformer. Ottesen-Jensen was born in Norway, but settled in Sweden in 1919. She worked as a journalist in the syndicalist press in the 1920s, and founded Riksförbundet för sexuell upplysning (the Swedish Association for Sex Education, RFSU), in 1933. As president, Ottesen-Jensen led this organisation through its first 25 years; it advocated access to contraceptives, abortion and sex education, as well as the legalisation of homosexual contacts. Ottesen-Jensen's and RFSU's position was that homosexuality was an innate 'variation' or 'deviation' of the sexual instinct.

In her extensive political and educational activity, Ottesen-Jensen repeatedly brought up the topic of homosexuality. She popularised the scientific opinion of the time, pleaded for tolerance and agitated against discriminatory laws. In the early 1930s, she arranged for the gay iron industry worker Eric Thorsell to visit Magnus HIRSCHFELD's Institute for Sexual Science in Berlin for a period of eight months. From the many letters she got from gays and lesbians, asking her for help and advice, she created an informal gay network, providing names, addresses and tips on meeting-places. She also encouraged the founding of Riksförbundet för sexuellt likaberättigande (Swedish Federation for Lesbian and Gay Rights, RFSL) in 1950. In Sweden, homosexual contacts were decriminalised in 1944.

D. H. Linder, *Crusader for Sex Education: Elise Ottesen-Jensen (1886–1973) in Scandinavia and on the International Scene*, Lanham, 1996; Elise Ottesen-Jensen archive and RFSU archive, at Labour Movement Archives and Library, Stockholm.

Lena Lennerhed

Ovid (Publius Ovidius Naso) (43 BC–AD 17), Roman poet. Born in Sulmo in the Appennines, east of Rome, Ovid studied grammar and rhetoric in Rome, and grew up in a period of civil war which followed the assassination of Julius Caesar, coming to maturity in the 20s BC when Augustus was establishing himself as the ruler of Rome.

Intended for a public career, Ovid held several minor positions in the magistrature but preferred to concentrate his efforts on poetry, and published his first collection, the *Amores*, maybe as early as 20 BC. A revised edition, issued around 2 BC, survives. Of all the Latin love poets, of whom he personally knew Horace, Propertius and Tibullus (for whom he wrote an elegy, *Amores* III. 9), Ovid is the one who most consistently deals with heterosexual relations, though he is aware that boys were potential objects of desire. The detail he provides of relations between men and

women is a major source for expectations of a Roman man in the field of sexual behaviour, and while it is no longer generally believed that all his personal poetry is strictly autobiographical, it may be supposed that the success of Ovid as a poet depended on the appeal of his description of these relationships. His *Ars Amatoria* (*The Art of Love*), published in 1 BC, treats love as a skill which can be taught, the practical application of which ran counter to the revival of traditional virtues promoted by Augustus. Ovid's lack of seriousness in this area – and perhaps some offence to a member of the emperor's family – contributed to his banishment by Augustus in AD 8 to Tomis, on the western shores of the Black Sea, where he eventually died, all his attempts at securing his return unsuccessful. This exile coincided with the banishment of Augustus's granddaughter Julia for adultery, which has prompted speculation that Ovid was somehow connected with Julia's activities; he blames a 'poem' (*carmen*), assumed to be the *Ars*, and a 'blunder' (*error*). Ovid's poetry from exile includes tender verses addressd to his wife, as well as affectionate poems to friends.

Ovid was not homosexual and did not express praise for homosexuality as his own sentiment. The only mention, indeed, of a favourable view is a passage in the *Amores* in which he laments having neither a boy nor a girl about whose love he can speak. In the *Ars amatoria* (III. 681–7) Ovid indicated that he dislikes a union which cannot give the same pleasure to both partners, adding that for this reason the love of boys attracts him less than the love of women. Furthermore, Ovid shared his contemporaries' contempt for the man who gives himself to other men.

Interestingly, however, when Ovid spoke of SAPPHO he explicitly took account of her 'lesbianism', if only in order to condemn it. In the *Heroides*, fictional letters from heroines to men who had deserted them, one whole letter, XV, is given to the legendary love of Sappho for the cruel

Phaon. In one verse, Sappho admits having loved women '*non sine crimine*' ('not without crime'), and in another Ovid says that because of her love of women, Sappho's reputation has been tarnished. An ambiguous phrase in *Tristia* (II. 365) – in which, listing the ways in which classical poets spoke of love, Ovid asks, 'What did Sappho teach if not to love women?' – should therefore be seen in light of this view.

Ovid, along with VIRGIL, was a major influence on later literature. *Metamorphoses*, the source for countless well known mythological stories such as the changing of Daphne into a laurel tree when pursued by Apollo (Book I), the self-obsession of Narcissus (Book III), and the flight of Daedalus and Icarus (Book VIII). Ovid's true contribution to homosexual imagination appeared in *Metamorphoses*, which for centuries ranked among the most widely read and beloved of classical texts. Ovid's accounts of homosexual myths, whether in the original work or in anthologies, were the most accessible and familiar to writers, painters and sculptors and to the public. Along with the best known myths – Orpheus creating the love of men, Cyparissus and Apollo, Zeus and GANYMEDE, Hyacinth and Apollo (all in Book X of the *Metamorphoses*) – are less well known ones — Poseidon and Pelopes, Cycnus and Filius, Minos and Milaetus. Important because of its rarity was also the myth of Iphis, who though born a woman fell in love with another woman and whom the goddess Isis, moved to pity, changed into a man. Mention of the mythological love of Bacchus and Ampelos also appears in the *Fastorum libri* (III. 407–14), an account of Roman festivals.

Ovid is consistently entertaining as a poet, whether through wit or ability as a story-teller. His devotion to the practice of poetry is paramount, and he pushed the parameters of different genres to their limits.

Ovid, *The Love Poems*, trans. A. D. Melville,

Oxford, 1990; S. Lilja, *Homosexuality in Republican and Augustan Rome*, Helsinki, 1983.
                    Giovanni Dall'Orto and Roger Pitcher

Owen, Wilfred (1893–1918), British poet. Born near Oswestry, Shropshire, into a middle-class family of limited means, from an early age Owen showed an interest in literature, and his keen intelligence allowed him to excel at the Birkenhead Institute in Liverpool, Shrewsbury Technical School and University College, Reading. His mother, with whom he was particularly close, hoped that Owen might be ordained, so he spent a few months as a lay assistant to a minister at Dunsdan. Around this time, in early 1913, Owen began to write poems heavily influenced by the Romanticism of Shelley and Keats, including the homoerotic 'Anateus'. In that same year he left for Bordeaux to teach English at the Berlitz School, then became a tutor for the children of Madame Léger. His poetry from this period, including 'Maundy Thursday', treats, albeit fitfully, male–male desire.

In 1915 Owen returned to England and enlisted in the Artist's Rifles. He was sent to the Somme as an officer with the 2nd Battalion Manchester Regiment in January 1917. By May he was diagnosed as having shell-shock and was sent to Craiglockhart War Hospital in Scotland. There he met the older poet Siegfried SASSOON, who was so impressed with Owen and his verse that he quickly befriended and decided to mentor him. This relationship was dramatised by Stephen MacDonald in his 1983 play *Not About Heroes*, and fictionalised by Pat Barker in her novel *Regeneration* (1991). Sassoon encouraged Owen to pursue further his graphically descriptive style, notable in poems such as 'Dulce et Decorum Est' and 'Disabled'. Owen was discharged from Craiglockhart in October 1917 and spent a three-week leave in London. Equipped with a letter of introduction from Sassoon, he met Robert Ross, who had been Oscar WILDE's intimate friend. Ross provided Owen with an entrée into the English literary scene.

Owen returned to France in August 1918 and in October earned the Military Cross. A week before the Armistice was signed he was killed while leading his men across the Sambre Canal. Owen is arguably the most significant poet of World War I, and his main theme, 'the pity of war' rather than its heroism, mirrors the pessimism of the modern moment. As Paul Fussell has persuasively contended, Owen occupies as well a firm place in the tradition of homoerotic war poetry, epitomised by his early 'It was a Navy Boy' and the more mature 'Sonnet: To My Friend, with an Identity Disc' and 'Strange Meeting'. Only five of his poems appeared in print in his lifetime; Owen's war poetry was posthumously published first by Edith Sitwell and later by Sassoon.

K. Van Comer, Strange Meetings: Walt Whitman, Wilfred Owen and the Poetry of War, Lund, Sweden, 1996; P. Fussell, The Great War and Modern Memory, New York, 1975; J. Stallworthy, Wilfred Owen, Oxford, 1974; M. Taylor, 'Introduction', Lads: Love Poetry of the Trenches, new edn, London, 1998.

George Piggford

P

Pandoni, Giannantonio de' ('Il Porcellio') (before 1409–after 1485), Italian humanist. Il Porcellio was born in Naples, but the first documents concerning him date from his period as a lecturer at the University of Rome. In 1434 he took part in an uprising which chased Pope Eugene IV from Rome, and he then participated in a mission to the Council of Basel. After the restoration of the pope, however, Il Porcellio was imprisoned for ten years. On his release, he began to move from court to court, writing Latin poems and historical works designed to ingratiate himself with various Italian luminaries; in Naples, he was appointed to diplomatic posts and in 1452 was made poet laureate to Emperor Frederick III. He lived subsequently in Rimini (1456) and Milan (1456–1459), then again in Naples and finally in Rome, where he taught at the university, and where he died sometime after 1485.

Although he was married and had at least one child, Il Porcellio throughout his life had a reputation as a sodomite. The most overt testimony to his behaviour was a short story published in 1554, after his death, by Matteo Bandello (1485–1561), recounting his years in Milan at the court of Duke Francesco Sforza. According to Bandello, Il Porcellio married late in life at the insistence of the duke, who wanted to distract him from young men. One day Il Porcellio fell ill, and his wife, believing him to be near death, summoned a confessor. When the priest left his room, she enquired whether her husband had confessed to the sin of sodomy. The priest admitted that he had not, whereupon he twice returned to ask Il Porcellio if he had committed the crime against nature, which he denied. Eventually, since Il Porcellio's wife kept insisting, the priest told him straightforwardly: 'You deny having sinned against nature, yet I am assured you are a thousand times fonder of boys than goats are fond of salt.' Il Porcellio, shaking his head, shouted: 'Oh, oh, reverend father, you did not ask me properly. Amusing myself with boys is to me more natural than eating or drinking to humankind, yet you asked me whether I had sinned against nature! Go away, go away, sir, since you do not know what a desirable thing is.'

Other contemporary testimonies to Il Porcellio's sexuality exist. For instance, the poet Francesco Filelfo, in Milan, played host to Il Porcellio, his son and two boys travelling with them; Filelfo and Il Porcellio later argued and Filelfo, in *De jociis et seriis* (1458–1465), published a series of venomous Latin epigrams about the man he called 'Porcellus Porcellius' ('Piggy Pig') and also accused him of sodomy in a Latin letter. Filelfo's 'Eulogium in Porcellium Porcellum Grammaticum' is a make-believe epitaph for the humanist in which he says: 'Piggy Porcellius, renowned for every / vice, is now ashes in this place. / In fact, having been unique as a bugger [*paedico fuit unicus*], his destiny was being burned by fire / or, poor him, after death: thus the gods decreed.' In another composition, Filelfo said that Il Porcellio's reputation for sodomy was known all over Lombardy in spite of his advanced age. The reputation was confirmed by a student, 'Pierangelo Siciliano', who between 1470 and 1480, lamented the wickedness of students in Rome (who, according to him, were also guilty of homosexuality). He also complained that students drew phalluses on the back of their teacher's chair, writing in Latin verse that they were for his lecherous anus.

As for Il Porcellio's own work, one poem, 'In Petrutium adolescentem', tells of young Petruccio who flees the poet's love verses. Yet, Il Porcellio argued, poetry was loved by Apollo, GANYMEDE, Hylas, the Muses and Jove; therefore he who wants to be numbered among the learned must also love poetry. The allusion to Ganymede, Jove's beloved, and Hylas, Hercules' lover, provides evidence of the explicit homoerotic interest of the poem's author.

M. Bandello, *Le novelle*, Turin, 1974, part I, section 6; *Carmina illustrium poetarum italorum*, Florence, 1719–1726: Vol. 7; U. Frittelli, *Giannantonio de' Pandoni detto 'il Porcellio'*, Florence, 1900; C. de' Rosmini, *Vita di Francesco Filelfo da Tolentino*, Milan, 1808: Vol. 3, pp. 32–4, 44 and 161–3.

                 Giovanni Dall'Orto

Parnok, Sophia Yakovlevna (1885–1933), Russian poet. Parnok, Russia's only self-identified, openly lesbian poet, was born in Taganrog, Russia, the first child of a physician mother who died when she was 6 years old. Parnok's father, a pharmacist, remarried shortly after his first wife's death. Friction with her stepmother and, later, with her father, who strongly disapproved of her lesbianism, cast a shadow over Parnok's youth, but tempered her in moral courage and independence. From the age of 6 she took refuge in writing, and

during her last two years at the *gymnasium* (1901–1903) she wrote extensively, especially about her lesbian sexuality and first love affairs. Her creativity would remain closely linked with her lesbian experience throughout her poetic life as she struggled to make her unique voice heard in an anti-lesbian literary culture.

In 1905, Parnok left home with an actress lover and spent a year in Europe. For a time, she studied at the Geneva Conservatory, but a lack of funds forced her to return to her hated father's house. To become independent of him, she married a close friend and fellow poet, and settled in St Petersburg. She began publishing her poems in journals, but marriage soon stifled her creativity and also hampered her personal life. In January 1909, she braved social censure and financial ruin, deciding to leave her husband in order to make what she termed 'a new start'. After her divorce, Parnok settled in Moscow, became marginally self-supporting, and made a modest career as a journalist, translator, opera librettist and poet. At the beginning of World War I, she met the young poet Marina TSVETAEVA, with whom she became involved in a passionate love affair that left important traces in the poetry of both women. Parnok's belated first book of verse, *Stikhotvoreniia* (*Poems*), appeared shortly before she and Tsvetaeva broke up in 1916. The lyrics in *Poems* presented the first, revolutionarily non-decadent lesbian voice to be heard in a book of Russian poetry.

Parnok and her new lover, Lyudmila Erarskaya, an actress, left Moscow in late summer 1917 and spent the Civil War years in the Crimean town of Sudak. There Parnok was inspired by her new love to write one of her masterpieces, the dramatic poem and libretto for Alexander Spendiarov's opera *Almast*. The physical deprivations of the Sudak years took their toll on Parnok's precarious health (she was a lifelong sufferer from Grave's disease), but the time she spent in the Crimea was a period of spiritual and creative rebirth. Under the aegis of her poetic 'sister', SAPPHO, and her 'Sugdalian sibyl', Eugenia Gertsyk (an intimate, platonic friend), the seeds of Parnok's mature lesbian lyricism were sown and yielded a first harvest in the collections *Rozy Pierii* (*Roses of Pieria*, 1922) and *Loza* (*The Vine*, 1923), which she published on her return to Moscow. Shortly after the appearance of *The Vine*, she met Olga Tsuberbiller, a mathematician at Moscow University, with whom she lived in a permanent relationship from 1925 until her (Parnok's) death. The Soviet censorship soon decided that Parnok's poetic voice was 'unlawful', and she was unable to publish after 1928. Nor did her work find favour with her similarly repressed fellow poets, who were embarrassed by her personal politics of the poet's soul and her straightforward, non-metaphoric expression of lesbian love and experience. Parnok's last two collections, *Muzyka* (*Music*, 1926), and *Vpolgolosa* (*Half-voiced*, 1928), attracted no notice from the official literary establishment.

During the last five years of her life, Parnok eked out a living doing translations. She was frequently bedridden and wrote poetry exclusively for 'the secret drawer'. Her isolation from readers and her status as an 'invisible woman' in Russian poetry became constant themes in her late and best verse. In late 1931, she met Nina Vedeneyeva, a physicist. The two middle-aged women fell impossibly in love, and their affair inspired Parnok's greatest lesbian work, the 1932–1933 lyrical cycles 'Bol'shaia medveditsa' ('Ursa Major') and 'Nenuzhnoe dobro' ('Useless Goods'). Parnok's health collapsed under the 'passionate burden' of her love affair, and she died after a heart attack in a village outside Moscow.

Diana L. Burgin

Pater, Walter (Horatio) (1839–1894), British scholar. An Oxford University don from 1864 to 1894, Pater's writings were formative texts in the late-Victorian phenomena of 'Aestheticism', 'Decadence' and 'Hellenism'.

Pater's first book was a collection of impressionistic essays titled *Studies in the History of the Renaissance* (1873). The Renaissance was for Pater not an historical period but an attitude of expansive intellectual and aesthetic receptiveness, an attitude most vividly demonstrated by 'the last fruit of the Renaissance', the eighteenth-century German Hellenist Johann Joachim WINCKELMANN. Winckelmann's achievement was to move beyond the dead classicism of his time, past Christian guilt and shame, and to fully experience the 'Greek spirit' through the appreciation of the sensuous male beauty of ancient Greek statues. The infamous 'Conclusion' advocated an aesthetic criticism that was not based on abstract theories but on trying to understand one's personal response to a particular object. Pater argued that 'Not the fruit of experience, but experience itself, is the end', and thus, that life should ideally be a series of exquisite moments of sensual experiencing: 'To burn always with this hard, gemlike flame, to maintain this ecstasy, is success in life.'

The book aroused controversy in Oxford because of its percieved relativism, agnosticism, amorality and paganism, but was to prove highly influential with the writers of the 1890s, including William Butler Yeats, Arthur Symons and Oscar WILDE, who said of it, 'It is my golden book; . . . but it is the very flower of decadence: the last trumpet should have sounded the moment it was written.' Wilde and his contemporaries were to popularise Pater's aestheticism within a 'decadent' context, as in 'art for art's sake', the separation of art from morality, and the celebration of surfaces and sensuality.

Revised editions of Pater's first book appeared in 1877 and 1888, the last being *The Renaissance* (1893). Among the changes was the addition, to the first chapter (concerning the medieval tale 'Aucassin and Nicolette'), of a discussion of the medieval legend of the comradeship of Amis and Amile, whose love for each other takes consideration over their lives and those of their families.

Pater's other works include a novel, *Marius the Epicurean* (1885), and collections of essays, stories and lectures: *Imaginary Portraits* (1887), *Appreciations* (1889), *Plato and Platonism* (1893), and the posthumously published *Greek Studies* (1895) and *Miscellaneous Studies* (1895).

Two homoerotic stories, 'Denys L'Auxerrois' (in *Imaginary Portraits*), and 'Apollo in Picardy' (in *Miscellaneous Studies*), recount the appearance, in medieval France, of Greek gods in mortal form. They incorporate retellings of classical myths, with Denys (Dionysius) inspiring an artistic flowering then bacchanalian frenzy that ultimately leads to his being torn apart by villagers, and Apollyon (Apollo) accidentally killing the acolyte Hyancinthus with a discus excavated from an ancient settlement.

D. Donoghue, *Walter Pater: Lover of Strange Souls*, New York, 1995; L. Dowling, *Hellenism and Homosexuality in Victorian Oxford*, Ithaca, 1994.

Jason Boyd

Paul, St (?–*c.* AD 64), biblical figure. Founder of Christianity as a world religion distinct from Judaism, Paul (also known by his Jewish name of Saul), a native of Tarsus, capital of Cilicia (a province of Asia Minor on the Mediterranean), was born around the beginning of the Christian era, and probably martyred during the Neronian persecution of the Christian movement in the mid-60s. His father was a Pharisee, and a Roman citizen.

Paul was responsible for two of three New Testament texts specifically interpreted in the modern period as condemnations of homosexuality, and for the only reference in the Bible taken to refer explicitly to lesbianism. The third reference commonly attributed to Paul is in 1 Tim-

othy, penned by a later writer (late first century or early second century) in Paul's name.

Paul's writings were all occasional correspondence with Christian communities, written amidst controversy, and addressing specific pastoral issues in the infant churches. His ethical teaching parallels, in both form and content, catalogues of 'virtues and vices' in the 'Wisdom' tradition of Judaism, and in Greco-Roman popular ethical teaching. Paul, it has been said, puts a 'Hellenistic dress on a rabbinic body'.

His first letter to the Corinthians was written from Ephesus *c.* 55. He states that neither *malakoi* nor *arsenokoitai* will inherit the kingdom of God. The linguistic meaning and cultural reference of these two Greek words remain uncertain. A bewildering variety of translations has been offered since the publication of the Tyndale Bible (1525). Only with the publication of the Revised Standard Version of the New Testament in 1946 did the word 'homosexual' become applied to this text. *Malakoi* (literally 'soft') was generally understood in later Christian discourse to refer to masturbation, or a self-indulgent and voluptuous way of life. *Arsenokoitai* appears to have been coined by Paul, and the word appears very infrequently after Paul. It means, literally, 'male fucker', and is most likely a prohibition on pederasty (sexual relations between adult males and post-pubertal male youths) or 'active' male prostitution ('active' with either men or women). Since the 1950s, the text has been used by Christian right-wing groups to justify discrimination against gay people both within the churches and in civil society.

Paul's letter to the Romans was penned from Corinth to Christians in Rome in 56–58. This provides the only passage in the New Testament that condemns both male and female homogenital activity in an explicitly theological context. The text appears within an extended argument and serves a rhetorical purpose: homogenital activity, which 'everyone knows' is 'against nature' (*para physin*), is assumed to be intrinsically lustful, compromising of proper gender relations in a patriarchal society, and potentially extinctive of the human species. On this set of assumptions, Paul appeals first to the judgmentalism of his Jewish Christian readers (see how wicked are the Gentiles!), but then pulls a 'sting' operation to condemn judgmentalism: 'For there is no distinction, since all have sinned and fall short of the glory of God.'

The specific occasion was controversy over ritual requirements of the Jewish law, especially male circumcision and dietary regulations. Paul chose homogenital activity for his rhetorical purpose precisely because, in his contemporary context, it was uncontroversial, meeting with widespread disapproval in both Jewish and Hellenistic thought.

Curiously to the modern mind, Paul interprets homogenital activity not as a sin worthy of punishment, but itself as divine punishment for the sin of idolatry, a consequence of God's decision to 'give up' rebellious creatures to follow their own futile thinking and desires. The specific acts that are considered to be 'against nature' are not specified. In the modern period they have been read as homosexual. Earlier in the history of the Christian tradition, they have been read as including non-procreative heterosexual acts, including oral and anal sex.

In our time, the text from Romans has been used as a key 'proof text' in the Christian Right's case against gay people, and is seen by some as offering theological justification for the HIV/AIDS pandemic ('Men committed shameless acts with men and received in their own persons the due penalty for their error'). There is no doubt that Paul himself would have been appalled by this judgmentalism, as of any selective and self-justifying morality.

A number of scholars, including S. Tarachow, H. Fischer, and J. S. Spong, have suggested that Paul himself may have been homosexual. In general, his life was dedicated to an understanding of the Christian message as universal, radically inclusive and transcending the constructed dualisms of human culture – Jew/Gentile, slave/free, male/female. His letter to the Galatians is a passionate appeal for responsible freedom.

1 Corinthians 6: 9; Romans 1: 1–3: 31; 1 Timothy 1: 10; J. Boswell, *Christianity, Social Tolerance, and Homosexuality: Gay People in Europe from the Beginning of the Christian Era to the Fourteenth Century*, Chicago, 1980; P. Coleman, *Christian Attitudes to Homosexuality*, London, 1980; V. P. Furnish, *The Moral Teaching of Paul: Selected Issues*, Nashville, 1985; R. Scroggs, *The New Testament and Homosexuality*, Philadelphia, 1983.

David J. Bromell

Pessoa, Fernando (1888–1935), Portuguese poet. Pessoa was born into a middle-class Lisbon family of mixed Jewish, aristocratic and Azorean descent. His father died when he was 5 and two years later his mother married the Portuguese consul in Durban, South Africa, where Pessoa spent his teens. He was educated at Durban High School and became fluent in English. Pessoa returned to Portugal in 1905 and never left it again. He soon abandoned his university studies and from then on maintained himself by translating commercial correspondence into English, which allowed him to live modestly but adequately. His external life was uneventful and he died in relative obscurity. He devoted his main energies to poetry and was involved in the major literary controversies of the day. Towards the end of his life he began to be recognised by the next generation of poets and since then his reputation has grown both in Portugal and internationally. Today he is recognised as one of the great European modernist poets. In Portugal he is regarded as the greatest poet of the twentieth century and has been accorded the status of a national hero.

Pessoa published relatively little in his

lifetime. Most of his poetry appeared in literary magazines and was only collected after his death. He left a famous trunk full of manuscripts which have been gradually published posthumously. Many of his early works were written in English and it appears that he initially hoped to make a literary reputation in Britain. Later works were written in Portuguese, but critics have noted an English influence in their syntax and rhythm, which forms part of their special appeal. Pessoa is best known now for his avant-garde and modernist works written in the 1910s and 1920s, and particulary for his invention of three heteronyms, Alberto Caeiro, Ricardo Reis and Álvaro de Campos. These were more than pseudonyms, since Pessoa invented separate identities for each of them and maintained an elaborate fiction that they wrote independently of their creator. He wrote different styles of verse under the three heteronyms, as well as under his own name. In 1934 he published a collection of mythical nationalistic poems called *Mensagem* (*Message*), which was exploited after his death by the conservative Salazar regime.

There is no direct evidence that Pessoa was homosexual, but the fact that he never married (despite a tentative courtship when he was in his thirties), his friendship with a number of openly gay writers and the evidence of his own work point in this direction.

In 1918 Pessoa published *Antinous*, a long poem written in English under his own name. This poem described the emperor HADRIAN mourning over the dead body of his young Greek lover, ANTINOUS, and promising to raise a marble sculpture in memory of their love which would act as an inspiration to their brothers yet to be born. Although the English is rather stilted, there are some fairly explicit descriptions as Hadrian remembers their physical love-making, dispelling any lingering belief that Pessoa was a purely intellectual poet. Pessoa sent review copies of the poem to various British newspapers,

which regarded it as something of a southern curiosity. In 1921 he published a revised version in a collection titled *English Poems*. This retained the same structure, but among other changes, Pessoa radically excised words such as 'vice' and 'crime' which suggested that the relationship was wrong. In the other major work in *English Poems*, 'Epithalamium', the poet imagined himself as a bride on her wedding morning, thinking of the pains and pleasures of the wedding night yet to come.

English Poems was published under the imprint of Olisipo, Pessoa's own shortlived publishing house. The following year he published the second edition of *Canções* (*Songs*), a collection of love poems by the openly gay poet António BOTTO, and wrote an article defending Botto's aestheticism for a leading literary and artistic magazine, *Contemporanea*. This engendered a major controversy, with book seizings and public demonstrations, and involving other writers, such as Raul Leal. Botto kept quiet throughout this period but both Pessoa and Leal issued leaflets attacking their opposition, before the controversy fizzled out.

The best-known of Pessoa's work with homoerotic aspects is the poem 'Ode Marítima' (Maritime Ode), first published in 1915 under the heteronym of the supposed engineer, Álvaro de Campos. In this lengthy work the poet pictures himself on the Lisbon quayside watching steamers heading out to sea. Gradually this prosaic scene is transformed into a sado-masochistic fantasy of attacks by pirate ships in the age of sail. The poet dreams of being a woman raped by pirates and the pleasures to be gained from the sufferings of others. The impetus of the poem is governed by the image of a fly-wheel which accelerates and then slows down, returning the poet to the mechanical world of the quayside. In another poem of the same period signed by Álvaro de Campos, 'Saudação a Walt Whitman' ('Greeting to Walt Whitman'), the poet refers to WHITMAN as a 'great pederast' and says, 'I am one of yours'. Because the poem is ostensibly written by Campos these views cannot be directly attributed to Pessoa.

This was not a form of simple closetry, however – since Pessoa's most forthright writings appeared under his own name – but rather part of an extended reflection on the meaning of personality and the role of the poet. The sincerity of Pessoa's expressed views has been the subject of much academic debate. Pessoa himself referred to his heteronymic writings as a 'drama in people'. The idea of multiple personalities and identities, with the associated image of the mask, has many philosophical connections, but has a particular resonance for gay readers looking for survival strategies in a hostile environment. Thus, while homoerotic themes are treated directly in a number of specific poems, they can also be seen to underlie much of Pessoa's work.

F. Pessoa, *Selected Poems*, trans. J. Griffin, Harmondsworth, 1982; F. Pessoa, *A Centenary Pessoa*, ed. E. Lisboa with L. C. Taylor, Manchester, 1995; F. Pessoa, *Poemas Ingleses*, ed. J. de Sena, Lisbon, 1974; J. Blanco, *Fernando Pessoa: Esboço de uma Bibliografia*, Lisbon, 1983; R. W. Howes, 'Fernando Pessoa, Poet, Publisher and Translator', *British Library Journal*, 9, 2 (Autumn 1983): 161–70.

Robert Howes

Petersen, Clemens (1834–1918), Danish critic. Petersen made his début as an actor in 1851, but failed. In 1857 he was the first to obtain a degree in aesthetics at the University of Copenhagen. Denmark's leading literary figure of the former generation, J. L. Heiberg (d. 1851), became his patron, and in 1856 he struck up a close friendship with the Norwegian author Bjørnstjerne BJØRNSON. At the same time he began a brilliant career as reviewer for the culturally and politically important daily newspaper *Fædrelandet*. His reviews, however, generated a largely hidden enmity, for example from the grand lady of the Danish theatre, Johanne Luise

Heiberg. In March 1869 Petersen suddenly left Denmark.

Hans Christian ANDERSEN wrote in his diary: 'Clemens Petersen has supposedly left town at the request of the police; there are strange rumours around' – 'It is said that he has interfered with boys at the school where he teaches. I wish it were a lie! What will happen now to the poor man, without money, alone in a strange land?' – 'All over town they speak ill of Clemens Petersen; he is rejected by everybody; he will probably kill himself!' After a short stay in Vienna, Petersen emigrated to the US where he remained for the next 35 years, living in near-poverty from poorly paid literary jobs on Danish emigrant newspapers. Soon after his arrival in the New World, he briefly became acquainted with Walt WHITMAN, who vaguely and circumspectly reported his presence in the US to his correspondent in Denmark, Rudolf Schmidt.

The press was silent on the matter. Petersen was determinedly forgotten as 'an aesthete now living in America', or 'the critic who was helped from gaol to America'. The exiling of Petersen signalled the installation in Denmark of the homosexual man, an unmentionable, artistic, double-faced and hysterical abuser of boys with tendencies to commit suicide or emigrate to America. In certain circles a 'clemens' became the polite synonym for a pederast. In 1904 literary friends financed his return to Denmark, but he remained forgotten.

Clemens Petersen i 'Fædrelandet', Copenhagen, 1975; H. C. Andersens Dagbøger 1825–1875 VIII, Copenhagen, 1975: 186; W. von Rosen, *Månens Kulør. Studier i dansk bøssehistorie 1628–1912*, Copenhagen, 1993: 540–5.

Wilhelm von Rosen

Petronius Arbiter (d. AD 66), Roman novelist and poet. Petronius Arbiter was the author of the *Satyrica*, often regarded as the first Western European novel. If, as most now accept, he is to be identified with the Petronius of whom Tacitus gives an account in *Annals*, he led a life of apparent idleness, sleeping by day and working and enjoying himself by night, neither a debauchee nor a spendthrift but an expert in luxury. However uninhibited and nonchalant his words and deeds, they found acceptance for their air of simplicity. He proved himself active and capable as proconsul in Bithynia and afterwards as consul. He was admitted to the circle of NERO's intimates, becoming Arbiter of Elegance, the one who decided for Nero what was chic and what was not. His sway with Nero earnt him the jealous enmity of Tigellinus, the brutal co-commander of the Praetorian Guard, who played on his master's cruelty to turn him against his arbiter. When Petronius learnt how things stood, rejecting the delays of fear and hope, he committed suicide, taking the time to write out an account of Nero's vices and the names of his partners, male and female, which he sent under seal to the emperor. We are ignorant of his date of birth, his origins, and the circumstances of his upbringing and education, although the literary qualities of the *Satyrica* establish that he had enjoyed a thorough Roman education. We do not know if he had a wife or children, though his decision in departing this life not to flatter a cruel and vindictive emperor might suggest that he had no one whom he needed to protect.

As it survives, the *Satyrica* (traditionally but incorrectly known as *The Satyricon*) consists of extensive fragments of Books 14–16, perhaps only a sixth or even a tenth of the original. It takes the form of a first-person narrative by Encolpius, an itinerant teacher living by his wits, who recounts his escapades with his young boyfriend, Giton, and their friend, Ascyltos, another teacher. One strand of the action concerns the ups and downs of the lovers' affair and the efforts of Ascyltos and Eumolpus, a self-important poet they meet, to wrest Giton from Encolpius. The rest the story, in all its fragmentariness, revolves around the travellers' adventures with the various

people they encounter: Agamemnon, a rhetorician; Trimalchio, the *nouveau-riche* (ex-slave) millionaire and his wife, Fortunata, whose dinner Encolpius mocks for its vulgarity; Circe, a rich and beautiful woman attracted to rough trade (Encolpius); and Quartilla and Oenothea, priestesses of Priapus.

As a fictional narrative the *Satyrica* is a comic homoerotic inversion of the form of prose fiction then known, the Greek romance, in which heterosexual lovers undergo precarious trials and tribulations in foreign parts before their love is consummated in marriage. A further unifying comic motif is Petronius's satire of the epic theme of divine anger best known from Homer (where Odysseus has to overcome Poseidon's fury). Encolpius's problems with his lover, who is flighty though ultimately faithful, are compounded by his having offended the ithyphallic god Priapus, who exacts divine revenge on the hero in the form of impotence.

Formally, Petronius wrote in a mode that combines verse and prose, known as Menippean satire. Its realistic, loose-knit, conversational qualities suited his purposes, not least because it allowed him opportunities to exercise his considerable poetic skills in a wide variety of ways. However, Petronius seems to lack the firm moral convictions of the satirist, and his standard of judgement is in the end aesthetic, as befits, perhaps, an arbiter of elegance. He would have appreciated camp, as the 1969 film of the book by Federico Fellini amply demonstrated, with only marginal exaggeration.

Petronius, *Satyrica*, trans. and ed. R. Bracht Branham and D. Kinney, London, 1996; J. P. Sullivan, *The Satyricon of Petronius*, London, 1968; H. D. Rankin, *Petronius the Artist: Essays on the Satyricon and its Author*, The Hague, 1971.

Gary Simes

Philippe, Duc d'Orléans (1640–1701), French prince. 'Monsieur' as he was simply called (being Louis XIV's only brother) shares with his uncle Gaston (also only brother to a king, Louis XIII) and his son Philippe (1674–1723) the strange destiny of having been labelled, like them, a 'debauch'. Only-brothers to the reigning king were seen, because of the sibling rivalries that marred the previous Valois dynasty in the Renaissance, as dangerous to the throne. Labelling them 'débauchés', and ensuring that they would pursue their natural inclinations unhindered, was part of monarchical strategy to avoid any challenge to the legitimate ruler. Cardinal Mazarin, who well understood this policy, is credited with having arranged the deflowering of both Louis (by one of his nieces, Olympe) and Philippe (at the hands of Philippe Mancini, Mazarin's own nephew, Duc de Nevers [1641–1707]).

This explains how and why both Gaston d'Orléans (1608–1660) and Philippe d'Orléans (as young brothers of the king, they incidentally carried the same title) could freely indulge in homosexual practices. They both offer an insight into the pragmatic interplay of power and sex in early modern France. This being said, it is undeniable that Philippe d'Orléans was a homosexual and that, for political reasons, his woman-mad and later bigot brother gave him free rein to indulge his desires. One must note that a similar treatment was reserved to the two princely Vendôme brothers who were direct descendants of Henri IV, Louis' and Philippe's grandfather, and who may have also posed a threat to the reigning branch of the House of Bourbon. One was a general who exerted himself – and his aides-de-camp – on the battlefields. The other, Philippe de Vendôme, who enjoyed immunity as Grand Hospitaller and Grand Prior of Malta, assembled around him a happy circle of *libertins*, poets, writers, painters – and one should add 'hustlers' – a group that prepared for the Regency. His famous '*nuits*' met in the Rue du Temple, in the Marais, a street near today's

Parisian gay district. There definitely was a royal policy of letting any possible contender to the legitimate monarch run free, and so discredit himself.

In that respect, the myth of 'Philippe', the man in the iron mask, is interesting in so far as it was a popular attempt at inventing a purer brother to Louis, a good Philippe whose life at Pignerol fortress would have spared him the debauchery the real sibling indulged in – while finding an alternative to a monarch who was to become the embodiment of tyranny. Significantly, in the first film of *L'Homme au masque de fer*, Jean Marais camped it up as a muscular, virile and somewhat populist d'Artagnan, who tries in vain to rescue a virginal, fragile and politically inept Philippe (played by effete Jean-François Porée), and yet manages at the end to convince Louis to be a good king – as if the director had exactly understood both the homoerotic and the socially redemptive subtexts of the myth (a dimension that eludes the recent Hollywood remake). Philippe's homosexual stature in French royal history is only rivalled by HENRI III's. It is extraordinarily well documented. Monsieur's life therefore offers an excellent gauge to evaluate some aspects of homosexual culture during the second half of the seventeenth century.

The physical descriptions of Monsieur all tend to reinforce a constrast between him and the king. He is often presented as physically grotesque, 'a pot-bellied man, raised on his high heel shoes as if on stilts' (Duc de Saint-Simon's *Memoirs*), a camp figure, 'adorned like a woman, dripping with rings, bracelets, precious stones, stuffed with ribbons, embalmed with perfumes, and meticulously clean'. By contrast, the king is well turned, graceful, well tempered. Where accounts differ, however, is with regard to his social abilities, which all indicate that he could have outshone his elder brother. A soldier who gained the military's admiration for his physical courage on the battlefield and his tactician's gifts, a courtier who, for being 'the silliest woman around' (according to Saint-Simon), yet knew the art of behaving at court, and how to charm everyone, he is often belittled for his indiscretions, his inability to attend state councils and his ineptitude. What must be read behind those conflicting descriptions is that Monsieur was a real threat to the king (as evidenced in the great care he took in marrying his daughters well and giving his son the best education possible), though his critics drew on an enduring stock of clichés to characterise effeminacy. Monsieur was a sort of catalyst for later public narration or rhetoric about homosexuals. Yet, when Venetian ambassadors noted that, at court, he was the image of the perfect prince, noble without affectation (unlike his brother), 'a prince from the olden days', they meant that he was cast in the mould of a Renaissance prince, not a modern autocrat like Louis.

Being given liberty and endless spending money by his brother, he made his château at Saint-Cloud the first *libertin* court, a model which opposed Versailles and its Spanish-inspired etiquette, a forerunner of the Vendôme's Temple, and of his son's, the Regent's, artistic and modern court – in brief an anticipation of eighteenth-century culture. There, he pursued his adolescent love affair with his contemporary Philippe, Chevalier then Prince de Lorraine. When married, he preyed on bright-eyed German princelings – for all to see, including his two wives.

He first married Henrietta, daughter of Charles I of England (1661), whom he made utterly unhappy (he discovered that she was having an affair and was then accused of having her dispatched by his own lover, Lorraine) then, after her unexpected death (1670), the Princess Palatine (Liselotte), a great-granddaughter of JAMES I of England (1671). The Princess Palatine has left in her own witty letters many amused accounts of her husband's liaisons and straightforward if startled descriptions of his adventures – while loving him very much and making sure that

Monsieur would not dissipate the Orléans' wealth on boys. Her letters, together with Italian adventurer Primi Visconti's *Memoirs*, are essential readings on Monsieur and his entourage.

But, being (a homosexual) of royal blood, Monsieur did fulfil his marital duties towards his two consorts. His first two daughters reigned in Spain and Savoy while, out of his happy marriage to the Princess Palatine, came a sovereign consort of Lorraine and the Regent of France who, by all accounts, was better groomed and educated to exercise power than his cousins – a fact he proved under the Regency. By an interesting twist, it was descendants of 'that silly woman' who became France's last reigning king, Louis-Philippe (reigned 1830–1848), and the current royal pretenders.

E. Spanheim, *Relation de la Cour de France en 1690*, Paris, 1973; *Letters from Liselotte*, trans. and ed. M. Kroll, New York, 1971.

Philippe-Joseph Salazar

Philippe IV le Bel (1268–1314), king of France. Born in Fontainebleau, Philippe ascended the French throne in 1285; his reign witnessed the confirmation and strengthening of the power of the French monarchy, the development of the bureaucracy and increased administrative centralisation.

Philippe used homosexuality as a political weapon to attain his objectives. In a conflict with the papacy, he used reports his envoys gathered from Roman aristocrats to accuse Pope Boniface VIII of sodomy. He then used the same accusation against the Knights Templar, a religious order created in 1119 to protect pilgrims to the Holy Land. The Templars had rapidly become a powerful and wealthy international force, securing the funds which they had collected in their fortresses and thus becoming veritable bankers. However, in 1291, they suffered defeat by the Muslim mamluks at Saint-Jean d'Acre, and the military disaster reinforced criticisms of the order for heresy and sodomy, which had already circulated. Philippe, chronically in need of funds, coveted the order's treasure and decided to take advantage of their lack of popularity to have all the Templars in French territory arrested on 13 October 1307. Their trial lasted seven years. The Templars, often tortured and facing a choice between confession and death, mostly admitted to the charges for which they were indicted, notably homosexual practices. According to witnesses' statements, new Templars were initiated by being kissed on various parts of their bodies, including the mouth, the penis and the anus; they were told that if they were consumed with lust they could ask fellow members to satisfy their passions, favours they must reciprocate if asked.

Most historians who have studied this affair, whether favourable or hostile to the Templars or to homosexuality, have concluded that such practices were highly probable, given the agreement between various eyewitness accounts, and confirmed by other available information on medieval knighthood and religious orders.

The order of the Knights Templar was abolished by Pope Clement V in 1312 and its grand-master, Jacques de Molay, along with other leaders, were burned at the stake in 1314, the same year in which King Philippe died. The successful attack on the Templars marks the beginning of effective repression of homosexuality by the French state, as trials of sodomites continued from the fourteenth century until the Revolution.

J. Favier, *Philippe le Bel*, Paris, 1979; A. Demurger, *Vie et mort de l'ordre du Temple*, Paris, 1985.

Didier Godard

Philips, Katherine (née Fowler) (1632–1664), English poet. Philips was born into a successful London cloth merchant's family and attended Mrs Salmon's Presbyterian boarding school for girls. Her mother,

Katherine Oxenbridge, was widowed three times between 1642 and 1648. She married her third husband, Sir Richard Philips, in 1646 and the family moved to Picton Castle in Pembroke, Wales. In 1648 the young Katherine was married to her step-father's 54-year-old relative, Colonel James Philips, a prominent Welsh politician, and took up residence at her husband's house, Cardigan Priory. James Philips served as an MP (1653–1656 and 1660–1662) and was an appointee to the High Court of Justice.

Katherine Philips began to write poetry as a young woman. Despite her strongly puritan background and marriage, her sympathies and tastes were royalist. Her friends and admirers included the cavalier poets Henry Vaughan and Abraham Cowley, and Sir Charles Cottterell, Master of the Ceremonies to both Charles I and Charles II. Philips's élite literary practice is shaped by courtly, neoclassical ideals of retired life governed by the ties of ardent friendship. However, in Philips's poetry, this traditionally male, homosocial ideal is thoroughly feminised. Her verse is conceived as written for and circulating within the bounds of a coterie 'Society of Friendship', a manuscript circle whose core members are close female friends, some from her days at boarding school. Calling herself 'Orinda', Philips addressed passionate epistles to 'Lucasia' (Anne Owen), 'Rosania' (Mary Aubrey) and other women, usually from the solitude of her home in Wales. In this she was influenced by the cult of platonic love associated with Charles I's consort, Queen Henrietta Maria. Familiar to her from her youth, the discourse of perfect friendship was repopularised as a sign of continuing loyalty to the royalist cause during the interregnum. The fact that Francis Finch's treatise *Friendship* (1653) was dedicated to 'noble Lucasia-Orinda' suggests the iconic potential of Philips's 'Society' and the inseparable female couple for Cavalier men.

At their most ecstatic, Philips's poems celebrate the sublime 'mysteries' of love between women: 'Whose thoughts and persons chang'd and mixt are one, / Enjoy content or else the world has none' ('Content'). But in poems such as 'On Rosania's Apostacy, and Lucasia's Friendship' that love is also figured as hazardous, vulnerable to betrayal and jealousy. In one of her letters to Cotterell ('Poliarchus'), Philips wrote: 'There are few Friendships in the World Marriage proof'. Philips's poem to the newly married Mary Aubrey reaffirms the intimate reciprocity between them and suggests a sexualised exchange of secrets, tears and sighs: 'Thy heart locks up my secrets richly set, / And my brest is thy private cabinet. / Thou shed'st no tear but what my moisture lent, / And if I sigh, it is thy breath is spent.'

More commonly, though, Philips is eloquent in abjection, as in 'Orinda to Lucasia parting': 'Adieu, dear object of my Love's excess, / And with thee all my hopes of happiness, / With the same fervent and unchanged heart / Which did its whole self once to thee impart, / (And which, though fortune has so sorely bruis'd, / Would suffer more, to be from this excus'd) / I to resign thy dear Converse submit, / Since I can neither keep, nor merit it. / Thou hast too long to me confined been, / Who ruin am without, passion within.'

Philips's reception amongst contemporary feminist and queer readers stresses the primacy of relations between women in her poetry, focusing especially on the embodied erotics and fraught dynamics of her 'friendship' poems addressed to women, compared with the less sublime and more formal character of those addressed to her husband and other men. It is precisely the extremity of affection between women in Philips's poetry, and its explicitly autobiographical character, which has led critics, including Hobby, to argue that it is appropriate to call Philips a lesbian poet.

Her play, *Pompey*, a translation of Corneille, was published anonymously and performed in 1663. Following its success, a pirated edition of Philips's *Poems* was issued in January 1664 and subsequently withdrawn from sale by the publisher after protests by Philips and her well placed friends. Philips died suddenly of smallpox in London. Sir Charles Cotterell published a folio edition of her works in 1667. She had a son, Hector, who died in infancy (1655), and a surviving daughter, Katherine, born in 1656.

The Collected Poems of Katherine Philips, ed. E. Hageman, London, 1997; *The Collected Works of Katherine Philips*, ed. P. Thomas, London, 1990; E. Hobby and C. White (eds), *What Lesbians Do In Books*, Milford, Conn., 1991; H. Andreadis, 'The Sapphic-Platonics of Katherine Philips', *Signs*, 15 (1989): 34–60; C. Easton, 'Excusing the Breach of Nature's Laws: The Discourse of Denial and Disguise in Katherine Philips' Friendship Poetry', in A. Pacheco (ed.) *Early Women Writers 1600–1720*, London, 1997; C. Barash, *English Women's Poetry 1649–1714*, Oxford, 1996.

Kate Lilley

Pico, Giovanni (Count Mirandola, Giovanni Pico della Mirandola) (1463–1494), Italian philosopher. After becoming dissatisfied with studies of canon law in Bologna, Pico began humanist studies, first in Florence (where he made friends with Poliziano), then in Ferrara and, from 1480 to 1482, in Padua. Aided by a famously prodigious memory, he studied Arabic literature and Hebrew cabalistic texts, as well as Latin and Greek classics – developing a special affection for PLATO. Pico tried to reconcile Greco-Roman, medieval-Aristotelian and Judeo-Arabic thought, and even the hermeticism of the *Corpus hermeticum*, with Christian teaching and his own deeply held religious beliefs. Such efforts were cut short by his early death, but were synthesised in 1486 in the 900 theses of his *Conclusiones philosophicae, cabalisticae et theologicae*. A committee of theologians, however, found this work suspect of heresy and, when Pico confirmed his views, Pope Innocent VIII condemned it all. Pico, therefore, fled to

France in 1488, where he was arrested. He finally effected a reconciliation with the pope and returned to Florence, where he spent the remainder of his life drafting philosophical and theological studies. In later life, Pico's mysticism drew him towards the supporters of the reformist friar Girolamo Savonarola.

Much influenced by Plato, Pico accepted the ideal of *amor socraticus* between men popularised by Marsilio FICINO. He described it thus: 'In heavenly love . . . everything tends and aims to the spiritual beauty of the soul, and of the mind, which is much more perfect among men than among women, as it happens with any other kind of perfection; therefore, those who were inflamed by this type of love, mostly loved some generously spirited young man, whose virtue was all the more appreciated when it was contained in a handsome body, and they did not make themselves effeminate by chasing a herd of whores.'

Pico experienced this type of heavenly love with Girolamo Benivieni (1453–1542), ten years his junior, himself a fervent Christian and Neoplatonic, who ardently reciprocated his affections. Theirs was, they declared, a fervent but chaste love kept under watch by rigorous morality and Christian mysticism. However, during a sermon after Pico's death, Savonarola made a revelation which caused a sensation: Pico's soul had not immediately gone to paradise, but was consigned for a time to the flames of purgatory because of certain sins, which he did not wish to name.

Popular opinion assumed that Pico had kept a female lover or a secret concubine. Five centuries later, it is impossible to know the truth, but the probability that Pico had a *male* lover, perhaps Benivieni himself, is now less unbelievable, as documents emerge showing the significance of homosexuality in the circle of Pico's friends (such as Ficino and Poliziano). The circumstances of Pico's death also raise questions. He died suddenly, only two months after the equally sudden death of

Poliziano, who himself died shortly after a young male prostitute had accused him of infecting him (even though the converse is more likely true). Past historians hinted at death by poisoning, but more recent scholars suspect that Poliziano and Pico numbered among the first victims of the large-scale epidemic of syphilis – marked by acute symptoms and very rapid physical deterioration – which broke out in Europe in 1493 and 1494.

It will never be known whether or not Pico remained celibate, or if his love for Benivieni was consummated. What is known is a delicate testimonial to this love: the tomb in which they decided to be buried together, and which can still be seen in the church of San Marco in Florence. The original tombstone, in Latin, reads: 'Here lies Giovanni Mirandola; known both at the Tagus and the Ganges [rivers] and maybe even the antipodes. He died in 1494, and lived for thirty-two years. Girolamo Benivieni, to prevent separate places from disjointing after death the bones of those whose souls were joined by Love while living, provided for this grave where he too is buried. He died in 1542, and lived for eighty-nine years and six months.' Such was their love, still alive after half a century of separation.

G. Dall'Orto, '"Socratic Love" as a Disguise for Same-Sex Love in the Italian Renaissance', in K. Gerard and G. Hekma (eds) *The Pursuit of Sodomy: Male Homosexuality in Renaissance and Enlightenment Europe*, New York, 1989: 33–65; J. Jacobelli, *Quei due Pico della Mirandola*, Rome, 1993; G. Pico della Mirandola, *Commento alla canzone di G. Benivieni: 'Dell'amore celeste e divino'*, Lucca, 1731, especially chapter 3.

Giovanni Dall'Orto

Platen, August Graf von (1796–1835), German poet. The seventh child, and second son, of a family in the lower nobility, Platen was sent at the age of 10 to a military academy. Although he suffered under its strict regime, he did enjoy his time as a page at the Munich royal court of the Bavarian king. With an initial goal of a diplomatic career, Platen received a three-year leave from military service. He studied law first at the university in Würzburg and then in Erlangen. In 1820, he broke off his law studies to pursue interests in languages and philosophy. He then travelled to Italy where he stayed too long, which led to a four-month sentence for being absent without leave.

He had already been writing poetry and plays while attending university, and his publishing success (*Ghaselen* [*Ghazels*, 1821], *Vermischte Schriften* [*Mixed Writings*, 1822]) led him to pursue a career as author. His best-known work appeared in 1825, *Sonette aus Venedig* (*Sonnets from Venice*), and included the famous poem 'Tristan'. He moved to Italy in 1826, living in various cities at different times and continuing to write. In late 1835, he tried to avoid a cholera epidemic in Naples by fleeing to Sicily. He became ill with colic, but thought it was cholera and tried to treat himself. These self-administered, large doses of various medicines killed him. He was 39 years old.

Platen has played a significant role in the history of German gay literature. His poems, the best of which arise from his (usually unrequited) love for men, were understood by his contemporaries to express male–male desire in ways that, even for the Romantic era when same-sex friendships were at their most effusive and most treasured, went beyond the bounds of friendship and into the realm of love. For this, Platen was viciously attacked by the great German poet Heinrich Heine who, in a classic fit of homophobia, tinged perhaps with professional jealousy, decried Platen's work as effeminate, artificial and unnatural.

Such attacks could not efface Platen's works, but they did influence his reception. He has long been seen by mainstream literary criticism as an aesthete, a stylist and rather unoriginal. The two-volume publication of his diaries in 1896 and 1900

led gay critics from the turn of the century onwards to renewed interest in him. In the diaries ('Memorandum of My Life'), he describes his desires for many handsome males. Typically, he would become enraptured by the person's beauty and fall in love from afar, but rarely form more than an acquaintance, at best, with him. In 1817, Platen wrote: 'My whole life long I shall carry this unstilled yearning for an intimate, inseparable Friend in whom I would be able to forget myself' (Mattenklott, 81).

He did find someone whom he thought would be that Friend, in Eduard Schmidtlein, a fellow student in Würzburg and a year younger than Platen. Their relationship lasted about one year (1819), during which Platen detailed the emotional highs and lows he experienced as he wooed Schmidtlein, whom he called 'Adrast' in his diary. The two young men did indeed form a close, tender relationship that also included passionate kisses and embraces. This took place at a time when such physical exchanges between men might be acceptable as expressions of heterosexual friendship. Schmidtlein seems to have seen them as such, although Platen was certain his friend was as homosexual as he. Thus, Platen was crushed when Schmidtlein called the love Platen offered him 'disgusting lust' that he 'despised'. It was for this reason that Platen left Würzburg for Erlangen.

Platen may never have found the Friend for whom he yearned, but he also never questioned the validity of his desire for men. In the twentieth century, Platen became an icon for two major German authors precisely because of his homosexuality. In 1930, Thomas MANN wrote an influential essay 'August von Platen', in which he reads the poet's work as an expression of his unfulfilled desires. That Mann saw much of himself in Platen became clear not just with the posthumous publication of his own diaries but already in the novella *Death in Venice* (1912), a kind of hymn to the unrequited homosexual love Platen personified for Mann. More recently, Hubert Fichte wrote an essay ('I can't get no satisfaction. Zur Geschichte der Empfindungen des Grafen August Platen von Hallermünde' ['On the History of Sensibilities of Count August Platen von Hallermünde', 1985]) in which he views Platen as a gay 'revolutionary', the first in German literature to write openly about his love for men.

G. Mattenklott and H. Schmidt-Bergmann (eds), *August von Platen. Memorandum meines Lebens: Eine Auswahl aus den Tagebüchern*, Frankfurt am Main, 1988; C. Mücke (ed.) '. . . bleibe doch wunderbar unglüklich.' *August von Platens Aufenthalt in Würzburg 1818–1819 und seine Liebe zu 'Adrast': Tagebücher – Gedichte – Briefe*, Würzburg, 1993.

James W. Jones

Plato (*c*. 427–347 BC), Greek philosopher. Born in Athens, Plato was the most famous student of SOCRATES, founder of the Academy and probably the most influential philosopher in the Western tradition. Plato holds an important but highly ambivalent position in the history of sexuality. On the one hand, both he and Socrates, the subject of many of his philosophical dialogues, had intense and apparently homosexual friendships with men. They shared the ancient Greek view of the normality of 'pederastic' relationships between older and younger men. Over the centuries Plato's *Phaedrus* and *Symposium*, in particular, have assumed canonic status for those holding out against the prevailing homophobia of Western culture. The *Symposium* is most often remembered for ARISTOPHANES' mythical explanation of love, which tells us that originally there were three sexes of 'doubled' human beings, each with two sets of limbs, heads, genitals and so on. One sex was male, one female and one 'man–woman'. But as a punishment for conspiring against the gods these doubles were eventually split into their parts, resembling the human beings we know today. And ever since, each part has longed to be reunited with its 'other half'. This beguiling explanation of love as 'the desire and pursuit of the whole' seems if anything to regard homosexual relationships between men or between women as preferable to heterosexual ones. Young men interested in other men are 'the best of boys and youths, because they have the most manly nature'. The story is even radical in the context of Greek culture, because it implies that love between men of the same age is as natural as the socially approved, pederastic relationship between an older 'lover' and a younger 'beloved'.

More problematically, though, some aspects of the Socratic and Platonic teachings on love helped to prepare the ground for subsequent Western contempt for sex and the body, and even sexual relations between men. Although the *Symposium* includes a wide range of opinions on love, both serious and humorous, it is Socrates, the last contributor to the discussion, who presumably comes closest to representing Plato's own views, which reflect his more general attitude to things earthly, contingent and particular as mere shadows of the eternal Ideas or Forms. Through his recollection of the sayings of the priestess Diotima, Socrates presents an idealising view of love as an almost mystical force. Love finds its proper purpose only when it leads us upwards from particular beautiful things, such as young men, to the abstract and higher Platonic Ideas of beauty and goodness: 'And the true order of going or being led by another to things of love, is to use the beauties of earth as steps along which he mounts upwards for the sake of that other beauty, going from one to two, and from two to all fair forms, and from fair forms to fair actions, and from fair actions to fair notions, until from fair notions he arrives at the notion of absolute beauty, and at last knows what the essence of beauty is.' The ideal love is a spiritual communion between souls. The sexual expression of love, like the body, is correspondingly devalued. Virtue consists in self-control, the control of soul over body, of reason over desire, for the sake of truth and goodness.

In Plato's last dialogue, *The Laws*, the prizing of virtue as manly self-control in the face of disruptive bodily passions approaches the later Christian doctrine that sex is acceptable only as a means of procreation. Whilst admitting that his argument may not be well received in Crete and Sparta, Plato refers to 'nature's rule' and the evidence of animals, where 'the males do not have sexual relations with each other, because such a thing is unnatural'. Plato's preferred law of sexual conduct would prohibit the sowing of 'illegitimate and bastard seed in courtesans, or sterile seed in males in defiance of nature'. Even his more pragmatic alternative, which only insists that privacy be maintained in matters adulterous and perverse, still casually proposes 'suppressing sodomy entirely'. Still, as John Boswell points out, Plato's hostility to sexual relations 'beyond nature' is tempered by his conviction that human beings are superior to animals and his acceptance that sexual relations between men are rife. Whatever Plato's attitude to sexual love between men, his elevation of soul, reason and 'Platonic' love above body, desire and lust, provided the homophobic prejudices of Judaism and Christianity with metaphysical cement.

Plato, *On Homosexuality: Lysis, Phaedrus, and Symposium*, trans. B. Jowett, selectively retranslated and introduced by E. O'Connor, Buffalo, NY, 1991; Plato, *The Laws*, trans. T. J. Saunders, London, 1970; J. Boswell, *Christianity, Social Tolerance, and Homosexuality*, London, 1980.

David West

Plomer, William (1903–1973), South African writer. Born in Pietersburg, Northern Province, he studied at Rugby, and on return to South Africa became a farmer and rural trader. With Laurens van der Post he began an anti-racist magazine, *Voorslag*, which was banned. He served in the Royal Navy in World War II. He travelled in Greece, Japan and the UK, and worked as an editor at Jonathan Cape in London. His novels include *Turbott Wolfe* (1926), *Sado* (1931) and *Ali and the Lion* (1936), his published collections of short stories *I Speak of Africa* (1928) and *Paper Houses* (1929); his collected poems were published in 1960. Plomer did not reveal his homosexuality in his works.

Ken Davis

Pomponio-Leto, Giulio (1428–1498), Italian humanist. Pomponio-Leto (the humanistic pseudonym by which he was known) was born in Diano, in Lucania, the illegitimate son of one Sanseverino, Prince of Salerno. He moved to Rome to study with the humanist Lorenzo Valla, then taught there himself. Pomponio yearned to reconstruct classical Rome and, around 1464, even set up in his own house the Roman Academy, which developed a fanatical and quasi-religious cult of pagan antiquity. Filippo Buonaccorsi and Niccolo Lelio Cosmico, among other humanists, attended the institute. Pomponio was admired by his contemporaries for his great erudition and in 1466 obtained a position at the University of Rome. The next year, he left for Venice with the intention of journeying further east to learn Greek and Arabic

He stopped in Venice, teaching the two sons of Andrea Contarini and Luca Michiel, two noblemen. However, a double catastrophe struck in 1468. First, Pomponio was brought under investigation by Venice's Council of Ten on suspicion of having seduced his students, whom he was said to have praised with excessive ardour in some Latin poems (now lost). Pomponio's accusers in the Council of Ten, according to Vladimiro Zabughin, referred 'to a 'dishonourable book' which had been annotated in his hand, and to certain indiscretions which he had let escape his lips'.

Meanwhile, in Rome, the pope alleged that Pomponio's academy, most improbably, was organising a pagan and republican *coup d'état*. Pomponio and Buonaccorsi figured among the principal suspects. The pope asked the Republic of Venice to extradite Pomponio to Rome for trial. This was, paradoxically, to save his life, since according to Gioacchino Paparelli, 'In its hearing, the Council of Ten decided that . . . Pomponio should be returned to the [Venetian] Republic, if he were not sentenced to capital punishment, . . . there to be punished for the crime of sodomy . . . which in Venice carried the death sentence. . . . This judgement was not executed and Pomponio's extradition proved his salvation'. He was incarcerated in the Castel Sant'Angelo until spring 1469, but was then acquitted and freed. Pomponio wisely decided not to set foot in Venice again and, for greater security, soon married.

While in prison, Pomponio had defended himself with a famous Latin peroration (published by Isidoro Carini), in which he said that he had indeed sung the praises of his students with love, but with the paternal and 'Socratic' love of a teacher. Zabughin comments perspicaciously: 'From the evidence in the court register of the Council of Ten, this was not an effective defence but rather a digression.'

Once freed, Pomponio reopened his academy (which would survive his death) and returned to his position at the University of Rome, teaching, among others, Girolamo BALBI. Pomponio's importance in cultural history lies mostly in his role as a teacher; his publications are largely composed of lectures and commentaries on classical works, and lack the philological rigour of the other great humanists of the Renaissance. On his death he was buried in the church of San Salvatore in Lauro in Rome. The existence in the Biblioteca Marciana in Venice of two Latin epigrams with sodomitical themes written by Pomponio (in Latin manuscript 4689) suggests that other writings of this sort may be rediscovered.

I. Carini, 'La "difesa" di Pomponio Leto', in *Nozze Cian-Sappa-Flandinet*, Bergamo, 1894: 153–93; G. Paparelli, *Callimaco Esperiente*, Salerno, 1971: 59–71; V. Zabughin, *Giulio Pomponio Leto*, Rome, 1909.

Giovanni Dall'Orto

Pontormo, Jacopo Carucci da ('Il Pontormo') (1494–1557), Italian painter. Born in Portormo, Tuscany, he studied painting with Fra Bartolomeo and, in 1510–1511, with Andrea Del Sarto. Pontormo was one of the major exponents of Tuscan Mannerism and in recent years has been rediscovered and revalued both by critics (by whom he had never been entirely forgotten) and by the public. Particularly successful was the last phase of his artistic work, characterised by an extraordinarily audacious use of colour. The most virtuoso examples are a *Deposition* in Santa Felícita in Florence, dating from 1525–1528, and a *Visitation*, in the Pieve in Carmignano (from around 1529–1530), which show an almost psychedelic colour treatment.

The past two decades have also witnessed a rediscovery of a homosexual dimension in Pontormo's life and work. This aspect of Pontormo cannot be reconstructed from personal accounts – almost nothing is known of his sexual life – nor can it be inferred from his painting. Two types of documents, however, suggest Pontormo's homosexuality. One is a series of 50 drawings, most of which are now in the Uffizi in Florence, which the artist made in preparation for painting his most important, but no longer extant work – frescos in the church of San Lorenzo in the Tuscan capital. In these drawings, which were not intended for public viewing or judgement, the usual formalistic and hieratic figures – which are typical of Pontormo's other work – appear less often, whereas there are male nudes which are so vibrant and sensual that many commentators have remarked on their homoeroticism. Jean-Claude Lebensztejn quotes an observation of G. R. Hacke: 'It can be said that, like LEONARDO DA VINCI and MICHELANGELO,

Pontormo identified his artistic ideal with the Platonic ephebe – but not just the "Platonic" one. The emphasis should be keenly placed on this aspect of sexual inversion.' (Hacke, incidentally, is wrong on one point: Pontormo's drawings do not celebrate languid ephebes, for his youths have already passed through adolescence and are endowed with a virile musculature.) Corrado Levi has even compared Pontormo's drawings with the leathermen of Tom of Finland.

The other evidence for Pontormo's sexuality is the diary in which the artist, suffering from stomach problems in 1554–1556, recorded his diet. He also included notes about his work in San Lorenzo and about his assistant Battista Naldini (1537–1591). Lebensztejn has published a (psycho)analysis of the diaries and remarked that, in 1555, Pontormo had such an attachment to Naldini that he suffered from psychosomatic attacks each time the young man did not return to sleep in his room or quarrelled with him and shut himself up in his own room: 'What the diary clearly reveals is that Pontormo loved Battista, and the fact that this was, simultaneously, the love of a lover for his beloved, of a parent for a child, of a master for his disciple and servant, is surprising only because in our eyes today a relationship of love has become so circumscribed.'

Pontormo died in Florence and is buried in the cloister of the church of the Santissima Annuziata; a funerary monument stands in the chapel of Santa Lucia in the same church.

G. Balin, 'Pontormo, peintre maniériste toscan', *Masques*, 20 (Winter 1983): 24–40; J. Cox Rearick, *The Drawings of Pontormo*, Cambridge, 1964; J.-C. Lebensztejn, 'Specchio nero', *Bullettino storico empolese*, 8 (1985): 199–268 (especially pp. 219–25); C. Levi, 'Madame Pontormo', *Dalle cantine frocie* (June 1977), insert; J. Pontormo, *Pontormo's Diary*, trans. R. Mayer, New York, 1982.

Giovanni Dall'Orto

Porter, Cole (1891–1964), American composer and lyricist. Porter was born in Peru, Indiana, the son of Katie Cole, daughter of millionaire J. O. Cole, and Sam Porter, a successful pharmacist. Although his precocious talent was ignored by his father and discouraged by his grandfather, Cole's mother encouraged his musical gifts, often extracting financial support from her father in order to free him to pursue a career. In 1909, Porter entered Yale University, where his talent for composing clever, rousing football songs made him exceedingly popular, and sealed his ambition to be a songwriter. There, he began a lifelong friendship with actor-director Monty Wooley, with whom he shared not only his passion for the theatre, but haunting male brothels in Harlem. A brief stint at Harvard Law School was abandoned in order to try his hand at composing musical shows.

Following the flop of his first show, *See America First* (1916), Porter sailed for Europe in 1917. He led a shadowy wartime existence until emerging as a popular entertainer at fashionable Parisian nightspots. In 1919, he met and married Linda Lee Thomas, a wealthy divorcée 15 years his senior. Together in residences in Paris, Venice and the Côte-d'Azur, they hosted glittering parties for members of the European and American 'smart set', a heady mixture of gay, lesbian, bisexual and heterosexual artists, composers, performers and aristocrats. Through the auspices of friends Gerald and Sara Murphy, Porter composed *Within the Quota* (1923), a successful ballet for Les Ballets Suédois, and in 1924 hosted a performance by DIAGHILEV's Ballets Russes in Venice, which led to a passionate affair with Diaghilev's secretary and confidant Boris Kochno.

During this expatriate period, Porter occasionally wrote for American musical shows, including scores for *Hitchy Koo* (1919 and 1922) and *Greenwich Village Follies* (1924), but other than the rather banal 'An Old Fashioned Garden' (which sold 500,000 copies), none was a hit. Kitty

Carlisle Hart proposes that, fearing failure, Porter 'preferred giving the impression of being a talented amateur who wrote and played for his smart European friends'. On trips to Europe, Richard Rodgers, George Gershwin and Irving Berlin, admirers of Porter's music, urged him to write for Broadway.

Returning to New York City, he had a genuine hit with 'Let's Do It' (Paris, 1928). The following year, Wake Up and Dream produced 'What is this Thing Called Love' and Fifty Million Frenchmen gave 'You Do Something to Me'. A string of Broadway successes followed in the 1930s: The New Yorkers (1930), Gay Divorcée (1932), Nymph Errant (1933), Anything Goes (1934), Jubilee (1935) and Red Hot and Blue (1936). In 1934, Porter began a long association with Hollywood, with The Gay Divorcée and Anything Goes (1936) and original film scores for Born to Dance (1936), Rosalie (1937) and Broadway Melody of 1940 (1939). Luxuriating in the film capital's lifestyle, Porter took over Hollywood's gay set with flamboyant nightclubbing and lavish, often orgiastic, pool parties, which nearly ruined his marriage.

The whirlwind pace of Porter's life came to a sudden halt in 1937 when both legs were crushed in a riding accident. Crippled for the rest of his life, his condition required more than 50 operations. Porter lived in frequently excruciating pain which he bore with stoic grace, but this led to a dependency on drugs and alcohol.

Not yet fully recovered, Porter returned to Broadway with the hits Leave it to Me (1938) and DuBarry was a Lady (1939). In the 1940s his Broadway hits included Panama Hattie, Let's Face It, Something for the Boys and Mexican Hayride; he closed the decade with arguably his best score, Kiss Me Kate, in 1948. His film scores produced only a few genuine hits. In the 1944 biopic Night and Day Cary Grant ludicrously portrayed the diminutive, somewhat effete Porter as tall, debonair, and straight. Increased illness and the loss

of his mother and wife in the early 1950s slowed Porter's output, but he continued to travel and produce memorable scores for Broadway (Can Can, Silk Stockings) and Hollywood (High Society, Les Girls). In 1958, surgery required the amputation of his right leg, after which he never wrote again and gradually retreated into seclusion.

In addition to the pervasive gay subtext and risqué innuendo in his lyrics ('Find Me a Primitive Man', 'Love for Sale', 'I'm a Gigolo', 'Anything Goes'), which often were challenged by censors, Porter's music is replete with contagious and erotic rhythms. His songs reveal a desperate need for love tempered by the constant fear of inconstancy and solitude ('In the roaring traffic's boom / In the silence of my lonely room / I think of you / Night and Day'). His deceivingly simple melodies convey the most complex of human emotions and relationships while sparkling with wit, grace and the blasé air of the sophisticate. Writer and critic Ethan Mordden has linked the voice in many Porter songs to the composer's artistic stance as a 'smart yet alienated commentator', an appropriate description for a genius who remained an avid yet publicly closeted homosexual.

Despite his marriage and debonair demeanour, Porter possessed a rapacious sexual appetite satisfied by an endless succession of paid sex with 'rough trade', preferably sailors, truck drivers and male prostitutes. By 1920 he already had contracted and was treated for syphilis. Yet there were attempts at meaningful relationships and a number of Porter's memorable songs were inspired by his male lovers, including Kochno, architect Ed Tauch ('Night and Day', 'In the Still of the Night') and dancer and choreographer Nelson Barclift ('You'd Be So Nice to Come Home To').

W. McBrien, Cole Porter: A Biography, New York, 1998; J. Morella and G. Mazzei, Genius and Lust: The Creative and Sexual Lives of Cole Porter and Noel Coward, New York, 1995;

C. Schwartz, *Cole Porter: A Biography*, New York, 1977.

A. M. Wentink

Porter, William (1805–1880), South African administrator. Porter practised as an advocate in Belfast in the present Northern Ireland until 1839, when he was appointed as Attorney General to the Cape Colony. He was accompanied to the Cape by his lifelong companion, Hugh Lynar, with whom he lived and worked throughout his adult life. A biographer described a typical scene: 'It was a common sight to see them on the way to the station, Porter striding ahead with Lynar a long way behind carrying the lunch basket.' Porter played an active and influential role in the public life of the colony, earning the accolade of 'the father of Cape Liberalism'. His influence on public life increased when he became a member of the Legislative Assembly in 1869. His reputation as a liberal thinker rested on his views on a colour-blind, qualified franchise, his stance against capital punishment and his conviction that Church and State should be separate. At the time of Lynar's death in 1873, the *Cape Argus* described their friendship as 'all but unprecedented in the annals of friendship'. Porter left the Cape Colony permanently three weeks later and died in Ireland in his seventy-fifth year.

W. Porter, *The Touwfontein Letters of William Porter (May–July 1845)*, ed. K. Schoeman, Cape Town, 1992; J. L. McCracken, *New Light at the Cape of Good Hope: William Porter, The Father of Cape Liberalism*, Belfast, 1993.

Graeme Reid

Powell (Brown), Evelyn (1893–unknown) and **Parkinson, Mary** (*c*.1880–unknown), Australian public figures. Evelyn Powell, born in Western Australia, worked as a stenographer, typist and clerk. Mary Parkinson was proprietor of the Perth Roneo Company, a duplicating and typewriting service. In 1916, Powell married Ernest Brown, a soldier in the Australian Forces. During the honeymoon, she refused to

have sex because she did not want to be a mother while Brown was away at war. On his return in 1919, Powell refused to sleep with him or even share his room. Meanwhile, Powell and her friend Parkinson shared the one bed at Powell's parents' house. Brown confronted Powell, who said that she did not intend to live with him as his wife. He engaged solicitors who filed a petition for 'Restitution of Conjugal Rights' at the Supreme Court of Western Australia. In 1920, the case came before the Divorce and Matrimonial Causes Court. Brown alleged that Powell refused to have a sexual relationship or live with him and lived instead with a female friend. He presented as evidence a passionate love-letter from Parkinson to Powell. The Judge granted Brown a decree for 'Restitution of Conjugal Rights', ordering that Powell 'return home to the Petitioner and render to him conjugal rights'. Powell did not return.

The Australian press reported the case extensively and reprinted Parkinson's love-letter. The respectable press made innuendoes about the women's relationship: 'An Unnatural Wife, Soldier's Short-Lived Happiness'. However, the sensationalist – and 'sexationalist' – press asserted that the women's relationship was sexual and deviant. *Perth Truth*'s headline declared: 'Bilked by a Bilker – A Sour Honeymoon and Unconsummated Marriage – Advent of the "Female Lover". Was it "69"? Curiously perverted correspondence'. *Melbourne Truth*'s headline 'Lesbian Love: Wife Loves Another Woman', made explicit reference to 'lesbian' – the first time in the Australian press. *Truth* described Parkinson's 'queer erotic letter' as a 'curious missive for one woman to write to another' and reported that 'events revealed a strange state of affairs, strongly suggestive of what the psychologist terms homosexuality'.

Whether Powell and Parkinson had a sexual relationship is not known, but Powell's actions and Parkinson's love-letter suggest a relationship that was intimate, deeply passionate and exclusive. Parkinson wrote: 'Sweetheart Mine? . . . With me it is *all or nothing* and you cannot blame me for hesitating where angels fear to tread. Were I to open the flood-gates it is you that would pause and perhaps count the cost: Are you willing and ready to give the same return? Let there be no reserve sweetheart but just as I say all or nothing unreserved and true. It lays in your hands. For you are the dearest, truest in this world to me. Yours always, M.' As well as adopting romantic language and the genre of the love-letter, she used imagery from classical mythology and drew on the notion of the ennobling quality of love between women. She also represented herself as an active desiring subject using figurative references to masculinised lust and sexuality, such as 'sailor like in every port' and 'floodgates'. Her letter challenges the view that the construction of the 'lesbian' and 'gender invert' by medicine and sexology played an exclusive part in the formation of 'lesbian' women's identities at this time. Rather, women drew on a wide range of romantic discourses to understand their love for women as exclusive, possessive and sexual. The letter, striking in its erotic language and embodied desire, also shows how women appropriated a tradition of asexual women's romantic friendship, re-encoding it with erotic and sexual meanings.

Ironically, for Powell and Parkinson, it was the letter's declarations of love which were used to expose their relationship and stigmatise and ostracise them as 'lesbian' nationwide. We know little of what happened to them after the scandal of the court case. Parkinson moved out of Powell's parents' house and changed the location of her business, but both women remained living in Perth until the late 1940s.

R. Ford, '"Lady-Friends" and "Sexual Deviationists": Lesbians and Law in Australia, 1920s–1950s', in D. Kirkby (ed.) *Sex Power and Justice: Historical Perspectives on Law in Aus-*

tralia, Melbourne, 1995; R. Ford, 'Harems, Floodgates and Love Letters: Declarations of Women's Same-Sex Passion in Early Twentieth Century Australia', forthcoming.

Ruth Ford

Prados, Emilio (1899–1962), Spanish poet. Prados is among the most intense poets in the Spanish canon. He is still among the lesser known members of the poetic group known as 'Generación del 27' ('Generation of 27'), and one of the least studied. Given that his work is notoriously difficult, sensitive and honest readings have been few and critics have contented themselves with preserving mystery rather than attempting to explore the still highly sensitive issue of the poet's sexuality. Biographical sketches present Prados as a hyper-sensitive boy, with severe health problems, subject to drastic mood swings, who never felt completely at ease either among other children or with adults. He seems to have gone through serious crises throughout childhood and adolescence, often waking up in the middle of the night, suffering from nightmares and acute terror. He then went to Madrid to continue his education in the prestigious Residencia de Estudiantes, a liberal institution which became a hotbed of artistic and intellectual talent. Other alumni include Salvador Dalí, Luis Buñuel and Federico García LORCA, whom Prados met and with whom he became close friends during their years at the Residencia. He felt a strong attachment to Lorca, verging on idol-worship, and later acknowledged a strong influence from his work. It is about this time, around 1923, that he devoted himself seriously to poetry. He also helped to create (with fellow poet Manuel Altolaguirre) *Litoral*, a leading literary magazine that published the early work of some members of the 'Generation of 27'. He also felt close to the Surrealist aesthetic, which he took steps to promote in collaboration with Vicente Aleixandre and Luis Cernuda.

From 1930, however, there was a move

towards more politically commited writing. These were times of conflict in Spain, and Prados felt the need to contribute actively to the cause of the left, abandoning some of his previous aesthetic ideals. He fought for the Republic during the Spanish Civil War (1936–1939), participating in the defence of Madrid and moving to Valencia when the capital was taken by the fascist army. In 1939, after facing extreme poverty, he crossed the French border into exile, later travelling to Mexico. The first years in this country were very difficult and he went through painful crises which he only overcame after 1942. At this time he adopted the orphan Francisco Sala, whom he had come to regard as a son. A new period of creativeness had started and he produced two of his best collections, *Jardín Cerrado* (*Closed Garden*, 1946) and *La piedra escrita* (*Carvings on Stone*, 1961). These are difficult, obscure works, of a highly personal significance. It would be simplistic to suggest that obscurity is the effect of a repression of sexual identity, but no doubt there is an element of awareness of the pressures to which his desire is subjected. The clearest instance of an attempt to deal with his sexuality is *Cuerpo perseguido* (1928), his one work focusing on the erotic experience. Even when references are characteristically ambiguous and there is nothing explicitly homosexual in any of his works, some critics (notably Ángel Sahuquillo) have described an awareness of desire under threat that may point towards expression of homosexuality. The very title, roughly translatable as 'The Pursued Body', contains a clue for the meaning of the sometimes painful, often physical, poems it contains. Yet, the critical establishment has been notoriously adverse to any homosexual interpretation of his work: no studies exist in which this is done systematically, and biographical information has been wilfully concealed as far as possible. A recent editor even goes so far as to leave the whole question open and suggest that the actual object of desire in *La piedra escrita* might well be a woman. Whether this is caused by bad faith or by ignorance will never be known, but the fact that the critic in question claims to have been the poet's 'good friend' (a boast all too common in Spanish literary criticism, as if personal relationships guaranteed reliable criticism; the opposite is often true) suggests the former. By denying or contributing to conceal Prados's emotional biography, critics think they honour the poet's memory. But trying to save a traditional notion of a good name distorts the reading of Prados's work.

Á. Sahuquillo, *García Lorca y la cultura de la homosexualidad masculina: Lorca, Dalí, Cernuda, Gil-Albert, Prados y la voz silenciada del amor homosexual*, Alicante, 1991.

Alberto Mira

Primavera, Giovan Leonardo (*c.* 1540/45– after 1585), Italian composer. Primavera was born in Barletta. By 1560 he was in Naples serving as a musician in the household of Fabrizio Gesualdo, who that same year had married the sister of the local archbishop, Cardinal Carlo Borromeo. Fabrizio's son, to become the composer Carlo Gesualdo, was also born around this time. Primavera remained in Naples for most of his life, though he appears to have been working further into the north of Italy, probably in and around Milan, Florence and Venice from about 1565 to 1578, and, around 1570, in Loreto. The last known reference to Primavera comes in 1585 with the publication of his final book of madrigals, dedicated to Carlo Gesualdo. Primavera's 12 published collections, all issued in Venice, consist entirely of secular vocal music, and include seven books of madrigals (1565–1585), settings of poems and sonnets by Petrarch, Tasso, Sannazaro and others (there are also a few to Primavera's own texts). There are also serveral volumes of such lighter style pieces as his so-called *canzone napolitane* and *villote*. Undoubtedly his most famous piece during his lifetime and since was a madrigal, *Nasce la gioja mia*, based on an arguably homoerotic poem addressed, unusually, in the masculine, to 'il mio bel sole' (my beautiful sun). This work, which first appeared in print in 1565, also circulated in numerous manuscript copies across Europe in the late sixteenth century, and was further immortalised when Palestrina used it as the theme for his *Missa Nasce la gioja mia* (published in 1590).

Though a popular composer in his time, Primavera's music is little known today. His greatest claim to notoriety, instead, comes from his participation in an incident 'of enormous ugliness' uniquely recorded in the correspondence of Guido Della Rovere, cardinal protector of the shrine of Loreto (and discovered there by the musicologist Richard Sherr). In March 1570, Rovere's governor in Loreto, Roberto Sassatelo, wrote to his master to report that, during a visit to the town by a party from Venice, one of their number, 'a musician and composer called Il Primavera', had slept in the same bed 'and also did worse' with a choirboy from the local basilica. The boy, Luigi Dalla Balla, probably about 16 at the time (Primavera was in his mid- to late twenties), already had a record of sexual contact with men, and himself admitted to having been the passive partner in anal sex (though while he was asleep) with Primavera, as well as with several others. These included his music teacher, Luigi Fontino, a singer and canon of the Loreto basilica. Fontino, a priest, was duly convicted of sodomy, defrocked, handed over to the secular authorities and executed (by decapitation). The boy, Dalla Balla, 'whipped and banned from the papal states' for his part in the crime, went on to make a small name for himself as a composer; two vocal pieces probably by him appear in collections of *canzonette* published in Venice in 1584 and 1587. Primavera, however, escaped by sea (presumably back to Venice) and thus, apparently, avoided any penalty, despite Sassatelo's intention that he, too, be 'given the pun-

ishment that such a scoundrel merits'. Predictably for this era, no other mention of Primavera's sexual activities or interests is known to have survived.

D. G. Cardamone, 'Primavera', in *The New Grove Dictionary of Music and Musicians*, London, 1980; R. Sherr, 'A Canon, a Choirboy, and Homosexuality in Late Sixteenth-Century Italy: A Case Study', *Journal of Homosexuality*, 21, 3 (1991): 1–22.

Graeme Skinner

Proust, Marcel (1871–1922), French writer. Proust was born to a successful doctor and a cultivated Jewish mother. He was subject to indifferent health throughout his life, and was indulged by female relatives. Though undoubtedly a social climber, he failed to scale the heights of society to the extent his writings might suggest. The discovery of his homosexuality may well be linked to his friendship with the composer Reynaldo Hahn.

Perhaps the greatest French stylist of the twentieth century, a refined observer of mores, Proust devoted almost all his efforts to literature, leaving the paradoxical impression that he had written a great deal, not just one book. The paradox may be resolved in two ways: *À la recherche du temps perdu* (*Remembrance of Things Past*) is indeed a very long book, and he wrote much besides, though many texts were published only posthumously. Worthy of mention are his *Pastiches et mélanges* (1919), imitations of famous authors, showing him as a conscious stylist, and his *Nouveaux Mélanges* (*Contre Sainte-Beuve*) published in 1954, attacking Sainte-Beuve's view that biography is a clue or key to literary creation.

Proust was a Jewish, dilettante, homosexual snob, and *À la recherche* – which is peopled with aristocrats, social climbers, homosexuals of assorted gender, Jews and pro- and anti-Dreyfusards (the Dreyfus affair, in which nationalist reactionaries engineered the conviction of a totally innocent Jewish officer on charges of complicity with a foreign power, divided French society, and placed socially successful Jews, in particular, in an agonisingly invidious position) – does little to disprove Sainte-Beuve's hypothesis. However, those traits in Proust's character are spread, in the novel, among a variety of characters: the aristocratic Guermantes family, the *arriviste* Verdurins, Baron Charlus, the lesbian Albertine, and Bloch, the Jewish parvenu. The fact that the novel is in the first person might be assumed to give it a confessional dimension; however, the narrator – curiously devoid of personality and feelings – is often a kind of voyeur. Nowhere is this more evident than in *Sodome et Gomorrhe*, when he sneaks into an empty shop to spy on Charlus and Jupien – strange behaviour for a heterosexual. The meeting is likened to a bumble-bee fertilising an orchid, a curious natural analogy reminiscent of GIDE's *Corydon*. Homosexuality is a social transgression, so Charlus does not want sex with his social equals. In the strict sense, homosexuality is degradation. The word 'homosexuality' is used, but not approved. The term 'inversion' is preferred, and same-sex desire explained in terms of false femininity. Homosexuals are a 'race' and the connotations are not fortuitous, for there are many clear and sustained comparisons with Jews. If inverts are a race condemned to live a lie, then *À la recherche* is the illustration of that lie. Though there is much more than a description of homosexuality in the book, the true gay dimension of *À la recherche* is not that it offers a convincing defence of homosexuality, but that it gives a view of society peculiar to those excluded from it (Jews or gays). Resolutely old-fashioned in his portrayal of a lost world of social privilege, Proust is nevertheless among the first to have dealt with the great twentieth-century themes of childhood, time and memory.

In a repressed age, homosexual men often succeeded in seeking each other out and in networking. There was no such complicity between the great contemporaries Proust and André Gide. Gide may have been the braver activist: Proust, undoubtedly, is the finer stylist and chronicler of an age. There may have been an element of jealousy, but more probably it was the kind of tension that exists today between those on either side of the closet door (it is no doubt Gide's great public visibility that accounts for the fact that it was he and not Proust who became the great emblematic figure of French homosexuality, although Gide's own life contained many compromises with bourgeois respectability). In any event, Gide, who was working for a publisher, turned down *Du côté de chez Swann*, the first volume of *À la recherche*, and Proust paid for it to be printed. About the same time, Proust engaged a chauffeur named Agostinelli, with whom he had a tempestuous affair, but who was killed in 1914. Increasingly, Proust became a recluse preoccupied only with his herculean literary task. As financial pressures finally impinged upon him, he moved to more exiguous lodgings, and retired to a cork-lined chamber, where he arose only at night to write.

J.-Y. Tadié, *Marcel Proust: Biographie*, Paris, 1996; R. Hayman, *Proust: A Biography*, London, 1990; J. E. Rivers, *Proust and the Art of Love: The Aesthetics of Sexuality in the Life, Times and Art of Marcel Proust*, New York, 1980; G. Florival, *Le Désir chez Proust: à la recherche du sens*, Paris, 1971.

David Parris

Puttkamer, Marie Madeleine von (1881–1944), German poet. Marie Madeleine (she used these names as her pseudonym) was born Marie Günther in Eydtkuhnen, East Prussia (now Russia). At age 19 she married the much older Major-General and Baron Georg Heinrich von Puttkamer, and moved to Berlin.

In the same year she published her first poetry collection, called *Auf Kypros* (*On Cyprus*, 1900). Although most of its poems are heterosexual in tone, some are clear depictions of lesbianism. This volume of erotic verse became extremely popular, and appeared in 37 editions to 1910, while its author acquired a sales-enhancing reputation among literary critics as 'shameless' and 'perverse'. In fact Marie Madeleine's lesbians have their literary predecessors in the work of established male poets such as Baudelaire; they are decadent, exotic constructions who burn with destructive passion.

Undeterred by her critics, Marie Madeleine had published six further successful collections of poetry by 1920, as well as plays, short stories, and novels. In *Taumel* (*Dizziness*, 1920), she created a type of female Don Juan, who voraciously pursues and conquers.

From 1905 Puttkamer lived mainly in Baden-Baden and in Nice. Her other writings include *Die drei Nächte* (*Three Nights*, 1901); *An der Liebe Narrenseil* (*A Puppet on Love's String*, 1902); *In Seligkeit und Sünde* (*In Bliss and Sin*, 1905); *Die Kleider der Herzogin. Roman* (*The Duchess's Clothes, a Novel*, 1906); *Katzen: Drei Liebesspiele* (*Cats: Three Plays about Love*, 1910); *Die rote Rose Leidenschaft* (*The Red Rose of Passion*, 1912).

P. Budke and J. Schulze, *Schriftstellerinnen in Berlin 1871 bis 1945: Ein Lexikon zu Leben und Werk*, Berlin, 1995; L. Fadermann (ed.) *Chloe Plus Olivia: An Anthology of Lesbian Literature from the Seventeenth Century to the Present*, New York, 1994; M. M. von Puttkamer, *Die rote Rose Leidenschaft. Gedichte und Prosa*, ed. S. Kaldewey and A. Kind, Munich, 1977.

Sarah Colvin

R

Rabelais, François (?1494–c. 1553), French writer. Born near Chinon, Rabelais is considered the major Renaissance prose writer in French, alongside MONTAIGNE. Of the five books in his suite of novels, published between 1532 and 1564, the most famous are *Gargantua* and *Pantagruel*, which quickly became European bestsellers. His chequered career led him from the Franciscan order to being a physician of repute and an aide to two cardinal-diplomats until, thanks to royal favour, he was given the living of Meudon, near Paris (a good vicarage which, in the spirit of the times, did not carry many ecclesiastical duties).

If *Pantagruel* and *Gargantua* (the story of giants, set in Renaissance Europe) are acknowledged to be an all-embracing allegorical satire of political struggles and social changes at the time, the remaining books are much more ferocious in their attacks on established orders, the university, parliament and church. Rabelais died, in unexplained circumstances, shortly after the *Fourth Book* – a violent attack against the church – had been condemned by the Sorbonne faculty of theology, the supreme arbiter in these matters (1552).

However, Rabelais's case sheds light on the difficulty of understanding homosexual thought in the Renaissance. Calvin had a clear perception of Rabelais's intentions. Whereas, indeed, most Renaissance poets who cultivated the arts of the 'civilis-ing process' shunned the exuberant style of Rabelais and his 'gay fooleries' and condemned him as 'obscene' (a label which simply meant a complete disregard for the codes and rules of gentility), Calvin in his *Treatise on Scandals* (*De Scandalis*, 1550) calls him a pig and a dog – and simply a materialist. It is established that Rabelais, in dangerous times, did stand for ideas that would make *libertinage* so prevalent in a later period, and with them, a complete disregard for set sexual rules. In this respect Rabelais must be set in the context of humanism. Calvin, who knew his real adversaries were not the papists but the humanists, bundled up Rabelais with Etienne Dolet (1509–1546), the atheist humanist and orator, trained in Padua like most *libertins*, who was burnt at the stake on the Place Maubert – ostensibly accused of blasphemy, and in all likelihood of sodomy. Dolet is credited with having reshaped the dry philological reading of Cicero's treatises into a theory of the Beautiful. Later, and in contrast, Pierre de la Ramée (or Ramus, 1515–1572), the greatest professor of rhetoric of his time and a keen 'amateur' of boys like MURET, was to develop rhetoric towards logic, and cultivate a 'virile' ideal of speech. In Dolet's case, male beauty was an extension of oratorical sublimity, in Ramus's case it was a 'virile' strategy of power, in Rabelais's instance an exuberant celebration of sex. Dolet and Ramus met the executioner's flame and sword, Rabelais disappeared. Their works should be read as strategies of concealment.

However, although Rabelais's works are not about sex and certainly not about homosexuality, it is striking that the main character who recurs throughout the novels and, from the *Third Book* onwards, takes over, is a strange young man called Panurge. Panurge (in Greek, a rascal) appears right at the beginning, as a pedantic fop, a swishy young man who follows the latest fashion in clothes and ideas, and who tries to impress country bumpkin Pantagruel with his knowledge. As Pantagruel turns into a Renaissance 'giant' and a wise prince, Panurge becomes his factotum, the mercurial side of Apollonian Pantagruel – the 'feminine' side of the New Man the kind giant is representing (women are conspicuously absent or relegated to secondary roles). As this all-male narrative unfolds (with a stupendous array of characters, like Friar Jean), the plot shifts to finding a wife for Panurge, a human panacea to his unnerving bachelorhood (while they think they have found the physical panacea, the *Pantagruelion*, marijuana). To do so, they embark on yet another navigation, this time to consult the oracle of the Holy Bottle. As to finding an answer, the only advice they receive from Bacbuc the priestress is 'Trinch!' ('Drink!'). That is, let Panurge be himself, loosened up by wine, and then decide whether he really likes women. The suite of novels ends on that high note. In all five books, Panurge, the real hero, has never touched a woman. To take the full measure of Rabelais's extraordinary courage in siting Panurge at the centre of his satire, one has to recall that in Aristotelian terms (with which he was fully acquainted) *panourgia* or unscrupulousness differs from wisdom (*phronesis*) in so far as those who practice *panourgia* use exactly the same energy (*dynamis*) to achieve their aims as those who exercise *phronesis*, yet without the Good as their intention, the Good being in Aristotle's argument the

civic common good. Seen in that light, Panurge is an upsetting figure, both sexually and socially. No surprise then that Calvin and the Sorbonne alike, who knew of the reshaping of Aristotle by the Paduan school, condemned Rabelais, and Panurge, to a man.

Taking all these elements into consideration, Rabelais's example does illustrate that, more often than not with early modern texts, the assessment of homosexuality or queerness follows cultural routes that need great care in being unravelled: Dolet's aesthetic oratory, Ramus's unbending belief in logic and Rabelais's 'gay fooleries' are strategies of concealment for change – social and sexual – firmly rooted in their readings of the Classics.

L. Febvre, *The Problem of Unbelief in the Sixteenth Century*, London, 1982.

Philippe-Joseph Salazar

Raffalovich, Marc-André (1864–1934), Russian-British writer, poet and patron of the arts. Born in Paris into a wealthy and cultivated Russo-Jewish family, Raffalovich came to England in 1882. His original intention had been to take his degree at Oxford University, but instead he settled in London. There, in his mansion in Mayfair, he entertained on a lavish scale with the object of founding a *salon* for writers and artists. Oscar WILDE and others were amused by his attempt to push himself into the literary world through dinner parties. Wilde's jibe became famous: 'Dear André! He came to London to found a salon and only succeeded in opening a saloon.' Wilde also mocked Raffalovich's ugliness: his beady eyes, thick lips, hooked nose and gutteral accent. Undeterred, and exemplifying the newly fashionable notion of homosexual as poet, Rafflovich continued to pursue his literary interests. Between 1884 and 1896 he published five volumes of verse, two novels and many articles, none of which received much recognition. In 1892 he met and fell in love with John GRAY. The couple then dropped out of Wilde's circle. Raffalovich became one of Wilde's critics. In 1895 he wrote an essay on *L'Affaire Oscar Wilde*, published in Paris, in which he discussed the recent scandal and attacked Wilde for encouraging vice in others. In the following year he published, in Lyon, *Uranisme et Unisexualité*, which won him the reputation of being the leading French expert on homosexuality. In this, and numerous articles and reviews in the *Archives de l'Anthropologie Criminelle*, he expounded the idea that a homosexual orientation is equal to heterosexuality as an expression of sexuality, although homosexual practices are sinful.

In 1896 Raffalovich was received into the Roman Catholic Church, taking the baptismal name Sebastian. For the rest of his life he was a devout Catholic and a benefactor of the Dominican order. He gave financial support to the dying artist Aubrey Beardsley and was instrumental in his conversion to Catholicism in 1897. When Gray went to Rome in 1897 to study for the priesthood, Raffalovich paid his expenses. In 1905 he followed Gray to Edinburgh. There he financed the building of St Peter's Church in Morningside, where Gray had been appointed rector and where he attended Mass each morning. The two men maintained separate households. Their friendship was intimate, though in public they treated each other with studied formality and detachment. In London Raffalovich had been a social failure, but in Edinburgh, with less competition, he succeeded in founding a *salon*. His elegant luncheons and evening dinner parties for Edinburgh residents and visitors of literary interests became quite famous. He retained his interest in Uranian literature; for his own collection, the artist Eric Gill designed a bookplate depicting a coiled snake.

Raffalovich's exposition of the view that a homosexual orientation is both natural and morally neutral was a notable contribution to late nineteenth-century literature on the subject. But it was a mixed message, deeply impregnated with Roman Catholic moralism. In 1905 he wrote: 'I have defended [unisexuals] against prejudice and ignorance; I have proclaimed that, like other men, they can be virtuous, chaste, passionate or dissolute, and that there is no line of demarcation between them and others; I have often written that they can rise above themselves and above their brothers by renouncing sexuality and pledging themselves to celibacy.'

P. W. J. Healy, 'Uranisme et Unisexualité: A Late Victorian View of Homosexuality', *New Blackfriars*, 59, 693 (1978); V. A. Rosario, *The Erotic Imagination: French Histories of Perversity*, New York, 1997; B. Sewell (ed.) *Two Friends: John Gray & André Raffalovich: Essays Biographical and Critical*, Aylesford, Kent, 1963; B. Sewell, *Footnote to the Nineties: A Memoir of John Gray and André Raffalovich*, London, 1968.

David Hilliard and Michael Sibalis

Rapinett, Guglielmo (1843–1912), Maltese politician. Rapinett, a lawyer, was elected to the Council of Government in 1871, and shortly afterwards was appointed a magistrate; he was also a Professor of Law and Economics at the University of Malta. In 1884 he was arrested by a military policeman for having attempted to seduce a young British soldier in Valletta. Charged with making indecent and immoral proposals to and indecently assaulting a man, he was found guilty and suspended from the office of magistrate.

Rapinett admitted to entering into a conversation with the soldier, who he said had asked him for a shilling; Rapinett claimed to have refused this and had even threatened to report him. According to Rapinett, the soldier then arrested him. Rapinett admitted that he was greatly worried by the 'terror of publicity' of the inquiry. He was upset at the 'sneers and jibes of the evil-minded, the innuendoes of friends and enemies, the political capital which the opposition papers [make]'.

Nevertheless after Rapinett was found guilty, all the elected members of Malta's Legislative Council, the Archbishop of Malta and 3,000 citizens petitioned for his release.

G. Rapinett, *The Case of Dr Rapinett of Malta – Stated by Himself*, n.p, n.d.

Joseph Chetcuti

Rasmussen, (Niels Carl) Gustav (Magnus) (1895–1953), Danish diplomat and foreign minister. After graduating in law, Rasmussen in 1921 entered the Danish foreign service. His career was brilliant. As an advocate for Denmark at the International Tribunal in The Hague, Rasmussen played a decisive role in the Danish–Norwegian dispute over Greenland (1932–1933). During World War II he was deputy to the Danish minister in London. When the Danish Legation in London in 1941 declared itself independent of the government of Denmark (under German occupation), Rasmussen was dismissed from the foreign service. After the war he was reinstated and although he had no experience or background in party politics, he was appointed foreign minister in the traditionalist-agrarian *(Venstre Party)* government (1945–1947). The prime minister, Knud Kristensen, who was a farmer, is said to have been surprised and disgusted when told that Rasmussen was a practising homosexual and that he lived with his chauffeur. Rasmussen continued as minister of foreign affairs in the Social Democratic government (1947–1950), but had no decisive influence on Denmark's entry into the Atlantic Pact in 1949. In parliament Rasmussen attacked Kristensen, the former prime minister, for his inadequate understanding of foreign policy. It was, on the other hand, Rasmussen's weakness that, as a career diplomat, he had little understanding of party politics.

When the Permanent Under-Secretary of State had to resign in 1948 after having 'taken over' the wife of a newly wedded colleague in the foreign service, Rasmussen appointed his close friend, Jens Rudolph Dahl (1894–1977), Permanent Under-Secretary. Dahl was a homosexual and two years later he too had to resign after having made homosocial advances to a young diplomat.

After the fall of the Social Democratic government in October 1950, Rasmussen was appointed ambassador in Rome. Dahl also settled in Rome and took up a career as a newspaper commentator. Although it was widely known that Gustav (aka 'Gysse') Rasmussen was a homosexual, the general public was not aware of it. However, in December 1950 Rasmussen was attacked in a provincial newspaper affiliated with the Venstre Party for having appointed Dahl. A well known former diplomat wrote that homosexuals had a natural tendency to form cliques and coteries closed to 'normal' people, declaring that the US House Committee on Un-American Activities was decidedly correct in its view of homosexuals as 'particularly dangerous persons'. However, according to younger colleagues, Dahl, after his resignation, retained to an amazing degree the respect and affection of his former colleagues, whom he regularly visited at the Foreign Ministry.

That the Foreign Ministry (but not foreign policy) during the post-war years was led by homosexual civil servants may in the longer perspective have contributed to the relaxed attitude towards homosexual personnel which has since characterised the Danish foreign service.

T. Kaarsted, 'Gustav Rasmussen', *Dansk Biografisk Leksikon*, Vol. 12, Copenhagen, 1982: 27–9; *Sorø Amtstidende*, 16 December 1950; *Lørdags-Avisen*, 30 December 1950.

Wilhelm von Rosen

'Raucourt' (Marie Antoinette Josèphe Françoise Saucerotte) (1756–1815), French actress. The most notorious lesbian of her day, born in Paris on 3 March 1756, as Françoise Saucerotte, who later adopted the name Raucourt, was trained in acting

by her father, himself a minor actor. Her
début at the Comédie Française in December 1772 (she was 16) was sensational.
According to a chronicle of the time,
'Nothing similar has ever been seen in
man's memory.' Her talent, beauty and
enchanting voice won her countless admirers and she was soon leading the high
life in Paris with a series of lovers, both
male and female, including the opera singer Sophie Arnould (1740–1802), whom she
allegedly 'married'. Her expensive tastes
brought her to bankruptcy in June 1776, in
part (it was said) because her lesbianism
deprived her of the financial support from
rich men that most other actresses could
count on. Despite declining popularity, she
continued to act at home and abroad with
the protection of Queen Marie Antoinette.
Her private life remained the subject of
public gossip and pamphleteers published
apocryphal defences of lesbianism under
her name. She supposedly presided over
the Anandryne Sect, a wholly imaginary
association of man-hating lesbians.

Imprisoned as a Royalist in 1793–1794
during the Reign of Terror, she returned
to the theatre after her release in August
1794 and settled down with Henriette
Simonnot-Ponty, whom she had met in
prison. She died in Paris in 1815. She was
to cause yet one final scandal. When the
curé of Saint-Roch refused her church burial (because she was an actress), a large
mob broke down the doors to the church
and triumphantly bore in her coffin.

J. de Reuilly, *La Raucourt et ses amies*, Paris,
1909; M.-J. Bonnet, *Les Relations amoureuses
entre les femmes*, Paris, 1995; J. Merrick, 'The
Marquis de Villette and Mademoiselle de Raucourt', in J. Merrick and B.T. Ragan (eds)
Homosexuality in Modern France, Oxford,
1996: 30–53; O. Blanc, *Les Libertines: Plaisir et
liberté au temps des Lumières*, Paris, 1997.

Michael Sibalis

Redl, Alfred Victor (1864–1913), Austrian
Army intelligence officer/spy. Born in
Lemberg (Lvov), in Austrian Galicia

(Poland), the son of a railway freight clerk,
Redl was the ninth of 14 children. An exceptionally bright student, he passed the
examination for cadet school at 14, and
two years later enlisted in the army. Determined to succeed, Redl advanced steadily through the ranks and was promoted to
battalion adjutant by 1889. His extraordinary loyalty, conscientiousness and
exemplary manner were observed by superiors who urged him to take the War
College examinations. Passing the entrance examination with honours, he
graduated a first lieutenant twenty-eighth
in his class. Following two years of service
in Hungary and one year at home in Lemberg, he was appointed to a post in the
Russian city of Kazan which, although
labelled a cultural attaché position, was in
reality the beginning of Redl's career in
intelligence and counter-intelligence.

In 1900, Redl was recalled to Vienna
and appointed Chief of the Russian Section of the Intelligence Bureau of the General Staff. In addition to routine
information-gathering tasks, Redl's responsibilities as Chief of the Operations
Section was undercover work, recruiting,
training and dispatching agents, and the
dissemination of information to other
agencies. An obsessive dedication to this
position resulted in short order with an
efficiency plan for the division which so
impressed the Intelligence Bureau chief
that Redl was appointed Chief of the
Operations Section and Chief of Counter-
intelligence. After successful implementa-
tion of the recommendations of his plan,
Redl demonstrated a marked behavioural
change. Confident in the close ties between
Counter-intelligence and the Imperial
Police, he began to spend lavishly and increase his homosexual activities and transvestism which, until this time, had been
discreet. The efficacy of Redl's counter-
intelligence policies so decimated the
ranks of Russian agents that he became a
major target of Russian intelligence. Following the failure of a female operative to
break Redl's silence, Russia's best agent

was assigned to the case. When confronted with voluminous and damaging reports on his gay activities, Redl agreed to become a paid agent of the Russian government. As part of his treasonous agreement, Redl delivered plans for Austrian military outposts in return for the names of expendable Russian agents, whose capture only enhanced his position. In 1904, when Austrian intelligence was informed that one of their high-ranking officials was a paid Russian agent, Redl managed with his Russian connections to evade discovery, and was promoted to major in 1905. For his indispensable service during the Balkan Crisis of 1908, Redl was promoted to lieutenant-colonel and nearly became Intelligence Bureau Chief. Instead he became the trusted aide to Colonel Urbanski. In 1911, Redi was assigned command of the 4th Battalion in Vienna, where he became a much admired and beloved officer. He was promoted to colonel in 1912, and after service in Bosnia prior to an expected invasion of Serbia, he was appointed Chief of Staff of the Eighth Army Corps in Prague.

The Prague assignment proved his undoing. In Prague, Redl spent lavishly on his young lover, Stefan Hromodka, and lived in a state of 'sybaritic sensuality' in a luxurious apartment, where he hid his women's clothes and wigs as well as nude photographs of himself and young male lovers. In April 1913, German intelligence contacted Austrian intelligence with a plan to reveal the identity of 'Herr Nikon Nizetas', a suspected agent in the Austrian service. The over-confident Redl walked into the trap. Confronted in his apartment, Redl confessed and was given the option of suicide, which he accepted by shooting himself on 25 May 1913. The discovery not only of Redl's duplicity but of the secret life revealed by the contents of his apartment shook the Austrian military and intelligence establishment to the core. Attempts at an Austrian government cover-up failed and the truth was revealed in less than a week. Redl was buried in

disgrace and his last lover, Hromodka, was incarcerated for 'unnatural prostitution'.

While Redl's downfall resulted from an internal tangle of feelings of inferiority, overweening ambition and decadent sexual tastes, his example has been cited as a case in point by enemies of gays in military service and sensitive government service. Played out against the backdrop of a fading Hapsburg Empire riddled by corruption and collapsing social order, the story of Redl's tragedy has inspired a number of important theatrical works including John Osborne's play *A Patriot for Me* and Istvan Szabo's 1985 film *Colonel Redl*.

N. L. Garde, *Jonathan to Gide: The Homosexual in History*, New York, 1964.

A. M. *Wentink*

Reich, Wilhelm (1897–1957), Austro-Hungarian psychoanalyst and sexual liberationist. Reich was born to non-practising Jewish parents in Dobrzcynica (now in the Ukraine). His youth was traumatic. After he informed his father of his mother's liaison with his tutor, she committed suicide; his father died soon afterwards. After serving in the defeated Austro-Hungarian army during World War I, Reich entered medical school in Vienna and joined Sigmund FREUD. Initiated into Freud's inner circle, he married fellow psychoanalyst Annie Pink; they had two children and divorced in 1933. In 1945 he married Ilse Ollendorff; they had one child and divorced in 1951. Reich was a compulsive heterosexual with little sympathy for other sexualities.

Among orthodox Freudians Reich's *Character Analysis* (1933) had greatest acceptance, with its description of 'character armor' – the defences of the uptight against their feelings. Combining Marx and Freud, Reich's theories of revolution influenced subsequent sex radicals. Reich attempted in his theories to psychologise communism and revolutionise psychoanalysis. For his efforts, the German

Communist Party expelled him in 1933, as did the International Psychoanalytic Association in 1934.

Reich's *Mass Psychology of Fascism* (1933) offered an influential psycho-social interpretation of Hitler's Germany. He argued that the sexual repression that Freud had identified in individuals also operated in the wider society, creating individual as well as mass psychoses. Freeing one's self from repression would liberate one's sexuality as well as society in general. In 1942, Reich predicted, 'Just as tsarist oppression unleashed the "hunger" revolution in Russia [with Lenin], sexual hypocrisy will unleash the sexual revolution in the USA.'

While his *Function of the Orgasm* (1927) celebrates the male heterosexual orgasm, it misinterprets the female orgasm. He believed that only the electrical energy between male and female could bring the male to healthy ejaculation. His ideas that there could never be sexual electricity between two women, between two men or in masturbation now seem outdated. His assertion, however, that sexuality underlies our whole life energy from cradle to grave has found numerous champions.

Despite Reich's misunderstandings of homosexuality, many gay liberationists found others of his ideas useful. During the 1960s, Reich (along with Herbert Marcuse) provided a missing link between personal and social analysis. Theorists such as Mario Mieli in Italy, Guy Hocquenghem in France, Paul Goodman or Gayle Rubin in the United States, Juliet Mitchell in Britain, Klaus Theweleit in Germany and a host of others mined Reich's *Sexual Revolution* (1936) for its critique of traditional sexual morality and its affirmation of the genital impulse. Reich's work likewise influenced gay literature. William Burroughs reflected Reichian theory in *Naked Lunch* (1959) as did the Living Theater in *Paradise Now* (1971).

Perhaps people know Reich's work best today only indirectly through Michel Foucault's *La Volonté de Savoir* (1976, translated as *The History Of Sexuality, Vol. I*). Foucault lashed out against Reich's 'essentialist' formulation of sexuality and broke sharply with Gilles Deleuze and Felix Guattari who had attempted to modernise Reich in their *Anti-Oedipus: Capitalism And Schizophrenia* (1972). Foucault's histories provided a more respectable theory for lesbian and gay males seeking to legitimise their movement by delegitimising sexuality and repudiating madness or revolution.

After Hitler came to power in Germany, Reich fled first to Oslo and then in 1949 to the United States, where he met a humiliating end. The Food and Drug Administration arrested him for selling orgone machines, and sent him to prison where he died. The FDA burnt many of his manuscripts, but the Harvard Medical School has since archived his surviving papers.

J. Weeks, *Sexuality and its Discontents*, London, 1985.

Charley Shively

Reid, Forrest (1875–1947), Irish writer. Besides sixteen (including two rewritten) novels and two story collections concerning boys and boyhood, Reid also published two autobiographies, *Apostate* (1926) and *Private Road* (1940), a number of books of criticism, and a translation, *Poems from the Greek Anthology* (1943). Reid spent his entire life in Belfast, Ireland, save for a period of study at Cambridge (1905–1908).

Reid's novels were praised for their perceptive recreation of the mindset of boyhood, which Reid drew from his remembrance of the 'lost paradise' of youth, according to Brian Taylor, 'lost for ever, yet ... approachable through desire and through memory'. An important theme developed throughout Reid's novels is the rejection of Christianity and the society and morality it created in favour of Hellenic paganism and the 'Greek ideal' of male friendship. Many of Reid's boy heroes live or find refuge within this Hellenic dream-world, and are frequently destroyed as a result of their inability to cope with the evils of modern society.

The Garden God: A Tale of Two Boys (1905) is a 'lyrical romance' of boyhood friendship remembered and lost. This novel ended Reid's friendship with its dedicatee, Henry JAMES, who was alarmed by the pagan eroticism of the relationship between the boys. *The Bracknels* (1911), rewritten and published as *Denis Bracknel* (1947), is about a sensitive boy who attempts, by means of pagan moon-worship involving rites of propitiation, to mitigate the evil that he witnesses in the world but cannot explain, which ultimately results in his derangement and death. *Demophon: A Traveler's Tale* (1927), based on the classical myth of Demeter and Demophon, chronicles the adventures of the hero in his ultimately successful quest to reunite with his divine playmate, the boy-god Hermes. *Brian Westby* (1934), which shares narrative similarities to Thomas MANN's *Death in Venice*, concerns a novelist's inspiring and revitalising reunion with his young son, a relationship which proves to be ultimately fleeting. The 'Tom Barber Trilogy', consisting of *Uncle Stephen* (1931), *The Retreat* (1936) and *Young Tom* (1944), linked by the theme of the search for the eternal friend, charts the development of the sensitive and highly imaginative Tom from the age of 10 to 15. This trilogy partakes heavily of the marvellous, involving nature worship, guardian angels, ghosts, magic arts and the bridging of the dream and real worlds.

Brian Taylor has remarked about Reid's entire *œuvre*, 'Reid's best work was always the result of ... resistance' to explicitly writing about erotic and sexual love between boys or between men and boys. However, as a consequence, his 'work was always, in a sense, incomplete'.

R. Burlingham, *Forrest Reid: A Portrait and a Study*, London, 1953; M. Bryan, *Forrest Reid*, Boston, 1976; B. Taylor, *The Green Avenue: The Life and Writings of Forrest Reid, 1875–1947*, Cambridge, 1980.

Jason Boyd

Reinhard, Joachim (Joakim) (1858–1925), Danish writer. Reinhard belonged to the first generation of homosexual men in Denmark. He studied aesthetics at the University of Copenhagen (1876–1877). Some students took a dislike to his arrogant and affected manners and spread the rumour that he had attempted to seduce two of them. At the same time another student, Martin KOK, caused a scandal at a party in the Student Union by drunkenly groping a cross-dressing student under his skirt. Under the weight of these rumours Reinhard, on his nineteenth birthday, fled to the US under an assumed name. He had no means of support in New York and a few months later, when the scandal had died down, he returned to Denmark. Privately Reinhard denied having attempted to seduce his fellow students, but his name was forever connected to the first publicised homosexual scandal in Denmark. For a few years he lived discreetly in the countryside as a private teacher and a journalist on provincial newspapers. Under a pseudonym, he published two novels that were well reviewed. After his return to Copenhagen in 1883, he published several more novels and became a member of a coterie of young literary homosexuals around the talented author and journalist Herman BANG. He also became a flaming queen. Unwisely, in 1889 Reinhard in a newspaper article attacked Georg Brandes, the dominant figure of modern literary criticism and cultural opposition in Denmark. A few days later a newspaper, owned and edited by Brandes's brother, ridiculed Reinhard as Martin Kok's 'comrade-in-arms' (i.e. as a homosexual). Other newspapers hinted at Reinhard as a sexual pervert and in November 1889 he emigrated to the US. In the 1890s Reinhard taught at Purdue University, later at a Catholic college in Arkansas. At his death in 1925 he was working as a librarian in Brooklyn, New York.

A large number of letters from Reinhard to Arthur Feddersen, an older and fatherly adviser, and to his contemporary, the author Karl Larsen, are preserved. They illustrate closely, on the level of the individual, the workings of the social process that made Reinhard a feminine homosexual. In 1908 Reinhard's friend, Karl Larsen, anonymously published a book in Germany, *Daniel–Daniela. Aus dem Tagebuch eines Kreuzträgers von* *** (*Daniel–Daniela. From the Diary of a Man who Bears a Cross by* ***). Reviewers in Germany accepted the authenticity of this tragic and pitiable self-description of a feminine homosexual man who confesses his love to a young officer and is treated to the whip. In a preface to the Danish edition (1922) under his own name, Larsen admitted that the book was a pastiche and a *roman à clef* written in order to contribute to an educated debate, but not motivated by sympathy for this type of person. There is no evidence in Reinhard's letters to Larsen that he knew that he figured as the protagonist of his friend's literary portrayal of an enemy.

W. von Rosen, *Månens Kulør. Studier i danske bøssehistorie 1628–1912*, Copenhagen, 1993: 569–606; J. N. Katz, *Gay/Lesbian Almanac: A New Documentary*, New York, 1983: 324–6.

Wilhelm von Rosen

Rhodes, Cecil (1853–1902), British-South African political figure. 'I would annex the planets if I could', one of Rhodes's *bons mots*, sums up the ambitions of Britain's best-known imperialist. The son of a clergyman, Rhodes went to South Africa to join his brother, a cotton planter, in the early 1870s; both soon moved on to look for their fortunes in the recently discovered Kimberley goldmines. Except for episodic stays in Britain, where he completed a degree at Oxford, Rhodes remained in South Africa, becoming a wealthy gold and diamond magnate – he owned the De Beers diamond company. He also entered politics and served as prime minister of the Cape Colony from 1890 to 1896, when he was forced to resign because of the failure of the Jameson Raid on the Boer state. Nevertheless, through Rhodes's efforts, British imperial control was extended through what is now South Africa, Zambia and Zimbabwe (formerly called Rhodesia). Much of Rhodes's immense fortune was left to establish the Oxford scholarships which bear his name.

Rhodes never married, pleading that 'I have too much work on my hands' and saying that he would not be a dutiful husband. Queen Victoria reportedly asked him if he was a woman-hater, which Rhodes denied. During his life, he surrounded himself with young men (usually with blue eyes and athletic build), from whom he demanded complete loyalty and who were rewarded with Rhodes's patronage and affection. According to Thomas, the 'greatest love of Rhodes' life' was Neville Pickering, also the son of a clergyman, who had moved to South Africa with his family. Apprenticed to merchants, Pickering met Rhodes, four years his elder, in the early 1880s and soon was appointed secretary of De Beers. Rhodes and Pickering lived together in a cottage in what one government official referred to as 'an absolutely lover-like friendship'. Rhodes's devotion was evident when he rushed back from important negotiations for Pickering's twenty-fifth birthday in 1882; on that occasion, Rhodes drew up a new will leaving his entire estate to Pickering. Two years later, Pickering suffered a riding accident and developed a serious infection from the thorns of the bush into which he had fallen. Rhodes nursed him faithfully for six weeks, refusing even to answer telegrams concerning his business interests (and thus forsaking an option on land which later produced twenty million pounds sterling of gold). Pickering, after whispering 'You have been father, mother, brother and sister to me', died in Rhodes's arms; at his funeral, Rhodes wept hysterically. For Plomer, 'Nothing in his life is more distinguished than his devotion to the dying Pickering.'

Rhodes subsequently had several close friendships of a similar sort, though lesser intensity. Harry Currey, a handsome young man, also became secretary to Rhodes and several of his companies and accompanied him to London; Rhodes was extremely upset, and broke with Currey, when the latter married. Another favourite was Jack Grimmer, according to Plomer, 'originally a junior clerk in De Beers, known as one of 'Rhodes's lambs', i.e. one of about a dozen young men who went up country with Rhodes from Kimberley in the early days'. A later secretary, Philip Jourdan, confessed in his biography that he was in love with Rhodes.

There is no evidence that Rhodes had sexual relations with any of his companions, though his emotional ties (particularly to Pickering) were obvious. Rhodes may be seen as physically asexual, or his sexual energies may have been repressed or sublimated into his work; perhaps his young associates simply provided all of the emotional satisfaction that Rhodes needed. The bonds between Rhodes and his protégés may have been fully fledged sexual unions, unconsummated love or romantic friendships. In the Victorian age, the boundaries between such different arrangements and sentiments were perhaps not so clearly drawn as they would later become.

A. Thomas, *Rhodes*, London, 1996; W. Plomer, *Cecil Rhodes*, London, 1933.

Robert Aldrich

Ries, Leopold Abraham (1893–1962), Dutch civil servant. Ries was the son of a prosperous Jewish draper. During his law study, he formed firm bonds with the future Dutch Minister for Foreign Affairs Eelco van Kleffens, and with the future lawyer Harro Bouman. Being given to coolly analysing any situation, beginning with his own, as a young man he accepted

his homosexuality. Still at the university, Ries established contact with Jacob SCHORER, the founder of the Dutch branch of HIRSCHFELD's Scientific-Humanitarian Committee. For some time he financially contributed to it, like his bosom friend Bouman.

After his studies Ries moved to The Hague, where soon his star shone as a brilliant civil servant. When only 28 years old, he was awarded a decoration by Queen Wilhelmina, and in 1927 he became acting Chief Treasurer in the Ministry of Finance. In 1935 he was finally appointed Chief Treasurer, one of the topmost official positions in The Netherlands. In these years, as a financial expert he was a shrewd negotiator with the German Nazi government about financial and economic affairs.

On 25 May 1936, only one day after concluding particularly fruitful negotiations in Berlin, returning from a debriefing by Minister-President Colijn, Ries was arrested. A 17-year-old boy, Henk Vermeulen, had brought a charge of having had sexual relations for money with Ries. Although Vermeulen was known as a pathological liar, police and justice gave all credence to him; Ries's solemn denial of the accusations was ignored. His house was searched, and his personal letters were confiscated and read by many. The Ries case generated a huge amount of publicity. Together with Ries, eight others had been arrested on Vermeulen's evidence. The newspapers, probably tipped off by the police, suggested the expected arrest of many other higher officials. As usual with sex scandals, this did not happen. Ries was set free after a few days in prison. The examining magistrate turned out to be particularly prejudiced and lax: only after four months was Ries informed that all charges were dropped. Of the other suspects, eventually only two were given a (suspended) sentence. One of them, destroyed by the publicity, committed suicide.

Apart from his lawyer, Bouman, the Chief Treasurer had a staunch defendant in a Social-Democrat member of the Lower House, A. van der Heide. He and several others debated sharply with the Ministers of Justice and Finance about the Ries case. The ministers reacted astutely: all members of the Lower House were dumbfounded by reports, planted on top of the Vermeulen evidence, about allegedly *contemplated* homosexual acts by Ries and a soldier, 13 years earlier, and Ries's presence at a homosexual party. The intended effect, that anyone would think Ries a dirty homosexual, was strikingly attained.

His character smeared, Ries was released in December: honourably, but without a pension. He soon emigrated, and in 1941 went to New York, where he did a good job for Dutch anti-Nazi propaganda. Afterwards, he worked for a Dutch firm, Müller & Co. In New York, he met and valued Hans Lodeizen (1924–1950), the homosexual son of its managing director, and an experimental poet of great talent. After Lodeizen's early death of leukaemia, Ries sorted out his poems and promoted the publication of *Het innerlijk behang* (*The Inner Wallpaper*) in 1951. He never returned from New York. Deprived of all idealism, Ries had still an extraordinary talent for friendship, evidence of which comes from his many candid, beautifully written letters.

The Ries case suggests an eagerness to kill the reputation of a brilliant homosexual Jewish official by judicial and police authorities, who partly had Nazi sympathies in the second half of the 1930s in Holland. To this end, many rules of justice and humanity were bent or broken. Ries's spirit, however, remained upright.

E. W. A. Henssen, *Een welmenend cynicus*, Amsterdam, n.d.; P. Koenders, *Tussen christelijk réveil en seksuele revolutie*, Amsterdam, 1996.

Paul Snijders

Rimbaud, Arthur (1854–1891), French poet. Rimbaud is the symbolic centre of social, sexual and aesthetic revolt in nineteenth-century French poetry. His lonely and troubled childhood was marked by a father at first absent on military missions, then gone for good, and a narrow-minded mother who was harsh and domineering. Until the age of 16 the young Arthur was an entirely quiescent child and a model pupil at school, where he won every prize with consummate ease. Then, two months before his sixteenth birthday he ran away to Paris, where he was arrested for travelling without a valid ticket. He was already determined to become a poet and perceived the literary circles of the capital as the only thing which could help him fulfil his ambition. His schoolmaster and mentor, Georges Izambard, arranged for his release and looked after him at his house in Douai for a while until Mme Rimbaud summarily demanded her son's return.

After two or three more attempts of the same kind, in September 1871, when not yet quite 17, he managed to get himself invited to stay with the poet Paul VERLAINE, ten years his senior and newly married. It was the beginning of a tempestuous but artistically fruitful relationship. Rimbaud may already have experienced initiation into all-male sex at the hands of a group of Communard soldiers on one of his escapes to Paris. He was certainly as much in need of affection (particularly male) as Verlaine was of a strong companion on whom he could lean. He was also keen to be closely involved with a poet whose work was developing the more experimental dimensions of contemporary verse. At this stage of his life, he saw artistic experiment and changing the face of the world as one and the same thing. Earlier in 1871 he had written, in a letter to his friend Paul Demeny, that a poet makes himself a visionary by means of a vast, long, reasoned disordering of all the senses. The same letter also contains the famous phrase '*JE est un autre*', the turning of the self into an objective sounding-board for both language and experience, on which poetry would create itself without his conscious intereference.

Verlaine's technical contribution to Rimbaud's development as a poet can be seen in the 19 or so poems which the latter wrote during 1871–1872, in which the young poet is increasingly experimental in his use of language, metre and rhyme. But Rimbaud's quest to overthrow established order was not just aesthetic; it was a call to revolt against reality as currently constructed, and that revolt included sex. As he wrote in the section 'Délire 1' of *Une Saison en Enfer* (*A Season in Hell*): 'I do not like women. Love needs reinventing, as you know.' That the affaire with Verlaine, as turbulent as it was passionate, was a necessary if finite physical stage in that process is evidenced by three sexually explicit sonnets, known as the *Stupra*: one, jointly written by Rimbaud and Verlaine, is an open celebration of homosexual sex, another invokes anal sex somewhat more indirectly and the third denounces the way in which the modern world suppresses the frank and open role which sex had formerly played in life.

It was inevitable that Rimbaud would grow tired of Verlaine, not just because of the latter's reluctance to commit himself permanently to leaving his wife, or even because of the violent scenes which culminated in the shooting in a Brussels hotel, but because Verlaine's poetic revolt was as conservative in its adventurousness as his moral revolt. In the prose poetry of *Illuminations*, a collection only put together by Verlaine long after Rimbaud's departure from France, and in the prose sequence *Une Saison en Enfer*, written in 1873 when the affair was essentially over, Rimbaud first breaks the bounds of conventional writing with a series of surreal experiments in visionary poetry and then turns his back on both his own experimentation and his relationship with Verlaine. *Une Saison en Enfer* is a powerful expression of a sense of 'not belonging'. It attacks every strand of conventional morality and

values in European society. After it, Rimbaud fell silent.

In 1874 he taught in England but grew restless again. From 1875 to 1878 he wandered around Europe, eventually joining the Dutch colonial army and sailing to Java, only to desert on arrival and work his way back to Europe again. In the autumn of 1878 he set off for the Eastern Mediterranean, and from there moved south down the Red Sea, working as a trader for 12 years in Aden and Ethiopia. Little is known of his personal life during this period. In 1891 he fell ill, and returned to France in search of treatment, but died soon after his arrival.

F. d'Eaubonne, *La Vie passionnée d'Arthur Rimbaud*, Paris 1956; C. Chadwick, *Rimbaud*, London, 1979.

Christopher Robinson

Rocco, Antonio (1586–1653), Italian rhetorician. Born in Scurcula d'Abruzzo, the naturalised-Venetian Antonio Rocco belongs to the historiography of gay studies on account of a single book, the authorship of which was denied him until recently, *L'Alcibiade fanciullo a scola* (*Young Alcibiades Goes to School*, 1652).

The history of *L'Alcibiade*'s circulation is in fact an excellent example of how gay books from the early modern period follow modes of circulation different from those of heterosexual texts. Until 1951 *L'Alcibiade*'s author was thought to be Ferrante Pallavicino (1615–1644), author of *La retorica delle putane* (*The Whores' Rhetoric*, 1642) which, together with other erotic texts, brought him to the pyre in 1644 (in Avignon). Written in 1630, *L'Alcibiade* was published anonymously in 1652. It then travelled the underground of 'sodomitic' literature (being sometimes attributed to Pietro Aretino), and its rare extant copies would become the envy of zealous bibliomaniacs until Jules Gay published a reprint in 1862 in Paris. That run was nearly entirely destroyed following a legal injunction in 1863 and, in 1868, the

French translation published in Brussels in 1866 was also condemned to be shredded as 'an outrage to good morals'. The text, however, resurfaced in French in 1891 (Brussels), 1936 (Paris), 1995 (Montreal reprint of 1866 edition) and, in 1982, in German (Munich). Interestingly, Alfred Kinsey had copies of it. In sum, *L'Alcibiade* remains a book for pornographers, rejected as it were from mainstream literature ever since the eighteenthth century.

The attribution to Pallavicino of *L'Alcibiade* fitted very well indeed in the literature produced by the Academicians Incogniti, one of the two main Venetian academies, by and large inspired by the works of Paduan philosopher Cesare Cremonini. Pallavicino was a member of the Incogniti. Cremonini is one of the references for the *libertin* movement that particularly in France gained great momentum in the seventeenth century. For these new Aristotelians, 'erotic' was often a password to mean a non-sinful, non-Christian, non-regulatory approach to sex.

This also accounts for many of those *libertin* philosophers' calling themselves '*medici*', to underscore their physical, medical approach to matters such as sex. For that reason, 'sodomitic' literature often signifies literature about matters sexual that circumvent doctrinal rules and goes back to the sources, Aristotle, Hippocrates and, chiefly, Galen (in this case the aprocryphal yet influential treatise *On Sperm, De Spermate*). The epithet 'epicurean' was also often used by their enemies to encapsulate the same notion. That their authors often put into sexual practice what they theorised about is quite certain – but 'sodomitic' acts are to be seen as part of the reassessment of nature done by Paduan Aristotelianism.

It is in such a complex cultural context that Rocco finds his place. His life and works are well documented in the academic annals of Venice. He studied with Cremonini, became a friar in order to teach philosophy at San Giorgio Maggiore monastery in Venice and, a teacher of ex-

cellence, he was promoted to a chair in rhetoric. Rocco turned down chairs in Padua and Pisa, and gracefully ended his career and life, having the pleasure of seeing his *Alcibiade* released after nearly 20 years of unhindered dissemination in manuscript.

The 'execrable, detestable, abominable Sodomitic book that ought to have been burnt with its author' (in the words of German eighteenth-century compilers) was not put on the Index (whereas one of Rocco's metaphysical treatises had been). It did create a stir, because of the crudity of its language and the related accusation of Rocco's being an 'atheist'. Yet one cannot infer from the elliptical signature 'D.P.A.' on the title page (i.e. 'Da Padre Antonio') that Rocco was afraid of the Inquisition. Anyone who was someone in the Venetian establishment was able to interpret the elliptic 'D.P.A.'. Quite simply, Rocco, celebrated professor of rhetoric, could not possibly sign a booklet published as a 'Carnival book', a fun book.

As the title indicates, *L'Alcibiade* takes its theme from the fact that SOCRATES had been Alcibiades' lover and teacher. The commonplace of that divine pair, an ugly teacher with a beautiful soul and a gorgeous student with a not so beautiful soul (as Alcibiades' dismal political life shows), became the stock in trade of 'sodomitic' satires from the Renaissance. Second, the 'Socratic dialogue' was the most traditional pedagogic tool in Renaissance rhetoric. It was in the dialogue form that most students' manuals were written, at least in Catholic Europe. Dialogues purported to imitate oral teaching (still the only norm) by reproducing or anticipating a live situation. Most dialogues also served to dramatise the teaching relationship between master and student, which was conceived as at once love and training. If teachers' manuals (as opposed to pedagogical dialogues) put such emphasis on rhetoric, and the power or seductiveness of the teacher's voice, it was because the teacher had to lead ('seduction', in Latin) his students to the truth by making the path attractive and, at the end, by transforming, thanks to the sheer power of his questions and gentility of his eloquence, rough children into young men able to hold parliamentary, church or state offices; all required the same rhetorical mastery. An image sometime used to symbolise this teaching method was that of the female bear licking its young and giving it 'form', just as the tongue of the master licks the young soul into shape. Such similes abounded, striking a comparison between intellectual 'formation' and sexual activity. Comparisons between penis and tongue, saliva and semen, were neither scandalous nor far-fetched: they rested on the premise that the human being is made of analogies, and that, in this case, speech that helped teach also helped express desire.

This set of cultural conditions is essential to understand *L'Alcibiade* fully. They explain how Father Rocco, a professor of rhetoric and a master teacher, could write a dialogue about the art of teaching that ends on the following: 'And, while talking to him, the horny teacher carried on screwing the pretty student. And the boy, whenever his master's dick slipped out of his tight arse, would cry out, "Give it to me, more!", because he knew that this was the only way for him to become as well-accomplished a man as his master. Happy man, the master who, being slave to the desires of his gorgeous boy, reaches ecstasy.' The dialogue which precedes this climax can be summed up by the idea of penetration, by tongue and penis. Using the well worn simile that speaking is inseminating with words, the teacher Filotimo (the Lover of Virtue) wants to stick his tongue down young Alcibiade's throat (repeating Apollo's sacral spitting) and then his cock ('*cazzo*') up his bum (imitating generation, in this case, generation of ideas). Both are metaphors for teaching, saliva and sperm being analogous to speech and knowledge. However, Filotimo cannot be granted his wish readily. The point of the dialogue is that he has to persuade Alcibiade to consent, to become his pupils' 'slave'. The dialogue is then a sparring match between the master and the pupil, an exchange of arguments apparently about kissing and fucking boys – in reality about mastery. Indeed, as the *disputatio* progresses, the student acquires mastery of the art of speaking, gaining the same rank as his master, being then ready to move on in life. As a reward for such excellent tuition, he will offer his mouth and his *derrière* to his master – that is, he will acknowledge the pleasure of learning.

However, one can reverse the argument. Is it not possible that Rocco used the Socratic dialogue genre and the cultural commonplaces that sustain it to really write a pornographic and pederastic text? Elements of response vary in interpretation. First the carnivalesque timing may explain that Rocco, a Venetian, wanted to have fun, in the well established traditions of 'sodomitic satires', and contribute to Carnival. He chose to make fun of boring Jesuitic manuals by releasing a booklet for 'popular' use, inscribing his own profession in the spirit of Carnival. Second, regarding the reception of the text, the violence of attacks suffered by *L'Alcibiade* in the eighteenth century simply bear witness to the decadence of Renaissance teaching codes: comparisons had lost their meaning, and what was left was the bare sodomitic text. This cultural change explains how *L'Alcibiade* passed into underground pornographic literature – a turn of events that would have amused Rocco and comforted him in the hypocrisy of religion.

Either way – pederasty disguised in scholarship, or scholarship disguised in pederasty – *L'Alcibiade* is a benchmark in the historiography of gay studies as it raises the question of the cultural reception of homosexual texts and of the processes of obfuscation that have taken place ever since.

A. Rocco, *L'Alcibiade fanciullo a scola*, Rome, 1988, reprinted in *Sex Research*, 3, 4 (1983).

Philippe-Joseph Salazar

Roditi, Edouard (1910–1992), French-American writer. Edouard Herbert Roditi was born in Paris of a French mother and an Italian father who happened to have US citizenship. Educated in France and then England, for health reasons he had to abandon classical studies at Balliol College, Oxford, in 1929, and moved back to Paris where he was associated with the Surrealist movement. He became a partner in Éditions du Sagittaire, which published André Breton, Tristan Tzara and the openly homosexual novelists Robert Desnos and René CREVEL. His final book, *Choose your own World* (1992), was a collection of short prose fantasies and fictions displaying a Surrealistic bent. As a Jew he moved to the United States in 1937 and studied Romance languages at Chicago and Berkeley. During the war he worked in the French short-wave broadcasting service of the US Office of War Information, and then as a translator at the foundation of the United Nations, the Nuremburg war crimes trials, Unesco, the Council of Europe in Strasbourg and the European Common Market in Brussels. In 1954 he settled in Paris, which remained his base for the rest of his life.

After a number of liaisons with women, he became increasingly aware during a stay in Hamburg in 1930 of his greater sexual attraction to men; his seduction by Federico García LORCA the previous year had not been an isolated experience in a young man's development. His first book of poems, *Poems for F.* (1935), was dedicated to a successful Austrian portrait painter with whom he conducted a tempestuous affair for two years. In his later poetry he often dealt with Jewish themes and topics. In 1947 he published *Oscar Wilde*, a study that adopted the then bold stance of taking seriously the poet and dandy's philosophy and aesthetics, and delineating the place of his homosexuality in his life and writing. In 1962 came *De l'homosexualité*, an interesting but curiously dated book adopting some perspectives that would find little favour now. It skil-fully exposes the injustice and inhumanity of the traditional Judaeo-Christian legal and social persecution of homosexuals in the West but propounds a psychoanalytically derived psychopathological conception of homosexuality; in Roditi's view it is not an illness in itself but a symptom of underlying neuroses or of neuro-endocrinological disturbance. A sufferer from epilepsy, Roditi underwent a prolonged psychoanalysis in the United States in the 1930s and early 1940s. His memoirs, of which a selection was published in 1991, outline a rich and varied life and in particular an extraordinary range of friends and acquaintances, including many of the notable homosexuals of the century. They also give some idea of his translating activity, into French, English and German, and from a dozen languages, and of his ceaseless output of essays and studies.

'Edouard Roditi; 1910–', in *Contemporary Authors Autobiography Series*, Vol. 14, Detroit, 1991: 237–87; 'Edouard Herbert Roditi, 1910–1992', *Contemporary Authors*, New Revision Series, Vol. 50, Detroit, 1996: 378–80.

Gary Simes

Roellig, Ruth Margarete (1878–1969), German writer. Roellig was one of the most popular writers on the lesbian scene in Weimar Germany. She was born in Schwiebus, but moved at age 9 with her parents to Berlin. After leaving school, Roellig first helped in the family's hotel business, then in 1911–1912 took up an apprenticeship with a Berlin publisher, and from there moved into a post as editor. During this time she also published poems and short stories in various magazines and newspapers. Her first novel, *Geflüster im Dunkeln* (*Whispers in the Dark*), appeared in 1913.

After travelling in Finland, Germany and France, Roellig returned to Berlin in 1927, where she worked for two popular lesbian-feminist journals, *Die Freundin* (*The Girlfriend*), and *Garçonne*. Roellig produced a guide to lesbian Berlin in 1928, called *Berlin's lesbische Frauen* (*Berlin's Lesbian Women*; reprinted as *Lila Nächte: Die Damenklubs der zwanziger Jahre*, 1981 and 1994), which detailed 14 clubs and dance halls on the lesbian scene. Her contribution to Agnes Countess Esterhazy's collection *Das lasterhafte Weib* (*The Vices of Woman*, 1930) was titled 'Lesbians and Transvestites', and attacked current prejudices regarding female homosexuality. Roellig's story, *Ich klage an* (*I Accuse*, 1930), and her novel *Die Kette im Schoß* (*The Chain in the Lap*, 1931) both revolve around lesbian central characters.

Surprisingly, Roellig survived the Nazi regime untouched, and was never even banned from publishing; but only two books appeared during this time, a murder mystery called *Der Andere* (*The Other*, 1935), and a novel of World War I with nationalistic overtones and the title *Soldaten, Tod, Tänzerin* (*Soldiers, Death, and the Dancer*, 1937). When her flat was bombed during the Allied attacks on Berlin, Roellig moved to Silesia; she returned in 1945, and lived in Berlin until her death. Her others works include *Liane. Eine sonderbare Geschichte* (*Liane: A Strange Story*, 1919), *Traumfahrt. Eine Geschichte aus Finnland* (*Dream Journey: A Story from Finland*, 1919), *Lutetia Parisiorum* (1920), and a collection of short stories, *Die fremde Frau* (*The Stranger Woman*, 1920).

P. Budke and J. Schulze, *Schriftstellerinnen in Berlin 1871 bis 1945: Ein Lexikon zu Leben und Werk*, Berlin, 1995; C. Schöppmann, "Ich bin ein durch und durch deutsch fühlender Mensch'. Ruth Margarete Roellig (1878–1969)', *Zeit der Maskierung. Lebensgeschichten lesbischer Frauen im 'Dritten Reich'*, Berlin, 1993: 132–43.
Sarah Colvin

Röhm, Ernst (1887–1934), German Nazi leader. Röhm (or Roehm) was born in Munich. He joined the Imperial German Army in 1906, and served with distinction in World War I, reaching the rank of Captain and receiving severe facial wounds at Verdun in June 1916. After the war, while still an Army intelligence officer, he returned to Bavaria and was an early member of the German Workers Party, which became the Nazi Party. He secretly directed Army funds to the party and became a close associate of its leader, Adolf Hitler. He organised the party's paramilitary wing, the Sturmabteilung (SA).

Following the failure of the 1924 Nazi 'Beerhall Putsch', Röhm fell out with Hitler and went to Bolivia, where he worked as a military adviser. In 1931 he was asked by Hitler to return to Germany and become SA Chief-of-Staff. For the next three years he was one of the most powerful men in the Nazi Party. When Hitler became Chancellor in January 1933, Röhm became a minister in both the national and Bavarian governments, but he maintained his independent base in the SA. He took seriously the 'socialist' component of National Socialism, and saw the SA, a largely working-class organisation, as the means of 'completing the revolution' by taking over the Army.

This made Röhm a threat to both the Army and to Hitler's alliance with the industrialists and financiers who supported the Nazis but had no intention of allowing a 'revolution' of any kind in Germany. Through 1933 his relationship with Hitler, once very close, deteriorated as other Nazi leaders such as Göring, Himmler and Goebbels plotted against him. The Army leaders demanded that the undisciplined SA (now 2.5 million strong) be brought under control as their price for supporting Hitler's regime.

In early 1934 Hitler was persuaded by Himmler and others that the power of the SA and Röhm had to be broken. The Gestapo was directed to collect incriminating evidence on Röhm's personal life, of which there was plenty. Röhm was warned that his position was under threat, but he did not believe it. He thought his long association with Hitler and the political debt that Hitler owed him from the 1920s would protect him. In fact Hitler resented this debt, and saw Röhm and the SA as a threat to his personal authority. On 30 June Himmler's SS was launched against Röhm, who was arrested and shot along with dozens of others in the 'Night of the Long Knives'.

Röhm has become the central figure in an elaborate mythology about the Nazi regime. The fact that he was homosexual, and promoted a number of other homosexual men to leadership positions in the SA, has given rise to the belief that the Nazi movement was riddled with homosexuality, and that there was some kind of homosexual 'brotherhood' in the Nazi party and its paramilitary organs, the SA and the SS. There have also been persistent assertions that many of the Nazi leaders, including Hitler and Himmler, were homosexual or at least sexually ambiguous. The Nazi regime's taste for black leather, fancy uniforms and male *Kameradshaft* is sometimes seen as evidence for this mythology.

This mythology has no basis in fact: it is based on wartime anti-Nazi propaganda, Christopher Isherwood's Berlin novels and a misreading of Nazi symbolism from the perspective of 1970s gay male fetishism. Röhm was the only Nazi of any seniority who was homosexual. He did promote a homosexual circle in the SA, but this proved a weakness, not a strength, when the other Nazi leaders began plotting against him. The Nazi movement certainly placed strong emphasis on male bonding, but this made them ever keener to draw a sharp line between homosocial behaviour and homosexuality. Himmler was virulently anti-homosexual, and prescribed ferocious penalties for homosexual behaviour in the SS. The Nazi regime maintained all Germany's existing anti-homosexual laws, and added more of their own. And they enforced them: thousands of homosexual men died in police cells or concentration camps.

Röhm's attitude as a Nazi to his own sexuality was exceptional, indeed unique,

and he knew it. He saw both his homosexuality and his Nazism as part of his rejection of 'bourgeois morality', but he knew that his views were not shared by the wider Nazi movement. He developed a hypermasculine homosexual identity as a defence against allegations that homosexuals were effeminate – an identity which was not to be seen again until the 1970s. During the period of the Weimar Republic he tried to have it both ways, using the relative freedom that 'bourgeois democracy' gave him, while working to destroy it. He was actually a member of one of Germany's gay rights organisations, the Bund für Menschenrecht (BMR, or Human Rights League), while also belonging to a party which promised to shut the gay rights movement down if it came to power.

This was tolerated in the Nazi movement precisely because Röhm was seen as an isolated eccentric rather than as part of a larger and more threatening phenomenon – and also because Röhm was too powerful a figure to mess with. Hitler certainly knew of Röhm's homosexuality, and made it known that Röhm continued to enjoy his favour despite it: this kept Röhm safe until 1934. In fact, Hitler was always jealous of his subordinates and liked them to have personal vulnerabilities he could use against them if need be – thus he also tolerated Göring's drug addiction and Goebbels's adulteries. Röhm deceived himself when he thought that his closeness to Hitler would allow him to survive while other German homosexual men were being persecuted. Röhm was not murdered because he was homosexual, but the fact that he was so gave his enemies a means of turning Hitler against him and securing his destruction.

Röhm's fate is instructive. As a Nazi, he was contemptuous of liberal values and of 'bourgeois democracy'. The Nazis shared this contempt with the Communist Party – it is sometimes forgotten that part of the reason Nazis and Communists hated each other so much was that they had so much in common. Yet as a homosexual man in a homophobic society Röhm was dependent on the protection he received from such characteristics of 'bourgeois democracy' as the rule of law and respect for personal freedom, even in the limited form these took in Imperial and Weimar Germany. It was only when his old friend Hitler took power, and a legal system in which 'the will of the Führer was the highest law' was created, that Röhm, along with millions of others, found he had no protection at all.

A. Bullock, *Hitler and Stalin: Parallel Lives*, London, 1991; M. Gallo, *The Night of the Long Knives*, London, 1972; E. Hancock, 'Only the Real, the True, the Masculine held its value: Ernst Röhm, Masculinity, and Male Homosexuality', *Journal of the History of Sexuality*, 8, 4 (April 1998): 616–41; P. Padfield, *Himmler: Reichsführer SS*, London, 1990.

Adam Carr

Rolfe, Frederick William (1860–1913), British artist and writer. Born in London into a family which for many years had carried on a piano-making business, Rolfe received an elementary education before taking up employment as a schoolmaster. He taught at a series of schools in southern England; nowhere did he stay long. As a teacher he was especially successful with younger boys and wrote poems that he addressed or dedicated to his favourites. Having passed through the Anglo-Catholic wing of the Church of England, in 1886 he was received into the Roman Catholic Church. As an enthusiastic convert, with high expectations of his new church, he was determined to become a priest. His two attempts to achieve this goal were unsuccessful. After a year at St Mary's College, Oscott (Birmingham), in 1888 his superiors decided that he was an unsuitable candidate for the priesthood. After only four months at the Scots College in Rome in 1890 he was dismissed for his inability to conform to the strict seminary regime. He referred to this as the 'great disappointment' of his life. He never lost his sense of grievance at what he regarded as his unjust treatment by the church authorities. Remaining in Italy for the summer of 1890, Rolfe was given hospitality by the Duchess of Sforza-Cesarini and rambled through the Alban mountains with a group of boys he had befriended. These experiences provided the matter for 'Stories Toto Told Me', which were published in *The Yellow Book* in 1895–1896, and their sequel 'In His Own Image'.

Rolfe returned to England in 1890 styling himself Frederick, Baron Corvo. He claimed that the title had been conferred on him by the Duchess of Sforza-Cesarini, but it is equally likely that he invented it as a pseudonym. He had neither regular employment nor income, but eked out a precarious existence from short-term jobs and small commissions, using his Catholic contacts as fully as he could. He was rarely out of debt and was often homeless. His intimate friendships usually ended in acrimony. During this period he developed his skills in painting, photography and the writing of poetry. Many of his compositions were about saints and boys: he was fascinated by images of young men being martyred. Increasingly he devoted himself to writing. His best-known work is the novel *Hadrian the Seventh* (1904), in which he imagined himself (an idealised portrait) as Pope. In 1908 he left England to live in Venice, where he wrote novels, short stories and essays, quarrelled with almost everyone he met, begged for money and yearned for sexual encounters with attractive local youths. Only rarely did he achieve the latter. He died in Venice in poverty.

In his sexual interests, his romanticism, his reverence for traditional hierarchies and aristocratic titles, his ornate writing style, his delight in obscure corners of scholarship and his assurance of his own genius, Rolfe was one of the more eccentric figures among English 'Uranian' writers of the early twentieth century.

A. J. A Symons, *The Quest for Corvo: An Experiment in Biography*, London, 1934; T. d'Arch Smith, *Love in Earnest: Some Notes on the Lives and Writings of English 'Uranian' Poets from 1889 to 1930*, London, 1970; D. Weeks, *Corvo*, London, 1971; M. J. Benkovitz, *Frederick Rolfe: Baron Corvo. A Biography*, London, 1977.

David Hilliard

Römer, Lucien Sophie Albert Marie von (1873–1965), Dutch writer. Among the papers of von Römer's youth is already to be found notice of his love for a young man. As a student, he started to write learned articles on homosexual topics following the lead of Magnus HIRSCHFELD. He would become an 'Obmann' of Hirschfeld's 'Wissenschaftlich-humanitäre Komitee' and a regular contributor to its *Jahrbuch für sexuelle Zwischenstufen*. His first article for this Yearbook, a biography of King HENRI III of France and Poland, appeared in 1902. With long essays on androgyny and the history of the persecutions of sodomites in eighteenth-century Holland, he opened new terrain for gay studies. He was convinced by the theory of intermediary sexes and created a model that comprised 687,375 variations. He was the first to hold sex surveys among his fellow students and discovered that 2 per cent were exclusively homosexual, 20 per cent had enjoyed homosexual contacts and 85 per cent had masturbated: his statistics were not much different from those of today. He translated NIETZSCHE's *Thus Spake Zarathustra* (1905) and edited Rochester's seventeenth-century play *Sodom* (1904).

Because of his views he was regularly attacked by scholars and politicians, but he always riposted very firmly. For the Christian-Socialist Rein-leven (Pure Life) group he defended the purity of gay sex in a loving relationship, but no one supported him, not even ALETRINO. His view was harshly rebuffed in the name of a pure life. When the theoretical journal of the Dutch socialist party published a critical article on homosexuality, he wrote a reply. The rejection of his dissertation by the Faculty of Medicine of the University of Amsterdam may have been influenced by his staunch criticism of one of its professors. The official reasons were that the book was written in German and included offensive imagery and genealogies of sexual perversion in royal families. After this setback, von Römer retreated from sexual science. When SCHORER in 1912 founded a Dutch chapter of Hirschfeld's Wissenschaftlich-humanitäre Komitee, von Römer became a member. In 1910, he joined as natural scientist an expedition into the inland of New Guinea, where he discovered unknown plants, some of which received his name. Soon afterwards, he emigrated to the Dutch East Indies, where he married and fathered two sons. In his work as a physician, he kept to his social standpoint and specialised in public hygiene. After Indonesia's independence he stayed in the country, where he died. His papers are in the State Archives in The Hague; they contained a sealed package that was opened in January 2000, which included a booklet of poetry (*c.* 1894) about his love for a young man who died early, and other material relating to his sex studies.

M. van Lieshout, 'Stiefkind der natuur. Het homobeeld bij Aletrino en Von Römer', in M. Dallas *et al.* (eds) *Homojaarboek I*, Amsterdam, 1981: 75–105.

Gert Hekma

Roosevelt, Eleanor (1884–1962), American humanitarian reformer, diplomat and writer. One of the most influential figures of the twentieth century, Eleanor Roosevelt has left a lasting legacy through her humanitarian accomplishments as reformer, diplomat and writer. Her personal life also reflects a singular triumph of self-realisation in the face of formidable emotional and societal obstacles.

Anna Eleanor Roosevelt was born in New York City into a life of wealth and social privilege (her uncle was President Theodore Roosevelt). Shy, introverted and physically plain, she also suffered the loss of both parents at an early age. After her marriage to her distant cousin, Franklin Delano Roosevelt, in 1905, she spent the next several years as wife and mother to their six children.

In the post-World War I years Eleanor Roosevelt become independently active in a variety of political and social causes, such as the League of Women Voters, the Women's Trade Union League and the women's division of the Democratic Party. By the time of her husband's election as President in 1933, she was poised to assume an increasingly public role as spokesperson for a number of other groups: African-Americans, youth, the poor and others in need of a humane political voice.

As First Lady for an unprecedented 12 years, Roosevelt's behind-the-scenes influence was great. Additionally, her widely distributed syndicated newspaper column, radio show, formal press conferences and extensive travelling furthered her promotion of liberal humanitarian causes. Perhaps her most publicised activity in this regard was her resignation from the Daughters of the American Revolution when that group refused to allow African-American singer Marian Anderson to perform in the Constitution Hall in Washington (which was owned by the organisation). Anderson later appeared to widespread publicity and great acclaim at the Lincoln Memorial.

The Roosevelt marriage having evolved into an intellectual and political partnership, Eleanor Roosevelt subsequently developed her own circle of close women friends, several of whom were lesbians. Her most intense emotional attachment was with a prominent newspaper correspondent, Lorena Hickok; their surviving correspondence (about 3,500 letters) gives strong evidence of a lesbian relationship.

Following the death of Franklin in 1945, Eleanor Roosevelt maintained a highly visible and active life in national and international politics. Appointed in 1945 by President Harry S. Truman as a member of the United States delegation to the United Nations, she became chair of the committee that produced the Universal Declaration of Human Rights in 1948. She continued to write a variety of newspaper and magazine columns, as well as a number of books. Until the end of her life, Roosevelt was an influential member of the Democratic Party. She died in New York City.

Criticised during much of her public life for her outspoken liberal views, Roosevelt was virtually universally admired during her later years (Truman dubbed her 'first lady of the world'). In subsequent decades, that reputation has endured and further intensified.

B. Wiesen Cook, *Eleanor Roosevelt: Volume One, 1884–1933*, New York, 1992; D. Kearns Goodwin, *No Ordinary Time: Franklin and Eleanor Roosevelt: The Home Front During World War II*, New York, 1994; J. P. Lash, *Eleanor: The Years Alone*, New York, 1972; R. Streitmatter (ed.) *Empty Without You: The Intimate Letters of Eleanor Roosevelt and Lorena Hickok*, New York, 1998.

David Garnes

Rosai, Ottone (1895–1957), Italian painter. Born in Florence into a family of artisans, Rosai's artistic education was partly formal, partly that of an autodidact. By 1911 he was able to exhibit engravings; he then experimented with both Futurist and Cubist styles. After World War I, he sought inspiration from thirteenth- and fourteenth-century Florentine painting and from the works of Cézanne. Like many others, he also joined the Fascist movement then emerging in Italy.

Rosai's 'classical' period is that of the years 1919 to 1930, when his subjects were streets and alleys in France, country landscapes and his celebrated 'omini', portraits of 'defeated' humans shown in the simple, humble activities of ordinary folk. Although this work made Rosai's reputation, it also led to charges of provincialism, even sentimentality, concerning his painting. However, two things worked against a fairer apreciation of Rosai's *œuvre* and made him unpopular among both the politically left and the right: for the former, his adherence to Fascism, and for both, his homosexuality, which was the homosexuality of a married, 'respectable' man who sought clandestine liaisons with teenagers, mostly hustlers. Fascist police in 1938 gave him a strong-armed warning about his frequenting of male prostitutes, and he avoided deportation only because of his Fascist membership card.

If it is now possible to turn a blind eye to Rosai's adherence to Fascism, it is because his paintings were always diametrically opposed to the type of art favoured by the regime. His homosexuality, however, remains an obstacle to a calm assessment of Rosai's work by critics, especially since a crucial part of his *œuvre* is composed of portraits of male nudes. These were proletarian youths whom he met in the streets of Florence and who generally became his lovers as well as his models, as revealed in the biography written by his close friend Piero Santi. The art critic Giovanni Testori has observed that 'an exhibition of Rosai's "nudes" would mean . . . linking them to his homosexuality, but those who could organise [such an exhibition] are afraid of showing this connection'. Although there have been some hints in critical studies (such as those of Dario Trento) about this link, and although several of Rosai's nudes were exhibited on the centenary of his birth, the artist's homosexuality remains a handicap in the conservative world of Italian art criticism.

V. Patanè, 'Ottone Rosai. Firenze di notte', in G. Dall'Orto (ed.) *1895. C'era una volta un secolo fa*, supplement to *Babilonia*, 135 (July–August 1995): 36–40; P. Santi, *Ritratto di Rosai*, Bari, 1966; D. Trento, 'Le notti di Rosai', *Babi-*

lonia, 94 (November 1991): 56–7; L. Doninelli, *Conversazioni con Testori*, Milan, 1993.

Giovanni Dall'Orto

Rosenmüller, Johann (*c.* 1619–1684), German composer. Rosenmüller received his elementary education at the Lateinschule in his birthplace, Oelsnitz, near Zwikau in northeast Germany. He matriculated in the theological school at Leipzig University in 1640. By 1642 he was an instructor at the Thomasschule (where J. S. Bach served much later), engaged in the musical training of younger singing boys for the choirs of Leipzig's Lutheran churches. In 1645 the eminent Dresden composer Heinrich Schütz (1585–1672) contributed a congratulatory poem to the preface of Rosenmüller's first publication, of instrumental dance music. By 1650 he was leading assistant to the Cantor (musical director) Tobias Michael. He served additionally as organist of the Nicolaikirche (the city's leading church) from 1651, and in 1653 was promised eventual succession to Michael in the cantorate. However, in May 1655 he and several choirboys were arrested on suspicion of homosexual practices. Unfortunately, the sole source of information on this matter is August Horneffer's 1898 biography, the original documentation being currently untraceable. Rosenmüller is said to have 'escaped' imprisonment and was next heard of in Venice, where, by early 1658, 'Giovanni' Rosenmüller was listed among the trombonists at the ducal church of San Marco. A few years later he was listed as *maestro di coro* at the Pio Ospedale della Pietà, a school for 'foundling' (i.e. illegitimate) girls with a speciality in musical training (where Vivaldi later served). He evidently remained in this post until 1677, but thereafter was still paid as a 'composer' from 1678 to 1682. Around 1682, he returned to Saxony, and became Kapellmeister at the court of Wolfenbüttel, where he died soon after. His epitaph dubbed him 'the Amphion of his age', and more than a century later no less a figure than J. W. Goethe remarked that he was 'never to be forgotten in the history of music'.

As with most figures of this era, Rosenmüller's sexual orientation can be surmised only as a result of a single and extremely damaging instance of legal action against him. Julie Anne Sadie, in her *Companion to Baroque Music* (1990), concludes with a blanket denunciation: 'Sadly his reputation was hopelessly tarnished by his conviction for practising homosexuality with schoolboys . . .'. However, nothing more is known of his sexual interests or contacts, homosexual, pedophile or otherwise, before or after. His voluminous output contains, predictably, no music to overtly homoerotic texts. However, entirely in accord with the general trends of time and place, some of his motets for solo voices reflect the new personalised and, some would argue eroticised, approach to the choice and musical setting of sacred texts (e.g. *Salve mi Jesu, adoro te*, and *O Salvator dilectissime*).

Rosenmüller's musical reputation and the quality of his output are high. His escape to Italy after 1655 was not merely a choice of last resort. In two publications of German and Latin sacred vocal music issued in Leipzig, Rosenmüller had shown a clear interest in up-to-date Italian vocal idioms. In Venice, he composed mainly vocal music (masses, Magnificats, psalms and motets) and instrumental sonatas for the (Catholic) liturgy of the Pietà (his choir and orchestra there evidently made up entirely of young women 'inmates'). However, his Venetian compositions also created interest back in (Lutheran) north Germany during his lifetime, and thus he may be credited with a role in the ongoing dissemination there of Italian musical idioms. In recent years, a number of fine commercial recordings of Rosenmüller's sacred and instrumental compositions have enhanced his reputation as a noteworthy musical figure of his age.

K. Johnson Synder, 'Rosenmuller', in *The New Grove Dictionary of Music and Musicians*, London, 1980.

Graeme Skinner

Rovsing, (Ludvig) Leif (Sadi) (1887–1977), Danish tennis champion and author. Born Qvist (his mother's name), Rovsing was adopted in 1889. From the death of his father in 1910, he lived the life of a wealthy gentleman of independent means. Except for a high-school diploma, he received no formal education. Tennis was his primary and all-consuming interest. He won several Danish championships in doubles, and was Swedish and Norwegian International Champion in 1916 (men's single). In 1923 he reached the finals (doubles) at the Indoor World Championships in Barcelona. He was considered to have a strong serve and a good drive.

In the upper-class world of tennis, Rovsing's openness as a homosexual seems not to have caused problems. However, tennis tournaments were organised by and played in clubs that were primarily football (soccer) clubs. Consequently the Danish Lawn Tennis Association was a subdivision of the Danish Football Association. When, in 1917, the details of a visit to Rovsing's home by a young tennis player were reported to the Board of Directors of his tennis and football club (B.93) Rovsing was confronted with the working-class respectability of organised football. He argued that he had never committed a criminal act, but he was nevertheless excluded from all clubs and tournaments under the Danish Football Association. The exclusion was revoked in 1921. This caused opposition from the Copenhagen Football Association and in 1924 Rovsing was once more excluded from participating in tournaments in Denmark. His 'opinions and his conduct' precluded him 'from participating in tournaments with related access to the showers and locker rooms of young players'. In 1927 Rovsing himself financed and made preparations for a separate tournament. Most of the prominent tennis players agreed to participate. The

Lawn Tennis Association, however, declared that Rovsing could not participate. He now sued the Danish Football Association. The outcome was a foregone conclusion. The High Court upheld the exclusion from tournaments as justified by Rovsing's sexual conduct and by the duty of the Danish Football Association to protect its young members.

Rovsing, who had decided not to be a witness in the court case, published a pamphlet in which he claimed that he was in reality the accused in 'The Public' versus Rovsing. Neither the exclusion from tournaments nor the court case and the pamphlet seem to have been reported in the press. Although Rovsing's perception was somewhat paranoid, it contained a large nucleus of truth.

In Hellerup, a suburb in northern Copenhagen, Rovsing in 1919 built himself a house and a magnificent wooden tennis hall which became the home of his own tennis club, the Dansk Tennis Club (The Danish Tennis Club). It neither was nor is affiliated with the Danish Lawn Tennis Association. It is partly financed through a foundation created by Rovsing in his will.

Rovsing travelled in the Far East and lived for a long period in Bali. In his book, I tropesol og måneskin (Under the Sun and the Moon of the Tropics), he gave a first-hand account of the delights of Balinese youths as opposed to the drab and restricting conditions in Denmark. In the 1950s he became a prolific contributor of articles to the homophile journal, Vennen (The Friend), which he briefly supported financially. In 1955 his home was ransacked by the police, and he was arrested and held in custody for 15 days charged with having had sex with a minor, a prostitute under the age of 18. He denied the charges, which he saw as a revenge for his writings, but was given a suspended sentence of 30 days in jail for indecency.

Rovsing in the 1950s and 1960s published a number of privately printed pamphlets on religion, sex and society. They are incoherent and characterised by the learning of an autodidact and a man whose perception of the social realities of his times is ill focused.

L. Rovsing, Det Offentlige mod Leif Rovsing, Copenhagen, 1928; L. Rovsing, I tropesol og måneskin, Copenhagen, 1959; A. Axgil and H. Fogedgaard, Homofile kampår, Rudkøbing, 1985: 32–6.

Wilhelm von Rosen

Rozanov, Vasily Vasil'evich (1856–1919), Russian writer. Born in a small town in central Russia, he graduated from the Historical-Philological Faculty of St Petersburg University in 1880 and the same year married Appolinaria Suslova, 14 years his senior and the former mistress of Fyodor Dostoevsky, a writer whom he greatly admired. This unhappy marriage ended in separation six years later; however, she refused to grant him a divorce, making Rozanov unable to marry his second, common-law wife. In 1881 he published his first book, a lengthy philosophical treatise titled On Understanding. After living in obscurity as a schoolteacher in several small towns in central Russia, he became famous following the publication of his second book, Dostoevsky's Legend of the Grand Inquisitor: A Critical Commentary (1894), and soon moved to St Petersburg to work as a journalist. Over the next few years, be became one of Russia's most popular and prolific writers of non-fiction texts in a great variety of genres, and one of the brightest and most controversial figures in the Russian cultural landscape of his time. He was notorious for his frequently self-contradictory statements and for publishing his essays in both extreme right-wing and left-wing periodicals. However, his most important contribution to Russian literature are his books of fragments, Solitaria (1911) and Fallen Leaves (Part One, 1913, Part Two, 1915). In them, he developed an aphoristic style similar to that of NIETZSCHE combined with a tone of public intimacy and a focus on the mundane life, on the one hand, and on religion and sexuality, on the other. Finally, his last book, *The Apocalypse of Our Time* (1918), also structured as a series of fragments, is an impassioned indictment of the Bolshevik revolution.

It was Rozanov's unorthodox views on sexuality that made him scandalously popular in his lifetime and served as one of the main reasons for the ban on his work in the Soviet era. Though it would be difficult to summarise his extremely self-contradictory pronouncements on the subject, it would be safe to say that he held a very affirmative view of sex as such. He repeatedly attacked the institutions that propagated the ideologies that value chastity and abstinence and claimed that his own work was written not with ink or even blood, but with sperm. It was his interest in fecund sexuality that led him to write a highly speculative volume titled *People of the Moonlight* (1911, revised 1913) which until very recently remained the only influential book-length study on the subject of homosexuality in Russia. In this book, he did not draw on personal experiences but predominantly engaged in abstract speculation, which is occasionally interspersed with polemical comments on various, mostly obscure, sources. While Rozanov rejected some of the stereotypes about homosexuality – for example, that it is a result of a surfeit of heterosexual experience – he strongly subscribed to another one – the conflation of aversion to heterosexual acts with aversion to sexuality *per se*. This belief underlies his argument and largely accounts for many of his conclusions. For example, he believed that in nine out of ten cases the actual same-sex copulation does not take place (and lesbian sex is literally unthinkable to him), that homosexuals never masturbate, and that the receptive partner never ejaculates. He also conflated homosexuality with transsexuality, and both of them with androgyny. Finally, he proclaimed those who speak out against sex 'spiritual sodomites' and spent a lot of his ire attacking them.

It takes a great deal of untangling to separate these attacks on 'spiritual sodomites', whom he openly wishes to 'descend into the grave', from some of his insights remarkable for the time and the context in which they were made. Rozanov spoke out emphatically against the criminal persecution of homosexuals and was fairly sceptical about the possibility of a 'cure' for homosexuality. He was also very much against the advice to gays 'not to act upon their desires'. In addition to that, Rozanov was the first in Russia to emphasise the homoerotic aspect of Christianity, beginning with JESUS himself, who for Rozanov is a quintessential 'man-maiden', and particularly of the monastic tradition. While he admired the ideology of fecundity he saw in the Old Testament, he simultaneously asserted that the individual who violated natural laws (including that of procreation) created the possibility for culture to emerge, to the point of crediting gays for the birth of civilisation. Finally, one of his most remarkable insights was his belief that in homosexuality desire saturates the entire being, rather than being confined in a particular organ, that every move, every touch could be sexually charged.

Rozanov's legacy as a writer and a thinker is highly controversial. However, both his aesthetic and his ideas exerted an enormous influence on the later Russian writers, especially those of the dissident movement of the 1960s–1980s, among them the leading gay writer of that generation, Evgeny Kharitonov. Ultimately, it is his iconoclastic spirit and readiness to challenge the most authoritative opinions that continue to attract new generations of readers to his work.

K. Moss (ed.) *Out of the Blue: Russia's Hidden Gay Literature: An Anthology*, San Francisco, 1997; R. Poggioli, *Rozanov*, New York, 1962; G. F. Putnam, 'Vasilii V. Rozanov: Sex, Marriage and Christianity', *Canadian Slavic Studies*, 6 (1971): 301–26; S. Roberts (ed.) *The Four Faces of Rozanov: Christianity, Sex, Jews and the Russian Revolution*, New York, 1978; A.

Siniavsky, 'Rozanov', in R. Freeborn and J. Grayson (eds) *Ideology in Russian Literature*, New York, 1990: 116–33; L. F. Watton, 'Constructions of Sin and Sodom in Russian Modernism', *Journal of the History of Sexuality*, 4, 3 (1994): 369–94.

Vitaly Chernetsky

Ruth and **Naomi** (*c*. eleventh century BC), Biblical figures. Described as a 'tender and touching' tale by Biblical scholars, this story of the strong love bond between two women is one of few such in a book more often seen as underpinned by patriarchal values.

Naomi, an Israelite, lived with her husband, Elimelech, and her two sons, Mahlon and Chilion, in Bethlehem. Fleeing famine, the family moved to nearby Moab, where they settled. Here their life progressed, with the sons marrying Moabite women, Orpah and Ruth, and, eventually, Elimelech dying. However, when the sons themselves died, Naomi decided to return to her homeland, now no longer ravaged by famine. While Orpah went 'back to her people and her gods', Ruth refused to be parted from her mother-in-law, declaring 'where you go I will go, and where you lodge I will lodge; your people will be my people, and your God my God' (Ruth 1: 16). The two women then set out on what was, for those times and for two women travelling alone, a difficult and dangerous journey of several hundred kilometres, traversing mountains and valleys and encountering unfamiliar tribes.

Upon their eventual return to Bethlehem, they were confronted with that age-old problem for women who wish to be independent, how to live in a world dominated by patriarchal rules, which often saw women as chattels. In this case, there were indeed men who could claim, under a 'right of redemption', the hands of either widow. Naomi contrived for her daughter-in-law to marry a well-to-do and sensitive relative of her late husband, by means of him exercising that kinsman's 'right'. A son to this union was the grandfather of King DAVID, from whose house JESUS Christ was descended.

While gay historians have been quick to 'recuperate' the story of David's love for Jonathan, the son of King Saul (whom David replaced on the throne of Israel), women-focused historians have been less expeditious in interrogating this tale, one of the few recorded examples in the Judaeo-Christian tradition of what could be read as a love 'surpassing the love of man'.

Garry Wotherspoon

S

Sá-Carneiro, Mário de (1890–1916), Portuguese writer. Sá-Carneiro was born into a middle-class family in Lisbon. His mother died when he was two and his sense of loss later deepened when his father married a woman who had no sympathy for her stepson. At the age of 20 he suffered another severe blow when a school-friend, Tomás Cabreira Júnior, committed suicide. After an unsuccessful attempt to study at the traditional university of Coimbra, Sá-Carneiro published his first major collection of prose, titled *Princípio (Beginning)* in 1912. This met with a mixed critical reception and he left shortly afterwards for Paris, where he threw himself enthusiastically into the artistic and literary milieu of the last days of the *belle époque*. Back in Lisbon in 1915, he helped launch the avant-garde literary magazine *Orpheu (Orpheus)*. This only succeeded in publishing two issues, but the scandal it caused in the staid intellectual circles of Lisbon revolutionised Portuguese poetry.

Sá-Carneiro returned to Paris later in the year but his mental state, always precarious, began to deteriorate increasingly rapidly. A series of letters to his close friend Fernando PESSOA and his poetry of the period chart his agonised decline. In April 1916 he committed suicide in a Paris hotel room by swallowing strychnine.

Sá-Carnerio wrote some juvenile plays but is best known for his poetry and prose. His early verse reveals the influence of Symbolism. Published in 1914 under the title *Dispersão (Dispersion)* it describes the delirious rise and fall of his aspirations as well as his impossible hopes and fears. Later poems, published posthumously as *Indícios de Ouro (Traces of Gold)* show the increasing dissolution of his personality. The poems are painfully confessional, revealing an insecure and narcissistic writer in a state of delirious crisis. One poem, titled simply '7', has become famous: 'I am not I nor am I the other / I am some sort of intermediary / a pillar of the bridge of tedium / which goes from me to the Other'. Another begins with the line 'And I who am the king of all this incoherence'. Sá-Carneiro's final poems, frantically evoking the chaos of modern urban life, look forward to Futurism. In linguistic terms his verse was highly innovatory and full of verbal inventiveness. Some critics think that, had he lived, Sá-Carneiro would have been a greater poet than Pessoa, his contemporary and friend.

Some of Sá-Carneiro's mental instability may have been due to repressed homosexuality. He seems to have had a relationship with a French woman, although little is known about her. Homosexuality, although not mentioned by name, permeates his most remarkable prose work, *A Confissão de Lúcio (Lúcio's Confession)*, a short novel first published in 1914. This is presented as an account by a man wrongly imprisoned for killing his friend. With *fin de siècle* Paris and Lisbon as his setting, the narrator, Lúcio, tells the story of his friendship with a poet, Ricardo, who confesses that he cannot feel friendship, only tenderness and a desire to kiss and possess his friends. To be someone's friend he would first have to possess him, but since he cannot possess someone of the same sex, the only way he can be the friend of another man would be if one of them changed sex. Ricardo acquires a wife, Marta, in mysterious circumstances, a shadowy and unreal woman with whom the narrator becomes increasingly obsessed. The two of them have an affair but Lúcio never feels he fully possesses her. Ricardo appears blissfully ignorant of the affair although it is carried on under his nose, and Lúcio comes to despise the apparently complaisant husband, suspecting that Marta has other lovers as well. The novel reaches a climax when, confronted by Lúcio, Ricardo tries to explain that he created Marta in order to respond to Lúcio's friendship and affection without possessing him physically. Following this, Ricardo runs to his house and shoots Marta but then, mysteriously, it is Ricardo who is found dead, with his smoking revolver lying at Lúcio's feet, while Marta has disappeared.

The melodramatic ending belies the complex issues of gender, sexuality and personal identity which the novel raises. The insistent, almost desperate assertion that one cannot possess someone of the same sex, the references to feeling in a masculine or feminine way when the opposite might be expected, the difficulty of differentiating between friendship and desire, and the use of a heterosexual affair to mediate the relationship between two men all point to deep-seated anxieties about sexual identity. The novel is set some 20 years before the date of publication in the decadent atmosphere of the *fin de siècle*, reflecting the concerns of a specific historical period. The psychological difficulties of the poet Ricardo seem to have a special resonance for Sá-Carneiro, however, and

suggest that homosexuality was one of the questions which racked this tormented writer.

M. Aliete Galhoz, *Mário de Sá-Carneiro*, Lisbon, 1963; Biblioteca Nacional, *Mário de Sá-Carneiro, 1890–1916*, Lisbon, 1990.

Robert Howes

Sachs, Maurice (1906–1944), French writer. Born Maurice Ettinghausen, half-Jewish and with a multiplicity of nationalities in his family tree, Sachs was educated in an English-style boarding-school, where he early learnt to give free rein to his interest in his own sex. In 1919 he lived in London for a year with his mother and worked in a bookshop, but the following year he returned to Paris and gravitated to the *Boeuf sur le Toit* group of young artists which centred on COCTEAU. In 1925 he converted to Catholicism under the influence of the fashionable Catholic thinker Jacques Maritain, with Cocteau acting as his godfather at the baptism. He then decided to become a priest and entered a seminary in 1926, a vocation which melted away swiftly when he met an amenable young man on the beach at Juan-les-Pins. After involvement in a number of dubious business activities, he fled to New York, where he passed himself off as an art dealer. Returning to Paris, he haunted leading homosexual writers of the time – Cocteau, GIDE and the aging Cubist poet Max Jacob – with all of whom he had stormy relationships whose precise nature is unclear. His lifestyle became increasingly extravagant and his means of supporting it increasingly uncertain. In the late 1930s he became friendly with Violette LEDUC, who seems to have been fascinated by Sachs's capacity for unrequited passions, a capacity which matched her own.

Sachs was mobilised at the start of the war but was discharged for sexual misconduct. During the early years of the Occupation he made money out of helping Jewish families escape to the Unoccupied Zone. He may also have been an informer for the Gestapo. To avoid the numerous enemies he was making, and to escape investigation into his own racial background, in 1942 he retreated to Ancenis in Normandy, taking Leduc with him. There they ran a profitable black-market trade in fresh food and other scarce commodities. Eventually Sachs was drawn back to Paris, where he disappeared. He resurfaced in prison in Hamburg, and seems to have died there in 1944 or early in 1945, though the circumstances of his death are still unclear.

Although Sachs had published translations, a book on Gide and a *roman-à-clef*, *Alias*, before the war, his best-known works, the self-consciously scandalous but powerful autobiography *Le Sabbat* (*The Sabbath*, 1960), another *roman-à-clef*, *Chronique joyeuse et scandaleuse* (*A Gay and Scandalous Chronicle*), and two sets of wittily analysed but cruel chronicles of French society between the wars, *La Décade de l'Illusion* (*The Decade of Illusion*) and *Tableaux et moeurs de ce temps* (*Pictures of Today's Contemporary Manners*), were all published posthumously between 1946 and 1952. In his writing, as in his life, his sexuality is very much to the fore.

Christopher Robinson

Sackville-West, Vita (1892–1962), British writer. Known to many contemporary readers as much for her affairs – most famously with Virginia WOOLF and most scandalously with Violet Keppel TREFUSIS – as she is for her literary output, Vita Sackville-West published over 50 books in her lifetime, including 13 novels, over 20 works of nonfiction and 10 volumes of poetry – the best-known of which, *The Land*, won the 1927 Hawthornden Prize. Some readers even come to Sackville-West's work through an interest in horticulture, as she published numerous books on gardening, a passion she cultivated at Sissinghurst, a castle in Kent she and her husband purchased in 1930, now maintained by the National Trust and still in glorious bloom.

Born to one of England's oldest aristocratic families, Sackville-West grew up an only child at Knole in Kent and was greatly aggrieved that she could not inherit her ancestral home because of her sex; it went to a male cousin. Sackville-West's *Knole and the Sackvilles* (1922) records this patrimonial injustice, but Knole is on the literary map due largely to Virginia Woolf's *Orlando* (1928), a mock biography that Sackville-West's son Nigel Nicolson thought a 'unique consolation' for his mother's lost inheritance; Nicolson called *Orlando*, 'the longest and most charming love letter in literature'. The 1973 publication of Nicolson's *Portrait of a Marriage* helped to engender renewed interest in Sackville-West's writing, her lesbian relationships, and her mostly platonic but loving and enduring marriage to diplomat and writer Harold NICOLSON, who, like his wife, had numerous homosexual affairs. Included in Nigel Nicolson's portrait of his parents' marriage are edited excerpts from a manuscript he found after his mother's death in which she tells of her passionate affair with Trefusis. *Challenge*, Sackville-West's 1923 fictionalised account of their relationship, was successfully prevented from being published in England by the two women's families, even though Sackville-West had transformed the novel's lovers into her and Violet's heterosexual counterparts, Julian and Eve, respectively. Sackville-West's novels, with the exception of her last – *No Signposts in the Sea* (1961) – do not explicitly refer to lesbian relationships; however, *The Dark Island* (1934), which echoes her relationship with Gwen St Aubyn, depicts an erotic undercurrent between the novel's main female characters.

One of Sackville-West's most experimental works, the short novel *Seducers in Ecuador* (1924), not only aided in the seduction of the woman to whom it was dedicated – Virginia Woolf – but was the first publication in what proved to be a long and profitable venture between Sackville-West and the Woolfs' Hogarth

Press. Between 1924 and 1949 Leonard and Virginia Woolf's press published 13 of Sackville-West's works. Her best-selling novels tended to explore Edwardian social values – as in the aptly titled social satire *The Edwardians* (1930) and *Family History* (1932) – especially as those values related to sexual politics, as is the case with her most overtly feminist novel, *All Passion Spent* (1931).

Sackville-West's 1920 secret journal, discovered after her death from cancer in 1962, is her most direct and sustained treatment of her own sexuality; she was even somewhat cryptic in her letters. Yet Vita Sackville-West's life and work continue to offer many possibilities for tracing certain threads in the evolving narrative of the development of lesbian consciousness in the twentieth century, especially in upper-class British culture.

V. Glendinning, *Vita: A Biography of Vita Sackville-West*, New York, 1983; S. Raitt, *Vita & Virginia: The Work and Friendship of V. Sackville-West and Virginia Woolf*, New York, 1993.

Annette Oxindine

Sade, Donatien Alphonse François, Marquis de (1740–1814), French writer. The Marquis de Sade was born into one of the oldest noble families of Provence. At the time he was born, however, the family belonged to the poorer nobility. To counter a further downfall, his parents applied different strategies for upward mobility. The young Sade grew up in the house of the illustrious de Condé family and received his education with its son. Later his parents married him to Pélagie de Montreuil, daughter of a family whose nobility was recent but whose fortune was large. He started a military career and participated in the battle of Cleves. In his youth, Sade developed a reputation as a libertine, following in the steps of his uncle, an abbot, and his father, who was once arrested for cruising men. Shortly after his marriage, he was arrested for the

first time, but escaped a long prison sentence thanks to his influential parents-in-law. On similar future occasions, they were less inclined to help him out of trouble. Before this, the young couple had two sons and a daughter.

In 1768, Sade snatched the seamstress Rosa Keller from the streets, took her to his house and asked her to beat him up and spit on the cross. When she refused to do so, he set the example and himself spat on the image of Christ and whipped the young woman. She escaped and filed a complaint. Sade ended up for the second time in prison, and was banished to his castle in La Coste. He was, however, soon allowed to come back to Paris, and until 1772 he lived a rather quiet family life divided between his different homes. In that year, he visited a bordello in Marseille, gave the prostitutes some aphrodisiacs they thought were poison, and had his man-servant sodomise him. For these crimes the fugitive Sade and his man-servant were sentenced to death, and were burned 'in effigy' (their portraits were burned). This made Sade the most famous victim of the sodomy laws. In 1777 he was arrested after he had come back to Paris to visit his dying mother. He was held in prison until 1790 by means of a *lettre de cachet* requested by his family, after his capital punishment had been revoked. In prison in Vincennes and at the Bastille, he started to write the books that established his fame. His wife remained faithful to him nearly until the end of his prison term.

Sade claims to have called the people of Paris to arms from inside his prison on 2 July 1789, shouting that the prisoners in the Bastille were beaten mercilessly. He was transferred to Charenton, and 12 days later the destruction of his former jail would announce the beginning of the French Revolution. Sade served another year in his cell before he could arrive on the scene of the revolution in which he participated actively until the radical Jacobins took over. As a count of the

Ancien Régime, his life was now in real danger, and indeed he was arrested and condemned to death for a second time, now for treason. But two days after the judgement, the Jacobins lost power and themselves perished on the guillotine. Sade was again a free man. He found a new lover with whom he lived in poverty. Some of his books were published and his plays staged. But his freedom would not last for long. Soon after Napoleon took power, Sade was again arrested, now because of the obscenity of his work, and once more put in the Charenton institution, which had become an asylum. There he died, barely surviving Napoleon's reign. He had lived during five different regimes, and all of them had condemned him to prison. No picture of Sade has survived, and his grave has been lost, but his texts miraculously survived all efforts of destruction. And his words made his fame.

Sade's work is notorious because of its endless stories of atrocities and extreme sexual pleasures. He is unsurpassed for violence and depravity. No sexual variation escaped his attention. As in most erotic literature of his time, the sexual scenes are interrupted by political and philosophical discourses that denounce religion and state. He subverted the dichotomy of good and bad, underlining that the devout people will always suffer because of wickedness, while the amoral will enjoy bad and good equally. It is in human nature to enjoy all pleasures and not to care about victims of violence. Space is a central theme in his sexual utopia. Lust needs an architecture with castles and monasteries. Boudoirs and bordellos are ideal places for pleasure as they disrupt the dichotomy of public and private.

Sade was not a sadist, but a passive sodomite who wanted to be whipped. He became a sadist when his anger was aroused by pious people who opposed his sexual pleasures and blasphemous behaviour. He wanted to teach them the lessons of abjection: one had to go through hell to know heaven.

His most famous books are *The 120 Days of Sodom* (first published in 1904), *Justine* (1791), *Philosophy in the Boudoir* (which is not a bedroom), *Aline et Valcour* (both 1795) and *Juliette* (1797). There exist many translations as well as new editions in French.

L. L. Bongie, *Sade: A Biographical Essay*, Chicago, 1998; F. du Plessix Gray, *At Home with the Marquis de Sade: A Life*, New York, 1998; N. Schaeffer, *The Marquis de Sade: A Life*, New York, 1999.

Gert Hekma

Saint-Pavin, Denis Sanguin de (1595–1670), French political and religious figure. Son of the Cardinal de Guise, Saint-Pavin had an honourable career in politics and the Church despite his avowed atheism and ostentatious homosexuality, without falling foul of the authorities. In an age when repression forced many to hide their sexuality or express it through euphemisms, Saint-Pavin called himself the 'Prince of Sodom' and, in 1645, when a schoolmaster was burned at the stake, Saint-Pavin courageously wrote: 'Dear Vougeon, how sad your death will make me, and what a misfortune it is for a prick to live in a land where those noble desires that are only a crime for Queens are punished by fire.'

His longevity is explicable only by his extreme ugliness.

David Parris

Sappho of Lesbos (*c.* 620–*c.* 560 BC), Greek poet. One of the earliest and most respected of Greek lyric poets, Sappho composed in her native Greek dialect, Aeolic Greek, towards the end of the seventh and the beginning of the sixth centuries BC. She was born and apparently lived her life in Lesbos, a large Greek island in the Aegean sea, a few kilometres off the northwest coast of Asia Minor (modern Turkey), which was settled by Aeolian Greeks probably in the tenth century BC. Her work survives for us now in a very fragmentary form, having been preserved on scraps of papyrus and in quotations by other writers for centuries after her time.

What is told of her life, the context for her poetry, the circumstances of its original dissemination or performance, is later construction – arising in part from classical period comedies and rumours about her, but in greater part from assumptions and speculation of scholars both ancient and more recent. We hear of Sappho as mistress of a finishing school; Sappho as married woman; Sappho as whore; Sappho as fat, ugly and rejected by men; Sappho at the centre of either a 'thiasos' (a group of women belonging to a religious cult) or some other Sapphic community of women, and so on – some of it derives from homophobic anxiety, some from the need to 'normalise', some from sheer misogyny, some from visions of a lesbian utopia. In addition, the very fragmentary nature of her surviving poetry does not help – only one poem, the 'Hymn to Aphrodite', seems to be complete, and this by virtue of its having been quoted in full by the orator and historian Dionysios of Halicarnassus in the first century BC as an example of smooth style.

But, leaving aside any attempts at reading 'poetry as biography', what the surviving fragments of her work and their transmission do tell us is that Sappho was a lyric poet, greatly respected in the literary culture of men of the classical period of the fifth and fourth centuries BC, who composed solo songs and who also wrote choral works for private marriage ceremonies and songs of praise to individual women. Thus Sappho – just as other lyric poets around her time – wrote hymns, wedding songs and songs of praise and blame; however, what survives of her compositions stand out as extraordinary in the unique 'woman-centredness' they express, and most notable among them are her songs of love to other women.

Sappho's expression of love in her 'Hymn to Aphrodite' (as contained in Greek in the Lobel and Page edition) assumes a mutuality not found in the extant writings of ancient Greek men. Sappho, in person – that is, using her own name – prays to the goddess of love and sex, Aphrodite, to come down to her grove. The presence of the goddess is required to persuade a woman whom the singer loves and who has apparently rejected her, to return to her. She utters her feelings of pain and sorrow, and sings of Aphrodite's epiphany, of how the goddess smiles and questions her about her suffering and desires. The goddess speaks: 'Whom, this time again, am I to persuade / to come back into your affection? Who is it, / Sappho, who does you wrong? / For indeed if she flees, soon she will pursue, / and although she does not now accept your gifts, / she will give, / and if she does not now love, soon she will love, / even against her will . . .?'

Sappho is the first extant Greek poet to write expressly about the feelings generated by love. The best example of this is found in what is perhaps Sappho's most famous fragment – *phainetai moi* - which also stands apart from surviving love poetry written by men in that it talks about the physical manifestation of emotion.

The physical manifestation of love in Sappho's lyrics is not expressed as sexual. There is next to nothing in any of her fragments that mentions any sexual act between women – apart, perhaps, from a few fragmentary lines that could be interpreted as suggesting a bodily contact leading to some sort of sexual fulfilment. After a description of the great grief felt at parting from someone who is referred to in the feminine, Sappho (again using her own name) recalls special times they shared together: '. . . and on soft bedding . . . tender . . . you satisfied your desire'. Although this is the closest reference to sex in Sappho's surviving fragments, a great deal of her description of groves, flowers and fruit might be read as sexual imagery.

It was the power of Sappho's poetry about, and to, women that gave rise to the term 'lesbian' – originally the adjectival form of the place-name of the island Lesbos – in its now-accepted sexual meaning. But the word seems not to have had female same-sex sexual connotations until about nine centuries after Sappho's lifetime: probably not until around the second century AD. (This may be disputed by some scholars who interpret a problematic fragment by the later sixth century BC poet Anacreon as referring to female homosexuality on the part of a woman from Lesbos.)

E. Lobel and D. Page, *Poetarum Lesbiorum Fragmenta*, Oxford, 1955; J. McIntosh Snyder, *Lesbian Desire in the Lyrics of Sappho*, New York, 1997; H. Parker, 'Sappho Schoolmistress', *Transactions of the American Philological Association*, 123 (1993): 309–51; L. Hatherly Wilson, *Sappho's Sweetbitter Songs*, London and New York, 1996.

Suzanne MacAlister

Sargent, John Singer (1856–1925), American painter. Sargent's homosexuality exists more in the reclamatory efforts of art historians than in documentation from his life. He enjoyed a brilliant career as a society portraitist, yet remained reticent about his private concerns – he was the proverbial 'confirmed bachelor'. Sargent associated with notorious *fin de siècle* aesthetes and dandies such as Oscar WILDE, Robert DE MONTESQUIOU and Henry JAMES; and it is known that he kept an album overstuffed with photographs of 'primitive' male nudes. His personal papers were destroyed by his family at his death and little is known about the artist's 25-year relationship with Italian model-turned-valet Nicola d'Inverno. If Sargent was homosexual, his mastery of social proprieties served equally to obscure his amative interests and to fuel his often insightful, sometimes scandalous, artwork.

Although of American parentage, Sargent, who was born in Florence and died in London, spent most of his life in Europe – Venice, Paris, London – developing an acute awareness of the limits of social acceptability and the thin line separating public and private domains. His prescience was often manifest in calculated artistic transgressions producing momentary infamy and enduring success. With *El Jaleo* (1879), Sargent profited from the eroticism and exoticism of the Other in the climactic dance of a Spanish Moorish woman.

The famous full-length *Portrait of Madame X* (1884) strategically punctured the pretentious social façade of Paris by presenting American 'professional beauty' Virginie Gautreau as the agent of her own sexuality. Both works catapulted Sargent to international attention, eventually resulting in hundreds of portrait commissions. His lush surfaces and liquid brushwork were much admired, but his unsparingly candid brush eventually scared off all but the most fearless sitters. Far from depicting the *beau monde* as it wished to be seen, Sargent often depicted his sitters as who he perceived them to be: pretentious, insecure and awkward.

Any homoerotic aspects to Sargent's work are found in his genre paintings and in his preparations for a large-scale mural commission. The artist's European holiday travels with family and friends produced a series of spontaneous and intimate works of languid picnickers. Sargent often took up a viewing position which emphasised intertwined legs and male groins, transforming the figures' easy familiarity into a sensual one; the viewer's position becomes that of voyeur, and the artist's brush is an unwelcome intruder. Images of nude male youths are sprinkled throughout Sargent's *œuvre*, but they are concentrated in the numerous drawing studies for the unfinished Boston Public Library mural *Triumph of Religion* (1890–1919). So erotic was Sargent's jumbling of male bodies in a study for the mural's Hell scene that Andy Warhol asked if it was a 'gang-bang' when he saw it in a 1986 exhibition.

T. Fairbrother, 'Warhol Meets Sargent at Whitney', *Arts Magazine*, 61 (February 1987): 64–71; T. Fairbrother, 'Sargent's Genre Painting and the Issues of Suppression and Privacy', *Studies in the History of Art*, 37 (1990): 29–49; P. Hills *et al.*, *John Singer Sargent*, New York, 1986.

Michael J. Murphy

Sassoon, Siegfried (Louvain) (1886–1967), British writer. Born in Benchley, Kent, into a wealthy Jewish family, Sassoon spent much of his youth golfing, fox-hunting, playing cricket and writing verse in a Romantic vein. When he was 5 his parents separated, and he saw very little of his father, who died when he was 9. Sassoon attended Marlborough School, then Clare College, Cambridge, where he remained for only four terms. He privately published nine collections of poems between 1906 and 1912, and in 1913 met Edward Marsh, who introduced Sassoon to a wide literary circle, including the poet Rupert BROOKE. Sassoon was sexually attracted to other men from an early age, but began to make sense of his homosexuality only when he read and later met Edward CARPENTER. His intimate friends would include Robert Ross, Noel COWARD, and Stephen Tennant.

At the outset of World War I Sassoon rode off on his bicycle to join the Royal Welsh Fusiliers. He was sent to France and, after the death at Gallipoli of his lover, a young subaltern named David Thomas, Sassoon earned the nickname 'Mad Jack' because of his reckless bravery and intense hatred of the Germans. A poem titled 'Citizen-Soldier', discovered by Sassoon's biographer Jean Moorcroft Wilson in 1998, pays tribute to Thomas. Sassoon was also attracted to a 19-year-old soldier named Gibson, who was killed in action in the battle of the Somme. Slowly, Sassoon began to change his views on the war and began to blame the political leadership of Great Britain, rather than the Kaiser, for its continuing stalemate. After being wounded in the shoulder, he was invalided and returned to England in April 1917.

Disgusted with the naïvety of those at home, he threw the Military Cross ribbon that he had earned in 1916 into the River Mersey. After writing a letter of protest against the war to Members of Parliament, he avoided court-martial only through the intervention of the poet Robert Graves, who arranged to have him put into Craiglockhart War Hospital in Scotland for shell-shocked officers. There he met Dr W. H. R. Rivers, an innovative neurologist, and the young officer and poet Wilfred OWEN, whom he mentored and befriended. Sassoon's Craiglockhart experiences are documented and dramatised in Stephen MacDonald's 1983 play, *Not About Heroes*, and are fictionalised in *Regeneration* (1991), the first volume of Pat Barker's World War I trilogy. Both texts note the homoerotic character of the friendship between Owen and Sassoon. Upon leaving hospital, Sassoon determined that he could protest the war most effectively from the front, so he returned to France. He was wounded once more by an English NCO, who shot him by mistake.

Sassoon married in 1933 and had one son. The last 30 years of his life were spent writing poetry and memoirs, including *Memoirs of a Fox-Hunting Man* (1928) and *Memoirs of an Infantry Officer* (1930), and he claimed to find peace and comfort in his religious faith. In 1957 he was awarded the Queen's Medal for Poetry. He remains an enigmatic figure in gay history: in his younger years homosexual but later, like Lord Alfred DOUGLAS, he lived comfortably as a conservative, religious, aristocratic heterosexual.

M. Thorpe, *Siegfried Sassoon: A Critical Study*, Oxford, 1966; J. Moorcroft Wilson, *Siegfried Sassoon: The Making of a War Poet 1896–1918*, London, 1998.

George Piggford

Schoondermark, Jacobus (1849–1915), Dutch sexologist, author. After an unfinished education in medicine, he became a prolific writer on popular medical topics. His field ranged from dentistry, nursing and bathing to contraception and sexual 'perversion'. Most of the books that he often published under his own name were translations or concoctions of foreign authors like Havelock ELLIS. To amplify his status, he enriched his name with the titles of doctor and professor.

Schoondermark was a quack who also sold such titles to other parvenus. His main importance lay in authoring books that no one else dared to publish. The first book in Dutch on homosexuality that asked for pity, not rejection, was his *Van de verkeerde richting* (*Of the Wrong Direction*, 1894). Later books, derived from other authors, would have opposite messages. He is typical of a kind of author that popularised medical theories on homosexuality and sexual perversion in cheap booklets for a broad public. Schoondermark's books appeared with the publishers who also sold Jean Fauconney (alias Dr Jaf and Dr Caufeynon) or R. H. Hayes. Notwithstanding his dozens of books that were often reprinted, Schoondermark twice went bankrupt. The work of these underworld authors on sexual 'perversions' deserves more attention, as they contributed plainly to the dissemination of ideas on homosexuality and perversions and offered to many people models of sexual identification.

G. Hekma, 'J. Schoondermark. De windhandel met een hersenschim', in H. Hafkamp and M. van Lieshout (eds) *Pijlen van naamloze liefde. Pioniers van de homo-emancipatie*, Amsterdam, 1988: 68–73; A. McLaren, *The Trials of Masculinity: Policing Sexual Boundaries 1870–1930*, Chicago, 1997: 147–55.

Gert Hekma

Schopenhauer, Arthur (1788–1860), German philosopher and essayist. Schopenhauer was born in Danzig, then part of Poland. His philosophy, which was most strongly influenced by PLATO and Kant, was itself a major influence on the thought of Friedrich NIETZSCHE and the psychoanalysis of Sigmund FREUD. According to Schopenhauer, the ultimate metaphysical reality, which underlies the world as it appears to human beings, is a blind, purposeless, impersonal 'will'. This will manifests itself throughout the natural world as 'vital force' or 'will-to-life'. Schopenhauer's cynical philosophy is notable for its treatment of a topic ignored by most previous philosophers in the Western tradition after Plato, namely the 'metaphysics of sexual love'.

In the second volume of his major work, *The World as Will and Representation*, published in 1844, Schopenhauer explains how will-to-life is expressed in the human sexual instinct. Blind will-to-life is the reality underlying our subjectively compelling but thoroughly deceptive feelings of love and desire. Although we think we pursue the object of our desires for the sake of individual happiness, we are really slaves to the reproductive interests of the species: 'The true end of the whole lovestory, though the parties concerned are unaware of it, is that this particular child may be begotten.' In fact, our pursuit of love usually brings considerable suffering and sometimes even death, because we wrongly assume that the one we love is the only one who can give us sexual satisfaction or we naïvely believe that a marriage based on love is the recipe for eternal bliss. According to Schopenhauer, nature must delude us in all these ways in order to ensure the reproductive success of the species as one expression of the cosmic will-to-life. Interestingly, Schopenhauer also anticipates currently popular 'sociobiological' arguments when, for example, he explains that men are promiscuous because they could easily father a hundred offspring in a year, whereas women tend to be more faithful because they can have only one. His fundamental idea that the human will is the plaything of forces beyond its control or ken inspires Freud's central insight that the conscious will is often misled by the mind's unconscious motivations, which usually have something to do with sex.

Schopenhauer is well aware, however, that his philosophy of sexual love provides no obvious explanation of non-procreative sexual acts. Evidently, 'pederasty' makes no obvious contribution to the reproduction of the species and is condemned by Christian moralists for just that reason. Whilst referring in conventionally derogatory terms to this 'disgusting depravity of the sexual instinct', Schopenhauer is at pains to maintain what was obvious to the ancient Greeks, namely that homosexuality is so widespread and so resistant to persecution that it must be regarded as natural: 'The universal nature and persistent ineradicability of the thing show that it arises in some way from human nature itself'. Schopenhauer's explanation for this apparent anomaly is also thoroughly classical. Aristotle had observed that the offspring of men who are 'too young' or 'too old' are invariably 'inferior, feeble, defective and undersized'. So pederasty, which for Schopenhauer is almost always a relationship between adolescents and older men, is nature's ingenious way of preserving the health of the species by diverting the sexual attentions of poor breeders to relatively harmless outlets.

This explanation of pederasty may appear bizarre. It is certainly incomplete since, as Schopenhauer admits, there are many exceptions to his rule. Still, the claim that homosexuality is natural and that nature was amoral was a fundamental challenge to nineteenth-century homophobia. Schopenhauer realised that his unorthodox views might reinforce his neglect by the academic philosophers of the day. No doubt it would be idle to speculate about his personal motivations. Notorious for his misogynist views, Schopenhauer never married; declaring that young men 'really offer the height of human beauty', he maintained a long-term friendship with a younger man, Julius Frauenstädt. At his death a number of additional papers on sexual love were suppressed by his execu-

tors. It is surely a coincidence that his remarks on pederasty were published not long after his fifty-fourth birthday when, according to Aristotle, men enter their second pederastic phase.

A. Schopenhauer, *The World as Will and Representation*, Vol. II (1844), trans. E. F. J. Payne, New York, 1966; P. Gardiner, *Schopenhauer*, Harmondsworth, 1963.

David West

Schorer, Squire Jacob Anton (1866–1957), Dutch activist. Schorer was born into a patrician family from Zealand. He studied law in Leyden and became a lawyer and judge in Middelburg. In 1903, he left his home town to study sexual sciences with Magnus HIRSCHFELD in Berlin, where he became an 'Obmann' of the 'Wissenschaftlich-humanitäre Komitee' (WHK). Inspired by German examples, he published an article on homosexuality in a Dutch law journal. It endorsed Hirschfeld's perspective of homosexuality being natural and homosexuals as a third sex. His view was condemned by the president of the Dutch High Court, and the editors immediately apologized for their mistake of having published Schorer's article.

After the death of his father, in 1910 he returned to The Netherlands. He went to live with his mother in The Hague, where he would soon lead the movement against the proposal for a new criminal law which forbade same-sex relations between adults and minors under 21 years. In 1911 the article was adopted as the infamous 248-bis. One of the arguments to include an anti-homosexual article in the law again after 100 years of liberty was precisely the activities of defenders of homosexuals like ALETRINO, RÖMER and Schorer. A year later, Schorer founded a Dutch chapter of Hirschfeld's WHK and published a Dutch version of the German leaflet 'What Everybody Should Know About Uranism'. Although others gave their name to this Dutch chapter, it remained very much the private business of Schorer. In 1914, after the beginning of World War I, the Dutch chapter renamed itself NWHK (Nederlandsch Wetenschappelijk Humanitair Komitee) to stress its independence from the Germans. Schorer's major work was writing articles in support of homosexuals, bringing them into contact with each other, and publishing annual reports (*Jaarverslagen*, 1915–1920 and 1933–1940). These reports were sent to politicians, legal and medical specialists and also to students in these fields. This led to unsuccessful attempts to forbid the mailing of such material. Schorer also collected one of the most important homosexual libraries of the world. Its contents have been printed in a catalogue with several supplements.

After the Germans occupied The Netherlands in 1940, the library was swept away within a few months and never a trace of it has been recovered. With the invasion, Schorer dissolved the NWHK and destroyed its archives. In 1942, he was evacuated to Harderwijk in the eastern part of the country, where he would live the rest of his life. Efforts to retrieve the library or to get financial compensation were unsuccessful and remain so to this day. In 1957, he died as a nearly-forgotten pioneer of homosexual emancipation in a provincial town where even nowadays gay life is largely absent.

Hans van Weel and Paul Snijders, 'Levenslang strijden voor rechtvaardigheid', in Hans Hafkamp and Maurice van Lieshout (eds), *Pijlen van naamloze liefde. Pioniers van de homoemancipatie*, Amsterdam, 1988: 96–103.

                    Gert Hekma

Schouten, Hubertus Johannes (1865–1936), Dutch writer. Son of the the well-to-do clergyman Leendert Schouten (founder of the Biblical Museum in Amsterdam), he studied theology, and was appointed as a village parson. He was a prolific writer, initially of anti-Catholic pamphlets under various pseudonyms. His other main interest surfaced in 1891, when he published an article refuting the persistent legend that Jean Calvin was branded on the right shoulder with three French lilies for being a sodomite.

In the first years of the twentieth century Schouten suffered a nervous breakdown. After being cured, he relinquished his ministry. Possibly a gay self-consciousness started to unfold in these years. About 1904 he learned about the existence of Magnus HIRSCHFELD and his Scientific-Humanitarian Committee. His article about Calvin was published in the 1905 *Jahrbuch für sexuelle Zwischenstufen*. Between 1907 and 1914 he published several pseudonymous pamphlets about homosexual issues. In the first, *Het 'Hofschandaal' te Berlijn* (*The 'Court Scandal' in Berlin*), exhibiting his knowledge of homosexuality in the German nobility, he explained legal proceedings around EULENBURG, Moltke and BRAND.

In 1910 Schouten moved to Amsterdam. Shortly afterwards, a blackmail press scandal induced the ink in his fountain pen to boil again. Under his new pen-name, Mr. (meaning Master of Law) G. Helpman, he published *Over chanteurs en wat hun sterkte is* (*About Blackmailers and their Strength*), discussing homosexuals as too easy victims of the 'pissoir-scum'.

Probably Schouten knew what he was writing about. In Amsterdam he met a 16-year-old boy making quite a lot of money as a rent boy. Schouten was 'intimate' with him, and then tried to 'save' him. The boy's mother and sister, however, seeing their easy income threatened, created a scandal, and turned Schouten over to the police as the boy's seducer. However, no lawsuit took place.

Until 1911 Dutch law did not differentiate between homosexual and heterosexual activity: both were allowed from 16 years onwards. Then, Edmond Regout, the Minister of Justice, proposed a new law: any adult (21 or older) who had sex with someone of his own sex under 21 was to be punished with imprisonment up to four years. When the Dutch parliament was discussing this new morals law, in February 1911, Schouten issued his next pamphlet. It mainly consisted of a long list of homosexual kings, scientists, artists and generals. The majority of the Dutch Lower House, however, accepted the anti-homosexual law. In April, 'Helpman'/Schouten sent a second pamphlet to the members of the Upper House, in which Regout, in a clear, sharp style, was accused of ignorance and fanatism. Schouten pointed at the blackmail aspect of the law, and asked aptly 'if His Excellency perhaps, deep down, applauds the help of the blackmailers in making the homosexuals unhappy?' Only a few months after Regout's infamous Article 248-bis came into force, Schouten was made an unhappy man indeed. A boy accused him of sexual activity. Schouten could not prove his innocence and fled, probably to Germany. His room was searched and his family harassed. The police appear to have said that 'imprisonment of "Mr. Helpman" as the first victim of this law would earn the special gratitude of the Minister of Justice'.

This did not stop Schouten from publishing (as Mr. G. Helpman) a pamphlet in November 1911, *De Neiging tot het Eigen Geslacht* (*The Inclination to the Own Sex*), a summation of his other pamphlets, which sold widely. It supplied an uncanny insight into Regout's fanatical mind. In 1914 the last Helpman pamphlet was written, an uncharacteristically confused defence against the accusations of sex with minors. And in the same year, under the new pseudonym Mr. H. J. Leendertsz, Schouten issued another pamphlet about the value of child witnesses in court, obviously motivated by his own bitter experience. After this, battle-weary, Schouten returned to The Netherlands. He seems never to have appeared in court, or published other pamphlets. Probably he lived from genealogical research, partly supported by his family.

Schouten had a difficult character, brandishing his pen like a holy sword – but he was able to see through the fanatical Minister of Justice who burdened The Netherlands with an old-fashioned and harmful anti-homosexual law.

H. van Weel and P. Snijders, 'Een schande voor ons land. Mr. G. Helpman', in *Pijlen van naamloze liefde*, Amsterdam, 1988.

Paul Snijders

Schwarzenbach, Annemarie (1908–1942), Swiss journalist and novelist. Schwarzenbach was born into a wealthy Zurich family, and, after completing her schooling at a girls' finishing academy in the Alps, studied history at the universities of Zurich and Paris, and was awarded her doctorate in 1931 for a dissertation on the history of the Engadine. In the same year her first novel was published, *Freunde um Bernhard* (*Bernhard's Friends*, 1931, reprinted 1993).

Around this time Schwarzenbach became acquainted with Erika and Klaus MANN, and a close friendship developed between the two women. Schwarzenbach moved to Berlin to pursue her career as a writer, and gave an account of her experiences in that city in her *Lyrische Novelle* (*Lyrical Novella*, 1933, reprinted 1988). The story is one of unrequited love, told by a male first-person narrator; Schwarzenbach later explained that this was a cover for what is in fact a portrayal of lesbian love.

During the winter of 1933–1934 Schwarzenbach toured in the Middle East; she subsequently wrote a number of short stories and a novel, *Das glückliche Tal* (*The Happy Valley*, 1940, reprinted 1987 and 1991), inspired by the trip. In 1934 she travelled to Moscow with Klaus Mann to take part in the Soviet Writers' Congress, the same conference at which Maxim Gorky and others attempted to define the role of literature within the socialist revolution, from which socialist realism emerged.

In 1935, she married a French diplomat,

Claude Carac, in Persia; but they lived together only briefly, and as a journalist she continued to travel Europe, the US, and in 1939 Afghanistan.

While she was living in Berlin, Schwarzenbach had begun to use morphine to combat her bouts of depression. Now a psychological collapse necessitated clinical treatment; after her return to the US in 1939 she attempted suicide, and was committed to a New York clinic. The last journey she made was to Africa, where she found herself under suspicion of espionage in the Belgian Congo. Following her return to Switzerland in 1942, she died, aged 34, after an accident she had while cycling in the Engadine. After her death, her mother, with whom Schwarzenbach had a particularly difficult relationship, destroyed a quantity of her remaining papers, including letters from Erika Mann.

Schwarzenbach's work has been attracting renewed interest in recent years, and her selected works have been reprinted in five volumes. Other published writings by Schwarzenbach include *'Wir werden es schon zuwege bringen, das Leben': Annemarie Schwarzenbach an Erika und Klaus Mann. Briefe 1930–1942* ('We'll Manage Life in the End': The Letters of Annemarie Schwarzenbach to Erika and Klaus Mann, 1930–1945, 1993).

P. Budke and J. Schulze, *Schriftstellerinnen in Berlin 1871 bis 1945: Ein Lexikon zu Leben und Werk*, Berlin, 1995; A. Georgiadou, *'Das Leben zerfetzt sich mir in tausend Stücke': Annemarie Schwarzenbach: Eine Biographie*, Frankfurt, 1995; N. Müller and D. Grente, *Der untröstliche Engel: das ruhelose Leben der Annemarie Schwarzenbach*, trans. E. Hagedorn and B. Reitz, Munich, 1995; A. Schwarzenbach, *Ausgewählte Werke*, ed. R. Perret, Basel, 1988–1996.

Andrea Capovilla and Sarah Colvin

Scott, Sarah (née Robinson) (1723–1795), British writer. Scott was the anonymous author of six novels and three historical biographies. She and her sister, Elizabeth Montagu, whose salons earned her the title 'Queen of the Bluestockings', were educated at home in a wealthy and intellectual milieu. In 1751 Sarah married George Scott, tutor to the Prince of Wales, but separated from him after only a year. Lady Barbara Montagu, Sarah's close friend, accompanied the Scotts on honeymoon and lived with them for most of the brief marriage. Afterwards the two women lived together in and around Bath until Lady Barbara's death in 1765, and were known for their frugal habits and charitable deeds. Elizabeth Montagu commented in a letter: 'Their convent, for by its regularity it resembles one, is really a cheerful place.'

Scott was and is chiefly known for her semi-autobiographical utopian novel, *A Description of Millennium Hall* (1762) by 'A Gentleman on his Travels', a kind of fictional response to Mary Astell's *Serious Proposal to the Ladies* (1694). It details a community of six virtuous women with a particular commitment to the education of poor girls and charity for indigent gentlewomen. An enclosure within the grounds of the estate also provides 'asylum for those poor creatures who are rendered miserable from some natural deficiency or redundancy'. *Millennium Hall* offers an allegory of female perspicacity and self-sufficiency, 'rational cheerfulness and polite freedom', in which class differences and niceties are preserved intact. 'The social comforts of friendship' between women of a certain rank serve as an instructive 'curiosity' to the two men who are introduced into their midst as a convenient audience and marker of gender difference: 'You will pity us because we have no cards, no assemblies, no plays, no masquerades, in this solitary place . . . we do not desire to drown conversation in noise; the amusing fictions of dramatic writers are not necessary where nature affords us so many real delights; and as we are not afraid of showing our hearts, we have no occasion to conceal our persons, in order to obtain either liberty of speech or action.' The novel's sentimental framework offers the transparent openness of genteel female friendship as a form of naturally occuring and continuous solicitude. Within its compass, coextensive with the boundaries of the estate, women without men are valued as models of self-improvement, benevolent employers of servants and compassionate keepers of 'monsters'. This structure finds its formal corollary in a series of inset narratives which introduce each woman in turn, unfolding her prior history and the linked contingencies of women's fate as the precondition for the foundation of Millennium Hall.

Scott ordered that her personal papers be destroyed after her death.

G. Haggerty, '"Romantic Friendship" and Patriarchal Narrative in *Millennium Hall*', *Genders*, 13 (1992): 108–22; J. Spencer, *The Rise of the Woman Novelist*, Oxford, 1986; D. Macey Jr, 'Eden Revisited', *Eighteenth Century Fiction*, 9 (1997): 161–82; F. Nussbaum, 'Feminotopias', in D. Mitchell and S. Snyder (eds) *The Body and Physical Difference*, Ann Arbor, 1997.

Kate Lilley

Sebastian, St (late third century to early fourth century AD), Roman soldier and Christian saint. There are very few reliable sources concerning St Sebastian, whose legend appears to have been considerably embroidered with additions drawn from other Christian saints. He was reportedly born in Narbonne to a Milanese mother married to a Roman official. Allegedly a member of the praetorian guard at Rome, because of his loyalty he served as a personal guard to the emperors Diocletian and Maximian (late third and early fourth century). As a Christian, he consoled prisoners awaiting martyrdom, and succeeded in converting many members of the nobility including the brothers Marcus and Marcellinus, the couple Nicostratus and Zoe, and the Roman prefect Croma-tius along with his son Tiburtius, all of whom were eventually martyred. As a result of this missionary activity, he himself was apprehended, tied nude to a post and shot with arrows. The executioners believed they had left him for dead; but Irene, widow of the martyr Castulus, came to fetch his corpse and found him still alive. Nursed back to health, he was urged to flee from Rome. But Sebastian preferred to declare his faith in Christ during a pagan ceremony held by the two emperors at the temple of Hercules. Arrested by Diocletian, he was flagellated to death at the Hippodrome situated on the Palatine hill and his corpse was thrown into a sewer. Its location was revealed to a woman named Lucina, who had him buried beside Sts Peter and Paul at the Catacombs on the Appian Way.

Sebastian, whose feast in the West is 20 January, and 13 December in the Eastern Church, has long been considered the third patron saint of Rome. In addition to Rome, his relics are found in many other places, including Soissons, Fulda and Farfa. Since the seventh century, when his invocation allegedly brought about the immediate cessation of the plague at Rome, Sebastian has been invoked against pestilence throughout Christendom. This may derive from the similarity between the marks which appeared on those stricken with plague and the wounds which disfigured the saint's body; and just as Sebastian had been revived, so plague victims might be saved through the saint's invocation.

The identification of Sebastian with homosexuality has no documentary foundation. Nevertheless, Christians held that the plague was brought as a judgement against humanity due to the same 'wrath of God' (Ephesians 5: 6) which had led to the destruction of the people of Sodom and Gomorrah for their sexual perversion. The visual representation of Sebastian flourished beginning with the Black Plague of 1348–1349, when he also appeared prominently in courtly literature.

Although previously usually portrayed in the garb of a soldier, during the Renaissance Sebastian often appeared as a beautiful naked youth tied to a tree or post suffering the torments of piercing arrows. It has been argued that the inspiration for this physical image of the saint is taken from classical Greek and Roman depictions of the god Apollo.

[J.-P. Joecker (ed.)] *Saint-Sébastien, Adonis et martyr*, Paris, 1983; R. A. Kaye, 'Losing His Religion: Saint Sebastian as Contemporary Gay Martyr', in P. Horne and R. Lewis (eds) *Outlooks: Lesbian and Gay Sexualities and Visual Cultures*, London, 1996: 86–105.

Michael Goodich

Seneca [Lucius Annaeus Seneca, or Seneca the Younger] (*c.* 4 BC–AD 65), Roman political figure, writer, philosopher. Born in Spain, Seneca studied in Rome, where he began his political career around AD 31. Yet in 41 he was implicated in a court case concerning adultery which involved the imperial family and was banished to Corsica, where he remained until 49. On his return to Rome, Seneca was given responsibility for the education of Lucius Domitius Enobarbus, the future Emperor NERO. When Nero took power in 54, Seneca's star rose and he was appointed to various public positions. The situation changed, however, after the assassination of Agrippina, Nero's powerful mother, in 59. Nero then dispensed with the services of his former tutor who, finding himself isolated in the emperor's entourage, retired to private life three years later, whereupon he was suddenly accused of conspiring against Nero. Seneca successfully proved his innocence. However, in 65, he was unable to prove that he had not been involved in another conspiracy: the emperor then ordered him to commit suicide, and Seneca obeyed.

Seneca was a relatively prolific author and a number of his works survive. Many include references to homosexual behaviour, which he saw as a degrading act,

the result of violence and the exercise of power, and the result of a passion to which the Stoic philosophy in which Seneca believed could not give approval. Seneca insisted that the slave who was used as a sex object was none the less as much a human being as his master and ought not to be degraded by sexual abuse (though he said nothing about the abuses of servile labour). This view, like others of Seneca's attitudes, was similar to that of Christianity, which indeed took the larger part of its sexual ethics and many aspects of its morality from Stoicism. To such an extent did medieval Christians feel a kinship with Seneca that they invented the legend (supposedly evidenced by an apocryphal correspondence between him and ST PAUL) that he was himself a secret Christian.

Among the many discussions of homosexuality in Seneca's work, especially noteworthy are the repeated allusions in the *Letters to Lucilius* (now Seneca's most widely read work) and passages in *De beneficiis* which focus on a man's loss of dignity following acceptance of homosexual acts, especially oral sex. However, Dio Cassius (*c.* 155–240) affirms in his *Roman History* (LXI. 10. 4–6) that notwithstanding his ostentatious philosophical virtue, Seneca loved men and taught his vice to Nero.

Giovanni Dall'Orto

Serge and **Bacchus, SS** (fourth century AD), Christian martyrs. High-ranking soldiers and Roman citizens, Serge and Bacchus were friends of the pagan Emperor Maximian but were themselves Christians; according to an ancient manuscript, 'Being as one in the love for Christ, they were also undivided from each other in the army of the world, united not by the way of nature, but in the manner of faith.' Enemies denounced them to Maximian for their Christianity, and they refused to sacrifice to Zeus when the emperor took them to a temple. He publicly humiliated the two men then exiled them to an eastern province, where they again refused to recant. Tortured and executed, they were later declared Christian saints.

John Boswell characterises Serge and Bacchus as the 'quintessential "paired" military saints' – others include Polyeuct and Nearchos, and Felicitas and Perpetua – and the ones most often invoked in ceremonies of same-sex unions. Boswell argues that such ceremonies, most common in the early Eastern Christian Church (but also occasionally celebrated in the West), involved the blessing of partnerships between men by a priest. He claims that these were consensual unions which involved strong emotional bonds between men and which ought not to be assumed not to be erotic. Critics have responded that there is no real evidence that such unions were sexual, that homosexuality was illegal in most of the societies in which they were performed, and that such ceremonies, in any case, were not widely used. Boswell's carefully argued and scholarly impressive thesis attracted much attention by suggesting that the early Christian Church may have condoned homosexual 'marriage' despite the violent homophobia of later Christianity.

J. Boswell, *Same-Sex Unions in Premodern Europe*, New York, 1994.

Robert Aldrich

Settembrini, Luigi (1813–1876), Italian nationalist and writer. Settembrini was born in Naples, and participated in the movement for Italian unification, for which he was condemned to death by the Neapolitan king, Ferdinand II, in 1851. The sentence was commuted to life imprisonment, but Settembrini escaped from prison in 1859, thanks to his son, who directed to Ireland the ship that was supposed to take Settembrini and other exiles to America. He stayed successively in Ireland, Britain and Florence, where he remained active as a writer and political figure. With the unification of Italy in 1860, Settembrini obtained a teaching post at the University of Naples. In 1873, he was named a member of the Italian senate.

Settembrini is the author of a number of important works, including a memoir, (*Ricordanze della mia vita*), a study of Italian literature and the complete Italian translation of the works of Lucian.

Settembrini's homosexuality was first mentioned in 1977, when his short novel *I neoplatonici* (*The Neoplatonics*) was first published; the work is a homoerotic fantasy set in ancient Greece which Settembrini wrote while in prison soon after completing his translation of Lucian (in 1858–1859). He had then sent it to his wife, claiming it to be a translation of a classical Greek text. Left among his papers at his death, the manuscript was afterwards read by the historian and philosopher Benedetto Croce, who advised against publication.

The novel reveals the intimate erotic fantasies of its author; though it lacks a real plot, it tells the story of two youths who are in love with each other and become sexual partners. It ends with the (heterosexual) marriages of the two heroes. The work includes descriptions of anal intercourse between the two men which are unique in Italian literature of the time. Though the modesty of the novel excludes it from Settembrini's major works, it remains a worthy composition, marked by an agile and fresh style and a certain elegance. The absolutely positive and serene image it presents of homosexuality is noteworthy. The author takes up a particular conception of pre-Christian (homo)sexuality, and presents homosexual love as a form of human behaviour capable of giving joy and satisfaction. He also portrays it as a relationship with both emotional and erotic dimensions – a relatively rare approach in nineteenth-century writing.

When *I neoplatonici* was first published, certain authors connected it with homosexual encounters which Settembrini might well have experienced in prison, but this hypothesis is unsubstantiated.

L. Settembrini, *I neoplatonici*, Milan, 1977, including introduction.

Giovanni Dall'Orto

Seymour, George Francis Alexander, Earl of Yarmouth, 7th Marquess of Hertford (1871–1940), British aristocrat and Australian colonist. Seymour was educated at Eton (1885–1888), then became a Lieutenant in the Warwickshire regiment before joining the Black Watch. He became Earl of Yarmouth in 1884 and the 7th Marquess of Hertford in 1901. In 1895 he arrived at the sugar district of Mackay, Queensland, Australia, taking up a small mixed farm. Despite his senior rank and status, the local population showed him little respect, scandalised by his behaviour. The local paper called him a 'skirt dancer' and local memory is of him performing dances in a sequined outfit with butterfly wings and of hosting male-only parties on his isolated property. Seymour seems to have returned to England for Queen Victoria's Jubilee then travelled to the US, where he married Alice C. Thaw of Pittsburgh in 1903; their childless marriage was annulled in 1908. He filed for bankruptcy in 1910 and inherited Ragley Hall and its large Warwickshire estate in 1912, but never lived there, preferring the high life in London.

Clive Moore

Sgricci, Tommaso (1789–1836), Italian poet. Verse improvisation was a typically Italian phenomenon at the beginning of the nineteenth century, made possible by the fact that Italian poetic language of the time was very repetitive and formulaic; prefabricated phrases could thus be put together rapidly. Sgricci was the ultimate practitioner of the style just before it disappeared. No one was as capable as Sgricci in creating poetry in such a mechanical fashion and adapting it so spectacularly for the stage; his performances enjoyed a delirious reception among paying audiences throughout Italy. Sgricci declaimed verses at such great speed and with such a virtuosity that his listeners were unable to evaluate the true value of the poetry which they heard – as his contemporary Pietro Giordani cuttingly remarked in 1816. Sgricci was not the only improvisational poet, but he was the most famous, winning prizes and the sort of monetary reward that no 'serious' poet of his age was able to obtain.

Of modest origins, Sgricci began to improvise poetry at a young age. By 1813, he was able to make a living from this work by touring Italy and even giving performances abroad. In a typical performance, Sgricci invited the audience to write down themes; he then drew one from lot and, on the spot, composed a complete verse play, reciting all of the roles and sometimes pretending to faint at the end from the mental exertion. Sgricci's fame finds a parallel today in certain rock stars; like them, he took advantage of his reputation to behave scandalously and to escape censure – in his case, as a homosexual – as no one else was able to do.

Notoriety as a 'sodomite' helped create around Sgricci an aura of nonconformity which the public expected of an 'artist' of his time. Lord BYRON, who met Sgricci in Ravenna, wrote of him on 3 March 1820: 'Sgricci is here improvising away with great success – he is also a celebrated Sodomite, a character by no means so much respected in Italy as it should be; but they laugh instead of burning – and the Women talk of it as a pity in a man of talent.' The Englishman was right, as seen in a letter written on 22 February 1817 by the poet Vincenzo Monti. He recounted entering Sgricci's room unannounced and finding him in bed with a youth; his account reveals only amusement at the incident.

However, there were scandals. In a letter of 21 January 1817, Monti said that in Milan Sgricci's reputation had been ruined because he used make-up and especially because he made no attempt to hide his 'Greek love' for a young servant named Tognino. The biggest scandal occurred in

Rome when, at the height of his fame, Sgricci was to be awarded the great honour of being 'crowned' poet in the city's Campidoglio. Yet, on 17 April 1819, he was suddenly expelled from the Papal States. The Church's official explanation is that Sgricci criticised papal government; at the time, lampoons said that he was expelled becaused he had 'raped Apollo [the Greek god of poetry] from the rear'. Even this episode did not greatly harm Sgricci, however, as six years later he was made a member of the Arezzo nobility.

As his career declined, Sgricci returned to Florence, where, from 1826, he was placed under police surveillance. The protection of the grand-duke, one of his admirers, guaranteed his impunity from arrest. The powerless police agents complained in their reports that Sgricci picked up grenadiers from a near-by barracks and that he dressed and behaved like a prostitute. On his death, wits wrote that after having violated Apollo, Sgricci would now be raped by Satan. He left behind such a reputation that Oscar Giacchi, writing two generations later, still referred to him as a notorious sodomite.

G. Dall'Orto, 'Sodoma all'improvviso', *Babilonia*, 133 (May 1995): 68–70; E. Del Cerro, *Misteri di polizia*, Florence, 1890: 149–51; P. Giordani, 'Dello Sgricci e degl'improvvisatori in Italia', *Opere*, Florence, 1851: Vol. 1, pp. 445–58; L. A. Marchand (ed.) *Byron's Letters and Journals*, London, 1977: Vol. 7, pp. 49–51; V. Monti, *Epistolario*, Florence, 1928–9: Vol. 4, pp. 337, 343–4, 367; O. Giacchi, *Pazzi e birbanti*, Milan, 1885: 178–9; U. Viviani, *Un genio aretino, Tommasco Sgricci, poeta tragico improvvisatore*, Arezzo, 1928.

Giovanni Dall'Orto

Shakespeare, William (1564–1616), English playwright and poet. Born the son of a merchant in Stratford-on-Avon, one first catches sight of him in 1592 as an actor and playwright in London. The comedies and history plays that he wrote early in his life were followed by the tragedies of his later work and the romances of his last years. He married in 1582 and returned in retirement to the town where he had been born.

Several characters in Shakespeare's plays have been interpreted as homosexual, but the most telling moments are those where Shakespeare's plots explore the ambiguity of the transvestite conventions of the English theatre of his time, where the female roles were played by boy actors. In *As You Like It*, the female heroine, Rosalind (who would have been played by a boy), disguises herself as a youth and takes the name GANYMEDE, a contemporary term for a catamite. The passionate bond between Rosalind and her female companion Celia adds to the sexual ambiguity of the situation. *As You Like It* is not alone in this: in *Twelfth Night* the female heroine Viola disguises herself as a youth and takes the equally ambivalent name of Caesario; and the language of Helena and Hermia in *A Midsummer Night's Dream* is as erotically charged as that of Rosalind and Celia.

It is, however, around Shakespeare's Sonnets that centuries of speculation have been constructed. In 1609, when Shakespeare was an established dramatist, a volume of sonnets appears in his name. The first group of sonnets are addressed to a beautiful young nobleman. They begin as earnest counsel to the young man but develop into an apparently passionate love. With the second group of sonnets, a dark-favoured lady enters the erotic triangle. The first group of sonnets are transfigured by a transcendent love, the second by the poet's revulsion at the strength of his heterosexual desires.

Some commentators have interpreted the first group of sonnets as homosexual. The problem with this view is that as one extends the same interpretation elsewhere, the argument begins to collapse under its own weight. There is a similar homoeroticism in the poetry of the enigmatic Christopher MARLOWE, but it is also to be found in the poetry of the robustly heterosexual

John Donne and in that of the devoutly religious Richard Crashaw, where it is applied in a theological context. The homoeroticism of the court of King JAMES I has similarly been read as stemming from James's supposedly homosexual nature, without grasping that it was also one of the conventions of the court of his predecessor, Henry VIII. The homoerotic gesture is a commonplace in the friendship between the educated men of Shakespeare's time; and Shakespeare's Sonnets are only one – albeit breathtaking – moment in the convention that could first playfully propose, and then archly deny, a sexual interpretation to the intimacy of a patron and his humanist-educated 'secretary'.

The issue in Shakespeare's twentieth sonnet is the potentially sexual nature of the poet's love for the beautiful young nobleman: 'A womans face with natures owne hand painted, / Haste thou the Master Mistris of my passion'. So it begins – and ends – with a studiedly ambiguous couplet that can be read *both* as denying a physical interest, in the most elevated of terms, and in the same breath as affirming it, in the most bawdy. 'But since she prickt thee out for womens pleasure, / Mine be thy love and thy loves use their treasure.' Voice the 's' in 'use' (as the verb) and read 'loves' as a plural not a possessive, and see what happens to that suggestion that the young man was 'prickt' out for women's pleasure.

The final couplet is in fact a joke, a spectacular junction of the most elevated and the most bawdy of desires; and its context in society is the ambiguity that corresponds to it in Shakespeare's twenty-ninth sonnet. This is probably the most famous statement in all literature of that lifting of the spirit that comes when the lover thinks of the beloved. It can also be read – word by word and phrase by phrase – as an elegantly worded request by a seventeenth-century client for a financial subvention from his patron. The homoerotic gesture of Shakespeare's twentieth

sonnet that one finds throughout his culture was finely designed to exploit the instincts of his contemporaries in two complementary respects. The first was their unwillingness to take seriously the ambiguous borderline between homosexuality and the shared beds and emotional bonding of its male companionship. The second was their inclination to see the 'sodomite' in political terms as a traitor or heretic. The point was that if the similarity of the 'sodomite' to the intimacy of the humanist counsellor and his scholarly patron was not to be taken seriously, then neither was its proximity to the conspiracy that the 'sodomite' readily suggested. Shakespeare's England saw the rise to positions of influence and power of the humanist scholars as the companions and counsellors of their noble patrons. It also saw the accompanying suspicions that their growing influence aroused.

The homoerotic gesture was designed to allay those suspicions, and judged the prejudices of its audience to a fine degree: a separation of homoeroticism and politics that later generations have been eager to embrace. The ironic result, several centuries on, is the honoured place that the idyllic homoeroticism of the literature of Shakespeare's England – that engaging world of male friendship far from mundane concerns – has come to occupy in the canon of English literature.

A. Bray, *Homosexuality in Renaissance England*, New York, 1995; J. Barrell, 'Editing Out the Discourse of Patronage in Shakespeare's Twenty-Ninth Sonnet', in *Poetry, Language and Politics*, Manchester, 1988; A. Bray and M. Rey, 'The Body of the Friend', in T. Hitchcock and M. Cohen (eds) *English Masculinities 1660–1800*, London, 1999; E. Kosofsky Sedgwick, *Between Men: English Literature and Male Homosocial Desire*, New York, 1985; S. Orgel, *Impersonations: The Performance of Gender in Shakespeare's England*, Cambridge, 1996; A. Stewart, *Close Readers: Humanism and Sodomy in Early Modern England*, Princeton, 1997; V. Traub, 'The (in)significance of

"Lesbian" Desire in Early Modern England', in J. Goldberg (ed.) *Queering the Renaissance*, Durham, 1994.

Alan Bray

Sitwell, Osbert (1892–1969), British writer. With his sister, Edith, and brother, Sacheverell, Osbert constituted the 'Sitwell triumvirate' that created a sensation in London's artistic circles in the years after World War I.

Sitwell had varying success as a poet, novelist, essayist, satirist, short-story writer, dramatist and travel writer, but it was not until he turned to autobiography that he came into his own. His multivolume memoir, published under the uniform title *Left Hand, Right Hand!*, comprises *Left Hand, Right Hand!* (1945), *The Scarlet Tree* (1946), *Great Morning* (1948), *Laughter in the Next Room* (1949) and *Noble Essences* (1950), and it proved to be a resounding critical and popular success. The last volume contains brilliant portraits of Edmund GOSSE, Ronald FIRBANK, Wilfred OWEN, Rex Whistler and Oscar WILDE's beloved 'Sphinx', Ada Leverson.

This series was a portrait of an age, not a confession, and, although these books are drawn from Sitwell's experiences, there is no mention of his homosexuality, not even in veiled or oblique terms. Philip Ziegler remarks that, until the mid-1920s, when he met David Horner, who would become his long-time partner, there is no mention anywhere of Sitwell's sexuality. Discretion about his private life was almost absolute: Ziegler refers to a 1967 letter written from Venice by Osbert to a friend – 'I enjoyed it particularly at night with all the illuminations, which made everything look so gay(!)' – and comments, 'The "(!)" is of interest as being – presumably – the only overt reference to his homosexuality to appear in any of his letters.'

Sitwell's discretion did not seem to stem from shame or fear of the opinion of others: he was not furtive or deceptive about his homosexuality, and made no pretences about his relationship with the flamboyant Horner. His homosexuality seems to have been tacitly acknowledged by his wide circle of friends and acquaintances, who seem to have found it unremarkable, as he did himself. He also seems to have kept himself aloof from homosexual coteries (artistic or otherwise) and apart from whatever homosexual subcultures existed at the time. Ultimately, Sitwell seems not to have regarded his homosexuality as of any special importance for his self-identity or his role as an artist.

P. Ziegler, *Osbert Sitwell*, London, 1998.

Jason Boyd

Sixtus IV (Francesco Della Ròvere) (1414–1484), pope from 1471 to 1484. A member of the Friars Minor (Franciscans), he received a degree in theology in Padua in 1444. After teaching in various Italian universities, he served as head of the Franciscan Conventuals (1464–1469). In 1467, he was made a cardinal by Paul II, at whose death he was elected pope. Sixtus IV pursued policies aimed at buttressing the temporal powers of the Church, to which end he practised nepotism, appointing his relatives to key positions and elevating two of them (Giuliano Della Ròvere and Pietro Riario) to the cardinalate. In foreign policy his main objective, though it produced few results, was to organise a crusade against the Turks. He was the initiator of urban renewal in Rome; among his constructions was the Sistine Chapel.

Concerning the pope's homosexuality, the chronicler Stefano Infessura (*c.* 1440–*c.* 1500), recorded in his diary in 1484 a series of documented episodes and unsubstantiated gossip: 'He, as is handed down from the people, and the facts demonstrated, was a lover of boys and a sodomite. In fact, what he did for the lads who attended upon him in his room has been taught by experience: not only did he give them an income worth several thousand ducats, he even dared give them cardinalships and important bishoprics. In fact, was it for any other reason, as certain people say, that he held so dear Count Girolamo [Riario] and Pietro [Riario], his brother, and afterwards Cardinal of San Sisto, except for sodomy? And what about the barber's son? He, a child not yet twelve, continuously spent his time with [the pope], who granted him such riches and, it is rumoured, an important bishopric. Word is that he even wanted to make him a cardinal, contrary to any justice, although he was a child, but God put his desires to nought.' (In reality, Masini and Portigliotti have shown that the honours were given not to the youth but to his father, who became a high papal official.)

It is clear today that Sixtus favoured his relatives not from sexual interest but in order to have at hand faithful executors of his policies. However, the favours shown to the young Giovanni Sclafenato (who was indeed named a cardinal) appear suspect in the light of the epitaph which the pope had engraved on his tomb in 1497, in which it was said that he was made a cardinal 'for ingenuousness, loyalty, . . . and his other gifts of soul and body'. This is perhaps a unique case of a youth being made a cardinal for his physical endowments.

As can be seen, with little available material, it is impossible to clear up the doubt remaining about this pope. Yet in Protestant countries rumours spread that Sixtus IV gave satisfaction to the request of the cardinal of Santa Lucia who asked him – on behalf of his fellow cardinals – for permission to practice sodomy during the three hottest months of the year (on the grounds that it was less tiring than heterosexual intercourse). Such charges would have appeared unlikely even if Pierre Bayle had not demonstrated their falsehood in 1702. They amounted to simple Protestant propaganda spread to discredit 'papists'.

The superb bronze sepulchre of Sixtus, built in 1493 but removed from old St Peter's to make room for the present-day building, is now housed in the Vatican Museum. It is listed among the masterworks of Antonio del Pollaiuolo (1433–1498).

P. Bayle, *Dictionnaire historique et critique*, Rotterdam, 1702; entries 'Sixte IV' and 'Lettres', in *Oeuvres diverses*, The Hague, 1734: Vol. 4, Letter 303; S. Infessura, *Diario della città di Roma* (1303–1494), Rome, 1890): 155–6; M. Masini and G. Portigliotti, 'I fàmuli di Sisto IV', *Archivio di antropologia criminale*, 27 (1916): 462–81.

Gioavanni Dall'Orto

Smyth, Dame Ethel (1858–1944), British composer, writer and feminist. Ethel Smyth was born into a middle-class military household in Sidcup, England, the fourth child in a family of six. She seems to have revealed her independent spirit at a young age and by the time she was 12 she had decided that she was going to become a composer. Her father was strongly opposed to the idea; any kind of a career was unusual for a girl of Ethel's social class and music was not meant for serious study. But the 'stormy petrel', as her mother called her, was not to be dissuaded, and after a period during which she locked herself in her room and refused to leave it, she was finally given permission.

In 1877, at the age of 19, Smyth arrived in Leipzig to study composition at the renowned conservatory. Within a year she was smitten by the 'dazzling and bewitching' Lisl von Herzogenberg, the wife of the composer who was to become her music teacher, Heinrich von Herzogenberg. She was to spend seven of the happiest years of her life studying in Germany, returning to her parents, as promised, during the summer months. In 1883 she visited Lisl's sister Julia and her husband, Henry Brewster, in Florence. Although at first she was more interested in Julia, Ethel soon realised that she was in love with Brewster and the two remained regular correspondents and occasional lovers until Brewster's death in 1908.

A passionate woman for whom love and its pursuit and cultivation were primary pursuits, Smyth's affections were most often captured by beautiful women and despite her lifelong attachment to Brewster, she refused to marry him, even after his wife's death. A stubborn individualist, Smyth wore tweeds, ties and men's hats and smoked cigars; she also defied convention by frequently conducting performances of her own compositions.

The first English woman to tackle the composition of major orchestral works, Smyth's best-received works were her *Mass in D* (1891) and her opera *The Wreckers*, composed in 1904. She was convinced that her compositions were not given a fair chance because she was a woman, daring to invade a male sphere, and she turned to writing her series of celebrated autobiographical works, at least in part, to make public the extent of her struggles on behalf of her music. Surprisingly, she came late to the cause of women's suffrage, but once won over, after meeting Emmeline Pankhurst in 1910, she was characteristically single-minded. She announced that she was putting aside her music for two years in order to help win the vote and threw a stone at a cabinet minister's window in order to secure her imprisonment. Smyth composed the *March of the Women*, soon to become the suffragist anthem, in 1911 and conducted its most celebrated performance with a toothbrush from a window in Holloway Prison the following year.

Despite the profound deafness which afflicted her in her final years, she continued to actively promote her music until her death at the age of 86. Courageous, obstinate, sometimes a nuisance but never dull, Smyth may perhaps have been her own greatest admirer, but this boundless self-confidence cannot obscure her genuine and original literary and musical ability.

Dictionary of National Biography, 1941–1950,

Oxford, 1959; C. St. John, *Ethel Smyth: A Biography*, London, 1959.

Kathleen E. Garay

Socrates (*c.* 470–399 BC), Greek philosopher. Socrates is one of the most significant and enigmatic figures in the history of Western thought: significant, because he was seen as the first of the Greeks to subject ethical issues to philosophical scrutiny, and enigmatic, because he left no writings of his own. His views, therefore, have to be discerned in the distorting mirror provided by other writers, chiefly ARISTOPHANES, XENOPHON, PLATO and Aristotle: and these men (three of whom knew Socrates) present diverse pictures.

Son of a stone-mason or sculptor, Socrates was born around 470 BC. He married Xanthippe (a woman of reputedly shrewish temper) and had three sons. While his parents were not poor, his determination to pursue philosophy without the corruption (as he saw it) attendant upon accepting fees for his teaching led to a life of simple poverty and iron self-discipline. He saw active service in three campaigns of the Peloponnesian War between Athens and Sparta, and confirmed his reputation for unbending adherence to principle in negotiations following the Athenian defeat in the sea-battle of Arginusae (406 BC). Socrates alone among the relevant officials refused to agree to an illegal motion relating to the trial of the generals involved. Following seizure of power at the end of the war by a brutal Junta of Thirty (404 BC), Socrates was equally adamant in refusing a command from this body to carry out an illegal arrest. Nevertheless, when the Athenian democracy was restored a year or so later, Socrates was treated with circumspection. His teaching was suspected of oligarchic tendencies, not least because he had in earlier years counted Kritias (a leading member of the Thirty) and the brilliant but unstable Alcibiades among his disciples. He was charged with not recognising the state's gods and with 'corrupting the youth'. The charges were probably a cover for political animus, but Socrates was found guilty, and (ignoring opportunities for escape) drank the hemlock, while discoursing with his friends on the immortality of the soul (399 BC).

In philosophy, Socrates seems to have begun by following his philosophical predecessors, with speculation on the nature of the physical universe (as caricatured in Aristophanes' play *The Clouds*). But he later turned to the analysis of virtue and the proper goals of human life. Disclaiming knowledge for himself, he goaded others by persistent questioning into clarifying and defining their thoughts. Opposed to the scepticism and relativism disseminated by the 'Sophists' – the professional teachers of his day – he began the search for unvarying truth behind the multiplicity of particular appearances which was to result in Plato's theory of Forms. His most famous tenet, perhaps, was that 'virtue is knowledge', since no one, he thought, could perceive what is good and then deliberately act otherwise.

As for love, it is clear that he was deeply attracted to beautiful youths. He said, for example, that he was 'set on fire' by a glimpse inside the cloak of the young Charmides. Moreover, close companionship with his followers was important for him and provided the medium through which wisdom might be evoked in them. He often used the language of love – claiming, for example, that there never was a time when he was not in love. In particular, his name was linked with that of Alcibiades, and over the centuries it has been widely believed that they were lovers. Thus Christopher MARLOWE wrote (in *Edward II*): 'The Roman Tully lov'd Octavius; Great Socrates, wild Alcibiades'. Such a consummation would have been in character for Alcibiades, who both in his private and his political life merited the adjective 'wild'. By all accounts singularly beautiful, he enjoyed numerous sexual relationships with both sexes. One source, for example, accuses him in his boyhood of drawing husbands away from their wives, and as a young man, wives from their husbands. In politics he was an aristocrat with populist ambitions. He sponsored the great (and disastrous) Athenian naval expedition against Syracuse (415 BC) and was appointed one of its generals. But because of his alleged complicity with a mysterious public scandal ('the mutilation of the herms'), he was recalled. In consequence, he shifted his allegiance to Sparta, and in the constantly changing political and military fortunes of the ensuing years intrigued at different times with Sparta, Persia and Athens. He was rehabilitated at Athens (407 BC) only to be again rebuffed and subsequently murdered (404 BC).

The true relationship of this flamboyant and erratic character to the philosopher Socrates is difficult to determine. They were friends in their earlier careers, and Xenophon says that Socrates exercised a good influence on Alcibiades so long as they remained associates. But were they lovers in other than a spiritual sense? At the opening of Plato's dialogue *Protagoras*, Socrates exchanges some banter with his companion about 'hunting Alcibiades' beauty': but he goes on to recall that he had ignored and kept forgetting the handsome Alcibiades because he was so preoccupied with the beauty of a visiting philosopher's wisdom. In Xenophon's writings, Socrates condemns the physical love of boys in remarkably strong language (and in opposition, it seems, to his own feelings). He regularly exalts the love of soul above the love of body. Most notable of all is the famous account (in Plato's *Symposium*) of Alcibiades' attempt to seduce Socrates. The young aristocrat creeps under the philosopher's cloak, assuming that the latter will respond to this beauty as all other men have done, only to be mortified by Socrates' refusal to be aroused. It seems that within the Socratic circle '*eros* is not a desire for bodily contact but a love of moral and intellectual excellence' (K. J. Dover).

While therefore the love between Socrates and Alcibiades has been a significant icon for some in the Western literary tradition, one seems obliged to conclude, on the available evidence, that in sober fact Socrates, while highly susceptible to ephebic beauty, not only preached but also practised homosexual celibacy.

K. J. Dover, *Greek Homosexuality*, London, 1978; W. K. C. Guthrie, *Socrates*, Cambridge, 1971; R. J. Littman, 'The Loves of Alcibiades', *Proceedings of the American Philological Association*, 101 (1970): 263–76; P. A. Vander Waerdt (ed.) *The Socratic Movement*, Ithaca, NY, 1994; G. Vlastos, *Socrates: Ironist and Moral Philosopher*, Cambridge, 1991.

Clifford Hindley

Södergran, Edith Irene (1892–1923), Swedish-Finnish poet. Södergran, an early modernist, is a notable figure in the history of Swedish-language literature in Finland. She has also been a spiritual model for generations of female writers in Finland and in Sweden, and is widely known among academics as well. All her work is available in English.

Södergran lived most of her life in Raivola, a village in eastern Finland, in the area which Finland lost to the Soviet Union in World War II. Södergran went to school in the cosmopolitan city of Viborg. At the age of 16 she was diagnosed with tuberculosis – her father had died of tuberculosis only a year before – and she spent part of her young years at various sanatoria in Finland and in Switzerland.

In her early years Södergran became inspired by NIETZSCHE's philosophy; later she was interested in Anthroposophy and in Christianity. She was a pioneer in modernist poetry in Finland. Her poetic self is a powerful, self-conscious woman with an androgynous dimension. In one of her best-known poems, 'Vierge Moderne', she wrote: 'I am no woman. I am a neuter. / I am a child, a page-boy, and a bold decision, / I am a laughing streak of scarlet sun . . .' (trans. Stina Katchadourian). Contempor-

ary critics were mostly negative. One irritated male critic wrote that even if someone is mad it does not mean that she is a genius.

Södergran found a literary supporter in Hagar Olsson (1893–1978), a young woman writer and critic. Their friendship began through correspondence in January 1919. Biographers have been almost neurotically keen on Södergran having a potential male lover and they have ended up describing Olsson and Södergran's relationship only as intellectual friendship, yet other interpretations can be made as well. Södergran and Olsson met for the first time in February 1919, when Olsson visited Södergran's place in Raivola. Södergran was ravished. Inspired by Olsson, she wrote a series of 'sisterhood-poems' in her third poetry collection, *Rosenaltaret* (*The Altar of Roses*, 1919). Olsson and Södergran met only six times. In her letters Södergran begged Olsson to visit Raivola again, since Södergran's financial and health problems limited her own travelling. But Olsson was occupied with her work in Helsinki, where she also had other affairs during these years, both heterosexual and homosexual.

In the summer of 1923 Olsson was travelling in Italy when she received word of Södergran's death. Olsson has described it as a shock because she was not aware of the critical state of Södergran's health, and feelings of guilt were to follow Olsson all her life. Södergran had given Olsson a ring that she called 'the ring of sisterhood'. Olsson would carry the ring all her life, and she also wished to be buried with it. As her heritage for later generations of lesbian readers, Södergran has left the poems of sisterhood, where longing, jealousy and love between two women were given a virtuous expression.

E. Södergran, *Complete Poems*, Newcastle upon Tyne, 1984; D. McDuff (ed.) 'My Sister, My Life: Extracts from Correspondence between Edith Södergran and Hagar Olsson', *Books from Finland*, 2 (1992); G. C. Schoolfield, *Edith Södergran: Modernist Poet in Fin-*

land, Westport, Conn., 1984; G. C. Schoolfield and L. Thompson (eds.) *Two Women Writers from Finland, Edith Södergran (1892–1923) and Hagar Olsson (1893–1978)*, Edinburgh, 1995.

Johanna Pakkanen

Sodoma, Il [Giovanni Antonio Bazzi] (1477–1549), Italian painter. Bazzi is best known outside the speciality of Renaissance art by the nickname, used in his own time and since, of Il Sodoma. Generations of Italian art historians have tortuously tried to find any derivation for this name – searching hard in local dialects – except the obvious one, and even the leading authority on his work, Enzo Carli, admits only that he was 'a flamboyant and eccentric personality' and denies that the nickname had anything to do with his sexual practices. The great sixteenth-century biographer of artists, Giorgio Vasari, wrote that Sodoma was a 'gay, licentious man' who 'was always surrounded with young men and beardless youth, whom he loved beyond measure, and he acquired the nickname of Sodoma, which caused him neither trouble nor disdain – rather he gloried in it'. Carli responded that his 'character was ... blackened by Vasari'. Some other anecdotal evidence does point to Sodoma's homosexuality; he did marry and father a child, but this was not unusual for other sodomites of his time.

Sodoma was born in Vercelli, the son of a shoemaker. He worked in Milan and Rome but spent most of his life in Siena, where he became the official painter of the Sienese Republic. Sodoma completed paintings on canvas and panel, frescoes and altarpieces. His subjects included both scenes from the life of Christ and the saints and scenes of classical mythology. His most important work is, according to Carli, frescoes of the *Marriage of Alexander and Roxanne* and the *Family of Darius before Alexander* in the Farnesina palace in Rome, dating from 1516.

Sodoma's portrayal of men, sometimes semi-nude, is neither more frequent nor more erotic than is common in Renaissance Italian art. In an important *St Sebastian* (1525), now in the Palazzo Pitti in Florence, the arrows of martyrdom do not detract from the portrayal of a handsome, slender youth. Pictures of Christ emphasise, in a somewhat unusual way, his virile muscularity. Another work shows a bearded patriarch embracing a pubescent angel. Conclusions about any homosexual intent in such works, however, would be speculative.

E. Carli, 'Sodoma', in J. Turner (ed.) *The Dictionary of Art*, London, 1996: Vol. 29, pp. 1–4; A. Hayum, *Giovanni Antonio Bazzi – "Il Sodoma"*, New York, 1976; G. Dall'Orto, 'Chiametemi Sodoma', *Babilonia*, 146 (July–August 1996): 74–6.

Robert Aldrich

Solomon, Simeon (1840–1905), British painter and poet. Born in London of Jewish parents, Simeon was the youngest of eight children, two others of whom, Abraham and Rebecca, were also to become successful painters. A precociously talented draughtsman, he entered the Royal Academy School in 1856 and first exhibited at the Royal Academy the following year. Solomon's early work combined the pictorial style of the Pre-Raphaelites, particularly through the influence of Dante Gabriel Rossetti, with Hebraic (especially Old Testament) subject matter, and was already portraying sexually ambiguous scenes, e.g. *David Playing the Harp before Saul* (1859). By the mid-1860s the painter Edward Burne-Jones had displaced Rossetti's influence and Solomon developed a more monumental, and androgynous, figure style and increasingly depicted pagan and mythological themes.

Closely associated with the Aesthetic Movement, Solomon formed close friendships with figures such as the critic Walter PATER, the headmaster of Eton public school Oscar Browning, and the poet Algernon Charles Swinburne, and produced illustrations for two of Swinburne's works, the novel *Lesbia Brandon* and the epic flagellation poem *The Flogging Block*. In addition to the pervasive interest in ancient Greece among this circle, the association with Swinburne in particular may have encouraged Solomon's shift from Jewish themes to an idealised classicism typified by paintings such as *Sappho and Erinna in a Garden at Mytelene* (1864) and *Love in Autumn* (1866). Other striking works from this period include the drawing *Love Among the Schoolboys* (1865), one from a series probably drawn for Swinburne and later owned by Oscar WILDE, and another drawing, *The Bride, the Bridegroom, and Sad Love* (1865), which is amongst the most homoerotic of Solomon's images. Several trips to Italy between 1866–1870 further consolidated his classicising tendencies, and paintings from this period, such as *Bacchus* (1867), frequently depict youthful male figures of idealised, and often highly androgynous, beauty.

In 1871 Solomon published a limited edition of his prose poem *A Vision of Love Revealed in Sleep*. Based loosely upon the Song of Solomon, and combining Jewish mysticism with pagan themes, the poem met with a mixed reception. It provoked a particularly aggressive response from Robert Buchanan in 'The Fleshly School of Poetry' in the *Contemporary Review*, and Swinburne was at best lukewarm, stating that the poem 'seems to want even that much coherence which is requisite to keep symbolic or allegorical art from absolute dissolution or collapse'. However, a more sympathetic reading was offered by John Addington SYMONDS who observed that 'His love is not classical, not medieval, not oriental, but it has a touch of all these qualities – the pure perfection of the classical forms, the allegorical mysticism and pensive grace of the Middle Ages, and the indescribable perfume of orientalism' – a description that might apply equally to Solomon's art.

Solomon's career went into abrupt decline after he and a 60-year-old stableman, George Roberts, were arrested at a public urinal in London on 11 February 1873 and subsequently charged 'that they did unlawfully attempt feloniously to commit the abominable Crime of Buggery'. While Roberts was sentenced to eighteen months of hard labour, Solomon did not receive a prison sentence but was fined instead. Following the trial, Solomon was effectively denied the opportunity to exhibit at venues such as the Royal Academy and the Arts Club, and he was also disowned by many of his former circle. For Swinburne, Solomon became 'a thing unmentionable' and their association was especially strained in 1879 when Solomon began to sell potentially compromising letters he had received from the poet. Despite his social disgrace, Solomon was able to sell drawings to a few loyal supporters who, together with his family, tried to revive his career after the late 1880s. Despite these efforts, Solomon's life during the three decades after the trial was characterised by extreme poverty and vagrancy (including begging as a pavement artist), alcoholism and growing anonymity. He spent his final years at the St Giles Workhouse in London, where he died.

B. Reade (ed.) *Sexual Heretics: Male Homosexuality in English Literature from 1850 to 1900*, New York, 1970; S. Reynolds, *The Vision of Simeon Solomon*, Stroud, 1985; *Solomon: A Family of Painters*, London, 1985.

David L. Phillips

Solon (sixth century BC), Greek lawmaker. Solon, the Athenian lawgiver, was celebrated as a poet, political reformer and one of the Seven Sages of the ancient world. By the fourth century BC he had come to be regarded as the founder of Athenian democracy.

As a young man he played an important role in Athens's battles with neighbouring Megara for control of the island of Salamis. Meanwhile, Athenian society was suffering from increasing hostility between the wealthy and nobly-born ruling class and the peasants who worked the land, the financial stranglehold of the former reducing the latter to virtual, if not actual, slavery. Through his highly political poems, Solon campaigned against this state of affairs, determinedly seeking a middle way of reform through which rich and poor could live in harmony, with justice.

In 594/593 BC Solon was appointed by both sides to the unique position of *archon* (senior administrator) and mediator. He enacted agrarian and constitutional reforms of a most far-reaching kind. Debts were cancelled, financial encumbrances on the land removed, and those enslaved for debt set free – a great *seisachtheia* (shaking-off of burdens). Constitutionally, Solon abolished the rights of noble birth in favour of income-based qualifications for office, while giving the common people a share in the assembly. With these and other measures, Solon's reforms amounted to a complete code of law. The 'mediator', nevertheless, refused to accept sole power as tyrant. Having completed his work, he travelled abroad for ten years. He died probably in 560/559 BC.

In his *Life of Solon*, Plutarch comments that the reformer's susceptibility to youthful beauty can be inferred from his poetry. Only a few lines on this subject have survived, but it is a challenging marker of the difference between ancient Athenian society and our own, that this eminent statesman should include the following in his body of poetry: 'when amid the delectable flowers of youth he loves a boy, yearning for thighs and a sweet mouth' (Frag. 25). A speaker in Plutarch's *Dialogue on Love* (probably written early in the second century AD), finds it necessary to excuse the couplet as the product of hot youth. There is, however, no evidence to suggest that in its own day it would have provoked surprise or disquiet. It may be compared with Aeschylus's verses for ACHILLES' lament over Patroclus. Indeed, these two quotations, brief as they are, imply a vigorous celebration of male same-sex experience in archaic Greece as something compatible with serious achievement in war and politics.

K. J. Dover, *Greek Homosexuality*, London, 1978: 195 ff.; I. M. Linforth, *Solon the Athenian*, New York, 1971 reprint; R. Thomas, 'Law and the Lawgiver in the Athenian Democracy', in R. Osborne and S. Hornblower (eds) *Ritual, Finance, Politics*, Oxford, 1994.

Clifford Hindley

Solovieva, Poliksena Sergeevna (1867–1924), Russian poet, prose writer, children's writer, and editor and publisher of a children's magazine. Solovieva's most lasting contributions were in the area of children's literature: hers was the first complete translation of Lewis Carroll's *Alice in Wonderland* (1909) and she published and edited a new kind of Russian children's magazine, *Tropinka* (*The Path*).

Born in the old building of Moscow University of which her father, the historian Sergei Soloviev, was then rector, Solovieva was the twelfth and last child of this illustrious family of the Moscow intelligentsia. One of her childhood friends was the prose writer 'K. El'tsova', who also grew up in a Moscow professor's home. Educated at home, Solovieva learned to read at five, began writing shortly thereafter, and spent long hours in a private fantasy world imagining herself 'now a pirate, now a poor knight, now a troubadour'. She studied singing and attended the School of Painting, Sculpture and Architecture in Moscow.

Her father's death was a major blow to the 12-year-old. She drew closer to her older brothers, especially Vladimir (the philosopher, poet and 'spiritual father' of the Russian Symbolist movement), whom she adored with a cult-like devotion and whose religious philosophy had a major impact on her own spiritual life. Her first poems appeared in 1883; after this first success, Solovieva became disenchanted with her writing and turned to painting and singing instead. At the same time she underwent a religious crisis and for a brief time even felt she had lost her faith. It returned, she noted in a short autobiography, 'but transformed, liberated from everything generally accepted'.

In 1895 Solovieva – along with her mother – moved to St Petersburg to be near Natal'ia Manaseina (1869–1930), a children's writer and the poet's lifelong companion. Solovieva's literary connections facilitated her breaking into mainstream Russian literature, and from 1895 onwards, her poems appeared regularly (under the pen name 'Allegro') in leading journals. Solovieva was introduced to the poet Zinaida Gippius by the literary critic Zinaida Vengerova and was a frequent presence in the St Petersburg literary salons of Konstantin Sluchevskii, Viacheslav Ivanov, Aleksandr Blok and his family, and the Merezhkovskiis. Her three pre-revolutionary books of verse were dutifully and gently reviewed by her famous contemporaries Annenskii, Ivanov, Blok and others. In 1908 she was the recipient of the Pushkin Medal for her 1905 collection *Inei* (*Rime*).

In 1906 Solovieva and Manaseina began publication of a unique children's magazine, *The Path*. Well known writers and artists of the day were invited to contribute, lending it a high literary and artistic quality. The publishing house that followed attracted the works of many leading Symbolists. Solovieva wrote several children's works for the journal in the seven years of its existence and continued publishing in this area after *The Path* was forced out of business by competitors in the field it had opened.

Almost no information exists about the last seven years of Solovieva's life. After the death of Manaseina's husband in 1917, she and Solovieva lived together, mainly in the Crimea and the Caucasus. In 1923 Solovieva published her last (and best) collection of lyrics. Her health had been in decline for many years and she died in a Moscow hospital.

Solovieva left a rather voluminous and many-faceted body of work which includes several volumes of poetry, verse dramas, verse fairy tales and narratives, stories and numerous children's works. Unfortunately, out of the hundreds of lyrics she wrote, only a handful reveal more than run-of-the-mill competence. Overall, her work lacks personality, a drawback of which the poet herself was aware. Nominally a member of the Symbolist school, Solovieva typically writes about world weariness, inexplicable sadness, quietude and the ever-presence of death. A kind of elegiac dreaminess suffuses her lyrics, which were criticised for their unreality and anemia.

The one striking characteristic of Solovieva's lyrics is her exclusive use of a male persona. All contemporary and later critics draw attention to this, but none has noted that Solovieva most probably resorted to this mask in order to camouflage her lesbian orientation, and to express her sexuality and difference in her writing. Ironically, Solovieva's male persona seems to have had the opposite effect: rather than express her true self, it obscures her identity and makes it difficult for her to tap into her emotional centre and one possibly potent source of her creativity. Solovieva's friend the poet and critic Maksimilian Voloshin seems to sense this when he characterised her poetic voice as 'almost a male contralto with female chest notes'.

One of her more interesting works is the epistolary novel in verse, *Perekrestok* (*The Crossroad*, 1913), which contains eight letters from a brother to his sister. The action takes place on a country estate in summer. The theme of the novel is the near impossibility of changing basic human behaviour, though it also deals with the so-called woman question. In this latter theme and in its verse form, the novel anticipates a similar effort by the poet Liubov' Stolitsa, who published a novel in verse, *Elena Deeva*, in 1914.

Strangely enough, Solovieva's most noteworthy creative achievement has generally been unmentioned; it is her 1909 translation of Lewis Carroll's *Alice in*

Wonderland, the first complete Russian translation of this masterpiece. Solovieva resists the temptation to retell Alice as a Russian children's story (as many Russian translators have chosen to do, including Nabokov). She translates the original faithfully, and with flair, and comes up with convincing equivalents for the obviously untranslatable portions and complex linguistic puns.

D. Burgin, 'Laid out in Lavender: Perceptions of Lesbian Love in Russian Literature and Criticism of the Silver Age 1893–1917', *Sexuality and the Body in Russian Culture*, Stanford, 1993; Z. Gippius, 'Poliksena Solovieva', *Vozrozhdenie*, 89 (1959): 118–24.

Diana L. Burgin

Somerset, Lord Arthur (1851–1926), British public figure. Somerset was one of the key figures in the Cleveland Street scandal (also known at the time as the West End Scandals) of 1889–1890. In London in 1889, police questioning a messenger boy, employed at the Central Telegraph Office, who was in possession of a suspiciously large amount of money, found that he had gained his earnings working at a homosexual brothel situated at 19 Cleveland Street in the West End. He had procured other teenage boys from the telegraph office for the establishment operated by Charles Hammond. Among the patrons was Somerset, third son of the Duke of Beaufort, a serving military officer and equerry to the Prince of Wales. Subsequently it was alleged that others who had visited the brothel included the Earl of Euston and even Prince Albert Victor ('Prince Eddy'), the eldest son of the Prince of Wales.

Soon George Veck, a former Post Office employee who sometimes posed as a clergyman and who had lived with Hammond in the Cleveland Street premises, was put on trial, along with Henry Newlove, a 19-year-old telegraph messenger accused of homosexual offences and procuring. Both were convicted and sentenced to relatively short periods of imprisonment. Several

months later, Ernest Parke, a journalist who published a report saying that Euston had patronised the Cleveland Street brothel, was sued for libel by the earl; he, too, was found guilty. Somerset, meanwhile, had fled England when he learned that a warrant for his arrest would probably be issued.

Henry LABOUCHERE, a Liberal Member of Parliament, who had been responsible for introducing an amendent to the Criminal Law Amendment Bill of 1885 which had made illegal 'any act of gross indecency with another male person' (thus making all homosexual behaviour short of anal intercourse a misdemeanour), charged in the House of Commons that the government had tried to cover up the scandal. He suggested that the prime minister, the Marquess of Salisbury, had directly or indirectly allowed Hammond to escape to the United States, not wishing more details of the scandal to be made public, especially if they might involve the heir to the throne. Furthermore, he implied that the prosecution had been kept from extraditing Somerset or arresting him when he returned to England for his grandmother's funeral. The accusations earned Labouchere a temporary suspension from Parliament.

Somerset was certainly guilty of having had sexual relations with the 'telegraph boys'. Euston claimed that he had visited the Cleveland Street establishment only once because he believed that *poses plastiques* (strip-teases) might be viewed there. Prince Eddy may well have gone to the brothel, though Montgomery Hyde, author of the standard account of the scandal, says that he was not homosexual. However, Aronson presents circumstantial evidence of Prince Eddy's homosexuality, and demonstrates that Somerset did not return to England because he did not wish to give evidence against Prince Eddy in court.

The *affaire* clearly showed that a homosexual subculture, including rent-boys and organised brothels, existed in London, and that journalists, lawyers and blackmailers were only too eager to take advantage of the criminalisation of homosexual acts. It was also proof, as Labouchere rightly argued, that the British 'establishment' would and could protect its own members if they were caught in 'immoral' circumstances. An adolescent rent-boy, an earnest young journalist and Hammond's dubious partner went to prison, while the aristocrats went free. 'Prince Eddy' and Euston died before inheriting their father's titles; Somerset, after considering a move to Asia or Africa, settled in France, where he died and was buried, never again setting foot in Britain. The necessity for great discretion in homosexual encounters, and the recourse to flight if arrest threatened, were lessons which, only a few years later, Oscar WILDE had apparently not learned.

H. Montgomery Hyde, *The Cleveland Street Scandal*, London, 1976; T. Aronson, *Prince Eddy and the Homosexual Underworld*, London, 1994.

Robert Aldrich

Spender, Sir Stephen (Harold) (1909–1995), British writer. Spender, the consummate man of letters of his generation, was born in London and educated at University College School, Hampstead, and University College, Oxford. While at university he met, and grew to idolise, W. H. AUDEN, co-edited *Oxford Poetry* with Louis MacNeice, and forged literary relationships that would forever identify him as one of the 'Auden Group', poets whose 'collective text' during the inter-war years espoused the Marxist alternative, embraced Freudian psychology, warned against the rise of fascism, and celebrated the efficiency of the machine. Auden and Christopher Isherwood lured the shy and awkward Spender to Hamburg and Berlin in the waning days of the Weimer Republic where he befriended the photographer Herbert LIST and watched the 'Children of the Sun' at play. His autobiographical

novel, *The Temple*, written in 1929 but not published until 1988, gives a vivid portrait of this lost era and reveals its author's sexual ambivalence, drawn equally to 'boys gentle and soft' and girls 'finely moulded'. Spender was eventually to marry twice: to Inez Pearn, in 1936, and to Natasha Litvin in 1941. Litvin bore him a son, Matthew, and a daughter, Elizabeth, both the subject of some adoring late poems. In his memoir, *World Within World* (1951), Spender is candid about his tentative experimentation with bronzed German youth, and his relationship during the 1930s with 'Jimmy Younger' (T. A. R. Hindman), an unemployed working-class boy from Cardiff who became the poet's secretary and travelling companion. He also asserts his dislike of sexual labels, and his ultimate belief in the 'wholeness' of heterosexual love.

In 1937 Spender joined, briefly, the Communist Party and made two trips to Spain on behalf of the Republican cause. *Forward from Liberalism* (1937) reveals the politically divided man: seeking a position left of traditional liberalism, but fearing full commitment to the Communist cause. George Orwell considered him a 'sentimental sympathiser'. During the war he co-edited *Horizon* with Cyril Connolly, and began a gradual retreat from political action, though the events of 1968 were to revive his old passions.

In the post-war years Spender consolidated his reputation nationally and internationally as a critic, educator and humanist. He worked for UNESCO in Paris; co-edited *Encounter* from 1953 to 1967 (surviving the embarrassing revelation that the CIA had initially funded the journal); taught at Berkeley; translated Rilke, Schiller and Sophocles; served as consultant in poetry at the Library of Congress; was Professor of English Literature at University College London from 1970 to 1977; and in 1981 travelled to China with David Hockney. He was knighted in 1983.

Spender's *Collected Poems, 1928–85* (1985) reveal a poet 'always at the edge of being', uncertain and vulnerable, a position assailed by Thom Gunn in his poem 'Lines from a Book'. Spender's œuvre does not match the authority of Auden or MacNeice, though individual poems, such as 'Ultima Ratio Regum', with the dead Republican soldier 'a better target for a kiss', and 'One More New Botched Beginning', a farewell to friends lost, move us with their compassion and honesty. Yet his romantic sensibility is never quite able to contend with the complex century he otherwise magnificently survived. As a literary and cultural critic, and as a memoirist, his legacy is more permanent: *The Destructive Element* (1935), *The Struggle of the Modern* (1963), *Love-Hate Relations: A Study of Anglo-American Sensibilities* (1974), *The Thirties and After* (1978), *China Diary* (with David Hockney, 1982), *Journals 1939–83* (1985). David Leavitt used *World Within World* as a 'springboard' for *While England Sleeps* (1993), and Spender filed a copyright infringement suit. Leavitt's novel was withdrawn from sales but revised and reissued in 1995, the year of Spender's death.

H. David, *Stephen Spender*, London, 1992; S. Hynes, *The Auden Generation: Literature and Politics in the 1930s*, London, 1976; K. Weatherhead, *Stephen Spender and the Thirties*, Lewisburg, Penn., 1975; D. Leeming, *Stephen Spender: A Life in Modernism*, New York, 1999.
Roger Bowen

Stanislaw August II (1732–1798), Polish king. The last king of the Polish-Lithuanian Commonwealth was born Stanislaw Poniatowski, the son of a respected Polish diplomat of the minor aristocracy, and his wife, a member of the semi-royal Czartoryski family. His elected regency (1764–1795) followed a half-century of political near-anarchy under the Saxon Wettin dynasty. Despite his occasionally successful reforms, Stanislaw's position was dependent on Russia's formal protection of the Polish-Lithuanian polity, and the actual administration of government was done in uneasy convention with successive Russian ambassadors and in habitual discord with parliament (Sejm). It was during his reign that the Commonwealth's threefold partition by Prussia, Russia and Austria took place; Stanislaw is chiefly remembered for his weakness in the face of this political outrage, as well as for his lifelong emotional subservience to his former lover, Catherine the Great, who had arranged his election as regent.

Recent historians, however, have begun to reassess Stanislaw and his reign. In his own time, he was renowned throughout Europe as an exemplary, if inadequately tyrannical, Enlightened ruler; his personal kindness and generosity were legendary (see Casanova's lively account of Warsaw); and his court, which was a magnet for artists, architects and defrocked Jesuits, drew the attention of such luminaries as Voltaire and Rousseau. Stanislaw introduced to the Commonwealth educational reforms, a literary culture and public sphere, industry and a nascent sense of (Polish) national identity; he proclaimed the emancipation of Jews and supported that of peasants; and he declared the Constitution of 3 May 1791, the first national constitution of its kind in Europe; it affirmed Polish-Lithuanian sovereignty, threatened widespread political reform, and ultimately instigated the third and final dismemberment of the Commonwealth in 1795. Stanislaw abdicated in disgrace and died three years later in involuntary exile in St Petersburg.

By his own account, Poland's bachelor king was ambivalent about his sexuality: 'I did not feel that I was made for women; my first attempts seemed to me like a mere necessity to be accounted for by circumstances', he writes in his memoirs, describing himself before the famous affair with Catherine. The question of his personal life is, however, one that few historians have addressed with much objectivity. Prior to his life as monarch, the precocious, handsome and introspective Poniatowski, the diplomat's son, travelled widely throughout aristocratic Europe, establishing personal friendships and political alliances. The most important of these was with the English nobleman Sir Charles Hanbury Williams, a childhood friend of Henry Fielding and Horace WALPOLE, who was serving as ambassador to the court of FREDERICK the Great when Poniatowski met him, and was later transferred to Russia, where the future king joined him as his secretary. Williams, 24 years Poniatowski's senior, was a mentor and father-figure to the young Polish nobleman, educating him in the complexities of European diplomacy, and, in St Petersburg, aiding his dangerous liaison with the empress-to-be. Whether their own relationship was ever sexual is anybody's guess, but it is not implausible. Occasional suggestions to that effect have nevertheless inspired irate accusations of poor scholarship and 'rumour-mongering' that, not surprisingly, lay bare the accusers' own lack of insight into the complexity of human relations and the limits of historical interpretation. The lack of evidence corroborating either viewpoint makes it a pointless subject to dwell on, but the historiographical handling warrants a case study of its own. Neither man was a homosexual or a bisexual in a contemporary understanding of the term, but the emotional attachment they displayed for each other, recounted by Stanislaw in his memoirs, was intense even by eighteenth-century standards of friendship. The king continued to cherish the memory of Williams long after the latter's death, and had a portrait of his English friend in his boudoir at the time of his own death.

R. Butterwick, *Poland's Last King and English Culture*, Oxford, 1998; A. Zamoyski, *The Last King of Poland*, London, 1992; Stanislaw Poniatowski, *Die Memoiren des letzten Königs von Polen Stanislaw August Poniatowski*, Munich, 1917.

William E. Martin

Stanley, Sir Henry Morton (1841–1904), British explorer and writer. Stanley was the most famous nineteenth-century explorer, vaulted to world fame when, after a trek from Zanzibar to the shores of Lake Tanganyika, in 1871 he 'discovered' the missionary David Livingstone, who had been presumed lost forever in the heart of Africa. On subsequent expeditions in the 1870s, Stanley traced the Congo river from the African interior to the Atlantic coast and laid the ground for the establishment of the Congo Free State by the Belgian King Leopold II. In the late 1880s, he led an expedition to 'rescue' a European adventurer, Emin Pasha, who had secured a position as governor of Equatorial Sudan but had fallen into strife. Stanley's colourful accounts of his travels became instant bestsellers, and he was presented with numerous awards by geographical societies and given a knighthood by Queen Victoria; he was also elected to parliament.

Stanley's career began with humble origins, as he was born in Wales, the illegitimate son of a maid, and spent part of his childhood in a workhouse. He then found a job as cabin-boy on a ship which took him to New Orleans; he later fought on both sides during the American Civil War. In 1867 Stanley became a correspondent with a New York newspaper, working in Spain and Abyssinia before the editor sent him to 'find Livingstone'.

Stanley's biographers record that he was uneasy with any expression of sexuality. It is possible that he was sexually assaulted as an adolescent, and he fled in horror from a brothel to which a friend took him in New Orleans. While travelling in Turkey, he was closely linked to a youth whom he called his 'half-brother', a relationship which has been considered to have a homosexual aspect. He was three times engaged to be married, but in circumstances where the length of his absence overseas made intimate contacts impossible, and the engagements were broken off. Stanley finally married (an English painter) in 1890, though circumstantial evidence suggests that the union was never consummated.

In 1873, Stanley published his only novel, the now forgotten *My Kalulu, Prince, King and Slave*. The hero was modelled on an African boy whom Stanley had hired during one of his expeditions; the youth visited Europe with the explorer, who was evidently very fond of him, then accompanied Stanley back to Africa, where Kalulu drowned in an accident. The novel is the story of a close friendship between an African chief, Kalulu, and a Zanzibari 'Arab' prince, named Selim – the name of one of Stanley's translators. They brave warfare, animal attacks, slave-trading and other misfortunes, but swear undying loyalty to each other in a ceremony that reads almost as a caricature of a Christian marriage, and the book concludes with the pair together, presumably living happily ever after. The work, according to Stanley's preface, was written for 'those clever, bright-eyed, intelligent boys, of all classes, who have begun to be interested in romantic literature, with whom educated fathers may talk without fear of misapprehension'. A 'Boy's Own' tale, it also portrays the intimate friendship which Stanley never seems to have found in his own life.

A number of important figures in imperial history – Stanley, General George Gordon, Lord Kitchener, Cecil RHODES, LAWRENCE of Arabia, Sir Hector MACDONALD, Rajah Charles Brooke, among British political and military examples – seemed most at home in the masculine camaraderie of overseas expeditions, military barracks and colonial administrations. Some were emotionally attached to other European men, while others sought companionship among 'natives'. Several are known to have had homosexual liaisons, though others apparently redirected their physical urges. The empire provided sexual opportunities outside the bounds of European mores (for both homosexuals and heterosexuals), but the ethos of expansion – from the sports fields of public schools to the battlefields of foreign conquests – may well have had, for some, distinctly agreeable homosocial and homoerotic benefits.

F. McLynn, *Stanley: The Making of an African Explorer*, Oxford, 1991; J. Bierman, *Dark Safari: The Life Behind the Legend of Henry Morton Stanley*, London, 1990; R. Hyam, *Empire and Sexuality: The British Experience*, London, 1990; R. Aldrich, *Homosexuality and Colonialism*, London, forthcoming.

Robert Aldrich

Stein, Gertrude (1874–1946), American writer. Born in Pennsylvania, Stein lived most of her life in France (1902–1946). She was a student of the psychologist William James while at Radcliffe College and she also studied the anatomy of the brain at Johns Hopkins University. Unlike her modernist counterparts in the Bloomsbury group in London, who were interested in FREUD and psychoanalysis, Stein rejected Freud and favoured Havelock ELLIS's theory that the invert could never truly change any more than the object choice of heterosexuals could be changed to one that is homosexual. She and her partner of nearly 40 years, Alice B. TOKLAS, presided over a salon in the Rue de Fleurus in Paris from 1903 until 1937 which became an important meeting place for writers and painters of the time, including Ernest Hemingway, Sherwood Anderson, Pablo Picasso and Henri Matisse. Stein and Toklas moved to 5 Rue Christine (in the Odéon quarter of Paris) in 1938; the couple spent their summers in rural southeastern France in the 1930s, and moved there in 1939 when World War II broke out, remaining in this part of France, initially governed from Vichy following the Occupation in 1940, for the remainder of the war, even after Germany occupied all of France, which was potentially perilous for two Jewish American lesbians.

Though modernism as a distinct literary and artistic movement has generally lacked clear definition, the canon of literary modernists, with the exception of Virginia WOOLF, is still predominantly understood to consist of such representative male writers as D. H. LAWRENCE, T. S. Eliot, James Joyce, André GIDE, Ezra Pound, Marcel PROUST and W. B. Yeats. Many modernist writers, including lesbians, gay men, heterosexual women and people of colour have been misjudged, trivialised or altogether omitted from the study of modernism, including, for example, Vita SACKVILLE-WEST, Djuna BARNES, H. D. (Hilda DOOLITTLE) and Stein herself. It has also become common to associate (male) modernist writers with exile, as a means of escaping puritanical values and intense feelings of alienation from their homelands, families or religions. But as Karla Jay has pointed out, simply reading the early male modernists as 'rebels' and 'exiles' overlooks not only Pound's and Eliot's deep conservatism, but the ways in which exile was politically and artistically necessary for Sapphic modernists, like Stein, who were exiled by their gender, by their lesbo-erotic practices and by their growing sense of danger coming out of the legal and moral climates in England and the United States. Also important to consider are not only the abstract, innovative and highly experimental aspects of Stein's writing and her rupturing of conventional literary forms, which closely align her with other modernists, but the ways in which her own view of modernist writing and her avant-garde creative processes were intimately intertwined with her sexual identity and her gender.

Modernist lesbian writers like Stein did challenge conventional understandings of such categories as genre, narration and form, as well as standard forms of intelligibility, including grammar, meaning and language itself. But experimentation was not motivated merely by aesthetic 'art-for-art's sake' sentiments prevalent at the time, and by attention only to the literary work's textual features, a theory of literature developed by formalist critics in England (I. A. Richards) and later by the early American New Critics (John Crowe

Ransom). Stein's experimentation with language allowed her to carefully encode lesbian desire in her reformulations of language. If lesbian eroticism had to be written in a coded language, working within the code, as Margaret Dickie says, was a site of struggle in so far as Stein attempted to come to terms with her sexual identity and experience as she worked to find a means of writing it. *The Autobiography of Alice B. Toklas* (1933), which brought her international recognition, challenges conventional notions of genre in that it shifts *between* autobiography, biography and memoir, thereby successfully concealing the exact nature of Stein's relationship with Toklas, evident in the fact that many initial readers assumed that Toklas was either her secretary or a paid companion.

Other contemporary critics, such as Shari Benstock, have pointed out that Stein, similar to Woolf and H.D., often filtered the lesbian content of her writing through the grid of presumed heterosexual subject matter or through experimental literary styles. Stein's 'As a Wife Has a Cow: A Love Story', published in Paris in 1926, contains detailed depictions of lesbian sex, including orgasm, if the reader is able to carefully read and decode Stein's adverbial and participial style: 'Feeling or for it, as feeling or for it, came in or come in, or come out of there or feeling as feeling or feeling as for it. As a wife has a cow. Came in and come out. As a wife has a cow a love story.' 'Miss Furr and Miss Skeene', published in *Geography and Plays* (1922) and reprinted in *Vanity Fair* magazine in 1923, reveals that some women who had sex with other women in the 1920s did take on a lesbian identity and often referred to themselves as 'gay', as homosexual men did. But, as Lillian Faderman notes, the wide heterosexual readership of the story, especially when it was published in *Vanity Fair*, most likely assumed Stein's repetition of the word 'gay' was indicative of her quirky repetitive style or was an ironic commentary on the sad life of 'spinsters'. Stein writes: 'To be regularly gay was to do every day the gay thing that they did every day. To be regularly gay was to end every day at the same time after they had been regularly gay. They were regularly gay. They were gay every day. They ended every day in the same way, at the same time, and they had been every day regularly gay.' Another highly experimental work, *Tender Buttons* (1914) – especially the section 'Rooms' which blurs the distinction between poetry and prose – was an earlier attempt to work with substitution as a way of oscillating between what Stein wanted to conceal and reveal about lesbian eroticism and her relationship with Toklas. 'Rooms' begins: 'Act so that there is no use in a centre'; yet the other sections, 'Objects' and 'Food', also attempt to decentre (public) language and meaning and are interlaced with encodings of secret erotic passions in the bed(room) Stein shared with Toklas.

Stein also wrote an openly lesbian novel, *Q.E.D.*, very early in her literary career in 1903 though it was only published posthumously in 1950. Much of her writing is collected in *Selected Writings of Gertrude Stein* (1962). Stein died in 1946 and was buried in Père-Lachaise cemetery in Paris, as was Alice B. Toklas following her death in 1967.

S. Benstock, 'Expatriate Sapphic Modernism: Entering Literary History', in K. Jay and J. Glasgow (eds) *Lesbian Texts and Contexts: Radical Revisions*, New York, 1990: 183–203; M. Dickie, *Stein, Bishop, and Rich: Lyrics of Love, War, and Place*, Chapel Hill, NC, 1997; L. Faderman, 'What Is Lesbian Literature? Forming a Historical Canon', and K. Jay, 'Lesbian Modernism: (Trans)Forming the (C)Anon', in G. E. Haggerty and B. Zimmerman (eds) *Professions of Desire: Lesbian and Gay Studies in Literature*, New York, 1995: 49–59 and 72–83.
William J. Spurlin

Stiller, Mauritz (1883–1928), Swedish film and theatre director. Stiller was born a Jewish subject of imperial Russia, in Helsinki, Finland, to Hirsch Stiller and his wife Mindel (née Weissenberg). After the death of his parents early in his life, Stiller, along with his siblings, were scattered to different foster families. Stiller began his career in the theatre in Helsinki in 1899. He continued roles in local theatre until his arrest by and escape from the Russian army, which had determined to put him on trial for not fulfilling his military service. It was at this time, equipped with a false passport, that Stiller moved to Sweden, where he was to produce the lion's share of his cinematic work.

Stiller came to film after several years of sporadic theatrical employment both in Stockholm and in tours around the country, at which time he signed a contract with AB Svenska Biografteatern and began his impressive directorial career with six films in three months, including *När svärmor regerar* (*When Mother-In-Law Rules*) and *Vampyren* (*The Vampire*). This level of productivity continued unabated for the next three years with Stiller directing no fewer than five films per year until 1916.

In that year the film *Vingarna* (*The Wings*) was made, based on a novel, *Mikael*, by the celebrated Danish author and recognised homosexual Herman BANG. *Vingarna* is seen by many later viewers to be the first representation of homsexuality on film, though this interpretation is strongly disputed by other sources, including Gösta Werner, Stiller's Swedish biographer. Stiller's film is not a literal rendering of Bang's material but rather a film-within-a film, which frames the literary story with the meta-filmic additional story of a director (Stiller himself) seeking to cast and shoot the film of the same name. The story tells of an ageing artist whose younger protégé becomes enamoured of a beautiful woman upon whom he squanders much of his benefactor's fortune. Whether these relationships are disguised or encoded same-sex relationships, it is this interpretation which has ensured Stiller's mention in the history of homosexual representation in cinema. Despite the commercial failure of *Vingarna*, Stiller continued to produce an impressive number of films, and, together with Victor Sjöström, gave an international face to Swedish film.

One of Stiller's great strengths as a filmmaker lay in his understanding of the new medium's possibilities, and his films tell their stories with a visual directness and cohesion unusual for the time. In that period it was quite common for films to take their inspiration from literary and stage works, and to explain the images with textual exposition in the intertitles. Stiller used such titles sparingly and preferred to depict the action in energetic, dramatic sequences. Some of his most notable sequences are the man riding the log in *Sågen om den eldröda blomman* (*The Song of the Fire Red Flower*), the man dragged by a reindeer through the tundra in *Gunnar Hedessaga* (*The Saga of Gunnar Hede*), or the pursuit of Lars Hansson and Greta GARBO by a pack of 'wolves' over a frozen lake in *Gösta Berlingssaga* (*The Saga of Gösta Berling*). However, his temper was equal to his talent and there are many tales of tantrums thrown at all stages of production.

Stiller himself is still better known to cinema-goers as the man who discovered Greta Garbo, who became an international superstar after her appearance in Stiller's *Gösta Berlingssaga* in 1924. Stiller apparently had a Svengali-like role in Garbo's life, which included renaming her, and insisting on strict exercise and diet regimes. Rumours abounded at the time that the two were lovers; Garbo seems to confirm them in a ghost-written autobiography. The two travelled to the US together to pursue global fame through Hollywood. After some rocky episodes, Garbo achieved just that. Stiller was not so fortunate: after repeated conflicts with actors and studio executives, and now in failing health, he returned to Sweden, where he died.

Some of Stiller's other most enduring and remarkable works are *Thomas Graals bästa film* (1917), *Herr Arnes pengar* (1919) and *Erotikon* (1920).

Elizabeth De Noma

Stoddard, Charles Warren (1843–1909), American writer. Born in Rochester, New York, into a middle-class family that never understood his 'timid and sensitive' nature, Stoddard travelled throughout the United States with his family as his father sought employment. The Stoddards eventually settled in San Franscisco, where Charles was inspired by the literary life of the city. At an early age, he began publishing poems in the San Francisco magazine *Golden Era*, and through his connection with this publication he became friends with Bret Harte and Mark Twain. During this period, he also enrolled in San Francisco's City College, but soon found that the 'enticing diversions in San Francisco' proved too tempting and he never succeeded as a student.

Stoddard's first book, *Poems* (1867), edited by Bret Harte, was published prior to his South Pacific travels – travels that would inspire his future writing. During the 1870s, Stoddard journeyed to Hawaii and Tahiti, publishing *South-Sea Idyls* in 1873 (the 1874 English edition was titled *Summer Cruising in the South Seas*). These sketches may be read as merging fictional elements with Stoddard's autobiographical experiences in the South Seas; many of them are undoubtedly intended to evoke homosexual fantasy, while they also champion the sexual liberation that can be accessed in Hawaii and Tahiti. Hawaiian men are presented as primitive, effeminate and receptive to homosexual liaisons with American travellers. *South-Sea Idyls* was followed by *Hawaiian Life* (1894) and *The Island of Tranquil Delights* (1904), both of which represent the South Pacific as a 'golden space' where the nineteenth-century sexual tourist can indulge in 'forbidden delights'. Although they were at times marked by colonising rhetoric, Stoddard's South Sea sketches, published from 1873 to 1904, serve as important documents for tracking the development of a homosexual identity, for his sketches were influenced by, and influential on, turn-of-the-century sexual theories; Xavier MAYNE, for example, quoted from *South-Sea Idylls* in *The Intersexes*, his 1908 defence of homosexuality.

Stoddard's autobiographical novel, *For the Pleasure of his Company: An Affair of the Misty City* (1903), is the story of Paul Clitheroe's unsuccessful bout of writing, acting and love in turn-of-the-century San Francisco. Paul's life among the city's homosexual Bohemians proves unsatisfying, so he escapes American 'civilisation' by fleeing to the ideal South Seas accompanied by 'three naked islanders'. In this novel Stoddard implies that Paul's same-sex desires place him outside the norms of American culture; he must therefore seek out an alternative to the repressive patterns of nineteenth-century American thought and action.

Stoddard returned to the United States in 1885 to teach at the University of Notre Dame and the Catholic University of America. His other texts include *Mashallah!* (1880) and *A Cruise Under the Crescent* (1898), both of which chronicle his voyage to the Holy Land and Egypt; *Lepers of Molokai* (1885), about leper colonies in the South Pacific; and *A Troubled Heart* (1885), an autobiographical text which recounts his conversion to Catholicism.

R. Austen, *Genteel Pagan: The Double Life of Charles Warren Stoddard*, ed. John W. Crowle, Amherst, Mass., 1991.

Justin D. Edwards

Strachey, Lytton (1880–1932), British writer. Born to upper-class parents descended from aristocrats of the English Renaissance, the family was now at the end of its prominence; young Lytton grew up in a large household of many siblings and relatives. His mother, Lady Strachey, involved in many social issues, ran a weekly salon for relatives and friends, many of whom were intellectuals and scholars. Strachey was a precocious shy child who endured a miserable public school experience where he was harassed and physically abused because of his delicate physique, but once he arrived at Cambridge, he blossomed. He belonged to the élite society of the Apostles, which he and John Maynard KEYNES dominated. Bertrand Russell complained that the two men made 'homosexual infatuation' fashionable among the Apostles, which was 'unheard of' in his day. Strachey and Keynes were intimate friends; Strachey may have been in love with Keynes. Their intimacy broke over Duncan GRANT, Strachey's first lover, who left him for Keynes. Grant belonged to the Bloomsbury circle in which Strachey became a central figure. He and Virginia WOOLF were close friends, sometimes rivals. On one impulsive occasion, Strachey proposed marriage to Woolf, and to his amazement, she accepted. Both recovered quickly enough to realise their mistake. Later, Strachey met a young painter, Dora Carrington, who inexplicable fell madly in love with him despite his adamant claim that he could never love women sexually. Nevertheless, the two set up a country household and lived in mutual contentment with each other for the rest of their lives (Carrington committed suicide some months after Strachey's death from stomach cancer).

Strachey began book reviewing when he left Cambridge, living back in his parents' home, unable to entertain the idea of a conventional job. But the writing led to his first book (*Landmarks of French Literature*, 1912); encouraged, he embarked on his study of Victorian hypocrisy which took six years to write. *Eminent Victorians* (1918) was a huge international success, critically and financially, establishing Strachey as one of the most incisive, witty and iconoclastic historians. The royalties allowed Strachey, Carrington and her lover, Ralph Partridge, to live together and freed Strachey from money worries. His next book, *Queen Victoria* (1921), was a best-seller, as was *Elizabeth and Essex* (1928), though neither were critically admired.

While Strachey did not write about homosexuality, he articulated in his life and his work a sensibility that would later be called 'gay', founded on irony, disdainful wit, an ascerbic critical eye about society, that was the product of the writer's sense of alienation from the world he was born into. Strachey's voice, while inimitably his own, is like WILDE's, though Strachey's work and reputation were in a much more minor key. Like Wilde, he represented the spirit of his age, the Edwardians and Bloomsbury of the 1920s, and like Wilde, he died in his early fifties. But his was a life he rescued from the self-destructiveness that drove Wilde, and while he had much homophobic contempt to deal with, he enjoyed a freedom from fear and confusion about his sexuality that made him a forerunner of modern homosexual experience.

M. Holroyd, *Lytton Strachey, A Critical Biography*, 2 vols, London, 1967.

Seymour Kleinberg

Straton of Sardis (*fl. c.* AD 125), Greek epigrammatist. On the basis of an allusion in one of his poems (*AP* xi. 117), Straton is thought to have written in the reign of HADRIAN (117–138). A later manuscript annotation states that he came from the city of Sardis (Sardes) in the fertile Hermus valley in Asia Minor (present-day Turkey). All else that is known of Straton (also anglicised as Strato) derives from the collection of his pederastic epigrams known as the *Mousa Paidikē* (*The Boyish Muse*), which is preserved in Book XII of the Greek Anthology, and a few more of his epigrams misplaced in Book XI. Book XII gathers together 258 pederastic epigrams of which 94 are by Strato; it is headed *Straton the Sardian's Mousa Paidikē*, and the introduction by Cephalas seems to imply that all are by him. At some stage, an editor must have greatly expanded the

Stratonic corpus with pederastic poems by 28 named and an unknown number of anonymous poets, while retaining the original title, introduction and ending.

The final epigram in Book XII is a concluding poem by Straton, disclaiming the 'pains of love' recorded in his 'trifles' and pretending that he simply scribbled them off for 'this or that boy-lover (*philópais*)'. However, the reality is that Straton celebrates the love of 'boys', *paides*, adolescent or teenaged males; he declares proudly that he is a boy-lover and a 'lover of youth'. In one of his epigrams, he says: 'I delight in twelve-year-olds, while a thirteen-year-old is much more desirable; he who is twice seven years old is a sweeter flower of the Loves; he who is beginning his fifteenth year is still more delightful; the sixteenth is the year of the gods; to seek the seventeenth is not for me but for Zeus.'

In pithy, sometimes witty epigrams, he deals with the joys and trials, the disappointments and fulfilments of being a boy-lover, and the beauties, foibles and annoyances of beloved boys. In short, the poems allow readers to enter into the mind and world of a Greek pederast, one who has nothing on his mind but boys, love and sex (and who is to contemporary ways of thinking anti-woman). He is appreciative of all kinds of youthful male beauty and, like all Greeks, is especially responsive to a shapely arse, devoting two of his wittiest poems to the topic.

Traditionally Straton's epigrams have received scant and scornful attention from literary critics and historians not only because of their overt and exultant homoeroticism but also because of their sexual explicitness – their 'indecency', their 'pornographic' quality. Some poems treat foreplay; two poems deal with his boyfriend's penis. Another witty poem describes his discovery of two boys masturbating; another, a stunningly beautiful prickteaser with a gorgeous arse who keeps him awake at night, yearning and masturbating to gain relief. But by far the greater number of sexually explicit poems deal with anal intercourse, which was his goal in sexual relations. The tone varies from the blunt through the punning to the metaphorical and witty. He was so pleased with his conceit about Lucky Pierre – the paradox of having two active and two passive partners, yet only three players – that he wrote two versions of it.

In the Introduction to Book XII Cephalas insists on the literary quality of Straton's poems, and Straton himself in the concluding epigram seeks to underplay his work's autobiographical content. Writing in the early second century AD, Straton saw himself as continuing a poetic tradition that was already several centuries old, as is apparent from both the form and content of his work and deliberate echoes of earlier poets. It follows then that it would be mistaken to read each and every poem as the autobiographical record of a particular experience, though some epigrams may well be 'confessional'. Their truthfulness lies in their reflection of the mind and sentiments of a pederast, Straton, and their record of the sorts of things he and men like him felt and thought and did.

A. Reid (trans.) 'Strato's Anthology', *The Eternal Flame: A World Anthology of Homosexual Verse (2000 B.C.–2000 A.D.)*, New York, 1992: Vol. I, pp. 27–99; R. Peyrefitte (trans.) *La muse garçonnière*, Paris, 1973; P. G. Maxwell-Stuart, 'Strato and the Musa Puerilis', *Hermes*, 100 (1972): 116–40; A Cameron, *The Greek Anthology from Meleager to Planudes*, Oxford, 1993.

Gary Simes

Strayhorn, Billy (1915–1967), American jazz musician and composer. Born in Dayton, Ohio, William Thomas Strayhorn was raised in Hilsboro, North Carolina. Through his life, he always stood out from the crowd with his tiny frame and horn-rimmed glasses. He had several nicknames, but most friends called him 'Swee Pea' after the baby in the Popeye cartoons.

As a teenager, Strayhorn was a dandy who spoke fluent French, subscribed to the *New Yorker* and graduated from his Pittsburgh high school by playing Grieg's *A Minor Concerto* with the school orchestra. He was almost 20 before he heard the Duke Ellington Orchestra and, in 1938, he submitted work to Ellington, who soon began recording Strayhorn's compositions. In 1939, after Strayhorn had played piano in Mercer Ellington's band, he joined Ellington on a permanent basis as an assistant arranger, co-composer and occasional pianist. They were to remain 'soulmates' and collaborators for 28 years. Though he rarely appeared with the Duke Ellington Orchestra in public, Strayhorn was responsible for 'Life', 'Chelsea Bridge', 'Satin Doll', 'Johnny Come Lately' and 'Raincheck'.

In 1942 Strayhorn began a close and intimate friendship with the singer Lena Horne, and in 1965 she described their first encounter in her autobiography, *Lena*: 'A pixie, brown color, horn-rimmed glasses, beautifully cut suit, beautifully modulated speaking voice, appeared as if by magic and said "I'm Billy Strayhorn – Swee Pea". We looked at each other, clasped hands . . . and I loved him. We became one another's alter egos. . . . I had a friend.' In June 1993 Horne topped the bill at a tribute to Strayhorn in the JVC Jazz Festival in New York. She also featured several Strayhorn compositions on an album she recorded that year called *We'll Be Together Again*. These included 'Maybe', 'Something to Live For', 'A Flower is a Lovesome Thing', the celebratory 'You're the One', as well as a sassy 'Love Like This Can't Last'. Though Horne was always aware that Strayhorn was gay, she revealed in an interview at this time: 'We never discussed sexuality at all. I wasn't throwing off a lot of femininity and he wasn't throwing off a lot of macho. It was more like brother and sister.' Says Strayhorn's biographer, David Hajdu: 'He was in a minority among gay people in that he was open about his homosexuality in an era when social bias forced many men and women to keep their sexual identities secret.'

Ellington was devastated when Strayhorn became ill with cancer in 1965. 'Blood Count', Billy's final work, was written during the last stages of his final illness. He died in New York City at the age of 52. Three months later, Ellington included 'Blood Count' on a tribute album he recorded called *And His Mother Called Him Bill*. He also wrote the following eulogy: 'He was a beautiful human being, adored by a wide range of friends. . . . He had no aspiration to enter into any kind of competition, yet the legacy he leaves, his *œuvre*, will never be less than the ultimate on the highest plateau of culture. . . . God bless Billy Strayhorn.'

D. Hajdu, *Lush Life – A Biography of Billy Strayhorn*, London, 1996.

Stephen Bourne

Strindberg, August (1849–1912), Swedish writer and dramatist. In one of his earliest texts, Strindberg makes mention of sodomitical sin and vows to deal with it in his works. The first of his stories to stir public debate on this issue was 'The Rewards of Virtue' in *Getting Married I* (1884), in which one of the consequences of the unnatural separation of the sexes before marriage was homosexuality. In the follow-up to that work, titled *Getting Married II* (1886), Strindberg provided more comprehensive explanations for the existence of homosexuality in the short story 'Criminal Nature', such as his suggestions that it is an occupational illness among sailors and monks, and that homosexuality should not be a crime. The next year, in the article 'The Last Word on the Question of Women' (1887), he clearly indicated a rising concern that the levelling of difference between the genders could lead to same-sex desire between men and – for the first time – between women. Not surprisingly, the radical content of his writing did not go unnoticed. Well known

polemicists, such as John Personne, Emil Svensén, Seved Ribbing and Knut Wicksell, all tackled the problems of sexual immorality including homosexuality in Strindberg's texts. The reading public was also quick to notice that these concerns were very current in Strindberg's own life, as he went through a divorce from his first wife, Siri von Essen, claiming that her lesbian escapades made her an unfit mother.

The texts written prior to the crisis described in *Inferno* (1897) – a time marked by psychological instability, mysticism and lack of artistic productivity – sought not only to explain the existence of homosexuality, but also to provide clues on how to spot those who did indeed practise the vice. One example is the posthumously published essay written in French, titled 'Perverts' (1894). By writing in French, Strindberg also hoped to protect his children and those closest to him in Sweden when, among other indiscretions, he described his wife and her friends as lesbians (in *A Madman's Defence*, 1895). Strindberg's preoccupation with homosexuality caught the attention of certain foreign sexologists, such as Otto de Joux, whose insinuations that Strindberg himself was the prototype of an urning drove Strindberg to go on the defensive in *Legends* (1898).

The post-*Inferno* works shifted dramatically in that the tone, as opposed to seeking to explain or study homosexuality, now condemned and mocked it. Strindberg accused many of his closest friends of expressing unnatural intimacy towards him and provided fictive accounts of their actions in works such as *Black Banners* and *A Blue Book*. Strindberg was undoubtedly the influence which drove some of these same friends to depict homosexual characters in their own works prior to the fiery break-ups which ensued. Adolf Paul is one such friend; his short play in *The Ripper* (1892) called *You Know What They Say About* . . . is most likely the first play ever written in Swedish to focus on homosexuality. While scholars for the past one hundred years have at times attempted to explain Strindberg's own sexual inclinations by having recourse to his texts and biography, the work on exploring the impact Strindberg had on creating social debate and discussion surrounding the topic of homosexuality is only now beginning.

O. de Joux, *Die Enterbten des Liebesglücks oder Das dritte Geschlecht*, Berlin, 1897.

Matthew M. Roy

Stuart, Henry (1725–1807), Cardinal of York and last Stuart pretender to the English throne. Born in Rome (where he lived and died), the son of James Edward Stuart, the 'Old Pretender', he set out on an ecclesiastical career. Only when his brother Charles Edward, the 'Young Pretender', died childless did he succeed as claimant to the throne. His private life had no dramatic features other than the fact of his descent from a line of dispossessed sovereigns and a lack of discretion in his homosexual affairs.

Stuart's attachment to youthful favourites was known to those around him, as noted by the diarist Hester Lynch Thrale (1741–1821): 'Old Cardinal de [*sic*] York kept a Catamite publicly at Rome while I was there, tho' a man of the best character possible, for Piety & Charity: with which – as a Person said to me – that Vice has nothing to do. They consider it a matter of taste.' Such evidence was confirmed by the (homosexual) diplomat and writer Giuseppe Gorani (1740–1819), who met Stuart at his palace in 1793 – and, unlike Thrale, found him arrogant and despised by the populace: 'Everybody should shrink from making rash judgements: I like to unmask hypocritical people, but I want to have clear proof. Therefore I shall just tell what I saw without the pretension to draw conclusions from it. His palace seemed to me filled with young men of a very comely appearance, dressed as abbots. This led me to suspect that this Royal Eminence could have the taste with which some of his brethren are accused. Nevertheless, having

not had the opportunity to ask these young people, I did not gather any proof that could confirm my suspicion.' In reality, Gorani's 'suspicion' was a certainty, so well known that even the strongly pro-Catholic writer Gaetano Moroni could not cover up an incident which occurred in 1752 between the 27-year-old cardinal and his father (known among supporters as James III): 'King James III was displeased by the great favour accorded by the cardinal to Monsignor Lercari, his majordomo, therefore he let it be understood that he wanted him dismissed from his service. The cardinal, who loved him exceedingly, secretly continued in his friendship, meeting him in arranged places. This only further irritated the king, and he asked the pope to have Lercari sent far away from Rome.' In order to avoid scandal, Pope Benedict XIV asked Cardinal Lercari, the uncle of the young monsignor, to suggest that he return to his native Genoa for a while. When young Lercari declined, the pope ordered him to leave. 'The cardinal [York] considered himself much offended and the following night, he too left for Nocera, swearing never again to set foot in Rome unless Monsignor Lercari had been returned to him. . . . The pope sent letters pleading with him to consider a situation in which the heretics would triumph in seeing such discord between a cardinal of the holy church and a prince so . . . respected for . . . his virtue.' Faced with such pressure from the pope himself, the young cardinal had no choice other than to return to Rome and seek reconciliation with his father.

Only after the pope's death was Stuart able to pursue his loves. Moroni admitted that 'he liked having in his Court handsome and tall people, as is appropriate for great Princes'. Particularly close to him from 1769 onwards was Monsignor Angelo Cesarini, a nobleman from Perugia, who, thanks to Stuart's protection, won various honours, was made canon of the cathedral in Frascati (near Rome) and finally, in 1801, became bishop of Milevi.

When Stuart died, Cesarini was still at his side, just as he had been for 40 years. This suggests that their liaison represented one of the longest (and, one supposes, happiest) relationships between men known in history; even when their erotic relationship might have ended, Cesarini remained Stuart's friend and confidant.

The cardinal of York is buried in St Peter's basilica in the Vatican; a famous tomb in it was sculpted by Antonio Canova for the last three descendents of the Stuart family.

D. Anelli, *Storia romana di trent'anni, 1770–1800*, Milan, 1931: 98–108; G. Gorani, *Mémoires secrets et critiques des cours, des gouvernements et des moeurs des principaux états de l'Italie*, Vol. 2, Paris, 1793: 100–2; G. Moroni, *Dizionario di erudizione storico-ecclesiastica*, Vol. 103. Venice, 1861: 324–30; H. Lynch Thrale, *Thraliana: The Diary of Mrs Hester Lynch Thrale (later Mrs Piozzi)*, Vol. 2 Oxford, 1951: 874–5.

Giovanni Dall'Orto

Suetonius (Gaius Suetonius Tranquillus) (*c.* AD 70 – *after* 122), Roman biographer. Suetonius's official career in Rome culminated in an appointment at the imperial palace under Trajan, from which he was dismissed by HADRIAN in 121–122. This position gave access to the imperial archives, which Suetonius seems to have used extensively in the accounts he published of Julius CAESAR and Augustus. These are the first two of twelve 'Lives of the Caesars' chronicling Rome's emperors down to the death of DOMITIAN in 96. Characterised by a fondness for anecdote, these lives are a rich source for personal details intended to illustrate the virtues, or vices, of each individual. To Suetonius are owed details of the activities of TIBERIUS on Capri (*Tiberius* 43–4), the depravity of Caligula (*Gaius* 24, 36), NERO's 'marriages' to Sporus and Doryphorus (*Nero* 28–9), and more. He is especially informative about the appearance of each of his subjects, in accordance with contemporary views about physical traits revealing character. In addition to these 'Lives of the Caesars', Suetonius published lives of famous men, specifically grammarians, rhetoricians and poets, some of which survive. The life of VIRGIL attributed to him informs us that Virgil was prone to passions for boys, and even names two, Cebes and Alexander (*Virgil* 9). Of his own personal life, nothing is known beyond the allegation that his dismissal from the imperial service was in some way connected with an indiscretion involving the empress.

Suetonius does not satisfy modern expectations of historical accuracy in biography, so has very often been dismissed as a gossip with a taste for the unsavoury. True though this might be, it fails to take account of Suetonius's intention, which was to focus on the personal in order to reveal the complexity of individuals. The salacious details are never the whole story; they are used to provide evidence for the way in which vice tends to overcome virtue. This attitude is in accord with a Roman view of history which interprets the present as inferior to the past, and preserves stories (e.g. the rape of Lucretia) to illustrate the interconnections between personal morality and politics.

Suetonius, *Lives of the Caesars and Extracts from Lives of Illustrious Men*, trans. J. C. Rolfe, 2 vols, London, 1914; Suetonius, *The Twelve Caesars*, trans. R. Graves, Harmondsworth, 1957; A. Wallace-Hadrill, *Suetonius*, London, 1983.

Roger Pitcher

Suffren de Saint-Tropez, Pierre-André (1729–1788), French admiral. Suffren, born in Saint-Cannat, became one of the great seamen of the eighteenth century, notably as captain of a French ship during the American War of Independence, then as commander of the French fleet in the Indian Ocean. On several occasions he fought the British, near Cape Verde, off the coast of Madras, and elsewhere. In addition to his fame in battle, he was well known for the attention he gave to the conditions of sailors under his command, including provisions for food and medical care. This solicitude – rare among military leaders of his time – was perhaps not unconnected with the homosexuality which he openly and serenely practised.

The commander was always surrounded by handsome young sailors, 'Suffren's *mignons*'; he encouraged homosexuality aboard his ships and favoured 'cruising and campaign marriages' facilitated by the sharing of bunks between two seamen. Indeed, he enjoyed matching up older and younger sailors, declaring that 'men married to each other will behave the best in combat. They will help each other. They are always in good spirits.'

Suffren died in mysterious circumstances, killed by stab wounds in the gardens of Versailles.

C. Manceron, *Les Hommes de la liberté*, Paris, 1977; M. Bertrand, *Suffren de Saint-Tropez aux Indes*, Paris, 1991; F. Hulot, *Suffren, 'L'Amiral Satan'*, Paris, 1994.

Didier Godard

Symonds, John Addington (1840–1893), British art historian, literary critic, translator, unsuccessful poet and discreet advocate for homosexuality. Symonds was born the son of a wealthy doctor in Bristol. As with many men of his class, Symonds's attraction to men was denied any straightforwardly sexual outlet by the intense homophobia of his time. After early explorations with obliging male cousins, the sexual and emotional repression of his early years at Harrow and Oxford was interrupted only by brief but intense friendships with young men. His father's stern disapproval of such 'unseemly' relationships was fixed for ever in Symonds's mind by his own part in the downfall of Dr VAUGHAN, a former headmaster at Harrow. Vaughan had sexual relationships with a number of the boys in his charge, including a close friend of Symonds. When Symonds betrayed this secret to a family friend, the ensuing scandal led, partly at the insistence of Symonds senior, to Vaughan's resignation.

Symonds's long struggle to come to terms with his sexuality took place at first mainly through poetry and art. Here his feelings for men could be explored with some degree of safety. Poets like BYRON, Swinburne, TENNYSON – particularly the latter's *In Memoriam* – and, above all, Walt WHITMAN, all expressed feelings that seemed to reach beyond the bounds of socially accepted male friendship. As for so many before him, a second avenue of self-acceptance was provided by an early encounter with PLATO's *Symposium* and other works of classical Greek culture, which treated love between men as something unremarkable. Both influences played a role in Symonds's long-standing fascination with the Italian Renaissance, which revived the humanist learning and pagan culture of the ancient world along with its appealing ideals of male beauty. This period was to provide the subjects for much of his critical and historical writing, including his seven-volume *The Renaissance in Italy* (1875–1886), his translation of the *Autobiography* of Benvenuto CELLINI (1888) and the *Life of Michelangelo Buonarroti* (1892). After 1877 Symonds lived with his wife and children mainly in the Swiss spa town of Davos, hoping to alleviate his chronic tuberculosis. He also travelled frequently to Italy, where he could pursue his artistic, historical and sexual interests with greater convenience. The gondolier Angelo Fusato was his lover from 1881 until his (Symonds's) death.

Apart from his dogged literary endeavours, which never received the recognition achieved by acquaintances like Swinburne and Walter PATER, Symonds was able to make an important contribution to the understanding of 'homosexuality', a term whose use in English he also pioneered. Written in 1873, his essay *A Problem in Greek Ethics* addressed one of the central paradoxes of nineteenth-century British culture, which revered

Greek art, philosophy and literature whilst deploring its sexual mores. *A Problem in Modern Ethics* (1891) goes further, reviewing a wide range of religious, historical, anthropological and literary arguments on sexual 'inversion'. Symonds also discusses the growing psychological and medical literature, notably KRAFFT-EBING's *Psychopathia Sexualis* (1889), which tended to emphasise the 'inborn' or congenital nature of the 'inverted sexual instinct'. His own views are considerably influenced by Karl Heinrich ULRICHS's complex classification of sexual types and famous explanation of the homosexual behaviour or the 'Urning' as the manifestation of a 'female soul in a male body'. Arguing cautiously only for decriminalisation of this 'sport of nature', Symonds is at pains to emphasise the 'anti-sexual' bias of the Urning, who is more interested in intense friendships than in sodomy, who is not necessarily effeminate, and who has no inclination to corrupt minors.

It is difficult to estimate the influence of Symonds's privately printed and sparsely circulated pamphlets on 'the problem' of homosexuality. Their impact can scarcely be distinguished from the subtle personal influence Symonds was able to exert through a multitude of friendships and extensive, if carefully worded, correspondence with many eminent contemporaries. These included philosophers like Benjamin Jowett, T. H. Green and Henry Sidgwick, literary figures such as Walter Pater, Edmund GOSSE, Swinburne, Walt WHITMAN, Henry JAMES and Robert Louis Stevenson, as well as co-workers in the field of sexuality such as Karl Ulrichs and Havelock ELLIS. Although his wife Catherine and close friends Horatio Brown and Henry Sidgwick prudishly suppressed the more revealing passages of Symonds's autobiography, his life is amply documented in Phyllis Grosskurth's excellent biography.

J. A. Symonds, *A Problem in Greek Ethics: Being an Inquiry into the Phenomenon of Sex-*ual Inversion, 1883; J. A. Symonds, 'A Problem in Modern Ethics' (1891), in D. W. Cory, *Homosexuality: A Cross Cultural Approach*, New York, 1956: 3–100; P. Grosskurth, *John Addington Symonds: A Biography*, London, 1964; J. Weeks, *Coming Out: Homosexual Politics in Britain from the Nineteenth Century to the Present*, London, 1977: Chapter 4.

David West

Szymanowski, Karol (1882–1937), Polish composer. Born into a cultured landed family, the young Szymanowski was able to travel widely from his base at the family estate in Tymoszówka (Ukraine). His early compositions, influenced by Chopin and Scriabin, helped win him the close friendship of such contemporaries as conductor Gregor Fitelberg, violinist Paul Kochanski and pianist Arthur Rubinstein, all lifelong advocates of his music, and all heterosexual. However, it was in the company of the young heir to a chemical fortune, Stefan Spiess (Rubinstein referred to him as Szymanowski's 'close and helpful friend') that he undertook personally formative tours to Italy and Sicily, Algiers and Tunis. Of a visit to Taormina (probably in 1914), he told Rubinstein: 'I saw a few young men bathing who could be models for Antinous. I couldn't take my eyes off them.' From then on, a hitherto Germanic stamp in his music was replaced by the orientalising aesthetic of his middle period, epitomised in his *Third Symphony* (1914–1916) with its setting of a poem by the thirteenth-century Arab mystic Jalal'al-Din Rumi. Not without homoerotic overtones, the last lines of this exotic text read: 'Silence binds my tongue / But I speak without a tongue tonight.'

In autumn 1917, the Szymanowski estate at Tymoszówka was razed to the ground during peasant riots. Many of the composer's early works were destroyed, but Szymanowski himself was in Kiev at the time. On his return in 1918 he resettled with his family in nearby Elisavetgrad, a town he found ugly and the antithesis of his beloved Mediterranean, and remained there through the Austrian occupation until the end of 1919. Meanwhile, he took solace working on the scenario for his opera, *King Roger* (completed in 1926), an evocation of Sicily under the Norman king Roger II (1095–1154), his *Songs of the Infatuated Muezzin* (1918), and on a thematically related novel. Two years in the writing (1917–1919) and titled *Efebos*, the novel recalled his own visits to Italy in the travels and homosexual romances of his central character, Prince Ali Lowicki. Never published, the novel was thought to have been lost during World War II. However, an account of its plot was published by Szymanowski's cousin and collaborator on *King Roger* and the *Songs*, the poet Jaroslav IWASZKIEWICZ, in 1947, and a fragment was published by Teresz Chylinska (1981). Palmer reported on a further 150 pages discovered in Paris in Russian translation. The later stages of his sojourn in Elizavetsgrad were further ameliorated by the arrival of a young Russian refugee, Boris Kochno (1904–1991), and his mother. In later remarks to Rubinstein, Szymanowski makes it clear that he and Kochno ('a young man of extraordinary beauty') shared a brief affair, decisive for Szymanowksi's sexual self-image and work (referring probably to his work on *Roger*, he said: 'It's only thanks to our love that I could write so much music'). When Szymanowski finally engineered Kochno's escape to Warsaw, however, the pair totally lost contact, leaving the composer discon-solate. In October 1920 Szymanowski embarked on a European tour. Meeting him in Paris, Rubinstein found him greatly changed ('now he was a confirmed homosexual') and reeling from his recent love affair. Disappointment was in store, however, when during a meeting with DIAGHILEV, Szymanowski discovered that Kochno was now also in Paris as the impresario's secretary and, apparently, lover.

Rubinstein describes the mature Szymanowski as suffering from agoraphobia and hypersensitivity to noise. He also called him 'the victim of his family', and it was partly because of their financial needs that Szymanowksi unwillingly accepted the directorship of the Warsaw Conservatory in 1927 over a similar offer from Cairo. During this final 'Polish' period, fired by a renewed interest in national folklore and culture, he completed his *Stabat Mater* (1926), the *Veni Creator* (1930) and *Second Violin Concerto* (1933). By this time, financial stress and the effects of childhood tuberculosis were taking a heavy toll. He died in a sanatorium in Lausanne aged 54.

A. Rubinstein, *My Young Years*, New York, 1973; A. Rubinstein, *My Many Years*, London, 1990; B. M. Maciejewski, *Karol Szymanowski: His Life and Music*, London, 1967; T. Chylinska, *Szymanowski*, Krakow, 1981; C. Palmer, *Szymanowksi*, London, 1983.

Graeme Skinner

T

Tallemant des Réaux, Gédéon (1619–1690), French gossip. Tallemant was born in La Rochelle, the son of a Huguenot (Protestant) banker. He is considered (with the exception of the Duc de Saint-Simon) the wittiest anecdotalist in French literature. His razor wit bubbles through every vignette, but he was also a refined psychologist and analyst of human motivation. He was probably not gay, but is the source for much of what we know about homosexuals in the seventeenth century, and he was extremely attentive to the sexual mores of his contemporaries. Thus he reports, for example, that the Abbé BOIS-ROBERT boasted of having been sodomised twice by Madame de Piémont's lackey.

Tallemant is an important source of information on Louis XIII. He suggests that Marie de' Médici had deliberately attempted to enfeeble her son by rendering him effeminate (as it was suggested Anne of Austria later did in the case of PHILIPPE d'Orléans). The king's first affections were for Saint-Amour, his coach driver, then Haran, his kennel-master. After which came the Duc de Luynes, then Barradas and Monsieur de Cinq-Mars (allegedly selected for him as an amusement by Cardinal Richelieu). The king drew Cinq-Mars into bed as early as seven o'clock, Tallemant reported in his *Historiettes* (not published until 1834), and was seen covering his hands with kisses before he could get in. When at war, Louis XIII had reports of Cinq-Mars's health sent several times a day. None of this prevented Cinq-Mars being beheaded. Louis XIII did not often share a bed with Anne of Austria. Efforts were early made to interest him in women, but seem to have been largely unavailing. He did, however, profess love for women, but as a chaste admiration. On one occasion the Abbé Boisrobert was moved to celebrate such an infatuation in verse. The king objected to the words 'with desire' on the grounds that he desired nothing. Boisrobert obligingly amended the line to 'without desire'.

W. W. Victor, *Tallemant des Réaux: The Man through his Style*, The Hague, 1969; E. Gosse, *Tallemant des Réaux: or, The Art of Miniature Biography*, Oxford, 1925.

David Parris

Tardieu, Auguste-Ambroise (1818–1879), French medical doctor and forensic expert. Tardieu helped shape negative professional attitudes toward homosexuality in France. Born in Paris, son of a celebrated engraver, Tardieu received his medical degree in 1843. His was an illustrious career. He served on the Paris municipal council, received many awards and honours, including the Legion of Honour, and published numerous books and articles. He was appointed professor of forensic medicine at the Faculty of Medicine in Paris in 1861 and dean of the faculty three years later.

Tardieu was a social conservative. In 1871, writing under the pen-name 'Démophile', he advocated a heavy tax on bachelors and childless widowers over 30 in order to encourage population growth: 'The bachelor is not only a sterile being, he is also a bad example and even more an agent of corruption. . . . Whereas the family consolidates the social edifice, bachelorhood is an active agent of destruction.'

Tardieu is remembered chiefly for one book, *A Medico-Legal Study of Indecent Assaults*, the third section of which dealt with pederasty and sodomy (then the common words for what would later be termed homosexuality). It went through seven editions between 1857 and 1878, and found a prominent place on the bookshelves of doctors, jurists and policemen. Tardieu wrote in the context of stepped-up police surveillance of Parisian pederasts as a result of several public scandals in the 1840s and 1850s. His work also reflected growing concerns about the supposed link between homosexuality and criminality, and cited with approval the public prosecutor who declared in 1845 that 'in Paris pederasty is the school in which the most skilled and most daring criminals are formed'. Under these circumstances, the courts often called upon doctors to establish whether or not an arrested man was a pederast. Based on his examination of 300 homosexuals of various ages and professions, Tardieu argued that the bodies of almost all of them carried 'material traces' of their sexual activities. Those with 'passive habits' (receptive anal intercourse) displayed buttocks that were 'wide, protruding, often enormous and entirely feminine in shape', and especially a funnel-shaped deformation of the anus, which constituted 'the unique and only true mark of pederasty'. The sign of 'active habits' (penetrative anal intercouse) was either a 'dog-like' penis, excessively slender and narrowing to a point, or a thick club-shaped penis that was often also twisted and deformed. As for 'certain individuals who lower themselves to [per-

forming] the most abject services' (fellatio), they normally had crooked mouths, short teeth and thick lips.

Tardieu did not explore in any detail the causes of homosexuality, but he did not believe that homosexuals were mentally or physically ill. Pederasty was a 'moral perversion' for which men were entirely accountable: 'However incomprehensible, however contrary to nature and reason acts of pederasty may seem, they cannot escape the responsibility of their conscience, nor the just severity of the laws, nor, above all else, the contempt of upstanding people.'

Tardieu died in Paris. According to one obituary, 'He had conquered first place in forensic medicine, and intervened in all the famous trials [of his day]. . . . A life of hard work was crowned by a Christian death.'

Démophile, *Proposition d'un impôt sur le célibat*, Saint-Etienne, 1871; A. Tardieu, *Une Etude médico-légale sur les attentats aux moeurs*, Paris, 1857–1878; G. Vapereau, *Dictionnaire universelle des contemporains*, Paris, 1880; obituary in *Polybiblion: Revue bibliographique universelle*, January–June 1879; V. Rosario, *The Erotic Imagination: French Histories of Perversity*, New York, 1997.

Michael Sibalis

Tasso, Torquato (1544–1595), Italian poet. Son of the poet and scholar Bernardo Tasso, Torquato Tasso studied law in Padua and Bologna. In 1565, he entered the service of Cardinal Luigi d'Este, first in Ferrara, and then, in 1570–1571, in Paris, where he came into contact with the 'Pléiade' poets. In 1572 he joined the court of Duke Alfonso II d'Este, who appreciated his literary talents and made Tasso official historian of Ferrara in 1576. The previous year, however, Tasso began to display symptoms of paranoia and in 1577, claiming to be the victim of continuing conspiracies, he fled the court. He returned to Ferrara in 1579 but his behaviour proved so erratic that he was confined to an asylum, where he remained until 1586. He then began a period of frenetic travel around various Italian cities, the moves made possible partly by the fame which his poetry – especially the heroic epic poem *La Gerusalemme liberata* (1580) – had obtained for him. (Some of his verses were even set to music by the greatest composers of the era, such as Sigismondo d'India and Claudio Monteverdi.) Tasso was still on the move when he died in 1595 in the Sant'Onofrio monastery in Rome (where he is buried).

Tasso is considered one of the most important figures in Italian literature, a status which in the past guaranteed a hostile reception to any suggestion of his homosexuality. Only on the four-hundredth anniverary of his death (1995) did one scholar, Sandra Gianattasio, admit: 'Tasso had a stormy relationship with the young courtesan Orazio Orlando. ... He was a victim of the Counter-Reformation, both from the point of his sexual inclinations (which he was obliged to repress) and from an intellectual point of view.' The outbreak of his paranoia has been seen, in Freudian terms, as linked with the repression of his sexual impulses.

It is not surprising that a person such as Tasso, who suffered from a persecution complex and who presented himself before the Inquisition in Bologna fearing for his own doctrinal orthodoxy, exercised a fanatical reserve in his life and writings. Nevertheless, this self-censorship did not completely hide several traces of his feelings. In addition to a sonnet addressed 'A un leggiardo giovinetto' ('To a Handsome Lad'), not included in modern editions of his complete works, Tasso wrote a revealing letter on 14 December 1576, six months before coming down with mental illness. He confessed his love for the 21-year-old Orazio Ariosto: 'I love him, and I shall love him for some months, for too strong was the impression that Love made in my soul to erase it in a few days, though he offends me; nevertheless, I hope time will cure my soul from this lovesickness.

... I call this "love" rather than "benevolence" because, in sum, it is love, although I did not realise it previously, and I did not want to realise it, because I did not feel in me any of those appetites that Love usually brings, not even in bed, where we had slept together. But now I clearly realise that I have been and I am not a friend, but a very honest lover, for I feel deep sorrow not only for the fact that he hardly reciprocates my love, but also for the fact that I can no longer talk with him with the same freedom I enjoyed in the past, and his absence distresses me very much. Every time I wake in the night his image is the first one to come to my mind, and considering how much I loved and honoured him, and how much he did scorn and offend me. ... I became so distressed that two or three times already I very bitterly cried.'

This description clearly reveals a guilt-ridden and repressed homosexual tendency, in the light of which must be read a biography of Tasso written in 1621 by his friend Giovan Battista Manso. He repeatedly insisted that Tasso was chaste and said that the poet swore to him that for 16 years after he was first confined to an asylum he was 'completely chaste' – the biographer admitted, however, that Tasso affirmed nothing about the 35 years before his illness. Manso wrote about Tasso's contempt for sexual relations between men and women and his aversion to matrimony. One anecdote is illustrative. Once several friends tried to persuade Tasso to accompany them to the house of a woman courtesan, arguing that if he did not visit her he would go mad; Tasso replied that he would prefer to go mad rather than frequent women. In brief, Tasso's sexuality (or asexuality) has remained a taboo subject, but it is possible that unknown documents exist which can cast light on the shadowy private life of one of the most enigmatic of Italian poets.

V. Ferrarini [Giovanni Dall'Orto], 'Anche Torquato Tasso', *Babilonia*, 130 (February

1995): 76–7; C. Guasti (ed.) *Le lettere di Torquato Tasso*, Naples, 1856: 170, 177; G. B. Manso, *Vita di Torquato Tasso*, Rome, 1995: 212–13, 241, 243, 251; A. Solerti, 'Anche Torquato Tasso?', *Giornale storico della letteratura italiana*, Vol. 9 (1887): 431–40; A. Solerti, *Vita di Torquato Tasso*, Turin, 1895: Vol. 1, pp. 247–50.

Giovanni Dall'Orto

Taylor, Bayard (1825–1878), American writer. Taylor was born in Pennsylvania, where his family of predominantly English Quakers had lived since its earliest days. Chafing under the restrictions and dullness of rural American life, Taylor's wanderlust would, starting in 1844, take him to Europe, Africa, Asia and Central America; the record of those travels made him the most famous travel writer in nineteenth-century America. Described as a man who had travelled more and seen less than anyone else in the world, Taylor had his literary breakthrough with *Views Afoot* (1846) and published ten further volumes. Though he wrote in a wide variety of genres, Taylor considered himself first and foremost a poet, publishing nearly 20 volumes of poetry before his death in Berlin. His finest literary and intellectual achievement was a translation of both parts of Goethe's *Faust* (1870–1871).

Though Taylor was married twice and fathered one child, he poured his passion into his romantic friendships with a wide range of men. These included the friend of his youth, John B. Phillips, fellow writers George Henry Boker and Richard Henry Stoddard, the artist Jervis McEntee, his young admirer Charles Melancthon Jones, and a German businessman and Taylor's travel companion, August Bufleb, whose niece he married in 1857, after having been a widower for seven years. Taylor also felt a Whitmanesque attraction to working-class men, and poems such as 'Hylas', 'The Bath', and 'To a Persian Boy' indicate that he was not blind to the homoeroticism of the Orient. The last of his four novels, *Joseph and His Friend* (1870), is a

fascinating exploration of male romantic friendship in Victorian America.

R. K. Martin, *The Homosexual Tradition in American Poetry*, Iowa City, 1998; B. Taylor, *Selected Letters of Bayard Taylor*, ed. P. C. Wermuth, Lewisburg, 1997; P. C. Wermuth, *Bayard Taylor*, New York, 1973.

Axel Nissen

Tchaikovsky, Peter Ilyich (1840–1893), Russian composer. The greatest Russian composer of the nineteenth-century, Tchaikovsky embodied the idea of the Romantic artist. Composer of six symphonies, eleven operas (of which only a few survive), three ballets and a large body of orchestral, instrumental and chamber works, his music achieved unparalleled emotional expressiveness while also incorporating distinctively Russian folk elements.

For a long time, acknowledgment of Tchaikovsky's homosexuality was suppressed – first by a nationalist Russian musical orthodoxy which saw it as a 'fatal flaw', and then under the Soviets, who could not countenance homosexuality in a cultural hero. Only in recent years have large volumes of documentary evidence surfaced which record beyond doubt the composer's homosexuality, and the tensions this produced in an artist living within the constraints of nineteenth-century Russian society.

Born the son of a mining inspector in the Urals, Tchaikovsky was sent to a school of jurisprudence at St Petersburg at the age of 10. It was here that not only his musical talents were first recognised but where he was also thought to encounter homosexuality for the first time.

By the 1860s he was fully engaged in composition, and produced a number of early works. He also increasingly turned to music criticism, and regularly wrote for *Russkyie Vedomosti*, a Russian daily newspaper. Frequent trips abroad during the 1870s and 1880s not only brought him into contact with other musical influences, but exposed him to life in the metropolitan capitals of Paris, Berlin, Vienna and New York.

Though his work contains no specific homosexual themes, many incorporate notions of unattainable love or thwarted desire, pre-occupations which to some degree at least reflect his personal circumstances. It would, however, be misleading and reductive to see in his music and aesthetics an unmediated portrayal of such personal matters. In many ways Tchaikovsky's life, like those of BYRON, Shelley and others, has come to attain the aura of the 'Great Romantic Artist'. Narratives have accumulated around his life which say more about those constructing them than they do about the artist. Since the 1960s, for example, with the advent of gay liberation politics, a whole new mythology has developed around his life which sees Tchaikovsky as the tortured 'gay artist' who produced works – such as the *Pathétique* symphony – which directly conveyed his troubled homosexuality. The reality, however, is likely to have been considerably more complex. Recent scholarship which focuses, on the one hand, on a detailed analysis of the music, and on the other hand explores the social milieux of the composer's life, suggests a much more subtle relationship between the biographical elements and the artistic creations.

L. Kearney (ed.) *Tchaikovsky and his World*, Princeton, 1999.

C. Faro

Tchelitchev, Pavel (1898–1957), Russian painter and stage-designer. Born into an ancient, wealthy family of landed gentry near Kaluga, southwest of Moscow, Tchelitchev was educated privately by tutors and then at the Moscow Academy and Moscow University. In 1918 the Russian Revolution forced the family to flee to Kiev, where he studied art and stage-design. He later moved to Odessa, Sofia, Constantinople and Berlin, and arrived in Paris in 1923. There he met a Chicago-born pianist, Allen Tanner, with whom he had a relationship until 1933, when he fell in love with the handsome 23-year-old Charles Henri Ford, co-author with Parker Tyler of a stream-of-consciousness gay novel, *The Young and Evil* (1933). They remained lovers until Tchelitchev's death. In 1934 Tchelitchev and Ford visited Spain and Italy before travelling to the United States. They were based there till 1950 when they moved to Grotta Ferrata, near Rome, and later Frascati, which remained their home for the rest of Tchelitchev's life.

His earliest paintings were in a Russian Cubist style. Later claiming that the Ukrainian painter Mikhail Vrubel was his first master, followed by Uccello, Piero della Francesca and Seurat, he moved beyond these early influences, and in Paris joined a chic group of dandified young painters labelled the Néo-Humanistes (in English also the Neo-Romantics) who, rejecting Cubism, Surrealism and abstraction, returned to figurative representationalism. Tchelitchev became one of the finest portraitists of the inter-war period, his subjects including René CREVEL, James Joyce, Gertrude STEIN, Alice B. TOKLAS, Allen Tanner, George Platt LYNES, Lotte Lenya and Dame Edith Sitwell (who fell in love with him, inspiring the desperate comment from Tchelitchev to Allen Tanner, 'that old Sitvouka; to be left *alone* with her? *Non, mon cher!* What you want? I should be raped?'). He repeatedly painted Ford, and in 1937 did a remarkable triple portrait of Lincoln Kirstein. He loved circuses and painted circus figures, bullfighters and freaks.

His other work was much more individual, reflecting diverse influences such as Pythagoras, alchemy, astrology, magic and the Renaissance Neoplatonists. He painted symbolic landscapes, and between 1934 and 1937 worked on a vast vision landscape filled with sombre figures and freaks of all kinds (many are recognisable portraits of his friends and acquaintances); *Phenomena* presents a bleak hellish view of the cosmos. It was followed by another gentler symbolic puzzle-picture, *Cache-Cache* (*Hide and Seek*, 1940–1942), that combined his studies of trees and children using the technique of Arcimboldo. Seeking to provide a modern version of Vesalius's anatomical prints, he then turned to painting the veins, arteries and nerves in transparent bodies, producing a long series of what he called 'interior landscapes'. These were followed by paintings of interior structures of the head, which he sometimes surrounded by containing patterns of line. Some of his final canvases were intricate three-dimensional veiny structures within boxes, linear bodies and mandala-like patterns.

Between 1919 and 1942 Tchelitchev also engaged in stage-design, gaining a reputation for innovativeness from his use of colour, new materials and strong lighting. He did cabaret work in Berlin in 1921, then in 1923 designed a new production of Rimsky-Korsakov's *Coq d'Or* for the Berlin State Opera that nearly bankrupted the company; *Ode* for DIAGHILEV's Ballets Russes in Paris followed in 1928, and through the 1930s he did designs for Balanchine and Massine in Paris and New York. His final effort was two designs for Balanchine productions in Buenos Aires in 1942.

L. Kirstein, *Tchelitchev*, Santa Fe, 1994; P. Tyler, *The Divine Comedy of Pavel Tchelitchev; A Biography*, New York, 1967; E. Roditi, 'Pavel Tchelitchev', *Dialogues; Conversations with European Artists at Mid-Century*, London, 1990: 136–48.

Gary Simes

Tennyson, Alfred (1809–1892), British poet. Born to George Tennyson and Elizabeth Fytche at Somersby in Lincolnshire, Tennyson grew up in a crowded country parsonage, the fourth of 12 siblings with a cultured but tyrannical father whose emotional violence marred the psyches of all the children: more than one brother was institutionalised for madness. Alfred himself was to suffer all his life from fears and anxieties that he finally brought under control through a happy marriage and paternity. But until he married, he wrote of his tormented soul – a theme that was to establish him as the greatest poet of his day.

The focus of his suffering was the grief he could not assuage over the death of his beloved friend Arthur Hallam, whom he met while he was an undergraduate at Trinity College, Cambridge, which he entered in 1827. The men formed a friendship of such intensity that the word 'love' is barely adequate to describe it. When Hallam died suddenly in 1833, Tennyson was more than bereft; he entered a state of mourning and melancholia which were to last for 20 years, resolved finally by the completion of his masterpiece *In Memoriam*, a long poem detailing the 'voyage of his soul', as the poet himself described it, from despair to resignation and acceptance. When the poem was published in 1850, anonymously at first, it was a critical and popular success, particularly with Queen Victoria, who found in the poet's obsessive grief a mirror of her own. Within a short period, Tennyson succeeded William Wordsworth as Poet Laureate in 1850, and he found as well the determination to marry and begin a family after postponing his engagement to Emily Sellwood for 14 years. His success grew, as did his prosperity and personal happiness; he remained productive though many modern critics prefer the work of the earlier years before his marriage.

Tennyson's love for Hallam has remained until recent decades critically sacrosanct, the ideal friendship, a relationship of platonic perfection. This was partly the result of the prudery of academic critics and scholars, but also because all the letters between Hallam and Tennyson were burned by Hallam's father immediately after his son's death and because Tennyson's eldest son, his literary executor and first biographer, Hallam Tennyson, destroyed many more letters after his father's death. *In Memoriam* was viewed as a metaphysical poem laden with symbolic and allegorical meaning, and interpretations that might be regarded as psychological or personal were dismissed as irrelevant. Only since the reprinting of his early poems, hitherto either unpublished or never reprinted after their first appearance, have critics begun to reexamine the nature of Tennyson's love for Hallam. Now it seems clear that their relationship was both passionate and romantic, though it is doubtful that it was ever consummated.

Tennyson's love for Hallam, undeniably homoerotic, was also unselfconscious, that is, free from remorse or guilt or a sense of the illicit. The idea of homosexuality denoting a psychological identity did not yet exist, and since the men were chaste, they had nothing to reproach themselves for, regarding the sin of sodomy. Tennyson's love for Hallam represents an image of homoerotic desire in nineteenth-century British culture before the notoriety of the Oscar WILDE scandal inaugurated a new consciousness about homosexuality and defined a new kind of homophobia distinct from the idea of sodomy, distinct even from the idea of sexual behaviour. But to the end of his days, literally on his deathbed, Tennyson would proclaim that the greatest love of his life, the love that 'surpassed the love of women', was Hallam.

Alfred Lord Tennyson, *The Poems of Tennyson*, ed. C. Ricks, London, 1969; C. Ricks, *Tennyson*, London, 1972; R. B. Martin, *Tennyson: The Unquiet Heart*, Oxford, 1980.
Seymour Kleinberg

Thalbitzer, Sophus (1871–1941), Danish psychiatrist and medical doctor. Thalbitzer specialised in manic-depressive psychoses. In 1912 he was appointed consultant at the St Hans Women's Hospital near Copenhagen. Through two articles on homosexuality, published in juridical journals in 1924 and 1925, Thalbitzer suc-

cessfully influenced criminal legislation on homosexuality in Denmark. His well timed intervention, 'on behalf of science', provided legitimation for the lowering of the age of consent in the Civil Criminal Code of 1930 from the proposed 21 years to 18 years and for not making prostitution a criminal offence for the person who pays the prostitute. Thalbitzer, who claimed that his opposition to the proposed clauses of the bill was shared by 'all Danish psychiatrists', had not previously published anything on homosexuality or sexology. In his two articles he now deployed the words 'science' and 'scientists' with impressive frequency. He completely identified himself with the tactics and the sexual politics of the Wissenschaftlich-humanitäre Komitee (WHK), the dominant organisation of homosexual emancipation in Germany, and referred to Magnus HIRSCHFELD's *Die Homosexualität des Mannes und des Weibes* (1914) as the generally accepted standard volume on homosexuality, that is, he dressed up his emancipatory position and his juridical politics as scientific fact and expertise by posing as the disinterested spokesman for homosexuals.

It was not generally known that Thalbitzer in 1923 had become a member of the Advisory Board of Directors *(Obmänner)* of the WHK. Thalbitzer was not married. There are no sources supporting a hypothesis that Thalbitzer may have been a homosexual.

S. Thalbitzer, 'Forarbejder til den nye danske straffelov. En overflødig paragraf', *Nordisk Tidsskrift for Strafferet*, Copenhagen, 1924: 320–7; S. Thalbitzer, 'Straffelovsforslaget og de Homosexuelle', *Ugeskrift for Retsvæsen*, Copenhagen, 1925: 1905–9.
Wilhelm von Rosen

Theocritus (third century BC), Hellenistic Greek poet. A native of Syracuse in Sicily, Theocritus spent much of his life in Alexandria and on the island of Cos. Alexandria, founded in 331 BC, was already, by

Theocritus's time, a great city with famous cultural institutions (the Museum and the Library) and a sophisticated urban life. It was the capital of King Ptolemy II Philadelphus, who ruled Egypt 283–246 BC, and we know that Theocritus sought (and probably gained) the king's patronage.

Theocritus's poems (written for the most part in the poet's native western, or Doric, form of Greek) came to be known as 'idylls'. They cover various styles and genres, the largest single group comprising the 'bucolic' idylls, which (through VIRGIL) originated the European pastoral tradition. Theocritus is generally credited with inventing this genre, though he may have drawn upon popular traditions from his native Sicily. The bucolic idyll features, in idealised form, the life of shepherds, cowherds and so forth, their rural simplicity, their musical and poetical contests, and their loves. Besides the bucolic poems, there are mimes (a sort of 'mini-drama'), mythological tales, appeals for patronage and a handful of 'personal poems'.

A variegated vein of pederastic interest runs through the genres, and is central to some of the poems. Heterosexual themes, however, are also prominent, and Theocritus shares the common Greek view that the gender of the love object is a matter of indifference. The style and emotional temperature vary considerably, from the elegant (but artificial) exchange of flirtatious couplets, fired alternately by love for a boy and for a girl (Idyll 5), through the (as it seems) genuinely felt prayers for a male lover's success (Idyll 7) to the ironically deflationary mood of the narrative of Heracles' love for Hylas. Theocritus fixes on the point in this story at which, during the *Argo*'s voyage in search of the Golden Fleece, Hylas is abducted by water nymphs while going ashore to fetch water. Heracles, mad with love, jumps ship to go in search of him. But while Hylas ends up numbered among the immortals, Heracles is stigmatised as a deserter, and obliged to make his way to Colchis on foot. What price, then, the 'heroism' of the past?

Three of Theocritus's 'personal' (though not necessarily autobiographical) poems directly concern love for boys. Two of them (Idylls 29 and 30) are, exceptionally, written in Aeolic Greek, the language of Lesbos and its great lyric poets of the late seventh and early sixth century BC, SAPPHO and Alcaeus of Mytilene. Like Solon of Athens, Alcaeus combined poetry with politics (though without Solon's success in public affairs), and his poems covered a very wide range, including pederastic love. Sadly, not a single line of his in the latter vein survives. Theocritus's choice of the Aeolic dialect, however, suggests that his Idylls 29 and 30 may have been modelled on the love poetry of Alcaeus.

These idylls, together with Idyll 12, depict in various ways, through an ironic blend of humour and pathos, the misery of a middle-aged lover seeking to hold the love of a less-than-committed youth. In Idyll 29 the poet urges that the young man's true happiness lies in settling down in a single nest, rather than flitting from bough to bough. In Idyll 30, the older man, sick with love, remonstrates with himself over his folly. He knows he cannot keep up with his *eromenos* ('A boy's life has the pace of a running fawn' – transl. Wells). But he has no choice: he must yield to the god (Eros) who subdues both Zeus and Aphrodite. In Idyll 12, the boy has returned after two days' absence. The poet is delighted, and prays that together they may realise the ancient pederastic ideal in love which will be celebrated for ages to come. But he has been deserted once, and he recalls the kissing competition at the shrine of Diocles (lover of boys) where the fortunate but perplexed arbiter must find a touchstone to determine who gives the sweetest kiss. The poet, it seems, needs a similar touchstone to distinguish true from false love.

P. Green, *Alexander to Actium: The Hellenistic*

Age, London, 1990: chap. 15; R. Hunter, *Theocritus and the Archaeology of Greek Poetry*, Cambridge, 1996; T. G. Rosenmeyer, *The Green Cabinet*, Berkeley, 1969.

Clifford Hindley

Theognis (sixth century BC), Greek poet. Theognis of Megara lived during the latter half of the sixth century BC. There was an ancient dispute whether his home state was the Megara situated on the Greek mainland between Athens and Corinth, or Megara in Sicily, but modern opinion accepts the former. Little is known about Theognis's life other than that he was a landowner at a time of transition from aristocratic rule, through a period of tyranny, to a more broadly based (but probably conservative) government. During the later part of the century, populist leaders took charge of Megara's affairs. Theognis, along with others of his class, lost his lands and was forced into exile, where he reflected pessimistically on what he saw as the woes of the age.

Theognis seems to have been both happily married and also devoted to a young man named Cyrnus, to whom upwards of 50 of his poems are addressed. His poems reflect the role of the *erastes* as counsellor and guide, with little that is openly erotic. Theognis comments mordantly on the class divisions in the city, and urges Cyrnus to choose his friends carefully. He calls for sincerity in love, and contentment with modest wealth, while avoiding penury. He lyrically affirms the power of the poet to confer immortal memory upon the lovely youth even beyond the grave: 'A song for all generations to come, so long as sun and earth endure' (251).

The main group of Cyrnus poems occupies some 240 verses out of the 1,400 or so that have survived. Much of the rest express similar themes, though with increasing pessimism. The concluding 150 verses (designated 'Book II') comprise a collection of poems devoted to the love of boys. Still the stern moralist, even in this section Theognis (if it be he) admits little direct description of fleshly delight. But his poems taken together present an unequalled view of the emotional experience of love for boys in archaic Greece.

Here are some of the themes he treats: No man, however strong and wise, can escape the power of love (1388), the power which destroyed Troy (1231). It flows from a god-given grace, but for the afflicted lover it is hard to bear (1319). It is also short-lived – while the chin remains smooth (1327), its lovely flower fading faster than a foot-race (1305). Meanwhile, the lover, enjoying the delights of love for boys, may recall Zeus himself with GANYMEDE, and be proud to surrender to a beautiful soft-skinned youth (1341–1350). He will respect the boy, not requiring him to do anything he does not want (1237), but doing him service. In return he looks for (but by no means always receives!) 'favour' – presumably sex (1329–1334). Happiness is in the love of a boy: ' Happy is the man in love who exercises his body and, going home, sleeps the whole day long with a lovely youth' (1335).

The boy, however, is not always so compliant, and many lines recall the pain of unrequited love. Love is a yoke on the neck (1357): to court a lad is to put one's hand into a fire of vine-clippings (1359). For too often, a boy is fickle: like a swiftly wheeling kite he turns from one lover to another (1261).

Theognis's final address to Cyrnus sums it all up: 'Bitter and sweet, Cyrnus, alluring and cruel, is love for young men, until it be fulfilled; for if one brings it to fulfilment, it becomes sweet, but if one fails in the pursuit, it is more painful than any other thing' (1353–1356).

A. R. Burn, *The Lyric Age of Greece*, London, 1967; K. J. Dover, *Greek Homosexuality*, London, 1978.

Clifford Hindley

Thomson, Virgil (1896–1989), American composer and critic. Born in Kansas City, Missouri, son of a farmer turned postal worker, Thomson began his music studies at age 5 and by 12 was playing organ at the Calvary Baptist Church. He also demonstrated an early gift for writing. In his autobiography, Thomson reveals that as a cherubic young child he was taunted as a 'sissy'. Unwilling to compete and unable to lash back with physical violence, he vowed thereafter to cajole friends and lovers or destroy enemies at will with his intellectual superiority.

Thomson enlisted in the US Air Force in 1917, and was commissioned a lieutenant. In 1919, he entered Harvard University, where he studied with Edward Bulingame Hill and Archibald T. Davision. In less than a year, he became an assistant instructor in music, a position he held until 1925. In 1925 he went on a European tour as conductor of the Harvard Glee Club. Thomson remained in Paris to study with Nadia Boulanger. There he was introduced to the Dada movement, fell under the influence of Erik Satie and the avant-garde composers known as Les Six, and befriended Gertrude STEIN and Alice B. TOKLAS. Thomson and Stein spent the next several years on the creation of the iconoclastic opera Four Saints in Three Acts (1928). The opera was not produced until 1934, when with an all-black cast, outlandish cellophane sets by Florine Stettheimer, and John Houseman's direction, it became a smash success on Broadway. In his book Prepare for Saints, Steven Watson portrays Four Saints as a watershed work which 'defined modern taste and stylishnes' in Depression America. Like the promoters of modernism in DIAGHILEV's Ballets Russes, most of the creators and sponsors behind Four Saints in Three Acts were gay: Stein (libretto), Thomson (music), Maurice Grosser (scenarist), Frederick Ashton (choreographer), and the 'Harvard modernists' impresario Lincoln Kirstein and architect Philip Johnson. Thomson later collaborated on another American opera, Mother of Us All (1947), inspired by the life of lesbian suffragist Susan B. ANTHONY.

In the 1930s, Thomson composed scores for classic film documentaries of Depression America, The Plow that Broke the Plains (1936) and The River (1937), and the Americana ballet, Filling Station (1938), for Lincoln Kirstein's Ballet Caravan. Other film scores include The Spanish Earth (with Marc Blitzstein, 1937), Tuesday in November (1945), Louisiana Story (1947; Pulitzer Prize, 1949), and the feature film The Goddess (1957). In 1940, Thomson became music critic of the New York Herald Tribune, a position he held until 1954, and in this capacity became more widely known and influential than for his compositions. Thomson is perhaps America's most important 'unknown' composer, yet the deceptive simplicity and clarity of his music, often incorporating American folk and religious elements, laid the groundwork for future innovations in American music. Both as composer and critic he served as an influential colleague or mentor to American gay composers Aaron COPLAND, Marc Blitzstein, Henry Cowell, Paul Bowles, Lou Harrison, John Cage and Ned Rorem.

Alternately charming and courtly or condescending and catankerous, Thomson nevertheless succeeded in forming enduring friendships with both men and women. Although he engaged in numerous gay relationships during his long relationship with painter Maurice Grosser, Thomson confessed, 'I didn't want to be queer', and never came out publicly. Among his most significant companioins were Leland Poole, Briggs Buchanan and painter Roger Baker. Throughout his long life he succeeded in scrupulously removing every reference to his personal life not only in his own but in the reminiscences of friends and lovers, including Grosser.

Thomson's published works include The State of Music (1939); his collected Tribune reviews, Music Reviewed 1940–54 (1967), American Music since 1910 (1971); an autobiography, Virgil Thomson (1966), and the posthumous Music with Words: A Composer's View (1990).

A. Tommasini, *Virgil Thomson: Composer on the Aisle*, New York, 1997; S. Watson, *Prepare for Saints: Gertrude Stein, Virgil Thomson and the Mainstreaming of American Modernism*, New York, 1999.

A. M. *Wentink*

Thorsell, Eric (1898–1980), Swedish ironworker. Born in Surahammar, Sweden, Thorsell's thirst for learning brought him to Brunnsvik's Folkhögskola (people's high-school), where so many Swedish workers have gained a knowledge normally reserved for the upper classes. Aware of being a homosexual in his teens, Thorsell soon became interested in the issue of sexuality and the situation of homosexuals. His first mentors were the Swedish homosexual philosopher Pontus WIKNER and PLATO. Thorsell visited Germany and the HIRSCHFELD Institute. He also collaborated with Elise OTTESEN JENSEN, who for many years was the leader of the Swedish Organisation for Sexual Education (Riksförbundet för Sexuell Upplysning, RFSU). Later he got into contact with the Riksförbundet för Sexuellt Likaberättigande (RFSL), the Swedish national organisation for homosexuals, which was founded in 1950. But as early as 1933 he gave a lecture 'Are the homosexuals outlaws or criminals?', perhaps the first lecture on this subject in Sweden. Thorsell never appeared openly as homosexual, but he was uncompromising in his struggle for the rights of homosexuals. He wrote no book, his media being the article and the lecture. After his death a fund was created in his memory.

F. Silverstolpe, *En homosexuell arbetares memoarer*, Stockholm 1981.

Johan Hedberg

Thurman, Wallace (1902–1934), American author. Thurman was born and grew up in Salt Lake City, Utah, moving to Los Angeles as an adolescent. In the unpublished 'Notes on a Stepchild', Thurman portrays a precocious child suffering from frequent illness and from both inter- and intraracial prejudice against those with his very black skin. While a journalism student at the University of California in Los Angeles in 1923, Thurman discovered the work of the Nietzchean iconoclastic H. L. Mencken. He founded the *Outlet*, a West Coast New Negro magazine that lasted six months.

Moving to New York in 1925 'with nothing but his nerve', as Theophilus Lewis recollected, and being arrested for indecency in a subway toilet a few days later, within four months he was editor of the *Messenger*, one of the most important African-American publications. He became part of what he called a 'niggerati' that included Langston Hughes, Zora Neale Hurston, Dorothy West, and Aaron Douglas. He published early work by all of them. He also wrote (under various names) for *True Story*, some scripts for 'adults only' movies, and worked as an editor for mainstream – i.e. white (downtown from Harlem) – publishers. None the less, Thurman was chronically in debt, considerably worsened by the one issue of *Fire!!*, an anti-assimilationist celebration of jazz, paganism, androgyny, black beauty and homoeroticism (the last especially in Richard Bruce Nugent's "Smoke, Lilies, Jade') that he produced in 1926. Thurman's story from it, 'Cordelia the Crude', became the basis of a successful Broadway play he co-authored in 1929.

Earlier in the same year his first novel, *The Blacker the Berry*, focused on the problems a middle-class dark-skinned girl, Emma Lou, encounters with lighter-skinned Negroes in the Midwest, at the University of Southern California and even in the 'Promised Land' of Harlem. She suffers discrimination even there from lighter-skinned owners of business and housing. At various points she attempts to straighten her hair and lighten her skin, to rebel and consort with other dark-skinned pariahs, and finally accepts a white mentor's suggestion that she accept herself as an individual. (There is also a doomed homosexual side plot.) Also in 1929 Thurman tried (disastrously) marriage with a woman: it lasted for six months.

In addition to being a vehicle for presenting his views on art, race and quasi-Nietzchean rationale for individualism, the *roman à clef Infants of the Spring* satirised and seemingly attempted to bury the Harlem Renaissance epoch in which he had been a leader. Most of it is set in the 'Niggerati Manor' (267 W. 136th St.) in which Thurman and other *artistes* lived in 1926–1927. Raymond Taylor, the earnest but too easily debauched by drink character that is a version of himself, believes that Oscar WILDE is the greatest man who ever lived, also revering VERLAINE, RIMBAUD and WHITMAN. He is enamoured of a masculine white sailor (Stephen Jorgeson, modelled on Harald Stefansson, who had been Thurman's lover at the time written about in the novel). Thurman satirises everyone, but is especially contemptuous of the Alain Locke character, the would-be Queen Bee of the New Negro. Moreover, following the convention that openly – especially flamboyantly – gay characters must be murdered or kill themselves, Thurman has Paul Arbian (the saffron-coloured character based on Bruce Nugent, who actually outlived him by decades) kill himself in an overflowing bathtub that makes the ink on his magnum opus run.

Thurman died in the same Welfare Island City Hospital he had exposed in a muckraking novel (*The Interne*, 1934), of tuberculosis exacerbated by alcoholism.

M. G. Henderson, 'Portrait of Wallace Thurman', in A. Bontemps (ed.) *The Harlem Renaissance Remembered*, New York, 1972: 147–69.

Stephen O. Murray

Tiberius (Tiberius Claudius Nero) (42 BC – AD 37), Roman emperor (Tiberius Julius Caesar Augustus). Tiberius's mother Livia, when pregnant with his brother Drusus, divorced his father (also named Tiberius Claudius Nero) in 38 BC in order to marry Octavian, the future Emperor Augustus. Tiberius was just reaching puberty when he participated in Octavian's triumph (August, 29 BC) celebrating the victory over Cleopatra and Antony at Actium. Thereafter he embarked on a career which brought him military renown, particularly in Pannonia (12–9 BC) and Germany (9–7 BC, AD 4–6). Married first (*c*. 19 BC) to Vipsania, the daughter of Augustus's general Marcus Agrippa, betrothed to him in infancy, Tiberius was later (11 BC) required to divorce her to marry Agrippa's widow, Julia, the daughter of Augustus. This marriage was not happy. In 6 BC, for reasons not entirely clear, Tiberius retired from Rome to live in Rhodes, where he remained until AD 2. Two years later, following the deaths of the sons of Julia and Agrippa, Augustus adopted Tiberius as his son, thereby acknowledging him as his heir.

Tiberius succeeded Augustus in AD 14, being proclaimed emperor on 17 September. The following 12 years he lived in Rome. In 26 he retired to Capri, where he remained for the rest of his life, giving rise to stories of licence and luxury, and investing this island off Naples with a reputation which would persist into the modern era. Although for most of his life no scandal attaches to Tiberius, and SUETONIUS records (*Tib*. 21) that some believed Augustus disapproved of his austerity, the tales told of Capri and the emperor's depravities there have a surer hold on his posthumous reputation. Suetonius is the major source for these (*Tib*. 43–5), describing rooms decorated with erotic paintings and sculptures, and youngsters of both sexes whose sexual antics gave the emperor particular delight. While by no means interested in boys alone, Tiberius is said to have trained young boys whom he called *pisciculi* ('little fish') to accompany him when he went swimming, to lick and nibble him. These stories are an integral part of Suetonius's blackening of Tiberius, along with other instances of cruelty, such as the large number of treason trials and his suspicion of relatives which marred his reign. The other major source for Tiberius, Tacitus (*Annals* Books 1–6), similarly reflects Tiberius's decline into cruelty, succinctly summarised in the obituary given at 6. 51 which concludes: 'Finally, putting aside shame and fear, he simply indulged his own true nature: he broke out into crime and turpitude.'

Suetonius, 'Tiberius', in *Lives of the Caesars and Extracts from Lives of Illustrious Men*, trans. J. C. Rolfe, 2 vols, London, 1914; Suetonius, *The Twelve Caesars*, trans. R. Graves, Harmondsworth, 1957; Tacitus, *The Annals of Imperial Rome*, trans. M. Grant, Harmondsworth, 1971; B. Levick, *Tiberius the Politician*, London, 1976; R. Seager, *Tiberius*, London, 1972.

Roger Pitcher

Tilden, William Taten ('Bill') (1893–1953), American athlete. Born in Philadelphia into a wealthy family, and a sheltered child, Tilden was home-schooled until adolescence. As a child, he initially disliked tennis despite winning several tournaments and in college even failed to make the tennis team at the University of Pennsylvania. Tilden demonstrated a true talent for the game that made him a star only after a humiliating defeat in the 1919 US Nationals, after which he worked obsessively to develop a powerful topspin backhand drive and brilliant first serve. In 1920, he won his first major title at Wimbledon, the first American to do so, at age 27. He won again the following year and was the oldest man to win a Wimbledon singles title at age 37 in 1930. He won six consecutive Grand Slam singles titles. Tilden was ranked No. 1 in the world from 1920–1925, No. 1 nationally from 1920–1929. In amateur competition, 'Big Bill' accumulated an astounding 0.936 winning percentage and, turning pro, remained the biggest attraction on the professional tennis circuit for nearly 20 years.

Despite his triumphs in the game, Tilden's life and career were plagued by difficulties, many of which were of his own making. His arrogance increased with success and made him unpopular with the US Lawn Tennis Association, which barred him from competing in the US Nationals in 1928 for being paid to write about tennis. Shortly after losing his top world ranking to René Lacoste and Henri Cochet, he finally turned pro in 1930, and reportedly earned more than $500,000 before 1937. Very much the showman throughout his career, often making dramatic entrances to matches in full-length camel-hair coats, Tilden moved to Hollywood in the 1930s. Off the court, however, he was as unsuccessful as an actor, novelist and producer as he had been successful as a player on the court.

Even more than waning abilities and ill-advised business ventures, Tilden's homosexuality, an open secret for many years, became his greatest career liability. His choice to travel the circuit with adolescent ball boys lost him invitations to many of the best tennis clubs. In 1946, he was arrested for fondling a teenage hustler on Sunset Boulevard and convicted of contributing to the delinquency of a minor. He was sentenced to a year in prison, but released on probation after serving slightly more than seven months. Less than two years later, he was arrested again for making advances to a 16-year-old hitchhiker. He was sentenced to a year term, and served ten months. Despite these relatively light punishments, Tilden's reckless behaviour virtually destroyed an already fading career. His scandalous reputation cost him lucrative teaching opportunities and his last years were spent in obscurity and near poverty, forced to pawn his trophies in order to survive. He died of a heart attack in a Los Angeles rented room. His net worth was $88.11.

Despite his tragic personal life, Tilden's athletic prowess was undeniable. 'Tilden simply was tennis in the public mind', writes Frank Deford, his biographer. 'He is an artist', wrote Franklin Adams in 1921: 'It is the beauty of the game that Tilden loves. It is the chase always, rather than the quarry.' In 1950, he was unanimously voted the most outstanding tennis player of the first half of the twentieth-century by the National Sports Writers Association and was voted No. 45 among North American athletes of the twentieth-century by a SportsCentury panel. An articulate analyst of his sport, Tilden's books, *How to Play Better Tennis, The Art of Lawn Tennis* and *Match Play and the Spin of the Ball*, are considered classics in the field.

F. Deford, *Big Bill Tilden: The Triumphs and the Tragedy*, New York, 1975.

A. M. *Wentink*

Toklas, Alice B(abette) (1877–1967), American writer. Growing up in San Francisco's Jewish middle class, Toklas led what she later called a 'gently-bred' childhood. In 1897 her mother died, and she took charge of her father's household. Despite her domestic responsibilities, she continued to develop her interests in politics, music, fashion and the arts. At the age of 30, knowing that she did not wish to marry, Toklas left for Paris. The day after her arrival she met Gertrude STEIN. After nearly a year's courtship, Toklas and Stein decided to consider themselves 'married'. Throughout their lives, their marriage would be a working partnership. Toklas typed all of Stein's manuscripts, offering suggestions that Stein incorporated into her work. Toklas presided over Stein's salon, and determined who would have access to the couple. Stein drew freely, if enigmatically, on her life with Toklas for inspiration, discussing even the most private aspects of their relationship, such as lovemaking, in a 'coded' language. Toklas was a fierce advocate for Stein's work. After World War I, she founded the 'Plain Edition' press, which published several of Stein's books. Frustrated that Stein's growing critical acclaim

did not result in greater financial compensation, Toklas encouraged her to write her memoirs.

The result, *The Autobiography of Alice B. Toklas* (1933), reveals the close personal and professional ties between the two women, as Stein's memoirs were written in Toklas's voice and from Toklas's point of view. Building on the success of *The Autobiography*, Stein agreed to do a lecture tour in the United States in 1934, where Toklas was described in the press as her 'secretary'. After a successful six months, they returned to France, where the political scene was becoming ominous. Despite repeated requests from American friends to return home, they decided to stay in France for the duration of the war. Perhaps because of their positive experiences working for the relief effort during World War I, the couple did not seem aware of the danger that two Jewish-American lesbians would face in Nazi-occupied France. They survived the war thanks to the protection of friends in high places and to their neighbours at their summer house in Bellay. They spent the war years growing vegetables, passing messages for the Resistance and trying to hide their true identities from the German soldiers they were forced to billet.

Stein died of cancer in 1946. Toklas spent the rest of her life promoting Stein's work and safeguarding her memory. In addition, she began to write, publishing over the next 20 years articles on art and fashion in American magazines, two cookbooks, a collection of her letters and a memoir, *What is Remembered* (1963). In her later years, Toklas converted to Catholicism, saying it comforted her to believe that she and Stein would be reunited in heaven. Toklas died in 1967 and had her own epitaph inscribed on the back of Stein's headstone in the Père Lachaise cemetery in Paris.

A. B. Tolkas, *Staying on Alone: Letters of Alice B. Toklas*, ed. E. Burns, New York, 1973;

L. Simon, *The Biography of Alice B. Toklas*, Garden City, NY, 1977.

Victoria Thompson

Trefusis, Violet (1894–1972), British writer. Born Violet Keppel, Trefusis was a clever and spoilt child in a rich Edwardian family. She liked to suggest that she was the daughter of Edward VII, since her mother, Alice Keppel, had been the king's mistress. Edward often played with Violet and her sister when he visited their mother. When she was 10, Trefusis befriended another aristocratic child, Vita SACKVILLE-WEST. The girls met occasionally, abroad, at Knole (the Sackville house), and at the Trefusis family castle in Scotland. They were prolific letter writers and usually spoke in French to each other.

Their friendship warmed into something more in 1918, by which time Sackville-West was married, not unhappily, to the diplomat Harold NICOLSON and had given birth to three children. The antics of the next three years are described in their son's biography *Portrait of a Marriage*. The two women ran off to Monte Carlo together but could never really disentangle themselves from their respective families. Sackville-West returned to Nicolson and Violet married Denys Trefusis. Sackville-West then sabotaged the honeymoon by carrying Trefusis back to Monte Carlo. But it was not all fun and high romance, and when the two husbands finally flew across the Channel in a plane, the game was up.

Mrs Keppel contrived to keep her daughter and son-in-law in France. It suited them and they mingled widely. Although her husband died in 1929, Trefusis never remarried. She had become a renowned hostess in Parisian society with her own salon. She produced five novels (in French) and eventually two volumes of memoirs.

During World War II Trefusis was forced to live in England. Sackville-West, now happily gardening at Sissinghurst, kept her at bay. In one memorable letter she described Trefusis as her unexploded bomb.

Yet the post-war Trefusis sparkled on, dividing her time between France and the house in Florence inherited from her parents. There were glamorous costume balls and dinners, suitors and escorts (always men), and the odd postcard from Sackville-West. The French Government awarded her the Legion of Honour; she was also decorated by the Italian Government. When she died in Florence, some of her ashes were buried in France with the epitaph, 'English by birth, French at heart'.

V. Glendinning, *Vita, The Life of Vita Sackville-West*, London, 1983; P. Julian and J. Phillips, *Violet Trefusis, Life and Letters*, London, 1976; N. Nicolson, *Portrait of a Marriage*, New York, 1973.

J. Z. Robinson

Tsvetaeva, Marina Ivanovna (1892–1941), Russian poet, prose writer, dramatist. Widely considered one of the four greatest twentieth-century Russian poets and an innovative prose writer and dramatist, Tsvetaeva was born in Moscow. Her father was an art professor and her mother a gifted pianist of Polish descent, whose father had forbidden her a concert career. Although Tsvetaeva's mother wanted her daughter to become a pianist, Marina herself was drawn to words and began writing poetry at the age of six. Her first volume of poems, *Evening Album*, was published in 1910 and was composed entirely of verse she had written between the ages of 15 and 17. Aside from Tsvetaeva's youthful love affair with the poet Sophia PARNOK, her self-acknowledged bisexuality, her lesbianism – and the lesbian theme that runs throughout her poetry, prose, letters and journals – have all been ignored, or at best mentioned only in passing by most of her Western biographers. The majority of Russian Tsvetaeva scholars have tried, and continue to try, to deny the poet's lesbianism and its significance in her work.

Tsvetaeva revealed an attraction to her own sex from childhood, both in her reading and in her relationships with other children. She tells the story of her childhood love for another girl in her prose work 'The House at Old Pimen'. Despite her lesbian inclinations, or perhaps in an effort to neutralise the anxiety they clearly caused her, Tsvetaeva married young and immediately had a daughter. Then, at the beginning of World War I, she met Sophia Parnok and fell in love at first sight. This passionate affair was fraught with ambivalence for Tsvetaeva, but it inspired the most artistically mature work of her early period, the lyrical cycle 'Girlfriend' (1914–1915), a masterpiece of lesbian love poetry that was published only in the 1970s and has not yet been translated into English in its entirety. Although both Parnok and Tsvetaeva predicted that their love was doomed almost from the start, Tsvetaeva was traumatised by their break-up (in early 1916). She called the loss of Parnok the 'first catastrophe' of her young life, and nurtured vengeful feelings against Parnok until the end of her (Tsvetaeva's) life. In the aftermath of the affair, Tsvetaeva returned to her husband, and immediately became pregnant. Her second daughter was born in early 1917.

Tsvetaeva spent the 1917 Revolution and the ensuing civil war in Moscow, alone with her two young daughters – her husband was an officer in the White army. She was forced to put her infant daughter in an orphanage where the little girl died of starvation. In 1918–1920 Tsvetaeva's work with an avant-garde Moscow theatre group, the Third Studio, led to her intimacy with Sonya Holliday, an actress. Their apparently platonic, but intensely erotic love affair was described by Tsvetaeva much later in the prose work 'The Tale of Sonechka' (which has not yet been translated into English) and in a cycle of lyrics, 'Poems to Sonechka'. 'The Tale of Sonechka' must be read in part as an encoded rewriting of Tsvetaeva's affair with her first Sonya (Parnok).

Just after the publication of her most famous collection, *Mileposts I*, Tsvetaeva left the Soviet Union (in May 1922) and was finally reunited with her husband in Prague. In early 1925 their son was born, and later that year the family moved to Paris, where Tsvetaeva lived for the next 14 years. At first she was welcomed into Russian émigré literary life in Paris, but during the 1930s, when most of her prose works were written, she was increasingly isolated and criticised. Eventually, she was treated as an outcast, due in large part to her husband's pro-Soviet political activities, which included espionage for the Soviet secret police.

In the early 1930s Tsvetaeva met Natalie Clifford BARNEY, the famous expatriate American lesbian writer (the 'Amazon of Letters'), and gave a poetry reading at Barney's Rue Jacob salon, but neither she, nor her work, were given an enthusiastic reception. Feeling rejected, Tsvetaeva wrote (in French) her 'Lettre à l'Amazone' (1932, revised in 1934), a highly encoded, autobiographical and polemical work with two addressees: Barney, and Tsvetaeva's former lover and earlier rejector, Parnok. In 'Lettre's' story of a lesbian love affair between a young girl and an older woman, Tsvetaeva rewrote her and Parnok's affair for the third time. Simultaneously, she composed an ambiguous, intensely personal and moving epitaph to her lost 'girlfriend' (Parnok), the only lover she had had who had made it possible for her to have an orgasm, and to like her sexual self. 'Lettre à l'Amazone' also gives expression to Tsvetaeva's struggle with her own lesbianism. Her internalised homophobia led her to defend lesbian relationships against the censure of society, God and the State, while striking out at them as an offence to nature and Mother. Tsvetaeva's 'Lettre à l'Amazone' remains the only original theoretical work on lesbianism by a Russian writer.

At the end of the 1930s Tsvetaeva returned to Soviet Russia, where tragedy awaited her. First, her daughter was arrested (in August 1939) and sent to a concentration camp; then her husband was arrested and shot as an enemy of the people. Shunned by her poet colleagues in Moscow, she was sent to live outside the city (in Golitsyno). Despite her desperate situation in Moscow during the year after her return, she became involved in a relationship with Tatyana Kvanina, the wife of a minor writer. Part of their intimate correspondence has recently appeared in a Russian journal.

After the German offensive began in earnest, Tsvetaeva and her teenage son were evacuated to Yelabuga in the Tatar Autonomous Republic. There, the beleaguered, hounded poet could find no work or assistance. On 31 August 1941, finding herself alone in the house for a few hours, she hanged herself from a beam in the ceiling. She was buried in an unmarked grave in the Yelabuga cemetery.

D. Burgin, 'Mother Nature versus the Amazons: Marina Tsvetaeva and Female Same-Sex Love', *Journal of the History of Sexuality*, 6, 1 (July 1995): 62–88; S. Karlinsky, *Marina Tsvetaeva: The Woman, her World, and her Poetry*, Cambridge, 1985.

Diana L. Burgin

Tuke, Henry Scott (1858–1929), British painter. Born in York of Quaker parents, he moved with his family to London in 1874. In 1875 Tuke enrolled at the Slade School of Art and won a three-year Slade Scholarship in 1877. In 1880 he travelled to Italy and from 1881 to 1883 lived in Paris, enrolling in the studio of the French history painter Paul Laurens, where he met the American painter John Singer SARGENT and the playwright Oscar WILDE. Although Tuke had received a highly academic training, he favoured a style of painting that lacked 'finish', preferring also to paint *en plein air* (i.e. outdoors). In England he had looked to the work of the *plein air* painter Arthur Lemon and in Paris he met Jules Bastien-Lepage, whose own practice of applying varying degrees

of finish to different areas of the canvas was to be an important influence.

In 1883 Tuke moved to the fishing village of Newlyn in Cornwall, where he became a founder member of the Newlyn School, but in 1885 he settled in another Cornish town, Falmouth, where he was to live for the rest of his life. During the 1880s and early 1900s, Tuke produced numerous narrative and anecdotal paintings of Cornish fishermen, e.g. *All Hands to the Pumps!* (1888), and of recreational sailing (Tuke himself being a keen sailor), e.g. *The Run Home* (1901–1902), frequently using local youths as models and often basing several figures in a painting on one individual. With the exception of works such as *The Bathers* (1885), Tuke depicted his figures fully clothed in his early paintings. However, his commissioned portraits aside, the nude adolescent male, typically depicted either on the shoreline or in a boating scene, soon became Tuke's principal subject, earning him the epithet 'The Painter of Youth'.

Following a trip to Italy and Corfu in 1892, Tuke's palette brightened dramatically and he also developed a looser painting technique – the luminous brilliance of the painting *August Blue* (1893) being indicative of his mature style. Although Tuke attempted to paint mythological pictures (most of which he never completed or else destroyed), he clearly preferred painting directly from nature and aimed to evoke an atmosphere or feeling rather than illustrate a specific narrative. To this end, and following the precedent of the painter James McNeil Whistler, he often gave his paintings titles such as *Ruby, Gold and Malachite* (1901) or *Aquamarine* (1928–1929). Despite the homoerotic tenour of many of Tuke's paintings, e.g. *Noonday Heat* (1903, 1911), there is little evidence this created difficulties for him (indeed, the main criticism of his work was that it tended to be formulaic and repetitive), while his close friendships with many of his models gave no cause for scandal.

However, Tuke did have connections with the Uranian poets and writers and wrote a sonnet to youth that was published anonymously in the journal *The Artist*. Tuke also contributed an essay to another journal, the *Studio*, which, like *The Artist*, published Uranian verse as well as illustrated articles on the male nude, until the trials of Oscar Wilde drove much of this material underground.

Tuke was an accomplished portraitist and maintained a studio in London to work on his commissions, and his sitters included the cricketer W. G. Grace and the soldier and author T. E. LAWRENCE. In 1886 Tuke was a founder member of the New English Art Club and in 1911 became a member of the Royal Watercolour Society. Elected an Associate of the Royal Academy in 1900, he was elected to full membership in 1914. In his later years Tuke travelled extensively, visiting Jamaica and Central America in 1923, until forced to return to England due to illness, and the Mediterranean and North Africa in 1925. He died at Falmouth.

E. Cooper, *The Life and Work of Henry Scott Tuke*, London, 1987; D. Wainwright and C. Dinn, *Henry Scott Tuke, 1858–1929: Under Canvas*, London, 1989.

David L. Phillips

Turing, Alan Mathison (1912–1954), British scientist. Turing is perhaps most widely known as one of the progenitors of the modern computer. Although trained in mathematics, his interests and influence crossed into logic, philosophy of the mind, engineering, biology and cryptoanalysis. His name is now associated with two pioneering formulations in computing science: the Turing machine and the Turing test.

Conceived in India (his father was in the Indian Civil Service), Turing was born in London and raised, along with his brother, by his mother in England. His father continued to spend extended periods of time working in India throughout Turing's childhood. Turing was educated in the English public school system (Sherborne), from where he won a scholarship to Kings College, Cambridge, to study mathematics. At Sherborne, Turing had a formative relationship (in terms of both his sexual and intellectual future) with a schoolmate named Christopher Morcom, who died suddenly in 1930.

In 1936, whilst at Cambridge, Turing published a landmark paper ('On Computable Numbers, with an Application to the Entscheidungsproblem'), that laid down the mathematical and logical principles of computability through the exposition of a universal computing device: the so-called Turing machine. This was an abstract machine (a model of computation), rather than an actual device – electronic computing machines (the precursors of the modern computer) were not built until the 1940s.

During World War II, Turing was seconded from Cambridge to Bletchley Park in rural England, which was the centre of the British wartime efforts to break the German Enigma code. There, Turing played a crucial role in breaking the German cipher (for which he received an OBE), and he came into contact with the engineering of code-breaking machines. Following the war, Turing took up a position at the National Physical Laboratory, where he devised plans for an Automatic Computing Engine. In 1948 Turing shifted to a full-time academic position at the University of Manchester, where one of the early computers was being built. Turing was fond of referring to this work as the construction of an 'electronic brain', and during this period his interests in the philosophical aspects of computation (e.g. can machines think?) developed further. In 1950 he published a paper that came to be highly influential in the philosophical developments of computing science. 'Computing Machinery and Intelligence' discussed the possibilities and philosophical implications of intelligence in machines and suggested a method for testing machine intelligence – what became known as the Turing test.

In 1951 Turing was made a Fellow of the Royal Society. In the same year, Turing's house was burgled by an acquaintance of a young man with whom Turing had started an affair. When the burglary was reported to the police, the details of Turing's relationship with the young man came to light and Turing was arrested for gross indecency. Convicted of the charges, Turing was given the option of a one-year prison sentence or treatment of his homosexuality with 'organo-therapy' (injections of oestrogen). He chose the organo-therapy.

Shortly after, he entered into Jungian analysis to alleviate depression and anger. In June 1954, after more innovative work on morphogenesis and without warning, Turing committed suicide – seemingly by eating an apple that had been dipped in cyanide.

J. L. Britton, D. C. Ince and P. T. Saunders (eds) *The Collected Works of A. M. Turing (Mechanical Intelligence; Pure Mathematics; Morphogenesis)*, Amsterdam, 1992; A. Hodges, *Alan Turing: The Enigma of Intelligence*, New York, 1983.

Elizabeth A. Wilson

U

Ulrichs, Karl Heinrich (1825–1895), German sexologist. Ulrichs was born in Aurich (Kingdom of Hanover), Germany; he died in Aquila, Italy. His father, an architect in the civil service of Hanover, died when Ulrichs was 10 years old; Ulrichs then moved with his mother to the home of her father, a Lutheran superintendent. He studied law in Göttingen and Berlin and was in the civil service of Hanover from 1848 until 1854, when he resigned in order to avoid being disciplined. His homosexual activity had come to the attention of his superiors and, although homosexual acts were not then illegal in Hanover, as a civil servant he could be dismissed. For the next few years, Ulrichs earned his living as a reporter for the important *Allegemeine Zeitung* (Augsburg) and as secretary to one of the representatives to the German Confederation in Frankfurt-am-Main. He also received a small inheritance from his mother on her death in 1856.

Using the pseudonym Numa Numantius, he published in 1864–1865 five booklets under the collective title *Forschungen über das Räthsel der mannmännlichen Liebe* (*Researches on the Riddle of Male–Male Love*). They set forth a biological theory of homosexuality, the so-called 'third sex' theory, which he summed up in the Latin phrase *anima muliebris virili corpore inclusa* (a female psyche confined in a male body). He coined the term 'Urn-ing' for the (male) subject of this condition; adding a typical German ending, he called the female opposite number 'Urningin'. (The term 'homosexual', coined by Karl Maria KERTBENY, first appeared in 1869.)

Ulrichs's next booklet, now under his real name, described his appearance at a Congress of German Jurists in Munich on 29 August 1867, where he urged repeal of the anti-homosexual laws. He was shouted down and not allowed to finish, but this was the first time that a self-acknowledged Urning spoke out publicly for his cause. Thus Ulrichs was not only the first theorist of homosexuality, but also the first 'homosexual' to 'come out' publicly.

Ulrichs's series of booklets continued until 1879; there were 12 in all. His goal was to free people like himself from the legal, religious and social condemnation of homosexual acts as unnatural, and for this he invented a new terminology that would refer to the nature of the individual and not to the acts performed. But his impact on sexology was more significant for directing medical researchers' attention to the subject of homosexuality than in changing their view of it. Richard von KRAFFT-EBING, for example, whose book *Psychopathia sexualis* established the medical view of homosexuality, was first made interested in the subject by Ulrichs's writings.

Ulrichs was also a political activist; he

was twice imprisoned for his public protests against the invasion and annexation of Hanover by Prussia in 1866. And he fought not only for the equal rights of homosexuals, but also for the rights of ethnic and religious minorities, as well as the rights of women, including unwed mothers and their children. But his one-man campaign against the legal oppression of homosexuals was unsuccessful. Although he remained in Germany after the harsh Prussian anti-homosexual law was extended to the unified Germany in 1872, he left in 1880 for voluntary exile in Italy, where he devoted the last years of his life to promoting Latin as an international language through the publication of a little journal written entirely by himself in that language.

Ulrichs's originally simple biological theory of homosexuality had to be repeatedly revised by him as he continued to encounter a greater variety of homosexuals. The doctrine as he taught it has since been abandoned, but for more than a century some form of biological determinism has prevailed, both in the popular mind and in scientific circles; it has been adopted by both homosexual liberationists and their enemies. But ultimately, perhaps, Ulrichs will be best remembered for his courageous stand for the equal rights of all and, as Magnus HIRSCHFELD wrote, 'as one of the first and noblest of those who have striven with courage and strength in this field to help truth and charity gain their rightful place'.

H. Kennedy, *Ulrichs: The Life and Works of Karl Heinrich Ulrichs, Pioneer of the Modern Gay Movement*, Boston, 1988; H. Kennedy, 'Karl Heinrich Ulrichs, First Theorist of Homosexuality', in V. A. Rosario (ed.) *Science and Homosexualities*, London, 1997: 26–45.

Hubert Kennedy

Umberto II (1904–1983), last king of Italy. Born in Turin as the second son of King Victor Emmanuel III, Umberto had a military education but also took a degree in law. Climbing through the ranks, he became a general in 1936 and four years later held nominal command of the Italian armies attacking France. However, when the king provoked the fall of Mussolini and switched his support to the Allies in 1943, they vetoed his plan to place Umberto at the head of the Italian army of liberation. Meanwhile, Mussolini, who had been freed by Nazi troops, had proclaimed the Republic of Salò (with himself as president) in northern Italy, which remained under the control of Nazi and Fascist forces. Fascist newspapers now began to attack the royal house; at this time were printed the first accusations about the homosexuality of Prince Umberto, whom they called 'Stellassa' ('Ugly Starlet').

In 1944, after the liberation of Rome, Umberto began acting as regent for his father in an attempt to save the monarchy, which had been compromised by 20 years of support of Fascism. In May 1946, as the Italians prepared for a referendum to choose between a monarchy and a republic, Victor Emmanuel abdicated in favour of his son, who became King Umberto II. On 2 June 1946, voters decided in favour of a republic; 12 days later, Umberto left Italy. Hoping to regain his throne, he did not abdicate; his refusal to do so led to the inclusion of a clause in the constitution of republican Italy forbidding all first-born males of the royal family from returning to Italy. Umberto lived for the rest of his life in Cascais (Portugal) and in Geneva, where he died. He is buried in the Savoy family tomb in Haute-Combe, France.

Thanks to the mediocrity of the Savoy dynasty to which he belonged, Umberto found himself in the rare position of being despised by both the right – which accused the royal family of treason – and by the left – which reproached the Savoy rulers for their support for the Fascists and Nazis. Because of this, Umberto did not benefit from the usual law of silence which surrounds the private life of those in power; anti-monarchist groups even took full advantage of accusations about his homosexuality in the lead-up to the referendum.

Only the ever-diminishing number of monarchists then showed concern about a book which appeared in the post-war years containing revelations about Umberto II. Enrico Montanari's work told how in 1927, when he was a young lieutenant in Turin, he was insistently courted by the then Prince Umberto, who even gave him a silver cigarette lighter bearing the inscription 'Dimmi di sì!' ('Say yes to me!'). No scandal arose from the hints contained in the biographies of the film-director (and duke) Luchino Visconti concerning – in more or less explicit terms – his relationship with the prince at the time when Umberto was considered one of the most eligible bachelors in Europe's royal families. Yet in 1930 Umberto married Princess Marie José of the Belgian Royal family, with whom he had four sons (including the current claimant to the Italian throne, Vittorio Emanuele). Nevertheless, the fact that the first was born only after four years of the couple's marriage gave rise to much gossip and rumours that the children had been conceived by artificial insemination; it was also said that there were the sons of other fathers, among them the Fascist leader Italo Balbo. Even Count Ciano, Mussolini's son-in-law, wrote in his diary on the occasion of a new pregnancy of Marie José: 'I was left to understand that the child who will be born is his [Umberto's] without the intervention of doctors or syringes.' This does not prove that the rumours were true – even if Domenico Bartoli comments on Ciano's assertions: 'It can be seen that there were grains of truth to the gossip' – but they do indicate the sort of notoriety which followed Umberto through his life. (Similar rumours circulated about his brother-in-law, Ludwig von Hassen).

Umberto did little to avoid such a reputation. For instance, he spent his wedding-night and his entire honeymoon in Courmayeur not with his wife but with a group of Turin officials and 'friends', to whom Umberto presented diamonds in the shape of a 'U'. Afterwards, when Umberto called on his wife, he always had himself announced and visited her accompanied by someone else. It is not surprising that the Fascist secret police soon began to gather information about the 'pederasty' of the heir, either in order to blackmail him or as leverage to control him in the future, as Balbo himself disclosed to the king, in an attempt to safeguard himself from charges which enemies had circulated about his own relationship with Marie José. Furthermore, Umberto and his wife lived apart, except for a mimimun of contact necessary for the sake of appearances; they kept separate apartments, separate beds and separate friends.

Umberto, unlike his Savoy predecessors, was a fervent Catholic. He experienced his sexual transgressions, according to his biographers, as guilt-inducing erotic raptures. For Bartoli, 'The prince was a true believer and a practising Catholic almost to the point of fanaticism. Therefore, sensual urges had a satanic origin, yet he was unable to resist them. . . . Thus the consequences of his sins became a devastating burden. The exact nature of the sins, however, could only be whispered.'

Umberto liked to choose his partners from the military, with a preference for officers – Visconti was an officer at the time of their liaison – rather than common soldiers. Later, in exile in Cascais, where Bartoli says euphemistically that the ex-king enjoyed no 'female distractions', he again chose his friends from among young regimental officers. Even before his marriage, Umberto's custom of giving a fleur-de-lis made of precious stones – the fleur-de-lis was a symbol of the Savoy dynasty – to the young officials and lovers in his entourage was well known; they flaunted the gifts in public.

Among his supposed lovers at the time were the handsome French actor Jean Marais (later the companion of Jean COCTEAU) and the boxer Primo Carnera, who won the world boxing championship in

1933. In response to questions about why Umberto once wanted to meet him in private, Carnera (quoted in Petacco) simply answered that 'the prince had received him wearing a swimming costume and asked him to go for a swim with him in the pool. They then spent the afternoon alone together.' Clearly, bathing costumes are fit for a king – especially when the visitor is endowed with a fine physique.

D. Bartoli, *La fine della monarchia*, Milan, 1946; S. Bertoldi, *L'ultimo re, l'ultima regina*, Milan, 1992; E. Montanari, *La lotta di liberazione*, quoted in S. Rossi, 'Il vizio segreto di Umberto di Savoia', *Extra*, 1, 4 (25 March 1971: 1–4; A. Petacco, *Regina: La vita e i segreti di Maria José* Milan, 1997.

Giovanni Dall'Orto

V

Valentino, Rudolph (1895–1926), Italian-American actor. Virile yet effeminate, menacing yet charming, an *homme fatal* – Valentino remains a potent image, often used in advertising and in comedies about early Hollywood. His allure, which spanned a career of only six years, has never been successfully recaptured. Rudolf Nureyev – who had been named after Valentino – unconvincingly starred in an overblown, evasive screen biography in 1977. A version that was announced in the early 1990s, starring Antonio Banderas – who has been called the new Valentino – has never been made. Long discounted as something of a joke, Valentino is slowly being recognised as a skilled actor with balletic grace and a stylish wit. Yet he was derided as effeminate, a pseudo-woman.

Certainly no other male star has courted decadence quite so openly. His first wife, who was bisexual, left him on their wedding night. His second, Natacha Rambova, the former lover of Alla Nazimova who had co-starred with him in *Camille*, was responsible for the ornate sets and costumes in some of his films. In *The White Rajah* he wore little more than a jewelled jock-strap and pearls. Their life together was a whirl of extravagance, involving custom-made cars, a Doberman Pinscher, two Great Danes, lion cubs, pet snakes and three Pekinese. After their marriage broke up, he became involved with another bisexual actress, Pola Negri.

Valentino's appeal was potent enough for his sudden death from peritonitis to ignite worldwide mourning and overnight create a cult unequalled until those surrounding James Dean and Bruce Lee.

Rumours about Valentino's bisexuality have never been proved. He left no diaries. There were no major scandals, although it is surmised that he had been a gigolo to both men and women, and had slept with men (and women) to secure film work before his sensational starring début in *The Four Horsemen of the Apocalypse* in 1921. The dildo used in the 1966 murder of another screen Latin lover, gay Ramon Novarro, was popularly supposed to have been a gift from Valentino, cast from his own member.

His biographer, Alexander Walker, successfully, though somewhat disparagingly, crystallises his subject's extraordinary single-handed redefining of the male on screen in a way similar to what Montgomery Clift was to achieve 30 years later. 'Valentino's great talent lay', wrote Walker, 'in the completely natural way he was able to humanise this mythical type [of hero] in terms of his own sexuality – and if the latter quality contains a strong element of sexual ambiguity, this is not something that should entirely surprise us. Nor, on the evidence available, is it something we can confidently label.'

A. Walker, *Valentino*, London, 1976.

                                    Keith Howes

Van Vechten, Carl (1880–1964), American writer, photographer and critic. Born in Cedar Rapids, Iowa, Van Vechten was educated at the University of Chicago. He then became the music critic for the *New York Times* and drama critic for the *New York Press*. His critical articles from this period are collected in *Red* (1925) and *Excavations* (1926). In New York literary circles he helped rediscover Herman MELVILLE and introduced Ronald FIRBANK to the United States; he helped Langston Hughes and Wallace Stevens publish their first collections of poetry, and his tireless efforts on behalf of Gertrude STEIN are well known. He also helped countless African-American writers publish their work, and made a substantial contribution to the advancement of black scholarship in the James Welden Johnson Memorial Collection of Negro Arts.

In 1906 Van Vechten moved to New York City to free himself from the small-minded ideals of his hometown, a town which he comically depicts in *The Tattooed Countess* (1924). At this time he gave up critical writing and turned to fiction. Using his satirical eye, Van Vechten wrote campy novels; his first success was *Peter Wiffle* (1922), a text which captures the charm and excitement of pre-World War I Paris and New York. At this time he 'became violently interested in Negroes' almost to the point of an addiction. Subsequently, Van Vechten began visiting the parties, speakeasies, cabarets and nightclubs of Jazz-Age Harlem. Although he was married to the Russian actress Fania Marinoff, his trips to Harlem were frequently in the company of 'handsome black call boys'. These uptown journeys inspired Van Vechten to write *Nigger Heaven* (1926), a novel about 'authentic' black life in Harlem. This text reads as a voyeuristic gaze into a culture which the author believed was 'unrestricted by Nordic rationalism'. Sexual liaisons take up much of the novel's action: white men solicit African-American prostitutes while white patrons cruise the nightclubs in search of homosexual opportunities. Although this novel was a financial success, African-American leaders (such as W. E. B. Du Bois) condemned the novel as an unjust and racist representation of black culture. For Van Vechten, though, Harlem was a liberating space where, even during the prohibition years, he could drink freely and be open about his homosexuality. This sense of sexual liberation is presented on the opening pages of his novel *Parties* (1930), which introduces the two male protagonists as they awake in bed together and discuss their rendezvous in a Harlem speakeasy on the previous evening.

Van Vechten's other novels include *The Blind Bow-Boy* (1923), *Firecrackers* (1925) and *Spider Boy* (1928). These novels are interesting in that they utilise and develop an urbane and camp sensibility that is often associated with gay culture.

E. Leuders, *Van Vechten and the Twenties*, New York, 1955; E. Leuders, *Carl Van Vechten*, New York, 1965; B. Kellner, *Van Vechten and the Irreverent Decades*, New York, 1968.

                                    Justin D. Edwards

Varchi, Benedetto (1503–1565), Italian man of letters. Born in Florence, the son of a notary, Varchi spent his life in the study and teaching of literature. As a youth, he undertook in-depth study of Latin (though he never mastered Greek), then took a degree in law at Pisa. In 1524, on his father's death, Varchi began practising as a notary, a profession he soon abandoned for literature. In order to earn a living, he then worked as a secretary and tutor for various illustrious patrons. He allied with the opponents of the Médicis and in 1537 joined anti-Médici exiles in Padua, where he gained the protection of the Strozzi family. Having lost their favour, partly because of a homosexual scandal, Varchi moved to Bologna in 1540; precarious finances forced him to accept an invitation to return to Florence, and to a reconciliation with Duke Cosimo de' Médici, three years later. From this moment on, Varchi played the role of a key figure in Florentine cultural life, hailed as a philosopher and perhaps honoured beyond his just due.

His status, however, did not keep him from being arrested in 1545 for the rape of a female child, although according to his biographers this was nothing more than a set-up mounted in order to ruin him; Varchi nevertheless had to pay a fine and compensation to the family of the victim. His conviction did not deprive him of Cosimo's favour, and Varchi subsequently held important posts in the Florentine Academy and published on linguistics, aesthetics and popular philosophy. He also wrote hundreds of (rather tedious) Neoplatonic and Petrachian sonnets. Most appreciated today among his large number of works is a history of Florence (covering the period 1527–1538), the comedy *La suocera*, several brief works on figurative art and, in particular, a treatise on the Italian language, *L'Ercolàno*.

From a homosexual point of view, Varchi's work is noteworthy for an uncompromising – and towards the end of his life unfashionable – defence of Socratic love, as cast in the homoerotic formulation of Marsilio FICINO. Varchi's sonnets are explicit, though supposedly chaste, declarations of love, whilst his Latin compositions constitute such veritable confessions that they were damned as 'scandalous' by Scipione Ammirato in his *Opuscoli* (1637). Varchi was thus among the last humanist heralds of Socratic love, and contemporaries displayed open distrust of the 'chaste affection' which had inspired his sonnets, for instance those written for the youth Giulio della Stufa. A letter written by the youth reveals that his father expressly forbade him to frequent Varchi, since various rival poets, such as Antonfrancesco Grazzini and Alfonso de' Pazzi, circulated sonnets in which they took aim at Varchi's

homosexual tastes and his relationship with Giulio.

Varchi was perhaps the most significant exponent for a whole generation of homosexuals (which also included MICHELANGELO) of a Platonism which served as both affirmation and defence. Using this philosophical cover, Varchi left in his writings a real autobiography of his romances. His first documented love (around 1525) was for an adolescent called Giovanni de' Pazzi, whose father had Varchi attacked and stabbed when he found out that the youth was slipping out of the family house in the dead of night to meet his lover. The following year, Varchi fell in love with one Giulianino Gondi. When Gondi met his death in a street fight, his place in Varchi's affections was taken in 1527 by 10-year-old Lorenzo Lenzi – proof of Varchi's increasingly pedophilic tendencies, though their liaison was probably not a physical one. Varchi wrote many love sonnets for Lenzi, whom he called, with a reference to Petrarch's work, 'Lauro'. They remained friends for the rest of Varchi's life, and he bequeathed his library to Lenzi; in 1555, Lenzi had come to the aid of Varchi, then suffering financial constraints, by inviting him to Bologna.

Varchi's fourth love affair, in 1537, was with Giulio Strozzi and took place in Padua, where Varchi had followed Lenzi when he went to that city to study law. Piero Strozzi, head of the Florentine exiles in Padua, hired Varchi as a tutor for his younger brothers Lorenzo, Alessandro and Giulio. In his poetry Varchi increasingly openly proclaimed his love for Giulio (whom he called 'Carino' in his verses), and turned desperate after the youth's death. Varchi was fired, and the break with the family was so bitter that Strozzi had him ambushed in the street and beaten by one of his servants. Varchi thereupon left Padua for Bologna.

Upon returning to Florence, Varchi found a fifth love: a lad about whom nothing is known except that Varchi celebrated him in his poems with the pastoral name of Iola. From 1553 to 1555, still in Florence, Varchi lost his head to the 14-year-old Giulio della Stufa – the pair became the laughing-stock of the city. When this love came to an end Varchi consoled himself with Cesare Ercolani, a nobleman whom he had met when he was staying in Bologna in 1555; Varchi's *L'Ercolàno* is dedicated to him. Towards the end of his life, Varchi wrote yet another series of love sonnets (which, for obvious reasons, have remained unpublished) for a 10-year-old boy, perhaps an orphan named Palla de' Ruccelai, whose praises he sang under the name of Cirillo. This, and his other loves, are detailed in Manacorda's and Pirotti's explicit biographies of Varchi.

It should be said that with the passing of time, the 'chaste' and 'pure' nature of the love celebrated by Varchi in his sonnets was viewed with ever-increasing scepticism, and he was attacked in numerous verse and prose works by his contemporaries. Probably because of this, Varchi realised late in life that he had gone too far in confronting popular opinion, and he entered holy orders in order to save his reputation. The strategy apparently was successful, and at his death Varchi was buried with full honours in the Chiesa degli Angeli in Florence.

G. Dall'Orto, ' "Socratic Love" as a Disguise for Same-sex Love in the Italian Renaissance', in K. Gerard and G. Hekma (eds) *The Pursuit of Sodomy: Male Homosexuality in Renaissance and Enlightenment Europe*, New York, 1989: 33–65; G. Manacorda, 'Benedetto Varchi. L'uomo, il poeta, il critico', *Annali della R. Scuola normale di Pisa*, 17, 2, 1903: 1–161; U. Pirotti, *Benedetto Varchi e la cultura del suo tempo*, Florence, 1971; J. Wilhelm (ed.) *Gay and Lesbian Poetry. An Anthology from Sappho to Michelangelo*, New York, 1995: 313–15.

Giovanni Dall'Orto

Vaughan, Charles John (1816–1897). British headmaster and clergyman. Born at Leicester in England, Vaughan was educated at Rugby School under its famous headmaster Dr Arnold, and Trinity College, Cambridge University, where he graduated BA in 1838. In 1839 he was elected a fellow of Trinity and in 1845 was awarded the degree of Doctor of Divinity, though his scholarship was not profound. In 1841 he was ordained deacon and priest in the Church of England and succeeded his father as vicar of a parish in Leicester. Having failed in his application to succeed Dr Arnold at Rugby, in 1844 he was elected headmaster of Harrow School, which was then in a run-down condition. In 1850 he married Catherine Stanley, daughter of the Bishop of Norwich and sister of Arthur Penrhyn Stanley, later Dean of Westminster. From 1851 Vaughan was a chaplain to Queen Victoria and one of her favourite preachers.

A purposeful school reformer, Vaughan sought to turn Harrow into something like Rugby and to this end implemented many of Arnold's ideas. The school flourished and became famous. He established close relationships with his senior pupils, seeking to inspire them with his ideals of Christian duty and leadership. His friendship sometimes went further. In 1858 a Harrow pupil told a school friend, John Addington SYMONDS, that he had been having a love affair with Vaughan and had personal letters to prove it. This information eventually came to the knowledge of Symonds's father, a well known physician, who threatened to expose Vaughan unless he resigned as headmaster and agreed never to accept an important ecclesiastical post. In 1859 Vaughan resigned, claiming that after 15 years of service at Harrow he had outlived his usefulness.

Soon afterwards, in 1860, Vaughan accepted the prime minister's offer of the bishopric of Rochester, but then, to everyone's surprise, he withdrew his acceptance. The author of his entry in the *Dictionary of National Biography* records that it was 'commonly believed that offers of a like sort were renewed more than once; but even to his closest friends he never spoke of them; his determination had been taken once for all.' Gossip about his indiscretions at Harrow spread though the upper levels of government and church, though nothing was said publicly. Vaughan then became vicar of Doncaster in Yorkshire where he began, within his own household, the preparation for ordination of talented young men who were university graduates. For this he became famous. His pupils were popularly known in the church as 'Vaughan's doves'; many of them later achieved high office.

In 1869 he was appointed Master of the Temple, a prestigious post in the city of London which, from 1879 (after Dr Symonds's death), he held concurrently with the deanery of Llandaff in Cardiff. An eloquent preacher, he published many books of sermons. He was a trusted confidant of archbishops and bishops but never became a bishop himself and he played little part in the public life of the Church of England. Among senior Victorian ecclesiastics he was unusual in having no life and letters published after his death. This was due to his own strict instructions that no biography be written. Vaughan managed to avoid public scandal but his homosexuality prevented him from being appointed a bishop.

Obituary in *The Times*, 16 October 1897; 'Vaughan, Charles John', *Dictionary of National Biography*, Vol. 20 (1899), pp. 159–61; W. T. Gibson, 'Homosexuality, Class and the Church in Nineteenth Century England: Two Case Studies', *Journal of Homosexuality*, 21, 4 (1991): 45–55; P. Grosskurth, *John Addington Symonds: A Biography*, London, 1964; J. A. Symonds, *The Memoirs of John Addington Symonds*, ed. P. Grosskurth, London, 1984.

David Hilliard

Vendôme, Louis-Joseph (1654–1712), French general. Paris's Place Vendôme, one of the city's best-known squares, once contained a mansion, the Hôtel de Vendôme, popularly known among seventeenth-century Parisians as the 'Hôtel de Sodome'. It belonged to the

Dukes of Vendôme, descendants of an illegitimate son of King Henri IV. Several members of the family were famous both for their homosexuality or bisexuality and their military successes, especially César (1594–1655), who scored a brilliant victory over the Spanish, Philippe (1655–1717) and particularly Louis-Joseph, one of Louis XIV's best generals.

Louis-Joseph de Vendôme, reputed for his *sang-froid* in battle, won numerous victories in campaigns in Italy and Spain, where he died and was buried in the Escorial. According to contemporary accounts, notably that of the Duc de Saint-Simon, Vendôme 'plunged', throughout his life, 'more than anyone else', into sodomy: 'his valets and officers . . . always satisfied' his desires. His penchant was well known, and those seeking to win his patronage began by paying court to his favourites. Vendôme owned a chateau at Anet, near Paris, and another contemporary wrote that 'the peasant men of the environs of his fine property at Anet waited for him as he went out hunting, as he would often take them into the woods to fuck him, giving them a coin for their work. The money helped them pay their taxes.'

Louis XIV accepted the homosexuality of Vendôme and other members of the court, such as LULLY; indeed, Lully and Vendôme were close friends, and musicians first performed Lully's opera *Acis et Galatée* at Vendôme's chateau in 1686.

Duc de Saint-Simon, *Mémoires*, Paris, 1982; *Clairambault-Maurepas, Chansonnier historique du XVIIIème siècle*, Paris, 1879–1884.

Didier Godard

Verlaine, Paul (1844–1896), French poet. Verlaine had the kind of upbringing and social background which unfitted him to cope with a bisexual temperament in an age of sexual conformism. He was the spoilt child of a doting mother. Brought up in an atmosphere of indulgence, he made little attempt to achieve creditable results at school in Paris, where his family settled when he was seven, and in his brief attempt at university life (1862–1863) he spent more time in the cafés of the Latin Quarter than in the Law Faculty where he was enrolled. In 1864 under parental pressure he became a clerk in an insurance company, but his father's death the following year removed the only restraining influence on him. After having a few poems and articles accepted in magazines, he published his first volume of poetry, *Poèmes saturniens* (*Saturnian Poems*), in 1866 at his own expense, having obtained the money from his cousin Elisa. Her death in childbirth a few months later seems to have shocked Verlaine greatly and to have occasioned a bout of heavy drinking which marked the onset of the alcoholism that was increasingly to mar his life. His second volume of poetry, *Fêtes galantes* (1869), is marked by a sense of spiritual and emotional emptiness and a profound cynicism about all things erotic. The same year, in search of personal and social stability, Verlaine turned to marriage: he became engaged to a 16-year-old provincial, Mathilde Mauté, whose youth was matched by her ignorance and banality of mind, and married her the following year. The collection of poems in which he dutifully expressed his love for his fiancée, *La Bonne Chanson* (*The Good Song*), was the most banal and unconvincing verse he was ever to produce, and gives rise to the impression that, though he was certainly physically bisexual, emotionally he was never really drawn to women. The real direction of both his emotional inclinations and his poetic talent was about to be revealed by a very different relationship.

The months following his marriage marked a period of political and personal turmoil. During the siege of Paris which followed the disastrous Franco-Prussian war (1870–1871) Verlaine was a member of the National Guard, and in the civil upheaval which followed the armistice he sided with the rebellious Communards who had tried to establish their own form of republic. When the forces of the Commune were defeated, fearing reprisals, he left Paris and took Mathilde to his relatives at Fampoux, near Arras in northern France. Jobless, he then returned with his now-pregnant wife to the capital. It was at this point that he received a letter from another 16-year-old, the budding poet Arthur RIMBAUD, who was desperate to escape from his own provincial backwater in Charleville, near the Belgian frontier. Verlaine promptly invited the boy to come and stay with him in his parents-in-law's house in Paris. When Rimbaud made himself so unpleasant to his hosts that he was forced to move out, Verlaine took his side. In January 1872 Mathilde's father took her and her two-month-old son away, and from then until the middle of March Verlaine lived with Rimbaud. Letters and poems written within the early months of what was to be an extremely stormy relationship show that intense emotional ties existed between the two men from the outset. But with characteristic indecision Verlaine yoyoed between wife and lover. The marriage was patched up in mid-March 1872 and Rimbaud went back to Charleville. Then on 7 July Verlaine left for Belgium with the boy. In Brussels Mathilde persuaded her husband to return, only to have him leave the train at the Franco-Belgian frontier and go back to Rimbaud, with whom he set off for London in September. But their relationship too was becoming marked by violent quarrels, and the pattern of parting and rejoining, involving trips to and fro across the channel, continued until 3 July the following year, when Verlaine rushed off to Brussels alone, threatening suicide if he could not effect a rapprochement with his wife. This was replaced by an intention to go as a volunteer to fight in the newly pronounced Spanish Republic. But when Rimbaud, who joined him in Brussels a few days later, made it plain that he considered their relationship over, Verlaine bought a revolver and shot his lover in the wrist. Filled with remorse, he rushed the boy off to hospital to have his wound treated, but later the same day Rimbaud, fearing a repeat performance, was obliged to ask a policeman for help, and Verlaine was arrested. Though Rimbaud tried to have the charges dropped, Verlaine had to stand trial and was condemned to two years' imprisonment, a penalty whose severity was undoubtedly the result of prejudice against the homosexual nature of the relationship. An appeal failed and Verlaine was sent to Mons to serve out his sentence.

By this time Verlaine had already composed his fourth and most important collection of poetry, *Romances sans paroles* (*Songs without words*), and in prison he contrived to continue arranging for its publication (1874). This is the collection which is most marked by his sexual sensibilities, which are expressed through the desire to abdicate reponsibility for the self and to represent experience as something over which the individual has no control. Many of the poems, particularly those in the 'Ariettes oubliées' section, are best experienced as though they were music, whose sensuality conveys more than the apparent surface of the language. At the beginning of May 1894, he learnt that Mathilde had succeeded in gaining a legal separation from him. From this point onwards, both his life and his poetic career started to go downhill. He was converted to a Catholicism which wobbled between picture-postcard naïvety and the kind of algolagnia evident in English poets such as Swinburne and Ernest Dowson. The aesthetic product of his conversion was his collection *Sagesse* (*Wisdom*, 1880). The most constructive period of his life after leaving prison was from 1877 to 1883, when he formed a relationship with another adolescent, Lucien Létinois, who was initially his pupil at a school in Rethel in northern France. The couple even settled on a farm there with Lucien's parents, between March 1880 and the beginning of 1882, but the venture was a financial failure. After Lucien's death from typhoid in April 1883, Verlaine never formed another relationship of any note, and his life declined further into drunkenness and a general sordidness. He continued to publish large collections of verse, some of which was very important to the growing Decadent movement. There are also, in *Jadis et naguère* (*Once Upon a Time*, 1884) and *Parallèlement* (1889), fine poems looking back on the relationships with his two lovers. But most of this later verse was banal and facile. Only the two clandestinely published volumes of erotic poetry, *Femmes* (*Females*, 1891) and *Hombres* (*Males*, posthumous, 1903), with their frank evocation of sexual pleasure and the joys of the human body, added anything new. The end of his life was marked by poverty and constant illness, until death was a welcome release.

C. Chadwick, *Verlaine*, London, 1973; J. Richardson, *Verlaine*, London, 1971.

Christopher Robinson

Viau, Théophile de (1590–1626), French poet. Viau was often just called Théophile, nicknamed *le Prince des Poètes*. The prestige of the court of Louis XIV occasionally blinds us to the precursors and founders of Classicism earlier in the century. Though Malherbe may be considered as the great reformer of French poetry, Théophile's influence was scarcely less. In his early years, he was the lover of Jean-Louis GUEZ DE BALZAC, who is regarded as the originator of classical prose style. It would be only slight exaggeration to say that classical French prose and poetry stemmed from a single pair of lovers. Guez de Balzac was not the greatest love of Théophile's life, however, and during an escapade in The Netherlands, uncannily foreshadowing VERLAINE and RIMBAUD, they split up after a brawl. Théophile, a Protestant by birth and a libertine by conviction, was predestined to be persecuted, and he was often exiled. In 1609 he went to London, and unsuccessfully sought to be presented to JAMES I. In 1619 he was banished after publishing some licentious verses about Louis XIII's favourite, the

Duc de Luynes, although he was soon back in Paris. By this time, he had found the great love of his life, Jacques Vallée, Sieur des Barreaux, nine years his junior. Despite Théophile's having abjured Calvinism, there was a powerful clique of bigots and Jesuits plotting against him. Their opportunity came in 1622 when Théophile published his *Parnasse satyrique*: a sonnet on venereal disease ends: 'My closest friends will not come near me, and in this state, I do not even dare touch myself: Philis, I got this illness by f*cking you. God, I wish I had not lived so badly, and if your ire does not strike me down straight away, I vow only to f*ck arses from now on.'

In 1623 court proceedings were initiated against Théophile and a certain Berthelot who, despite the fact that he had been dead for eight years, was like Théophile condemned to be burned at the stake. Théophile – by now in hiding – sought to flee to England, but was apprehended and returned to Paris. While he was in prison, Théophile felt himself abandoned by those he loved, and his *Plainte à un sien ami* (*Complaint to a Friend*) foreshadows WILDE's *De Profundis*. However, des Barreaux did discredit the prosecution by testifying that while a schoolboy, he had been abused by one of Théophile's most zealous detractors. Théophile was spared the pyre, and was sheltered by the Duc de Montmorency at Chantilly. But his health was ruined, and he died there of tuberculosis, in des Barreaux's arms, in 1626. The street singers called des Barreaux 'Théophile's widow'.

Viau was but one of a number of so-called *libertins*. It would be wrong to present these as forming a coterie of gays analogous to pre-Nazi Berlin. For one thing, the term '*libertin*', like the term 'sodomite', could refer both to heterosexual and homosexual sexual athletes. The very fact that straight and gay were lumped together in a single category prevented this group from using sexuality as a mark of identity. Still, there were a con-

siderable number of homosexuals, including Jean-Louis Guez de Balzac, Denis Sanguin de SAINT-PAVIN, François le Métel de BOISROBERT and Charles Coypeau d'Assoucy.

G. Saba, *Fortunes et infortunes de Théophile de Viau: histoire de la critique suivie d'une bibliographie*, Paris, 1997; C. Rizza, *Libertinage et littérature*, Paris, 1996; M. Lever, *Les bûchers de Sodome*, Paris, 1985; F. Lachèvre (ed.) *La vie et les poésies libertines inédites de Des Barreaux, 1599–1673 [et de] Saint-Pavin, 1595–1670*, Paris, 1911; C. E. Scruggs, *Charles Dassoucy: Adventures in the Age of Louis XIV – the Life and Works of Dassoucy with Selected Narratives from his Adventures*, London, 1984.

David Parris

Villamediana, Juan de Tassis, Count of (1582–1622), Spanish poet and man-about-town. Juan de Tassis is one of the most colourful personalities of the Spanish Golden Age. His poetic output is in itself remarkable: a follower of the Baroque style of Góngora, he wrote satire but also poems meant to praise politicians. His reputation rests on two philosophical poems about the dangers of ambition, inspired by mythological figures such as Phaeton and Icarus. He knew what he was talking about. Contemporary accounts present a man with high aspirations, a restless self-publiciser with a talent for Machiavellian operations, a man who was both intelligent and vain, elegant and obscene, faithless and spiritual – eventually, one who would go one step too far in giving offence to people more powerful than himself and pay for his mistakes with his life. Tassis may have been one of the inspirations for Tirso de Molina's *El burlador de Sevilla*, one of the earliest theatrical manifestations of the myth of Don Juan, thereafter explored by BYRON, Molière and Mozart.

Villamediana belonged to a European family which held a monopoly on postal services in Spain. He received a careful humanistic education typical of noblemen at this time, as his family intended to place him in the court of Philip III. He arrived in Madrid in 1599, and diverse accounts show him obsessed with finding connections to help him climb up socially. He soon attempted to win the king's sympathy, but he had a strong enemy in the powerful and equally machiavellian Conde-Duque de Olivares. His satirical lyrics made things worse and he soon saw himself in a very dangerous situation to which only the king's death brought some relief. He then came into the service of Philip IV, but the new monarch was aware of the poet's reputation and never trusted him fully. Among ordinary people, he was known as a womaniser, and his alleged exploits made him into something of a living legend. It is difficult to tell which of the anecdotes about him are true and which are the product of the imagination of Madrid citizens. In any case, rumours about a liaison between him and the queen, and, even worse, about him boasting of making Philip IV into a cuckold, were frequent and may have been the cause of his death. He was murdered in highly suspicious circumstances in Madrid.

Records of a forensic investigation mention that the Count was a sodomite, and that this crime was proven. Even if evidence is not too abundant on this point, many specialists have simply wondered why he should not have been one. Accounts of sexual profligacy and both homosexual and heterosexual brothel consortiums run by individuals close to the court seem to be accurate. Homosexuality appears to have been common in Renaissance Spain, and in the case of Villamediana it is impossible to ignore homophobic jibes that are found in a satirical poem by Quevedo, an even more sharp-tongued satirist than the count himself.

N. A. Cortés, *La muerte del conde de Villamediana*, Valladolid, 1928; L. Rosales, *Pasión*

y muerte del Conde de Villamediana, Madrid, 1969.

Alberto Mira

Villaurrutia, Xavier (1903–1950), Mexican poet. Villaurrutia belongs to the avant-garde poetry group Contemporáneos. As a founder of the Ulises theatre organisation (1928), he attempted to renew the Mexican stage by writing modern plays, training actors who had been limited to melodrama and slapstick, and teaching a new public to understand the new artistic forms of modern times. He also founded Grupo de Orientación in 1932 and other small theatre groups in the 1930s and 1940s.

Nostalgia de la muerte (*Nostalgia of Death*, 1938) is his most famous collection of poems. 'Nocturno amor' ('Nocturnal Love') and 'Nocturno de los ángeles' ('Nocturne of the Angels') are among the best gay poems ever written. Other important poems are 'Nocturno Mar' ('Sea Nocturne') and 'Nocturno de la alcoba' ('Nocturne of the Bedroom'), and some of his epigrams.

In prose he wrote *Dama de corazones* (*Queen of Hearts*, 1928), a Proustian exercise. *El Amor es así* (*Love is This Way*) is a melodrama about the life of working-class immigrants in Mexico City. *Variedad* (*Variety*) is a key text to understanding the influence of André GIDE among the Contemporáneos group. *Cartas de Villaurrutia a Novo (1935–1936)* (*Letters from Villaurrutia to Novo*) is a collection of letters of high literary value that Villaurrutia sent Salvador NOVO while he was studying theatre at Yale University.

Autos profanos (1943) is a collection of one-act plays. *¿En qué piensas?* (*What are you thinking about?*, 1938) is a study about the modern woman. *Sea usted breve* (*Be Brief*, 1938) has absurdist elements and denouces an attempt by the authority to promote birth control without taking into account the opinion of women. *El asente* (*The Absent One*, 1943) criticises machismo in the working class and advocates the right of women to live by themselves. *La mulata de Córdoba* (*The Mulatto Woman from Cordoba*, 1939) is a melodram written by Villaurrutia and his male companion, the painter Agustín Lazo. It is written in the fashion of the scripts of the Mexican cinema of the 1930s, and uses the melodrama to try to resolve the social conflicts of the period. The opera version of this play elevates to the rank of high culture the popular culture of the Golden Age of Mexican cinema. *La hiedra* (*Ivy*, 1941) is a Victorian drama whose main purpose is to Mexicanise bourgeois European high culture. *La mujer legítima* (*The Legitimate Wife*, 1942), *Invitación a la muerte* (*Invitation to Death*, 1943), and *El yerro candente* (*The Burning Error*, 1944) are bourgeois dramas built around Greek myths, with powerful heroines. They are effective in depicting dysfunctional families, and at the same time presenting the family as the place where conflicts have to be resolved. *El pobre Barba Azul* (*Poor Blue Beard*, 1947) and *Juego peligroso* (*Dangerous Game*, 1950) are comedies similar to the previous melodramas. They present the same problems, family and gender construction, but in a comic way. Villaurrutia combined a deep knowledge of high and popular culture. He also wrote *género chico* (a hybrid genre akin to cabaret). As a film critic he wrote more than 500 movie reviews, and he published essays about literature and art.

F. Dauster, *Xavier Villaurrutia*, New York, 1971.

Salvador A. Oropesa

Villette, Marquis Charles-Michel de (1734–1793), French writer. Villette was the most famous sodomite in eighteenth-century France. A wealthy nobleman, born in Paris, Villette earned a law degree, but instead of practising his profession preferred to serve in the French army during the Seven Years War (1756–1763), before beginning a literary career with the support of VOLTAIRE, who was his mother's

friend. (Indeed, Villette liked to hint that he was Voltaire's illegitimate son.) He was rich, handsome (though very short) and witty, but contemporaries gossiped about his private life and mocked him in print as an aristocratic wastrel, coward and sodomite.

Satirical pamphlets published at the start of the French Revolution portrayed Villette as spokesman for the country's sodomites and an advocate of sexual liberty. For example, *The Children of Sodom before the National Assembly* (1790), supposedly signed by 'Charles, Marquis de Villette, High Commander of the Order', and purportedly the text of a meeting of an association of sodomites, announced that sodomy 'will henceforth become a science studied and taught in all classes of society'. Similarly, in *Les Petits Bougres au Manège* (1790), 'M. de V—, authorised Procurer of the Sodomitical Society', declared that 'my cock and balls belong to me, and so ... whether I put them in a cunt or an arsehole is of no business to anyone else'.

Villette supported the French Revolution from the beginning. He wrote for the *Chronique de Paris* from April 1789 to August 1792, when the department of the Oise elected him deputy to the National Convention. He adopted a moderate political position in the assembly, voting against the death penalty at the trial of Louis XVI. He died of natural causes.

J. Merrick, 'The Marquis de Villette and Mademoiselle de Raucourt', in J. Merrick and B. T. Ragan (eds) *Homosexuality in Modern France*, London, 1996: 30–53; 'Les Petits Bougres au Manège' and 'The Children of Sodom', in M. Blasius and S. Phelan (eds) *We Are Everywhere: A Historical Sourcebook of Gay and Lesbian Politics*, New York, 1997: 37–43.

Michael Sibalis

Villon, François (*c.* 1431–*c.* 1462), French poet. There can be no doubt that Villon was one of the few great French poets. But was he homosexual? It is not certain. The great themes of the *Testament* are the human condition and mortality. However, there is a small collection of ballads in *argot*, the forerunner of modern French slang. These have been recently reissued as *Ballades en argot homosexuel* by Thierry Martin with a translation and promise of a book on Villon's sexuality. Unfortunately, this slang – studied by, among others, the well respected linguist Pierre Guiraud – is all but impenetrable. On the other hand, the fairly frequent occurrence of the world *circoncis* (in modern French 'circumcised') makes it difficult to see them as entirely innocent. If Martin's hypothesis is correct, these ballads are about a refined system of homosexual relations which become comprehensible when one understands the basic rules. According to his interpretation, it was forbidden to sodomise a man who had an erection, so it was necessary to give one's potential partner his pleasure first by fellation. As both partners might be striving to achieve the same end, it was a race in which the slower won. In Martin's translation, *circoncis* means 'with glans exposed', that is, ready for sex.

Villon was born François de Montcorbier in or soon after 1431, raised by a cleric called Villon, and studied theology from 1443 to 1452. Having got in with a disreputable crowd, including the allegedly homosexual Colin de Cayeux, he inadvertently killed a priest in 1455 and fled, but he was pardoned and returned to Paris, only to flee again in 1457, when one of his cronies was hanged. This time he joined a troupe of wandering players. He may also have briefly enjoyed the friendship and patronage of the aristocratic poet Charles d'Orléans. Villon seemed unable to stay out of trouble, and in 1462 was condemned to death, and then pardoned. He died soon after, however, probably of the after-effects of torture. The first version of the *Ballades en argot* turned up in Stockholm in 1884. Another version had long formed part of the complete works.

M. Thierry (ed.) *Ballades en argot homosexuel*, Paris, 1998; J. Dufournet, *Nouvelles recherches sur Villon*, Paris, 1980; P. Guirand, *Le Jargon de Villon ou le gai savoir de la Coquille*, Paris, 1968.

David Parris

Virgil (Publius Vergilius Maro (70–19 BC), Roman poet. Details of the life of this poet, arguably the most significant of all Rome's poets, are very meagre. Born near Mantua (Mantova), he was one of a number of poets from this region who were to have an impact on the development of Latin poetry in the first century BC. His family suffered land confiscations in the aftermath of the civil war between Brutus and Cassius, and Octavian and Antony (44–42 BC), disruption which lies behind Virgil's earliest published verse, the *Eclogues*, poems which exploit pastoral themes in the Greek manner. The second *Eclogue* is a lament of a man who fails to win the love of a beautiful boy, and expresses in lyric style the disappointment of love. The *Georgics* (published *c.* 29 BC) deal with country matters, farming, animal husbandry and the like, while the *Aeneid* (completed *c.* 19 BC), Virgil's final work, turns to the legendary origins of Rome, specifically through Aeneas, who, as son of Venus, was an ancestor of the Julian family to which the emperor Augustus belonged.

Tradition asserts that Virgil, like his patron MAECENAS, preferred the love of men, and SUETONIUS provides some names. What emerges is that in the world of Augustan Rome the sexual preferences of men like Virgil and Maecenas were not an issue. Sexual relations are not central to Virgil's work (unlike OVID), though there are famous passages where the anguish of love is clearly depicted: the story of Orpheus and Eurydice (*Georgics* IV) prefigures Aeneas's loss of his wife Creusa in the flight from Troy (*Aeneid* II), and the parting of Aeneas from Dido is more powerfully described than their union (*Aeneid* IV). Similarly, Aeneas's killing of

Turnus in revenge for the death of Pallas is more important then the details of his relationship with Pallas.

Aeneas is the hero of the *Aeneid*, an epic poem in 12 books which recounts the fall of Troy to the Greeks and the subsequent flight of Aeneas and other Trojans to Italy, where they become the ancestors of the Romans. Aeneas was the son of Venus, goddess of love, and the Trojan Anchises, and was the husband of Creusa, one of the daughters of King Priam. It was the rape of Helen, wife of Menelaus of Sparta, by Priam's son Paris which precipitated the Greek expedition to Troy and the ten-year siege which ended only when the Greeks built a wooden horse inside which they hid soldiers and persuaded the Trojans to take the horse into their city. Fleeing from Troy, Aeneas is shipwrecked near Cathage, whose queen Dido falls in love with him. When he abandons her in order to fulfil his mission to found Rome, Dido commits suicide. On the banks of the Tiber Aeneas is entertained by Evander, whose son, Pallas, is awestruck by the visitor and joins the Trojans in their fight against the Rutulians, and is killed in battle by the Rutulian leader Turnus. The climax of the story is single combat between Turnus and Aeneas: having brought Turnus to his knees, Aeneas is on the point of sparing him, but the sight of Pallas's baldric stirs the anger of Aeneas and he kills Turnus on the spot. Thus the *Aeneid* ends with the hero exacting revenge for the life of Pallas, raising questions about the character of Aeneas and the behaviour appropriate to a hero.

The importance of Aeneas lies in his humanity and susceptibility to human emotions and feelings, as shown especially in his relationship with Dido. While there is no evidence of any sexual relationship with Pallas, the language used suggests an intensity of feeling which goes beyond that Aeneas shows to his own son, Ascanius, though similar to that he shows his father. Virgil's reticence on this may reflect contemporary values; while Aeneas has a faithful companion, Achates, he does not provide a primary emotional focus for Aeneas.

E. Oliensis, 'Sons and Lovers: Sexuality and Gender in Virgil's Poetry', in C. Martindale (ed.) *The Cambridge Companion to Virgil*, Cambridge, 1997: 294–311; M. C. J. Putnam, 'Possessiveness, Sexuality and Heroism in the *Aeneid*', in *Virgil's Aeneid: Interpretation and Influence*, Chapel Hill, 1995: 27–49.

Roger Pitcher

Vivien, Renée (1877–1909), Anglo-French poet. One of the major French lesbian poets of the turn of the century, Vivien was in fact the daughter of an English father of independent means and an American mother. Born in London, her real name was Pauline Mary Tarn. Her childhood was an unsettled one. The family moved to Paris when Vivien was one year old, but the death of her father in 1886 caused further upheavals. Vivien spent her adolescence moving between England and France, an oscillation which was matched by her difficult relationship with her mother – Mary Tarn seems to have been principally interested in getting her hands on as much as possible of her daughter's inheritance. In consequence, while still an adolescent, Vivien suffered such diverse experiences as being made a ward of court, being threatened with incarceration in a mental asylum, and being formally presented to Queen Victoria. The decisive influence of her childhood, however, was Violet Shillito, the daughter of an American industrialist, who both encouraged her in her reading and writing of poetry and fostered her deep dislike of men. In 1899, when Vivien had decisively re-established herself in Paris, Shillito introduced her to another American, also the daughter of an industrialist, Natalie Clifford BARNEY, who had just hit the gossip columns because of her lesbian relationship with the leading courtesan Liane de Pougy. Barney and Vivien were instantly attracted to one another, and by the following year were settled into a relationship which was to be central both to Vivien's poetic career and (eventually) to her physical and emotional disintegration.

By 1901 the tempestuous relationship with Barney had already apparently collapsed: Vivien found their 'open' marriage too stressful, though she herself was very far from monogamous in the ensuing period. But Barney never resigned herself to the separation and made strenuous efforts to get Vivien back, efforts which ended only with the latter's death. It was through Barney that Vivien met both the cream of Parisian lesbian society and a wide range of writers, both the established and the avant-garde. Her own first volume of poems, *Etudes et Préludes*, appeared under the ambiguous signature R. Vivien in 1901, receiving favourable if limited critical attention. A swift succession of other collections followed, of which the most successful was *Evocations* (1903) and the most challenging *La Vénus des aveugles* (*The Venus of the Blind*, also 1903), but it was her *Sapho, traduction nouvelle avec le texte grec*, incorporating all the most recently found fragments and offering a modern and intensely personal view of the Greek poet SAPPHO, which brought her the most critical attention. Attention of a rather different kind followed the publication of an autobiographical novel, *Une Femme m'apparut* (*A Woman Appeared to Me*), in 1904 (revised edition 1905), with its open hostility to male sexuality and its hatred of maternity, the former of which also figured largely in the collection of stories, *La Dame à la louve* (*The Lady with the Lorgnette*), which she published in the same year. At the same period she was also producing works under the pseudonym Paule Riversdale, some of them in collaboration with Baroness Hélène von Zuylen (with whom she had an affair almost as long-drawn-out and chequered as that with Barney). The stress of her lifestyle, with its endless travel, intense bouts of writing (her collections of poetry alone total a dozen in eight years), sexual indul-

gence and drugs finally took their toll. In 1908 she unsuccessfully attempted suicide (with laudanum, in the Savoy Hotel in London). The following year her health began to collapse generally – eye problems, dysentery, amnesia – and eventually she died from a bout of pneumonia.

The morbidity which marked her life is heavily imprinted on her writing, not least through the themes and images of pain, destruction and death which she shares with Baudelaire and the poets of the male Decadent tradition. There is, however, at the same time a quite different side to her writing, deriving from her interest in Sappho and the other Greek women poets, which tried to project a female world unsullied by masculine contact. Here the images are of light, warmth and purity. This can be linked to the importance which Mytilene (the modern name for the island of Lesbos) took on for her: she escaped to the island at regular intervals in the period 1905–1907. The aesthetic tension within her writing thus mirrors the tension between the desire for lesbian separatism and the constraints of social reality which marked her life.

S. Benstock, *Women of the Left Bank: Paris, 1900–1940*, London, 1986; K. Jay, *The Amazon and the Page: Natalie Clifford Barney and Renée Vivien*, Indianapolis, 1988; V. Sanders, *La Poésie de Renée Vivien*, Amsterdam, 1991.

Christopher Robinson

Vizzani, Catterina (1719–1743), Italian retainer. Vizzani was born in Rome, the daughter of a carpenter. At the age of 14, she fell in love with – and her sentiments were reciprocated by – Malgherita, a girl to whom she went each day to learn embroidery. Already she liked to dress in men's clothing, which also allowed her to pay court to her beloved at night by standing under her window. The relationship between the two girls lasted more than two years, until Malgherita's father confronted Vizzani and treatened to denounce her to the courts. Vizzani thereupon decided to move to Viterbo and definitively take on men's dress and identity (under the name of Giovanni Bordoni). Forced to return to Rome because of lack of money, she found work as a (male) retainer for a vicar in Perugia through the intermediary of a priest whom she had met near a Roman church. The vicar declared himself completely satisfied with the services of 'Giovanni' except for one thing for which he always reprimanded him: Giovanni ran after women too much. Vizzani's cross-dressing extended to wearing an artifical leather penis; claims of a venereal disease were used to justify to washerwomen the stains from menstrual blood on her clothing.

Giovanni's reputation as a great seducer spread rapidly. After the 'dissolute retainer' received a serious wound to the neck from a rival for one woman, the vicar decided to write to the Roman priest who had recommended Giovanni to him to complain about his intemperate behaviour. The priest spoke with Giovanni's father, Pietro Vizzani, and learned the truth, but decided to remain silent in order to protect the girl.

After three or four years, Vizzani left the vicar's employ and moved to Monte Pulciano, to the estate of Cavalier Francesco Maria Pucci. There she fell in love with the niece of the local priest; the girl was kept under strict surveillance by her uncle, but she found a way to escape and accept Giovanni's courtship, deciding to flee with her suitor to Rome, where he promised to marry her. She revealed her project to her sister, who threated to expose the two if they did not take her with them – the first hitch in their plan. The two girls rode the horse taken for their escape, while Giovanni followed them on foot. In Lucca the three fugitives picked up a gig, but it broke down during the journey; men sent by the girls' uncle in pursuit were able to catch up with them easily. One of them started a fire and struck Vizzani on the leg – he also killed a dog and injured a child. Vizzani's injury was neglected by the same doctor, Bianchi, who later recorded her story;

though not serious, the wound became infected and proved fatal. On her deathbed, Vizzani revealed her real sex to a nun and expressed a desire to be buried in women's clothes and garlanded as a virgin. Vizzani's funeral attracted a large crowd, partly as several religious figures had proclaimed her a saint because of her virgin death. Vizzani's virtue, in the eyes of her contemporaries, was her 'success' in maintaining strict heterosexual virginity notwithstanding her having lived in the constant company of young men. It was impossible for them to imagine a woman who simply had no interest in men. At the age of 24, Vizzani had paid with her life for her exclusive love for women.

G. Bianchi, *Breve storia della vita di Catterina Vizzani, romana, che per ott'anni vestì abito da uomo in qualità di Servidore, la quale dopo vari casi essendo in fine stata uccisa fu trovata Pulcella nella sezzione del suo cadavero*, Venice, 1744.

Maria Di Rienzo

Vladislas III of Varna (Władysław III Warneńczyk, Ulaszlo I) (1424–1444), king of Poland. From the Jagiellonian dynasty, and son of Vladislas II Jagiello, Vladislas was king of Poland from 1434 to 1444. In 1440, he was offered the crown of Hungary under the condition of marrying Queen Elisabeth, the pregnant widow of King Albrecht Habsburg. The queen soon gave birth to Vladislas the Posthumous and refused to marry her suitor, almost half her age, and decided to fight for the rights of her son. The struggle for the crown was waged for two years until Vladislas of Poland was finally recognised as king of Hungary, mainly because as a knight he would be able to defend the country against the Turks.

In 1443–1444, Vladislas III took part in the crusade against the Turks organised by Pope Eugene IV, during which the king was most probably killed in the Battle of Varna, though legends of his miraculous survival circulated for many years (as his body was never recovered). The lost battle ended any meaningful military attempts of helping Constantinople, which was finally taken by the Turks in 1453.

Though a defender of the faith and martyr, Vladislas was never beatified nor made a saint. Some sources claim that this happened under the influence of the Habsburgs, who did not want a new saint from a rival dynasty. The most popular explanation of the fact (already quoted about 1470 by Jan Długosz in his *Chronicles of the Kingdom of Poland*) is that Giulio Cesarini, the papal nuncio, hastened to inform the Holy See that the decisive battle had been lost due to sin committed by the late monarch. Vladislas supposedly spent the night before the battle in the tent of a good-looking Hungarian page. It is impossible to establish for certain whether Vladislas really was homosexual. It is clear, however, that faced with his possible homosexuality, the popes preferred not to take unnecessary risks by canonising him.

Paweł Jasienica, *Polska Jagiellonów*, Warsaw, 1986: 146–67; L. Stomma, *Królów polskich przypadki*, Warsaw, 1993: 82–7.

Krzysztof Fordoński

Vock, Anna ('Mammina') (1884–1962), Swiss journalist. Vock collaborated on the first, hectographed pages of the homosexual emancipationist *Freundschafts-Banner* (Zurich) in 1932. Publication ceased the same year, but then resumed in 1933 as *Schweizerisches Freundschafts-Banner*, with her name on the masthead as editor and publisher. She continued in this position through 1942, the year the new criminal code in Switzerland allowed homosexual sex between adult men, i.e. over age 20 (lesbian sex had not been criminalised). She several times lost jobs when the gutter press attacked her, publishing her name and address, but she persevered with the periodical, financing it herself when the number of subscribers was too

small to support it. Once she was accused of 'acting as a pander' because of the personal ads in the periodical, but her conviction was overturned by a higher court – and the judge who had convicted her was himself convicted half a year later of having relations with female defendants.

In 1937 Vock changed the name of the periodical to *Menschenrecht* (*Human Rights*), but the choice seemed unfortunate when she and her co-worker Karl 'Rolf' Meier were arrested on suspicion that the paper was a communist front. However, after spending some hours in jail, they were released. By the end of 1942, her finances could not keep the periodical afloat and it was taken over by a small group of men, headed by Meier, who changed the name again. With the new title *Der Kreis* (*The Circle*) in 1943, under the direction of Meier, who always used the pseudonym Rolf as editor, it lasted for 25 more years and became internationally famous as a unique trilingual gay male journal, publishing articles and stories not only in German, but also in French (from 1941) and in English (from 1952).

Affectionately known as 'Mammina' and revered by her comrades, male and female, this courageous lesbian was also a devout Roman Catholic, though not uncritical of her Church. Once when she was refused absolution because of her orientation and her attitude, she proudly left the confessional, to then get absolution nevertheless from an understanding bishop. In his obituary, Rolf recalled the role that she had played: 'Farewell Mammina. Your name will forever be bound with our cause in Switzerland. You prepared the ground on which we must build.'

Rolf [Karl Meier], *Wie es begann: Festliche Worte anlässlich der Jubiläumsfeier unserer Zeitschrift 'Der Kreis'*, 20. *Dezember 1952*, Zurich, 1952; Rolf [Karl Meier], 'Abschied von Mammina', *Der Kreis*, 31, 1 (1963): 6–7.

Hubert Kennedy

Voltaire (pen-name of François-Marie Arouet) (1694–1778), French writer and philosopher. Born in Paris, Voltaire became the leading French proponent of the intellectual movement known as the Enlightenment. Poet, playwright, essayist, amateur scientist and more, Voltaire was also a passionate advocate of reason, justice and human rights, who sought to dissipate prejudice and intolerance and who helped countless victims of injustice. He did little to defend homosexuals, however, although the formal penalty in France before 1791 (albeit rarely applied) was death by burning at the stake.

There is no proof that Voltaire ever had a homosexual experience. Most of the evidence for his occasional homosexuality in the four-volume biography by Roger Peyrefitte is fabricated. The story that Voltaire once had sexual relations with a Prussian soldier as an experiment, only to decline a second experience with the quip 'Once a philosopher, twice a sodomite', is certainly apocryphal. He attended the Jesuit college of Louis-le-Grand as a boy, and while visiting England years later reportedly remarked, 'Oh! those damned Jesuits . . . buggar'd me to such a degree that I shall never get over it as long as I live', but he was probably being facetious.

On the other hand, Voltaire certainly encountered many homosexuals during his lifetime. As a young man he frequented the 'libertines' (hedonists and freethinkers) who gathered at the Temple, Parisian headquarters of the Knights of St John, whose commander, Philippe de VENDÔME, was a notorious sodomite. In 1725, when Voltaire intervened with the government to obtain the release of the abbé Pierre-François-Guyot Desfontaines, incarcerated for seducing adolescent boys, another cleric wrote a note to the police implying that Voltaire shared the abbé's tastes: 'If you acquaint yourself with the life that this poet has led since graduating from the Jesuit college, and if you examine the people whom he frequents, you will not give any consideration to his entreaties

nor those of his friends.' He corresponded flirtatiously with the homosexual king of Prussia, FREDERICK the Great, writing in April 1740, for example, 'I dream of my prince the way one dreams of one's mistress', and even lived at Frederick's court from 1750 to 1753, but he explained to his niece: 'I know, my dear child, what they say about Potsdam throughout Europe . . . , but all that is none of my business.' He looked on the Marquis de VILLETTE, the most famous sodomite of his day, as a son and died in Villette's house in Paris.

And yet Voltaire's writings demonstrate little understanding or approval of homosexuality. In 'So-called Socratic Love', an entry in his *Philosophical Dictionary* (1764), Voltaire asked rhetorically how it came about 'that a vice destructive of mankind if it were general . . . is yet so natural?' He thought that many boys, raised and educated without the presence of girls and therefore 'not finding the natural object of their instinct, fall back on what resembles it. A young boy often looks like a beautiful girl for two or three years'. But Voltaire clearly condemned adult homosexuality: 'What seems merely a weakness in the young Alcibiades is a disgusting abomination in a Dutch sailor and a Muscovite camp-follower.'

His last word on the subject appeared in the short entry 'On Sodomy' in his study of criminal law, *Prix de la Justice et de l'Humanité* (1777). Here he described sodomy as 'the sin against nature', 'this filth', and 'this vice unworthy of man'. He did state, however, that sodomy ought not to be punished by death. A note by Marie-Jean-Nicolas de Caritat, Marquis de Condorcet, appended to later editions of Voltaire's book, adopted a more liberal yet no less hostile tone: 'Sodomy, when there is no violence involved, does not fall within the jurisdiction of criminal law. It does not violate the rights of any man. . . . It is a base and disgusting vice, best punished by [public] contempt.'

In his polemical writings Voltaire often tried to discredit his enemies by accusing them of sodomy and in his short stories he frequently jibed at the alleged homosexuality of clerics (especially the Jesuits). D. A. Coward has suggested that if public hostility to sodomy increased in the eighteenth century, this was partly due to growing anti-clericalism (people considered sodomy to be common among the clergy) and that Voltaire was to some extent responsible for this development. Voltaire's attitude towards homosexuality was quite typical of the Enlightenment. Homosexuality was a fact of life to be studied and explained by the philosopher, while homosexuals themselves were merely weak creatures deserving of contempt, but not criminals who merited harsh punishment.

E. Raynaud, 'Le dossier Voltaire', *Mercure de France*, 1 November 1927; Alain, 'Voltaire fut-il un "infâme"?', *Arcadie*, 1 (1954): 27–34; R. Pomeau, 'Voltaire, du côté de Sodome', *Revue d'histoire littéraire de la France*, 86 (1986): 235–47; D. A. Coward, 'Attitudes to Homosexuality in Eighteenth-Century France', *European Studies Review*, 10 (1980): 231–55; Voltaire, *Philosophical Dictionary*, ed. T. Besterman, Penguin Books, 1971.

Michael Sibalis

Walpole, Horace (Horatio) William, 4th Earl of Orford (1717–1797), British writer and antiquarian. The third son of Sir Robert Walpole, who was later prime minister, he studied at Eton and King's College, Cambridge. He was a member of parliament (1741–1768), but his principal interest was letter-writing. A voluminous and bitchy correspondent, he wrote with an eye to posterity, cataloguing the motives, appearance and manners of personalities of his day in 4,000 surviving letters. He published *Anecdotes of Painting in England* (1762–1771), *The Castle of Otranto* (1764, the first Gothic novel), and *Essays on Modern Gardening* (1785); his *Memoirs* of the reigns of George I and II was published posthumously. Walpole's most significant contribution to visual culture was his development and promotion of 'Strawberry Hill Gothick', a style which led to a new strand of English architecture. From 1753 to 1776 Walpole had his residence, Strawberry Hill, Twickenham, rebuilt in an asymmetrical pseudo-Gothic mode, which contradicted the Palladian pomposity of the architectural establishment of his youth and the Adamesque fantasies popular in the 1770s. Timothy Mowl has interpreted this as a war of style, in which the homosexual outsider Walpole attacked the values and norms of his father's generation, creating an introspective and fantastical retreat.

Despite plenty of evidence to the contrary, Walpole's homosexuality was ignored and even rebutted until the 1960s. His chief biographer of the inter-war years, W. S. Lewis, the famous Walpole memorabilia collector and editor of the 48-volume Yale edition of the *Letters*, interpreted Walpole's relationships as gentlemanly and platonic. Mowl's recent biography has rejected this position, indicating that Walpole had a loving teenage relationship with Henry Fiennes-Clinton, 9th Earl of Lincoln and later 2nd Duke of Newcastle-under-Lyme, who subsequently married; a group of personal letters survives. The pair were painted in Venice, in companion portraits, by Rosalba Carriera (1741). Walpole was part of a network of bachelors with same-sex inclinations, including the poet Thomas Gray, with whom Walpole took the Grand Tour between 1739 and 1741, and whose work Walpole published on his private press, and the architect John Chute, who designed part of Walpole's house.

In 1764 a political enemy, William Guthrie, published a pamphlet describing Walpole's character as 'by nature muleish, by disposition female, so halting between the two that it would very much puzzle a common observer to assign to him his true sex'. Lacking a contemporary framework and language to connect homosexual behaviour with personal identity, this was the very trope which had been used earlier in the century to attack 'mollies', sodo-motical working-class men, and in the 1760s and 1770s, the 'macaroni', a type of English fop who was also read as poten-tially sodomitical. Walpole never married and died in his London house in Berkeley Square.

W. S. Lewis (ed.) *The Yale Edition of Horace Walpole's Correspondence*, 48 vols, New Haven, 1937–1983; P. McNeil, ' "That Doubtful Gender": Macaroni Dress and Male Sexualities', *Fashion Theory*, 3, 4 (1999): 1–38; T. Mowl, *Horace Walpole, The Great Outsider*, London, 1996; W. Hunting Smith (ed.) *Horace Walpole: Writer, Politician and Connoisseur*, New Haven, 1967.

Peter McNeil

Waters, Ethel (1896–1977), American singer and actress. Born in Chester, Penn-sylvania, Waters was one of the most in-fluential African-American jazz and blues singers of her time. Perhaps the most famous among the many song classics she popularised was 'Stormy Weather', which she introduced at the Cotton Club in Harlem in 1933. She later described this as 'the theme song of my life'. Waters was also the first African-American woman to be given equal billing with white stars in Broadway shows, and to play leading roles in Hollywood films. Once she had estab-lished herself as one of America's highest-paid entertainers, she made a successful transition to dramatic roles. Almost single-handedly Waters shattered the myth that African-American women could perform only as singers. For example, in the early 1950s she played a leading role in the stage and screen versions of Carson McCullers's *The Member of the Wedding*. Waters's portrayal of a Southern mammy could have lapsed into racial stereotype, but in her capable hands, the character became a complex, multifaceted and fully rounded human being. However, in a career that spanned almost 60 years, there were few openings for an African-American woman of her class, talent and ability.

When singer Elisabeth Welch (who introduced 'Stormy Weather' to Britain in 1933, and performed it in Derek Jarman's film *The Tempest* in 1979) was interviewed in the August 1997 issue of the British les-bian magazine *Diva*, she remembered Waters with affection and respect: 'Ethel Waters was a great artist and loved by everyone. I met her in Paris in 1929. She was an ordinary person, not educated, and somewhat shy. I think she wanted to be friendly but didn't know how. I adored her.' In the 1920s, Waters lived in Harlem with her girlfriend Ethel Williams. Says Welch: 'They were known in Harlem as "The Two Ethels", but in those days it was scandalous for two women to live to-gether. Ethel Williams was skinny, light-skinned and red-haired. Ethel Waters was called a bull dyke, a terrible name. After she became famous, Ethel turned the other way, but her relationships with men were disastrous. They abused and exploited her. Eventually she turned her back on men, took up religion, and preached the word of God till the day she died. But, in doing so, I felt she lost her sense of humour, and became a sad person.'

Waters is rumoured to have had a li-aison with the lesbian novelist Radclyffe HALL. They met in Paris around 1929–1930 and Waters briefly recalled this encounter in her autobiography, *His Eye is on the Sparrow*, published in 1951. Hall wrote a manuscript about an inter-racial lesbian love affair that has never been found. In the late 1950s ill-health forced Waters into semi-retirement. A deeply religious woman, most of her later public appear-ances were restricted to Billy Graham's rallies. She died in Los Angeles, Califor-nia, at the age of 80.

D. Bogle, *Brown Sugar – Eighty Years of Amer-ica's Black Female Superstars*, New York, 1980; S. Bourne, 'Sophisticated Ladies', *Diva* (Lon-don), August 1997: 26–8; E. Waters with C. Samuels, *His Eye is on the Sparrow*, New York, 1951, 1989.

Stephen Bourne

Waugh, Evelyn (Arthur St John) (1903–1966), British writer. Born in London, Waugh attended Heath Mount preparatory school, where he bullied Cecil BEATON. After graduating, he was to have attended Sherbourne School, but the scandal caused by the publication of his brother Alec's *The Loom of Youth* (1917), a fictionalised exposé of homosexuality there, induced their father to send the younger Evelyn to Lancing. He claimed that, unlike his brother, he had no homosexual experiences before his undergraduate years.

Waugh by his own admission wasted his time at Hertford College, Oxford, before leaving in 1924 without finishing his degree. His life at College featured 'offal': meals of beer and cheese with friends. He affected a dandyish look, often donning tight-fitting blue tweeds and sea-green plus fours, and he began a habit of heavy drinking that would contribute to his death. His colourful circle of friends, all members of the 'Hypocrites Club', included the flamboyant homosexual Brian HOWARD; Robert Byron, who enjoyed dressing as Queen Victoria; Tony Bushell, a strikingly attractive actor; Peter Rodd, the inspiration for a character in Waugh's novel *Black Mischief* (1932); and Harold ACTON, the dedicatee of Waugh's first novel, *Decline and Fall* (1928). Waugh and Acton, a 'strenuous aesthete' who invented the loose trousers now known as 'Oxford bags', became close friends, sharing a love for the baroque and a disdain for the Bloomsbury aesthetics of Roger Fry. Acton introduced Waugh to the writers Edith Sitwell and Gertrude STEIN.

According to his biographer Douglas Patey, Waugh's main orientation from 1922 until late 1925 or early 1926 was homosexual. His first male love was Richard Pares, followed by Alastair Graham, who was the model for Sebastian Flyte in Waugh's putative masterpiece, *Brideshead Revisited* (1945). Waugh claimed that the 'aesthetic bugger', Anthony Blanche, in that novel was two-thirds Brian Howard

and one-third Harold Acton. In *A Little Learning* (1964) Graham returns as the character Hamish Lennox. Waugh claimed that he never regretted the liaisons of his homosexual period; he was convinced that most people grow up gradually and ought to explore a variety of possibilities while young.

After leaving Oxford, Waugh entered what Acton called his 'Dostoievski period', when he was intermittently employed in London, often returned to Oxford for weekend visits, and was almost invariably either drunk or hung-over. During this period he began to suffer from the depression and insomnia that would plague him for the rest of his life. By the late 1920s, when his sexual interest in men was diminishing, he began writing the bitingly satiric novels that first made him famous; in 1930, he converted to Roman Catholicism.

Waugh's first marriage, to Evelyn Gardner, lasted from 1927 to 1929. He and his wife were generally called 'He-Evelyn' and 'She-Evelyn'. In 1937 he married Laura Herbert, with whom he raised six children. Waugh, who travelled and wrote extensively beginning in the 1930s, suffered a breakdown in 1954, which he fictionalised in *The Ordeal of Gilbert Pinfold* (1957). Like Pinfold, Waugh heard disembodied voices during his psychotic episodes that accused him of being homosexual.

Charles Sturridge's 1981 television mini-series of *Brideshead Revisited* posthumously introduced Waugh to a large audience, including many gay men who viewed the close Oxford friendship between the characters Charles Ryder (Jeremy Irons) and Sebastian Flyte (Anthony Andrews) as homoerotic at the very least.

D. L. Higdon, 'Gay Sebastian and Cheerful Charles: Homoeroticism in Waugh's *Brideshead Revisited*', *Ariel*, 25, 4 (1994): 77–89; R. J. Kloss, 'My Brother Evelyn and Myself: Alec and Evelyn Waugh', in N. Kiell (ed.) *Blood*

Brothers, New York, 1983; D. L. Patey, *The Life of Evelyn Waugh: A Critical Biography*, Oxford, 1998.

George Piggford

Wedekind, Frank (1864–1918), German playwright. Born Benjamin Franklin Wedekind in Hanover, Germany, Wedekind became first a circus secretary, then an actor and finally an influential and controversial dramatist. He lived with his German-American father and Swiss mother (who had been an actress) in Switzerland from 1872 to 1884, and then moved to Munich, where he remained until his death in 1918.

The publication of his early tragedy, *Frühlings Erwachen* (*Spring's Awakening*), in 1891 caused a scandal. The play deals with the confused, intense sexuality of children at puberty, and includes scenes of both heterosexual and homosexual desire.

Wedekind's two famous 'Lulu' plays, which inspired Alban Berg's opera, were *Erdgeist* (*Earth Spirit*, 1895/1903) and *Die Büchse der Pandora* (*Pandora's Box*, 1904). They feature the lesbian Countess Geschwitz, who accompanies the heroine, Lulu, in her 'decline' from the position of (through marriage) society lady to London prostitute. She finally dies trying to protect Lulu from Jack the Ripper.

Geschwitz incorporates many of the stereotypical attributes of the emancipated 'New Woman' at the turn of the century. Her clothing is military or mannish in style; she is physically unattractive (her name could be translated as 'sweat'); she is intelligent, and has intellectual and artistic interests. Like the men in the play, she is unable to resist Lulu; but, unlike them, Geschwitz is exploited by, rather than seeking to exploit, the heroine. She catches cholera and is put in prison for Lulu's sake, in return for promises of passionate favours; but Lulu subsequently declares herself disgusted by the very idea. Jack the Ripper, before he kills Lulu, comments on her ingratitude towards Geschwitz.

In his introduction to the third edition of *Pandora's Box*, Wedekind makes the interesting claim that the tragic heroine of the play is not Lulu, but Countess Geschwitz. He notes that, in the furore of moral outrage that followed the appearance of the play, none of the judges called upon to pronounce on its legal status objected to 'the terrible fate of unnaturalness that weighs upon this human being' (i.e. Geschwitz's homosexuality). Wedekind claims that he chose to portray such a character because he felt inspired by the need to awaken public sympathy for homosexuality. But recent critics have read Wedekind's pious claims as subterfuge: an unconvincing attempt to obscure the central position of the amoral Lulu character, whose constant involvement with pimps and prostitution concerned the censors. In Georg Wilhelm Pabst's film version, *Die Büchse der Pandora* (1929), with Louise Brooks as Lulu, Alice Roberts's Geschwitz is a peripheral but explicitly lesbian character.

Other works by Wedekind include the plays *Der Liebestrank* (*The Love Potion*, 1899), *Der Marquis von Keith* (*The Marquis of Keith*, 1901), *König Nicolo oder So ist das Leben* (*King Nicolo, or Such is Life*, 1902/1911), *Tod und Teufel* (*Death and the Devil*, 1906/1909), *Musik* (1908), *Die Zensur* (*Censorship*, 1908), *Schloß Wetterstein* (1910), *Franziska* (1911), *Bismarck* (1916); the novel *Die Fürstin Russalka* (*Princess Russalka*, 1897); and *Mine-Haha oder über die körperliche Erziehung der jungen Mädchen* (*Mine-Haha: On the Physical Education of Young Girls*, 1903).

E. Boa, *The Sexual Circus: Wedekind's Theatre of Subversion*, Oxford, 1987; M. Morris, 'Admiring the Countess Geschwitz', in C. E. Blackmer and P. J. Smith (eds) *En Travesti: Women, Gender Subversion, Opera*, New York, 1995: 348–70.

Sarah Colvin

Weininger, Otto (1880–1903), Austrian writer. Weininger was born in Vienna, the son of a goldsmith. He attended school in Vienna and attracted attention as an unconventional student with extraordinary ideas and thoughts. In 1898 he began studies of philosophy at the University of Vienna, concentrating on the history of philosophy, psychology and educational sciences.

In 1900 Vienna was characterised by a vibrant atmosphere, which created bizarre and modern ideas at the same time. Sigmund FREUD's psychoanalytic concepts and his studies of hysteria drew attention from the conservative public. Contemporary anti-Semitic pamphlets were discussed, as was the reform movement of famous women's and children's rights activists like Ellen Key and Hedwig Dohm, who supported equal rights for women and a better education for children. In 1899 Magnus HIRSCHFELD, who founded a scientific institute for sexual reforms in Berlin, published a yearbook about sexual intermediate stages, which included a petition for the repeal of all sodomy laws. The progressive psychiatrist Richard von KRAFFT-EBING and the Viennese liberal playwright Arthur Schnitzler signed this petition.

In 1901 Weininger, who was very interested in these approaches, wrote his first essay, *Eros und Psyche*, which analysed the psychological differences between men and women. In 1903 his most important book, *Geschlecht und Charakter* (*Sex and Character*) was published. This book considered the constitution of sex and the bisexual nature of all men. Many contemporary artists and writers were fascinated by Weininger's theories and arguments. August STRINDBERG began an intimate correspondence with the young student, and the German novelist Thomas MANN confessed that he was impressed by the treatise.

A hundred years later *Sex and Character*, which has achieved more than 28 reprints, appears strange and sometimes ludicrous. Weininger, like many of his contemporary philosophers, was hostile towards the women's movement and believed that only a man can be a genius. In *Eros und Psyche* he wrote: 'All emancipated women, all famous and well known women have male characters.'

Although he endorsed the idea that every human being has a bisexual and androgynous orientation, he felt a strong ambiguity towards homosexuality. He described gay men and lesbian women as an intermediate gender, which includes female and male aspects. Although he himself was gay and of Jewish descent, he could not cope with his homoerotic feelings and developed a persistent resentment towards women and minorities.

His self-hate was so overwhelming that he became desperate and committed suicide by shooting himself in front of the opera in Vienna. His death at the age of 23 caused a shock in the public and led to an animated discussion about suicide and youth. His ideas and theories proved to be weird and strange. He was a premature genius destroyed by the morbid and confusing atmosphere in Vienna and the challenges of a new century.

J. Le Rider, *Der Fall Otto Weininger*, Vienna, 1985; A. Janik, *Essays on Wittgenstein and Weininger*, Amsterdam, 1985.

Gerald Pilz

Weirauch, Anna Elisabet (1887–1970), Romanian-German novelist. Anna Elisabet Weirauch was one of the few German authors of the 1920s to accord literary treatment to the topic of homosexuality.

She was born in Galatz in Romania. Her mother was a writer, her father the founder and director of the Bank of Romania. After his death, her German mother (who was also a writer) returned to her home country with the children, settling first in Thuringia and later, in 1893, in Berlin, where Anna Elisabet was educated at a private school and then began training as an actress. From 1904 to 1914 she was regularly employed at Berlin's German State Theatre.

Given this context, it is unsurprising

that her first literary experiments were with drama; some of her plays were performed as matinées at the State Theatre. But it soon became clear that her real interest and strength lay in the novel. Her first novel, *Die kleine Dagmar* (*Little Dagmar*) was published in 1918, and marked the beginning of a prolific career as a writer. Her first literary treatment of homoeroticism was published a year later, in the form of a novella called *Der Tag der Artemis* (*The Day of Artemis*, 1919). Her most famous work is the three-part novel *Der Skorpion* (*The Scorpion*, 1919–1931), which tells the story of a young German woman from a respectable family who is forced to come to terms with society's prejudice against her lesbian sexuality. Unlike Elisabeth DAUTHENDEY, who – writing just 20 years earlier – does not permit her heroine physical love with other women, Weirauch describes scenes of passionate love between her characters. In 1926 *Der Skorpion* was censored, classed as a potentially corrupting influence on young people.

From 1933, Weirauch lived in the town of Gastag in Upper Bavaria, but she returned to Berlin in 1961, and died there. Her numerous novels include *Ruth Meyer: eine fast alltägliche Geschichte* (*Ruth Meyer: Almost an Everyday Story*, 1922), *Lotte. Ein Berliner Roman* (*Lotte: a Berlin Novel*, 1932), *Das Rätsel Manuela* (*Manuela, the Enigma*, 1939) and *Die Ehe der Mara Holm* (*Mara Holm's Marriage*, 1949).

L. Fadermann and B. Eriksson, *Lesbians in Germany: 1890's–1920's*, Tallahassee, 1990 (1980); C. Schöppmann, '*Der Skorpion*': Frauenliebe in der Weimarer Republik, Hamburg, 1985; N. P. Nenno, '*Bildung* and Desire: Anna Elisabet Weirauch's *Der Skorpion*', in C. Lorey and J. L. Plews (eds) *Queering the Canon: Defying Sights in German Literature*, Columbia, SC, 1998: 207–21.

Sarah Colvin

Weiwha (1849–1896), Native American 'berdache'. Weiwha was born in the Zuni

pueblo, perched atop a Mesa plateau, in one of the oldest continually inhabited villages in the United States, certainly in New Mexico. Weiwha lived a remarkable life and was recognised both for her many contributions to the life of her village as well as for her generosity in sharing the Zuni culture. Encountered by many anthropologists and explorers, Weiwha was perhaps best known through the influence of Matilda Coxe Stevenson. Stevenson was one of the earliest women anthropologists and she wrote extensively about her interactions with Weiwha, eventually inviting her to Washington in 1866. After making quite an impression on Washington, Weiwha returned to Zuni, where she eventually died.

Weiwha was the subject of Will Roscoe's *The Zuni Man-Woman*, in which Roscoe explored the historical and cultural tradition of the Zuni *Ihamana*, or what anthropologists and ethnographers have termed the *berdache*. Berdachism, unlike contemporary gay or queer identity, has been found within a variety of indigenous cultures in both North and South America and dates as far back as the Spanish conquests. As a model, berdachism – generally associated with male-to-male sexual practices – is an important site from which to look at the cultural construction of gender. Berdachism can best be understood as an umbrella term for an entire set of cultural practices, and it must be noted that each native culture will have its own specific term for the berdache figure. In general, the majority of native terms refer to a combination of spiritual qualities most often translated as *ihe–shei* or 'halfman-halfwoman'. Currently referred to as transgendered, or even as a third or fourth gender, the berdache figure must primarily be recognised for its particular emphasis on community contributions over sexual behaviour. This is particularly significant at Zuni, where the berdache figure was generally understood to have a special link with the spirit world. Weiwha's social status as a berdache was frequently ranked closely with that of the medicine man, and as a result berdachism must be seen as part of a rich and complex cultural system which incorporated sexual preferences into a multi-dimensional framework involving economic, social and spiritual dimensions – all of which contributed to its overall acceptance and integration within the community. Among the Zuni, the *Ihamana*'s link to the spiritual world was particularly significant to anthropologists because it is reflected in numerous mythological stories usually emphasising the berdaches' primary characteristics. They are frequently represented as mediators between the sexes, as craftspeople, and as links with agricultural production. Each characteristic extends the berdache tradition beyond sexuality.

G. Herdt (ed.) *Third Sex, Third Gender: Beyond Sexual Dimorphism in Culture and History*, New York, 1994; W. Roscoe, *The Zuni Man-Woman*, Albuquerque, 1991; W. L. Williams, *The Spirit and the Flesh: Sexual Diversity in American Indian Culture*, Boston, 1986.

Ken Gonzales-Day

Welch, Denton (1915–1948), British writer. John Lehmann was convinced that had Maurice Denton Welch lived longer, he would have become 'an English GIDE, but a more delicate and exotic bird'. He was certainly an obsessive diarist, and in his fiction he is consistently dedicated to the self-portrait, but he lacked Gide's absolute candour about homosexual desire, and was denied, or denied himself, any breadth of experience. E. M. FORSTER, though admiring his work, wearied of his 'funking of intimacy ... and cockteasiness'.

Welch was born in Shanghai of Anglo-American parentage; his father was a wealthy company director and his mother a fifth-generation New Englander. At her death in 1926, the youngest of the three Welch sons was sent home to England to preparatory school and eventually Repton,

where he was wretchedly unhappy. He ran away at 16, travelling to China once more, before returning to London and enrolling at the Goldsmith School of Art. In 1935, at the age of 20, his youth and ambition were cut short by a devastating bicycle accident. A fractured spine and internal injuries taxed a less than robust constitution. The companionship of Eric Oliver, who served as nurse, secretary and eventually literary executor, eased the loneliness of his last years. He had turned from painting to autobiographical fiction and memoir, and in the productive final six years of his life he was championed by Edith Sitwell, and praised at his death by Stephen SPENDER. His *œuvre* slight, his range narrow, his remembrance of things past none the less remains vivid and compelling.

Maiden Voyage (1943) reconstructs his flight from boarding school back to the China he had shared as a child with an adored mother. 'Denton', the hypersensitive adolescent protagonist, records minutely a fearful and inconclusive quest for sexual maturation, his pilgrimage defined by masochism and voyeurism. Random encounters with strong male figures reveal equally attraction and revulsion. The author reappears as 15-year-old Orvil Pym in *In Youth is Pleasure* (1945), an isolated and conflicted boy, caught between the brutalities of boarding school and an unsympathetic family, and driven by a sexual curiosity compromised by shame. His best-known short story, 'When I Was Thirteen' – from *Brave and Cruel* (1948), a collection which relentlessly explores the alienation of the child and the adolescent – depicts the flowering and destruction of a schoolboy's sexual awakening. There is loss of innocence, but never growth; consummation remains out of reach, and perhaps beyond desire.

A Voice Through a Cloud (1950), a haunting account of his pain-ridden life as an invalid, evoking at once JOB and Kafka, was the first of his posthumous publications. Other works include *A Last Sheaf* (1951), short stories; *I Left My Grand-*

father's House (1958), another pilgrimage narrative; *Dumb Instrument* (1976), poems and fragments collected by Jean-Louis Chevalier; *The Journals of Denton Welch*, edited by Michael de la Noy (1984); and *Fragments of a Life Story: The Collected Short Writings of Denton Welch* (1987).

R. Phillips, *Denton Welch*, New York, 1974; M. de la Noy, *Denton Welch: The Making of a Writer*, London, 1984.

Roger Bowen

Welles, (Benjamin) Sumner (1892–1961), American diplomat. Born in New York City into a wealthy and socially prominent family, Welles was educated at Harvard University, graduating in 1914. At a loss for a career, Welles followed the advice of family friend Franklin D. Roosevelt and took the Foreign Service examination in 1915. Entering the diplomatic corps at a time when it was heavily dominated by the American upper class, Welles used his privileged birth, intelligence and dignified public presence to rise quickly through the ranks. His diplomatic work focused on Latin America and the Caribbean, where he was instrumental in developing Roosevelt's 'Good Neighbor' policy. He served briefly as US Ambassador to Cuba in 1933, but his public and controversial attempts to undermine a liberal regime there led to his ouster.

In 1937 he was promoted to Undersecretary of State and was one of Roosevelt's most trusted diplomatic advisers, playing a leadership role in the formation of the North Atlantic Treaty Organization in 1941. Secretary of State Cordell Hull came to resent Welles's influence over the President, which only grew as Hull suffered the effects of tuberculosis and the outbreak of World War II brought Roosevelt's attentions around to international relations.

Welles was the natural choice to succeed the aging Secretary of State, but Hull's personal dislike made him particularly receptive to rumours that Welles had frequently propositioned men for sex, most notably in an incident involving a railway car porter during an official government function in 1940. An official investigation initiated by FBI Director J. Edgar Hoover turned up evidence corroborating these events (since confirmed by historians), which usually coincided with Welles's occasional bouts of heavy drinking. Hull, under heavy pressure from Welles's rival, William Bullitt (himself aiming at the Secretary's portfolio), brought the investigation to the attention of Roosevelt in early 1943. Roosevelt, who personally disliked homosexuals and saw their presence in sensitive diplomatic posts as a 'security risk', had no choice but to accept the resignation of his trusted friend and adviser (although he did go to great lengths to destroy Bullitt's political career). Excluded both formally and informally from the foreign policy establishment, Welles lived quietly until his death.

Welles married three times, raised children and always denied any interest in homosexuality. His heavy drinking and preference for anonymous encounters reveal a deeply troubled sexual identity. More important is what the Welles resignation – which robbed the US of its likely Secretary of State in the middle of World War II – reveals about the damage homophobia did to mid-century American foreign policy.

I. F. Gellman, *Secret Affairs: Franklin Roosevelt, Cordell Hull, and Sumner Welles*, Baltimore, 1995; B. Welles, *Sumner Welles: FDR's Global Strategist*, New York, 1997.

Christopher Capozzola

Westermarck, Edward (1862–1939), Finnish scholar. Born into an upper-class Finnish-Swedish family in Helsinki, Westermarck spent a large part of his adult life in England, where he was a professor in sociology at the London School of Economics (1907–1930), and in Morocco, where he did fieldwork for nine years. He also had a chair in philosophy at the Helsinki University (1906–1918), and at the Åbo Akademi University (1918–1932).

With Alfred Cort Haddon and Bronislaw Malinowski, Westermarck was one of the founders of modern anthropology and a pioneer in anthropological fieldwork. He made his first voyage to Morocco in 1898. He was a critical evolutionarist in that he dismissed attempts to construct any unilinear grand theory of the history of humankind, but he sought to reconstruct developmental sequences of social forms and cultural phenomena on a more modest scale. Westermarck remains a major authority in the study of Moroccan religions and rituals, but among the topics of interest throughout his career were the history of marriage, the institutionalised patterns of sexual behaviour, sexual mores, sexual psychology and the nature of moral judgements. The studies he wrote on these subjects became classics in his own lifetime: *The History of Human Marriage* (1891, fifth revised and enlarged edition in three volumes, 1921) and *The Origin and Development of Moral Ideas* (two volumes, 1906–1908).

His studies of sexual mores and sexual practices focused on issues that also concerned contemporary sexologists. A thread running through his work was an ambition to show how the social, the psychological and the biological aspects interpenetrate in the formation of human sexual life. He admired the work of Havelock ELLIS on sexual psychology, and the two were close friends and held each other in high esteem. Westermarck appreciated the research and the sexual policy reforms that Ellis, Magnus HIRSCHFELD and many other sexologists were pursuing, but as for Sigmund FREUD, he was more dubious. The theory of the Oedipus complex and incest taboo became a topic of much heated debate between Westermarck and Freud and their followers.

Westermarck wrote also on homosexuality, in particular in *The Origin and Development of Moral Ideas*, in *The Future of Marriage in Western Civilisation* (1936) and in *Christianity and Morals* (1939). As an unmarried homosexual man he also had a personal stake in studying the issue. His sexual preferences seem to have been an open secret among his colleagues. Considering that many European men of art and culture with homoerotic leanings (such as André GIDE) were travelling in the Arab countries at the turn of the century and enjoying what they felt was a relaxed attitude to male homoeroticism, it is possible that Westermarck also found Morocco a particularly congenial environment.

In his studies Westermarck demonstrated that homosexual practices had been frequent and various around the world and throughout history. He suggested that a potential 'favourable organic [congenital] predisposition' to homosexual behaviour in some people is 'probably no abnormality at all, only a feature in the ordinary sexual constitution of man'. Thus he did not conceive of homosexuality as regression in psychosexual development but as a valid mode of human sexual desire in itself. He also suggested, on the basis of his observations in Morocco, that habit and practice can shape a person's previously heterosexual instinct into a genuine homosexual desire; hence sexual preferences may be more fluid and more prone to social scripting than the standard argument has often assumed.

Westermarck criticised the aggressively intolerant attitudes that were manifest in Western culture, which he regarded as a typical case of 'sentimental dislike'. As his theory of the nature of moral judgement suggested, such 'irrational aversion' is perhaps at the root of all moral judgements, but he argued that such emotions must not be accepted as a justification for public moral regulation in modern society. He saw institutionalised Christianity as largely responsible for the persistent oppression of homosexuals, and also in this respect he regarded the diminishing power of religious dogmas as a positive trend in Western culture. This critique can also be set in the context of Westermarck's position as a convinced atheist who fought actively for the legal rights of free-thinkers in Finland.

Though Westermarck conceptualised sexuality, culture and society in rather a static fashion, he helped pave the way for subsequent relativist studies of sexuality in anthropology, for example by Ruth BENEDICT and Margaret MEAD.

J. Ihanus, *Multiple Origins: Edward Westermarck in Search of Mankind*, Frankfurt am Main, 1998; T. Stroup, 'Edward Westermarck: A Reappraisal', *Man*, 19, 4 (1984): 575–92.

Jan Löfström

Wetterhoff, Adolf Fredrik (Fritz) (1878–1922), Finnish lawyer and historian. In the book *Die Homosexualität des Mannes und des Weibes* (1914) by Magnus HIRSCHFELD, there is a short but powerful section on homosexuality in Finland. Information for this section was provided by Fritz Wetterhoff, a Finnish lawyer, historian and unofficial diplomat in the service of the Finnish independence movement.

Wetterhoff was born in Helsinki into a military and civil servant's family of German descent, who had been living in Finland for several generations. Wetterhoff's mother died early, and Fritz Wetterhoff and his sister grew up in the custody of their aunts, Rosina and Fredrika Wetterhoff, who were both active in the Finnish women's movement.

Wetterhoff first studied history at the University of Helsinki, but probably never finished his studies. He trained as a technician in a weaving mill in Aachen, Germany, after which he moved back to Finland to teach in the textile technical college in Hämeenlinna, founded and run by his aunt. Later he studied law at the University of Helsinki and after graduating in 1909, he worked as the public prosecutor and mayor of Hämeenlinna, a small town 100 km north of Helsinki.

In 1911 the local newspaper denounced Wetterhoff's homosexuality. No names were mentioned in the article, but it was not necessary in a small town. Wetterhoff moved to Helsinki and worked as an attorney. Either because of the scandal surrounding his sexual orientation, or because of a new scandal about unclear financial business, he left Finland in 1913 and settled in Berlin, where he worked in a joint Scandinavian attorneys' office.

Wetterhoff's contribution on homosexuality in Finland to Hirschfeld's book is the earliest attempt to write about homosexual history and the current situation of gay men in Finland. He begins by discussing homosexual elements in Scandinavian Viking sagas and lists important eighteenth- and nineteenth-century personalities in Finnish aesthetics and contemporary literature, such as Gustaf Mauritz Armfelt (1757–1814), a military figure, diplomat and opera director and Fredrik Cygnæus (1807–1881), a writer, professor of aesthetics and contemporary literature and patron of the arts who, according to Wetterhoff, were homosexuals. Wetterhoff constructs a narrative history of the identity of Finnish homosexuals with the folklore and heroes of 'our own'.

Wetterhoff then continues with a detailed description (almost an ethnography) of the male homosexual subculture in Helsinki at the beginning of the twentieth century. He mentions the most important outdoor meeting places and discusses sexual° practices among men (according to him, anal sex was not very popular, but oral sex and mutual masturbation were).

Wetterhoff's contribution to Hirschfeld's book ends with his own theory of the reasons for homosexual conduct: 'homosexuals are not only "psychic", but also biological hermaphrodites, whose cell constitution differs from normal men and women'. He ends programmatically: 'Exact natural sciences will bring our vindication, it will be total and invincible.'

Apart from Finnish gay history, Wetterhoff is an important figure in the history of Finnish independence. Until 1917 Finland was an autonomous Grand

Duchy of Russia. Since the middle of the nineteenth century, there had been an increasing national movement demanding independence (Fredrik Cygnæus having been an important figure at this stage of the movement). At the beginning of the twentieth century, during the reign of the last Russian tsar, Nicholas II, the oppression of small nations which were under the rule of Russia became harsher.

The tsar had abolished the Finnish national army in 1905 and young men had no chance to receive military training in Finland. In 1914 young academics and students founded the so-called Jaeger movement, an organisation for armed resistance. They decided to turn to Germany in order to receive military training.

Wetterhoff had come to the same idea in Berlin and, after being authorised by the students, made use of his personal contacts with German high military officials, politicians and even members of the royal family. Wetterhoff succeeded astonishingly well, since in 1915 Wilhelm II signed an order to organise full military education for 2,000 Finnish men who illegally left Finland in order to become trained as Jaegers in Germany.

The written history of the Jaeger movement explains Wetterhoff's success through diplomatic skills, personal charm and an astonishing capability to persuade people and make the impossible possible. Some Jaegers have later, in unpublished interviews, assumed that Wetterhoff's success was due to his homosexuality. There were many homosexuals among the German senior officers and, according to the interviewees, the homosexuals were like Freemasons, always helping each other.

Wetterhoff became an unofficial diplomat, a kind of first Finnish 'ambassador' in Germany. His career was splendid, but short. Although young Jaegers considered it self-evident that Wetterhoff would be the leader of the national independence movement, elderly leaders of the independence movement did not consider him a proper model for the Finnish youth.

The written history gives two reasons for this: his unclear financial business, for which he was said to have left Finland in 1913 – and his homosexuality.

Wetterhoff's German rival, Major Maximilian Bayer, the officer who was in charge of the Finnish Jaeger battalion, managed to get Wetterhoff jailed on the basis of false accusations of Wetterhoff being a traitor to his country. However, no charges were raised against him, and after some months in pre-trial detention, he was sent to the German western front as an ordinary soldier.

Wetterhoff had taken German citizenship in 1914 in order to secure his position – as a Finnish citizen his activities for Finnish independence from Russia would have been a severe offence from the viewpoint of Tsar Nicholas II.

The Finnish executive group of the independence movement, based in Stockholm, displaced Wetterhoff from the leadership of the Berlin bureau of the Jaeger movement and his office – actually the first Finnish Embassy in Germany – was closed.

After the war Wetterhoff returned to Berlin and held a minor position in the new Finnish Embassy in Berlin. Later he returned to Finland, where he held an unimportant job in the press department of the Ministry of Foreign Affairs. He died in Helsinki in 1922 at the age of 44 of heart disease. In his lifetime Wetterhoff never received any ovations for his work for Finnish independence, despite his great effort for the Finnish Jaeger movement.

In his contribution to Hirschfeld's book, Wetterhoff describes Helsinki academic gay male circles at the beginning of the twentieth century as rather open and the atmosphere towards homosexuality as rather tolerant. This opinion probably sealed his own fate. He had probably been too open about his sexuality and the attitudes towards homosexuality had changed in the 1910s.

Kati Mustola

Whale, James (1889–1957), British film director. Born into a poor family in the English Midlands, Whale was determined not to enter a manual trade. While serving in World War I, he worked his way up to the rank of second lieutenant before the Germans captured him. He spent the remainder of the war organising a theatrical company and winning at cards in a POW camp.

After the Armistice, Whale used his poker winnings as a stake to enter the theatrical world. While learning production and design with groups – including the Oxford Players – Whale adopted speech patterns and mannerisms from his 'gentleman lovers'. Whale moved from acting into directing and took the World War I drama *Journey's End* to the top theatrical realms of London's West End and New York's Broadway. The sound motion picture required directors with skills at dialogue; Whale signed with Paramount as a dialogue director, then helmed the film version of *Journey's End* (1930) for Tiffany Studios.

Whale reached the pinnacle of his directing career at Universal Studios between 1930 and 1937. The director made two more war films, then directed his first classic in the horror genre, *Frankenstein* (1931). Critics observe that one key to this film's success involved giving the monster a personality. Whale wrote to his bisexual friend Colin Clive, who played the doctor/creator Henry Frankenstein, that 'Frankenstein would contain a great deal of us'. Marc Gatiss notes that Whale's homosexuality afforded him the insight to include a poignancy about being an outsider in society. After making a few other films, including *The Invisible Man* (1933), Whale directed *The Bride of Frankenstein* (1935). A sequel considered a classic in its own right, the film contained the director's dark humour and Ernest Thesiger's campy portrayal of the weird doctor who compels Frankenstein to make a mate for his creation. In 1936, Whale made what many consider to be the best version of the musical *Show Boat*. Perhaps because his sexual orientation made him aware of prejudice, Whale befriended performers Hattie McDaniel and Paul Robeson, and gave them realistic and warm representations, a rarity for African-Americans in motion pictures of the era.

During his first years in Hollywood, friends introduced Whale to David Lewis, a handsome assistant story editor who eventually became a producer. The pair dined regularly at the Brown Derby, a noted industry locale, and began a relationship that lasted over two decades. Whale and Lewis were one of the few homosexual couples of that era who attended industry affairs together. Unlike fellow homosexual directors Mitchell Leisen and Edmund Goulding, Whale did not host sexual parties during his career.

Whale's career floundered, then ended, in the early 1940s. Gatiss thinks Whale's aloofness, remoteness and homosexuality all played a part in his decline in Hollywood. Dennis Fischer asserts that Whale's homosexuality increased his sense of being distanced from the industry leaders. Whale spent much of his remaining time painting, directing plays and living off his investments. He ended his sexual relationship with Lewis in the early 1950s, and hosted pool parties attended almost exclusively by young gay men whom he tried to impress. He began a relationship with Pierre Fogel, a young man who had served as his chauffeur. After having a nervous breakdown, Whale explained he wanted to forgo old age and pain, and threw himself into the shallow end of his pool in May 1957.

J. Curtis, *James Whale*, Metuchen, NJ, 1982; D. Fischer, *Horror Film Directors, 1931–1990*, Jefferson, NC, 1991; M. Gatiss, *James Whale: A Biography or The Would-be Gentleman*, London, 1995.

Brett L. Abrams

Whitman, Walt (1819–1892), American poet. Whitman was born on a Long Island

(New York) farm to a typically heterosexual family. His father drank too much; his mother suffered; and his eight siblings did poorly except for two brothers. The poet idolised his mother, Louisa Van Velsor Whitman, and credited her with inspiring his poetry. From first to last, his writings applaud sexual love. 'Song of Myself', published in 1855, contains Section V, which celebrates the soul through the trope of fellatio: 'Loafe with me on the grass, loose the stop from your throat, / . . . Only the lull I like, the hum of your valved voice'. *Leaves of Grass*, the title Whitman gave his collected poems, pivots upon this dalliance with a young man in the grass. In 1889, the poet told an interviewer, 'Sex, sex, sex: sex is the root of it all.'

Readers have identified many Walt Whitmans: working-class, language poet, Bohemian, gay liberationist and celebrant of United States world supremacy. Unlike most other poets, Whitman both originated in and celebrated the working class. A farmer, then a typesetter, during the US Civil War a clerk and volunteer nurse, Whitman loved working-class lads. His notebooks contain numerous entries suggesting sexual liaisons. Edward CARPENTER (an English lover) wrote: 'The unconscious, uncultured, natural types pleased him best.' One of those types, Fred Vaughan, inspired Whitman to write the erotic Calamus sequence first included in the 1860 edition of *Leaves of Grass*. Whitman liked transport workers. In 1865, riding to the end of a District of Columbia streetcar route, he met the conductor; Peter Doyle recalled their first contact: 'We were familiar at once – I put my hand on his knee – we understood . . . . From that time on, we were the biggest sort of friends.'

During the Civil War, Whitman worked in Washington. An outraged Methodist fired him from the Interior Department after discovering a copy of *Leaves of Grass* in Whitman's desk, but Attorney-General James Speed quickly found him

another position. Speed's brother Joshua had spent four years sleeping with Abraham Lincoln in Illinois. Lincoln himself had read and admired the second edition of *Leaves of Grass*. One of the soldiers, Alonzo Bush, wrote Whitman about a friend who 'went down on your BK, both so often with me. I wished that I could . . . have some fun for he is a gay boy' (22 December 1863); 'BK' might mean 'buck' or 'book', but one writer suggests 'Big Cock'. The death of President Lincoln devastated Whitman. He wrote his last great poem, 'When lilacs last in the dooryard bloomed', for Lincoln. The poet himself suffered a stroke in 1873 and he moved to Camden, New Jersey, with his brother. The later poems became more abstract and less homoerotic, although Whitman's health recovered after he swam in Timber Creek with his lover Harry Stafford, Carpenter and other young men.

Whitman may now be the premier United States poet, but his work had to overcome much resistance. *Leaves of Grass* first appeared in a self-published edition in 1855 with few readers; it underwent multiple transformations before the so-called 'death-bed' edition in 1892. *Leaves of Grass* certainly marked the boldest departure from standard English prosody. Of the five reviews to the first edition, Whitman wrote three anonymous favourable ones. Another reviewer was lukewarm, but the other denounced 'that horrible crime not to be mentioned among Christians'. The fervently homoerotic 1860 edition with the Calamus cluster attracted little attention and the publisher quickly went bankrupt; the 1882 edition was banned in Boston.

As Whitman's powers, both physical and poetic, declined, his admirers increased. In 1868 William Rossetti published a bowdlerised selection that brought him English admirers in John Addington SYMONDS and Carpenter. Whitman's British reputation enhanced his standing in the US.

During the 1950s, biographer Gay Wilson Allen established Whitman as the philopietistic poet for what Henry Luce (head of the Time–Life conglomerate) called the 'American Century'. When the Roman Catholic authorities in New Jersey protested against naming a bridge from Camden to Philadelphia after the poet, Allen certified that Whitman was no queer. New Jersey later added a Whitman rest stop on their turnpike. Gay interpretations outraged traditional Whitman scholars; they excoriated Robert K. Martin, whose *Homosexual Tradition in American Poetry* (1979, 1998) declared, 'Whitman intended his work to communicate his homosexuality to his readers.'

Nearly a generation later, Gary Schimdgall in *Walt Whitman: A Gay Life* (1997) connects Whitman with Oscar WILDE. Wilde's mother read *Leaves of Grass* to her son. Wilde visited Whitman twice in Camden; they drank elderberry wine together, and the playwright wrote the poet that there was no American 'whom I love and honour so much'. Whitman's teenage assistant Billy Duckett compared himself to Wilde's lover. Duckett and Whitman both posed nude for the Philadelphia photographer Thomas EAKINS.

Good evidence supports the view that Whitman was an urban sophisticate. He followed theatre and opera and during the 1850s was associated with musical, dramatic and literary critics in New York City; 'my darlings my gossips', he called them. Whitman wrote in 1863, recalling these 'dear boys' company & their gayety & electricity, their precious friendship'. The poet claimed that contralto Marietta Alboni inspired his work; he attended her every performance in New York City. He encouraged his lover Peter Doyle to attend the theatre regularly; in Ford's Theater on 14 April 1865, Doyle saw actor John Wilkes Booth assassinate President Lincoln. Whitman was then visiting his mother in Brooklyn, where he wrote his extraordinary memorial to Lincoln, which follows the outline of an opera.

Allen Ginsberg traces an important side of Whitman: the seer, starting with William Blake, developing a vision of America, culminating in a world of universal love and freedom. Apocalyptic and sensual poetry would provide the sustenance to transform an oppressive society into a land of orgies, universally opening the doors of perception. One of Ginsberg's more fanatic followers, Schmidgall, claims: 'Whitman's doctrine quite simply was that cocksucking, butt-fucking and boy-loving were religious activities equal to what some Christians called "god's love".'

J. R. LeMaster and D. D. Kummings, *Walt Whitman: An Encyclopedia*, New York, 1998; J. Myerson, *Walt Whitman: A Descriptive Bibliography*, Pittsburgh, 1993.

Charley Shively

Wikner, Carl Pontus (1837–1888), Swedish philosopher and writer. Wikner was senior lecturer in philosophy at the University of Uppsala from 1864 and was appointed professor of philosophy and aesthetics in Christiania (Oslo) in 1884. He married in 1871.

Wikner sided with the liberal theological criticism of religious dogmas and was deeply influenced by his homosexual friend Nils Wilhelm Ljungberg's public attack in 1861 on the Church's dogmatic view of JESUS. Wikner's religiosity had a clear touch of mysticism and the figure of Christ was of central importance for him. He lived in many respects according to the slogan 'all or nothing' and his 'love for Jesus' often came into conflict with his 'love for a friend'. In situations where infatuation threatened to overturn ideals, he often chose to break off the relationship and flee into an exalted worship of Jesus.

Wikner's contribution to homosexual history consists foremostly, as Wilhelm von Rosen has pointed out, of producing the first description in the Nordic countries of the problematics about homosexual identity and the coming-out process. He deposited for future research at the medical faculty in Uppsala his

'Psychological Self-Confessions' from 1879 and diaries from 1853 to 1871. Wikner begins his confessions with a plea to the reader: 'You, man, who read these lines, they are written to you by a brother who has suffered much. My thoughts are pressed out of the deepest distress which yet tries to give itself in words.' Against the argument that homosexuality is unnatural, he answered that only that which according to the laws of nature cannot occur is unnatural. And nothing is bad which does not injure or harm any person. When the common opinion stamped homosexual love as being unnatural, it referred in reality to the fact that it is unacceptable according to existing social norms. To claim that heterosexual love is the only correct love is just as wrong as saying that the majority is always in the right over the minority. The Church's view on homosexuality as something unnatural and sinful comes, according to Wikner, from the laws in the Old Testament books by Moses, whose primitive view of humanity and tough retributional punishment had been abandonded long ago. Wikner points out that there are other parts of the Bible which can be used to claim a more positive view on homosexuality; for example, that Jesus loved John 'in a certain way'.

Wikner dimissed all arguments that homosexuality could be formed by masturbation or seduction, arguing that it is inborn and that it probably is physically or psychologically founded. He pleaded to all future readers to give homosexuals the right to get married. He thought that there should not be any unnecessary obstacles in the way of divorce, particularly since marriage between homosexuals does not carry any responsibility for support.

Wikner, after decades of doubt and inner struggle, managed to unite a Christian humanistic view of life with a positive homosexual identity. He seems even to have held some hopes that the prejudice would be lesser in a future society with a higher level of education.

P. Wikner, *Psykologiska självbekännelser*, ed. L. Johannesson, Stockholm, 1971; L. Johannesson, *Pontus Wikner, Dagböckerna berättar*, Avesta, 1982; W. von Rosen, *Månens Kulør, Studier i dansk bøssehistorie 1626–1912*, II, Copenhagen, 1993.

Åke Norström

Wilde, Oscar (Fingal O'Flahertie Wills) (1854–1900), British dramatist, poet, critic. Born in Ireland to affluent Protestant parents, William Wilde and Jane Elgee – who preferred to be known as Francesca Speranza, Lady Wilde – Oscar Wilde died in France five years after his trials and imprisonment, impoverished and largely alone, following a brilliant dramatic career and huge social success among the upper class and literati of London. Equally at home in the grand houses, the artistic salons and the *demi-monde* of the day, Wilde was adored for his dazzling conversation, for his wit, his aplomb, his good humor and liberality of spirit.

Wilde arrived at Oxford University in 1874 and distinguished himself as a student of Classics, flirted with conversion to Catholicism, and flung himself into the Oxford Movement, a circle of men in the Anglican Church who sought to link it more closely to Roman Catholicism. The movement originated in Oxford in 1833, and by Wilde's day it was noted for its religious fervour and also for its devotion to ideas about art and classical culture; at Oxford, the circle was also suspected of devotion to homosexual love. Even before he graduated and set off for London, Wilde had decided to be a poet, a dandy, and most of all, a celebrity. He wrote two verse tragedies, *Vera* and *The Duchess of Padua*, which no one would produce. By the time Gilbert and Sullivan parodied him in *Patience* as the figure of Bunthorne with a lily in his hand, Wilde had become much talked about as the symptom of everything wrong with the new aestheticism. His fame spread far enough for him to be invited in 1881 to give a continent-wide tour of America, lecturing on any subjects he chose. When he returned to England, he began a leisurely two-year courtship of Constance Lloyd, whom he married in 1884. In 1885 his son Cyril was born, in 1886 his son Vyvyan. Supported largely by his wife's income, Wilde became a journalist in the next few years and authored a book of fairy tales, *The Happy Prince and Other Tales* (1888). In 1891, he published four books – two volumes of short stories, one of critical essays, the novel *The Picture of Dorian Gray* – as well as his most famous political tract, 'The Soul of Man Under Socialism', and completed his first successful play, *Lady Windermere's Fan*, as well as most of *Salome*. In the next four years he wrote *An Ideal Husband, A Woman of No Importance* and his masterpiece, *The Importance of Being Earnest*.

At the height of his fame, he sued the Marquess of Queensbury, the father of his lover, Lord Alfred DOUGLAS, known as Bosie, for slander after he accused Wilde of 'posing' as a 'somdomite [*sic*]'. Wilde lost the suit, but because he perjured himself and because of the enormous scandal of the trial, he was indicted on charges of gross indecency. His first trial on these charges ended without a verdict, and friends urged him to flee to France before he could be retried, but his mother and Douglas persuaded him to stay, assuring him that he would be acquitted. The second trial led to a guilty verdict; the details about gay life among the upper classes and the *demi-monde* so outraged the judge that he imposed the maximum prison sentence of two years. When Wilde was released, he was broken, his health shattered. Bankrupted, bereft of wife and sons, most of his friends, his place in society and his theatre audience, he went into exile in Italy and later in France. He died and was buried in Paris.

While in prison for committing homosexual acts, he wrote *De Profundis*, an extraordinary letter, really a memoir, recounting how he came to destroy himself, which was published posthumously, and

'The Ballad of Reading Gaol', which was his last published work. Wilde often claimed that he put his talent into his writing but his genius into his life, which he wanted to make into a work of art. But he did not expect that the 'work of art' would be a tragedy, both personal and artistic. Exile was death for the artist, and the empty years led to despair and dissipation which finally completed the ruination of his health begun in prison.

Wilde's significance is twofold, as a writer whose sensibility helped define modernism, and as a figure whose victimisation ushered into consciousness the predicament of homosexual men in a society that would tolerate closetry but never openness. His ordeal helped bring to public attention not only the injustice visited upon homosexuals, but also the reason for that vicious homophobia: Wilde brought out of the closet not only the subject of sexual deviance, but the much larger subject of the nature of sexuality, his scandal challenging many of the received notions about sexual desire and behaviour. Like WHITMAN, Wilde never publicly acknowledged his homosexuality, but he remains for the history of homosexuality perhaps the most famous example of what would later be identified as 'gay'. Wilde himself discovered that his sexuality was not only a matter of behaviour or even desire; his sexuality gave him his identity, and ultimately the meaning of his life. His is one of the stories of the transformation of sexual desire into sexual identity, perhaps the best example of the creation of the idea of the homosexual in the nineteenth century.

R. Ellmann, *Oscar Wilde*, New York, 1988; V. B. Holland, *Oscar Wilde*, London, 1960, rev. edn., 1988; H. Montgomery Hyde, *Oscar Wilde, A Biography*, New York, 1975; N. Bartlett, *Who Was That Man?*, London, 1988; D. Coakley, *Oscar Wilde, The Importance of Being Irish*, Dublin, 1994; G. Schmidgall, *The Stranger Wilde: Interpreting Oscar*, New York, 1994; A. Sinfield, *The Wilde Century: Effeminacy, Oscar Wilde, and the Queer Movement*,

London, 1994; J. Nunokawa, *Oscar Wilde*, New York, 1995; M. S. Foldy, *The Trials of Oscar Wilde: Deviance, Morality, and Late-Victorian Society*, New Haven, 1997.

Seymour Kleinberg

William III (1650–1702), William of Orange, Statholder of The Netherlands, and later King William III of England, Scotland and Ireland. Born at The Hague, he was the son of William II, who died a few days before he was born, and he thus inherited his Dutch titles from birth. His mother was Mary Stuart, daughter of the late King Charles I of England, who had been executed in 1648. England was at this time a republic under Oliver Cromwell.

William was thus a central figure in European politics from the day of his birth. As head of the House of Orange, he was automatically Statholder of The Netherlands (a kind of hereditary princehood somewhere short of kingship), and one of the leaders of Protestant Europe in its endless wars with Catholic France and Spain. Should the English monarchy be restored, only Charles I's two sons, the exiled Charles II and his brother James, Duke of York, would have better claims to the English throne. Since Charles was childless and York a Catholic, William's chances of the succession seemed good. He reinforced his claim in 1677 by marrying James's daughter Mary.

In 1660 the English monarchy was restored, and Charles II came to the throne and reigned until 1685, leaving no legitimate children. York then succeeded as James II, despite the efforts of the Protestant Whig party to prevent a Catholic becoming king. James had two daughters, Mary and Anne, both Protestants and married to Protestant princes (Mary to William and Anne to George of Denmark), so the Protestant succession seemed assured. William, meanwhile, had grown to be a talented military and political leader, the champion of Protestantism against the Catholic imperialism of France's Louis XIV.

In 1688 James's second, Catholic, wife gave birth to a son, raising the prospect of a Catholic dynasty. The Protestant party in England called on William to invade England and claim the throne in the name of his wife, Mary. William agreed only on the condition that he and Mary would be joint monarchs, which meant in practice that he would rule. William's army landed in Devon in November and he marched on London. James had few supporters and fled to France. William and Mary were crowned joint King and Queen of England, Scotland and Ireland in January 1689. Mary died in 1694, and William then reigned alone until his death in 1702. They had no children, and the throne then passed to Mary's sister Anne.

William was an austere and dominating ruler, and his popularity with the English quickly faded. He fuelled their resentment by showing extraordinary favour to two of his Dutch associates. These were (first) Hans Willem Bentinck, whom he made Earl of Portland, and (later) Arnold Joost van Keppel, created Earl of Albemarle. Bentinck was a year older than William and had been his servant and companion since childhood. When William had smallpox in 1675, Bentinck risked his life to nurse the prince. His closeness to William naturally aroused jealousies, but there seems to have been no serious suggestion that there was anything improper about their relationship.

The same could not be said for Keppel, who was 20 years William's junior and strikingly handsome, and had risen from being a royal page to an earldom with suspicious ease. Now it was Portland's turn to be jealous, and he wrote to William in 1697 that 'the kindness which your Majesty has for a young man, and the way in which you seem to authorise his liberties ... make the world say things I am ashamed to hear'. This, he said, was 'tarnishing a reputation which has never before been subject to such accusations'. William replied, saying, 'It seems to me very extraordinary that it should be impossible to have esteem and regard for a young man without it being criminal.'

It is impossible after 300 years to know the truth of these matters, when royal courts were always surrounded by intrigue, gossip and propaganda. It is possible, though not likely, that William and Bentinck had been lovers in their youth, and possible also that his relationship with Keppel was sexual. It is also possible that William had homosexual tendencies which he never acted on, but which led him to favour attractive young men, especially if they were capable and loyal.

Several facts must be set against the theory that William III was homosexual. First, he was deeply devoted to his wife. Their marriage was childless, but they shared a bed, and had the marriage not been consummated such a scandal would have been reported. His grief at her death was spectacular. Second (and despite this), he was known to have had a long affair with an English lady-in-waiting, Elizabeth Villiers, which ended only in 1685 when it was discovered that James II was using the affair as a means of espionage and blackmail at William's court. Third, both Portland and Albemarle had well documented heterosexual affairs. None of these facts are conclusive, but they weigh heavily when there is no direct evidence to support the opposite view.

There are striking parallels between William's relations with his two favourites and those of two earlier monarchs with their favourites: King EDWARD II (with Piers Gaveston and Hugh Despenser) and JAMES I (with Robert Kerr and George Villiers). Both were suspected of homosexuality. Later, Queen Anne's close friendship with Sarah Churchill was to be the subject of similar speculation. In each case, while there may have been a sexual dimension to the relationship (overt or sublimated), the real value of these favourites was their loyalty to monarchs who felt (and were) friendless and surrounded by sycophants and conspirators. In William's case the verdict must be 'not proven'.

H. and B. van der Zee, *William and Mary*, London, 1973.

Adam Carr

Winckelmann, Johann Joachim (1717–1768), German scholar. Winckelmann has been called the father of both art history and modern archaeology. This admirer of Hellenic ideals wrote the epoch-making *Geschichte der Kunst des Altertums* (*History of the Art of Antiquity*) (1764), which ushered in an age of new classicism in European art. Winckelmann developed an entirely new kind of art criticism, showing how art styles reflected historical and political changes in different civilisations through the ages. He also sanctioned homoeroticism in art, stessing the beauty of the young male nude depicted in ancient Greek sculptures. Winckelmann took no great pains in concealing his homosexuality, as the vast collection of his personal correspondence confirms. His homosexuality has been publicly acknowledged since 1805, when one of Winckelmann's greatest admirers, the great German poet Johann Wolfgang von Goethe, broached the subject in *Winckelmann und sein Jahrhundert* (*Winckelmann and his Century*).

Winckelmann arose from impoverished surroundings as the son of a poor Prussian cobbler. Armed with sheer determination and an aptitude for classical Greek, he was able to receive an academic education, then usually reserved only for males of the privileged classes. He pursued university studies in theology, physics, medicine and anatomy in Halle and Jena. In 1742, as a private tutor in Magdeburg, he fell in love with his pupil, 14-year-old Peter Lamprecht, whom he described as his 'first love and friendship'. When Winckelmann accepted the post of schoolmaster in the small town of Seehausen in 1743, Lamprecht followed him, living with him intimately until 1746, when he returned to Magdeburg. Winckelmann remained in his position until 1748, when he became librarian for a nobleman near Dresden. He felt intellectually stifled there in provincial seclusion and converted to Roman Catholicism in 1754, presumably to facilitate a journey to Rome.

Winckelmann's first essay about Greek art, *Gedanken über die Nachamung der griechischen Werke in der Malerei und Bildhauerkunst* (*Thoughts on the Imitation of Greek Works*, 1755), was published a few months before he left Germany. This work, the best introduction to his aesthetic thought, praised Hellenic sculpture as humanity's highest achievement, worthy of imitation. Winckelmann asserted here that the essence of the Greek ideal was 'a noble simplicity and a calm grandeur', famous words which would exert immense influence on subsequent thinkers and writers, such as Goethe, for many decades to follow.

Winckelmann lived in Italy for 13 years, serving as librarian successively to two influential cardinals. He was befriended by the German Neoclassicist painter Anton Rafael Mengs, who introduced him to artistic circles in Rome. Winckelmann had a brief affair with one of Mengs's pupils, Franz Sander. Winckelmann had many other amours, and the legendary lover Giacomo Casanova once surprised him in a compromising situation with a young man. Winckelmann also had a burning, unconsummated passion for a young Latvian nobleman to whom he dedicated an artistic treatise emphasising homoerotic friendships, *Abhandlung der Empfindung des Schönen in der Kunst* (*Treatise on the Capacity for the Feeling of Beauty*, 1763).

The ruins of Pompeii and Herculaneum were discovered shortly before Winckelmann's arrival in Italy. He first visited the sites in 1762 and through his reports, he made the ruins internationally famous and gave scientists the first reliable information about the treasures unearthed there. He also proposed more efficient methods of excavation, raising archaeology, formerly only a hobby for rich dilettantes, to a science. His magnum opus, *Geschichte der*

Kunst des Altertums, soon followed, giving art history a new systematic basis. Winckelmann possessed a shrewd political, as well as artistic mind. This work criticised the despotic age in which he lived by subtly asserting that democratic ideals and political freedom were necessary prerequisites for great art to flourish.

Returning from Vienna in 1768, where he had been received at court, Winckelmann stopped in the harbour city of Trieste, where he was stabbed to death in an inn by Francesco Angeli, a common thief to whom he had trustingly shown some gold coins presented as gifts from the Empress of Austria.

Winckelmann's *Geschichte* remained the bible of art history for several decades, but its influence waned in the nineteenth century, when drier, more empirical evaluations of art prevailed. Nevertheless, Winckelmann's homoerotic aesthetic continued to be upheld in some corners, especially by Walter PATER in England, and by the disciples of the German poet Stefan GEORGE.

W. Leppmann, *Winckelmann. Ein Leben für Apoll*, Bern, 1982; A. Potts, *Flesh and the Ideal: Winckelmann and the Origins of Art History*, New Haven, 1994; D. M. Sweet, 'Winckelmann – Welcher Winckelmann? Etappen der Winckelmann-Rezeption', *Forum: Homosexualität und Literatur*, 4 (1988): 5–15.

Seán Henry

Winsloe, Christa (1888–1944), German-American-French writer. Winsloe was the scriptwriter of what has been called the most important pre-war lesbian film, *Mädchen in Uniform* (*Girls in Uniform*, 1931).

She was born in Darmstadt, Germany, and educated at the militaristically strict Kaiserin-Augusta-Stift in Potsdam before being sent to a Swiss finishing school. In 1909 Winsloe moved to Munich to study sculpture; misogynist attitudes to female sculptors are something she later described in her novels. Four years later she married a Hungarian baron, Lajos Hatvany, and lived mainly on his estate in Hungary until they divorced in 1924, when she returned to Munich and continued her work as a sculptor. On the literary scene, her first notable success was a play called *Ritter Nérestan* (*Nérestan the Knight*), first performed in Leipzig in 1930. For the subsequent Berlin production the title was changed to *Gestern und heute* (*Yesterday and Today*); this became the basis for *Mädchen in Uniform*.

Gestern und heute plays in a Prussian boarding-school not unlike the Augusta-Stift where Winsloe had her early schooling. In the play, a child called Manuela falls in love with her teacher, Fräulein von Bernburg, and comes to believe that her feelings are reciprocated. After drinking too much punch at a school celebration, Manuela declares her love before her assembled classmates and teachers. The response is drastic: the headmistress isolates her from the other girls in the belief that she is in the grip of an aberrant disorder. Fräulein von Bernburg fails to provide support, instead acquiescing in the general perception of events. In desperation, Manuela commits suicide by leaping from the window of her upstairs room.

Gestern und heute was filmed in 1931, under the direction of Leontine Sagan, as *Mädchen in Uniform*. The film is remarkable for its time in that it was written by a woman, directed by a woman and acted by women and girls. But in the process of its transformation for the cinema, the piece lost its tragic ending: Sagan's schoolgirls prevent Manuela's suicide. Much celebrated on its release, *Mädchen in Uniform* was seen as a critique of Prussian militaristic values; its lesbian theme, however, was largely overlooked. Winsloe's novel, called *Das Mädchen Manuela* (*The Child Manuela*), appeared in 1933 in Amsterdam and 1934 in Leipzig and Vienna, but was almost immediately blacklisted by the new Nazi government in Germany, and only reprinted in 1983.

Winsloe left Germany soon after the National Socialists came to power. Via Italy, Austria and Hungary, she eventually moved to the US, where her partner was the news correspondent Dorothy Thompson. She missed Europe, however, and returned there in 1938. A year later, in Paris, G. W. Pabst approached her to write the script for his film *Jeunes filles en détresse* (1939). Winsloe complied, and in the same year she moved to the Côte d'Azur, from where she offered temporary support and refuge for those fleeing Nazi Germany. But on 10 June 1944, she and her Swiss partner, Simone Gentet, were shot dead near Cluny. There are two versions of the circumstances surrounding Winsloe's death: the first is that she was killed by the *Résistance* for having contacts with German officers; the second only emerged in a post-war trial, and is that the murderers were ordinary criminals who subsequently pretended to have been carrying out an 'execution'.

Other works by Christa Winsloe include her comedy *Schicksal nach Wunsch* (*A Fate of Your Choice*, 1932); the novels *Life Begins* (published in England in 1935) and *Passagiera* (1938); and another comedy, *Der Schritt hinüber* (*Stepping Across*, 1940). Her unpublished works include a novel, *Halbe Geige*, about male homosexuality, and a play called *Sylvia und Sybille*.

C. Schöppman (ed.) *Im Fluchtgepäck die Sprache: Deutschsprachige Schriftstellerinnen im Exil*, Berlin, 1991; A. Stürzer, *Dramatikerinnen und Zeitstücke: Ein vergessenes Kapitel der Theatergeschichte von der Weimarer Republik bis zur Nachkriegszeit*, Stuttgart, 1993; R. Wall, *Lexikon deutschsprachiger Schriftstellerinnen im Exil 1933 bis 1945*, Freiburg i. Br., 1995.

Sarah Colvin

Witkiewicz, Stanisław Ignacy (1885–1939), Polish writer and painter. Known as Witkacy, he was a playwright, novelist, art theorist, philosopher and painter. Educated primarily by his father, the writer

Stanisław Witkiewicz, he studied art in Cracow, but travelled to Italy, Germany and France frequently. His circle of gay friends included the composer Karol SZYMANOWSKI and the noted anthropologist Bronisław Malinowski. His stormy affair with the actress Irena Solska was related in his 622 *upadki Bunga, czyli Demoniczna kobieta* (622 *Falls of Bungo, or The Demonic Woman*, written in 1910–1911, but only published in 1972). As a Russian subject, he served as an officer in the Russian army in World War I, witnessing the fall of the empire and the October Revolution. In 1918, he returned to Poland, where he lived in Zakopane. His painting initially was in the tradition of Art Nouveau but he became famous for his Expressionist works, with their strong sense of colour. Later he produced Symbolist works approaching the abstract. Although he gradually abandoned painting, he continued to paint portraits in pastels for money. A member of an avant-garde group, the Polish Formists (Formiści Polscy), he devoted most of his efforts to writing, especially dramas (over 30, some lost and most only published after his death). Between 1925 and 1932, he wrote three novels, although most of his energy was devoted to philosophy. He committed suicide upon the Soviet invasion of Poland.

According to Witkacy, civilisation was at a turning point: religion, philosophy, and art would be eliminated by this new modern era of equality, socialism and mechanisation, but the masses would be satisfied. His theories were avant-garde as well as catastrophic. Considering theatre to be the domain of pure form, his dramas were seldom performed in his lifetime. Usually included among his most significant plays are *Wariat i zakonnica, czyli Nie ma złego co by na jeszcze gorsze nie wyszło* (*The Madman and the Nun, or There's Nothing Bad that Couldn't Go Even Worse*, 1925), *Kurka wodna* (*The Water Hen*, 1922) and *Szewcy* (*The Shoemakers*, staged in 1957). His most important novel is often considered to be *Nienasycenie* (*In-*

satiability, 1930). Although he was not gay, he dealt with themes of decadence, sexual deviation and gender transfer. His novels are peopled by characters longing for the extreme in experience – erotic, narcotic and artistic. During his lifetime, Witkiewicz was treated seriously by only a few intellectuals. However, he is now regarded as a precursor of the theatre of the absurd and a visionary prophesying Europe's catastrophic fate, on the edge of World War II.

D. Gerould, *Witkacy: Stanisław Ignacy Witkiewicz as an Imaginative Writer*, Seattle, 1981; D. Gerould (ed.) *The Witkiewicz Reader*, Evanston, Ill., 1992; Witkiewicz, *Insatiability*, trans. L. Iribarne, Urbana, Ill., 1976; Witkiewicz, *The Madman and the Nun and Other Plays*, trans. D. Gerould and C. S. Durer, Seattle, 1968.

John Stanley

Wittgenstein, Ludwig (1889–1951), Austrian-British philosopher. Born in Vienna, the youngest of eight children of a wealthy Austrian industrialist, Wittgenstein was educated at home until age 14; he concentrated on mathematics and science at school and for two years studied mechanical engineering in Berlin. His early interests were in the field of aerodynamics, and while at the University of Manchester in England (1908–1911) he designed experimental aeroplanes that incorporated jet propulsion. The writings of philosophers Bertrand Russell and Gottlob Frege had a profound influence on young Wittgenstein, who abandoned engineering to pursue studies in mathematical logic at Cambridge University with Russell, who felt that the avid pupil 'soon knew all that I had to teach'. Leaving Cambridge in 1913, Wittgenstein traveled to Skjolden, Norway, to pursue his philosophical investigations in seclusion.

Enlisting in the Austrian army at the outbreak of World War 1, Wittgenstein distinguished himself in service on both the Eastern Front and in Italy, and by 1918 he had also completed the manuscript of a philosophical tract which he had worked on throughout the war. Eventually published with the help of Bertrand Russell in 1922, *Tractatus Logico-Philosophicus*, the philosophical essence of which was the nature and understanding of language, soon became regarded as a work of profound significance in the field. *Tractatus* offered the daring metaphysical proposition that the limits of language are the limits of thought, that one cannot speak of what cannot be said or thought and that there is a realm of existence about which nothing can be said.

Having adopted a Tolstoyan simplicity in his personal life, Wittgenstein gave away his large inheritance and between 1920 and 1926 worked as an elementary school teacher, during which time he was torn between suicidal tendencies and the joy derived from relationships with his pupils. In the controversial study *Wittgenstein*, W. W. Bartley III contends that during this period Wittgenstein indulged in promiscuous sex with 'rough young men ready to cater to him sexually' in Vienna's famous park, the Prater. In *The Misfits: A Study of Sexual Outsiders*, Colin Wilson asserts that these proclivities are the basis of Wittgenstein's philosophy. Ray Monk convincingly argues that despite elements of truth in Bartley's claims, Wittgenstein feared *any* sexual contact and though these young men *did* exist, his encounters with them transpired primarily in his mind. Throughout the decade, Wittgenstein had no formal association with philosophers but occasionally met with members of the 'Vienna Circle', the creators of 'Logical Postivism', and with the young British philosopher Frank Ramsey, with whom he had a brief sexual affair and contentious intellectual relationship, which ended with Ramsey's death at 26 in 1930.

Wittgenstein returned to the academic world in 1929, when he was made a fellow of Trinity College Cambridge, where his intellectual brilliance dazzled students who spread his revolutionary theories throughout the English-speaking world. For the next two decades, with an interruption for volunteer work during World War II, Wittgenstein maintained an antagonistic relationship with Cambridge. Despite being appointed in 1939 to G. E. Moore's chair in philosophy, he denounced the validity of academics while profoundly influencing the field through his ground-breaking work within the academy. He finally resigned from the 'living death' of academe in 1947. The remainder of his life was spent in ill-health, working in semi-seclusion in Ireland, and later in the US and England, on *Philosophische Untersuchungen* (*Philosophical Investigations*, 1953), which, at his request, were not published until after his death.

This work, his *magnum opus*, completely contradicted the propositions of *Tractatus*, proposing that there is no logical unity in thought, that all actions and reactions are interrelated, and that the task of philosophy is to untangle the tangled knots of our understanding.

Wittgenstein was blessed with genius, wealth, professional success and reasonably good looks. Yet, much of his life was spent in rejecting these gifts. Though his motivations were frequently generous and humane, he could be cruel and critical. Despite his acclaim as one of the great philosophers of the century, Wittgenstein, by his own admission, lacked the faith and courage to love. His greatest fear, rejection, led him to prefer the company and affection of brilliant but naïve and devoted male students. In addition to Ramsey, his most important companions were David Pinsent, Francis Skinner (who died of polio, aged 31 in 1941) and Ben Richards, Wittgenstein's companion until the philosopher's death in Cambridge.

A. Janik and S. Toulmin, *Wittgenstein's Vienna*, New York, 1973; R. Monk, *Ludwig Wittgenstein: The Duty of Genius*, London, 1990.

A. M. Wentick

Wolfe, Elsie de, later **Lady Mendl** (1865–1950), American interior decorator. Daughter of a New York doctor, de Wolfe spent her teenage years mixing with London society. She embarked upon a stage career in New York in 1886, where her high fashion wardrobe was better received than her acting. In 1905 she announced her services as an interior decorator, the first woman to undertake what previously had been reserved for amateurs, architects or tradesmen. A suffragette active in protests in 1912, she believed that women should be entitled to a place in the world of business. During World War I she served with French hospitals; for her efforts she was later awarded the Croix de Guerre and Legion of Honour. De Wolfe used the feminine domain of the home to build a powerful career. Her notoriety ensured success and she enjoyed a long international career. Her formula ousted dark Victorian gloom for a revival of eighteenth-century French furniture and light, pastel rooms. Her ideas were promoted in the ghost-written semi-autobiographical *The House in Good Taste* (1913). She became a millionaire from decorating the Henry Clay Frick mansion, New York, in 1916. In the 1930s she popularised new materials such as large plate-glass mirrors and lucite and camp, theatrical motifs such as leopard skin. She lived her life as a work of art and was part of an international social set which included creative homosexuals such as Cecil BEATON, a protégé. De Wolfe performed a type of hyper-femininity, with the house, clothes by Mainbocher and Chanel, hair-style and face-lift so perfect it verged on the parodic. Beaton, who held an exhibition at her 5th Avenue gallery, the Elsie de Wolfe Gallery, in 1929, upon drawing her portrait, noted, 'She is the sort of wildly grotesque artificial creature I adore'.

De Wolfe had a famous lesbian relationship with Elisabeth (Bessie) Marbury for thirty years from 1892; they were openly received in New York society. De Wolfe deployed the home and decorating as a female space in which women might refashion themselves from the restrictive spirit of their Victorian mothers. Surrounded by mirrors, light open spaces and delicate furniture, she promoted a new type of modernity which did not reject traditional languages of design. In New York she was part of a 'Sapphic enclave' which included Anne Morgan, Mrs Chauncey Olcott and Anne Vanderbilt. In 1905 Marbury bought for her the Villa Trianon near Versailles, where Elsie established her domain as one of the great international hostesses. In 1926 she married the diplomat Sir Charles Mendl, for companionship and his social connections. It is not regarded as a physical relationship. In old age her eccentricity extended to standing on her head every day and dyeing her hair blue, the original 'blue rinse'. Her life was described in the autobiography *After All* (1935). Her will established a foundation for young designers and charities. There has been a revival of interest in her work from the 1980s, when inter-war alternatives to modernism were reassessed by the market and academy alike. Aaron Betsky recently gave her a prominent position in his text *Queering Modernism* (1997).

N. Campbell and C. Seebohm, *Elsie de Wolfe. A Decorative Life*, New York, 1992; P. McNeil, 'Designing Women: Gender, Sexuality and the Interior Decorator *c.* 1890–1940', *Art History*, 17, 4 (December 1994), pp. 631–57; Jane S. Smith, *Elsie de Wolfe. A Life in the High Style*, New York, 1982.

Peter McNeil

Woolf, Virginia (1882–1941), British writer. Born in London into a large family of rather eminent Victorians, Virginia Woolf wrote ten novels, in addition to copious essays and short stories, which have secured her a place in the modernist canon afforded few other women writers. Her essay *A Room of One's Own* (1929) has become a feminist classic; from that essay, the sentence 'Chloe liked Olivia' has become shorthand for lesbianism – a case in point being Lillian Faderman's 1994 anthology of lesbian literature titled *Chloe Plus Olivia*. Nearly all of Woolf's novels and many of her short stories have been interpreted from a variety of feminist, lesbian feminist and queer critical perspectives.

Adeline Virginia Stephen was born to Julia Pattle Duckworth Stephen, whose Pre-Raphaelite beauty was captured in the famous photographs of her aunt, Julia Margaret Cameron. Sir Leslie Stephen, literary critic and editor of the *Dictionary of National Biography*, who although he did not believe in formally educating girls, made his voluminous library available to his precocious daughter Virginia. After her father's death in 1904, Woolf's intellectual powers flourished when she, her sister Vanessa and brother Thoby moved to London's Bloomsbury. There they formed what came to be known as the Bloomsbury Group, which included Clive Bell, Desmond MacCarthy, Roger Fry, Leonard Woolf, E. M. FORSTER, Duncan GRANT and Lytton STRACHEY – the latter three of whom were homosexual. Strachey once proposed to Virginia but successfully recanted 'before the end of the conversation', he confessed in a letter to Leonard Woolf, who was more serious and tenacious in his proposal. Although she admitted feeling no physical attraction for him, Virginia Stephen agreed to marry Leonard Woolf in 1912. All biographers agree that it was essentially a sexless marriage, but many also agree that on some levels it was a satisfying partnership for both. Their union is undoubtedly responsible for creating one of the most important presses in the history of twentieth-century literature: the Hogarth Press, which published some of the most important authors in the modernist canon, including T. S. Eliot – Woolf typeset *The Waste Land* herself – Gertrude STEIN and Katherine Mansfield, as well as translations of Sigmund FREUD. Hogarth Press, of course, also published Woolf's

novels from *Jacob's Room* (1922) to her final novel, *Between the Acts*, which was published in 1941 after Woolf committed suicide by drowning. 'I'm the only woman in England free to write what I like', wrote Woolf. Woolf's acute awareness of censorhip, however – especially in the case of Radclyffe HALL's banned lesbian novel *The Well of Loneliness* – has led some critics to examine Woolf's strategies of encoding the lesbian content of much of her fiction.

While many critics and biographers have insisted on viewing the intense emotional, erotically charged and sometimes sexual relationships that Woolf developed with women throughout her entire life as the result of one or more psychological wounds – her mother's early death when Virginia was 13 or her sexual abuse by a half-brother – critical and biographical perspectives have shifted to make significant space for the discussion of Woolf as a writer with a lesbian consciousness. Her most famous affair of the heart and the one to have been most physical was that with Vita SACKVILLE-WEST, for whom she wrote the novel *Orlando* (1928). Nearly all of Woolf's novels – including her first, *The Voyage Out* (1915); her more famous ones, *Mrs. Dalloway* (1925) and *To the Lighthouse* (1927); and her last two, *The Years* (1937) and *Between the Acts* (1941) – have been interpreted in light of their lesbian themes. Woolf's pronouncement that 'Women alone stir my imagination' has stirred the imagination of countless readers and scholars of her work.

E. Barrett and P. Cramer, *Virginia Woolf: Lesbian Readings*, New York, 1997; B. Wiesen Cook, '"Women Alone Stir My Imagination": Lesbianism and the Cutural Tradition', *Signs: Journal of Women in Culture and Society*, 4 (1979): 718–39; J. Marcus, *The Languages of Patriarchy*, Bloomington, 1987; S. Raitt, *Virginia & Vita: The Work and Friendship of V. Sackville-West and Virginia Wolf*, New York, 1993; H. Lee, *Virginia Woolf*, London, 1996.

Annette Oxindine

X

Xenophon (c. 430–c. 354 BC), Greek soldier-of-fortune and man of letters. Xenophon was born into a wealthy Athenian family about 430 BC. Perhaps because he lacked sympathy for the democracy which was restored to Athens in 403, he joined the army of Cyrus, claimant to the Persian throne, as a mercenary along with some 13,000 other Greeks. However, in the first battle of the campaign (at Cunaxa on the Euphrates, 401 BC), Cyrus was killed. Later, the Greek commanders were treacherously murdered, leaving the army leaderless. The hitherto untried Xenophon now emerged as one of the generals who led the army in an heroic march northwards through unknown country to the shores of the Black Sea and onwards to Byzantium and the kingdom of Seuthes in Thrace. However, instead of returning to Athens, Xenophon now joined forces with the Spartan army in campaigning against the local Persian governors of Asia Minor. It was here that he met (and came greatly to admire) the Spartan king, Agesilaus. Returning to Greece with Agesilaus in 394, Xenophon found himself fighting with the Spartans against the Athenians and Thebans. Now (if not earlier) exiled from Athens, he was installed by the Spartans in a country estate at Scillus in the Peloponnese. Here he lived with his wife and twin sons for some 20 years, when he moved to Corinth. He was reconciled with Athens, though he seems not to have returned there to live. He died some time after 354 BC.

During his long life Xenophon wrote on a remarkable variety of subjects. His importance here is as a transmitter of SOCRATES' teaching on same-sex love and his own (rather different) views on the subject. There are also sufficient clues in his narrative of the great march to invite speculation that he himself had found a male lover to accompany him at that time.

In the *Memoirs of Socrates*, Xenophon recalls how Socrates rebuked a handsome and wealthy young man named Critoboulus for kissing the beautiful young son of Alcibiades. Such a kiss, he says (humorously, but with serious intent), is like a poisonous spider's bite, hard to recover from and leading to all kinds of excess. But Xenophon declares that he also might take that risk for such a kiss, thus distancing himself from the ascetic teaching of Socrates. Later, in Xenophon's dialogue *The Symposium*, Critoboulus makes an ardent speech in praise of his beloved, Clinias, and of homosexual love in general: such love, he declares, makes a man modest, self-controlled, and even reverential towards that which he most desires. Similarly, the tyrant Hiero (in the dialogue which bears his name) declares that he will not force his sexual will on his beloved Dailochus, but that he seeks physical consummation within a responsive loving relationship which enhances erotic delight.

In these passages Xenophon combines the virtue of self-control with an acceptance of sexual pleasure in love between men. He also, by implication, contrasts Hiero's positive account of same-sex love with the negative strictures of Socrates against all-male sex reported in his (Xenophon's) *Symposium*. When Xenophon praises King Agesilaus for resolutely resisting sexual temptation (posed by the beautiful Persian youth, Megabates), it is because of the potential danger to the city's interests arising from a foreign liaison, not because of any moral condemnation of homosexual love.

Xenophon's *Symposium*, and PLATO's work of the same title, belong to a genre which the ancients recognised as 'discourses on love' (*erotikoi logoi*). They include a discourse attributed to the orator Lysias (died *c.* 380 BC) on the 'non-lover', which describes various aspects of love and friendship, while claiming that the advantage lies with a pursuit of sexual satisfaction without love. We also have (ascribed to Demosthenes, 384–322 BC) a high-minded letter in praise of a young man named Epicrates, from an older lover who assumes the role of moral guide and tutor. The records mention some seven or eight other works on *eros* emanating from within the Socratic tradition, none of which survive. They include treatises by Aristotle and Theophrastus, and a book 'On Love' by the cobbler Simon, a friend of Socrates, fragmentary remains of whose workshop have been found near the agora in Athens.

M. Foucault, *The Use of Pleasure*, Vol. 2 of *The History of Sexuality*, trans. R. Hurley, Harmondsworth, 1985; C. Hindley, 'Eros and Military Command in Xenophon', *Classical Quarterly*, NS, 44, 2 (1994): 347–66; C. Hindley, 'Xenophon on Male Love', *Classical Quarterly*, NS, 49, 1 (1999): 74–99.

Clifford Hindley

Y

Yourcenar, Marguerite (1903–1987), French novelist and poet. Born Marguerite de Crayencour, in Brussels, she was given her father's French nationality although her parents were both from old Flemish families. When she started publishing poetry in her late teens, she created her pen-name, an anagram constructed with her father's help, and registered it as her legal name in the US in 1947. Between the two wars she travelled widely in Europe, notably in Italy and Greece, and steadily established herself as a writer, notably with *Alexis or le Traité du vain combat* (*Alexis or Treatise on Fruitless Struggle*, 1929), a discreet psychological study of a young man who has to leave his wife and baby son when he comes to terms with his real sexual orientation, and *Denier du rêve* (*Coinage of Dreams*, 1934), the story of a failed attack on the life of Mussolini (a novel she eventually revised in 1959). In 1936 she published a series of prose poems, *Feux* (*Passions*), mostly playing on motifs from antiquity, in which her own passion for an ungendered lover is reflected through a series of images many of which have homoerotic connotations. In 1937 she met an American, Grace Frick, who was to be her lifetime companion as well as the principal translator of her works. In 1939 she prepared a series of translations from the poetry of the contemporary homosexual Greek poet CAVAFY and wrote a prefatory essay to accompany them, though the work was not to appear in volume form until 1958.

Yourcenar was in the US in June 1940 when the Germans invaded France, and there she was to remain for most of her life, setting up house with Frick on the coast of Maine. There she wrote the book which was to bring her to international attention, *Mémoires d'Hadrien*. She had started to work on a novel based on the Roman emperor HADRIAN in the 1930s but completely re-worked the material. As soon as it appeared in 1951 the *Mémoires* was a major critical and popular success, receiving a prize from the Académie Française the following year. This was only the first of many such examples of public recognition. In 1962 her collection of essays *Sous bénéfice d'inventaire* (*The Dark Brain of Piranesi and Other Essays*, trans. R. Howard, 1984), which included the Cavafy preface, won the Prix Combat, and *L'Œuvre au noir* (*Working in Darkness*), a work set in sixteenth-century Europe, was awarded the Prix Fémina in 1968. She was elected to the Royal Belgian Academy in 1970, awarded the Légion d'honneur in 1971, and the Grand Prix of the Académie Française in 1974. She then became the first woman to be elected to the Académie Française in 1980. This is probably the most distinguished literary career of any woman writer in the West in modern times.

Yourcenar neither spoke of nor denied

her sexuality, but it is an important fact of her work that she wrote constantly about *male* homosexual characters – Alexis, Eric in *Le Coup de grâce* (1939), Hadrian and Antinous, Zeno in *L'Œuvre au noir* – and translated works by Europe's most overtly homoerotic poet, Cavafy. By looking at a male-centred world she was able to study issues of power and marginalisation, and to look at such questions as the separation of emotion and physical desire, all of which are reflected in overtly lesbian French writers from Natalie BARNEY onwards, but without committing herself to their alternative values. By projecting herself into her gay male heroes, she has also been able to examine the nature and limits of masculinity and femininity in an ostensibly objective way, while using first-person narration. The result, however 'politically' contentious, is thought-provoking writing of the highest quality, equally accessible to a gay and straight readership.

M. Yourcenar, *Archives du Nord*, Paris, 1977; C. Robinson, *Scandal in the Ink*, London, 1995.
Christopher Robinson

Z

Zahle, Vilhelmine (1868–1940), Danish writer and teacher. Zahle wrote the first explicit tale in Danish literature of a young woman's attraction to another woman. A young girl, Martha, has been 'madly in love' for seven years with her best friend Edith. Martha loses herself in depression when Edith marries and Martha finally resigns herself to a loveless marriage with a cousin of her beloved. The storyteller explains that for some people who are not strong enough to overcome grief, repression is the obvious response to painful self-knowledge. The tale 'Ogsaa en Kærlighedshistorie' ('Also a Love Story') was published in 1890, together with another short story under the title *Vildsomme Veje (Pathless Ways)*.

Zahle was born in Copenhagen to the vicar and member of parliament Peter Christian Zahle and his second wife, Clara. Her mother died when she was 7 months old and she grew up with her maternal grandparents. Zahle's mother had been musically talented and she inherited these traits. The literary skills can be attributed to her father, who was a very productive writer.

As a young girl she dreamed of becoming an actress, but the fact that she was quite near-sighted turned out to be an insurmountable obstacle. However, at the age of 16 she started studying with a celebrated actress from the Royal Theatre in Copenhagen, Agnes Nyrop, a woman of the world. Zahle was clearly attracted to the older woman, and this infatuation was a strong motivation for her wanting to become an actress. After the death of Nyrop, Zahle frankly related the story of this first love in an obituary.

The tale of Martha's love for Edith in 'Ogsaa en Kærlighedshistorie' seems in many ways to build on the personal experience of the 16-year-old Zahle and with the 21-year-old writer's attempt to find answers to questions such as, 'Could it be that there exists some strangely endowed women who are only capable of loving one of their own sex?' Neither Martha nor the author solves this identity dilemma or finds any support or role models. Furthermore, the surrounding society – represented by Martha's hermit-like father, the local vicar and the family doctor – is equally ignorant. When she acts naturally, they find her odd, and when she forces herself into a more emotionally retricted role, they find her natural.

In spite of the controversial topic of the short story, the book never received much attention. In a review in the daily *Politiken* in 1890, Edward Brandes praised the handling of the topic for its 'necessary discretion'. The portrait of Martha is clearly not a description of a dangerous *femme fatale* or the physical anomaly of the hermaphrodite as in Balzac's 'Seraphita' from the mid-1840s. Martha is in many ways a very ordinary girl, almost dull and bashful. The words 'homosexuality' or 'lesbianism' or similar terms are never mentioned. Maybe this is because the young author did not have any words for her reality, or could not imagine a sexual relationship between two women. Her own story resembles the tale of Martha beyond the narrative.

In 1891, Zahle married a young grocer, Frederik Vilhelm Gjøl Korch. It turned out to be an unhappy marriage, and in 1899 she left her husband, taking along her daughter Gertrud. In the following years she earned her living as a private tutor and journalist, and the family settled in Germany from 1913 to 1917. They returned to Denmark when the tragedy of World War I made it impossible to earn a living in Germany.

Zahle ended her life as a well respected though rather unorthodox teacher in the town of Vejle in Jutland, where she arrived around 1921. She never referred to her own literary work in her teaching, but pupils have reported that if homosexuality was mentioned, she recommended Radclyffe HALL's *The Well of Loneliness*. In her own life she never found love outside the world of fiction.

Zahle's short story is the first defence in Danish literature of the right to love whom you choose regardless of gender. The fact that the book was published under her own name is a rare indication of self-integrity and courage at the turn of the centrury – but also a sign of ingenuousness. Homosexuality between women in Denmark was simply invisible – and thus silenced – whereas homosexuality between men was a matter of criminal law and punishment. In the tale of Martha the Church is seen as the most significant hindrance to the expression of female homosexuality, but the reader notices the emerging scrutiny of the medical profession, symbolised in Edith's husband, Stein. The word 'homosexual' appeared for the first time in Denmark in 1892 in a medical journal. The journey from sin to sickness had begun, and in Danish litera-

ture it would take almost two generations before feminist writers decisively revolted against this new stereotyped view of the lesbian as a sexual deviant.

V. Zahle, *Vildsomme Veje*, Copenhagen, 1890 and 1982; P. Dahlerup, 'Det moderne gennembruds kvinder', Copenhagen, 1983; H. Jarlmose, *Kærligheden, der ikke kendte sit eget navn. Om kvindelig homoseksualitet i litteraturen 1890–1940*, Copenhagen, 1992.

Helle Jarlmose

Zahrtmann, (Peter Henrik) Kristian (1843–1917), Danish painter. Zahrtmann was educated at the Royal Danish Academy of Fine Arts and made his début in 1869. He was a pupil of Wilhelm Marstrand, one of the painters of the Golden Age of Danish painting. Zahrtmann was uninfluenced by Impressionism; his work concentrated on historical painting and Italian folklore. From 1884 to 1913 he regularly visited Civita d'Antino near Rome (where he was made an honorary citizen in 1902), often accompanied by students from his School of Painting ('Zahrtmann's School'). His selection of male students was sometimes motivated solely by their beauty and youth.

Zahrtmann's historical paintings are theatrical and often invite the viewer to interpret the depicted person's state of mind. Sometimes they are bizarre; the nude *Bathing Susanna* (1906–1907) is seen from behind, literally upside down, in a handstand. Many of his later works are homosocial all-male situations, often including naked and eroticised male bodies (*Socrates and Alcibiades*, 1907 and 1911). There is no Eve in *Adam in Paradise* (1914), but there is a bunch of bananas and a snake between the sitting Adam's muscular spread legs. Adam's futile attempt to hide his genitalia with a branch of leaves turns him into a passive sex object aware of the viewer's penetrating look. At various intervals Zahrtmann painted the historical figure Eleonora Christina, the daughter of a king of

Denmark and the author of a celebrated autobiography who was held in jail for 22 years for treason. Zahrtmann's interpretation of her as *the* tragic, slightly absurd, *grande dame* 'demonstrates a homosexual sensibility or attitude to gender that is rooted in traditional concepts, but at the same time transcends the boundaries of gender-roles by defining them as roles' (M. St. Hansen).

Zahrtmann was a loner in Danish art. Although he was well known as a painter and became a media personality, his art was never accepted by the critics or the general public. Some of his paintings are in museums in Denmark and Norway, but by far the largest number, including all the late paintings of males, are privately owned. This seems to mirror a curatorial distaste for Zahrtmann's self-conscious, ironic and less than respectable treatment of gender and sexuality, his subversive comment on his own identity and on Denmark's bourgeois culture at the turn of the century. For more than ten years (*c*. 1983–1993) his large 'historical' painting *Prometheus* (1904) hung in Cosy Bar, one of Copenhagen's sleazier after-hours gay bars: a chained and writhing naked man about to be ravaged by a huge eagle. This painting is also represented on walls in the background of a number of Zahrtmanns's other paintings, such as his self-portrait (1917). Zahrtmann was unmarried. He cross-dressed on a number of semi-public occasions. Nothing is known about actual sexual relations.

S. Danneskiold-Samsøe, *Kristian Zahrtmann*, Copenhagen, 1942; B. Jørnæs, 'Kristian Zahrtmann', *Dansk Biografisk Leksikon*, Vol. 16, Copenhagen, 1984: 128–31; M. S. Hansen, 'Kristian Zahrtmanns sene historiemalerier. En kontrærseksuel kunstners persona i Danmark ved århundredskiftet', *Periskop. Forum for kunsthistorisk debat*, 4 (1995): 43–64.

Wilhelm von Rosen